Fisheries Regulation in the Central Arctic Ocean

Queen Mary Studies in International Law

Edited by

Malgosia Fitzmaurice

VOLUME 56

The titles published in this series are listed at *brill.com/qmil*

Fisheries Regulation in the Central Arctic Ocean

Background, Motivations and Aspirations of the 2018 CAOF Agreement

By

Lena J. Haas

BRILL | NIJHOFF

LEIDEN | BOSTON

Library of Congress Cataloging-in-Publication Data

Names: Haas, Lena J, author.
Title: Fisheries regulation in the Central Arctic Ocean : background, motivations, and aspirations of the 2018 CAOF Agreement / by Lena J Haas.
Description: Leiden ; Boston : Brill/Nijhoff, 2025. | Series: Queen Mary studies in international law ; volume 56 | Includes bibliographical references and index. | Summary: "Since time immemorial, the Arctic has been a white spot on the map - an ocean that was largely inaccessible for humanity. Until the very recent past, humanity was compelled to accept this inaccessibility, plain and simple. Literally, the Arctic has been white due to a metres thick permanent ice layer covering the entire region. Yet, for some time now, more and more colour has been added to the region: due to climate change, the layer of ice is melting at an alarmingly rapid pace, offering multiple options for human impact on a hitherto virtually untouched natural environment
Identifiers: LCCN 2024050124 | ISBN 9789004700666 (hardback) | ISBN 9789004700673 (ebook)
Subjects: LCSH: Fishery law and legislation–Arctic Ocean. | Law of the sea–Arctic Ocean. | Marine resources conservation–Law and legislation–Arctic Ocean. | Arctic Ocean–International status.
Classification: LCC KZA1667 .H33 2025 | DDC 343.07/692–dc23/eng/20241022
LC record available at https://lccn.loc.gov/2024050124

Typeface for the Latin, Greek, and Cyrillic scripts: "Brill". See and download: brill.com/brill-typeface.

ISSN 1877-4822
ISBN 978-90-04-70066-6 (hardback)
ISBN 978-90-04-70067-3 (e-book)
DOI 10.1163/9789004700673

This book is printed on acid-free paper and produced in a sustainable manner.

Contents

Preface

Writing this book has been an extraordinary journey that began several years ago with the desire to further deepen my keen interest in international maritime and environmental law. The uniqueness of the CAOF Agreement as a fisheries agreement in force before fishing occurs in a particular area, its wide relevance in the context of climate change and as a multinational (model) agreement in difficult times made it a topic worth looking at more closely and presenting to the public. The process was both challenging and rewarding, as it opened up new perspectives and broadened my understanding not only of the legal aspects involved, but especially of global geopolitical and environmental developments.

As a result – and this is what distinguishes this work from others in the field – this book offers a deeper insight into the scientific aspects of the subject and links them to the legal aspects of the Agreement. A large part of my objective is to give those who otherwise deal with the subject in a more analytical and theoretical way an understanding of these scientific developments.

I would like to thank everyone who has supported me in the process of this work, much of which was written under difficult circumstances with challenging research and working possibilities due to the COVID-19 pandemic. I am deeply grateful to my husband Simon, my parents, sisters and friends for their unconditional encouragement, and to my Ph.D. supervisor Daniel Khan and colleagues for their invaluable feedback and insightful guidance, especially Clemens Hufeld, Philip Nedelcu, Nick Applegarth, and Kevin Li. Furthermore, I would like to thank the institutions, networks and fellow scholars that provided essential resources for my research, in particular Erik J. Molenaar and the UArctic Thematic Network on Arctic Law. Many thanks also go to Malgosia Fitzmaurice and De Gruyter Brill, whose interest in my work initiated the publication and makes it accessible to a wider audience.

As you explore the CAOF Agreement through this book, I invite you to consider not only the immediate implications for Arctic fisheries, but also the broader lessons it holds for international cooperation, environmental protection, and the ever-changing relationship between humanity and the natural world. May this work inspire greater awareness and action towards the sustainable management of our shared marine resources.

Lena J. Haas
Munich, June 2024

Figures

Abbreviations

2030 Agenda	United Nations 2030 Agenda for Sustainable Development
ACIA	Arctic Climate Impact Assessment
AEPS	Arctic Environmental Protection Strategy
the Agreement	2018 Agreement to Prevent Unregulated High Seas Fisheries in the Central Arctic Ocean, unless otherwise indicated
Agreement Area	The single high seas portion of the central Arctic Ocean that is surrounded by waters within which Canada, the Kingdom of Denmark in respect of Greenland, the Kingdom of Norway, the Russian Federation and the United States of America exercise fisheries jurisdiction
AMAP	Arctic Monitoring and Assessment Programme
Arctic Five	Arctic coastal States Canada, the Kingdom of Denmark (acting on behalf of Greenland and the Faroe Islands), the Kingdom of Norway, the Russian Federation, and the United States of America
AWI	Alfred-Wegener-Institut
Barcelona Convention	Convention for the Protection of the Mediterranean Sea Against Pollution
BBNJ treaty	International legally binding instrument under the United Nations Convention on the Law of the Sea on the conservation and sustainable use of marine biological diversity of areas beyond national jurisdiction, also referred to as the biodiversity beyond national jurisdiction treaty
BEAC	Barents Euro-Arctic Council
BRC	Barents Regional Council
CAFF	Conservation of Arctic Flora and Fauna Working Group of the Arctic Council
CAMLR Convention	Convention on the Conservation of Antarctic Marine Living Resources
CAO	Central Arctic Ocean
CAOF Agreement	2018 Agreement to Prevent Unregulated High Seas Fisheries in the Central Arctic Ocean
Cartagena Protocol	Cartagena Protocol on Biosafety to the Convention on Biological Diversity
CBD	United Nations Convention on Biological Diversity
CCAMLR	Commission for the Conservation of Antarctic Marine Living Resources

CCCC	Climate Change and Carrying Capacity
CDS	Catch documentation schemes
CITES	Convention on International Trade in Endangered Species of Wild Fauna and Flora
CMS	Convention on the Conservation of Migratory Species of Wild Animals
the Convention	United Nations Convention on the Law of the Sea, unless otherwise indicated
COP	CBD conference of the parties
CWP	FAO's Coordinating Working Party on Fishery Statistics
Decision V/6	Decision V/6 of the COP to the CBD
the Directive	2008 EU Marine Strategy Framework Directive
DWF State	Distant water fishing State
EBSAS	Ecologically or biologically significant marine areas
EEZ	Exclusive Economic Zone
EIA	Environmental impact assessment
EPPR	Emergency Prevention, Preparedness and Response Working Group of the Arctic Council
EU	European Union
FAO	Food and Agriculture Organization of the United Nations
FAO Code of Conduct	FAO Code of Conduct for Responsible Fisheries
FAO Compliance Agreement	1993 Agreement to Promote Compliance with International Conservation and Management Measures by Fishing Vessels on the High Seas
FiSCAO	Scientific Experts on Fish Stocks in the Central Arctic Ocean
Five-plus-Five	The ten parties to the CAOF Agreement
FPZ	Fisheries Protection Zone
FSP Guidelines	FAO Voluntary Guidelines for Flag State Performance
IAD framework	Institutional Analysis and Development framework
ICC	Inuit Circumpolar Council
ICCAT	International Commission for the Conservation of Atlantic Tunas
ICCPR	International Covenant on Civil and Political Rights
ICES	International Council for the Exploration of the Sea
ICJ	International Court of Justice
ILO	International Labour Organization
ILO Convention No. 169	International Labour Organization Convention concerning Indigenous and Tribal Peoples in Independent Countries (No. 169)

IMO	International Maritime Organization
IPCC	Intergovernmental Panel on Climate Change
IPHC	International Pacific Halibut Commission
IPOA	International Plan of Action
IPOA-CAPACITY	International Plan of Action for the Management of Fishing Capacity
IPOA-IUU	International Plan of Action to Prevent, Deter and Eliminate Illegal, Unreported and Unregulated Fishing
IPY	International Polar Year
ITLOS	International Tribunal for the Law of the Sea
IUU fishing	Illegal, unreported and unregulated fishing
IWC	International Whaling Commission
Johannesburg Plan of Implementation	Plan of the Implementation of the World Summit on Sustainable Development
JointFish	Joint Norwegian-Russian Fisheries Commission
JPSRM	Joint Program of Scientific Research and Monitoring
MARPOL	International Convention for the Prevention of Pollution from Ships
MFG Guidelines	FAO Voluntary Guidelines on the Marking of Fishing Gear
MOSAiC expedition	Multidisciplinary drifting Observatory for the Study of Arctic Climate expedition
MSY	Maximum sustainable yield
NAFO	Northwest Atlantic Fisheries Organization
NAFO Convention	Convention on Cooperation in the Northwest Atlantic Fisheries
Nagoya Protocol	Nagoya Protocol on Access to Genetic Resources and the Fair and Equitable Sharing of Benefits Arising from their Utilization to the Convention on Biological Diversity
NASCO	North Atlantic Salmon Conservation Organization
NEAFC	North-East Atlantic Fisheries Commission
NEAFC Convention	Convention on Future Multilateral Cooperation in North-East Atlantic Fisheries
NEMURO	North Pacific Ecosystem Model for Understanding Regional Oceanography
NEMURO.FISH	NEMURO For Including Saury and Herring

New Delhi Declaration	International Law Association's New Delhi Declaration of Principles of International Law Relating to Sustainable Development
(N)GO	(Non-)governmental organization
NIS	Non-indigenous species
NOAA	National Oceanic and Atmospheric Administration
Oslo Declaration	2015 Declaration Concerning the Prevention of Unregulated High Seas Fishing in the Central Arctic Ocean
OSPAR Convention	Convention for the Protection of the Marine Environment of the North-East Atlantic
Other Five	Parties to the CAOF Agreement except the Arctic Five, namely China, Iceland, Japan, the Republic of Korea and the European Union
PAME	Protection of the Arctic Marine Environment Working Group of the Arctic Council
the Parties	The ten parties to the CAOF Agreement, listed in Article 9(1) CAOF Agreement
PICES	North Pacific Marine Science Organization
Polar Code	International Code for Ships Operating in Polar Waters
Preamble	Preamble of the CAOF Agreement
PSCG	Provisional Scientific Coordinating Group
PSMA	Agreement on Port State Measures to Prevent, Deter and Eliminate Illegal, Unreported and Unregulated Fishing
PSSA	Particularly Sensitive Sea Area
RFB	Regional Fishery Body
RFMA	Regional Fisheries Management Arrangement
RFMO	Regional Fisheries Management Organization
Rio Declaration	Rio Declaration on Environment and Development
SAO	Senior Arctic Officials
SDGs	UN Sustainable Development Goals
SOLAS	International Convention on Safety of Life at Sea
SPRFMO	South Pacific Regional Fisheries Management Organisation
SRFMA	Subregional Fisheries Management Arrangement
SRFMO	Subregional Fisheries Management Organization
SSF Guidelines	FAO Voluntary Guidelines for Securing Sustainable Small-Scale Fisheries in the Context of Food Security and Poverty Eradication
Stockholm Declaration	1972 Declaration of the United Nations Conference on the Human Environment
TAC	Total allowable catch

TACC	Total allowable commercial catch
UN	United Nations
UNCED	United Nations Conference on Environment and Development
UNCLOS	United Nations Convention on the Law of the Sea
UNDRIP	United Nations Declaration on the Rights of Indigenous Peoples
UNFCCC	1994 United Nations Framework Convention on Climate Change
UNFS Agreement	Agreement for the Implementation of the Provisions of the United Nations Convention on the Law of the Sea of 10 December 1982 relating to the Conservation and Management of Straddling Fish Stocks and Highly Migratory Fish Stocks
VCLT	Vienna Convention on the Law of Treaties
WCPFC	Convention on the Conservation and Management of Highly Migratory Fish Stocks in the Western and Central Pacific Ocean
WSSD	World Summit on Sustainable Development

Text of the Agreement and Outline of Provisions

Text of the Agreement

AGREEMENT TO PREVENT UNREGULATED HIGH SEAS FISHERIES IN THE CENTRAL ARCTIC OCEAN[1]

The Parties to this Agreement,
RECOGNIZING that until recently ice has generally covered the high seas portion of the central Arctic Ocean on a year-round basis, which has made fishing in those waters impossible, but that ice coverage in that area has diminished in recent years;
ACKNOWLEDGING that, while the central Arctic Ocean ecosystems have been relatively unexposed to human activities, those ecosystems are changing due to climate change and other phenomena, and that the effects of these changes are not well understood;
RECOGNIZING the crucial role of healthy and sustainable marine ecosystems and fisheries for food and nutrition;
RECOGNIZING the special responsibilities and special interests of the central Arctic Ocean coastal States in relation to the conservation and sustainable management of fish stocks in the central Arctic Ocean;
NOTING IN THIS REGARD the initiative of the central Arctic Ocean coastal States as reflected in the *Declaration Concerning the Prevention of Unregulated High Seas Fishing in the Central Arctic Ocean* signed on 16 July 2015;
RECALLING the principles and provisions of treaties and other international instruments relating to marine fisheries that already apply to the high seas portion of the central Arctic Ocean, including those contained in:

> the *United Nations Convention on the Law of the Sea* of 10 December 1982 ("the Convention");

> the *Agreement for the Implementation of the Provisions of the United Nations Convention on the Law of the Sea of 10 December 1982 relating to*

1 The Agreement's text can inter alia be found on the website of the Government of Canada, the depositary, see 'Agreement to Prevent Unregulated High Seas Fisheries in the Central Arctic Ocean (Ilulissat, 3 October 2018)' <https://www.dfo-mpo.gc.ca/international/documents/pdf/EN-CAO.pdf> accessed 9 July 2021.

the Conservation and Management of Straddling Fish Stocks and Highly Migratory Fish Stocks of 4 August 1995 ("the 1995 Agreement"); and

the 1995 Code of Conduct for Responsible Fisheries and other relevant instruments adopted by the Food and Agriculture Organization of the United Nations;

UNDERLINING the importance of ensuring cooperation and coordination between the Parties and the North-East Atlantic Fisheries Commission, which has competence to adopt conservation and management measures in part of the high seas portion of the central Arctic Ocean, and other relevant mechanisms for fisheries management that are established and operated in accordance with international law, as well as with relevant international bodies and programs;

BELIEVING that commercial fishing is unlikely to become viable in the high seas portion of the central Arctic Ocean in the near future and that it is therefore premature under current circumstances to establish any additional regional or subregional fisheries management organizations or arrangements for the high seas portion of the central Arctic Ocean;

DESIRING, consistent with the precautionary approach, to prevent the start of unregulated fishing in the high seas portion of the central Arctic Ocean while keeping under regular review the need for additional conservation and management measures;

RECALLING the 2007 United Nations Declaration on the Rights of Indigenous Peoples;

RECOGNIZING the interests of Arctic residents, including Arctic indigenous peoples, in the long-term conservation and sustainable use of living marine resources and in healthy marine ecosystems in the Arctic Ocean and underlining the importance of involving them and their communities; and

DESIRING to promote the use of both scientific knowledge and indigenous and local knowledge of the living marine resources of the Arctic Ocean and the ecosystems in which they occur as a basis for fisheries conservation and management in the high seas portion of the central Arctic Ocean,

HAVE AGREED as follows:

Article 1: Use of Terms

For the purposes of this Agreement:

(a) "Agreement Area" means the single high seas portion of the central Arctic Ocean that is surrounded by waters within which Canada, the Kingdom of Denmark in respect of Greenland, the Kingdom of Norway, the Russian Federation and the United States of America exercise fisheries jurisdiction;

(b) "fish" means species of fish, molluscs and crustaceans except those belonging to sedentary species as defined in Article 77 of the Convention;

(c) "fishing" means searching for, attracting, locating, catching, taking or harvesting fish or any activity that can reasonably be expected to result in the attracting, locating, catching, taking or harvesting of fish;

(d) "commercial fishing" means fishing for commercial purposes;

(e) "exploratory fishing" means fishing for the purpose of assessing the sustainability and feasibility of future commercial fisheries by contributing to scientific data relating to such fisheries;

(f) "vessel" means any vessel used for, equipped to be used for, or intended to be used for fishing.

Article 2: Objective of This Agreement

The objective of this Agreement is to prevent unregulated fishing in the high seas portion of the central Arctic Ocean through the application of precautionary conservation and management measures as part of a long-term strategy to safeguard healthy marine ecosystems and to ensure the conservation and sustainable use of fish stocks.

Article 3: Interim Conservation and Management Measures Concerning Fishing

1. Each Party shall authorize vessels entitled to fly its flag to conduct commercial fishing in the Agreement Area only pursuant to:

(a) conservation and management measures for the sustainable management of fish stocks adopted by one or more regional or subregional fisheries management organizations or arrangements, that have been or may be established and are operated in accordance with international law to manage such fishing in accordance with recognized international standards; or

(b) interim conservation and management measures that may be established by the Parties pursuant to Article 5, paragraph 1(c)(ii).

2. The Parties are encouraged to conduct scientific research under the framework of the Joint Program of Scientific Research and Monitoring established pursuant to Article 4 and under their respective national scientific programs.

3. A Party may authorize vessels entitled to fly its flag to carry out exploratory fishing in the Agreement Area only pursuant to conservation and management measures established by the Parties on the basis of Article 5, paragraph 1(d).

4. The Parties shall ensure that their scientific research activities involving the catching of fish in the Agreement Area do not undermine the prevention of unregulated commercial and exploratory fishing and the protection of healthy marine ecosystems. The Parties are encouraged to inform each other about their plans for authorizing such scientific research activities.
5. The Parties shall ensure compliance with the interim measures established by this Article, and with any additional or different interim measures they may establish pursuant to Article 5, paragraph 1(c).
6. Consistent with Article 7 of the 1995 Agreement, coastal States Parties and other Parties shall cooperate to ensure the compatibility of conservation and management measures for fish stocks that occur in areas both within and beyond national jurisdiction in the central Arctic Ocean in order to ensure conservation and management of those stocks in their entirety.
7. Other than as provided in paragraph 4 above, nothing in this Agreement shall be interpreted to restrict the entitlements of Parties in relation to marine scientific research as reflected in the Convention.

Article 4: Joint Program of Scientific Research and Monitoring

1. The Parties shall facilitate cooperation in scientific activities with the goal of increasing knowledge of the living marine resources of the central Arctic Ocean and the ecosystems in which they occur.
2. The Parties agree to establish, within two years of the entry into force of this Agreement, a Joint Program of Scientific Research and Monitoring with the aim of improving their understanding of the ecosystems of the Agreement Area and, in particular, of determining whether fish stocks might exist in the Agreement Area now or in the future that could be harvested on a sustainable basis and the possible impacts of such fisheries on the ecosystems of the Agreement Area.
3. The Parties shall guide the development, coordination and implementation of the Joint Program of Scientific Research and Monitoring.
4. The Parties shall ensure that the Joint Program of Scientific Research and Monitoring takes into account the work of relevant scientific and technical organizations, bodies and programs, as well as indigenous and local knowledge.
5. As part of the Joint Program of Scientific Research and Monitoring, the Parties shall adopt, within two years of the entry into force of this Agreement, a data sharing protocol and shall share relevant data, directly or through relevant scientific and technical organizations, bodies and programs, in accordance with that protocol.
6. The Parties shall hold joint scientific meetings, in person or otherwise, at least every two years and at least two months in advance of the meetings of

the Parties that take place pursuant to Article 5 to present the results of their research, to review the best available scientific information, and to provide timely scientific advice to meetings of the Parties. The Parties shall adopt, within two years of the entry into force of this Agreement, terms of reference and other procedures for the functioning of the joint scientific meetings.

Article 5: Review and Further Implementation

1. The Parties shall meet every two years or more frequently if they so decide. During their meetings, the Parties shall, *inter alia*:

(a) review implementation of this Agreement and, when appropriate, consider any issues relating to the duration of this Agreement in accordance with Article 13, paragraph 2;

(b) review all available scientific information developed through the Joint Program of Scientific Research and Monitoring, from the national scientific programs, and from any other relevant sources, including indigenous and local knowledge;

(c) on the basis of the scientific information derived from the Joint Program of Scientific Research and Monitoring, from the national scientific programs, and from other relevant sources, and taking into account relevant fisheries management and ecosystem considerations, including the precautionary approach and potential adverse impacts of fishing on the ecosystems, consider, *inter alia*, whether the distribution, migration and abundance of fish in the Agreement Area would support a sustainable commercial fishery and, on that basis, determine:

  (i) whether to commence negotiations to establish one or more additional regional or subregional fisheries management organizations or arrangements for managing fishing in the Agreement Area, and

  (ii) whether, once negotiations have commenced pursuant to subparagraph (i) above and once the Parties have agreed on mechanisms to ensure the sustainability of fish stocks, to establish additional or different interim conservation and management measures in respect of those stocks in the Agreement Area;

(d) establish, within three years of the entry into force of this Agreement, conservation and management measures for exploratory fishing in the Agreement Area. The Parties may amend such measures from time to time. These measures shall provide, *inter alia*, that:

  (i) exploratory fishing shall not undermine the objective of this Agreement,

(ii) exploratory fishing shall be limited in duration, scope and scale to minimize impacts on fish stocks and ecosystems and shall be subject to standard requirements set forth in the data sharing protocol adopted in accordance with Article 4, paragraph 5,

(iii) a Party may authorize exploratory fishing only on the basis of sound scientific research and when it is consistent with the Joint Program of Scientific Research and Monitoring and its own national scientific program(s),

(iv) a Party may authorize exploratory fishing only after it has notified the other Parties of its plans for such fishing and it has provided other Parties an opportunity to comment on those plans, and

(v) a Party must adequately monitor any exploratory fishing that it has authorized and report the results of such fishing to the other Parties.

2. To promote implementation of this Agreement, including with respect to the Joint Program of Scientific Research and Monitoring and other activities undertaken pursuant to Article 4, the Parties may form committees or similar bodies in which representatives of Arctic communities, including Arctic indigenous peoples, may participate.

Article 6: Decision-Making

1. Decisions of the Parties on questions of procedure shall be taken by a majority of the Parties casting affirmative or negative votes.
2. Decisions of the Parties on questions of substance shall be taken by consensus. For the purpose of this Agreement, "consensus" means the absence of any formal objection made at the time the decision was taken.
3. A question shall be deemed to be of substance if any Party considers it to be of substance.

Article 7: Dispute Settlement

The provisions relating to the settlement of disputes set forth in Part VIII of the 1995 Agreement apply, *mutatis mutandis*, to any dispute between Parties relating to the interpretation or application of this Agreement, whether or not they are also Parties to the 1995 Agreement.

Article 8: Non-parties

1. The Parties shall encourage non-parties to this Agreement to take measures that are consistent with the provisions of this Agreement.

2. The Parties shall take measures consistent with international law to deter the activities of vessels entitled to fly the flags of non-parties that undermine the effective implementation of this Agreement.

Article 9: Signature

1. This Agreement shall be open for signature at Ilulissat on 3 October 2018 by Canada, the People's Republic of China, the Kingdom of Denmark in respect of the Faroe Islands and Greenland, Iceland, Japan, the Republic of Korea, the Kingdom of Norway, the Russian Federation, the United States of America and the European Union and shall remain open for signature for 12 months following that date.
2. For signatories to this Agreement, this Agreement shall remain open for ratification, acceptance or approval at any time.

Article 10: Accession

1. For the States listed in Article 9, paragraph 1 that have not signed this Agreement, and for the European Union if it has not signed this Agreement, this Agreement shall remain open for accession at any time.
2. After the entry into force of this Agreement, the Parties may invite other States with a real interest to accede to this Agreement.

Article 11: Entry into Force

1. This Agreement shall enter into force 30 days after the date of receipt by the depositary of all instruments of ratification, acceptance, or approval of, or accession to, this Agreement by those States and the European Union listed in Article 9, paragraph 1.
2. After entry into force of this Agreement, it shall enter into force for each State invited to accede pursuant to Article 10, paragraph 2 that has deposited an instrument of accession 30 days after the date of deposit of that instrument.

Article 12: Withdrawal

A Party may withdraw from this Agreement at any time by sending written notification of its withdrawal to the depositary through diplomatic channels, specifying the effective date of its withdrawal, which shall be at least six months after the date of notification. Withdrawal from this Agreement shall not affect its application among the remaining Parties or the duty of the withdrawing Party to fulfill any obligation in this Agreement to which it otherwise would be subject under international law independently of this Agreement.

Article 13: Duration of This Agreement

1. This Agreement shall remain in force for an initial period of 16 years following its entry into force.

2. Following the expiration of the initial period specified in paragraph 1 above, this Agreement shall remain in force for successive five-year extension period(s) unless any Party:

(a) presents a formal objection to an extension of this Agreement at the last meeting of the Parties that takes place prior to expiration of the initial period or any subsequent extension period; or

(b) sends a formal objection to an extension to the depositary in writing no later than six months prior to the expiration of the respective period.

3. The Parties shall provide for an effective transition between this Agreement and any potential new agreement establishing an additional regional or subregional fisheries management organization or arrangement for managing fishing in the Agreement Area so as to safeguard healthy marine ecosystems and ensure the conservation and sustainable use of fish stocks in the Agreement Area.

Article 14: Relation to Other Agreements

1. The Parties recognize that they are and will continue to be bound by their obligations under relevant provisions of international law, including those reflected in the Convention and the 1995 Agreement, and recognize the importance of continuing to cooperate in fulfilling those obligations even in the event that this Agreement expires or is terminated in the absence of any agreement establishing an additional regional or subregional fisheries management organization or arrangement for managing fishing in the Agreement Area.

2. Nothing in this Agreement shall prejudice the positions of any Party with respect to its rights and obligations under international agreements and its positions with respect to any question relating to the law of the sea, including with respect to any position relating to the exercise of rights and jurisdiction in the Arctic Ocean.

3. Nothing in this Agreement shall prejudice the rights, jurisdiction and duties of any Party under relevant provisions of international law as reflected in the Convention or the 1995 Agreement, including the right to propose the commencement of negotiations on the establishment of one or more additional regional or subregional fisheries management organizations or arrangements for the Agreement Area.

4. This Agreement shall not alter the rights and obligations of any Party that arise from other agreements compatible with this Agreement and that do not affect the enjoyment by other Parties of their rights or the performance of their

obligations under this Agreement. This Agreement shall neither undermine nor conflict with the role and mandate of any existing international mechanism relating to fisheries management.

Article 15: Depositary

1. The Government of Canada shall be the depositary for this Agreement.
2. Instruments of ratification, acceptance, approval or accession shall be deposited with the depositary.
3. The depositary shall inform all signatories and all Parties of the deposit of all instruments of ratification, acceptance, approval or accession and perform such other functions as are provided for in the 1969 *Vienna Convention on the Law of Treaties*.

DONE at Ilulissat on this 3rd day of October 2018, in a single original, in the Chinese, English, French and Russian languages, each text being equally authentic.

Outline of Provisions

The Agreement to Prevent Unregulated High Seas Fisheries in the Central Arctic Ocean (CAOF Agreement; the Agreement) consists of a preamble with 12 paragraphs and 15 Articles.

Contextual Provisions: Preamble and Article 1

The preamble of the CAOF Agreement (Preamble) sets forth the underlying motivation for the conclusion of the Agreement. It highlights the status quo in the Arctic region, recalls the responsibilities and aspirations of the parties to the CAOF Agreement (Parties) and the forward-looking approach concerning fisheries and fish stocks in the Central Arctic Ocean (CAO). The Preamble has not been specifically adopted.

Article 1 defines the most relevant terms of the Agreement, *inter alia* the Agreement Area and different types of fishing.

Article 2: Objective of the Agreement

Article 2 displays the objective of the CAOF Agreement. Its main goal is to prevent unregulated fishing in the Agreement Area. The implementation of this approach is to be achieved by the application of precautionary conservation and management measures, which are further specified in Article 3 of the Agreement. Through these measures, a long-term strategy to safeguard healthy marine ecosystems and to ensure the conservation and sustainable use of fish stocks should be achieved.

Articles 3 and 4: Measures and Programs

Article 3 presents specific interim measures necessary to ensure the safeguarding of healthy marine ecosystems and the conservation and sustainable use of fish stocks. The different subparagraphs deal with commercial fishing, scientific research, exploratory fishing, and the relation and compliance of multiple activities that may be conducted under the Agreement.

As an implementation of cooperation, Article 4 specifies the requirements of a joint program of scientific research and monitoring that should be established by the Parties.

Article 5: Review and Further Implementation

Article 5 sets forth the elements of review, considerations and determinations. *Inter alia*, the Parties should determine whether the distribution, migration and abundance of fish in the CAOF Agreement area would support a sustainable commercial fishery. To this effect, Article 5(1)(c)(i) CAOF Agreement, considered the "trigger clause" of the Agreement, demands the Parties to ascertain whether to commence negotiations to establish one or multiple additional regional or subregional fisheries management organizations or arrangements for managing fishing in the agreement area.

Articles 6–10: Decision-Making, Dispute Settlement and Member Policy

Articles 6 and 7 CAOF Agreement contain general provisions on decision-making and dispute settlement.

Article 8 of the Agreement sets forth the behaviour towards non-parties, and Article 9 lists the (associations of) States for which the Agreement is open for signature. These are Canada, the People's Republic of China, the Kingdom of Denmark in respect of the Faroe Islands and Greenland, Iceland, Japan, the Republic of Korea, the Kingdom of Norway, the Russian Federation, the United States of America and the European Union (the Parties). Article 10 regulates the accession to the Agreement of these States and the European Union (EU), in case they have not yet signed the Agreement, and other States.

Articles 11–15: Final Provisions

Articles 11, 12 and 13 deal with the entry into force, withdrawal and duration of the Agreement, which should remain in force for at least 16 years after its entry into force. Article 14 entails a disclaimer to not prejudice any duties and rights stemming from other compatible agreements. Article 15 names the depositary, Canada, and its function. The Agreement's closing wording accepts versions in Chinese, English, French and Russian as equally binding.

CHAPTER 1

Introduction

Since time immemorial, the Arctic has been a white spot on the map – an ocean that was largely inaccessible for humanity. Until the very recent past, humanity was compelled to accept this inaccessibility, plain and simple. Literally, the Arctic has been white due to a metres thick permanent ice layer covering the entire region. Yet, for some time now, more and more colour has been added to the region: due to climate change, the layer of ice is melting at an alarmingly rapid pace, offering multiple options for human impact on a hitherto virtually untouched natural environment. It is therefore not surprising that the vision of new shipping routes, enhanced research, military activities and profitable economic exploitation has brought the region to the top of the international political and, eventually, legal agenda. Emerging conflicts of interest of various stakeholders are almost inevitable and call for new and possibly innovative forms of governance in a region that has hardly known any before. Predominantly part of the high seas, and thus beyond the reach of national sovereignty,[1] for this area such a regulatory regime can only be established at the international level.

Despite its harsh and hostile conditions, the Arctic Ocean is home to a great variety of living resources, which offer promising economic prospects for the future. New possibilities for access might enable fisheries, should there be sufficient fish stocks. As, due to the freedom of the high seas, the high seas portion of the Arctic Ocean is originally "accessible to the commercial fishing fleets of any jurisdiction",[2] all States interested could take up such opportunities. This in turn bears the risk of overfishing, which is already a considerable problem in international waters. In the last 10–15 years, one-third of global fish stocks have been constantly overexploited,[3] and two-thirds are in

1 See Article 89 'United Nations Convention on the Law of the Sea (Montego Bay, 10 December 1982) – UNTS Vol. 1833, No. 31363' <https://treaties.un.org/doc/Publication/UNTS/Volume 1833/volume-1833-A-31363-English.pdf> accessed 30 March 2022.

2 'Preventing Unregulated Commercial Fishing in the Central Arctic Ocean (CAO) – A Compilation of Reports from Meetings of Experts in Shanghai (China), Incheon (Korea) & Sapporo (Japan)' (2017) 2 <https://oceanconservancy.org/wp-content/uploads/2018/09/Preventing-Unregulated-Commercial-Fishing-CAO.pdf> accessed 23 July 2020.

3 See Food and Agriculture Organization of the United Nations, 'The State of World Fisheries and Aquaculture 2020: Sustainability in Action' 48;54 <https://doi.org/10.4060/ca9229en> accessed 4 April 2022; Food and Agriculture Organization of the United Nations, 'The State

 | DOI:10.1163/9789004700673_002

decline.[4] Additionally, one must bear in mind that the Arctic Ocean is a unique and delicate environment, and much of its functioning is not yet fully understood. Little is known about prospective effects of climate change on ecologically important species, and the information available mostly stems from short-term laboratory experiments. Interactions of different actors, activities and species can therefore not be investigated to a sufficient extent.[5] Increased effort needs to be put into understanding the ecosystem and fish and their health in the central Arctic Ocean (CAO) when developing new fishing grounds. Moreover, the conquest of new territories naturally leads to conflicts between littoral States and other international actors such as other States, communities and indigenous peoples who have an interest in the area.

In principle, several approaches of governance are possible. Regulating a specific area could follow a strict multilateral approach or a unilateral one, relying on coordinated but sovereign action. Another option, often chosen for fisheries, is the establishment of a governance regime. Further, with specific regard to Arctic fisheries, in order to prevent devastating impacts on the Arctic ecosystem caused by excessive or illegal, unregulated and unreported (IUU) fishing, several options are conceivable. These range from a fishing ban to a long-term oriented cooperative strategy. However, the introduction of a regulation usually also entails the restriction of a freedom, in this case the freedom of the high seas. Since the Arctic is one of the last largely untouched marine areas and the CAOF Agreement regulates future fisheries in this area, it could herald the end of the freedom of the high seas. In addition, new activities causing changes in the CAO environment will most likely affect weather and climate worldwide. Therefore, actions need to be taken with utmost care and extreme caution. Here, a proactive approach is considered helpful and appropriate.

The 2018 Agreement to Prevent Unregulated High Seas Fisheries in the Central Arctic Ocean (CAOF Agreement; the Agreement) as such an approach

---

of World Fisheries and Aquaculture 2016: Contributing to Food Security and Nutrition for All' 5 et seq. <https://www.fao.org/3/i5555e/i5555e.pdf> accessed 5 December 2021.

4 Bradley Turner, 'Iceland Offers a Model for Arctic Fisheries Management' *The New Humanitarian–Arctic Deeply* (9 December 2016) <https://deeply.thenewhumanitarian.org/arctic/articles/2016/12/09/iceland-offers-a-model-for-arctic-fisheries-management> accessed 20 October 2020.

5 See Samuel SP Rastrick and others, 'Using Natural Analogues to Investigate the Effects of Climate Change and Ocean Acidification on Northern Ecosystems' (2018) 75 ICES Journal of Marine Science 2299, 2306 <https://academic.oup.com/icesjms/article/75/7/2299/5133274> accessed 10 December 2020.

of governance was created just in time. Currently, new projects such as the exploration of fishing grounds are envisaged but not yet thoroughly planned or the circumstances are not (yet) suitable. They depend on the results of research that still needs to be conducted and on the possibility of carrying out new activities, possibly after adapting to the unknown extreme conditions of the Arctic. This is where the CAOF Agreement comes into play: it regulates fishing and requires prior research before any potentially harmful action can be taken, making it a unique fisheries regime as it came into force before actual fishing is carried out. With this approach, it might develop a new international standard for Regional Fishery Bodies (RFBS), the primary tools of fisheries management,[6] and may serve as a model for the modernization of existing agreements or for future engagements.[7]

This study provides a critical analysis of the CAOF Agreement. The Agreement is considered in the context of economic development, sociological realities, environmental conditions and climate change. Of particular relevance is how modern fisheries management deals with climate change in hitherto sparsely regulated areas. In order to get an overview of the environment in which the agreement came into being, the characteristics and situation of the Arctic region are first presented (Chapter 2). These include the Arctic climate and environment and the fish living in it. In this regard, it is important to understand the far-reaching and diverse changes that climate change is causing in the Arctic, which is often not given sufficient attention in the legal context. Further, the process of the Agreement's development is described, starting with the initial motives of its creation. For a better understanding of the individual motivation of the various stakeholders, an overview of their political interest in the Arctic Ocean is provided (Chapter 3). Subsequently, the existing regime of fisheries law and governance in the Arctic, including the resulting level of environmental protection, is presented and assessed. Additional cooperative mechanisms and various governance options are proposed (Chapter 4). This correlates with a broader analysis of general standards and principles in fisheries management, and the extent to which the Agreement implements them to achieve effective management under international law (Chapter 5). Specific

6 See specifically on the classification of RFBS Chapter 4 Section 3, 3.2 *infra*.

7 Although geographical coverage of RFBS is getting close to being comprehensive, general RFBS can be (additionally) established in areas where species-specific RFBS are managing fisheries, and the other way around. Further, the approach developed by the CAOF Agreement can be useful for other pristine areas like the deep seabed.

interim conservation and management measures that can be taken under the CAOF Agreement are then presented (Chapter 6). The work concludes with a presentation of current developments (Chapter 7) and a summary of considerations and possible implications of the Agreement for international law (Chapter 8).

CHAPTER 2

The Area: Characteristics and Challenges

The Central Arctic Ocean is an integral part of a larger social-ecological system, commonly referred to by the term "Arctic". This northernmost region of the northern hemisphere is a unique, most fragile and not yet fully explored ecosystem, featuring specific climatic conditions that cannot be found anywhere else in the world. Therefore, first, a brief look at the region as a whole is taken (Chapter 2 Section 1), before narrowing the perspective to its geographical centrepiece, the Arctic Ocean (Chapter 2 Section 2). The analysis then turns to the territorial scope of the CAOF Agreement, which encompasses only the central maritime parts of the Arctic (Chapter 2 Section 3). This introductory chapter concludes by addressing the two key issues of climate and fisheries central to the following analysis, both with specific reference to the region at stake (Chapter 2 Section 4).

1 Definition of the Arctic

The word Arctic stems from the Greek ἀρκτικός (arktikos), meaning "near the bear" or "northern".[1] Analogies with Antarctica (meaning "opposite to the Arctic", "opposite to the north")[2] have to be drawn with utmost care: from a geological point of view, the two are fundamentally different, as the Arctic is essentially an ice-covered sea surrounded by landmasses, whereas Antarctica consists of a nearly fully glaciated bedrock.[3] Therefore, whereas similarities exist in terms of climatic conditions and the (crucial) function of both polar regions for climate worldwide, the legal regimes governing both areas have virtually nothing in common: the central part of the Arctic is governed by the

1 'Henry George Liddell, Robert Scott: A Greek-English Lexicon | Ἀρκτικός' <http://www.perseus.tufts.edu/hopper/text?doc=Perseus%3Atext%3A1999.04.0057%3Aentry%3D%23l5193&redirect=true> accessed 2 September 2021.

2 Bernadette Hince, *The Antarctic Dictionary: A Complete Guide to Antarctic English* (CSIRO Publishing 2000) 6 <https://books.google.de/books?id=upcoFJXWT38C&hl=de> accessed 2 September 2020.

3 S McLoughlin, 'The Breakup History of Gondwana and Its Impact on Pre-Cenozoic Floristic Provincialism' (2001) 49 Australian Journal of Botany 271, 272 et seq. <https://www.publish.csiro.au/bt/bt00023> accessed 8 April 2022.

 | DOI:10.1163/9789004700673_003

International Law of the Sea, whereas the area adjacent to the South Pole is subject to a specific Antarctic Treaty System.[4]

Uncertainty prevails when it comes to defining the Arctic.[5] Several definitions exist that focus on different characteristics related to astronomy or geography,[6] temperature, vegetation,[7] the extent of ice or political boundaries.

Especially politically there is no universally accepted definition of the Arctic, which reflects the fragmented governance of the area[8] and ongoing disagreement about sovereignty in the Arctic. Nevertheless, fortunately, the disputed borders of the Arctic do not necessarily impair resource management, as, *inter alia,* the joint Norwegian-Russian management[9] of the Barents Sea illustrates.[10]

The Arctic can also be characterised by focusing on its marine area. The Arctic marine boundary lies along the convergence of cool, less saline surface waters from the Arctic Ocean and warmer, more saline waters from southern

---

4 See 'Antarctic Treaty (Washington, 1 December 1959) – UNTS Vol. 402, No. 5778' <https://treaties.un.org/doc/Publication/UNTS/Volume402/volume-402-I-5778-English.pdf> accessed 4 April 2022.

5 See a compilation of definitions at Kjetil S Grønnestad, 'What Is the Arctic?' *BarentsWatch* (21 January 2016) <https://www.barentswatch.no/en/articles/Hva-er-Arktis/> accessed 5 December 2021.

6 Geographically, the Arctic is defined as the region above the Arctic Circle at approximately 66°34'N; see Conservation of Arctic Flora and Fauna (CAFF) Working Group, 'Arctic Flora and Fauna: Status and Conservation' (2001) 21 <https://oaarchive.arctic-council.org/bitstream/handle/11374/169/Arctic_Flora_Fauna_Status_Trends_2001%281%29.pdf?sequence=1&isAllowed=y> accessed 4 April 2022.

7 Depending on climate and vegetation, the Arctic can be divided into three zones, the High Arctic, the Low Arctic and the Sub-Arctic, see EP Hoberg and others, 'Arctic Biodiversity: From Discovery to Faunal Baselines – Revealing the History of a Dynamic Ecosystem' (2003) 89 Journal of Parasitology 84 <https://www.researchgate.net/publication/285855224_Arctic_biodiversity_From_discovery_to_faunal_baselines_-_Revealing_the_history_of_a_dynamic_ecosystem> accessed 1 March 2022. Grønnestad (Chapter 2, n 5). cf. 'National Snow and Ice Data Center | What Is the Arctic?' <https://nsidc.org/cryosphere/arctic-meteorology/arctic.html> accessed 5 December 2021.

8 See e.g. a defintion of the Arctic Council's working group AMAP at Arctic Monitoring and Assessment Programme (AMAP), 'AMAP Assessment Report: Arctic Pollution Issues' (1998) 9 et seq. <https://www.amap.no/documents/doc/amap-assessment-report-arctic-pollution-issues/68> accessed 10 August 2021.

9 See e.g. the Joint Russian-Norwegian Fisheries Commission (JointFish), Chapter 6, Section 1, 1.2, 1.2.1 *infra*.

10 Richard A Barnes, 'International Regulation of Fisheries Management in Arctic Waters' (2011) 54 German Yearbook of International Law 193, 197 < https://papers.ssrn.com/sol3/papers.cfm?abstract_id=3676485 > accessed 2 November 2024.

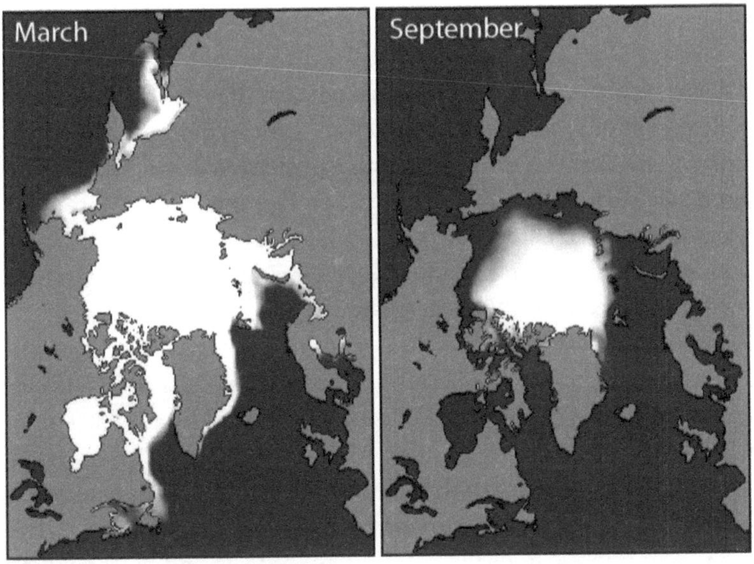

FIGURE 1 Maximum extension of ice in the Arctic in March and September 2016
SOURCE: GRØNNESTAD (CHAPTER 2, N 5)

oceans,[11] which usually also corresponds to the boundary of ice-covered to ice-free areas.[12]

Put simply, the marine Arctic is the sea area that was covered with ice during the maximum extent of ice cover in May. This definition is dynamic and subject to constant change as the area's ice coverage varies from year to year, with a tendency to shrink due to global warming.[13] The marine definition is not to be confused with the definition of the Arctic Ocean,[14] which usually excludes adjoining seas like the Barents Sea or Beaufort Sea.

11 Arctic Monitoring and Assessment Programme (AMAP) (Chapter 2, n 8) 10.
12 Grønnestad (Chapter 2, n 5).
13 Courtenay Strong and others, 'On the Definition of Marginal Ice Zone Width' (2017) 34 Journal of Atmospheric and Oceanic Technology 1565, 1565 <www.ametsoc.org/PUBSReuseLicenses> accessed 1 March 2021. X Liu, H Chen and T Feng, 'Multi-Scale Change Analysis Of Sea Ice Extent In Arctic' (2018) XLII–3 The International Archives of the Photogrammetry, Remote Sensing and Spatial Information Sciences 1153, 1153 et seq <https://doi.org/10.5194/isprs-archives-XLII-3-1153-2018> accessed 5 December 2021.
14 For a definition of the Arctic Ocean, see Chapter 2 Section 2 *infra*.

2 Definition of the Arctic Ocean

The Arctic Ocean can be considered the centrepiece of the Arctic. While there is no formal legal definition of the Arctic Ocean, various definitions exist in relevant international instruments. For instance, the Food and Agriculture Organization of the United Nations (FAO), when defining Arctic waters for Fishing Area 18 in the FAO system for defining Major Fishing Areas, excludes waters such as the Labrador Sea and Baffin Bay, but includes Hudson Bay, which is part of the seasonal ice zone.[15] The definition of the Arctic Monitoring and Assessment Programme (AMAP) extends to the Faroe Islands and Southern Greenlandic waters.[16] Although the exact size of the Arctic Ocean depends on the respective definition, the Arctic Ocean is considered the smallest ocean in the world with an area of just over 14 million km^2 (5,5 million mi^2).[17]

The CAOF Agreement itself refers to the Arctic Ocean multiple times without offering a definition. Rather, the Agreement regards the marine area in the context of a broader approach, respecting that ecosystems and marine living resources do not adjust to formal delimitations.[18] As it nevertheless differentiates between the Arctic Ocean, central Arctic Ocean and the high seas portion of the central Arctic Ocean,[19] two implications can be made: the central Arctic Ocean consists of a high seas portion and adjacent maritime zones of coastal States, and the Arctic Ocean consists of the central Arctic Ocean and adjacent waters.[20]

The central Arctic Ocean, the CAO, is defined purely in legal terms, without reference to natural criteria such as ice coverage. It is considered to be the high seas beyond 200 nautical miles (NM) from the baseline of the coastal

---

15 'FAO | FAO Major Fishing Areas: Arctic Sea (Major Fishing Area 18)' <http://www.fao.org/fishery/area/Area18/en> accessed 5 December 2021.

16 Barnes (Chapter 2, n 10) 197.

17 North Pacific Fishery Management Council, 'Fishery Management Plan for Fish Resources of the Arctic Management Area' (2009) 48 <https://www.npfmc.org/wp-content/PDFdocuments/fmp/Arctic/ArcticFMP.pdf> accessed 5 December 2021.

18 See especially differentiations made in the Preamble and Articles 1(a), 14(2) CAOF Agreement.

19 The Agreement Area comprises only a single high seas portion of the central Arctic Ocean, see Article 1(a) CAOF Agreement. For details on the Agreement Area, see Chapter 2 Section 3 *infra*.

20 See Erik J Molenaar, 'The CAOF Agreement: Key Issues of International Fisheries Law' in Tomas Heidar (ed), *New Knowledge and Changing Circumstances in the Law of the Sea* (Brill | Nijhoff 2020) 449; Erik J Molenaar, 'International Regulation of Central Arctic Ocean Fisheries' in Myron H Nordquist, John Norton Moore and Ronán Long (eds), *Challenges of the Changing Arctic: Continental Shelf, Navigation, and Fisheries* (Brill | Nijhoff 2016) 431.

States.[21] Article 86 of the United Nations Convention on the Law of the Sea (UNCLOS) defines the high seas as "all parts of the sea that are not included in the exclusive economic zone, in the territorial sea or in the internal waters of a State, or in the archipelagic waters of an archipelagic State". During the drafting process of the CAOF Agreement, participants agreed that only five States border the central Arctic Ocean and are therefore central Arctic Ocean coastal States: Canada, the Kingdom of Denmark (by virtue of Greenland), the Kingdom of Norway, the Russian Federation and the United States (by virtue of Alaska)[22] – although Iceland still claims to be at least a coastal State of the Arctic Ocean, if not of the central Arctic Ocean.[23] In line with Article 57 UNCLOS, all CAO coastal States have established Exclusive Economic Zones (EEZs)[24] that extend 200 NM north of the baselines from which the breadth of their territorial sea is measured.[25] The waters in between, the waters of the CAO, share borders with several marginal seas, namely the Barents Sea, Kara Sea, Laptev Sea, Chukchi Sea, Beaufort Sea, Wandel Sea (McKinley Sea) and Lincoln Sea.[26] The CAO has an average depth of 1.205 m (3.363 ft) with its

21 Njord Wegge, 'The Emerging Politics of the Arctic Ocean: Future Management of the Living Marine Resources' (2015) 51 Marine Policy 331, 332.

22 See references to coastal States in the Preamble of the CAOF Agreement to the Declaration Concerning the Prevention of Unregulated High Seas Fishing in the Central Arctic Ocean issued by these five States; 'Declaration Concerning the Prevention of Unregulated High Seas Fishing in the Central Arctic Ocean (Oslo, 16 July 2015)' <https://www.regjeringen.no/globalassets/departementene/ud/vedlegg/folkerett/declaration-on-arctic-fisheries-16-july-2015.pdf> accessed 10 August 2021.

23 Erik Jaap Molenaar, 'Participation in the Central Arctic Ocean Fisheries Agreement' in Akiho Shibata and others (eds), *Emerging Legal Orders in the Arctic-The Role of Non-Arctic Actors* (Routledge 2019) 137.

24 Concerning Spitsbergen (Norwegian: "Svalbard"), Norway has established a 200 NM Fisheries Protection Zone. On the issue of Svalbard's maritime zones, see Chapter 2 Section 3 *infra*.

25 'United Nations | Maritime Space: Maritime Zones and Maritime Delimitation – Canada' <https://www.un.org/Depts/los/LEGISLATIONANDTREATIES/STATEFILES/CAN.htm> accessed 2 March 2021; 'United Nations | Maritime Space: Maritime Zones and Maritime Delimitation – Denmark' <https://www.un.org/Depts/los/LEGISLATIONANDTREATIES/STATEFILES/DNK.htm> accessed 2 March 2021; 'United Nations | Maritime Space: Maritime Zones and Maritime Delimitation – Norway' <https://www.un.org/Depts/los/LEGISLATIONANDTREATIES/STATEFILES/NOR.htm> accessed 2 March 2021; 'United Nations | Maritime Space: Maritime Zones and Maritime Delimitation – Russian Federation' <https://www.un.org/Depts/los/LEGISLATIONANDTREATIES/STATEFILES/RUS.htm> accessed 2 March 2021; 'United Nations | Maritime Space: Maritime Zones and Maritime Delimitation – United States' <https://www.un.org/Depts/los/LEGISLATIONANDTREATIES/STATEFILES/USA.htm> accessed 2 March 2021.

26 See Figure 2 *infra*. The Wandel Sea and the Lincoln Sea are located north of Greenland and are not specifically indicated in Figure 2.

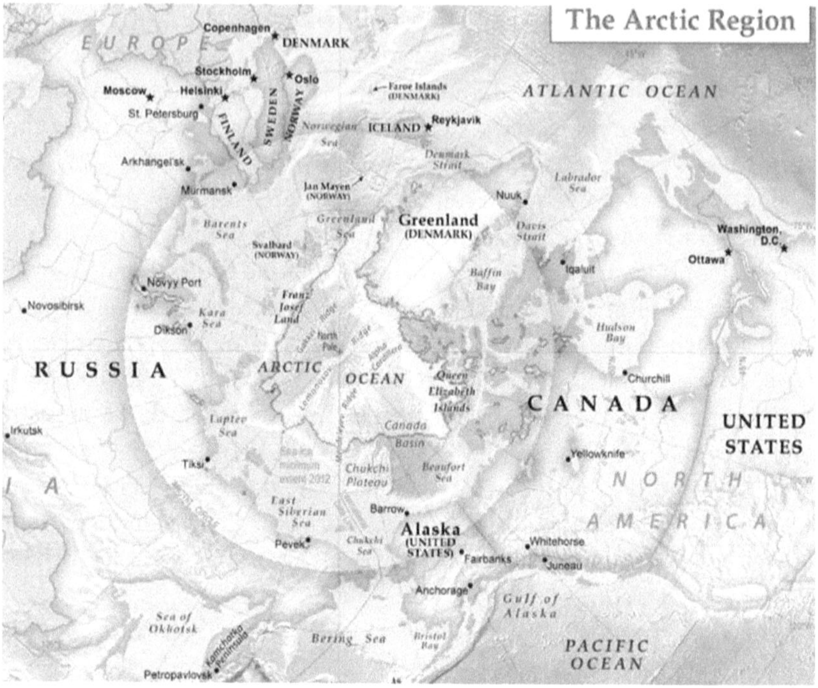

FIGURE 2 Arctic Ocean and bordering countries, Arctic Circle, and minimal extent of summer sea ice cover
SOURCE: 'VISI47TNORDIC | ARCTIC CIRCLE MAP' <HTTPS://WWW.VISITNORDIC.COM/EN/ARTICLE/ARCTIC-CIRCLE-MAP> ACCESSED 4 MAY 2024

deepest point being the Fram Basin at 4.665 m (15.305,12 ft).[27] Concerning fisheries, the CAO hence partly provides for a fishable depth, which usually ranges up to 1.500m to 2.200m (4.921 ft to 7.218 ft).[28]

The geographic North Pole is located slightly offset in the middle of the Arctic Ocean. Since almost all year round, the central part of the Arctic Ocean is covered by floating polar ice with an average thickness of three metres, the North Pole is situated in frozen waters.[29] In terms of sovereignty, it should be

27 Amanda Briney, 'Arctic Ocean or Arctic Seas' *ThoughtCo.* (6 November 2019) <https://www.thoughtco.com/arctic-seas-overview-1435183> accessed 10 August 2021.

28 'Marine Conservation Institute | Marine Protection by Country: High Seas' <http://www.mpatlas.org/map/high-seas/> accessed 23 July 2020.

29 Briney (Chapter 2, n 27).

noted that the central part of the Arctic "belongs to humanity; its challenges are the responsibility of all nations".[30]

Besides other smaller ridges, the deep seabed of the Arctic Ocean is characterised by a submarine ridge, the Lomonosov Ridge, which separates the 4.000–4.500 m (13.124–14.764 ft) deep Eurasian (or Nansen) Basin and the 4.000 m (13.124 ft) deep North American (or Hyperborean) Basin.[31] As in any other ocean, there is a continuous exchange of water in the (central) Arctic Ocean. 90 % of water inflow comes from the Atlantic Ocean via the Norwegian Current,[32] and the largest outflow of cold Arctic water comes from the East Greenland Current.[33] This heat transfer has profound effects on the marine environment and living marine resources: colonisation of new regions by immigrant species is more likely on the Atlantic side of the Arctic Ocean than on the Pacific side.[34]

3 Agreement Area

The CAOF Agreement defines its agreement area (Agreement Area) as

> the single high seas portion of the central Arctic Ocean that is surrounded by waters within which Canada, the Kingdom of Denmark in respect of Greenland, the Kingdom of Norway, the Russian Federation and the United States of America exercise fisheries jurisdiction.[35]

---

30 Michael Byers, 'Rules for the North Pole' *The New York Times* (18 August 2011) <https://www.nytimes.com/2011/08/19/opinion/19iht-edbyers19.html> accessed 10 January 2020.

31 'MarineBio Conservation Society | Ocean Geography' <http://marinebio.org/oceans/geography/> accessed 5 December 2021.

32 Norwegian name of Spitsbergen; used since the Spitsbergen Treaty became effective in 1925, see 'Besitzergreifung von Spitzbergen (Svalbard) Durch Norwegen' (1925) 31 Geographische Zeitschrift 300, 300 <https://www.jstor.org/stable/27811470?seq=4#metadata_info_tab_contents> accessed 10 August 2021.

33 Sarah Gibbens, 'The Arctic Ocean, Explained' *National Geographic* (29 March 2019) <https://www.nationalgeographic.com/environment/oceans/reference/arctic-ocean/> accessed 5 December 2021; Grønnestad (Chapter 2, n 5).

34 Tore Haug and others, 'Future Harvest of Living Resources in the Arctic Ocean North of the Nordic and Barents Seas: A Review of Possibilities and Constraints' (2017) 188 Fisheries Research 38, 39 <https://linkinghub.elsevier.com/retrieve/pii/S0165783616304131> accessed 5 December 2021.

35 See Article 1(a) CAOF Agreement.

It therefore comprises only a part of the central area of the Arctic Ocean and only areas beyond national jurisdiction. As mentioned above, under Article 57 UNCLOS and as recognised[36] by customary international law,[37] all the States mentioned above have established EEZs up to 200 NM from their baselines in which they may exercise fisheries jurisdiction[38] or respectively an equally measured Fisheries Protection Zone (FPZ).[39]

The definition of the Agreement Area chosen for the CAOF Agreement can be considered a political compromise, as it does not answer any territorial controversies. In particular, disagreement exists over the use of Svalbard's FPZ. Although Norway holds undisputed sovereignty over Svalbard, questions and tensions arise over Svalbard's maritime zones, as the geographical scope of the 1920 Spitsbergen Treaty[40] itself is difficult to clarify.[41] The Spitsbergen Treaty, later referred to as the Svalbard Treaty, was created when maritime zones around the world were not as well defined as they are now under UNCLOS. It is therefore unclear whether the Spitsbergen Treaty applies in Svalbard's territorial sea, internal waters, FPZ and on Svalbard's continental shelf. An overlap of UNCLOS and the Spitsbergen Treaty raises several issues: *inter alia*, the question arises whether Norway may regulate fisheries within the territorial waters and the FPZ around Svalbard, or whether Svalbard creates its own maritime zones that may be equally accessed by the parties to the Spitsbergen Treaty. Essentially three different views on these issues exist: the FPZ is either open only to Norwegian fishing vessels, or is open to everyone, rendering the FPZ basically non-existent, or the FPZ is completely legal and every State party has

36 See *Case Concerning the Continental Shelf (Libyan Arab Jamahiriya v Malta), Judgment of 3 June 1985, ICJ Reports 1985, p 13* [34].

37 It is important to emphasise the customary status of the Article, as the US, party to the CAOF Agreement, is not a party to UNCLOS and therefore its Articles are not per se binding on the country.

38 See Article 56 (1)(a) and (b) UNCLOS.

39 Norwegian Ministry of Foreign Affairs, 'Decree No. 6 of 1977 Relative to the Fishery Protection Zone of Svalbard' <http://extwprlegs1.fao.org/docs/html/nor12764.htm> accessed 2 March 2021.

40 'Treaty Relating to Spitsbergen (Svalbard) (9 February 1920)' <https://www.spitzbergen.de/wp-content/uploads/2020/01/Spitsbergen-treaty_English.pdf> accessed 2 March 2021.

41 For an overview of the problem, see also Valentin Schatz, Alexander Proelß and Nengye Liu, 'The 2018 Agreement to Prevent Unregulated High Seas Fisheries in the Central Arctic Ocean: A Critical Analysis' (2019) 34 International Journal of Marine and Coastal Law 195; for a display of the vayring positions, see EJ Molenaar, 'Fisheries Regulation in the Maritime Zones of Svalbard' (2012) 27 International Journal of Marine and Coastal Law 3, 10 et seq.; see also Andreas Østhagen, 'Managing Conflict at Sea: The Case of Norway and Russia in the Svalbard Zone' (2018) 9 Arctic Review on Law and Politics 100.

the same possibility to fish within 200 NM of Svalbard.[42] Against this background, it is not surprising that the definition of the CAOF Agreement Area was considered problematic and discussed until one of the last meetings.[43] The definition ultimately chosen for the Agreement Area wisely avoids deciding on existing discrepancies. It does not refer to the maritime waters of States, but to the zones in which States exercise fisheries jurisdiction, which thus includes the waters around Svalbard.

The resulting Agreement Area beyond these 200 NM limits, within the blue lines in Figure 3 above, measures approximately 2,8 million km^2 (1,08 million mi^2), which is roughly the size of the Mediterranean Sea.[44] It overlaps slightly with the North East Atlantic Fisheries Commission (NEAFC) convention area, which is marked within the dashed red lines above. The overlap is substantial, as the NEAFC also deals with the regulation of fisheries. In order to avoid possible conflicts in this regard, the CAOF Agreement emphasises

> the importance of ensuring cooperation and coordination between the Parties and the North-East Atlantic Fisheries Commission, which has competence to adopt conservation and management measures in part of the high seas portion of the central Arctic Ocean.[45]

The five Arctic coastal States noticed that problems could arise from the overlapping of the treaty areas and noted this in their 2015 Declaration Concerning the Prevention of Unregulated High Seas Fishing in the Central Arctic Ocean (Oslo Declaration),[46] a draft document for the CAOF Agreement.[47] They stated that possible interim measures that may be taken under the Oslo Declaration "will neither undermine nor conflict with the role and mandate of any existing international mechanism relating to fisheries, including the North East Atlantic

42 Andrew Yerkes, 'Whose Fish? Looking at Svalbard's Fisheries Protection Zone' *The Polar Connection* (4 December 2016) <https://polarconnection.org/svalbard-fisheries-protection-zone/> accessed 2 March 2021.

43 'Chairman's Statement, Fifth Meeting on Central Arctic Ocean Fisheries (Reykjavik, 15–18 March 2017)' 2 <https://2017-2021.state.gov/remarks-and-releases-bureau-of-oceans-and-international-environmental-and-scientific-affairs/meeting-on-high-seas-fisheries-in-the-central-arctic-ocean-5/#fn1> accessed 2 November 2024.

44 'Chairman's Statement, Sixth Meeting on Central Arctic Ocean Fisheries (Washington D.C., 28–30 November 2017)' <https://oceanconservancy.org/wp-content/uploads/2017/11/Chairmans-Statement-from-Washington-Meeting-2017.pdf> accessed 10 August 2021.

45 See Preamble CAOF Agreement.

46 'Declaration Concerning the Prevention of Unregulated High Seas Fishing in the Central Arctic Ocean (Oslo, 16 July 2015)' (Chapter 2, n 22).

47 On the drafting process of the Agreement, see Chapter 3 Section 2 *infra*.

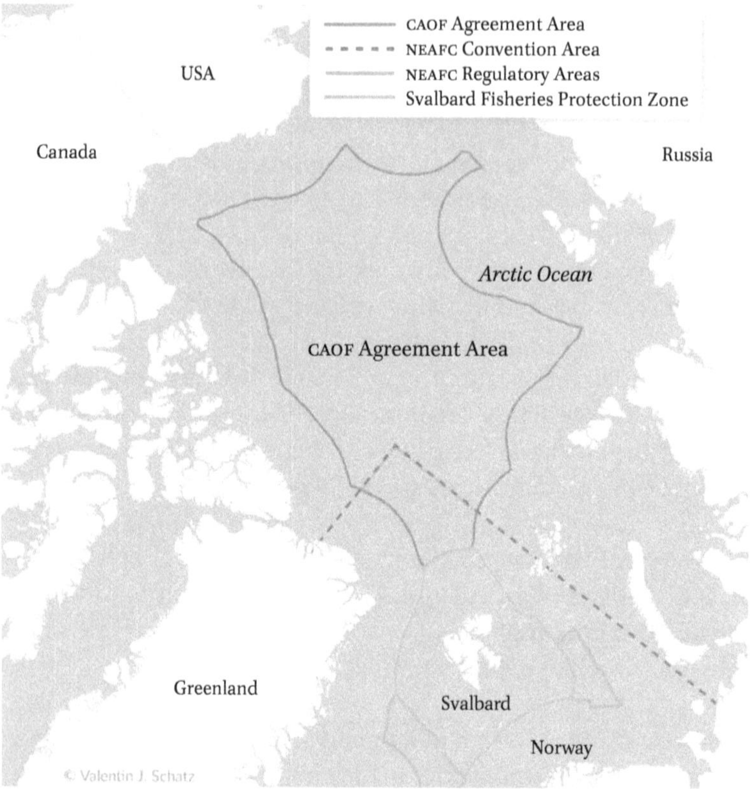

FIGURE 3 CAOF Agreement Area, North-East Atlantic Fisheries Commission (NEAFC) Convention Area, NEAFC Regulatory Area and Svalbard Fisheries Protection Zone
SOURCE: SCHATZ, PROELß AND LIU (CHAPTER 1 N 41) 200

Fisheries Commission."[48] Similarly, although the direct reference to the NEAFC was deleted in the drafting process, the final Article 14(4) CAOF Agreement states that the Agreement "shall neither undermine nor conflict with the role and mandate of any existing international mechanism relating to fisheries management". All NEAFC contracting members[49] are also parties to the CAOF Agreement and participated in the Agreements negotiations. Therefore, a

48 'Declaration Concerning the Prevention of Unregulated High Seas Fishing in the Central Arctic Ocean (Oslo, 16 July 2015)' (Chapter 2, n 22).

49 Contracting members are Denmark in respect of the Faroe Islands & Greenland, the EU, Iceland, Norway, the Russian Federation and the United Kingdom, see 'NEAFC | Becoming a Contracting Party' <https://www.neafc.org/becomingacp> accessed 10 August 2021.

serious conflict between the two regimes seems unlikely.[50] However, the overlap of areas jeopardises the consistency of decisions and measures in the area either developed by NEAFC or adopted under the CAOF Agreement. This problem can be avoided by the parties to the CAOF Agreement (Parties) adopting no or very few future conservation and management measures in the overlap area.[51]

The CAOF Agreement makes further reference to additional regimes by emphasising the importance of ensuring cooperation and coordination between the Parties and

> other relevant mechanisms for fisheries management that are established and operated in accordance with international law, as well as with relevant international bodies and programs.[52]

It is striking that the preambular paragraph refers to the NEAFC having "competence to adopt conservation and management measures in part of the high seas portion of the central Arctic Ocean", while the reference to "other relevant mechanisms for fisheries management" is inserted without reference to competence in this area. Furthermore, rather than making reference to Regional Fisheries Management Arrangements (RFMAs) or Regional Fisheries Management Organizations (RFMOs),[53] also referred to as RFBs as the primary instruments of fisheries management, reference is made to "mechanisms". Looking at the drafting process of the Agreement, the meaning of these different references becomes clear: the wording chosen includes, *inter alia*,[54] the Joint Norwegian-Russian Fisheries Commission (JointFish), on which the Parties disagreed as to whether it constitutes an RFMA/O.[55] Moreover, although JointFish mostly focuses on the Barents Sea and the Norwegian Sea, it lacks an explicit geographic mandate in its founding instrument but claims

50 See Schatz, Proelß and Liu (Chapter 2, n 41) 215; Tomas Heidar, 'The Legal Framework for High Seas Fisheries in the Central Arctic Ocean' in Myron H Nordquist, John Norton Moore and Ronán Long (eds), *International Marine Economy: Law and Policy*, vol 20 (Brill | Nijhoff 2017) 197.

51 Molenaar, 'The CAOF Agreement: Key Issues of International Fisheries Law' (Chapter 2, n 20) 457.

52 See Preamble CAOF Agreement.

53 On the distinction of RFMAs and RFMOs, see Chapter 4 Sections, 3, 3.2 *infra*.

54 For other regimes that could possibly adopt conservation and management measures in the CAO, see Chapter 6 Sections 1, 1.2 *infra*.

55 Cf. Molenaar, 'International Regulation of Central Arctic Ocean Fisheries' (Chapter 2, n 20) 442, 445.

that its regulatory area covers the entire Arctic Ocean and therefore technically overlaps with the CAOF Agreement Area.[56] Thus, the wording chosen ensures that a determination on both the status of JointFish and its regulatory area is avoided. Further, it makes clear that fisheries under the auspices of JointFish in the CAO are not an exception to the qualified abstention of commercial fisheries to be established by the CAOF Agreement.[57] The fact that the only two parties to JointFish, Russia and Norway, are also parties to the CAOF Agreement, already indicates that they support a multilateral rather than a bilateral approach to fisheries management in the CAO. It is therefore unlikely that the two States will authorise commercial fisheries in CAO waters exclusively under the leadership of JointFish.[58]

According to Article 13(1) CAOF Agreement, the duration of the CAOF Agreement is limited, and so is the definition of the Agreement Area. The initial period of the Agreement's validity is set out for 16 years after its entry into force, which occurred in June 2021.[59] Hence, its first re-negotiation will optionally take place in 2037. Since most researchers and institutions predict[60] – even if the predictions vary by a few years – that the Arctic will be almost ice-free at least in summer by the middle of the 21st century,[61] it is very likely that the water in the Arctic has warmed drastically by the time the CAOF Agreement

56 ibid 438–441, 452–454.

57 See Molenaar, 'The CAOF Agreement: Key Issues of International Fisheries Law' (Chapter 2, n 20) 458–459.

58 See also Erik J Molenaar, 'The Oslo Declaration on High Seas Fishing in the Central Arctic Ocean' (2015) 2015 Arctic Yearbook 427, 428.

59 'European Union | Arctic: Agreement to Prevent Unregulated Fishing Enters into Force (25 June 2021)' <https://ec.europa.eu/oceans-and-fisheries/news/arctic-agreement-prevent-unregulated-fishing-enters-force-2021-06-25_en> accessed 25 March 2022; David A Balton, 'No. 9 | The Arctic Fisheries Agreement Enters into Force' *Polar Points* (25 June 2021)<https://www.wilsoncenter.org/blog-post/no-9-arctic-fisheries-agreement-enters-force> accessed 30 June 2021.

60 On Arctic warming and melting ice, see also in detail Chapter 2 Sections 4, 4.1, 4.1.2 and Chapter 2 Sections 4, 4.1, 4.1.3 *infra*.

61 'NASA Earth Observatory | World of Change: Arctic Sea Ice' <https://earthobservatory.nasa.gov/world-of-change/sea_ice.php> accessed 9 July 2021; Andy Isaacson, 'Extreme Research Shows How Arctic Ice Is Dwindling' *National Geographic* (1 January 2016)<https://www.nationalgeographic.com/magazine/2016/01/arctic-ice-environment/> accessed 5 December 2021; European Commission, 'Joint Communication – Developing a European Union Policy towards the Arctic Region: Progress since 2008 and next Steps (2012) – JOIN(2012) 19 Final' <https://op.europa.eu/de/publication-detail/-/publication/70245d63-201c-47e8-9091-d5c07b96d964> accessed 5 December 2021; Muyin Wang and James E Overland, 'A Sea Ice Free Summer Arctic within 30 Years?' (2009) 36 Geophysical Research Letters 1, 1.

might be renegotiated, and the distribution of fish shoals in the fisheries jurisdiction zones of the participating States and in the Agreement Area itself will have changed considerably. These changes could lead to the need to revise the Agreement Area. During the negotiation process of the Agreement,[62] the focus has permanently shifted from general fisheries in the Arctic Ocean to exclusive fisheries in only its central part.[63] Yet, the current definition of the Agreement Area does not take into account that marine species are not confined to boundaries. Rather, they move within an ecosystem and therefore need to be managed "in their entirety", pursuant to Article 7(2) of the Agreement for the Implementation of the Provisions of the United Nations Convention on the Law of the Sea of 10 December 1982 relating to the Conservation and Management of Straddling Fish Stocks and Highly Migratory Fish Stocks (UNFS Agreement).[64] Compatibility between the measures adopted in the maritime zones of coastal States and those adopted for the conservation and management of fisheries on the high seas that might affect the same fish stock present in both zones should therefore be ensured. The States concerned are required, in accordance with the duty to cooperate,[65] to develop measures that do not prejudice each other.[66] In addition, States should take into account the interdependence of stocks and the impact on species associated with or dependent on targeted species.[67] The implementation of such a comprehensive

62 For the drafting history of the CAOF Agreement, see Chapter 3 Section 2 *infra*.

63 Molenaar, 'International Regulation of Central Arctic Ocean Fisheries' (Chapter 2, n 20) 450.

64 Cf. Alex G Oude Elferink, 'The Impact of Article 7(2) of the Fish Stocks Agreement on the Formulation of Conservation and Management Measures for Straddling and Highly Migratory Fish Stocks' (1999) 4 FAO Legal Papers Online 1, 5 <https://www.fao.org/documents/card/fr/c/04b8e10e-bd4f-4072-9057-daae852e4c8f/> accessed 3 September 2020; United Nations General Assembly, 'United Nations Conference on Straddling Fish Stocks and Highly Migratory Fish Stocks, Second Session (New York, 12–30 July 1993), Chairman Statement Held on 12 July 1993 – A/CONF.164/11' 3 <https://documents-dds-ny.un.org/doc/UNDOC/GEN/N93/403/51/pdf/N9340351.pdf?OpenElement> accessed 3 September 2021.

65 See more on the duty to cooperate in the context of fisheries management at Chapter 3, 1, 1.2, 1.2.2 and Chapter 5 Section 2, 2.2 *infra*.

66 See Article 7(1) and (2) of the Agreement for the Implementation of the Provisions of the United Nations Convention on the Law of the Sea of 10 December 1982 relating to the Conservation and Management of Straddling Fish Stocks and Highly Migratory Fish Stocks (UNFS Agreement) and reference in Article 3(6) CAOF Agreement; see 'Agreement For The Implementation Of The Provisions Of UNCLOS Relating To The Conservation And Management Of Straddling Fish Stocks And Highly Migratory Fish Stocks (New York, 4 August 1995) – UNTS Vol. 2167, No. 37924' <https://documents-dds-ny.un.org/doc/UNDOC/GEN/N95/274/67/PDF/N9527467.pdf?OpenElement> accessed 1 July 2021.

67 See Article 61(2) and (3) UNCLOS.

ecosystem approach, as applied *inter alia* by Article 5(e) UNFS Agreement that calls upon States to "adopt, where necessary, conservation and management measures for species belonging to the same ecosystem or associated with or dependent upon the target stocks", is indeed not an easy task, but not impossible. The Convention on the Conservation of Antarctic Marine Living Resources (CAMLR Convention) is a good example of establishing a spatial focus while implementing the ecosystem approach.[68] It applies to Antarctic marine living resources in the area south of 60°S and in the area between that latitude and the Antarctic Convergence that are part of the Antarctic marine ecosystem.[69] Accordingly, should the timeframe of the Agreement be extended and fisheries be able to take place in the waters of the CAO, a possible adaptation of the Agreement Area is conceivable in order to increasingly address changes that have occurred in the habitats of living resources and the ecosystems in the Arctic Ocean.

4 Climatic and Ecological Conditions and Developments

A few decades ago, conducting fisheries in the Arctic was deemed absolutely impossible. Changes due to climate change in the Arctic gradually altered this assumption. The continuous warming of the Arctic and the associated melting of ice create new possibilities. Already in 1955, Pharand had a visionary eye and anticipated a continuing warming trend that could make navigation in the Arctic a real possibility.[70] Also decades later, the polar regions and climate change are closely interrelated. In Antarctica, which consists of a bedrock covered with ice, the consequences of global warming leading to the melting of Antarctic ice would have fierce effects. However, since the Arctic consists only of sea ice and water, global warming may lead to its complete disappearance, which will have a major impact on the global climate. The vast sea and land spaces of the Arctic region are vital and vulnerable components of the earth's

68 'Convention on the Conversation of Antarctic Marine Living Resources (Canberra, 20 May 1980)' <https://www.ccamlr.org/en/organisation/camlr-convention-text>.

69 See Article 1(1) CAMLR Convention.

70 See Suzanne Lalonde, 'Donat Pharand – The Arctic Scholar' in Suzanne Lalonde and Ted L McDorman (eds), *International Law and Politics of the Arctic Ocean: Essays in Honor of Donat Pharand*, vol 44 (Brill | Nijhoff 2015) 50–51, in french; freely translated by the author: Navigation, in the true sense of the term, is not yet possible at the North Pole itself, with the exception of submarine navigation, but it is very likely that it will become possible. The general warming that we have been talking about is not only causing the surface ice to shrink but also decreases in thickness.

environment and climate system,[71] shaped by geological histories, warm and cold ocean currents and distinct weather patterns.[72] Especially the Arctic marine environment is potentially fragile. Arctic waters host a unique ecosystem that includes both the environment and living species.[73] The drastic change in temperature, the resulting loss of ice and the implementation of new fishing activities may trigger the disappearance of species that depend on the cold Arctic environment, such as fish stocks. This can lead to a continued loss of biodiversity: dwindling fish stocks, which are an integral part of the Arctic food chain, could cause its collapse. Past experience has shown that once a food chain collapses, it recovers very slowly – if at all. In fact, a collapse usually leads to the extinction of a species even though it was not primarily targeted by an action or affected by an event.[74] Such extinction must be avoided at all costs. It is always easier to protect an ecosystem in advance than to rebuild it after it has been destroyed. This underscores the importance of protective legal instruments in sensitive areas. The CAOF Agreement has recognized this scenario and therefore seeks to regulate fisheries in the Arctic before they can even take place.

In order to gain a better understanding of the existing conditions and thus to be able to better assess the effectiveness of the CAOF Agreement, the climatic and ecological situation of the Arctic and the status quo of Arctic fisheries is presented. Further, the effects of climate change on Arctic fisheries and the scope of the Agreement's subject are discussed.

4.1 *Arctic Climate*

Climate changeis a challenge for all societies in the world, and its drivers and impacts have been specifically assessed and identified for years. The Intergovernmental Panel on Climate Change (IPCC), the United Nations (UN) body responsible for the scientific assessment of climate change, found that climate change is "unequivocal"[75] and concluded that human activities are

71 'National Snow and Ice Data Center | Climate Change in the Arctic' <https://nsidc.org/cryosphere/arctic-meteorology/climate_change.html> accessed 12 August 2021.

72 Barnes (Chapter 2, n 10) 207.

73 ibid.

74 See Edoardo Calizza, M Letizia Costantini and Loreto Rossi, 'Effect of Multiple Disturbances on Food Web Vulnerability to Biodiversity Loss in Detritus-Based Systems' (2015) 6 Ecosphere 1 <http://doi.wiley.com/10.1890/ES14-00489.1> accessed 10 August 2021.

75 Intergovernmental Panel on Climate Change, 'Climate Change 2013: The Physical Science Basis – Contribution of Working Group I to the Fifth Assessment Report of the Intergovernmental Panel on Climate Change' (2013) 4 <https://www.ipcc.ch/site/assets/uploads/2018/02/WG1AR5_all_final.pdf> accessed 4 April 2022.

most likely the "dominant cause"[76] of climate change.[77] Concerning the Arctic, the Arctic Climate Impact Assessment (ACIA) reports submitted by Arctic Council working groups assume that the Arctic serves as an indicator of climate change, as impacts tend to occur earlier in this region and warming will be proportionally higher than in other parts of the world.[78] In addition, climate change in the Arctic will have impacts on the environment worldwide, e.g. as melting glaciers and thermal expansion leads to sea level rise, or thawing permafrost affects infrastructure.[79] Increasing human activities, such as the introduction of fishing, can further drive climate change and threaten the ecological and climatic balance in the region.[80]

4.1.1 General Remarks

In terms of weather and climate, the Arctic is a unique place. Both depend on many variables, including latitude, temperature and the relationship between land and water. Sunlight is one of the most important factors.[81] Furthermore,

---

76 ibid 17; IPCC Intergovernmental Panel on Climate Change, 'Climate Change 2014-Synthesis Report-Summary for Policymakers' (2014) 4 <https://www.ipcc.ch/site/assets/uploads/2018/02/AR5_SYR_FINAL_SPM.pdf> accessed 26 March 2020.

77 See Intergovernmental Panel on Climate Change, 'Climate Change 2022: Impacts, Adaptation and Vulnerability – Working Group II Contribution to the Sixth Assessment Report' (2022) 11 <https://www.ipcc.ch/report/ar6/wg2/downloads/report/IPCC_AR6_WGII_SummaryForPolicymakers.pdf> accessed 13 April 2022; similarly, see Intergovernmental Panel on Climate Change, 'Climate Change 2007: Synthesis Report – Contribution of Working Groups I, II and III to the Fourth Assessment Report' (2007) 5–6 <https://www.ipcc.ch/site/assets/uploads/2018/02/ar4_syr_full_report.pdf> accessed 26 March 2020.

78 Arctic Monitoring and Assessment Programme (AMAP), Conservation of Arctic Flora and Fauna (CAFF) Working Group and International Arctic Science Committee (IASC), 'Arctic Climate Impact Assessment' (2005) 45, 215, 220, 365, 482 <http://www.amap.no/documents/doc/arctic-arctic-climate-impact-assessment/796> accessed 10 August 2021; similiar, see E Carina H Keskitalo, Timo Koivurova and Nigel Bankes, 'Climate Governance in the Arctic: Introduction and Theoretical Framework' in Timo; Koivurova, E Carina H; Keskitalo and Nigel; Bankes (eds), *Climate Governance in the Arctic* (Springer 2009) 1.

79 Keskitalo, Koivurova and Bankes (Chapter 2, n 78) 2.

80 See Christian TKH Stadtländer, 'A Book Review on International Governance of the Arctic Marine Environment: With Particular Emphasis on High Seas Fisheries' (2014) 1 Frontiers in Marine Science 10, 2; European Union, 'Communication from the Commission to the European Parliament and the Council – The European Union and the Arctic Region (20 November 2008) – COM/2008/0763 Final' 2 <https://eur-lex.europa.eu/legal-content/EN/TXT/?uri=celex:52008DC0763> accessed 5 December 2021; 'National Snow and Ice Data Center | Climate Change in the Arctic' (Chapter 2, n 71).

81 Arctic Monitoring and Assessment Programme (AMAP), 'Arctic Pollution Issues: A State of the Arctic Environment Report' (1997) 14 <https://www.amap.no/documents/download/68/inline> accessed 10 August 2021. ibid 5; 'National Snow and Ice Data Center |

these factors interact with each other to create weather patterns and climate feedbacks. These have far-reaching effects both within the Arctic region and in other parts of the world,[82] and determine the balance of heat in the Arctic region, whereas the Arctic region acts as a heat sink for the earth.[83] Over the course of the year, warm air, water and moisture[84] flow northward from temperate regions into the Arctic, and heat partially escapes into the atmosphere.[85] As a snow–covered area, 90% of the incident solar energy is reflected back into space by snow and ice, and additionally, heat is released through the ice from the water below.[86]

The interdependence of different factors makes it difficult to reliably predict further climatic developments.[87] Although most observations project an overall warming of the globe, some scientists anticipate that a decrease in sea ice in the Arctic could lead to more intense, colder winters instead of warmer ones: Warmer temperatures in the Arctic may cause instability of the polar vortex, a circulating Arctic jet stream, and send this cold Arctic air south.[88] Therefore, changes in the Arctic, such as declines in sea ice, should be observed with extreme caution as they are likely to affect, or are already affecting,[89] climate and weather patterns in other parts of the world.[90]

Climate vs. Weather' <https://nsidc.org/cryosphere/arctic-meteorology/climate_vs_weather.html> accessed 12 August 2021.

82 'National Snow and Ice Data Center | Effects of Arctic Weather and Climate' <https://nsidc.org/cryosphere/arctic-meteorology/effects_of_climate_weather.html> accessed 5 December 2021.

83 'National Snow and Ice Data Center | Effects of Arctic Weather and Climate' (Chapter 2, n 82).

84 Arctic Monitoring and Assessment Programme (AMAP) (Chapter 2, n 8) 14.

85 'National Snow and Ice Data Center | Factors Affecting Arctic Weather and Climate' <https://nsidc.org/cryosphere/arctic-meteorology/factors_affecting_climate_weather.html> accessed 29 January 2022.

86 Arctic Monitoring and Assessment Programme (AMAP) (Chapter 2, n 8) 14.

87 'National Snow and Ice Data Center | Climate Change in the Arctic' (Chapter 2, n 71).

88 Gibbens (Chapter 2, n 33).

89 Changing atmospheric flow systems over the northern hemisphere are for example already affecting weather patterns in Europe, see Federal Foreign Office Germany, 'Germany's Arctic Policy Guidelines – Assuming Responsibility, Creating Trust, Shaping the Future' (2019) 11 <https://www.arctic-office.de/fileadmin/user_upload/www.arctic-office.de/PDF_uploads/Germany_s_Arctic_Policy_Guidelines_2019_Web.pdf> accessed 2 Novmeber 2024.

90 'National Snow and Ice Data Center | Climate Change in the Arctic' (Chapter 2, n 71).

4.1.2 Warming

The Arctic has been warming faster than any other place on the planet,[91] twice the global average,[92] and temperatures are rising steadily.[93] In June 2020, record temperatures for the area above the Arctic Circle of 100°F (38°C) were recorded in Verkhoyansk, a city in north-eastern Siberia, showing just the tip of the iceberg of months of unprecedented warmth in the region.[94]

This continuing long-term increase in Arctic air temperatures, which is indicative of climate change rather than mere variation, is a direct cause of the decline in Arctic sea ice cover. As an example, the IPCC projects that, with a global warming of 1,5°C (2,7°F), the Arctic Ocean will be ice-free in one summer every century, while with a warming of 2°C (3,6°F), the time frame is significantly reduced to one ice-free summer every decade.[95] It is therefore of utmost importance to minimize global warming, even below the 1,5–2°C (2,7–3,6°F) target envisaged in Article 2(a) Paris Agreement.[96]

4.1.3 Melting Ice

Not long ago, the Arctic was covered with ice all year round and extended to the continental shelves of most Arctic coastal States. However, it has become

91 Matthew P Humphreys, 'Climate Sensitivity and the Rate of Ocean Acidification: Future Impacts, and Implications for Experimental Design' (2017) 74 ICES Journal of Marine Science 934, 938.

92 European Union, 'Communication from the Commission to the European Parliament and the Council – The European Union and the Arctic Region (20 November 2008) – COM/2008/0763 Final' (Chapter 2, n 80) 2; Sabrina Shankman, 'Arctic Report Card 2019: Extreme Ice Loss, Dying Species as Global Warming Worsens' *Inside Climate News* (10 December 2019) <https://insideclimatenews.org/news/10122019/arctic-report-card-2019-bering-sea-ice-extent-greenland-melt-permafrost-indigenous-impact> accessed 20 January 2020.

93 'National Snow and Ice Data Center | Climate Change in the Arctic' (Chapter 2, n 71). Shankman (Chapter 2, n 92). Arctic Monitoring and Assessment Programme (AMAP), Conservation of Arctic Flora and Fauna (CAFF) Working Group and International Arctic Science Committee (IASC) (Chapter 2, n 78) 100.

94 Carolyn Gramling, '4 Ways to Put the 100-Degree Arctic Heat Record in Context' *Science News* (1 July 2020) <https://www.sciencenews.org/article/climate-new-high-temperature-heat-record-arctic-siberia-context> accessed 4 September 2020. 'National Snow and Ice Data Center | Arctic Sea Ice News & Analysis, 16 July 2020: Siberian Downward Slide' <http://nsidc.org/arcticseaicenews/> accessed 23 July 2020.

95 Intergovernmental Panel on Climate Change, 'Special Report 2018: Global Warming of 1.5°C – Summary for Policymakers' (2018) 8 <https://www.ipcc.ch/sr15/chapter/spm/> accessed 8 April 2022.

96 'Paris Agreement (Paris, 12 December 2015) – UNTS Vol. 3156, No. 54113' <https://treaties.un.org/doc/Treaties/2016/02/20160215 06-03 PM/Ch_XXVII-7-d.pdf> accessed 5 April 2022. On the Paris Agreement, see also Chapter 4 Sections 1, 1.4, 1.4.5 infra.

unlikely that the Arctic climate will ever return to such previous conditions:[97] modern projections[98] predict virtually unanimously (almost) sea ice-free summers by the middle of the 21st century.[99] In September, the month that marks the end of the summer melt season, compared to the average sea ice extent between 1981–2010, the extent of Arctic sea ice gradually decreases[100] by roughly 13,3% per decade.[101] In the last summers, 30–40% of the sea ice in the Arctic has melted into open water.[102]

The rate of decline started with the new century, although the decline in sea ice does not have to be steady. Just as global temperature rises with a few colder or warmer years in between, sea ice extent fluctuates between years or decades and has partially increased in recent years, although the ice decreases overall.[103] In September 2002, the minimum ice extent in summer was the lowest it had been since 1979 and marked the beginning of a series of record sea-ice lows in the Arctic.[104] In 2019, Greenland's ice sheet lost about 1 million

---

97 'National Snow and Ice Data Center | Arctic Sea Ice News & Analysis, 16 July 2020: Siberian Downward Slide' (Chapter 2, n 94); see also Nicola Scafetta and Adriano Mazzarella, 'The Arctic and Antarctic Sea-Ice Area Index Records versus Measured and Modeled Temperature Data' (2015) 2015 Advances in Meteorology 481834, 6 <http://dx.doi.org/10.1155/2015/481834> accessed 27 March 2020.

98 'NASA Earth Observatory | World of Change: Arctic Sea Ice' (Chapter 2, n 61); Isaacson (Chapter 2, n 61); European Commission, 'Joint Communication – Developing a European Union Policy towards the Arctic Region: Progress since 2008 and next Steps (2012) – JOIN(2012) 19 Final' (Chapter 2, n 61); Wang and Overland (Chapter 2, n 61) 1.

99 James E Overland and Muyin Wang, 'When Will the Summer Arctic Be Nearly Sea Ice Free?' (2013) 40 Geophysical Research Letters 2097, 2097; see Scafetta and Mazzarella (Chapter 2, n 97) 6.

100 A visualization from NASA shows the changes of perennial sea ice – ice that lasts throughout the summer – from 1979 to 2014. Video by NASA/Goddard Space Flight Center Scientific Visualization Studio, retrievable at 'NASA Earth Observatory | World of Change: Arctic Sea Ice' (Chapter 2, n 61); A vivid interactive graph for Arctic sea ice extent with data from 1979 until today can be found at 'National Snow and Ice Data Center | Charctic Interactive Sea Ice Graph' <https://nsidc.org/arcticseaicenews/charctic-interactive-sea-ice-graph/> accessed 9 July 2021.

101 Scafetta and Mazzarella (Chapter 2, n 97) 6.

102 Liu, Chen and Feng (Chapter 2, n 13) 1153.

103 ibid. Marius Årthun, 'The Arctic Sea Ice Extent May Increase despite the World Getting Warmer' *The Nansen Legacy* (6 May 2019) <https://arvenetternansen.com/2019/05/06/arctic-sea-ice-extent-may-increase-despite-the-world-getting-warmer/> accessed 10 August 2021; see Marius Årthun, Tor Eldevik and Lars H Smedsrud, 'The Role of Atlantic Heat Transport in Future Arctic Winter Sea Ice Loss' (2019) 32 Journal of Climate 3327 <https://journals.ametsoc.org/view/journals/clim/32/11/jcli-d-18-0750.1.xml> accessed 2 November 2024.

104 Dan Liu, 'The 2015 Oslo Declaration on Arctic High Seas Fisheries: The Starting Point Towards Future Fisheries Management in the Central Arctic Ocean' (2017) 2017 Arctic

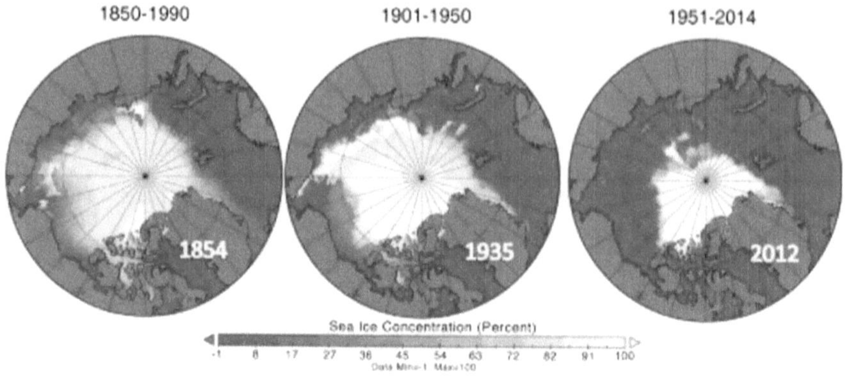

FIGURE 4 Arctic sea ice concentration maps
Individual maps show Septembers of 1854, 1935 and 2012, which are the months of minimum ice coverage, during the three indicated subperiods. Concentrations are color-coded according to the bar at the bottom of the figure.
SOURCE: JOHN E WALSH AND OTHERS, 'A DATABASE FOR DEPICTING ARCTIC SEA ICE VARIATIONS BACK TO 1850' (2017) 107 GEOGRAPHICAL REVIEW 89, 99

tonnes of ice every minute. There are fears that the loss has passed the point of no return, as annual snowfalls are no longer sufficient to restore the snow and ice lost during the summer melt.[105]

As regards recent developments, Arctic sea ice extent in mid-July 2020 was at a record low since the time of satellite observations for this time of year. In the first half of July 2020, sea ice decreased by an average of 146,000 km^2 (56,371 mi^2) – about the size of Bangladesh – per day. This represents an increase of almost 70% in sea ice decline over 10 years. The Northern Sea Route along the Russian coast was almost open. On the contrary, the sea ice extent north of Alaska was in the average range. Such evidence is an important indication of greater variability in the Arctic climate, but nevertheless supports the prediction of a continuing trend towards Arctic sea ice retreat and increasing temperature.[106]

Yearbook 1, 3 <https://arcticyearbook.com/images/yearbook/2017/Scholarly_Papers/21_The_2015_Oslo_Declaration_on_Arctic_High_Seas_Fisheries.pdf> accessed 6 March 2020.

105 'NASA Earth Observatory | World of Change: Arctic Sea Ice' (Chapter 2, n 61).

106 Rory Carroll, 'Arctic Time Capsule from 2018 Washes up in Ireland as Polar Ice Melts' *The Guardian* (5 November 2020) <https://www.theguardian.com/world/2020/nov/05/arctic-time-capsule-from-2018-washes-up-in-ireland-as-polar-ice-melts> accessed 10 August 2021.

Not only is the total extent of sea ice shrinking, but the quality of the sea ice is also decreasing: Multi-year sea ice in the Arctic is continuously disappearing.[107] As a result, today's sea ice cover in the Arctic is much more vulnerable to melting, causing further decline.[108]

The decline in the extent and thickness of the Arctic sea ice cover is directly linked and negatively correlated to the persistent increasing air temperatures[109] and certain weather events such as intense winds.[110]

The rapid decline of Arctic sea ice further triggers feedback mechanisms that accelerate global warming, also known as Arctic amplification: when white sea ice melts in summer, areas of dark, open water are exposed to the sun. These can absorb more of the sun's heat, which in turn causes even more ice to melt, leading, *inter alia*, to a rapid and significant rise in sea level.[111] In addition, soot particles from exhaust gases produced by burning fossil fuels, also known as black carbon, are deposited on the ice, increasing the thawing of the ice.[112] In addition,

107 National Oceanic and Atmospheric Administration, 'Arctic Report Card 2019: Arctic Ecosystems and Communities Are Increasingly at Risk Due to Continued Warming and Declining Sea Ice' (2019) <www.arctic.noaa.gov/Report-Card> accessed 27 March 2020; National Oceanic and Atmospheric Administration, 'Arctic Report Card 2018: Effects of Persistent Arctic Warming Continue to Mount' (2018) <www.arctic.noaa.gov/Report-Card> accessed 27 March 2020.

108 Shankman (Chapter 2, n 92).

109 National Oceanic and Atmospheric Administration, 'Arctic Report Card 2019: Arctic Ecosystems and Communities Are Increasingly at Risk Due to Continued Warming and Declining Sea Ice' (Chapter 2, n 107) 2–3; see Liu (Chapter 2, n 104) 2; Scafetta and Mazzarella (Chapter 2, n 97) 4; Stadtländer (Chapter 2, n 80) 1.

110 Carroll (Chapter 2, note 106).

111 Edward Struzik, 'Welcome to the Arctic Ocean, Mysterious Fish' *The New Humanitarian – Oceans Deeply* (12 May 2017) <https://deeply.thenewhumanitarian.org/oceans/articles/2017/05/12/welcome-to-the-arctic-ocean-mysterious-fish-2> accessed 8 April 2022. National Oceanic and Atmospheric Administration, 'Arctic Report Card 2019: Arctic Ecosystems and Communities Are Increasingly at Risk Due to Continued Warming and Declining Sea Ice' (Chapter 2, n 107) 6; Jianmin Ma, Hayley Hung and Robie W Macdonald, 'The Influence of Global Climate Change on the Environmental Fate of Persistent Organic Pollutants: A Review with Emphasis on the Northern Hemisphere and the Arctic as a Receptor' (2016) 146 Global and Planetary Change 89 <http://dx.doi.org/10.1016/j.gloplacha.2016.09.011> accessed 5 December 2021; Wang and Overland (Chapter 2, n 61) 4; Barnes (Chapter 2, n 10) 194; European Union, 'Communication from the Commission to the European Parliament and the Council – The European Union and the Arctic Region (20 November 2008) – COM/2008/0763 Final' (Chapter 2, n 80) 2; 'National Snow and Ice Data Center | Climate Change in the Arctic' (Chapter 2, n 71); Gramling (Chapter 2, n 94); Stadtländer (Chapter 2, n 80) 1.

112 Federal Foreign Office Germany (Chapter 2, n 89) 11.

exploitation of Arctic resources is likely to result in further release of greenhouse gases.[113]

In summary, predicting the Arctic climate is difficult. Some changes in the Arctic may have negative feedback effects, or effects that reduce the amount of warming. However, for the most part, available evidence indicates that the positive feedback effects outweigh the negative effects, suggesting a constant decline in Arctic ice. Most observations can be summarised into three central assessments: at no time in the last 150 years has sea ice extent in the Arctic been as low as in recent years. Moreover, the rate of sea ice retreat in recent years is also unprecedented in the historical record. Further, the natural fluctuations in sea ice over several decades are generally smaller than the year-to-year fluctuations, indicating a continuous trend.[114] Although this ongoing trend of Arctic sea ice retreat will negatively affect climate and the environment worldwide, it is not considered a poor development by all nations.[115] Several States are vying for access to a new Northwest Passage that runs from Greenland to Canada to Alaska,[116] and the melting of Arctic ice is enabling expanded exploration and exploitation of fish and other natural resources, such as oil and gas.[117] A new ocean is emerging and suddenly becoming accessible, presenting itself as attractive to a wide range of activities and actors. Whether the Arctic ecosystem can support such activities remains to be seen.

4.1.4 Ecological Changes in Food Web and Environment in the Arctic Marine Area

Both the presence and melting of ice largely influence ecological conditions in the Arctic. Climate variability and human activities have already caused rapid shifts in the organization of arctic marine ecosystems.[118] Most Arctic species

113 International Arctic Science Committee (IASC) AMAP, CAFF, *Arctic Climate Impact Assessment* (Cambridge University Press 2005) 34 <http://www.amap.no/documents/doc/arctic-arctic-climate-impact-assessment/796>.

114 Arctic Monitoring and Assessment Programme (AMAP), Conservation of Arctic Flora and Fauna (CAFF) Working Group and International Arctic Science Committee (IASC) (Chapter 2, n 78) 34.

115 Andrew C Revkin, 'Arctic Climate Change Revealed in a Luxury Cruise and Haunting Wreck' *Dot Earth New York Times Blog* (23 September 2016) <https://dotearth.blogs.nytimes.com/2016/09/23/arctic-change-revealed-in-a-luxury-cruise-and-a-haunting-wreck/?searchResultPosition=3> accessed 11 December 2020.

116 'US Climate Objections Sink Arctic Council Accord in Finland' *BBC News* (7 May 2019) <https://www.bbc.com/news/world-europe-48185793> accessed 7 May 2021.

117 Gibbens (Chapter 2, n 33).

118 Arctic Monitoring and Assessment Programme (AMAP), Conservation of Arctic Flora and Fauna (CAFF) Working Group and International Arctic Science Committee (IASC) (Chapter 2, n 78) 659. Rafael Cereceda, 'How Summer 2019 Was Hellish for the Arctic, the Frontline of Climate Change and Global Warming' *Euronews* (24 September 2019)

depend on the presence of sea ice for the maintenance of their habitat, both above and below water.[119] Climate change and with it the increase in temperature and decrease of sea ice in the Arctic therefore affects Arctic animals and the Arctic food chain.[120]

Regarding the specific effects of climate change in the Arctic, on the one hand, climate change has an impact on the distribution of marine animals.[121] Many plankton and fish species are expanding northwards.[122] Capelin, for example, has replaced Arctic cod as the dominant prey fish in Hudson Bay.[123]

Global warming is also driving changes in oceanographic conditions in the Arctic Ocean and adjacent continental slopes. This results in favourable conditions for increased biological production in waters adjacent to northern continental shelves, although production in the CAO will continue to be limited for the time being by light levels and reduced nutrient availability.[124] Increasing temperatures and light in the Arctic in spring result in a burst of plant growth in the form of an ice edge bloom, supporting large populations of fish, marine mammals and birds.[125] Altered timing and duration of the ice edge bloom increases the possibility of a discrepancy in productivity, resulting in grave impacts throughout the ecosystem.[126] This shows that one cannot simply say

---

<https://www.euronews.com/2019/09/18/how-2019-was-hellish-for-the-arctic-the-frontline-of-climate-change-and-global-warming> accessed 10 August 2021; Edward Struzik, 'Fire and Ice: Arctic Responses to Climate Change and Lessons for the Rest of Canada' (2019) 5 <https://ppforum.ca/wp-content/uploads/2019/06/ArcticResponsesToClimateChangeAndLessonsForTheRest-of-PPF-JUNE2019-EN.pdf> accessed 12 March 2022.

119 See Arctic Monitoring and Assessment Programme (AMAP), Conservation of Arctic Flora and Fauna (CAFF) Working Group and International Arctic Science Committee (IASC) (Chapter 2, n 78) 659.

120 Gibbens (Chapter 2, n 33); see Edward Struzik, 'Welcome to the Arctic, Fish' *Hakai Magazine* (16 August 2016) <https://www.hakaimagazine.com/article-long/welcome-arctic-fish?utm_content=buffer2ad70&utm_medium=social&utm_source=twitter.com&utm_campaign=buffer> accessed 4 August 2022.

121 For Arctic fisheries and climate change see specifically Chapter 2 Sections 4, 4.2, 4.2.2 and 4.2.3 *infra*.

122 KF Drinkwater, FJ Mueter and SI Saitoh, 'Shifting Boundaries of Water, Ice, Flora, Fauna, People, and Institutions in the Arctic and Subarctic' (2017) 75 ICES Journal of Marine Science 2293, 2294 <https://academic.oup.com/icesjms/article-abstract/75/7/2293/5256682> accessed 15 January 2020.

123 Struzik, 'Fire and Ice: Arctic Responses to Climate Change and Lessons for the Rest of Canada' (Chapter 2, n 118) 5–6.

124 Haug and others (Chapter 2, n 34).

125 'OSPAR Commission | Region I: Arctic Waters' <https://www.ospar.org/convention/the-north-east-atlantic/i> accessed 20 May 2020.

126 CBD Conference of the Parties and Conservation of Arctic Flora and Fauna (CAFF) Working Group, 'Arctic Regional Workshop to Facilitate the Description of Ecologically

that the survival and growth of a species is higher in years with early sea ice retreat and increased production. Several factors are significant. In very warm years with little sea ice for example, there was more cannibalism among pollock than in colder years with more sea ice and increased predation due to prey-switching in the diet of other species, like juvenile salmons, to pollock.[127] Hence, in years with exceptionally early sea ice retreat, there are likely to be weak year classes of pollock.[128] This demonstrates only a small part of the complex relationship of water temperature, sea ice, and the existence of fish in Arctic waters.

The melting of the ice also causes salinity and Arctic water temperatures to vary.[129] The resulting halocline, a vertical zone between layers of different salinity, separates the fresher water from the saltier water and keeps warmer, deeper water from reaching the surface, affecting the existence of marine life in the different layers.[130]

Recent developments in Arctic climate have further led to profound biogeochemical and ecological changes in Arctic waters: rising global CO_2 emissions are raising the partial pressure of CO_2 in the atmosphere. Almost a quarter of annual CO_2 emissions dissolve in the oceans, where they react and lower the pH level of the oceans in a process commonly known as ocean acidification.[131] Since the beginning of the Industrial Revolution about 250 years ago, ocean acidity has increased by 30%. Previous hyperthermal events associated with ocean acidification led to major extinction events for marine calcifiers, e.g. corals and crustaceans.[132] Ocean acidification is further believed to be an additional stressor for some Arctic fish species,[133] e.g. Arctic Cod, in the near future.[134]

---

or Biologically Significant Marine Areas (Helsinki, 3–7 March 2014)' 55 <https://www.cbd.int/doc/meetings/mar/ebsaws-2014-01/official/ebsaws-2014-01-05-en.pdf> accessed 10 August 2021.

127 GL Hunt and others, 'Climate Impacts on Eastern Bering Sea Foodwebs: A Synthesis of New Data and an Assessment of the Oscillating Control Hypothesis' (2011) 68 ICES Journal of Marine Science 1230, 1233, 1236 <https://academic.oup.com/icesjms/article-abstract/68/6/1230/703602> accessed 15 January 2020.

128 ibid 1241.

129 'MarineBio Conservation Society | Ocean Geography' (Chapter 2, n 31).

130 Arctic Monitoring and Assessment Programme (AMAP) (Chapter 2, n 8) 10 et seq.

131 Intergovernmental Panel on Climate Change, 'Special Report 2019: The Ocean and Cryosphere in a Changing Climate' (2019) 52 <https://www.ipcc.ch/srocc/chapter/summary-for-policymakers/> accessed 4 April 2022; Humphreys (Chapter 2, n 91) 934; see Drinkwater, Mueter and Saitoh (Chapter 2, n 122) 2294.

132 Humphreys (Chapter 2, n 91) 934.

133 See specifically on impacts for fish stocks Chapter 2 Sections, 4, 4.2, 4.2.2 *infra*.

134 Naomi Harada, 'Review: Potential Catastrophic Reduction of Sea Ice in the Western Arctic Ocean: Its Impact on Biogeochemical Cycles and Marine Ecosystems' (2016) 136 Global

Additionally, as another example, melting of the Greenland ice sheet is promoting the rapid dissolution of mercury, presumably from a geological source of mercury at the ice sheet bed, with expected but not yet fully assessed impacts on Arctic and global ecosystems. Mercury ingestion by fish, which in turn are eaten by marine mammals, indirectly puts humans, especially local communities, at risk.[135]

Changes in sea ice have further direct impacts on humans. Both the retreat and thinning of Arctic sea ice makes it increasingly dangerous for Arctic residents to use the ice sheet as a transportation and hunting platform.[136] As a result, traditionally used sled dogs are being dispatched in many communities as boats can be used year-round. To be near buyers, many fishermen are moving from coastal villages to cities.[137] Climate change thus impacts native communities[138] by lowering productivity, altering food web dynamics, and modifying habitat complexity.[139]

In this context, given the multiple impacts of progressive climate change, both locally and globally, Pugh rightly notes that "[w]e need to save the Arctic not because of the polar bears, and not because it is the most beautiful place in the world, but because our very survival depends upon it."[140]

---

and Planetary Change 1 <http://dx.doi.org/10.1016/j.gloplacha.2015.11.005> accessed 5 December 2021. 'Report of the Fourth FiSCAO Meeting on Central Arctic Ocean Fisheries (Tromsø, 26–28 September 2016)' 26 <https://apps-afsc.fisheries.noaa.gov/documents/Arctic_fish_stocks_fourth_meeting/508_Documents/508_FourthFiSCAOreportfinalJan26_2017.pdf > accessed 2 November 2024.

135 Jon R Hawkings and others, 'Large Subglacial Source of Mercury from the Southwestern Margin of the Greenland Ice Sheet' (2021) 14 Nature Geoscience 496 <http://www.nature.com/articles/s41561-021-00753-w> accessed 26 May 2021.

136 Aisha Abdelhamid, 'Climate Change Deniers vs Climate Scientists – Who's Right on Arctic Sea Ice?' *PlanetSave* (25 July 2016) <https://planetsave.com/2016/07/25/climate-change-deniers-vs-climate-scientists-whos-right-arctic-sea-ice/> accessed 30 June 2021.

137 Denis Loctier, 'Protecting Life in the Arctic Seas' *Euronews* (20 March 2020) <https://www.euronews.com/2019/10/10/protecting-life-in-the-arctic-seas> accessed 12 August 2020; Struzik, 'Fire and Ice: Arctic Responses to Climate Change and Lessons for the Rest of Canada' (Chapter 2, n 118) 5.

138 See more on native communities Chapter 3 Sections 4, 4.2 *infra*.

139 Farrah T Chan and others, 'Climate Change Opens New Frontiers for Marine Species in the Arctic: Current Trends and Future Invasion Risks' (2019) 25 Global Change Biology 25, 26 <https://onlinelibrary.wiley.com/doi/abs/10.1111/gcb.14469> accessed 12 August 2021.

140 'Conserve Energy Future | Various Tundra Animals' <https://www.conserve-energy-future.com/various-tundra-animals.php> accessed 22 December 2021.

4.2 *Arctic Fisheries*

Mainly due to large ice coverage, there is currently no (commercial) fishing conducted in CAO waters. In general, Arctic fisheries have never been conducted on a large scale,[141] although this has increased over the past decade: while there were no significant commercial fisheries north of the Bering Strait in 2011, and only limited subsistence or small-scale artisanal fisheries near the coast,[142] sub-Arctic areas support larger regional fisheries today. These comprise fisheries for Cod, Halibut, and Shrimp in the North Atlantic, including the Barents Sea (Norway/Russia), North Pacific, including the Bering Sea (Russia/US), Davis Straight (Canada/Greenland),[143] and, although not on a large commercial scale, fisheries within the EEZs of the Arctic coastal States.[144]

The problem of (Arctic) fisheries lies in the subject matter itself: fish stocks are considered a common good and a renewable resource that is not spatially confined.[145] In particular, the northward shift of the range of many fish stocks from tropical regions towards polar regions[146] calls for effective cooperative regulations that prevent overfishing and economic inefficiencies.[147] Similarly, in a report that assessed ongoing climatic changes in the Arctic and their global implications with respect to fisheries, the Arctic Council concluded that climate change is likely to have less impact on fish stocks than effective management and enforcement of fisheries policies.[148] Regulation, such as the CAOF Agreement, is therefore considered crucial to prevent stock collapse.

141 Arctic Monitoring and Assessment Programme (AMAP), Conservation of Arctic Flora and Fauna (CAFF) Working Group and International Arctic Science Committee (IASC) (Chapter 2, n 78).

142 Barnes (Chapter 2, n 10) 201.

143 Maya Gold, 'Negotiating the International Agreement to Prevent Unregulated Fishing in the High Seas of the Central Arctic Ocean (Arctic Biodiversity Congress, 10 October 2018)' (2018) 4 <https://www.arcticbiodiversity.is/index.php/program/presentations2018/402-the-cao-fishing-agreement-negotiations-and-next-steps-maya-gold/file> accessed 23 July 2020.

144 Molenaar, 'Participation in the Central Arctic Ocean Fisheries Agreement' (Chapter 3, n 32) 133.

145 Erik Jaap Molenaar, 'The Concept of "Real Interest" and Other Aspects of Co-Operation through Regional Fisheries Management Mechanisms' (2000) 15 International Journal of Marine and Coastal Law 475, 477.

146 Haug and others (Chapter 2, n 34) 43 et seq.

147 Molenaar, 'Participation in the Central Arctic Ocean Fisheries Agreement' (Chapter 2, n 23) 133.

148 Arctic Monitoring and Assessment Programme (AMAP), Conservation of Arctic Flora and Fauna (CAFF) Working Group and International Arctic Science Committee (IASC) (Chapter 2, n 78) 770.

To gain an understanding of the status of fish stocks in the Agreement Area and adjacent waters, their current status and changes related to climate change that have occurred or are currently occurring are considered. Furthermore, the substantive scope of the regulating CAOF Agreement is shortly presented.

4.2.1 Current Status of Fish Stocks and Fisheries in the Central Arctic Ocean

Currently, only 10% (63) of the total (633) fish species of the Arctic Ocean and adjacent seas occur in the Arctic. Only a few are considered commercially relevant:[149] in the North Atlantic, these include[150] Atlantic salmon, North-East Arctic cod, Norwegian spring-spawning herring, haddock, and red king crab. North Pacific fish species *inter alia* comprise Pacific cod, Alaska pollock, snow crab and multiple Pacific salmon species. Important circumpolar species to mention are Greenland halibut, capelin and northern shrimp. Arctic char and Polar cod are also found circumpolar, but are harvested mostly for purposes of subsistence.[151]

Arctic species have adapted to live in a fluctuating environment. Most fish live in a narrow temperature range, are largely bottom-dwellers, and do not undertake long distance migrations. This makes them particularly vulnerable to climate change, invasive species and fisheries.[152]

With the development of fisheries, fish stocks in the northern seas are also steadily declining. The demand for fish is increasing, mostly due to changing eating habits or the awareness that fish is a rich source of protein.[153] It is

149 European Parliament, 'Report on an Integrated European Union Policy for the Arctic (2017) – A8-0032/2017' 31 <https://www.europarl.europa.eu/doceo/document/A-8-2017-0032_EN.html> accessed 29 January 2022; European Union, 'Policy Department B: Fisheries Management And The Arctic In The Context Of Climate Change – Study' (2015) 14 <http://www.europarl.europa.eu/RegData/etudes/STUD/2015/563380/IPOL_STU(2015)563380_EN.pdf> accessed 10 August 2021.

150 For detailed lists of species of fish documented to occur within the high seas area, including their potential for future commercial harvests, see 'Report of the Fourth FiSCAO Meeting on Central Arctic Ocean Fisheries (Tromsø, 26–28 September 2016)' (Chapter 2, n 134) 59 et seq.

151 Molenaar, 'International Regulation of Central Arctic Ocean Fisheries' (Chapter 2, n 20) 431.

152 European Union, 'Policy Department B: Fisheries Management And The Arctic In The Context Of Climate Change – Study' (Chapter 2, n 149) 14.

153 Food and Agriculture Organization of the United Nations, 'The State of World Fisheries and Aquaculture 2016: Contributing to Food Security and Nutrition for All' (Chapter 1, n 3); Yoshifumi Tanaka, *The International Law of the Sea* (Cambridge University Press 2015) 231 et seq.

possible that fisheries will also expand to the CAO sooner or later: moderate warming and associated ice melt improves conditions for important commercial species such as Atlantic cod, herring, pollock[154] and capelin[155] and opens up new fishing grounds as climate change progresses,[156] as the majority of species prefer water masses with temperatures above 0°C (32°F).

Thus, although currently only few species have the potential to migrate into the Arctic Ocean, if the water warms to temperatures above 0°C (23°F), migrations of fish stocks become more likely. In view of rapidly progressing climate change, this is a possible scenario and can even be already observed to some extent, as presented in the following.

4.2.2 General Changes for Fish Stocks Resulting from Climate Change

The existence of progressive climate change and climate variability has become an established fact and are likely to have significant impacts on marine species,[157] some of which are addressed below.[158]

Determining exact long-term implications for fish stocks remains difficult to predict in light of potential changes to water temperature, salinity, and complex systems interactions.[159] However, most experts agree on one implication: fish are gradually moving northwards. The potential ranges of fish stocks already vary due to the natural movements of these fishes, without humans directly influencing their distribution through intentional or

154 Barnes (Chapter 2, n 10) 201.

155 Protection of the Arctic Marine Environment (PAME) Working Group, 'PAME Factsheet Series 13/18: Central Arctic Ocean LME' (2016) 5 <https://www.pame.is/index.php/document-library/ecosystem-approach-to-management-documents/large-marine-ecosystems/398-13-central-arctic-ocean-lme/file> accessed 12 March 2020.

156 Efthymios Papastavridis, 'Fisheries Enforcement on the High Seas of the Arctic Ocean: Gaps, Solutions and the Potential Contribution of the European Union and Its Member States' (2018) 33 International Journal of Marine and Coastal Law 324, 359.

157 Arctic Monitoring and Assessment Programme (AMAP), Conservation of Arctic Flora and Fauna (CAFF) Working Group and International Arctic Science Committee (IASC) (Chapter 2, n 78) 659; Henry P Huntington and others, 'A New Perspective on Changing Arctic Marine Ecosystems: Panarchy Adaptive Cycles in Pan-Arctic Spatial and Temporal Scales' in Salvatore Aricò (ed), *Ocean Sustainability in the 21st Century* (Cambridge University Press 2015) 109.

158 European Union, 'Policy Department B: Fisheries Management And The Arctic In The Context Of Climate Change – Study' (Chapter 2, n 149).

159 Arctic Monitoring and Assessment Programme (AMAP), Conservation of Arctic Flora and Fauna (CAFF) Working Group and International Arctic Science Committee (IASC) (Chapter 2, n 78) 520, 717; Barnes (Chapter 2, n 10) 194.

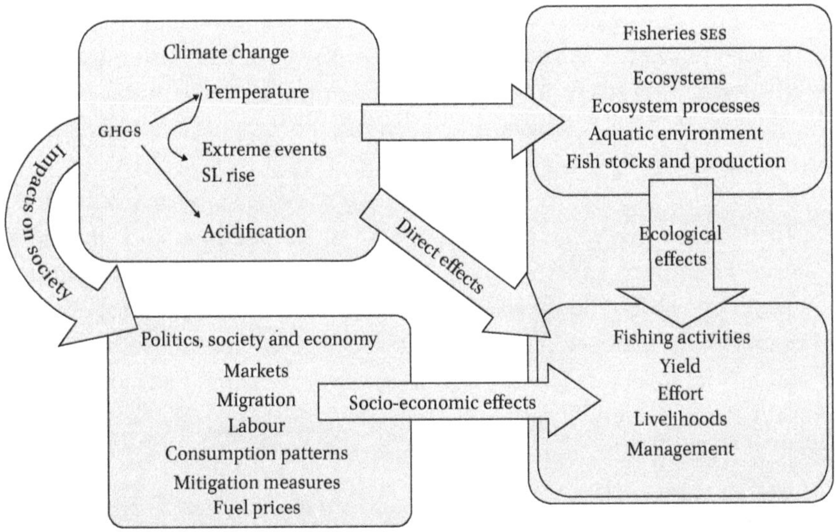

Ecological impacts	Direct impacts	Socio-economic impacts
Change in yield Change in species distribution Increased variability of catches Changes in seasonality of production	Damaged infrastructure Damaged gears Increased danger at sea Loss/gain of navigation routes Flooding of fishing communities	Influx of migrant fishers Increasing fuel costs Reduced health due to disease Relative profitability of other sectors Resources available for management Reduced security Funds for adaptation

FIGURE 5 Ecological, direct and socio-economic impacts of climate change on fisheries
SOURCE: EUROPEAN UNION, 'POLICY DEPARTMENT B: FISHERIES MANAGEMENT AND THE ARCTIC IN THE CONTEXT OF CLIMATE CHANGE – STUDY' (CHAPTER 2, N 149); K COCHRANE AND OTHERS, 'FAO FISHERIES AND AQUACULTURE TECHNICAL PAPER 530: CLIMATE CHANGE IMPLICATIONS FOR FISHERIES AND AQUACULTURE' (2009) 123 <HTTP://WWW.LIS.EDU.ES/UPLOADS/07483FB7_72A2_45CA_B8E7_48BF74072FD3.PDF> ACCESSED 24 APRIL 2020

accidental introductions.[160] Evidence further indicates that with the summer retreat of sea ice and the warming of ocean waters, plankton and fish

160 BA Block and others, 'Tracking Apex Marine Predator Movements in a Dynamic Ocean' (2011) 475 Nature 86, 1 <http://dx.doi.org/10.1038/nature10082> accessed 10 August 2021; cf. Cindy Chu, Nicholas E Mandrak and Charles K Minns, 'Potential Impacts of Climate Change on the Distributions of Several Common and Rare Freshwater Fishes in Canada' (2005) 11 Diversity and Distributions 299, 302 <http://doi.wiley.com/10.1111/j.1366-9516.2005.00153.x> accessed 12 August 2021.

species are undergoing northward distributional shifts,[161] including commercially important ones.[162] Already in the US Senate Joint Resolution that provided the initial impetus for the CAOF Agreement, the United States pointed to the likelihood of fish stocks moving north towards Arctic waters into new habitats:

> [F]ish stocks are migratory throughout their habitats, and changing ocean conditions can restructure marine habitats and redistribute the species dependent on those habitats; [Whereas] changing global climate regimes may increase ocean water temperature, creating suitable new habitats in areas previously too cold to support certain fish stocks, such as the Arctic Ocean.[163]

---

161 See Drinkwater, Mueter and Saitoh (Chapter 2, n 122) 2294; Liu (Chapter 2, n 104) 3; 'Report of the Fifth FiSCAO Meeting on Central Arctic Ocean Fisheries (Ottawa, 24–26 October 2017)' 14–15 < https://apps-afsc.fisheries.noaa.gov/documents/Arctic_fish_stocks_fifth_meeting/508_Documents/508_Final_report_of_the_5th_FiSCAO_meeting.pdf> accessed 2 November 2024; 'Report of the Fourth FiSCAO Meeting on Central Arctic Ocean Fisheries (Tromsø, 26–28 September 2016)' (Chapter 2, n 134) 16, 25–26; Molenaar, 'International Regulation of Central Arctic Ocean Fisheries' (Chapter 2, n 20) 431; 'Report of the Second FiSCAO Meeting on Central Arctic Ocean Fisheries (Tromsø, 28–31 October 2013)' 14 <https://archive.fisheries.noaa.gov/afsc/Arctic_fish_stocks_third_meeting/Report of 2nd Scientific Meeting on Arctic Fish Stocks 28 31 October 2013.pdf> accessed 10 August 2021; Anne Babcock Hollowed, Benjamin Planque and Harald Loeng, 'Potential Movement of Fish and Shellfish Stocks from the Sub-Arctic to the Arctic Ocean' (2013) 22 Fisheries Oceanography 355, 355 <http://doi.wiley.com/10.1111/fog.12027> accessed 6 March 2020; United States Senate, 'Hearing: Defending U.S. Economic Interests in the Changing Arctic: Is There a Strategy? (112. Congress, First Session, 27 July 2011)' 12, 66 <https://www.govinfo.gov/content/pkg/CHRG-112shrg72568/pdf/CHRG-112shrg72568.pdf> accessed 10 December 2021; 'Report of the First FiSCAO Meeting on Central Arctic Ocean Fisheries (Anchorage, 15–17 June 2011)' 3 <https://archive.fisheries.noaa.gov/afsc/Arctic_fish_stocks_third_meeting/First Meeting Sci Experts Arctic Fisheries 30 Aug 2011.pdf> accessed 10 August 2021; GA Rose, 'Capelin (Mallotus Villosus) Distribution and Climate: A Sea "Canary" for Marine Ecosystem Change' (2005) 62 ICES Journal of Marine Science 1524, 1528 <https://academic.oup.com/icesjms/article-lookup/doi/10.1016/j.icesjms.2005.05.008> accessed 5 December 2021.

162 Gregory K Silber and Jeffrey D Adams, 'Vessel Operations in the Arctic, 2015–2017' (2019) 6 Frontiers in Marine Science 573, 12 <https://www.frontiersin.org/article/10.3389/fmars.2019.00573/full> accessed 29 May 2020.

163 United States Congress, 'Senate Joint Resolution No.17 (4 October 2007) – 122 STAT. 1569' <https://www.congress.gov/bill/110th-congress/senate-joint-resolution/17/text> accessed 8 April 2022.

Changes in fish distribution associated with increased water temperatures are already being observed in Greenland. While the most profitable catch, halibut, is migrating to colder areas, an increasing number of different species such as mackerel, herring, Atlantic bluefin tuna and cod are entering Arctic waters and finding their way to Greenland's shores[164] to seek more favourable conditions,[165] posing an additional threat to Arctic species by potentially displacing them or making them prey.[166] In 2012, an assessment of the potential for 17 fish or shellfish stocks or stock groups to move from the sub-Arctic areas into the Arctic Ocean came to the conclusion that two thirds of the fish analysed have potential or high potential to move or expand in the high Arctic, with one third bearing the necessary characteristics to establish viable resident populations.[167]

By way of example, capelin, a cold-water fish species with a circumpolar distribution in the boreal waters of the North Pacific and North Atlantic, resides in waters sometimes as cold as −1,5°C (29,3°F).[168] Capelin are pelagic, migratory, planktivorous fishes, and changes in their physical and biological environment can have severely affect their abundance, migrations, distribution and growth.[169] They appear to respond rapidly to such environmental changes. Thus, the fishes act as an early-warning of (climatic) changes that may also affect other species and the ecosystem.[170] Currently, capelin are predicted to make shifts of approximately 400–1800 km (250–1120 miles), corresponding to 4–16° latitude, based on the scenario of a 2–4° C (3,6–7,2°F) temperature increase in the 21st century and a strict northward shift.[171] However, climate changes at different rates and in different directions in different places, and

164 On the introduction of non-indigenous species, see Chapter 2 Sections, 4, 4.2, 4.2.3 *infra*.

165 Loctier (Chapter 2, n 137).

166 Conservation of Arctic Flora and Fauna (CAFF) Working Group, 'State of the Arctic Marine Biodiversity: Key Findings and Advice for Monitoring' (2017) 6, 17 <https://oaarchive.arctic-council.org/handle/11374/1945> accessed 4 April 2022.

167 Hollowed, Planque and Loeng (Chapter 2, n 161) 1.

168 See Viðar Engilbertsson, 'Energy Dynamics and Recruitment of Icelandic Capelin' (University of Iceland 2014) 30 <https://skemman.is/bitstream/1946/19866/1/MS_ritgerd_vidar.pdf> accessed 5 December 2021; Hjálmar Vilhjálmsson, 'Capelin Biology and Ecology Capelin (Mallotus Villosus) in the Iceland-East Greenland-Jan Mayen Ecosystem' (2002) 59 ICES Journal of Marine Science 870, 878; Rose (Chapter 2, n 161) 1526.

169 Vilhjálmsson (Chapter 2, n 168) 871.

170 Rose (Chapter 2, n 161) 1528.

171 ibid; see Morgan Kelly, 'Movement of Marine Life Follows Speed and Direction of Climate Change' *Princeton University* (12 September 2013) <https://www.princeton.edu/news/2013/09/12/movement-marine-life-follows-speed-and-direction-climate-change#:~:text=Details of the surveys revealed,38 miles north per decade> accessed 8 April 2022.

regional factors such as winds, can actually counteract warming waters and lead to cooler seas. Therefore, another global climate scenario predicts widespread cooling as a result of the weakening of the Gulf Stream and the North Atlantic heat pump.[172] Under this scenario, southern movements of capelin, as observed in the Northwest Atlantic in the 1990s, are expected to occur.[173]

In the western Arctic Ocean, a potential habitat for chum salmon, i.e. an area with a positive growth rate for chum salmon, was located taking into account monthly changes in water temperature under global warming scenarios.[174] Accordingly, the potential habitat of chum salmon was predicted to expand under current climate conditions due to increased water temperatures and zooplankton density. Yet, under predicted climate conditions in 2095, the area of potential habitat south of 71°N will shrink in summer due to an increase in temperature beyond the optimal range (4–12°C/39–54°F) for chum salmon. However, because these results are based only on predicted temperatures, a fish resource variability model[175] needs to be developed for the Arctic Ocean. This needs to evaluate the effects of multiple environmental stressors on fishes. Further, such a model should attempt to predict how the distribution and migration routes of higher trophic level organisms will be altered by increased temperatures and Arctic freshening and acidification,[176] as well as changes in the community of grazing organisms like zooplankton.[177]

The parties to the CAOF Agreement have expressed their belief that "commercial fishing is unlikely to become viable in the high seas portion of the

172 Bob Dickson and others, 'Rapid Freshening of the Deep North Atlantic Ocean over the Past Four Decades' (2002) 416 Nature 832, 836 <http://www.nature.com/articles/416832a> accessed 17 January 2022; Bogi Hansen, William R Turrell and Svein Østerhus, 'Decreasing Overflow from the Nordic Seas into the Atlantic Ocean through the Faroe Bank Channel since 1950' (2001) 411 Nature 927, 929 <http://www.nature.com/articles/35082034> accessed 7 September 2020; Sirpa Häkkinen and Peter B Rhines, 'Decline of Subpolar North Atlantic Circulation during the 1990s' (2004) 304 Science 555, cf. <https://www-jstor-org.emedien.ub.uni-muenchen.de/stable/3836715?seq=1#metadata_info_tab_contents> accessed 7 September 2020.

173 Rose (Chapter 2, n 161) 1529.

174 Seokjin Yoon and others, 'Potential Habitat for Chum Salmon (Oncorhynchus Keta) in the Western Arctic Based on a Bioenergetics Model Coupled with a Three-Dimensional Lower Trophic Ecosystem Model' (2015) 131 Progress in Oceanography 146, 149 et seq. <http://dx.doi.org/10.1016/j.pocean.2014.12.009> accessed 5 December 2021.

175 See e.g. NEMURO.FISH model, Chapter 6 Section 6 *infra*.

176 Harada (Chapter 2, n 134) 13; Yoon and others (Chapter 2, n 174).

177 Nicolas Dupont, 'Polar Cod Have Become Larger in the Barents Sea over the Last 30 Years' *The Nansen Legacy* (3 July 2020) <https://arvenetternansen.com/2020/07/03/polar-cod-have-become-larger-in-the-barents-sea-over-the-last-30-years/> accessed 22 July 2020.

central Arctic Ocean in the near future".[178] Nevertheless, sea ice retreat, a resulting dispersal of species and varying stock patterns and changes in distribution may also support the emergence of and access to fisheries sites that were previously inaccessible. In this regard, the US Joint Resolution, the driving force for the CAOF Agreement,[179] recognizes that the potential for habitat expansion and migration increases the likelihood of (commercial) fishing in the area.[180] This in turn raises issues of access rights, environmental impacts on fisheries and coordination of these and other activities in the region.[181] For example, industrial fisheries already operating on many Arctic shelves are believed to be having a radical impact on local fish species, as they catch the latter as unprecedented bycatch.[182]

Nevertheless, fish migration routes, much more than human behaviour, follow temperature and thus climate velocity.[183] The trio of impacts – temperature increase, sea-level rise and ocean acidification – mutually impinges sensitive ecosystems and species and causes fish stocks and phytoplankton to adapt their distribution, abundance and locations.[184] Hence, fish distributional shifts will most likely increase in the future due to the drastic effects of climate change.[185]

4.2.3 Introduction of Non-indigenous Species

Physical and biological barriers usually set the geographical limits of biota. The position and effectiveness of these barriers vary due to the modification of

---

178 See Preamble CAOF Agreement.

179 On the motivations for the CAOF Agreement and its drafting history, see Chapter 3 Section 1 and Section 2 *infra*.

180 United States Congress (Chapter 2, n 163).

181 Barnes (Chapter 2, n 10) 194.

182 Jørgen S Christiansen, Catherine W Mecklenburg and Oleg V. Karamushko, 'Arctic Marine Fishes and Their Fisheries in Light of Global Change' (2014) 20 Global Change Biology 352, 352 <https://onlinelibrary.wiley.com/doi/full/10.1111/gcb.12395> accessed 12 August 2021; cf. Arctic Monitoring and Assessment Programme (AMAP), Conservation of Arctic Flora and Fauna (CAFF) Working Group and International Arctic Science Committee (IASC) (Chapter 2, n 78) 749 et seq.

183 Kelly (Chapter 2, n 171).

184 See Séverine Alvain and others, 'Rapid Climatic Driven Shifts of Diatoms at High Latitudes' (2013) 132 Remote Sensing of Environment 195 <http://dx.doi.org/10.1016/j.rse.2013.01.014> accessed 10 August 2021; Seoung-Yong Hong and Jon M Van Dyke, 'Publications on Ocean Development' in Jon M Van Dyke (ed), *Maritime Boundary Disputes, Settlement Processes, and the Law of the Sea* (Brill | Nijhoff 2009) 37.

185 David A Balton, 'Considering Future Arctic Fisheries' in Myron H Nordquist, Tomas H Heidar and John Norton Moore (eds), *Changes in the Arctic Environment and the Law of the Sea* (Martinus Nijhoff Publishers 2010).

climate and configuration of water bodies and landmasses by tectonic upheavals over time. When this barrier between biotas with long separate histories breaks down, species invade from one biotope to another. This is intensified by deliberate or accidental introduction through global trade and by creating opportunities for dispersal where such barriers existed before.[186] This can also be observed in the Arctic Ocean and adjacent seas: the increasing area of open waters enables biotas to mix and leads to increased human activities, resulting in an introduction of non-indigenous species (NIS), i.e. an expansion of species due to an extension of their suitable habitat, and the fisheries that they attract.[187]

As outlined above,[188] one factor in fish stocks changing their habitat is the rising water temperature of the oceans. Fish are generally very sensitive to even a small change in temperature of 0,5°C (0,9°F).[189] Native polar species live in very low temperature ranges, with most of them unable to manage basic activities at more than 3°C (37,4°F). This temperature is likely to be maintained in deep Arctic waters, but will certainly be exceeded in coastal areas in future summers. Therefore, due to poor physiological adaptability and extended generations of cold-water species, it is very likely that they will also be displaced in Arctic waters by temperate NIS entering the Arctic high seas due to increased ocean temperatures and anthropogenic activities.[190]

The invasion of species into the Arctic Ocean is already occurring,[191] promoted by merchant shipping[192] and an increased Pacific-Atlantic connectivity due to melting sea ice[193] and resulting distribution shifts. An average invasion

186 Geerat J Vermeij, 'When Biotas Meet: Understanding Biotic Interchange' (1991) 253 Science 1099, 1099.

187 Marit Reigstad, Tor Eldevik and Sebastian Gerland, 'The Nansen Legacy' *The Nansen Legacy* (11 April 2019) <https://arvenetternansen.com/2019/04/11/the-nansen-legacy/> accessed 22 July 2020; Chan and others (Chapter 2, n 139) 33.

188 See Chapter 2, Sections 4, 4.2, 4.2.2 *supra*.

189 Cf. European Union, 'Policy Department B: Fisheries Management And The Arctic In The Context Of Climate Change – Study' (Chapter 2, n 149) 14.

190 Chan and others (Chapter 2, n 139) 26–33.

191 Intergovernmental Panel on Climate Change, 'Climate Change 2022: Impacts, Adaptation and Vulnerability – Working Group II Contribution to the Sixth Assessment Report ' (Chapter 2, n 77) 21.

192 Molenaar, 'International Regulation of Central Arctic Ocean Fisheries' (Chapter 2, n 20) 431.

193 Mary S Wisz and others, 'Arctic Warming Will Promote Atlantic-Pacific Fish Interchange' (2015) 5 Nature Climate Change 261 <http://www.iobis.org> accessed 11 March 2020.

of two species per 0,5° latitude was predicted for the Arctic Ocean.[194] The discovery of NIS per year has quadrupled in the marine Arctic since the 1960s,[195] especially near the Icelandic shelf, in the Barents Sea and in the Norwegian Sea with more than 10 discoveries since then. Nearly 40% of these NIS were introduced by ships, a quarter were introduced by aquaculture, but a third were actually introduced by natural spread into the new habitat.[196] The survival of such NIS in previously unsuitable habitats can subsequently be enhanced by changes in temperature, sea ice cover or ocean currents.[197]

Although not all NIS are significantly harmful per se, every introduction of a new species necessarily leads to a change in the existing ecosystem: it alters the food web by making local species prey, competes with native species and changes the respective community structure.[198] The introduction of invasive NIS can therefore cause massive economic and ecological damage and is considered one of the biggest threats to biological diversity, especially in geographically and evolutionary isolated ecosystems.[199]

Hence, based on historical examples,[200] it is assumed that such interchanges in the Arctic will have significant and partly unknown effects[201] on species composition and trophic structure in Arctic ecosystems with low species diversity.[202] In this context, fisheries management is expected to be the determining factor for future Arctic Ocean fisheries: changes in migration patterns have put existing regimes to test and led to conflicts between participants in fisheries by changing the balance of quota exchange and access, as has happened e.g. with the northward shift of mackerel stock from Norwegian and

194 Miranda C Jones and William WL Cheung, 'Multi-Model Ensemble Projections of Climate Change Effects on Global Marine Biodiversity' (2015) 72 ICES Journal of Marine Science 741 <http://www.iobis.org/> accessed 10 December 2020.

195 Chan and others (Chapter 2, n 139) 29.

196 ibid 25.

197 ibid 26.

198 Conservation of Arctic Flora and Fauna (CAFF) Working Group, 'State of the Arctic Marine Biodiversity: Key Findings and Advice for Monitoring' (Chapter 2, n 166) 6, 17; Cynthia H McKenzie and others, 'ICES Cooperative Research Report No. 335: Alien Species Alert: Didemnum Vexillum Kott, 2002: Invasion, Impact, and Control' (2017) 9, 16 <http://doi.org/10.17895/ices.pub.2138> accessed 20 January 2020.

199 CBD Conference of the Parties, 'COP 6 Decision 23: Alien Species That Threaten Ecosystems, Habitats or Species (The Hague, 7 – 19 April 2002)' para 1(2) <https://www.cbd.int/doc/decisions/cop-06-dec-23-en.pdf> accessed 10 August 2021.

200 Dor Edelist and others, 'Restructuring the Sea: Profound Shifts in the World's Most Invaded Marine Ecosystem' (2013) 19 Diversity and Distributions 69, 74.

201 European Union, 'Policy Department B: Fisheries Management And The Arctic In The Context Of Climate Change – Study' (Chapter 2, n 149) 83–84, 92.

202 Wisz and others (Chapter 2, n 193) 262.

EU waters to Faeroese, Greenlandic and Icelandic waters.[203] The strategy is therefore to prevent damage by promoting robust biosecurity plans and avoiding the introduction of NIS rather than controlling or eradicating them.[204] Thus, with projected warming and subsequent potential developments, policy and management efforts are urgently needed to minimize invasion opportunities in high latitudes such as the Arctic Ocean[205]– a matter that should be considered during the implementation of the Agreement.

4.2.4 Fish in the Sense of the CAOF Agreement

The CAOF Agreement, as a fisheries agreement, logically revolves around fish. For the purposes of the Agreement, the term is defined in Article 1(b) CAOF Agreement. Fish in this context refers to species of fish, molluscs and crustaceans other than those that are sedentary species as defined in Article 77 UNCLOS. According to Article 77(4) UNCLOS, these are "organisms which, at the harvestable stage, either are immobile on or under the seabed or are unable to move except in constant physical contact with the seabed or the subsoil". Such sedentary species are often considered to belong to the ocean floor or subsoil, rather than to marine waters as such, and therefore correspond to "crops in a field."[206] About 300–400 deep-sea sedentary species live in the CAO, such as bryozoans, bristle worms, and bivalves. However, most of them do not play a role in fisheries,[207] probably as they are unlikely to move off the

203 Arctic Centre University of Lapland, 'Strategic Assessment of Development of the Arctic – Assessment Conducted for the European Union' (2014) <http://library.arcticportal.org/1905/> accessed 10 August 2021.

204 Elizabeth Cook and others, 'Marine Biosecurity: Protecting Indigenous Marine Species' (2016) 5 Research and Reports in Biodiversity Studies 1, 1 <https://www.researchgate.net/publication/290474067_Marine_biosecurity_protecting_indigenous_marine_species> accessed 12 August 2021.

205 Catherine E de Rivera and others, 'Potential for High-Latitude Marine Invasions along Western North America' (2011) 17 Diversity and Distributions 1198, 1198 <http://doi.wiley.com/10.1111/j.1472-4642.2011.00790.x> accessed 20 January 2020.

206 Harald Sakarias Brøvig Hansen, 'The Challenging Barents Sea Snow Crab' in Svein Rottem and Ida Soltvedt (eds), *Arctic Governance Volume 2: Energy, Living Marine Resources and Shipping* (IB Tauris 2018) 168.

207 'Arctic Ocean Diversity | Sea-Bottom Diversity: An Overview of the Benthic Realm' <http://www.arcodiv.org/SeaBottom_overview.html> accessed 17 January 2022; cf. Harald Sakarias Brøvig Hansen, 'Snow Crab (Chionoecetes Opilio) in the Barents Sea. Diet, Biology and Management' (UiT The Arctic University of Norway 2015) <https://munin.uit.no/bitstream/handle/10037/7746/thesis.pdf?sequence=2&isAllowed=y> accessed 14 April 2022.

continental shelf with high food availability and benthic biomass[208] outside the Agreement Area.[209]

One kind of sedentary species, but of great importance to fisheries in Arctic waters, is snow crab.[210] The snow crab is a subarctic, relatively recently discovered species that was first discovered in the eastern Barents Sea in 1996[211] and is gradually spreading throughout the waters of the Northern Hemisphere as a fairly invasive species.[212] The species prefers cold water temperatures and is found in a wide depth range from 20 to 2000 meters, usually on sandy or muddy bottoms.[213] Beginning as incidental bycatch by groundfish vessels, snow crab fisheries increased rapidly and shifted from primarily nearshore to offshore in the early 2000s.[214] Its biomass in the Barents Sea in 2016 was estimated to be ten times that of red king crab and about half that of shrimp.[215] This gives snow crab a high economic potential, exceeding even that of cod – the most valuable fishery in the Norwegian EEZ – and makes it one of the most valuable fisheries in Canada and the United States.[216]

Although snow crabs share several characteristics of both fish and sedentary species, there is more or less agreement that snow crabs should be classified as sedentary species and therefore excluded from the scope of the

208 Cf. VV Fedyakov and AD Naumov, 'Marine Bivalvia of the Arctic Ocean' in Yvonne Herman (ed), *The Arctic Seas* (Springer US 1989).Mats Walday, 'European Environment Agency: Europe's Biodiversity – Biogeographical Regions and Seas: The Arctic Ocean' (2008) <https://www.eea.europa.eu/publications/report_2002_0524_154909/regional-seas-around-europe/arctic_ocean.pdf/view> accessed 4 April 2022. Arctic Ocean Diversity, 'Sea-Bottom Diversity. An Overview of the Benthic Realm' (2010) <http://www.arcodiv.org/SeaBottom_overview.html> accessed 4 July 2019.

209 Cf. Hansen, 'Snow Crab (Chionoecetes Opilio) in the Barents Sea. Diet, Biology and Management' (Chapter 2, n 207) 21.

210 Molenaar, 'Participation in the Central Arctic Ocean Fisheries Agreement' (Chapter 2, n 23).

211 Andreas Østhagen and Andreas Raspotnik, 'Crab! How a Dispute over Snow Crab Became a Diplomatic Headache between Norway and the EU' (2018) 98 Marine Policy 58, 60.

212 Brooks A Kaiser, Melina Kourantidou and Linda Fernandez, 'A Case for the Commons: The Snow Crab in the Barents' (2018) 210 Journal of Environmental Management 338 <https://doi.org/10.1016/j.jenvman.2018.01.007> accessed 5 December 2021.

213 'Government of Canada | Snow Crab' <https://www.dfo-mpo.gc.ca/species-especes/profiles-profils/snow-crab-crabe-neiges-atl-eng.html> accessed 5 December 2021.

214 ibid.

215 Østhagen and Raspotnik (Chapter 2, n 211) 60; MM Mcbride and others, 'Joint Norwegian-Russian Environmental Status 2013: Report on the Barents Sea Ecosystem Part II' (2016) <https://www.barentsportal.com/barentsportal/index.php/en/joint-norwegian-russian-environmental-status-2013-report-on-the-barents-sea-ecosystem-part-ii-complete-report-published-2016> accessed 5 December 2021.

216 Østhagen and Raspotnik (Chapter 2, n 211); Hansen, 'Snow Crab (Chionoecetes Opilio) in the Barents Sea. Diet, Biology and Management' (Chapter 2, n 207).

CAOF Agreement. Moreover, as the species generally has potential to colonize CAO waters, classifying snow crab as a sedentary species is more beneficial to most fishing States: it is relevant for their rights to harvest and manage the species, since most fishing occurs outside the EEZs but within the continental shelf. If the species is considered sedentary, belonging to the seafloor, it would be managed under continental shelf regulations,[217] and States could enjoy sovereign fishing rights over snow crab.[218] However, if it is considered a fish – more specifically, a straddling stock – it would be subject to high seas regulations,[219] and the coastal States involved would be required to cooperate in managing the population.[220] The matter of classification[221] has been part of several disputes in the past.[222] For instance, Norway addressed the issue in a 2015 fishing ban[223] for snow crab on the Norwegian continental shelf,[224] and both Norway and Russia, which cooperate in the management of living marine resources in the Barents Sea, chose to treat crab as a sedentary species rather than a shared stock.[225] This may have had consequences for the CAOF Agreement: supported by the Arctic coastal States[226] and the

---

217 See UNCLOS Part VI.

218 See Article 77(1) UNCLOS.

219 See UNCLOS Part VII.

220 Hansen, 'Snow Crab (Chionoecetes Opilio) in the Barents Sea. Diet, Biology and Management' (Chapter 2, n 207) 73.

221 Harald Sakarias Brøvig Hansen, 'Three Major Challenges in Managing Non-Native Sedentary Barents Sea Snow Crab (Chionoecetes Opilio)' (2016) 71 Marine Policy 38, 42 <http://dx.doi.org/10.1016/j.marpol.2016.05.013> accessed 5 December 2021.

222 See European Commission, 'Letter from the Director General for Maritime Affairs and Fisheries (MARE) – Subject: Snow Crab Fisheries in the NEAFC Regulatory Area (5 August 2015)' <https://www.politico.eu/wp-content/uploads/2017/06/SPOLITICO-17061514340.pdf> accessed 8 September 2020.

223 'Norwegian Directorate of Fisheries | (Utgått) Forskrift Om Forbud Mot Fangst Av Snøkrabbe, J-280-2014 [(Expired) Regulation Concerning Ban of Catching of Snow Crab)]' <https://www.fiskeridir.no/Yrkesfiske/Regelverk-og-reguleringer/J-meldinger/Utgaatte-J-meldinger/J-280-2014> accessed 8 September 2020; Norwegian Parliament, 'Skriftlig Spørsmål Fra Helga Pedersen (A) Til Fiskeriministeren [Written Question from Helga Pedersen (A) to the Fisheries Minister]' (2017) <https://www.stortinget.no/no/Saker-og-publikasjoner/Sporsmal/Skriftlige-sporsmal-og-svar/Skriftlig-sporsmal/?qid=68730> accessed 8 September 2020.

224 From Norway's point of view, this includes Svalbard. On the maritime issues around Svalbard, see Chapter 2 Section 3 *supra*.

225 Hansen, 'Three Major Challenges in Managing Non-Native Sedentary Barents Sea Snow Crab (Chionoecetes Opilio)' (Chapter 2, n 207) 42.

226 'Notes of Phone Call with Erik J. Molenaar, Assistant Professor of Law, Economics and Governance at Utrecht University and EU Representative in Consultations for the CAOF Agreement, on 16 October 2020, on File with the Author'.

EU,[227] it was quite clear from the beginning that the Agreement should not address the snow crab fishery, and as a result, sedentary species are not subject to protection under the CAOF Agreement either.

This result may be comprehensible, yet problematic concerning the Agreement's aim to prevent potential overfishing or IUU fishing. Therefore, the need to protect certain species should have been another consideration to be taken into account when defining the scope of the CAOF Agreement. Snow crabs are managed internationally by the National Oceanic and Atmospheric Administration (NOAA) Fisheries and the North Pacific Fishery Management Council through harvest criteria and harvest limits designed to ensure sustainable reproduction,[228] and additional national management.[229] Beyond that, snow crabs and sedentary species in general are not usually considered in international fishery protection and management regimes, although they would certainly benefit from them. Although the current open-access fishery for snow crab in international waters has developed a positive spin-off by curbing the westward spread of the invasive species into fragile benthic ecosystems,[230] the inclusion of snow crab in the scope of the Agreement would have supported an all-encompassing ecosystem approach.[231] It is therefore concerning that sedentary species have been excluded from the scope of the CAOF Agreement for political reasons in order to avoid conflicts in the ongoing debate about the outer limits of the continental shelves of the Arctic coastal States. Nevertheless, this is understandable given the overarching goal of achieving a binding multi-stakeholder agreement.

4.2.5 Fishing in the Sense of the CAOF Agreement

The CAOF Agreement was created to encounter the potential threat of overfishing and IUU fishing in Arctic waters, as the number of fishing vessel operations steadily increased over the last years.[232] In this context, it is necessary to clarify what the word "fishing" in the Agreement actually means.

Fishing is described three times in the Agreement. The single term "fishing" is defined in Article 1(c) CAOF Agreement to mean "searching for, attracting,

227 European Commission, 'Letter from the Director General for Maritime Affairs and Fisheries (MARE) – Subject: Snow Crab Fisheries in the NEAFC Regulatory Area (5 August 2015)' (Chapter 2, n 222).

228 'NOAA Fisheries | Alaska Snow Crab' <https://www.fisheries.noaa.gov/species/alaska-snow-crab> accessed 5 December 2021.

229 See for example Canada: 'Government of Canada | Snow Crab' (Chapter 2, n 213).

230 Kaiser, Kourantidou and Fernandez (Chapter 2, n 212).

231 On the ecosystem approach specifically, see Chapter 5 Sections 2, 2.1, 2.1.2 *infra*.

232 Silber and Adams (Chapter 2, n 162) 8, 11–12.

locating, catching, taking or harvesting of fish or any activity that can reasonably be expected to result in the attracting, locating, catching, taking or harvesting of fish." This definition differs from and clarifies the original meaning of the term, which is often referred to simply as "the sport or occupation of catching fish."[233] While sport fishing understandably plays only a minor role in the CAO, commercial or exploratory fishing are of great importance in the Arctic and are defined in subsections (d) and (e) of Article 1. The categorization of the different types of fishing is necessary as different rights and obligations are assigned to each of them.[234] The definition of "fishing" in Article 1(c) CAOF Agreement is very broad and already includes the first steps of the activity to catch fish: searching for, attracting or finding fish is considered fishing, as is any activity that can reasonably be expected to result in these activities. The actual catching of fish is not necessary for an activity to fall within the definition, although catching, taking and harvesting are further included in the definition, which supports a more general understanding of the term. The broad definition ensures the widest possible regulatory scope, paving the way for comprehensive and effective protection of fish stocks.

Fishing is currently only possible up to a certain depth, the so-called fishable depth, which is determined for the regulatory area of an RFB by each RFB itself. It usually reaches up to roughly 1500m to 2200m (4921 ft to 7218 ft).[235] Figure 6 above illustrates the current possibilities for fisheries in the CAO in international waters and fishable depths. These are currently located in the section of the Agreement Area near Russia and the United States. The remaining Agreement Area is regularly covered in ice, or the waters are too deep to conduct fishing at present.

The Agreement further distinguishes between commercial and exploratory fishing. Article 1(d) CAOF Agreement defines "commercial fishing" as fishing for commercial purposes. Commercial fishing will be of great importance to the parties to the CAOF Agreement, should it be possible in the CAO one day, as the Parties represent roughly 75% of the worlds GDP[236] and contribute to a large extent to fishing.[237]

---

233 'Cambridge English Dictionary | Fishing' <https://dictionary.cambridge.org/dictionary/english/fishing> accessed 5 July 2019.

234 For example, Article 3 CAOF Agreement distinguishes between the terms "commercial fishing" and "exploratory fishing" by devoting a separate subsection to each term with specific conditions that must be met in order to conduct each type of fishing; see Chapters 6 Sections 1 and 2 *infra*.

235 'Marine Conservation Institute | Marine Protection by Country: High Seas' (Chapter 2, n 28).

236 Loctier (Chapter 2, n 137).

237 European Union, 'Policy Department B: Fisheries Management And The Arctic In The Context Of Climate Change – Study' (Chapter 2, n 149) 92.

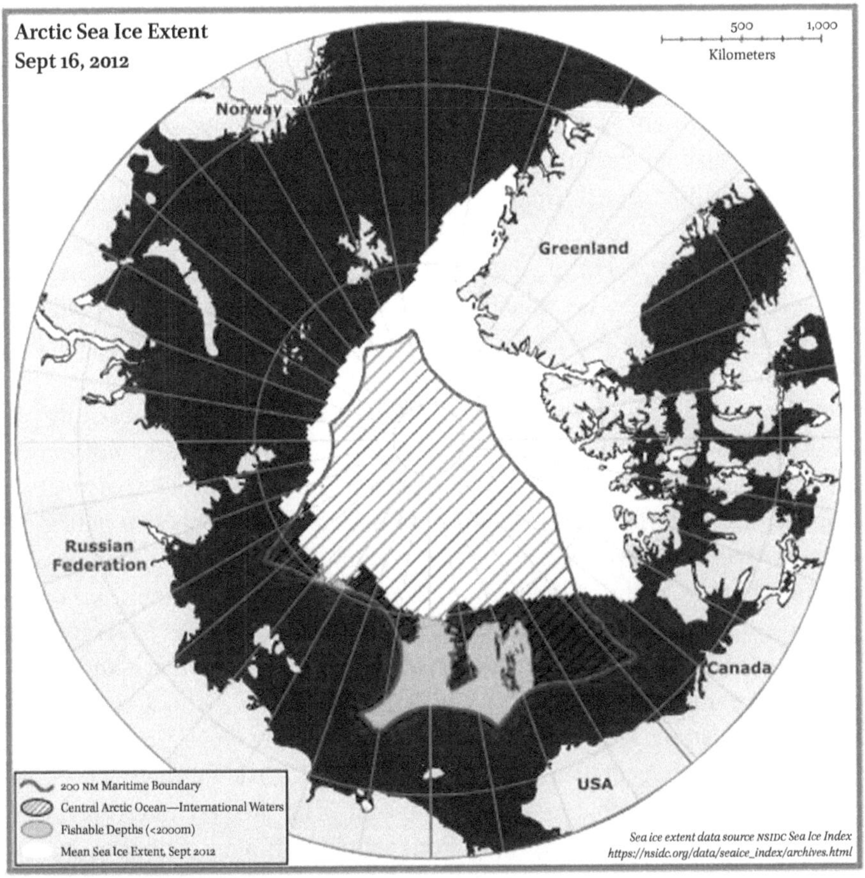

FIGURE 6 Arctic EEZs, 2012 summer sea ice extent and fishable depths
SOURCE: 'PREVENTING UNREGULATED COMMERCIAL FISHING IN THE CENTRAL ARCTIC OCEAN (CAO) – A COMPILATION OF REPORTS FROM MEETINGS OF EXPERTS IN SHANGHAI (CHINA), INCHEON (KOREA) & SAPPORO (JAPAN)' (CHAPTER 1, N 3) 18, WITH REFERENCE TO THE DATA SOURCE OF THE NATIONAL SNOW AND ICE DATA CENTER (NSIDC)

The manner in which the CAOF Agreement should address exploratory fishing was not clear from the beginning.[238] Regarding commercial fishing, there

238 'Chairman's Statement, Fourth Meeting on Central Arctic Ocean Fisheries (Tórshavn, 29 November – 1 December 2016)' 2 <https://apps-afsc.fisheries.noaa.gov/documents/Arctic_fish_stocks_fifth_meeting/508_Documents/508_Chairman_s%20Statement%20from%20Torshavn%20Meeting%202016.pdf> accessed 2 November 2024.

seemed to be a large consensus to ban it for the time being. Yet, the issue to allow exploratory fishing, especially under what circumstances, was a lot more complex. The Parties ultimately agreed to define exploratory fishing in Article 1(e) CAOF Agreement as "fishing for the purpose of assessing the sustainability and feasibility of future commercial fisheries by contributing to scientific data relating to such fisheries". This definition reflects the scientific and forward-looking approach of the Agreement.[239]

Although the inclusion of Arctic residents and their communities, including indigenous peoples, is explicitly mentioned in the Agreement's Preamble, the two definitions in Article 1(d) and (e) of the CAOF Agreement lack reference to fisheries conducted by indigenous peoples for other than commercial or exploration purposes. Local communities typically practice harvesting for subsistence purposes only and often hunt in traditional ways by foot or, for longer distances, by snowmobile or dog sled instead of by boat.[240] This practice supports their traditional understanding of having a high respect for nature.[241] The lack of technical equipment can however impair local communities reaching harvest areas offshore, where there is no ice on which hunters can move and hunt.[242] Yet, although climate change may affect one type of hunting, it may enable another: this has happened, for example, in West Greenland in the early 20th century when seals moved further north but cod, halibut, and shrimp moved into warmer local waters and allowed the development of a cod fishery.[243] In any case, local communities may be forced to adapt their harvesting techniques and equipment to ensure food security for their community.

Hence, although fisheries by indigenous people will not be conducted extensively on a large scale, they should nevertheless be considered. It seems reasonable that the CAOF Agreement does not qualify subsistence and recreational

239 On this approach and its implementation in the CAOF Agreement, see Chapter 5 Sections 2, 2.1 *infra*.

240 Arctic Monitoring and Assessment Programme (AMAP), Conservation of Arctic Flora and Fauna (CAFF) Working Group and International Arctic Science Committee (IASC) (Chapter 2, n 78) 662.

241 Cf. Lipton Matthews, 'Did Native Peoples Live in Harmony with Nature? It' s Complicated.' *Mises Wire* (10 April 2020) <https://mises.org/wire/did-native-peoples-live-harmony-nature-its-complicated> accessed 4 April 2022.

242 Timo Koivurova, Henna Kervo and Adam Stępień, 'Arctic Transform Background Paper: Indigenous Peoples in the Arctic' (2008) 12 <https://www.arctic-transform.eu/download/IndigPeoBP.pdf> accessed 5 December 2021.

243 Arctic Monitoring and Assessment Programme (AMAP), Conservation of Arctic Flora and Fauna (CAFF) Working Group and International Arctic Science Committee (IASC) (Chapter 2, n 78) 662–663.

fisheries as commercial fishing.[244] Yet, strictly speaking, such fisheries also do not fall under the definition of fishing for scientific reasons or exploratory fishing. An adaption of the Agreement to regulate this specific case would therefore be desirable, if alone to give more visibility to native peoples. This does not mean that subsistence fishing must be restricted. Explicitly permitting traditional hunting by local communities is one possible way to protect the interests of indigenous peoples. Furthermore, where there is no regulation, there is often room for abuse. With respect to hunting rights of local communities, for example, this is currently the case with the exception of polar bear hunting, which is granted to foreigners when guided by an indigenous person in Canada. Whereas in all other countries in which polar bears occur, hunting of polar bears was severely restricted by the 1973 International Agreement for the Conservation of Polar Bears[245] after it became endangered throughout its range, hunting is now only possible for aboriginal people and their purposes[246] in Canada. Hunting by non-aboriginal people and non-citizens is permitted when guided by an Inuit as part of the polar bear hunt – which is readily accepted by hunting enthusiasts.[247] This illustrates the need for indigenous peoples to be part of resource regulation agreements to ensure comprehensive protection of the resource in question. Concerning fish stocks in the CAO, this may not be a current threat. Nevertheless, the inclusion of indigenous peoples within the scope of the CAOF Agreement is a necessary approach to ensure adequate long-term protection and control of overfishing in the CAO.

4.3 *Further Developments in the Arctic*

The development of the Arctic creates opportunities not only for fisheries, but also for other economic activities. In a probabilistic approach, it is estimated that the Arctic region holds about 30% of the world's untapped gas[248]

244 See Seamus Ryder, 'The Declaration Concerning the Prevention of Unregulated High Seas Fishing in the Central Arctic Ocean' *The University of Calgary Faculty of Law Blog* (31 July 2015) 4 <https://ablawg.ca/2015/07/31/the-declaration-concerning-the-prevention-of-unregulated-high-seas-fishing-in-the-central-arctic-ocean/> accessed 27 November 2020.

245 'Agreement on the Conservation of Polar Bears (Oslo, 15 November 1973) – UNTS Vol. 2898, No. 50540' <https://treaties.un.org/pages/showDetails.aspx?objid=0800000280363c19> accessed 30 June 2021.

246 'Polar Bear Range States | National Management' <https://polarbearagreement.org/polar-bear-management/national-management> accessed 5 December 2021.

247 'Polar Bears in Canada | Guided Hunting in Canada' <https://www.polarbearscanada.ca/en/management/harvest/sport-hunting-in-canada> accessed 8 April 2022.

248 Federal Foreign Office Germany (Chapter 2, n 89) 31.

and 13% of its oil.[249] Engaging in their production supports a long-term sustainable energy supply. Germany, for example, gets most of the oil and gas it needs from Norway and Russia, both of which already produce raw materials in the Arctic.[250] Further, as sea ice melts, a year-round ice-free North Sea route would provide the shortest shipping route between European ports in the North range and East Asian ports. This would save time, fuel and money, and create interesting opportunities for shipbuilders and tourism,[251] although problems such as the unpredictability of the ice, inadequate emergency rescue capabilities and the lack of suitable transport vessels for the Arctic remain.[252]

Political developments in the Arctic are difficult to calculate. Overlapping interests among Arctic littoral States are likely, which may lead to a geopolitical race[253] for sovereign rights or rights to use the Arctic seabed and its natural resources.[254] Therefore, the integration of the Arctic region into a system of multilateral stability, trust, and cooperation is crucial.

---

249 Parliament of Iceland Althingi, 'Parliamentary Resolution on Iceland's Arctic Policy (Reykjavík, 28 March 2011)' <http://library.arcticportal.org/1861/> accessed 10 August 2021.

250 See Federal Foreign Office Germany, 'Guidelines of the Germany Arctic Policy – Assume Responsibility, Seize Opportunities' (2013) 6 <https://www.arctic-office.de/fileadmin/user_upload/www.arctic-office.de/PDF_uploads/Germanys_Arctic_policy_guidelines.pdf> accessed 4 April 2022.

251 See Eleanor Huffines, 'Most Large Ships Transiting Arctic Use New Routes That Help Protect Environment and Communities' *The Pew Charitable Trusts* (20 May 2020) <https://www.pewtrusts.org/en/research-and-analysis/articles/2020/05/20/most-large-ships-transiting-arctic-use-new-routes-that-help-protect-environment-and-communities> accessed 11 December 2020.

252 Federal Foreign Office Germany (Chapter 2, n 250) 10.

253 As an example, several unresolved issues are mentioned in Iceland's Arctic policy: "(1) The United States and Canada are involved in a dispute over the Northwest Passage and a part of the Beaufort Sea which is estimated to hold vast oil deposits. The United States considers the Northwest Passage as an international strait whereas Canada considers the route its internal waters. (2) Denmark and Canada, on the one hand, and Russia, on the other hand, disagree on jurisdiction over the Lomonosov Ridge in the Arctic Ocean. (3) Most nations reject Norway's claim of a 200 nautical miles zone around Svalbard on the basis of conditional sovereignty over the island and have refused to recognise their "fisheries protection zone" around it. (4) A dispute is ongoing between Canada and Denmark over Hans Island, which is located in the strait that separates Ellesmere Island from Northern-Greenland and connects Baffin Bay with the Lincoln Sea."

254 Parliament of Iceland Althingi (Chapter 2, n 249).

5 Summary

The Arctic comprises a unique, fragile area that is subject to varying definitions, depending on the application of different characteristics such as climate, temperature, sea ice extent or political views. The Arctic Ocean is considered to be the open waters between the areas of the High Arctic, the northernmost part of the Arctic. The CAOF Agreement Area includes only a portion of the central part of the Arctic Ocean, and thus only the part of the high seas surrounded by waters where Canada, the Kingdom of Denmark with respect to Greenland, the Kingdom of Norway, the Russian Federation, and the United States exercise fisheries jurisdiction. This avoids touching upon the issue of maritime zones around Svalbard, but may conflict with the ecosystem approach to fisheries, where an entire stock within an ecosystem should be protected regardless of boundaries.

Climate change and the Arctic are unfortunately inextricably linked. The continuing rise in Arctic temperatures leads to regional and global consequences. Arctic sea ice is melting. Moreover, not only is the extent of sea ice decreasing, but also its quality, measured in terms of age and thickness. Greenhouse gases are gradually being released into the atmosphere, exacerbating further warming. Changes in the food web and environment for aquatic life and indigenous peoples are the result.

As far as fishing is concerned, there is currently no fishing in CAO waters, as fish stocks are low and fishing is difficult due to sea ice. However, as temperatures rise in the Arctic Ocean region and the ice sheet decreases, fish stocks are gradually moving northward to colder areas. In addition, NIS are introduced by vessels, aquaculture and natural dispersal. It is likely that this trend will continue to spread into central Arctic waters, opening up new opportunities for fisheries in the future. The CAOF Agreement distinguishes between fisheries for scientific purposes, commercial fisheries and exploratory fisheries. Subsistence and recreational fisheries are not specifically mentioned in the Agreement but are assumed to be at least outside the scope of commercial fisheries. In addition to fisheries, ongoing changes in the Arctic offer new opportunities for, *inter alia,* shipping and the exploitation of resources such as gas and oil. All in all, the Arctic is subject to constant change, and emerging opportunities call for regulation.

CHAPTER 3

Foundations and Political Drivers of the CAOF Agreement

The CAOF Agreement is the first regional fisheries agreement to have been adopted before fisheries actually began in a given area. Due to these exceptional circumstances, it is particularly worthwhile to take a closer look at the motivations that led to the adoption of the Agreement (Chapter 3 Section 1) and influenced its drafting process (Chapter 3 Section 2). Moreover, fundamental for understanding the Agreement are the diverse composition of the Parties (Chapter 3 Section 3) and the specific way in which the Agreement seeks to bring together the interests of a large and heterogeneous group of stakeholders (Chapter 3 Section 4).

1 Motivations for the CAOF Agreement

The CAOF Agreement's overarching objective is to prevent IUU fishing in the Agreement Area.[1] In this regard, two interests must be reconciled: the freedom of the high seas and the conservation of marine resources.

In areas beyond national jurisdiction, which usually means beyond State's EEZs, the concept of the freedom of the high seas applies. The concept was significantly shaped by Hugo Grotius, a Dutch scholar, philosopher and jurist, whose work *Mare Liberum* (The Free Sea)[2] had a major impact on the modern understanding of international law, especially the law of the sea.[3] Grotius regarded the sea as a public good, a shared resource of "common use" for the benefit of mankind, "common to all, proper to none", just like the air or the sun.[4] This understanding has fortunately remained valid to this day and has

1 See Article 2 CAOF Agreement.

2 Hugo Grotius, *Mare Liberum: Sive de Iure Quod Batavis Competit Ad Indicana Commercia Dissertatio* (Lodewijk Elzevir 1609).

3 Julia Martine Van Ittersum, 'Hugo Grotius: The Making of a Founding Father of International Law' in Anne Orford and Florian Hoffmann (eds), *The Oxford Handbook of the Theory of International Law* (Oxford University Press 2016) 2.

4 Robert Feenstra, *Hugo Grotius Mare Liberum 1609–2009 – Original Latin Text and English Translation* (Brill | Nijhoff 2009) 62 et seq. <https://brill.com/view/title/16983> accessed 8 July 2020.

 | DOI:10.1163/9789004700673_004

been accepted as customary international law.[5] The triumph of Grotius *mare liberum* idea over the contradicting *mare clausum* theory in the 17th century ensures that today we

> evaluate the propriety and legitimacy of individual claims against the international community interest, rather than the opposite process of carving an area of community concern from a myriad of conflicting claims to ownership of the seas.[6]

Nowadays, this approach contributes largely to the sharing of resources, such as fishing in the high seas. The understanding has been incorporated by UNCLOS, of which Article 136 stipulates that the area of the high seas and its resources "are the common heritage of mankind". The concept of the freedom of the high seas itself has been implemented in Article 87 UNCLOS, which specifically mentions the "freedom of fishing".[7] Taking that into account, Article 116 UNCLOS fundamentally guarantees all States the right for their nationals to engage in fishing on the high seas.

But this freedom is not unconditional. On the one hand, the freedom of the high seas should be exercised under the conditions laid down by UNCLOS and by other rules of international law.[8] Furthermore, each State must accept restrictions on its own freedom of action resulting from the equal freedom of other States, which requires a balancing of interests in the use of the seas.[9] The conditions to exercise the freedom of fishing are hence determined by the international community. In this context, Article 117 UNCLOS provides for the duty of States to cooperate with other States to take necessary conservation measures for the living resources of the high seas.[10] The preferred means of cooperation should be (sub)regional fisheries management organizations,

---

5 Tanaka (Chapter 2, n 153) 23; J Ashley Roach, 'Today's Customary International Law of the Sea' (2014) 45 Ocean Development and International Law 239; cf. James Crawford, *Brownlie's Principles of Public International Law* (9th edn, Oxford University Press 2019) 282, who advocates in favour of a general principle of international law.

6 Eric Wilson, 'Mare Liberum and Opinio Iuris: A Grotian Reading of the North Sea Continental Shelf Cases' (2002) 2 Monash University Law Review 299, 325 <http://www.austlii.edu.au/au/journals/MonashULawRw/2002/13.pdf> accessed 3 September 2020.

7 See Article 87(1)(e) UNCLOS.

8 See Article 87(1) UNCLOS.

9 Douglas Guilfoyle, 'Article 87 – Freedom of the High Seas' in Alexander Proelß (ed), *United Nations Convention on the Law of the Sea: A Commentary* (Nomos 2017) para 3,9.

10 See already *Fisheries Jurisdiction (United Kingdom v Iceland), Judgment of 25 July 1974, ICJ Reports 1974, p 3* [72]; *Fisheries Jurisdiction (Federal Republic of Germany v Iceland), Judgment of 25 July 1974, ICJ Reports 1974, p 175* [64].

hence RFBs.[11] These have been considered[12] and proven to be (more or less) effective instruments to cooperatively balance the interests of fisheries and conservation of fish stocks. However, these regimes so far followed a reactive approach. Until now, they only came into play when a fish species was already endangered due to long-term excessive fishing and the fishery had to be controlled as a result.

Regimes like RFBs mainly target the prevention of IUU fishing. Fishing in areas beyond national jurisdiction on the high seas is considered one of the main threats to the conservation and sustainable use of marine biodiversity in these areas.[13] Where this is conducted illegally and in an unregulated manner, the effects are conceivably even worse. The fight against IUU fisheries[14] is a recurring issue on the international stage.[15] In this context, regional fisheries regimes are seen as a useful tool to combat IUU fisheries by providing a framework that must be respected if fishing should take place in a given area, e.g. through setting up reporting obligations and other regulations.[16]

Uncontrolled or ineffectively controlled fishing often correlate with overfishing.[17] Overfishing describes a situation where stock abundance is fished to below the level that can produce a maximum sustainable yield (MSY), which has devastating consequences for marine wealth. It negatively impacts biodiversity and ecosystem functioning and reduces fish production, which subsequently leads to negative social and economic consequences.[18] In addition, where the exploitation of newly accessible natural resources – like fish – precedes scientific research and effective management measures, these

11 See Article 118 UNCLOS. Similiar, see Article 63(2) UNCLOS and Article 8(4) UNFS Agreement.

12 See Article 8(1) UNFS Agreement.

13 Erik J Molenaar and Richard Caddell, 'Options and Pathways to Strengthen International Fisheries Law in an Era of Changing Oceans', *Strengthening International Fisheries Law in an Era of Changing Oceans* (Hart Publishing 2019) 424.

14 See e.g. the FAO's International Plan of Action to Prevent, Deter and Eliminate Illegal, Unreported and Unregulated Fishing of (IPOA-IUU), Chapter 4 Sections 1, 1.3, 1.3.3 *infra*.

15 'United Nations General Assembly Resolution 64/72, Sustainable Fisheries (Adopted 4 December 2009)' 10; European Commission, 'Commission Regulation (EC) No 1010/2009 Laying down Detailed Rules for the Implementation of Council Regulation (EC) No 1005/2008 (22 October 2009) – OJ L 280/5' <https://eur-lex.europa.eu/legal-content/EN/TXT/PDF/?uri=CELEX:32009R1010&from=DE> accessed 12 August 2021.

16 'United Nations General Assembly Resolution 64/72, Sustainable Fisheries (Adopted 4 December 2009)' 10.

17 Food and Agriculture Organization of the United Nations, 'The State of World Fisheries and Aquaculture 2020: Sustainability in Action' (Chapter 1, n 3) vi.

18 ibid 54.

resources are even more prone to overexploitation, especially internationally shared fish stocks in high sea waters.[19] Currently, more than one-third of global fish stocks are overfished, an even lager number are in decline, and the numbers are steadily increasing.[20] On the high seas, the situation is even more critical for highly migratory, straddling and other fisheries resources:[21] compared to the 1950s, catch on the high seas increased from under two million tonnes to over ten million tonnes in 2006.[22]

The case of the Bering Sea "Donut Hole" fisheries was therefore a particular impetus for the CAOF Agreement.[23] As common in the 1970s and subsequent years, the United States and the Soviet Union, later Russia, made claims[24] to extend fisheries jurisdiction in their respective coastal waters up to 200 NM.[25] These claims, however, did not cover the whole Bering Sea but left a substantial part of its waters without national fisheries jurisdiction. The remaining high seas portion of the Bering Sea became known as the "Donut Hole".

For a few years, little attention was paid to the area, as fishing was still possible in the zones under US and Soviet jurisdiction. However, with the growing national fleets of the US and the Soviet Union, fishing opportunities diminished. As a result, China, Japan, Poland and South Korea engaged in large-scale

---

19 'European Commission | The EU Joins Forces with Nine Countries for Future Science-Based Management of the High Seas of the Central Arctic Ocean (13 February 2020)' <https://www.europarl.europa.eu/cmsdata/196428/Trawler%20February%202020.pdf> accessed 2 November 2024.

20 Food and Agriculture Organization of the United Nations, 'The State of World Fisheries and Aquaculture 2016: Contributing to Food Security and Nutrition for All' (Chapter 1, n 3) 5 et seq.; Turner (Chapter 1, n 4).

21 Food and Agriculture Organization of the United Nations, 'The State of World Fisheries and Aquaculture 2020: Sustainability in Action' (Chapter 1, n 3) 48–54.

22 Sarika Cullis-Suzuki and Daniel Pauly, 'Failing the High Seas: A Global Evaluation of Regional Fisheries Management Organizations' (2010) 34 Marine Policy 1036, 1036 <https://www.sciencedirect.com/science/article/abs/pii/S0308597X10000540> accessed 12 August 2021.

23 On the 'Donut Hole' fisheries, see in detail David A Balton, 'The Bering Sea Doughnut Hole Convention: Regional Solution, Global Implications' in Olav Schram Stokke (ed), *Governing High Seas Fisheries: The Interplay of Global and Regional Regimes* (Oxford University Press 2001).

24 United States Department of State, 'Public Notice 2237: Exclusive Economic Zone and Maritime Boundaries; Notice of Limits' (1995) 60 Federal Register 43825, 43827 <https://www.govinfo.gov/content/pkg/FR-1995-08-23/pdf/95-20794.pdf> accessed 28 March 2021; United Nations Office for Ocean Affairs and the Law of the Sea, 'The Law of the Sea: Baselines: National Legislation With Illustrative Maps' (1989) 353 et seq. <https://www.un.org/depts/los/LEGISLATIONANDTREATIES/PDFFILES/publications/E.89.V.10.pdf> accessed 29 March 2021.

25 These zones later became Exclusive Economic Zones (EEZs).

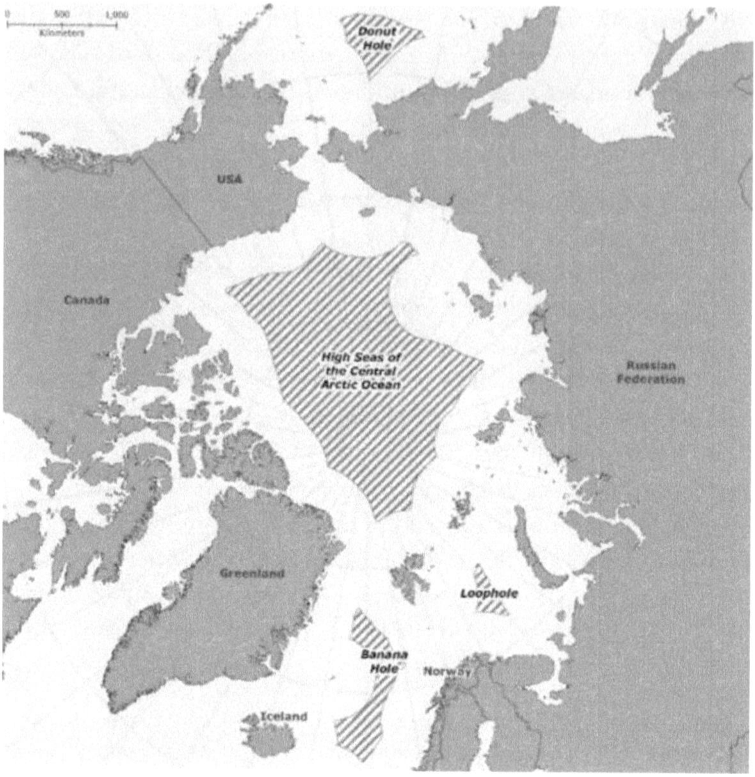

FIGURE 7 High seas pockets in the marine Arctic
SOURCE: MOLENAAR, 'PARTICIPATION IN THE CENTRAL ARCTIC OCEAN FISHERIES AGREEMENT' (CHAPTER 2, N 23) 136

pollock fisheries in the "Donut Hole", which became one of the largest single-species fisheries in the world. The inadequate control and rapid growth of the fishery raised concerns about its collapse, which would have affected not only the "Donut Hole" itself but also fisheries in the adjacent US and Soviet fisheries jurisdiction zones. These concerns led to negotiations on a convention in the early 1990s.[26] But unfortunately, two years before the successful conclusion of the 1994 Convention on the Conservation and Management of Pollock

26 David A Balton, 'Implementing the New Arctic Fisheries Agreement' in Tomas Heidar (ed), *New Knowledge and Changing Circumstances in the Law of the Sea* (Brill | Nijhoff 2020) 429–431.

Resources in the Central Bering Sea,[27] the pollock stock had collapsed and has never fully recovered since.[28]

In this regard, the Summary of the Roundtable on Ecosystem and Fisheries Issues in the Central Arctic Ocean, held in March 2016, concluded that

> [t]he collapse of Pollock stocks in the "Donut Hole" of the Bering Sea, and the decimation of Northern Cod in the Northwest Atlantic were presented as unfortunate precedents to be avoided ... key practical examples of 'the tragedy of the commons'.[29]

Similar concerns about the development of uncontrolled fisheries in the high seas part of the Arctic Ocean arose as the initial situation in Arctic waters is somewhat similar to the previous situation in the Bering Sea: fishing jurisdictions of coastal States surround a high seas portion, in this case the central part of the Arctic Ocean. Although commercial fishing in Arctic waters was not possible for a long time, rising temperatures and growing ice-free areas brought this possibility into the near future. The process in research that provided new insights into the value of potentially accessible resources led to a drastic change in the calculations of Arctic littoral states towards the interests of the rest of the world. A strong tendency to territorialise resources that were originally considered beyond the control of a State's national jurisdiction came to light.[30] The unaltered high demand for fishery products causes countries to constantly look for alternative sources of supply. With receding sea ice, the number of trips, especially fishing vessel operations, in Arctic waters has continuously increased over the last years.[31] In the Arctic, however, the idea is to do better and to show that it is possible to learn from mistakes: in order

27 'Convention on the Conservation and Management of Pollock Resources in the Central Bering Sea (Washington D.C., 16 June 1994)' <https://www.ecolex.org/details/treaty/convention-on-the-conservation-and-management-of-pollock-in-the-central-bering-sea-tre-001217/> accessed 12 August 2021.

28 Don Bowen, Jake Rice and Robert J Trumble, 'MSC Final Report and Determination for Alaska Pollock – Bering Sea-Aleutian Islands' (MRAG Americas 2015) 18 <https://cert.msc.org/FileLoader/FileLinkDownload.asmx/GetFile?encryptedKey=v5NAojNkiUZRzn52Lf/KM5Ylxb3g6nRc8mRKhTsxOdE4pwpZXgAkpouYs6bJWuLB> accessed 10 August 2021.

29 'Preventing Unregulated Commercial Fishing in the Central Arctic Ocean (CAO) – A Compilation of Reports from Meetings of Experts in Shanghai (China), Incheon (Korea) & Sapporo (Japan)' (Chapter 1, n 2) 9.

30 Christopher R Rossi, 'Tradition, Tendency, Temptation', *Sovereignty and Territorial Temptation–The Grotian Tendency* (Cambridge University Press 2017) 6.

31 Silber and Adams (Chapter 2, n 162) 8, 11–12.

to avoid IUU fishing, basic research on the widely unknown Arctic ecosystem should be conducted, and future scenarios about fishing areas should be developed, e.g. on the Atlantic or Pacific side of the Arctic Ocean and within coastal State marine areas or in international waters. Further assessed should be dates, species, and fishing techniques for potential target species but also possible impacts for non-target species[32]- all points that were missed to address in relation to the Bering Sea pollock fishery at the time. Hence, the CAOF Agreement, which was largely influenced by Russia and the USA, the two major players involved in overfishing in the "Donut Hole", can be seen as a signal that a lesson has been learned: the general opinion was that the scenarios mentioned above needed to be thought through and managed appropriately before fisheries take place, preferably under the auspices of an internationally binding agreement such as the CAOF Agreement.

Along with the objective of preventing IUU fishing, the Agreement was created to protect healthy Arctic marine ecosystems and ensure the conservation and sustainable use of fish stocks.[33] This was not considered sufficiently guaranteed under the existing framework conditions.[34] UNCLOS provides a framework that sets out the obligations of States to (cooperatively) protect and conserve the marine environment,[35] but does not elaborate further. Post-UNCLOS innovations have taken a step further and developed the duty to cooperate to encompass a broader concept of the marine environment: it requires an integrated and coherent approach to management, taking into account the full range of activities and impacts on the marine environment.[36] This approach is found in the efforts on the creation of an international legal framework relating to the conservation and sustainable use of marine biodiversity

32 Timo Koivurova and Erik J Molenaar, 'International Governance and Regulation of the Marine Arctic – Three Reports Prepared for the WWF International Arctic Programme' (2009) 51 <https://wwfint.awsassets.panda.org/downloads/overview_and_gap_analysis.pdf>.

33 See Article 2 CAOF Agreement.

34 European Union, 'Communication from the Commission to the European Parliament and the Council – The European Union and the Arctic Region (20 November 2008) – COM/2008/0763 Final' (Chapter 2, n 80); European Commission, 'Joint Communication – Developing a European Union Policy towards the Arctic Region: Progress since 2008 and next Steps (2012) – JOIN(2012) 19 Final' (Chapter 2, n 61).

35 See *inter alia* Preamble, Articles 117 et seq., 145 et seq., 192 et seq. UNCLOS.

36 Kristina M Gjerde, Nichola A Clark and Harriet R Harden-Davies, 'Building a Platform for the Future: The Relationship of the Expected New Agreement for Marine Biodiversity in Areas beyond National Jurisdiction and the UN Convention on the Law of the Sea' (2019) 33 Ocean Yearbook Online 3, 42 <https://brill.com/view/journals/ocyo/33/1/article-p1_1.xml> accessed 5 December 2021.

in areas beyond national jurisdiction (so called biodiversity beyond national jurisdiction (BBNJ) treaty).[37] The aim of the treaty is to achieve a consensual outcome of high quality that would allow for universal participation and bring coherency to conservation in areas beyond national jurisdiction,[38] which is very much supported internationally.[39] Initially in June 2015, the UN General Assembly adopted Resolution 69/292 on the development of a respective legally binding instrument under UNCLOS.[40] Although envisaged to be completed after four intergovernmental conferences, due to the COVID-19 pandemic, the last session was postponed[41] multiple times and has been scheduled to take place in early 2022.[42] In the meantime, delegations have submitted

37 For discussion on the process see Vito De Lucia, 'The Question of the Common Heritage of Mankind and the Negotiations Towards a Global Treaty on Marine Biodiversity in Areas Beyond National Jurisdiction: No End in Sight?' (2020) 16 McGil International Journal of Sustainable Development Law & Policy 138 <https://www.ssrn.com/abstract=3542384> accessed 17 January 2022; For the history on a pontential new agreement see Holly Matley, 'Developments in International Fisheries Law and Their Contribution to Improving the Effectiveness of RFMOs and Other Environmental Regimes' in Neil Craik and others (eds), *Global Environmental Change and Innovation in International Law* (Cambridge University Press 2018) 120 et seq.

38 De Lucia (Chapter 3, n 37) 17.

39 See for example Federal Foreign Office Germany (Chapter 2, n 89) 18; 'Government of Canada | Marine Biodiversity in Areas beyond National Jurisdictions: New International Treaty Negotiation' (25 July 2018) <https://www.canada.ca/en/environment-climate-change/services/sustainable-development/strategic-environmental-assessment/public-statements/international-treaty-marine-biodiveristy.html> accessed 11 December 2020; Katherine Zischka and others, 'Marine Biodiversity Beyond National Jurisdiction – Australia's Continuing Role' (2017) <https://d3n8a8pro7vhmx.cloudfront.net/edonsw/pages/5428/attachments/original/1513316783/Marine_BBNJ_Report_%28FINAL%29.pdf?1513316783> accessed 11 December 2021; National University of Singapore Centre for International Law, 'Workshop on the "Conservation and Sustainable Use of Marine Biological Diversity of Areas beyond National Jurisdiction: Preparing for the PrepCom" – Executive Summary' (2016) <https://cil.nus.edu.sg/wp-content/uploads/2015/10/BBNJ-Workshop-Executive-Summary-Final.pdf> accessed 2 November 2024.

40 'United Nations General Assembly Resolution 69/292, Development of an International Legally Binding Instrument under UNCLOS on the Conservation and Sustainable Use of Marine Biological Diversity of Areas beyond National Jurisdiction (Adopted 19 June 2015)'.

41 United Nations, 'Fourth Session of the BBNJ Intergovernmental Conference: Letter from the President of the General Assembly (9 March 2020)' <https://www.un.org/bbnj/sites/www.un.org.bbnj/files/bbnj-letter-from-president-of-the-bbnj-conference.pdf> accessed 4 February 2022.

42 United Nations General Assembly, 'Draft Decision: Intergovernmental Conference on an International Legally Binding Instrument under the United Nations Convention on the Law of the Sea (9 June 2021) – A/75/L96' <https://www.undocs.org/en/A/75/L.96> accessed 28 June 2021.

textual proposals for a BBNJ treaty to be considered at the fourth intergovernmental conference.[43] Further, in order to maintain the momentum of the process, the President of the BBNJ Intergovernmental Conference introduced an intersessional work program[44] to delegations that should be conducted until the negotiation process may continue.[45] In addition, a high ambition coalition has been launched to gather parties that are committed, at the highest political level, to achieve an ambitious outcome of the ongoing negotiations.[46] The session in March 2022 did however not yet lead to the conclusion of a treaty.[47] A framework agreement was and is therefore still not laid down in a single treaty, which shows, among other things, the need for the CAOF Agreement.

As a result, the current framework still consists of a multitude of global, regional and bilateral legally binding and non-legally binding instruments and provisions – UNCLOS, various regional and sub-regional agreements, national laws and soft-law instruments. This creates a decentralized, sectoral framework that consequently suffers from spatial and substantive gaps and actual and potential overlaps. This gave rise to a range of inconsistent or insufficient mandates in existing agreements and institutions, uncovering an overall lack of coordination and cooperation both within and across the various sectors.[48] Apart from the envisaged BBNJ treaty, there is no regime for assessing cumulative impacts over time and across all different sectors and for coordinating activities that take place between the waters of the high seas and the waters of the coastal States' extended continental shelf. This last point is of

43 United Nations, 'Textual Proposals Submitted by Delegations by 20 February 2020, for Consideration at the Fourth Session of the Intergovernmental Conference on an International Legally Binding Instrument under UNCLOS – A/CONF.232/2020/3' (2020) <https://www.un.org/bbnj/sites/www.un.org.bbnj/files/textual_proposals_compilation_article-by-article_-_15_april_2020.pdf> accessed 13 August 2020.

44 United Nations, 'Updated Programme of the BBNJ Intersessional Work (9 November 2020)' <https://www.un.org/bbnj/fr/node/963> accessed 11 December 2020.

45 United Nations, 'Letter from the President of the BBNJ Intergovernmental Conference to Delegations (10 September 2020)' <https://www.un.org/bbnj/sites/www.un.org.bbnj/files/intersessional_work_-_bbnj_president_letter_to_delegations.pdf> accessed 11 December 2020.

46 'European Commission | Protecting the Ocean, Time for Action: High Ambition Coalition on Biodiversity Beyond National Jurisdiction' <https://ec.europa.eu/oceans-and-fisheries/ocean/international-ocean-governance/protecting-ocean-time-action_de> accessed 6 April 2022.

47 See 'United Nations | Intergovernmental Conference on Marine Biodiversity of Areas Beyond National Jurisdiction' <https://www.un.org/bbnj/> accessed 6 April 2022.

48 Christopher R Rossi, 'The Club within the Club: The Challenge of a Soft Law Framework in a Global Arctic Context' (2015) 5 Polar Journal 8, 171; Lilly Weidemann, *International Governance of the Arctic Marine Environment* (Springer 2014).

considerable importance in the Arctic, as the claims of coastal States to the outer or extended continental shelf potentially affect all but a tiny portion of the CAO's high seas areas.[49] In addition, although regional regimes relating to fisheries and protection of the marine environment exist – *inter alia* the NEAFC, the North Atlantic Salmon Conservation Organization (NASCO) and the Oslo-Paris Conventions (OSPAR)[50] – there are gaps in participation and the geographic scope of regimes. Furthermore, a regulatory instrument for transboundary environmental impact assessment is missing:[51] for instance, although the OSPAR Commission is tasked with declaring marine protected areas, it has not yet declared the Arctic Ocean to be such an area with special protection status.[52] Given the current lack of fishing in the high latitudes, this is perhaps not surprising. However, it is precisely this current lack of activity that provides a useful window of opportunity for the international community to take precautionary action and ensure the protection of vulnerable Arctic marine ecosystems.

Indeed, there have been thoughts on how this "window" should be used. Although critical voices claim that the Arctic needed to be "saved" from sovereign politics,[53] most scientists believe that changes in the Arctic marine environment require adequate international governance for protection, development and management.[54] Similar in structure[55] to the comprehensive Antarctic treaty regime,[56] the Arctic was considered "a role model for necessary

---

49 Rosemary Rayfuse, 'Protecting Marine Biodiversity in Polar Areas beyond National Jurisdiction' (2008) 17 Review of European Community and International Environmental Law 3, 7.

50 ibid 8; Stadtländer (Chapter 2, n 80) 1.

51 Weidemann (Chapter 3, n 48) 119 et seq.

52 See Annex V 'Convention for the Protection of the Marine Environment of the North-East Atlantic (OSPAR Convention) (Paris, 22 September 1992) – UNTS Vol. 2345, No. 42279' <https://treaties.un.org/doc/Publication/UNTS/Volume2354/v2354.pdf> accessed 12 August 2021.

53 Rossi, 'The Club within the Club: The Challenge of a Soft Law Framework in a Global Arctic Context' (Chapter 3, n 48) 171.

54 Erik J Molenaar, 'Managing Biodiversity in Areas beyond National Jurisdiction' (2007) 22 International Journal of Marine and Coastal Law 89, 95 et seq.; see also Rayfuse, 'Protecting Marine Biodiversity in Polar Areas beyond National Jurisdiction' (Chapter 3, n 49) 7; Stadtländer (Chapter 2, n 80) 1; Laetitia M Navarro and others, 'Monitoring Biodiversity Change through Effective Global Coordination' (2017) 29 Current Opinion in Environmental Sustainability 158, 166.

55 Koivurova and Molenaar (Chapter 3, n 32) 95.

56 'Convention on the Conversation of Antarctic Marine Living Resources (Canberra, 20 May 1980)' (Chapter 2, n 68).

adaptations and improvements"[57] and a "test case for the legal framework for high seas fisheries governance, or more broadly, for integrated and comprehensive ocean governance".[58] Sector- and area-based measures, an Arctic-wide environmental impact assessment and regional, cross-sectoral binding agreements were proposed as possible measures.[59] The envisaged instrument should be regional and comprehensive but not focus on specific target species. Above all, it should cover areas beyond national jurisdiction and ensure cooperation between various actors.[60] Regional soft-law regimes, which merely focus on Arctic cooperation among the littoral States, were believed not to compensate for the lack of a comprehensive treaty to ensure environmental protection.[61] This created a gap for the management of Arctic fisheries. The stalled negotiations on the BBNJ treaty put the Arctic coastal States on notice, forcing them to take timely action to fill the presented gap with the CAOF Agreement – with the nice side effect that the Arctic coastal States were able to determine the conditions of membership. Thus, although the CAOF Agreement is not the comprehensive treaty regime that some have called for, it is a step in the right direction and a possible component of effective governance in the Arctic region.

2 Drafting History and Framework Conditions

The lack of comprehensive regulation concerning both IUU fishing in CAO high sea waters and the protection of biodiversity in areas beyond national jurisdiction visibly demanded for an arrangement in the Arctic. Despite this external pressure, the drafting period of the CAOF Agreement[62] took almost

57 Stadtländer (Chapter 2, n 80) 1.
58 Weidemann (Chapter 3, n 48) 195.
59 ibid 199 et seq.
60 Molenaar, 'Managing Biodiversity in Areas beyond National Jurisdiction' (Chapter 3, n 54) 95 et seq.; see also Rayfuse, 'Protecting Marine Biodiversity in Polar Areas beyond National Jurisdiction' (Chapter 3, n 49) 7; Stadtländer (Chapter 2, n 80) 1; Navarro and others (Chapter 3, n 54) 166.
61 Stadtländer (Chapter 2, n 80) 1; Weidemann (Chapter 3, n 48) 119 et seq.
62 Specifically on the drafting process, see inter alia Molenaar, 'The CAOF Agreement: Key Issues of International Fisheries Law' (Chapter 2, n 20) 452 et seq.; Balton, 'Implementing the New Arctic Fisheries Agreement' (Chapter 3, n 26) 429–435; Alexander N Vylegzhanin, Oran R Young and Paul Arthur Berkman, 'The Central Arctic Ocean Fisheries Agreement as an Element in the Evolving Arctic Ocean Governance Complex' (2020) 118 Marine Policy 104001, 6–7; Schatz, Proelß and Liu (Chapter 2, n 41) 204 et seq.; Heidar (Chapter 2, n 50) 191 et seq.; Jianye Tang, 'Conservation of Marine Living Resources in the Central Arctic Ocean: Five Arctic Coastal States' Initiatives' in Myron H Nordquist, John Norton Moore and Ronán Long (eds), *International Marine Economy: Law and Policy*, vol 20

ten years – much longer than initially assumed. The creation of an Arctic fisheries agreement was discussed in multiple fora. Especially within the Arctic Council, the so-called "Arctic Five", the grouping of the five Arctic coastal States,[63] initiated meetings of Senior Arctic Officials (SAO) and permanent participants. Further, ministerial meetings and meetings of scientific experts (FiSCAO) were held.[64]

The case of the "Donut Hole" fisheries still in mind,[65] concerns about the development of an uncontrolled fishery in the high seas part of the Arctic Ocean led to a call for action. The initiative was originally driven by US commercial fishing interests, Alaskan Native groups, environmental organizations, and others.[66] It resulted in the first ever US Arctic Fisheries Management Plan. The plan was adopted in order to establish a management framework for commercial fishing in the US Arctic Management Area[67] and to prevent potential adverse effects on the Arctic marine environment from IUU commercial fishing.[68] Additionally, it supported the initial impulse of the CAOF Agreement, the adoption of United States Joint Resolution No. 17 in 2007, which calls upon the United States of America to

> initiate international discussions and take necessary steps with other Arctic nations to negotiate an agreement or agreements for managing

---

(Brill | Nijhoff 2017) 220 et seq.; Molenaar, 'International Regulation of Central Arctic Ocean Fisheries' (Chapter 2, n 20) 446–450; Wegge (Chapter 2, n 21) 335; partially EJ Molenaar, 'Arctic Fisheries Conservation and Management: Initial Steps of Reform of the International Legal Framework' (2013) 1 The Yearbook of Polar Law Online 427, 453; see also Mark Nuttall, Torben R Christensen and Martin Siegert, *The Routledge Handbook of the Polar Regions* (Routledge 2018).

63 Canada, Denmark (in respect of Greenland and the Faroe Islands), Norway, the Russian Federation, and the United States of America.

64 See a chronological overview of all meetings in the Arctic Five and Five-plus-Five processes at Molenaar, 'The CAOF Agreement: Key Issues of International Fisheries Law' (Chapter 2, n 20) 453.

65 On the "Donut Hole" fisheries see Chapter 3 Section 1 *supra*.

66 Balton, 'Implementing the New Arctic Fisheries Agreement' (Chapter 3, n 26) 432–433.

67 National Oceanic and Atmospheric Administration, 'Fisheries of the United States Exclusive Economic Zone Off Alaska; Fisheries of the Arctic Management Area; Bering Sea Subarea' (2009) 74 Federal Register 56734 <https://www.federalregister.gov/documents/2009/11/03/E9-26452/fisheries-of-the-united-states-exclusive-economic-zone-off-alaska-fisheries-of-the-arctic-management>.

68 National Oceanic and Atmospheric Administration, 'Fisheries of the United States Exclusive Economic Zone Off Alaska; Fisheries of the Arctic Management Area; Bering Sea Subarea' (2009) 74 Federal Register 27498, 27499 <https://www.govinfo.gov/content/pkg/FR-2009-06-10/pdf/FR-2009-06-10.pdf> accessed 6 April 2021.

> migratory, transboundary and straddling fish stocks in the Arctic Ocean and establishing a new international fisheries management organization or organizations for the region.[69]

Early intergovernmental discussions about the management of fisheries in the CAO were held later that year in November 2007 at the first meeting of the eight Arctic Council SAOs in Narvik, Norway.[70] Among the Arctic Council SAO's, the creation of an Arctic fisheries management agreement, as proposed by the US within the context of existing mechanisms, found great support.[71] This suggests that most Arctic States did not want the Arctic Council, which had previously not specifically dealt with fishing, to be directly involved in managing Arctic fisheries,[72] and to keep a future instrument exclusive. Accordingly, an EU counter-proposal to extend the mandate of existing RFB's such as the NEAFC as the preferred solution to the creation of a new instrument[73] was not sufficiently supported.[74] In addition, immediate action to implement a fisheries moratorium in unregulated Arctic waters was demanded by academics, scientists and non-governmental organizations (NGOs), e.g. the participants of the 2009 International Arctic Fisheries Symposium[75] and scientists at an International Polar Year meeting in Montreal in 2012.[76]

In a next step, following a meeting of the Foreign Ministers of the Arctic Five in Ilulissat, which was considered controversial due to the exclusion of fellow Artic Council States Finland, Iceland, Sweden and permanent participants

69 United States Congress (Chapter 2, n 163).

70 Molenaar, 'International Regulation of Central Arctic Ocean Fisheries' (Chapter 2, n 20) 446.

71 'Report, SAO Meeting (Narvik, 28–29 November 2007)' 12 <https://oaarchive.arctic-council.org/bitstream/handle/11374/380/ACSAO-NO02_Narvik_FINAL_Report.pdf?sequence=1&isAllowed=y> accessed 11 March 2020.

72 Molenaar, 'Arctic Fisheries Conservation and Management: Initial Steps of Reform of the International Legal Framework' (Chapter 3, n 62) 451.

73 European Union, 'Communication from the Commission to the European Parliament and the Council – The European Union and the Arctic Region (20 November 2008) – COM/2008/0763 Final' (Chapter 2, n 80) 9.

74 Molenaar, 'International Regulation of Central Arctic Ocean Fisheries' (Chapter 2, n 20) 446; Molenaar, 'Arctic Fisheries Conservation and Management: Initial Steps of Reform of the International Legal Framework' (Chapter 3, n 62) 456–458.

75 Balton, 'Implementing the New Arctic Fisheries Agreement' (Chapter 3, n 26) 433.

76 David Barber and others, 'An Open Letter from International Scientists' (2012) <https://www.pewtrusts.org/~/media/legacy/oceans_north_legacy/page_attachments/international-arctic-scientist-letter-with-sigs-522012.pdf?la=en> accessed 10 August 2021.

representing Arctic indigenous peoples,[77] the non-binding Ilulissat Declaration was adopted in May 2008.[78] Although the document mainly reiterates the predominant role of the Arctic Five in Artic matters, it also recognizes the ongoing rapid change in the Arctic due to global warming and calls for enhanced management efforts in particular fields.[79] The former Danish Minister for Foreign Affairs Møller stated in this regard that

> With the Ilulissat Declaration we have created a solid political framework for a peaceful development in the Arctic Ocean in the years ahead. We have sent a clear political signal to the local inhabitants and the rest of the World that we will act responsibly when addressing the development in the Arctic Ocean.[80]

In 2009, the US delegation to the 28th Session of FAO's Committee on Fisheries hosted a side event on Arctic fisheries. There, it was proposed to conduct an intergovernmental meeting the same or following year at which the participants adopt a non-legally binding instrument on Arctic fisheries. There was no indication as to whether the meeting should take place within the framework of the FAO or whether other participants should be involved.[81] In any case, it quickly became apparent that US efforts were on the pulse of time: Arctic fisheries and possible new regulations became a hot topic during the negotiations on the 2009 UN General Assembly Resolutions "Oceans and the Law of the Sea" and "Sustainable Fisheries"[82] that followed various EU proposals to include provisions on Arctic fisheries. The Resolutions, *inter alia,* raised the UN

77 See more on tensions between the Arctic Five and other States at Chapter 3 Section 3 *infra*.

78 'Arctic Ocean Conference Ilulissat Declaration (Ilulissat, 28 May 2008)' <https://cil.nus.edu.sg/wp-content/uploads/2017/07/2008-Ilulissat-Declaration.pdf> accessed 14 April 2022.

79 Brooks B Yeager, 'The Ilulissat Declaration: Background and Implications for Arctic Governance' (2008) 3 <https://www.arctic-report.net/wp-content/uploads/2012/01/2008.11-Ilulissat-Background-and-Implications.pdf> accessed 4 April 2022.

80 'Ministry of Foreign Affairs of Denmark | Conference in Ilulissat, Greenland: Landmark Political Declaration on the Future of the Arctic' <https://fnnewyork.um.dk/en/denmark/denmarks-engagement-with-the-un/statements/newsdisplaypage/?newsid=3d153209-5740-4b81-ba8b-f89cd39ca4fc> accessed 12 August 2021.

81 Molenaar, 'International Regulation of Central Arctic Ocean Fisheries' (Chapter 2, n 20) 446; Koivurova and Molenaar (Chapter 3, n 32) 73.

82 'United Nations General Assembly Resolution 64/71, Oceans and the Law of the Sea (Adopted 4 December 2009)'; 'United Nations General Assembly Resolution 64/72, Sustainable Fisheries (Adopted 4 December 2009)'.

General Assembly's deep concern about the delicate Arctic Ocean ecosystem and promoted enhanced international cooperation relating to the conservation and sustainable use of marine biodiversity in areas beyond national jurisdiction. The prevailing view of the Arctic Five was, however, that a regional fishery framework does not fall within the remit of the UN General Assembly and should not be demanded by it.[83]

In principle, the Arctic Five came to the conclusion that if a new international instrument to regulate Arctic fisheries should be adopted, this should take place outside the framework of existing mechanisms and form a new independent regime.[84] Due to the wide membership and institutional rules that had to be followed under existing frameworks like the FAO, coastal States like the Arctic Five and key flag States would have otherwise risked to be deprived of the principal role they commonly have in drafting processes to establish RFBs.[85] The understanding of a key role of the Arctic Five to exercise governance in fisheries in the Arctic grew with ongoing discussions and was expressed at several occasions throughout the process.[86]

Increasing climatic variations in the Arctic added pressure to the scene. In May 2011, within a letter to the US Secretary of State, Alaska's Senators supported the negotiation of an exclusive international Agreement, stating that the

> waters north of the U.S. and Russian EEZs are experiencing significant loss of multi-year sea ice. Much of this area is of fishable depth, the waters are open for several months each year now, and research is being conducted in these waters by non-coastal states already. Exploratory fishing may not be far behind. As a first step, we believe now is the time to secure an international agreement that prevents commercial fishing in these international waters.[87]

Thus, the basis for the Agreement was created. No further Arctic Five Foreign Affairs ministerial meetings took place, but concerning Arctic fisheries, the

83 Molenaar, 'International Regulation of Central Arctic Ocean Fisheries' (Chapter 2, n 20) 447; see Schatz, Proelß and Liu (Chapter 2, n 41) 204.

84 Molenaar, 'The CAOF Agreement: Key Issues of International Fisheries Law' (Chapter 2, n 20) 452; see Wegge (Chapter 2, n 21) 335–336.

85 Erik J Molenaar, 'Arctic Fisheries Management' in Erik J Molenaar, Alex G Oude Elferink and Donald R Rothwell (eds), *The Law of the Sea and the Polar Regions:: interactions between global and regional regimes* (Koninklijke Brill NV 2013) 246–248.

86 On the leading role of the Arctic Five, see Chapter 3 Section 3, 3.1 *infra*.

87 See Vylegzhanin, Young and Berkman (Chapter 3, n 62) 6.

Arctic Five continued to meet multiple times on an SAO level for questions of policy in a next step. This has been considered as the formal beginning of the Arctic Five process, which presented a factual preparatory procedure for the subsequent broader process.[88] Simultaneously to the SAO meetings, scientific FiSCAO meetings were conducted. SAO meetings took place in Oslo in June 2010, Washington in 2013 and 2014 in Nuuk. Among other things, discussed was the importance of gathering scientific information to increase scientific certainty on fish stocks.[89] FiSCAO meetings were convened in Anchorage in June 2011,[90] Tromsø in October 2013[91] and in April 2015 in Seattle.[92]

On 16 July 2015, the Arctic Five met at an ambassadorial level to sign the Declaration Concerning the Prevention of Unregulated High Seas Fishing in the Central Arctic Ocean, the Oslo Declaration. Therein, the Arctic Five recognized the differences in ice distribution and associated changes in the CAO environment, but expressed that only provisional measures and no additional RFB needed to be established. The declaration already contained key elements of the CAOF Agreement: its geographical scope, namely only the "high seas portion of the central Arctic Ocean", and the commitment to conduct high seas commercial fishing "only pursuant to one or more regional or subregional fisheries management organizations or arrangements that are or may be established to manage such fishing". Also the establishment of a joint program of scientific research, and cooperation with "relevant scientific bodies", including but not limited to the International Council for the Exploration of the Sea (ICES) and the North Pacific Marine Science Organization (PICES) were already mentioned in the Oslo Declaration.[93]

The Oslo Declaration provided for an opening of the process towards States with an interest in preventing IUU fisheries in the CAO through "working with

88 Molenaar, 'The CAOF Agreement: Key Issues of International Fisheries Law' (Chapter 2, n 20) 446–447.

89 'Chairman's Statement, Third Meeting on Central Arctic Ocean Fisheries (Nuuk, 24–26 February 2014)' <http://www.pewtrusts.org/~/media/assets/2014/09/arcticnationsagreetoworkoninternationalfisheries-accord.pdf?la=it> accessed 10 August 2021.

90 'Report of the First FiSCAO Meeting on Central Arctic Ocean Fisheries (Anchorage, 15–17 June 2011)' (Chapter 2, n 161).

91 'Report of the Second FiSCAO Meeting on Central Arctic Ocean Fisheries (Tromsø, 28–31 October 2013)' (Chapter 2, n 161).

92 'Report of the Third FiSCAO Meeting on Central Arctic Ocean Fisheries (Seattle, 14–16 April 2015)' <https://www.research.kobe-u.ac.jp/gsics-pcrc/sympo/20151218/documents/03Ocean/03Ocean_03Science2015.pdf> accessed 10 August 2021.

93 'Declaration Concerning the Prevention of Unregulated High Seas Fishing in the Central Arctic Ocean (Oslo, 16 July 2015)' (Chapter 2, n 22).

them in a broader process".[94] Consequently, in December 2015 in Washington D.C, first discussions took place on establishing an international fisheries agreement among the Arctic Five and countries or regions that have a history of distant water fishing and are likely to join such an agreement due to a real interest[95] – China, the EU, Iceland, Japan, and South Korea.[96] The meeting marked the beginning of the broader process, also referred to as the Five-plus-Five process, which involved the Arctic Five and the "Other Five", the four other States and the EU. Further governance meetings with the same constellation were conducted in Washington, D.C. in April 2016, and in Iqaluit in July 2016. In November of the same year, negotiations continued in Tórshavn on the Faroe Islands. Discussions were held on the basis of a Chairman's Text circulated in October 2016 that was formatted as a legally binding agreement, and successful outcome was expected.[97] However, it took, two more meetings, one in Reykjavík in March 2017, the other one in Washington, D.C in November 2017, before an agreement to prevent unregulated fishing in the high seas of the CAO was reached in principle.

Additional FiSCAO meetings were conducted in parallel to support diplomatic discussions. The fourth FiSCAO meeting took place in Tromsø in 2016, with the primary goal to develop a Joint Scientific Research and Monitoring Plan based on the draft version of a plan that summarized the outcome of the prior three meetings. The intent was to offer guidance for further workshops and meetings to ensure effective implementation of the plan and to provide advice on the potential of sustainably harvesting commercial species in the CAO.[98] Another meeting was held in Ottawa in October 2017, which, among other things, dealt with the likelihood of conducting fisheries in the CAO, e.g. by analysing the possibility of northward expansion of fish stocks.[99]

---

94 ibid.

95 On the concept of real interest, see Chapter 3 Section 3, 3.2 *infra*.

96 See Erik J Molenaar, 'The December 2015 Washington Meeting on High Seas Fishing in the Central Arctic Ocean' *The JCLOS Blog* (5 February 2016) <https://research-portal.uu.nl/en/publications/the-december-2015-washington-meeting-on-high-seas-fishing-in-the-> accessed 2 November 2024.

97 'Chairman's Statement, Fourth Meeting on Central Arctic Ocean Fisheries (Tórshavn, 29 November – 1 December 2016)' (Chapter 2, n 238) 1.

98 'Report of the Fourth FiSCAO Meeting on Central Arctic Ocean Fisheries (Tromsø, 26–28 September 2016)' (Chapter 2, n 134) 81.

99 'Report of the Fifth FiSCAO Meeting on Central Arctic Ocean Fisheries (Ottawa, 24–26 October 2017)' (Chapter 2, n 161).

Although the United States has tended to stay away from international agreements during Trump's term in office,[100] this was not the case for all agreements: after a legal and technical review meeting in February 2018 in Washington D.C., finally, on 3 October 2018, the Arctic Five and the Other Five signed the Agreement to Prevent Unregulated High Seas Fisheries in the Central Arctic Ocean in Ilulissat, Greenland.[101] The participants in the CAOF Agreement negotiations were able to agree on a package deal on four components: decision-making, the requirements for entry into force, the duration of the CAOF Agreement, and the recognition of the special responsibilities and interests of the Arctic Five in the central Arctic Ocean.[102] The Agreement now provides a framework for all Parties to work together to better understand the ecosystems of the area and prevent commercial fishing until adequate scientific information is available to inform management measures. In particular, the CAOF Agreement calls on its parties to take into account indigenous and local knowledge, to cooperate in science and research in the CAO, to establish appropriate conservation and management measures, and to ensure the participation of Arctic indigenous peoples.[103] With the end of negotiations and the entry into force of the Agreement[104] in June 2021,[105] an "institutional phase"[106] begins, in which meetings must be held and decisions on conservation and management measures must be made.

100 Oona Hathaway, 'Reengaging on Treaties and Other International Agreements (Part I): President Donald Trump's Rejection of International Law' *Just Security* (2 October 2020) <https://www.justsecurity.org/72656/reengaging-on-treaties-and-other-international-agreements-part-i-president-donald-trumps-rejection-of-international-law/> accessed 13 April 2021.

101 'Government of Canada | International Agreement to Prevent Unregulated High Seas Fisheries in the Central Arctic Ocean' <http://www.dfo-mpo.gc.ca/international/arctic-arctique-eng.htm> accessed 5 December 2021.

102 See Molenaar, 'Participation in the Central Arctic Ocean Fisheries Agreement' (Chapter 2, n 23) 168; Erik J Molenaar, 'PPP: The CAOF Agreement: Key Issues of International Fisheries Law' (2018), on file with the author.

103 'Government of Canada | International Agreement to Prevent Unregulated High Seas Fisheries in the Central Arctic Ocean' (Chapter 3, n 101).

104 On the requirements of entry into force, see Chapter 6 Section 3 *infra*.

105 See 'European Union | Arctic: Agreement to Prevent Unregulated Fishing Enters into Force (25 June 2021)' (Chapter 2, n 59).

106 Molenaar, 'The CAOF Agreement: Key Issues of International Fisheries Law' (Chapter 2, n 20) 454.

3 Participation in the CAOF Agreement

International agreements depend on their members, either through (political) will, finances, or compliance. The question of participation is therefore a constitutive issue, as the success of the respective arrangement will depend on it. Among regional fisheries arrangements, there appears to be a tendency to limit participation and therefore access to fisheries.[107] States and organizations seem to be aligned on two sides: there are the "ins", the States that already participate in the respective regime or play another superior role in decision-making, e.g. due to the regional proximity of their territory to the respective regulatory area, or because upcoming regulations pose a greater risk of exceptional interference for them. Further, there are the "outs", against which the "ins" often ally to restrict or discourage their entry. Although Article 116(b) UNCLOS highlights the right for a State's nationals to engage in fishing on the high seas, and to especially consider the rights and duties of coastal States, the "ins" often try preventing new States to participate.[108]

The drafting process of the CAOF Agreement already shows that there have been at least two categories of participants and draw the picture of a "club within the club".[109] There were the "Arctic Five", the five Arctic coastal States as the inner circle, and somehow separated the "Other Five", mostly distant water fishing (DWF) States. The situation was even more complex: in particular, the role of the Arctic Five in respect to the "Arctic Eight", namely the eight States of the Arctic Council including the Arctic Five plus Finland, Iceland, and Sweden, was one of the main issues in the Agreement's development process.[110] But

107 Andrew Serdy, 'The Bioeconomics of High Seas Fishing: New Entrants and the Tragedy of the Commons', *The New Entrants Problem in International Fisheries Law* (Cambridge University Press 2016) 4 <https://doi.org/10.1017/CBO9780511736148.001> accessed 11 September 2020; see Erik J Molenaar, 'Participation in Regional Fisheries Management Organizations' in Richard Caddell and Erik J Molenaar (eds), *Strengthening International Fisheries Law in an Era of Changing Oceans* (Hart Publishing 2019).

108 This is independent of the composition of the "ins": the Northwest Atlantic Fisheries Organization (NAFO) for instance is numerically dominated by DWF States, and the NEAFC by coastal States, see Andrew Serdy, 'Postmodern International Fisheries Law, or We Are All Coastal States Now' (2011) 60 International and Comparative Law Quarterly 387, 416 <https://www.cambridge.org/core/product/identifier/S002058931100008X/type/journal_article> accessed 5 December 2021.

109 See Christopher R Rossi, 'Problems of Governance: The Arctic and the Club Within the Club', *Sovereignty and Territorial Temptation–The Grotian Tendency* (Cambridge University Press 2017).

110 Andreas Kuersten, 'The Arctic Five Versus the Arctic Council' (2016) 2016 Arctic Yearbook 389, 390 <https://papers.ssrn.com/sol3/papers.cfm?abstract_id=2861269> accessed 8 April 2022; Schatz, Proelß and Liu (Chapter 2, n 41).

also the accession of other States to the Agreement after its entry into force is subject to arguable prerequisites.

3.1 *The Club within the Club: Leading Role of the Arctic Five*

The Arctic Five is the grouping of the five Arctic coastal States Canada, Denmark (in respect of Greenland and the Faroe Islands), Norway, Russia, and the United States of America addressing Arctic affairs in meetings and negotiations in an *ad hoc* manner.[111] These five States consider themselves to play a key role when it comes to regulating Arctic fisheries. Their proclaimed leading role in Arctic Ocean matters was already expressly stated in the Ilulissat Declaration, although the declaration did not specifically deal with a fisheries regime.[112] Further, during the plenary debates on the 2009 UN General Assembly "Oceans and the Law of the Sea" and "Sustainable Fisheries" Resolutions,[113] Norway, itself part of the Arctic Five, indicated that the Arctic Five "have a special responsibility" in "balancing the protection of the Arctic environment with the orderly and sustainable use of its resources".[114] The Chair's Summary of the Arctic Five ministerial meeting in Chelsea in March 2010 expressed a similar view by highlighting that the Arctic Five have "a unique interest and role to play in current and future efforts for the conservation and management of fish stocks" in the Arctic Ocean. Both statements show that the Arctic Five were of the view that, should some sort of fisheries arrangement be established in the Arctic, they should have a leading role in the development and implementation of it.[115]

From a legal perspective, Article 87(2) UNCLOS establishes the duty to have regard to the interests of others (including coastal States) while exercising the freedom of the high seas stated in Article 87(1) UNCLOS – a freedom that is "open to all States, whether coastal or land-locked." Similar, when determining the nature and extent of participatory rights of new members to an RFB, Article 11 UNFS Agreement merely encourages States to "take into account" the interests of new members. Furthermore, according to Article 116(b) UNCLOS,

111 Kuersten (Chapter 3, n 110) 390; Schatz, Proelß and Liu (Chapter 2, n 41).

112 'Arctic Ocean Conference Ilulissat Declaration (Ilulissat, 28 May 2008)' (Chapter 3, n 78).

113 'United Nations General Assembly Resolution 64/71, Oceans and the Law of the Sea (Adopted 4 December 2009)'; 'United Nations General Assembly Resolution 64/72, Sustainable Fisheries (Adopted 4 December 2009)'.

114 United Nations General Assmebly, 'Official Records of the 56th Plenary Meeting (New York, 4 December 2009) – A/64/PV.56' 16 <https://digitallibrary.un.org/record/672710/files/A_64_PV.56-EN.pdf>.

115 Molenaar, 'International Regulation of Central Arctic Ocean Fisheries' (Chapter 2, n 20) 447.

fishing on the high seas should take into account the special rights and duties and interests of coastal States. Even though the provisions therefore suggest a special treatment of coastal States, they do not support a coastal State monopoly status in respect of fish stocks.[116] Hence, both UNCLOS and the UNFS Agreement do not acknowledge any exclusionary privilege for coastal States in the management of fish stocks on the high seas. It is nevertheless universally accepted that coastal States play a decisive role in regional fisheries regimes. This is not least because high seas fisheries are strongly associated with the adjacent coastal States' fisheries conservation and management measures, and coastal States' monitoring and surveillance in high seas is facilitated due to their territory's proximity.[117]

Also in Arctic fisheries, the Arctic Five base their legitimacy to take a leading role – which was conveniently associated with substantially shaping the material outcome of the broader process – on their status as coastal States and thus on their geographic proximity and unique interest and role in the potential regulatory area.[118] In principle, the categorisation of States has been supported by the 2009 UN General Assembly Sustainable Fisheries Resolution. It encourages States, where there is no regional fisheries regime that establishes conservation and management measures for straddling or highly migratory fish stocks, to establish an RFB for that task.[119] Further, the resolution explicitly distinguishes between "relevant coastal States and States fishing on the high seas", referring to two competent categories, like the Arctic Five and the Other Five. In fact, this is not unusual for RFBs: when looking at the membership of various RFMOs, most usually include all relevant coastal States and only some developed distant water fishing States and entities.[120]

The Arctic Five held several meetings without the other five subsequent parties to the CAOF Agreement.[121] The meetings took place in times of surging

116 Serdy, 'Postmodern International Fisheries Law, or We Are All Coastal States Now' (Chapter 3, n 108) 420.

117 Leilei Zou and Henry P Huntington, 'Implications of the Convention on the Conservation and Management of Pollock Resources in the Central Bering Sea for the Management of Fisheries in the Central Arctic Ocean' (2018) 88 Marine Policy 132, 136 <https://doi.org/10.1016/j.marpol.2017.11.019> accessed 4 April 2022.

118 Molenaar, 'The Oslo Declaration on High Seas Fishing in the Central Arctic Ocean' (Chapter 2, n 58) 430 et seq.

119 'United Nations General Assembly Resolution 64/72, Sustainable Fisheries (Adopted 4 December 2009)' 17.

120 Molenaar, 'Participation in Regional Fisheries Management Organizations' (Chapter 3, n 107) 128.

121 See drafting history at Chapter 3 Section 2 *supra*.

interest from various sides in the Arctic.[122] There were differing views on the role of the Arctic Five, especially in relation to the role of the Arctic Eight, the eight member States of the Arctic Council, which additionally to the Arctic Five include Finland, Iceland, and Sweden. Views reached from considering the Arctic Five format a "necessary" and "preferable forum", to the opinion of it not being inclusive enough. Canada for example expressed that where the other three Arctic Council States have an interest, it would be preferable to include them in discussions.[123] It should be clarified here that the meetings focused on general Arctic issues and not yet specifically on the conservation of marine biological resources in the CAO, for which the three States have transferred their competence to the EU[124] and thus direct participation in the CAOF Agreement would not have been possible anyway. The round of eight in the Arctic Council was nevertheless sometimes considered to be "unwieldy for political discussions",[125] and an attempt was made to create a political Arctic forum through Arctic Five meetings. Further criticized was the non-inclusion of indigenous participants of the Arctic Council in discussions of the Arctic Five. Again, concerns were, *inter alia,* raised by Canada: the State took the view that "[k]eeping the group limited to the five littoral states also risks appearing to exclude the indigenous permanent participants of the Arctic Council".[126] Also Pharand, in his treaty proposal for the establishment of an Arctic Regional Council, advocates in favour of a superior role of the Arctic Eight towards other States in respect of Arctic matters, stating that due to

> the geographic location of their territories (bordering the Arctic Ocean or the adjacent seas) and the fact that all indigenous peoples are located on

122 In that context it seems worth mentioning that the first Arctic Five meeting took place shortly after Russia's flag was planted on the seabed on the North Pole and was initiated mostly to deal with extended continental shelves and to settle maritime disputes; see Torbjørn Pedersen, 'Debates over the Role of the Arctic Council' (2012) 43 Ocean Development and International Law 146, 8 et seq.

123 ibid 154.

124 See Article 3(1)(d) 'Treaty on the Functioning of the European Union (Consolidated Version) (Lissabon, 1 December 2009)' <https://eur-lex.europa.eu/legal-content/EN/TXT/PDF/?uri=CELEX:12012E/TXT&from=EN> accessed 9 July 2021.

125 'Deputy Secretary's Meeting with Norwegian Fm Stoere in Greenland, Cable to the U.S. Secretary of State (11 June 2008) – Ref 08COPENHAGEN337' para 4 <https://wikileaks.org/plusd/cables/08COPENHAGEN337_a.html> accessed 11 September 2020.

126 'Deputy Secretary's Meeting with Canadian Resource Minister Lunn in Greenland, Cable to the U.S. Secretary of State (11 June 2008) – Ref.08COPENHAGEN338' para 7 <https://wikileaks.org/plusd/cables/08COPENHAGEN338_a.html> accessed 11 September 2020.

> most of those territories, the eight Arctic States [...] have special interests and responsibilities.[127]

Yet, an additional exclusive ministerial-level meeting of the Arctic Five, labelled as "Ilulissat II", took place in Chelsea in March 2010. As to the content of the meeting, Canada indicated – perhaps to legitimise meeting in the round of five – to address "issues of particular relevance to the roles, responsibilities and jurisdiction of those [five] states".[128] The Arctic Council's other three members Finland, Iceland, and Sweden and its permanent participants criticised both the holding of the Ilulissat ministerial meetings itself and the adoption of its declaration to undermine the Arctic Council.[129] In particular, Iceland, who considers itself an Arctic coastal State as "the northern part of the Icelandic Exclusive Economic Zone falls within the Arctic and extends to the Greenland Sea adjoining the Arctic Ocean", felt that it should be entitled to take part in Arctic issues.[130] The meeting report of the Arctic Council SAO Meeting in Ilulissat in April 2010 explains that the three States

> pointed to the lack of inclusiveness at this meeting, and noted that after the Ilulissat Declaration they had the understanding that there would be no more Arctic Coastal States meetings. It was underlined that the AC [Arctic Council] is, and should continue to be, the central body for discussion of Arctic issues, with full participation of all Members. To strengthen the AC, one should avoid fragmentation.[131]

Also, then Secretary of State Clinton expressed a strong desire to include States with "legitimate interests in the region"[132] in significant international discussions and denounced the appropriateness of inclusive meetings, thus

127 Donat Pharand, 'The Case for an Arctic Region Council and a Treaty Proposal' (1992) 23 Revue générale de droit 163, 192.

128 'Report, SAO Meeting (Ilulissat, 28–29 April 2010)' 20 <https://oaarchive.arctic-council.org/bitstream/handle/11374/979/SAO_report_illulissat_Apr_2010.pdf?sequence=1&isAllowed=y> accessed 12 March 2020.

129 Molenaar, 'International Regulation of Central Arctic Ocean Fisheries' (Chapter 2, n 20) 449.

130 Parliament of Iceland Althingi (Chapter 2, n 249).

131 'Report, SAO Meeting (Ilulissat, 28–29 April 2010)' (Chapter 3, n 128) 20.

132 Mike Blanchfield, 'Clinton Rebukes Canada on Arctic Meeting' *The Globe and Mail* (29 March 2010) <https://www.theglobeandmail.com/news/politics/clinton-rebukes-canada-on-arctic-meeting/article1210187/> accessed 10 August 2021.

effectively rejecting the Arctic Five forum.[133] Indeed, no further Arctic Five ministerial meetings were held, and the support for the Arctic Council was restored and even intensified.[134] This was confirmed in the 2011 Nuuk ministerial meeting: the Arctic Eight agreed to "strengthen the capacity of the Arctic Council to respond to the challenges and opportunities by establishing a standing Arctic Council secretariat" and welcomed "the increased cooperation among the Arctic States and peoples in order to address the new challenges and opportunities".[135]

Although no further Arctic Five ministerial meetings took place concerning Arctic fisheries, the Arctic Five continued to meet on a senior official level for questions of policy and further held several scientific meetings, as it was considered "appropriate for the States whose exclusive economic zones border the high seas area in question to take the initiative on this matter."[136] Rumours circulated that Russia would not accept the involvement of non-Arctic States and entities when it comes to regulation Arctic fisheries at all.[137] In this regard, it has to be kept in mind that the Agreement had to be developed under challenging circumstances. No historic parallels of how to manage an ocean where fishing has never occurred existed, and an organization taking a leading role in the management was absent or turned out not to be the ideal forum.[138] It was therefore apparent that some forum had to take a leading role. Yet, in order to achieve far-reaching international support, a broader process that would include additional States was envisaged,[139] and further joint meetings with the Other Five were held – although it should be noted that with the exception of one meeting in Reykjavik, all meetings of the drafting process took place on the territory of the Arctic Five,[140] further reinforcing their continued leadership role. Nevertheless, the three remaining Arctic Council States Iceland,

133 Pedersen (Chapter 3, n 122) 12; Molenaar, 'International Regulation of Central Arctic Ocean Fisheries' (Chapter 2, n 20) 449.

134 Molenaar, 'International Regulation of Central Arctic Ocean Fisheries' (Chapter 2, n 20) 449.

135 'Arctic Council Nuuk Declaration (Nuuk, 12 May 2011)' 1–2 <https://oaarchive.arctic-council.org/handle/11374/92> accessed 12 March 2022.

136 'Chairman's Statement, Third Meeting on Central Arctic Ocean Fisheries (Nuuk, 24–26 February 2014)' (Chapter 3, n 89).

137 Molenaar, 'The CAOF Agreement: Key Issues of International Fisheries Law' (Chapter 2, n 20) 466–467.

138 Cf. Wegge (Chapter 2, n 21) 336.

139 'Chairman's Statement, Third Meeting on Central Arctic Ocean Fisheries (Nuuk, 24–26 February 2014)' (Chapter 3, n 89).

140 See Molenaar, 'The CAOF Agreement: Key Issues of International Fisheries Law' (Chapter 2, n 20) 453.

Sweden, and Finland (the latter via the European Union) were involved in the process, which resolved the issue of the Arctic Five vs. the Arctic Eight.

In the final text of the CAOF Agreement, the Preamble recognizes the "special responsibilities and special interests of the central Arctic Ocean coastal States in relation to the conservation and sustainable management of fish stocks in the central Arctic Ocean". Nevertheless, the Arctic Five and the Other Five are encouraged to cooperate in order to "ensure the compatibility of conservation and management measures for fish stocks" in their entirety. The conclusion of the Agreement thus allows all interested Parties to participate equally, at least factually, in an Arctic instrument, free of the status of an Arctic Council State, Arctic coastal State or DWF State.[141]

3.2 *Accession of States*

Membership in the CAOF Agreement is hence not confined to geographical boundaries. It nevertheless has certain limits. Although an international legal framework for admitting members to an RFB does not yet exist, and generally accepted criteria for membership are therefore missing, the concept of real interest has been developed to tackle this problem.

Many regional fisheries regimes will sooner or later be confronted with the question of what criteria should be used to welcome new members, so-called new entrants, to the club. Unfortunately, in most cases, a transparent and orderly process for the acceptance of new members is missing.[142] As in general, the principle of the freedom of the high seas comprises the freedom of fishing "both for coastal and land-locked States",[143] criteria for the admission of new members to a regional fisheries regime must not be chosen arbitrarily. Therefore, it makes sense that the UNFS Agreement[144] states that membership to regional fisheries regimes must be open. Members to such regimes or participants of a group of States conducting fisheries in a certain area must be prepared to welcome new entrants. Article 11 UNFS Agreement provides for several considerations that may be taken into account when determining whether the accommodation of new entrants in the fisheries concerned is

141 See Vylegzhanin, Young and Berkman (Chapter 3, n 62) 8; Molenaar, 'The CAOF Agreement: Key Issues of International Fisheries Law' (Chapter 2, n 20) 466.

142 Schatz, Proelß and Liu (Chapter 2, n 41) 237; Generally on the new entrants problem, see Andrew Serdy, *The New Entrants Problem in International Fisheries Law* (Cambridge University Press 2016).

143 See Article 87(1) UNCLOS.

144 See Articles 8–11 UNFS Agreement.

possible.[145] Based on this framework, it is argued that new entrants can only be welcomed if there is a "large surplus of the stock and other interests geographically more closely related have been ensured an adequate share of the available resources."[146] Moreover, it is supported that new entrants should not be principally excluded from fisheries but offered a "just and reasonable share of the TAC [total allowable catch] available".[147]

Article 8(4) UNFS Agreement[148] establishes that States are not forced to join an existing RFB. However, it becomes clear from the duty to cooperate expressed in UNCLOS and the UNFS Agreement[149] that where RFBs exist and have the authority to establish conservation and management measures in respect of straddling or highly migratory fish stocks, coastal and fishing States must either become members of the body or agree to apply its conservation and management measures.[150] Where such measures are set in place, the exercise of free fishing, guaranteed by the freedom of the high seas, in the regulatory area is no longer possible – especially, where the regulations foresee the allocation of all total allowable catch (TAC) and effort limits for the stocks managed to the RFB's participants. States thus have two options: either joining the RFB and conducting fishing according to the body's regulations, or refraining from fishing in the regulatory area.[151]

145 Article 11 UNFS Agreement suggests to consider (a) the status of the stocks, the existing level of fishing effort in the fishery, (b) the respective interests of new and existing members, (c) the respective contributions of new and existing members to conservation and management of the stocks and (d)–(f) the needs of (coastal) developing States and dependant communities.

146 Francisco Orrego Vicuña, *The Changing International Law of High Seas Fisheries* (Cambridge University Press 1999) 211.

147 Peter Örebech, Ketill Sigurjonsson and Ted L McDorman, 'The 1995 United Nations Straddling and Highly Migratory Fish Stocks Agreement: Management, Enforcement and Dispute Settlement' (1998) 13 International Journal of Marine and Coastal Law 119, 123; Cf. Molenaar, 'The Concept of "Real Interest" and Other Aspects of Co-Operation through Regional Fisheries Management Mechanisms' (Chapter 2, n 145) 497.

148 Non-members and non-participants that are claiming the privileged position granted by Article 8(4) UNFS Agreement, such as the application of Part IV UNFS Agreement, will have to prove the customary status of these provisions.

149 See Articles 63, 64, 117, 118 UNCLOS and Article 8 UNFS Agreement.

150 Rosemary Rayfuse, 'Article 118 – Cooperation of States in the Conservation and Management of Living Resources' in Alexander Proelß (ed), *United Nations Convention on the Law of the Sea: A Commentary* (Nomos 2017) para 27.

151 Northwest Atlantic Fisheries Organization, 'Report of the Working Group on Allocation of Fishing Rights to Contracting Parties of NAFO and Chartering of Vessels Between Contracting Parties (Halifax, 13–15 April 1999)' 16 <https://www.nafo.int/Portals/0/PDFs/gc/1999/GC-99-004.pdf> accessed 6 March 2020.

Although membership should hence remain open, RFBS usually have a limited number of participants, often due to their regional character. This favours the decision-making process within the respective body and compliance with the regime. It further ensures that members are actively concerned and involved. The question that hence remains is how to determine whether a State or other international actor like an NGO is qualified to become a member of such body.

In this regard, the 2009 UN General Assembly Sustainable Fisheries Resolution requests RFBS to lay down participation criteria and consider, when establishing such criteria, the status of the fish stocks in question and the applying States' interests in the fishery.[152]

With regard to the CAOF Agreement, the drafting process of a possible CAOF agreement gradually opened,[153] initially in order to streamline fishing practice and develop an international standard for potential CAO fisheries,[154] towards the inclusion of non-Arctic nations with large fishing fleets. For instance, China harvests most fish globally and accepts significantly greater distances to fulfil its demand of fish, which rendered the State a highly plausible candidate to engage in fishing in the CAO whenever this will be possible.[155]

Where participation in the final Agreement is concerned, Article 10 CAOF Agreement regulates the possible accession[156] of States to the Agreement.[157] According to Article 10(2) CAOF Agreement, the Agreement's signatories may "invite other States with a real interest" to accede to the Agreement after its entry into force. It is assumed that the Parties jointly decide on an invitation.[158]

---

152 'United Nations General Assembly Resolution 64/72, Sustainable Fisheries (Adopted 4 December 2009)' 19.

153 Molenaar, 'International Regulation of Central Arctic Ocean Fisheries' (Chapter 2, n 20) 458.

154 Cf. Molenaar, 'The Oslo Declaration on High Seas Fishing in the Central Arctic Ocean' (Chapter 2, n 58) 430.

155 Gloria Dickie, 'International Accord Bans Fishing in Central Arctic Ocean, Spurs Science' *The New Humanitarian – Oceans Deeply* (4 December 2017) <https://deeply.thenewhumanitarian.org/oceans/community/2017/12/01/an-app-and-volunteer-army-are-improving-local-tidal-flood-forecasts> accessed 20 October 2020.

156 Accession in international law generally refers to the affirmation of the Agreement through signature or ratification, showing its consent to be bound by a treaty, Article 2(1)(b) Vienna Convention on the Law of Treaties (VCLT).

157 Article 10(1) CAOF Agreement, which deals with the accession to the Agreement of the States and the EU that are listed in Article 9(1) of the Agreement and have not signed it yet, has become relatively meaningless after the Arctic Five and the Other Five have all signed the Agreement in 2018.

158 For the process of internal decision-making, see Article 6 CAOF Agreement.

It is noted that although Article 10(1) CAOF Agreement differentiates between States and the EU, Article 10(2) CAOF Agreement only mentions States and not associations of States as possible new members. Regardless of the underlying incentive to exclude associations, e.g. keeping the decision-making process and functioning of the regime simple, no association of States that has the competence of concluding binding agreements for its member States in the field of fisheries will likely join the Agreement soon.

Further excluded by the wording are governmental and non-governmental organizations. Participation for them is only possible through delegations of members. In principle, to reduce the odds of denied ratification of an agreement, it has proven beneficial to involve different domestic players from the start.[159] Nevertheless, and although organizations like Greenpeace and the Pew Charitable Trust showed interest in participating already in the Agreement's drafting process as observers, the Arctic Five, while valuing their scientific input, decided against direct participation.[160] Representatives of civil society are further considered critical drivers of transparency and effectiveness of RFBs. Also from a legal perspective, Article 12 UNFS Agreement calls on States to provide for transparency in decision-making processes and other RFBs' activities, and states the right of (N)GOs to participation and access to information. Regardless, it is not uncommon that NGO participation is either restricted from the start, or, when granted, to limit access where sensitive and contentious issues are at stake.[161] But also as participants of national delegations, NGOs can make an impact. Usually following a certain conviction, NGOs have an incentive to monitor delegates' actions and may thus influence internal delegation decisions. Additionally, as a positive side effect for the respective national government, in this way delegates can be detected who stray too far away from the preferred governmental line.[162] Either way, the consideration of interests of NGOs in any manner seems beneficial. However, this does not necessarily mean that they should be included as parties to an agreement. Experience suggests that broad membership in regional fisheries bodies likely favours adverse impacts on cooperation and effective operation.[163] While

159 Kal Raustiala, 'States, NGOs, and International Environmental Institutions' (1997) 41 International Studies Quarterly 719, 731 <http://www.jstor.org/stable/2600859> accessed 4 August 2022.

160 Wegge (Chapter 2, n 21) 335.

161 Cf. Matilda T Petersson, 'Transparency in Global Fisheries Governance: The Role of Non-Governmental Organizations' (2022) 136 Marine Policy 104128, 8 <https://doi.org/10.1016/j.marpol.2020.104128> accessed 8 April 2022.

162 Cf. Raustiala (Chapter 3, n 159) 729.

163 Örebech, Sigurjonsson and McDorman (Chapter 3, n 147) 123.

through the participation of various (N)GOs, transparency might be enhanced, for some issues a narrow decision-making process excluding NGOs can be more efficient.[164] With this in mind, for the time being, indirect participation of non-State actors in the CAOF Agreement seems sufficient and expedient while the Agreement is on its way of being implemented. Nevertheless, the option of granting (N)GOs observer status or similar participation rights could be pursued in the future. Enhanced participation of new actors could also be regulated separately, e.g. by a new RFB, when fishing can be conducted in CAO waters and the regime may benefit from the involvement of several actors.

Article 10(2) CAOF Agreement further sets up a second criterion for participation: in addition to being invited by members, States that wish to join the CAOF Agreement must have a real interest to accede to the Agreement. However, the prerequisite of a real interest is not further established. The wording is in fact commonly used as a condition for acquiring membership status in regional fisheries regimes.[165] Yet, there is no unanimity as to what real interest includes, and a distinct description of the concept is missing. To make the concept more tangible, it is worth looking at its origins.

In legal fisheries frameworks, the concept of real interest is first mentioned in the UNFS Agreement.[166] In its Article 8(3), the UNFS Agreement establishes a State's "real interest in the fisheries concerned" as a prerequisite for joining RFBs that have the competence to establish conservation and management measures for particular straddling fish stocks or highly migratory fish stocks. Yet, it does not outline the condition further and leaves it to the RFB to define it.[167] It is however noted that the wording "may become members" contained in Article 8(3) UNFS Agreement should not be read as a "mere discretionary option but as an expression of entitlement" for States with a real interest to join an RFB. Partly it is even claimed that Article 8 UNFS Agreement refers to membership being mandatory, thus giving effect to a State's duty to cooperate.[168]

164 Petersson (Chapter 3, n 161) 1–3, 8.

165 As an example, in its proposal agreement for the establishment of an Arctic Regional Council, Pharand states that the membership to the Arctic Regional Council should be open to "all those with sufficient interest", referring to States or organizations of States, NGO's, or territorial governments and regional governments upon favourable recommendation of the Arctic Regional Council Commission, but does also not characterise the concept any further; see Pharand (Chapter 3, n 127) para 192.

166 The CAOF Agreement recalls, in its Preamble, the provision of the UNFS Agreement that already apply to the CAO.

167 Örebech, Sigurjonsson and McDorman (Chapter 3, n 147) 122.

168 Orrego Vicuña (Chapter 3, n 146) 208.

Further, States that plan to cooperate through RFBs should inform other States with a real interest in the RFB's work of such cooperation.[169]

Reference to UNFS Agreement provisions to outline an international concept is no problem where interest States are members to the UNFS Agreement. Although it is assumed that the CAOF Agreement encompasses all States that might conduct fisheries in the CAO when this will be possible, provisions of a treaty they have not acceded to or that do not constitute customary international law do not bind potential new members, by implication of the principle of *pacta sunt servanda* as enshrined in Article 26 Vienna Convention on the Law of Treaties (VCLT). However, Article 8(3) UNFS Agreement invites all States fishing for straddling or highly migratory fish stocks to agree to apply the conservation and management measures established by a regional fisheries body, irrespective of their participation in the respective body or the UNFS Agreement.[170] This is not considered to be contrary to the pacta tertiis rule as embodied in Article 34 VCLT, which generally excludes a third-party effect of treaties. It is rather seen as an invitation to comply – well aware that the regulations are not per se binding for a third party due to the aforementioned principle. It is argued that this fundamental idea of international law must also apply to the introduction of a concept and hence to the concept of real interest.

As demonstrated above, the concept of real interest is widely used. In a next step, the substance of the concept must be carefully determined. Although development and change are considered easier within a relatively small circle of members,[171] which supports the application of strict criteria, the bar should be set reasonably and not too high: a repelled State might ignore management measures and endanger the effectiveness of the respective arrangement.[172] Several suggestions for the concept of real interest have been made. For instance, Orrego Vicuña is firmly convinced that the requirement of a real interest "can only be taken to mean the conduct of actual fishing operations of significance in the region concerned", going on to say that "[t]he fact of having fished in the past or the intention to do so in the future is not enough to qualify for membership or participation under the real interest criteria".[173] Hence, in

169 See Article 9(2) UNFS Agreement.

170 Örebech, Sigurjonsson and McDorman (Chapter 3, n 147) 124.

171 Cf. Tore Henriksen, Geir Hønneland and Are Sydnes, *Law and Politics in Ocean Governance-The UN Fish Stocks Agreement and Regional Fisheries Management Regimes* (Brill | Nijhoff 2006) 130.

172 Molenaar, 'The Concept of "Real Interest" and Other Aspects of Co-Operation through Regional Fisheries Management Mechanisms' (Chapter 2, n 145) 493.

173 Orrego Vicuña (Chapter 3, n 146) 208; similarly, see David A Balton, 'Strengthening the Law of the Sea: The New Agreement on Straddling Fish Stocks and Highly Migratory Fish

summary, real interest States include relevant coastal States and other States participating in the fishery.[174] The Northwest Atlantic Fisheries Organization (NAFO) suggests a slightly broader definition. Accordingly, a real interest State is a State that has an interest in participating in a respective fishery, including those States presently fishing in the area, and the relevant coastal States.[175] Where this is not the case, NAFO distinguishes that "a State could in principle have a real interest in a managed fishery that did not include a direct fishing interest, such as concern for bycatch species or for the environmental effects of using a particular fishing gear".[176] Indeed, confining membership to the existence of a real interest in fisheries excludes States that do not have a particular interest in fishing but in conservation and effective ocean management. Some authors therefore assert that non-participating States may claim non-user interests to legitimize participation. Claims may be based on individual rights, on behalf of the international community, or on both. Possible interests are hence the protection and preservation of the marine environment and safeguarding of marine biodiversity, or to safeguard adherence of coastal States with regulations in the Arctic marine area.[177] However, it cannot be denied that States usually participate in RFB's not due to ethical, but economic reasons. In theory, most participants want to secure maximum benefit for themselves with minimal regulation.[178]

Where no fisheries have been conducted yet, as in CAO waters, a broad interpretation of the concept is suggested, meaning that all States that are interested in fishing in CAO waters, provided this would be possible, have a real interest in the sense of Article 10(2) CAOF Agreement.[179] Limiting the broader process to include no other States than the Other Five – considered as "wholly

---

Stocks' (1996) 27 Ocean Development & International Law 125, 139 <https://www.tandfonline.com/doi/abs/10.1080/00908329609546078> accessed 10 August 2021.

174 Northwest Atlantic Fisheries Organization (Chapter 3, n 151); Molenaar, 'The Concept of "Real Interest" and Other Aspects of Co-Operation through Regional Fisheries Management Mechanisms' (Chapter 2, n 145).

175 Northwest Atlantic Fisheries Organization (Chapter 3, n 151) 16.

176 ibid.

177 Koivurova and Molenaar (Chapter 3, n 32) 65.

178 Matley (Chapter 3, n 37) 106.

179 Rosemary Rayfuse, 'Regulating Fisheries in the Central Arctic Ocean: Much Ado About Nothing?' in Niels Vestergaard and others (eds), *Arctic Marine Resource Governance and Development* (Springer 2018) 48; Heidar (Chapter 2, n 50) 186; Schatz, Proelß and Liu (Chapter 2, n 41) 241, 243.

consistent with State practice and international law"[180] – expressed the view of the Arctic Five that only the Other Five have a real interest in potential CAO fisheries, or at least declared a clear interest in the issue. This seems reasonable: by the inclusion of the EU and Iceland, the three additional States of the Arctic Council, Sweden, Finland, and Iceland, joined the Agreement. China, Japan, South Korea and the EU as significant DWF actors are represented. Also included are all NEAFC contracting States, whose regulatory area overlaps slightly with the CAOF Agreement Area, and the Convention on the Conservation and Management of Pollock Resources in the Central Bering Sea with an adjacent regulatory area.[181] From the current point of view, the question of real interest will likely only become relevant in the future in very few cases: the UK is likely to become an additional member post Brexit,[182] and Ukraine and Taiwan might claim a real interest,[183] although participation will likely provoke difficulties with the CAOF Agreement participants Russia and China due to the generally known existing foreign policy tensions. In these cases, as outlined above, a broad interpretation of the concept should be followed.

In summary, there seems to be consensus that a real interest exists if States are or would be active in the relevant fishery if fishing were possible. However, there is no agreement on whether, exceptionally, other reasons, such as a general conservation interest, are also sufficient for a real interest within the meaning of Article 8(3) UNFS Agreement. A clear and general determination of the requirement can therefore not be made and depends on the respective RFB. For the CAOF Agreement, an exact determination does not have to be made yet. Requirements may nevertheless be reassessed where States issue their interest in taking part in the Agreement.

---

180 Rayfuse, 'Regulating Fisheries in the Central Arctic Ocean: Much Ado About Nothing?' (Chapter 3, n 179) 48; Cf. Molenaar, 'International Regulation of Central Arctic Ocean Fisheries' (Chapter 2, n 20) 460.

181 Heidar (Chapter 2, n 50) 196.

182 Cf. Andreas Østhagen, 'Swimming Away! Arctic Fisheries and International Cooperation' *The Arctic Institute* (22 October 2019) <https://www.thearcticinstitute.org/swimming-away-arctic-fisheries-international-cooperation/> accessed 14 September 2020; 'UK Arctic Policy after Brexit: What Might Change?' *Over the Circle* (13 January 2019) <https://overthecircle.com/2019/01/13/uk-arctic-policy-after-brexit-what-might-change/> accessed 14 September 2020.

183 See Molenaar, 'Participation in the Central Arctic Ocean Fisheries Agreement' (Chapter 2, n 23) 146; Molenaar, 'The December 2015 Washington Meeting on High Seas Fishing in the Central Arctic Ocean' (Chapter 3, n 96) 2.

Concerning membership in the CAOF Agreement, one last question remains: How will the membership of new members be structured, and will there be different categories of members? RFB's try to regulate the issue of membership in existing fisheries mostly to prevent implicit "free-riding" of new entrants. Participation in RFBs is commonly linked to a share in the TAC[184] – an idea that could be pursued by a potential follow-up agreement of the CAOF Agreement, should sustainable commercial fisheries be possible in CAO waters. Yet, where RFB members take effective measures to rebuild the stocks administered, DWF nations are able to profit from the management by agreeing to comply with the established system while at the same time demanding pro rata shares of the net economic benefit from the RFB's fisheries, without bearing any of the regime's establishment and investment costs. This bears the possibility of undermining cooperative resource management arrangements.[185]

The involvement of new members must therefore be well considered. When welcoming new members, RFB's are often increasing the TAC rather than reducing the share of existing members. This can however only be considered as a temporary measure, as due to increased competition, this practice will reduce the original members' expected economic returns from the RFB fisheries over time. To counteract this issue, prospective new members can be treated as cooperating non-members, not as full new members. Upholding the duty to cooperate,[186] these cooperating non-members agree to the RFB's regulating framework and enjoy some benefits without bearing full costs and obligations of membership. One approach, *inter alia* followed by NAFO and NEAFC, is accepting new members with the notice that currently managed stocks are fully allocated and fishing opportunities are likely to be limited to new fisheries. An alternative approach is to allocate a meaningful grant on members in the hope of persuading them to refrain from conducting IUU fishing. Otherwise, as States are generally not bound by treaties to which they did not consent to be party,[187] there is a possibility that these States will engage in IUU fishing that provides them with the benefit of the member States'

184 Molenaar, 'The Concept of "Real Interest" and Other Aspects of Co-Operation through Regional Fisheries Management Mechanisms' (Chapter 2, n 145) 493.

185 Michael W Lodge and others, 'Recommended Best Practices for Regional Fisheries Management Organizations – Report of an Independent Panel to Develop a Model for Improved Governance by Regional Fisheries Management Organizations' (Chatham House 2007) 16 <https://repository.oceanbestpractices.org/bitstream/handle/11329/1456/39374297.pdf?sequence=1&isAllowed=y> accessed 2 November 2024.

186 See specifically on the customary duty to cooperate Chapter 4 Sections 1, 1.2, 1.2.2 *infra*.

187 See Article 34 VCLT.

restraint. This in turn furthers the deterrent effect for the latter not to accept that very restraint at all.[188] There is hence a risk of the right TAC allocation: if too generous, the grant might impede cooperation of existing members, and if not generous enough, the approach might backfire and new members might opt out and engage in fisheries as they please. A suggested solution proposes the sale of quotas of existing RFB members to new members.[189] This ensures both adherence with the cooperative approach and compliance of new members with regulations of the RFB while staying within the limits of TAC and MSY.[190] Indeed, when used along with other policy measures like sustainable catch quotas, and where effectively enforced, catch shares feature a feasible instrument to achieve sustainable fisheries management.[191] Deviating from the common practice of single-species management, a broader view on management bears the chances of increasing performance through enhanced coordination.[192] Although for the CAOF Agreement, these specific considerations on participation are still up in the air and need to be implemented only if high seas Arctic commercial fishing can be conducted, these observations should be kept in mind for the future.

4 Diversity of Interests

Concluding international agreements does inevitably involve several actors with varying interests. Parties may further follow different instructions and have different possibilities when implementing an agreement.[193] Within the

188 Serdy, 'The Bioeconomics of High Seas Fishing: New Entrants and the Tragedy of the Commons' (Chapter 3, n 107) 3.

189 Andrew Serdy, 'Quota Trading in International Fisheries Commissions: An Idea Whose Time Has Come?', *The New Entrants Problem in International Fisheries Law* (Cambridge University Press 2016) <https://doi.org/10.1017/CBO9780511736148.005> accessed 9 May 2020.

190 Lodge and others (Chapter 3, n 185) 16–17.

191 For a detailed analysis, see Michael C Melnychuk and others, 'Can Catch Share Fisheries Better Track Management Targets?' (2012) 13 Fish and Fisheries 267 <http://doi.wiley.com/10.1111/j.1467-2979.2011.00429.x> accessed 14 July 2020.

192 Sam Cunningham, Lori S Bennear and Martin D Smith, 'Spillovers in Regional Fisheries Management: Do Catch Shares Cause Leakage?' (2016) 92 Land Economics 344, 360 et seq. <https://papers.ssrn.com/sol3/papers.cfm?abstract_id=2467161> accessed 12 August 2021.

193 Cf. 'First International Meeting on the Establishment of the South Pacific Regional Fisheries Management Organisation (Wellington, 14–17 February 2006) – SP/01/Inf5' para 13 <http://www.sprfmo.int/assets/Meetings/Meetings-before-2013/International-Consultations-2006-to-2009/IntCons-1-2006-Wellington-New-Zealand/SPRFMO-InfConf-1-2006-Interim-Measures.pdf> accessed 20 July 2020.

realm of the CAOF Agreement, these actors are both linked to the Arctic and to fisheries. In order to better understand the task of the Agreement to streamline the interests of Arctic stakeholders, these interests must first be identified. This is of special importance as several decisions will have to be made in the course of the Agreement's implementation.[194] Stakeholders include not only the Arctic Five and the Other Five, but also Arctic residents like local communities and indigenous peoples. Further, interests of other international actors that do not (yet) participate in the CAOF Agreement are worth looking at.

4.1 *Interests of CAOF Agreement Participants: Political Positions and National Approaches*

Increasing development in the North,[195] including new economic opportunities, furthered different conceptions on the status of the Arctic,[196] and also prompted many States to want to secure a slice of the pie. For instance, Arctic littoral States have made claims on the extension of the Arctic Ocean continental shelves. If all claims were approved, 88% of the Arctic Ocean would be under the control of Canada, Russia, Norway, Denmark (respectively Greenland) and the United States, and the States could potentially benefit far more from resources if they acted alone.[197] By contrast, other States, e.g. China, may not claim sovereignty in the Arctic but manifest national interests through membership in the Arctic Council.[198] Nevertheless, although sovereign claims by Arctic littoral States have not been withdrawn, it is all the more encouraging to see that Arctic issues were for the most part approached "in a spirit of cooperation, with outstanding disputes managed peacefully".[199]

Not only Arctic issues in general, but also the CAOF Agreement involves different stakeholders. The ten signatories to the Agreement are listed in Article 9(1) CAOF Agreement. On paper, these nine States plus the EU seem like equal

194 Such as *inter alia* the decision to found a new RFMA/O or to start commercial fishing in the CAOF Agreement Area.

195 For the development of Northern geopolitics, see Lassi Heininen, 'Northern Geopolitics: Actors, Interests and Processes in the Circumpolar Arctic' in Richard C Powell and Klaus Dodds (eds), *Polar Geopolitics?: Knowledge, Resources and Legal Regimes* (Edward Elgar Publishing 2014).

196 See Klaus Dodds, 'The Ilulissat Declaration (2008): The Arctic States, "Law of the Sea," and Arctic Ocean' (2013) 33 SAIS Review of International Affairs 45.

197 Linda Jakobson, 'China Prepares for an Ice-Free Arctic' (2010) 2 SIPRI Insights on Peace and Security 1, 10 <http://news.xinhuanet.com/ziliao/2006->.

198 Maxime C Casteleyn, 'China and the Arctic: An Opportunity for the U.S.' (Air University–Maxwell AFB, AL 2017) 9 <https://apps.dtic.mil/sti/citations/AD1038063> accessed 2 November 2024.

199 Jakobson (Chapter 3, n 197) 12.

Parties.[200] However, as the Agreement's text recognizes the special responsibilities and interests of the Arctic Five in the CAO, this is only factually the case. The Arctic Five used their special status of "stewardship over ocean issues"[201] in the Arctic, claimed in the 2008 Ilulissat Declaration and through their position as initiators of the CAOF Agreement process, to pursue their interests and set forth the conditions under which commercial fisheries in the CAO may take part. As declared in the 2015 Oslo Declaration, the conditions of agreement were the geographical scope to be limited to the high seas portion of the CAO, and the qualified abstention from commercial high seas fishing. The Arctic Five were able to prevail: both were approved by the Other Five during the drafting process and therefore found their way into the final Agreement.[202]

Although in the end, most interests align within the group of the CAOF Agreement's parties, the issue of interests is much more complex. It is not the case that the Arctic Five oppose the remaining five Parties. For example, the Kingdom of Denmark fulfils a hybrid function as being part of the Arctic Council, an Arctic coastal State in respect of the Faroe Islands, and a central Arctic coastal State in respect of Greenland. Denmark is further part of the European Union. Iceland, which likes to be considered as another Arctic Ocean coastal State, has similar interests as the Arctic Five and is often added to this group in other fora. Hence, these States can be considered as six Arctic States with aligning interests. The EU is acting in factual capacity of high seas fishing States, but at the same time representing three Arctic Council States (Denmark, Finland and Sweden). China, the EU, Japan and the Republic of Korea all have a(n) (*de facto*) observer status in the Arctic Council.[203] The Parties' views on a topic and the interests involved can therefore vary depending on the issue in question.

Within the drafting process of the CAOF Agreement, different tendencies towards a stricter or less strict preservation approach existed. Yet, especially the Arctic Five shared broad agreement on most substantive issues like the need to acquire more scientific knowledge in order to determine the sustainability of fisheries. Further, all States principally rejected both a complete ban of

200 Which is further indicated e.g. by the fact that the Chinese, English, French and Russian versions of the Agreement have equal standing.

201 Rossi, 'Problems of Governance: The Arctic and the Club Within the Club' (Chapter 3, n 109) 170.

202 Molenaar, 'Participation in the Central Arctic Ocean Fisheries Agreement' (Chapter 2, n 23) 140.

203 Molenaar, 'PPP: The CAOF Agreement: Key Issues of International Fisheries Law' (Chapter 3, n 102).

commercial fisheries and the implementation of a special Arctic treaty regime, while not ruling out an agreement on fisheries that would pave the way towards an RFMO.[204] Hence, the Arctic Five's utilization-oriented[205] approach deviated from the more conservative view of other participants like Finland[206] and the EU:[207] the latter advocated in favour of a network of Arctic conservation areas, similar to the Natural Resources Defense Council[208] or Greenpeace, who even called for a strict "moratorium on all industrial activities there – including fishing".[209] But the Arctic Five did not only have concurrent interests: while it was clear – and even legally demanded[210] – for the US delegation to work towards the conclusion of an international agreement, this understanding was not initially shared by all Arctic Five States. Doubts about the necessity of an agreement were raised by Russia and Norway in particular. The two States had much better data and estimates of CAO waters and their living beings than Canada, Greenland and the United States, since their national adjacent waters were more easily accessible and therefore fishing could be conducted closer to the CAO. Therefore, the two States did not initially consider an agreement necessary. The will to work towards an agreement developed only gradually.[211] Moreover, there was disagreement among the Arctic Five about issues of participation of other (non-)Arctic States and indigenous peoples, and about whether to issue a ban of specific fishing gear. Different views existed also on the explicit wording of the provisional abstention from commercial fishing. Whereas the United States favoured the term "moratorium", Canada, Russia

204 Wegge (Chapter 2, n 21) 335.
205 ibid 337.
206 Government of Finland, 'Finland's Strategy for the Arctic Region 2013 – Government Resolution on 23 August 2013 (Prime Minister's Office Publications 16/2013)' (2013) 14, 57 et seq. <https://vnk.fi/documents/10616/1093242/J1613_Finland's+Strategy+for+the+Arctic+Region.pdf/cf80d586-895a-4a32-8582-435f60400fd2?version=1.0> accessed 14 April 2022.
207 'European Parliament Resolution on the EU Strategy for the Arctic (12 March 2014) – P7_TA(2014)0236' para 38 <https://eur-lex.europa.eu/legal-content/EN/TXT/PDF/?uri=CELEX:52014IP0236&from=EN> accessed 29 January 2022.
208 Natural Resources Defense Council, 'NRDC Is Reviving Our Oceans' (2013) <https://www.nrdc.org/sites/default/files/reviving-our-oceans-FS.pdf> accessed 8 April 2022.
209 'Greenpeace | Expedition Launch: Arctic Under Pressure – Greenpeace Heads to Arctic to Investigate Urgent Ocean Threats' <https://wayback.archive-it.org/9650/20200403092926/http://p3-raw.greenpeace.org/international/en/news/features/arctic-under-pressure120510/> accessed 29 January 2022.
210 See United States Congress (Chapter 2, n 163).
211 Cf. Wegge (Chapter 2, n 21) 336.

and Norway objected to the use of "moratorium" or "ban" for the temporary closure.[212]

The geographical scope of the CAOF Agreement and the content of the temporary ban of commercial fishing under the CAOF Agreement are the two key elements that in any case create a fundamental difference between the CAO fisheries interests of the Arctic Five and the Other Five. These interests stem from different concepts. While the interests of the Arctic Five are based on sovereign rights and jurisdiction over fisheries in their respective national maritime zones,[213] and only additionally originate from the concept of the freedom of fishing on the high seas,[214] the fisheries interests of the Other Five are based on the latter concept only.

The Arctic Five have two possibilities to conduct fishing in the CAO: within their adjacent maritime zones, and within the high seas portion of the CAO. Yet, it is expected that the Arctic Five will only engage in the latter where its coastal State interests are not at stake. In this regard, collective interests in two categories emerge: on the one hand, an allowance of fishing in the high seas portion of the CAO might conflict with utilization-oriented interests – where a CAO coastal State has allowed for commercial fishing in its own maritime zones near the CAO, it is only natural that such State will try to restrain the allowance of fishing on the CAO high seas. Further, the coastal States are in a position to decelerate a northward expansion of the respective fish stocks into the high seas of the CAO, as fish would first have to pass through the coastal States maritime zones and can be caught there.[215] On the other hand, where coastal States pursue conservation-oriented interests, an allowance of fishing in the Agreement Area might conflict with a possible prohibition of fishing that is set up in the respective maritime zones of a coastal State. Also under the second scenario, in line with the ecosystem approach, coastal States are unlikely to support the start of fisheries in the high seas portion of the CAO.[216]

It is therefore likely that the Other Five will be more inclined to favour the commencement of high seas fishing than the Arctic Five, as for them, access to Arctic fish stocks will only be possible in the high seas portion of the CAO. Further, if commercial fishing in the CAO might be allowed at some time, the

212 ibid.
213 See Articles 2(1), 49(1), 56(1)(a), 77(1) UNCLOS.
214 See Article 166 UNCLOS.
215 Cf. Zou and Huntington (Chapter 3, n 117) 135.
216 Molenaar, 'The CAOF Agreement: Key Issues of International Fisheries Law' (Chapter 2, n 20) 462–463; see Molenaar, 'International Regulation of Central Arctic Ocean Fisheries' (Chapter 2, n 20) 462–463.

Other Five rely on the goodwill of the Arctic Five: the biophysical and legal features of the Arctic Ocean render (safe) engagement in fisheries for non-Arctic states impossible if none of the Arctic coastal States is willing to provide support through access to its coastal infrastructure, communication and navigational facilities and search and rescue institutions.[217] Contrary, the Arctic coastal States are technically free to access stocks within their EEZs much earlier and without the need of TAC sharing. The Arctic Five will therefore presumably only support the commencement of commercial CAO fisheries if either they intend to participate in high seas fishing themselves, or if such fishing would not significantly conflict with their coastal State interests.[218]

It seems safe to say that commercial viability of fisheries within coastal State maritime zones will be reached earlier than on the high seas. Yet, the diverse interests of the Arctic Five and the Other Five must be aligned, and credibility and compatibility among coastal States and States fishing on the high seas[219] must be ensured for the Agreement to be successful. Hence, the Arctic Five's task is to set up appropriate regulation in their own maritime zones "in accordance with 'recognized international standards', with particular reference to new and exploratory fisheries", similar as for instance Canada did[220] or the United States has adopted with its "freeze of fishing effort" in their Alaskan EEZ near the CAO.[221]

Thus, although there are different interests, a cooperative, regional approach is mostly taken in Arctic fisheries. Besides the CAOF Agreement, there are bilateral agreements between some of the States that focus on fisheries, for example the Agreement between the Government of Iceland, the Government of Norway and the Government of the Russian Federation Concerning Certain Aspects of Cooperation in the Area of Fisheries from 1999,[222] or the "Northern

217 Vylegzhanin, Young and Berkman (Chapter 3, n 62) 6.

218 Molenaar, 'Participation in the Central Arctic Ocean Fisheries Agreement' (Chapter 2, n 23) 140 et seq.; Molenaar, 'The CAOF Agreement: Key Issues of International Fisheries Law' (Chapter 2, n 20) 462.

219 See Article 7 UNFS Agreement; see more on compatibility at Chapter 5 Sections 2, 2.5 *infra*.

220 'Government of Canada | News Release: Minister Aglukkaq Announces the Signature of the Beaufort Sea Integrated Fisheries Management Framework (17 October 2014)' <https://www.canada.ca/en/news/archive/2014/10/minister-aglukkaq-announces-signature-beaufort-sea-integrated-fisheries-management-framework.html> accessed 29 November 2021; see Balton, 'Implementing the New Arctic Fisheries Agreement' (Chapter 3, n 26) 433.

221 Molenaar, 'The Oslo Declaration on High Seas Fishing in the Central Arctic Ocean' (Chapter 2, n 58) 431.

222 'Agreement between the Government of Norway, the Government of Iceland and the Government of the Russian Federation Concerning Certain Aspects of Cooperation in the

Agreements" between the EU and the Faroe Islands and the EU and Norway.[223] Nevertheless, the ten parties to the CAOF Agreement have not only grouped national interests but also individual national interests, that are mostly shaped by their traditions of conducting – or not conducting – fishing near CAO waters. As the North is becoming more and more important strategically, most States have developed their own "Northern" or "Arctic" strategy.

With Norway starting in 2006,[224] all of the Arctic Five States have adopted "Northern" or "Arctic" strategies that have partly been supplemented or renewed over time.[225] The five States mostly take an economic approach and focus on

---

Area of Fisheries (Saint Petersburg, 15 May 1999) – UNTS Vol. 2073, No. 35869 ' <https://treaties.un.org/doc/Publication/UNTS/Volume 2073/v2073.pdf> accessed 7 April 2022.

223 'Agreement on Fisheries between the European Economic Community, of the One Part, and the Government of Denmark and the Home Government of the Faroe Islands, of the Other Part (Brussels, 15 March 1977) – OJ L 226/12' <https://eur-lex.europa.eu/LexUriServ/LexUriServ.do?uri=CELEX:21977A0315(01):EN:HTML> accessed 30 June 2021; 'Agreement on Fisheries between the European Economic Community and the Kingdom of Norway (Brussels, 29 August 1980) – OJ L 226/48' <https://eur-lex.europa.eu/LexUriServ/LexUriServ.do?uri=CELEX:21980A0227(05):EN:HTML> accessed 30 June 2021.

224 Norwegian Ministry of Foreign Affairs, 'The Norwegian Government's High North Strategy' (2006) <https://www.regjeringen.no/globalassets/upload/ud/vedlegg/strategien.pdf> accessed 13 April 2022; supplemented by Norwegian Ministry of Foreign Affairs, 'New Building Blocks in the North – The next Step in the Government's High North Strategy' (2009) <https://www.regjeringen.no/globalassets/upload/ud/vedlegg/nordomradene/new_building_blocks_in_the_north.pdf> accessed 22 April 2020; Norwegian Ministry of Foreign Affairs, 'Norway's Arctic Policy – Creating Value, Managing Resources, Confronting Climate Change and Fostering Knowledge. Developments in the Arctic Concern Us All' (2014) <https://www.regjeringen.no/globalassets/departementene/ud/vedlegg/nord/nordkloden_en.pdf> accessed 13 April 2020; superseded by Norwegian Ministries, 'Norway's Arctic Strategy – between Geopolitics and Social Development' (2017) <https://www.regjeringen.no/contentassets/fad46f0404e14b2a9b551ca7359c1000/arctic-strategy.pdf> accessed 13 April 2020.

225 For the Russian Federation, see ARCTIS, 'Russian Federation Policy for the Arctic from 2008 to 2020 (English Translation)' (2009) <http://www.arctis-search.com/Russian+Federation+Policy+for+the+Arctic+to+2020> accessed 10 August 2021; for Canada, see Government of Canada, 'Canada's Northern Strategy: Our North, Our Heritage, Our Future' (2009) <https://publications.gc.ca/collections/collection_2009/ainc-inac/R3-72-2008.pdf> accessed 2 November 2024; P Whitney Lackenbauer and Ryan Dean, 'Canada's Northern Strategy under Prime Minister Stephen Harper: Key Speeches and Documents, 2005–15' (2016) <www.sju.ca/cfpf> accessed 13 April 2020; 'Government of Canada | Canada's Arctic and Northern Policy Framework' <https://www.rcaanc-cirnac.gc.ca/eng/1560523306861/1560523330587#s4> accessed 13 April 2020; for Denmark, see 'Denmark, Greenland and the Faroe Islands: Kingdom of Denmark Strategy for the Arctic 2011–2020' (2011) <http://library.arcticportal.org/1890/1/DENMARK.pdf> accessed 13 April 2022; Marc Jacobsen, 'Denmark's Strategic Interests in the Arctic: It's the Greenlandic Connection, Stupid!' *The Arctic Institute* (4 May 2016)

new possibilities in the Arctic that emerge from climate change. Security issues and the wish to foster (ecological) cooperative Arctic development are further addressed. The strategies' focus on security and broad cooperation further bears positive side effects for some countries. As an example, for the United States, cooperating with multiple States in the region, e.g. China, follows economic interests[226] and additionally weakens Arctic-dominant Russia.[227]

The Other Five share the fate of being geographically further away from the CAO, and thus have similar – limited – fishing opportunities. Most have issued Arctic policy papers that promote close cooperation in new emerging activities in the region. For instance, Japan and South Korea especially focus on building close international and bilateral cooperative relationships concerning Arctic matters.[228] Otherwise, the motivation to participate in the Agreement partly differs. New opportunities to access Arctic resources offer States the chance to provide and grow their populations. This is of special relevance for States that are likely to be particularly affected by climate change,[229] and where dependence on resources is therefore complicated, like China.

China is a major fish producer and exporter of fish but also a large-scale importer as a result of increasing national consumption of non-domestic produced species and outsourcing of processing from other countries. The country is therefore forced to look for multiple sources to fulfil its need for fish resources.[230] Pollution and warming ocean temperatures led to a decrease in fish stocks in China's waters, and the country hence expanded its distant-water

---

<https://www.thearcticinstitute.org/denmark-interests-arctic-greenland-connection/> accessed 13 April 2020; and for the United States, see The White House, 'United States National Security Presidential Directive NSPD-66 on Arctic Region Policy' (2009) <https://fas.org/irp/offdocs/nspd/nspd-66.htm> accessed 2 April 2022; The White House, 'United States National Strategy for the Arctic Region' (2013) <https://obamawhitehouse.archives.gov/sites/default/files/docs/nat_arctic_strategy.pdf> accessed 22 April 2021.

226 The White House, 'National Security Strategy' (2010) 50 <http://unipd-centrodirittiumani.it/public/docs/USA_NSS_2010.pdf> accessed 5 December 2021.

227 Casteleyn (Chapter 3, n 198) 18.

228 Government of Japan, 'Japan's Arctic Policy (Provisional Translation)' (2015) <https://www8.cao.go.jp/ocean/english/arctic/pdf/japans_ap_e.pdf> accessed 7 April 2022; Ministry of Oceans and Fisheries of the Republic of Korea, 'Policy Framework for the Promotion of Arctic Activities of the Republic of Korea 2018–2022' (2019) <http://www.koreapolarportal.or.kr/data/Policy_Framework_for_the_Promotion_of_Arctic_Activities_of_the_Republic_of_Korea-2018-2022.pdf> accessed 7 April 2022.

229 See Figure 8 *infra*.

230 See Food and Agriculture Organization of the United Nations, 'The State of World Fisheries and Aquaculture 2016: Contributing to Food Security and Nutrition for All' (Chapter 1, n 3) 6.

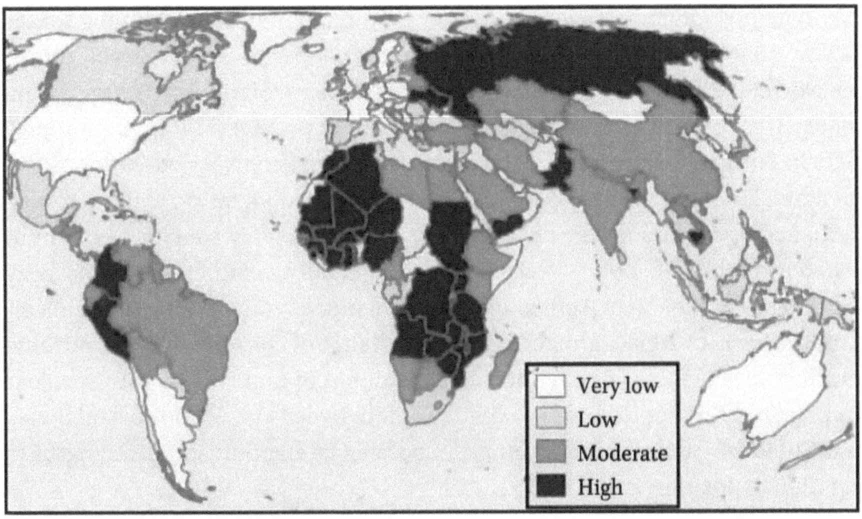

FIGURE 8 Comparative vulnerability of national economies to climate impacts on fisheries
SOURCE: K COCHRANE AND OTHERS, 'FAO FISHERIES AND AQUACULTURE TECHNICAL PAPER 530: CLIMATE CHANGE IMPLICATIONS FOR FISHERIES AND AQUACULTURE' (2009) 123 <HTTP:// WWW.LIS.EDU.ES/ UPLOADS/07483FB772A245CAB8E748BF74072 FD3.PDF> ACCESSED 24 APRIL 2020, 134

fishing fleet and invested in overseas fisheries.[231] The State actively seeks access to resources, including fish that are or will soon be available in the Arctic Ocean, to maintain China's economic growth and development and consequently legitimize and sustain the power of the ruling Chinese Communist Party.[232] As a global big player, it finds itself in a difficult position: on the one hand, China wants to position itself to be considered in Arctic affairs while not contradicting its usual strong uphold of respecting State sovereignty. On the other hand, it attempts to prevent alarming the Arctic Five and causing the formation of an alliance of Arctic States. Broader cooperation with Nordic countries is therefore envisaged.[233] In particular, the strong role of Russia, as being an Arctic coastal State and having control of shipping routes, can be alleviated through cooperation with other Arctic States. An economic route through the Northwest Passage or Northern Sea Route would enable China's economy to grow further, or at least sustain its economic growth.[234] China considers the Arctic as one of

231 Casteleyn (Chapter 3, n 198) 5.
232 ibid 1.
233 Cf. Jakobson (Chapter 3, n 197) 12–13.
234 Casteleyn (Chapter 3, n 198) 6.

the "blue economic passages". The State even renamed Arctic shipping routes as the "Polar Silk Road" and initiated economic cooperation with Russia, due to the Northwest Passage being along the Russian coast. Significantly orientating themselves towards the Arctic, Chinese investors promote infrastructure projects in European countries.[235] Additionally, China is only a non-voting-rights member State in the Arctic Council. Other ways of cooperation with increased influence in Arctic matters are therefore understandably sought. China published its first Arctic policy white paper in 2018, only a couple of months away from the date the CAOF Agreement was concluded, with specific thoughts on Arctic fisheries. China highlighted the importance of conservation and rational use, but nevertheless favoured the establishment of an RFMO in the CAO, and emphasized the importance of cooperation between the Arctic coastal States and China.[236] All these endeavours can be seen as an approach to strengthening China's position in the Arctic.

Also Iceland uses the Agreement to secure its position in the Arctic. It adopted an Arctic policy in 2011, in which it opposes a strict geographical definition of the Arctic region but advocates that it "rather be viewed as an extensive area when it comes to ecological, economic, political and security matters". Thus, it reaffirms its view of being an Arctic coastal State. The country further strongly criticises the Arctic Five meetings that excluded other Arctic Council States, stating that if "consultation by the five States develops into a formal platform for regional issues, it can be asserted that solidarity between the eight Arctic States will be dissolved and the Arctic Council considerably weakened."[237]

As for the EU, it has special ties to the Arctic by a combination of history, geography, economy and scientific achievements. Three of its member States' territories lie above the Arctic Circle (Denmark by virtue of Greenland and the Faroe Islands, Finland, and Sweden), and Iceland and Norway are part of the European Economic Area. Canada, Russia and the United States are further important strategic partners for the EU.[238] Where the relevance of fisheries is

235 Sanna Kopra, 'China and Its Arctic Trajectories: The Arctic Institute's China Series 2020' *The Arctic Institute* (17 March 2020) <https://www.thearcticinstitute.org/china-arctic-trajectories-the-arctic-institute-china-series-2020/> accessed 5 August 2020.

236 State Council of the People's Republic of China, 'China's Arctic Policy' (2018) <http://english.www.gov.cn/archive/white_paper/2018/01/26/content_281476026660336.htm> accessed 12 August 2021.

237 Parliament of Iceland Althingi (Chapter 2, n 249).

238 European Union, 'Communication from the Commission to the European Parliament and the Council – The European Union and the Arctic Region (20 November 2008) – COM/2008/0763 Final' (Chapter 2, n 80) 2.

concerned, in 2013, already about half of the fish caught in polar seas was consumed in the EU.[239] In addition to the individual Arctic strategies of each country,[240] the EU has developed a strategy over the years. First steps were taken in 2008,[241] followed by a Joint Communication in 2016, which has been continuously adapted.[242] Only recently, it was replaced by a Joint Communication in 2021, which especially focuses on cooperation in Arctic matters.[243] To further strengthen this commitment, the position of Special Envoy/Ambassador at Large for the Arctic was introduced in 2017.[244]

In terms of competences, the European Union is exclusively in charge to manage the conservation of marine biological resources for its Member

239 Federal Foreign Office Germany (Chapter 2, n 250) 6.

240 For example for Finland, see Government of Finland, 'Finland's Strategy for the Arctic Region (Prime Minister's Office Publications 8/2010)' (2010) <https://arcticportal.org/images/stories/pdf/J0810_Finlands.pdf> accessed 14 April 2022; Government of Finland (Chapter 3, n 206); for Germany, see Federal Foreign Office Germany (Chapter 2, n 250); Federal Ministry of Education and Research Germany, 'Rapid Climate Change in the Arctic: Polar Research as a Global Responsibility' (2012) <https://www.fona.de/medien/pdf/Rapid_Climate_Change_in_the_Arctic.pdf> accessed 10 August 2021; Federal Foreign Office Germany (Chapter 2, n 89).

241 European Union, 'Press Release: The Arctic Merits the European Union's Attention – First Step towards an EU Arctic Policy (20 November 2008) – IP/08/1750' <http://europa.eu/rapid/press-release_IP-08-1750_en.htm> accessed 12 August 2021.

242 European Commission, 'Joint Communication – Developing a European Union Policy towards the Arctic Region: Progress since 2008 and next Steps (2012) – JOIN(2012) 19 Final' (Chapter 2, n 61); 'European Parliament Resolution on the EU Strategy for the Arctic (12 March 2014) – P7_TA(2014)0236' (Chapter 3, n 207); European Union, 'Council Conclusions on the Arctic: Foreign Affairs Council (20 June 2016) – 10400/16' <http://data.consilium.europa.eu/doc/document/ST-10400-2016-INIT/en/pdf> accessed 4 April 2022; European Economic and Social Committee, 'Opinion: An Integrated European Union Policy for the Arctic (14 December 2016) – JOIN (2016) 21 Final, REX/470' <https://eur-lex.europa.eu/legal-content/EN/TXT/PDF/?uri=CELEX:52016AE4426&rid=4>; European Union, 'Opinion of the European Committee of the Regions – Union Policy for the Arctic (8 February 2017) – OJ C 207/17' <https://eur-lex.europa.eu/legal-content/EN/TXT/PDF/?uri=CELEX:52016AR4295&from=NL> accessed 23 April 2020; 'European Parliament Resolution on an Integrated European Union Policy for the Arctic (16 March 2017) – P8_TA(2017)0093' <http://www.inuitcircumpolar.com/uploads/3/0/5/4/30542564/> accessed 23 April 2021.

243 European Commission, 'Joint Communication – A Stronger EU Engagement for a Peaceful, Sustainable and Prosperous Arctic (13 October 2021) – JOIN(2021) 27 Final' <https://www.ipcc.ch/report/ar6/wg1/> accessed 25 March 2022.

244 Cf. 'European Parliament Parliamentary Questions, VP/HR – EU Policy on the Arctic and the Successor to the Special Advisor/Ambassador at Large for the Arctic (17 April 2019)' <https://www.europarl.europa.eu/doceo/document/P-8-2019-001961_EN.html> accessed 25 March 2022.

States.[245] This happens through both its participation in RFBs and other relevant fora, and indirectly via the Member States themselves.[246] In particular, cooperation between northern States has been an important issue and has been promoted through the introduction of the joint "Northern Dimension" policy of the EU, Russia, Norway and Iceland.[247] Interests outlined in this policy need to be considered by EU States like Sweden, Finland and Denmark besides national decision-making processes.[248] Other initiatives, like the Barents Euro-Arctic Council, a forum for intergovernmental collaboration in the Barents Sea,[249] have been initiated already in 1993.[250] Another long-standing objective of the EU has been to become an observer in the Arctic Council. This initiative was however blocked by Canada in response to the EU regulation banning the trade of seal products in 2008,[251] and has been complicated to pursue ever since.[252] Concerning Arctic fisheries, the EU acknowledges the sensitivity of the area, its importance for biodiversity and the impacts of climate change that allow for possible fisheries that should be approached with precaution in a collaborative way.[253] In addition, the EU is party to the NEAFC, with the European Fisheries Control Agency monitoring the implementation

245 See Article 3(1)(d) Treaty on the Functioning of the European Union.

246 Barnes (Chapter 2, n 10) 199.

247 See 'Northern Dimension Institute | About ND' <http://www.northerndimension.info/northern-dimension> accessed 30 June 2021.

248 Keskitalo, Koivurova and Bankes (Chapter 2, n 78) 3.

249 The Barents Euro-Arctic Council was initially established in 1993 to ensure security in the region around the Barents Sea as an international organization consisting of subnational or regional governments, intended to enhance regional cooperation between the northern member States. The BEAC meets at Foreign Minister level of the eight parties Denmark, Finland, Iceland, Norway, Russia, Sweden and the European Commission. There is also coordination with the relevant activities of the Nordic Council of Ministers, the Council of the Baltic Sea States, the Arctic Council, and the Northern Dimension where appropriate. See ibid 6; 'Barents Euro-Arctic Cooperation | About Us' <https://www.barentscooperation.org/en/About> accessed 30 June 2021.

250 'Declaration on Cooperation in the Barents Euro-Arctic Region (Kirkenes, 11 January 1993)' <https://barents-council.org/files/459_doc_KirkenesDeclaration.pdf > accessed 2 November 2024.

251 European Union, 'Policy Department: The Outcome of the Ninth Arctic Council Ministerial Meeting' (2015) <http://www.arctic-council.org/index.php/en/about-us/arctic-council/observers> accessed 23 April 2020.

252 Elena Conde Pérez and Zhaklin Valerieva Yaneva, 'The European Arctic Policy in Progress' (2016) 10 Polar Science 441 <https://linkinghub.elsevier.com/retrieve/pii/S1873965216300536> accessed 12 August 2021.

253 European Parliament (Chapter 2, n 149); European Union, 'Policy Department B: Fisheries Management And The Arctic In The Context Of Climate Change – Study' (Chapter 2, n 149).

of the EU's NEAFC obligations. At an NEAFC Meeting in 2019, the EU issued a statement on its contribution to the implementation of the CAOF Agreement, especially through providing funds for research activities and support for the European consortium of researchers in the international Multidisciplinary drifting Observatory for the Study of Arctic Climate (MOSAiC) expedition.[254]

The incentive for each of the other five participants to join the CAOF Agreement might therefore have been very different in part. It can nevertheless be summed up to symbolise the individual wish of the Other Five to keep one foot in the door when it comes to Arctic issues. In the broader domain of international fisheries law, the international law of the sea and the international law relating to the Arctic, some of the Other Five had concerns on "multilateral creeping coastal State jurisdiction".[255] These concerns were raised both in the BBNJ treaty process[256] and within the Five-plus-Five process that led to the CAOF Agreement,[257] stemming from the assertion of special roles, interests or rights within the processes.[258] China, the EU, Japan and South Korea especially expressed dissatisfaction with their inferior participatory status in the Arctic Council, the Arctic Council System and in new peripheral Arctic bodies.[259] The CAOF Agreement solved the issue, at least for Arctic fisheries, by settling for a compromise: it refrained from granting proposals like allocating special decision-making rights or an exceptional role concerning the entry into force of the Agreement to the Arctic Five,[260] but recognizes "the special

254 North-East Atlantic Fisheries Commission, 'Statement by the EU Regarding the EU's Contribution to the Implementation of the International Agreement to Prevent Unregulated High Seas Fisheries in the Central Arctic Ocean (12–14 November 2019) – AM 2019–95' <https://www.neafc.org/system/files/AM-2019-95_EU-statement-on-Arctic_Final.pdf> accessed 10 August 2021.

255 'United Nations General Assembly Resolution 72/249, International Legally Binding Instrument under UNCLOS on the Conservation and Sustainable Use of Marine Biological Diversity of Areas beyond National Jurisdiction (Adopted 24 December 2017)'.

256 Negotiation process on an "international legally binding instrument under the UNCLOS on the conservation and sustainable use of marine biological diversity of areas beyond national jurisdiction", in short biodiversity beyond national jurisdiction (BBNJ) process.

257 Molenaar, 'Participation in the Central Arctic Ocean Fisheries Agreement' (Chapter 2, n 23) 144–145.

258 See e.g. Ilulissat Declaration: „the five coastal states are in a unique position"to address possibilities and challenges in the Arctic Ocean; SAO Report to Ministers (Nuuk, May 2011) 3; „key role of the Arctic States"; similar, see 1973 Agreement on the Conservation of Polar Bears: States recognized "the special responsibilities and special interests of the States of the Arctic Region in relation to the protection of the fauna and flora".

259 ibid 146 et seq.

260 Molenaar, 'The CAOF Agreement: Key Issues of International Fisheries Law' (Chapter 2, n 20) 474–475.

responsibilities and special interests of the central Arctic Ocean coastal States in relation to the conservation and sustainable management of fish stocks in the central Arctic Ocean" in its Preamble. This compromise seems, at least for the time being, to have reconciled all interests, satisfied all Parties and made it possible to conclude the Agreement.

4.2 *Position of Arctic Communities and Indigenous Peoples*

Further relevant for addressing Arctic issues is the exceptional group of local communities, including indigenous peoples. The circumpolar region is extremely sparsely populated, and the number of Arctic inhabitants varies with the definition of the term, sometimes referring to indigenous peoples or simple inhabitants. According to the Arctic Human Development Report's definition of the Arctic,[261] in 2010, Arctic areas – the map above considers the territories of the eight Arctic Council States – were home to approximately four million people, with indigenous peoples being a minority in most countries.[262] While the highest number of indigenous peoples can be found in Murmansk and Alaska, the highest share of the indigenous population compared to the total population can be found in Greenland and in Canadian Nunavut and Nunavik.[263] Following a broader definition, according to the University of the Arctic Atlas, approximately 13,1 million people, not necessary indigenous, live in the area of the circumpolar North.[264] The EU considers around four million people inhabiting the Arctic, of which less than 10 % are indigenous.[265]

Indigenous groups like the Inuit in Canada and Greenland, and the Yu'pik, Iñupiat, and Athabascan in Alaska are believed to have lived in the Arctic for twenty thousand years.[266] European and Russian Arctic exploration began much later, only in the 11th and 12th century and peaked in the 18th century.[267]

There is a tendency of portraying life in Arctic regions as harsh and difficult, and it is true that local residents naturally face a number of difficulties in the Arctic. The progressive change of local ecosystems significantly interferes with the natural basis of existence and culture of indigenous peoples and forces communities to adapt to new living conditions. Furthermore, the right of

---

261 See Figure 9 *supra*.
262 'National Snow and Ice Data Center | Arctic People' <https://nsidc.org/cryosphere/arctic-meteorology/arctic-people.html> accessed 10 August 2021.
263 See Figure 9 *supra*.
264 Joan Nymand Larsen and Gail Fondahl, 'Arctic Human Development Report' (2015) <http://urn.kb.se/resolve?urn=urn:nbn:se:norden:org:diva-3809> accessed 5 December 2021.
265 European Parliament (Chapter 2, n 149) 7, letter R.
266 'National Snow and Ice Data Center | Arctic People' (Chapter 3, n 262).
267 ibid.

FIGURE 9 Indigenous population in the Arctic regions

SOURCE: 'NORDREGIO | INDIGENOUS POPULATION IN THE ARCTIC' <HTTPS://ARCHIVE.NORDREGIO.SE/EN/MAPS/01-POPULATION-AND-DEMOGRAPHY/INDIGENOUS-POPULATION-IN-THE-ARCTIC/INDEX.HTML> ACCESSED 5 DECEMBER 2021

indigenous peoples to self-determination and freedom in their living environment constantly collides with the interests of national States over sovereign rights.[268] However, besides its certainly difficult climatic conditions, the Arctic is also a quest to harness opportunities and achieve well-being and happiness, and provides a home for its inhabitants, true to the Yakutian expression "We don't survive – we live here".[269] It is hence considered essential to be aware of the exceptional situation of Arctic residents, to guarantee local residents participation in dynamic international processes, perceive their interests, and acknowledge local communities' specific rights within international agreements like the CAOF Agreement.

4.2.1 Exceptional Situation of Arctic Residents

Local residents, especially indigenous peoples, share a strong spiritual, cultural, social and economic relationship with their traditional lands and the environment in general. They have developed the understanding that wildlife is a "shared resource that must be protected and managed in a manner that maintains the delicate ecological balance of the region, whilst responding to the needs of the people".[270] Consequently, native communities are accustomed to take from nature "only what is necessary for their survival today, so that nature will still be there for them tomorrow".[271] Traditional laws, customs and practices express an affiliation to land and a responsibility for preserving such lands for the use by future generations,[272] thus practicing a form of ecosystem based management for centuries.[273] Whereas it is often emphasized that indigenous peoples follow the approach of living in harmony with nature, this is not unconditionally the case. Just like individuals in contemporary societies, indigenous peoples, by putting their interests above those of other species, have altered their environment and engaged in religious or agricultural activities, some of which are considered unsustainable and most of which are not for the benefit of animals.[274]

---

268 Federal Foreign Office Germany (Chapter 2, n 250) 13.

269 'We Don't Survive – We Live Here!' *Arctic Anthropology* (27 September 2019) <https://arcticanthropology.org/2019/09/27/we-dont-survive-we-live-here/> accessed 10 August 2021.

270 Pharand (Chapter 3, n 127) 175.

271 ibid.

272 United Nations Office of the High Commissioner for Human Rights, 'Leaflet No. 10: Indigenous Peoples and the Environment' (2008) 2 <https://www.ohchr.org/Documents/Publications/GuideIPleaflet10en.pdf> accessed 6 April 2020.

273 'Report of the Second FiSCAO Meeting on Central Arctic Ocean Fisheries (Tromsø, 28–31 October 2013)' (Chapter 2, n 161) 19.

274 See Matthews (Chapter 2, n 241).

Nevertheless, when regulating activities such as resource exploitation, a distinction should be made between life-sustaining practices – as fishing is for most traditional Arctic communities – and commercial motives. Most indigenous peoples are directly dependant on renewable resources and ecosystems.[275] Traditionally, Arctic native people lived primarily from hunting, fishing, herding and gathering wild plants for food. Although many of them live in modern houses using modern appliances nowadays, they follow a strong approach of passing on traditional knowledge and skills.[276] Many Arctic communities still practice subsistence harvesting of marine mammal and fish, which is an expression of their tradition and direct dependence on renewable resources, and their inextricable link to the Arctic environment and its wildlife.[277]

Climate related changes in the Arctic environment therefore have a direct impact on Arctic residents much earlier than in the rest of the world: for them, climate change is not a future phenomenon – it is already happening. Changes in the distribution of fish in Arctic waters have implications for the economies of many small, remote Arctic settlements in terms of hunting, trapping and fishing.[278] The same applies to the continuous decline of sea ice. Among other things, the resulting rise of sea levels favours eroding coastlines, which are forcing native villages in Alaska to consider relocating.[279] Sea ice has become an increasingly unreliable hunting platform. Rising temperatures impact the life cycles and abundance of prey species. As a result, some indigenous communities face an aggravation of food shortages and poor nutrition. For example, in 2015, due to difficulties in walrus hunts, the US government had to ship in frozen fish to Alaskan communities. In the north of Greenland, hunters see themselves forced to kill their dogs as they can no longer hunt for seals on sea ice. In Canada, studies suggest that between one- to two-thirds of households in the extensive lands of Nunavut lack access to safe and healthy food.[280] Also the Inuit Circumpolar Council (ICC), an NGO that represents all Inuit from Alaska, Canada, Greenland, and Chukotka on matters of international

275 See also para. 26.3(a)(iv) Agenda 21.

276 'National Snow and Ice Data Center | Arctic People' (Chapter 3, n 262).

277 Pharand (Chapter 3, n 127) 175–176.

278 See Arctic Monitoring and Assessment Programme (AMAP), Conservation of Arctic Flora and Fauna (CAFF) Working Group and International Arctic Science Committee (IASC) (Chapter 2, n 78) 659.

279 Henry Fountain, 'The Arctic Is Shifting to a New Climate Because of Global Warming' *The New York Times* (14 September 2020) <https://www.nytimes.com/2020/09/14/climate/arctic-changing-climate.html?searchResultPosition=2> accessed 11 December 2020.

280 Struzik, 'Welcome to the Arctic, Fish' (Chapter 2, n 120).

importance, states in its 2018 Utqiaġvik Declaration that the health of the Inuit people is connected to the health of the animals and overall Arctic environment, and although climate-related changes provide opportunities, they also cause challenges to food security. Changes in temperatures, sea ice coverage and movement, thawing permafrost, increase in storm surges, shifts in animal migration patterns, and arrival of new species is resulting in a need to adjust hunting strategies and ways of storing food.[281] Further problematic in the context of fishing is that the anti-harvesting lobby movement increasingly threatens the subsistence of local communities, especially as animal welfare and conservation issues have become more openly debated. Arctic communities therefore depend on governments to recognize their harvesting rights of renewable resources and to directly include these communities in the development and implementation process of any measures for the protection and conservation of Arctic species and habitats.[282]

Besides the aspect of nutrition, the traditional lifestyle of indigenous peoples is of great importance in another context. Due to the native populations' strong link with the environment, preventing them to continue their traditional lifestyle bears a devastating effect. The suicide rate amongst indigenous peoples in the Arctic is among the highest suicide rates in the world, often 4–6 times higher than compared to the rest of the population in the respective State,[283] and has even increased in the last decades.[284] The main trigger of this is not considered the cold or the dark in the North. Besides general suicide risk factors, suicide among indigenous peoples is seen as a result of colonization, dispossession, culture loss and social disconnection.[285] Distracting indigenous peoples and Arctic residents to follow their traditional lifestyle and engage in cultural activities, like traditional fishing techniques, may hence have severe consequences.[286] Fortunately, the importance of physical and mental health

281 Inuit Circumpolar Council, 'Utqiaġvik Declaration (Utqiaġvik, 19 July 2018)' 4 <https://www.arctictoday.com/wp-content/uploads/2018/07/2018-Utigavik-Declaration.pdf> accessed 8 April 2020.

282 Pharand (Chapter 3, n 127) 175–176.

283 T Kue Young, Boris Revich and Leena Soininen, 'Suicide in Circumpolar Regions: An Introduction and Overview' (2015) 74 International Journal of Circumpolar Health 27349 <https://doi.org/10.3402/ijch.v74.27349> accessed 8 April 2020.

284 Eduardo Chachamovich and others, 'Suicide Among Inuit: Results From a Large, Epidemiologically Representative Follow-Back Study in Nunavut' (2015) 60 Canadian Journal of Psychiatry 268, 269.

285 Michael J Kral, 'Suicide and Suicide Prevention among Inuit in Canada' (2016) 61 Canadian Journal of Psychiatry. Revue canadienne de psychiatrie 688, 688 <http://www.ncbi.nlm.nih.gov/pubmed/27738249> accessed 8 April 2020.

286 ibid 691.

of indigenous peoples is more and more recognized and addressed, e. g. in the 2011 Nuuk Declaration: the eight Arctic Council States recognized "the continued health challenges and note the need to improve physical and mental health and well-being and empowerment of indigenous peoples and residents of Arctic communities".[287]

In order to take due account to the exceptional situation of Arctic residents, especially to ensure food security, it is claimed, in line with the ICC, that a healthy environment and, among other things, access to resources, physical and mental health, recognition of culture and participation in management are necessary.[288]

4.2.2 Participation of Arctic Residents

An essential aspect towards food security and sustainable development is participation,[289] which has been internationally recognized from various sides. The ICC, for example, emphasizes that the Inuit, as primary users of marine life, should be considered competent partners in addressing international issues including commercial fishing. Their traditions and customs should be part of any Arctic renewable resource management regime. For both economic and cultural reasons, prospective commercial activities should not undermine Inuit subsistence hunting, harvesting and navigation, and awareness is necessary regarding the pollutant discharges from fishing and hunting vessels as well as from increased commercial shipping and offshore drilling.[290] Similar to the International Labour Organization (ILO) Convention concerning Indigenous and Tribal Peoples in Independent Countries (No. 169)[291] (ILO Convention No. 169),[292] Molenaar and Koivurova emphasize the need for socio-economic benefits for present and future generations.[293] Speakers of the Permanent Forum on Indigenous Issues stressed the importance of including indigenous peoples in high-level decision-making and even called for their observer status in the

287 'Arctic Council Nuuk Declaration (Nuuk, 12 May 2011)' (Chapter 3, n 135) 2.

288 Inuit Circumpolar Council, 'Utqiaġvik Declaration (Utqiaġvik, 19 July 2018)' (Chapter 3, n 281) 1; similar also Pharand (Chapter 3, n 127) 175–176.

289 'We Don't Survive – We Live Here!' (Chapter 3, n 269).

290 Inuit Circumpolar Council, 'Inuit Arctic Policy' (2010) <http://library.arcticportal.org/1898/1/g100765_Inuit_Arctic_Policy-June02.pdf> accessed 25 April 2020.

291 International Labour Organisation, 'Indigenous and Tribal Peoples Convention No. 169 (Geneva, 27 June 1989)' <https://www.ilo.org/dyn/normlex/en/f?p=NORMLEXPUB:12100:0::NO::P12100_ILO_CODE:C169> accessed 7 April 2020.

292 See Articles 13 et seq. ILO Convention No. 169.

293 Koivurova and Molenaar (Chapter 3, n 32) 106.

UN General Assembly.[294] Also under EU law, the importance of protection of Arctic indigenous populations and cultures is highlighted.[295] The 2017 EU Report on an integrated European Union policy for the Arctic specifically notes that Arctic indigenous populations have the right to use natural resources in their home areas and should therefore be parties to any future plans for commercial fishing. Further, any fisheries activity in the Arctic region must take place in compliance with historical fishing rights.[296] Accepting Arctic indigenous peoples as competent partners and involving them in an international process is hence considered vital.

In particular, the values of indigenous peoples, traditional knowledge and resource management practices should be studied and taken into account when implementing integrated management systems. This is especially helpful for environmentally sound and sustainable development and management of natural resources.[297] Indigenous knowledge especially bears one main advantage compared to knowledge gathered via general research activities: it usually outclasses scientific knowledge in depth and time.[298] However, the CAOF Agreement signatories did not recognize the value of such knowledge at first. Indigenous participants were not included in the conclusion of the Ilulissat Declaration in 2008. To address the disappointment about their exclusion, indigenous Inuit communities issued a paper called "A Circumpolar Inuit Declaration on Sovereignty in the Arctic" that emphasized the importance of the Inuit's role as active partners, especially in relation to their unique knowledge of Arctic ecosystems and their sustainable use. The paper also urged the consideration of Inuit consent, expertise and perspectives on future

294 United Nations, 'Press Release: Indigenous Peoples Must Be Part of High-Level Decision-Making, Speakers Stress, Calling for Observer Status in General Assembly, as Permanent Forum Continues (26 April 2019)' <https://www.un.org/press/en/2019/hr5435.doc.htm> accessed 5 December 2021.

295 See for example on the special protection of the Arctic Saami population in Norway, Finland and Sweden: European Union, 'Act Concerning the Conditions of Accession and the Adjustments to the Treaties on Which the European Union Is Founded, Protocol No 3 – on the Sami People (29 August 1994) – 11994N/PRO/03' <https://eur-lex.europa.eu/legal-content/BG/TXT/?uri=CELEX:11994N/PRO/03> accessed 6 April 2021.

296 European Parliament (Chapter 2, n 149) 9, lit. AF, AG.

297 United Nations Conference on Environment and Development, 'Agenda 21 (Rio de Janerio, 3–14 June 1992)' paras 8.5(d), 26.3(a)(iii) <https://sustainabledevelopment.un.org/content/documents/Agenda21.pdf> accessed 7 April 2022.

298 TI Van Pelt and others, 'The Missing Middle: Central Arctic Ocean Gaps in Fishery Research and Science Coordination' (2017) 85 Marine Policy 79, 80; cf. Valentin Schatz, 'Incorporation of Indigenous and Local Knowledge in Central Arctic Ocean Fisheries Management' (2019) 10 Arctic Review on Law and Politics 130, 131.

commercial fisheries.[299] Six years later, the ICC adopted its 2014 Kitigaaryuit Declaration that recognizes the importance of fisheries for Inuit life and calls upon States to include Inuit representatives on all bodies dealing with Arctic fishing issues.[300] As a result, some States included indigenous representatives in their delegations to conclude a future CAOF Agreement,[301] and the value of indigenous peoples' and local knowledge was increasingly taken into account.[302] *Inter alia,* FiSCAO Meetings continuously acknowledged the importance of fishing for the economic viability and social health of indigenous communities and the value of traditional knowledge in general.[303] Indigenous knowledge was considered "a valuable source of information for understanding and monitoring changes in Arctic fisheries" which could "greatly enhance an ecosystem-based understanding of potential changes".[304] Especially the traditional understanding of the interconnections between trophic levels has shaped the scientific process as to consider the entire food web to better understand ongoing changes and the consequences of decisions, and to extend research beyond economically important species.[305] It was anticipated that there was limited traditional knowledge for the high seas portion of the CAO due to the distance between traditional communities and the high seas. Nevertheless, it was highlighted that traditional communities could provide valuable data from adjacent regions. They can especially be of help when deriving diet data and information on trigger variables,[306] such as historic and

299 Inuit Circumpolar Council, 'A Circumpolar Inuit Declaration on Sovereignty in the Arctic' (2009) paras 3.4–3.5 <https://iccalaska.org/wp-icc/wp-content/uploads/2016/01/Signed-Inuit-Sovereignty-Declaration-11x17.pdf> accessed 7 April 2020.

300 Inuit Circumpolar Council, 'Kitigaaryuit Declaration (Kitigaaryuit, 24 July 2014)' paras 20, 22 <https://iccalaska.org/wp-icc/wp-content/uploads/2016/01/2014-Kitigaarguit-Declaration-Final-Signed.pdf > accessed 2 November 2024.

301 Schatz (Chapter 3, n 298) 132.

302 See for example 'Arctic Council Nuuk Declaration (Nuuk, 12 May 2011)' (Chapter 3, n 135) 3; 'Preventing Unregulated Commercial Fishing in the Central Arctic Ocean (CAO) – A Compilation of Reports from Meetings of Experts in Shanghai (China), Incheon (Korea) & Sapporo (Japan)' (Chapter 1, n 2) 3.

303 'Report of the First FiSCAO Meeting on Central Arctic Ocean Fisheries (Anchorage, 15–17 June 2011)' (Chapter 2, n 161) 3. 'Report of the Third FiSCAO Meeting on Central Arctic Ocean Fisheries (Seattle, 14–16 April 2015)' (Chapter 3, n 92) 13, 16.

304 'Report of the Fifth FiSCAO Meeting on Central Arctic Ocean Fisheries (Ottawa, 24–26 October 2017)' (Chapter 2, n 161) 18.

305 'Report of the Second FiSCAO Meeting on Central Arctic Ocean Fisheries (Tromsø, 28–31 October 2013)' (Chapter 2, n 161) 18 et seq.

306 'Report of the Fourth FiSCAO Meeting on Central Arctic Ocean Fisheries (Tromsø, 26–28 September 2016)' (Chapter 2, n 134) 19. 'Report of the Fifth FiSCAO Meeting on Central Arctic Ocean Fisheries (Ottawa, 24–26 October 2017)' (Chapter 2, n 161) 18.

contemporary baseline data on species distributions and abundances, and environmental conditions in the CAO or adjacent waters. Participants of the FiSCAO meetings recommended continued engagement and involvement of indigenous peoples, and ongoing development of the mapping and monitoring programs with indigenous representation.[307]

As regards the monitoring process, existing organizations and programs in particular were identified as being able to provide relevant information. This included the ICC, which already expressed its determination on its own initiative to "utilize indigenous knowledge to advice all future processes of the Central Arctic Ocean Moratorium on Commercial Fisheries".[308] Further included were the Exchange for Local Observations and Knowledge of the Arctic, and regional programs like the Nunavut Coastal Resource Inventory in Canada, and Alaskan native organizations that work cooperatively with US federal government agencies through cooperative agreements.[309] As an example, although the ICC was not present at the 2017 FiSCAO meeting in Ottawa, it was invited to submit comments, which were offered to be included in the full meeting report.[310]

4.2.3 Specific Rights of Local and Arctic Residents

Nowadays, local or native residents, especially indigenous peoples, enjoy special rights that should pay tribute to their exceptional situation compared to other residents of a country. These include fishing rights and rights that protect their special relationship with the environment.

Although there is not yet a specific international regulation on native peoples' fishing rights, in most cases they are already part of agreements that take into account their indigenous status. Article 27 of the International Covenant on Civil and Political Rights (ICCPR), to which all CAOF Agreement parties are parties,[311] ensures that people belonging to ethnic, religious or linguistic

307 'Report of the Fifth FiSCAO Meeting on Central Arctic Ocean Fisheries (Ottawa, 24–26 October 2017)' (Chapter 2, n 161) 11.

308 Inuit Circumpolar Council, 'Utqiaġvik Declaration (Utqiaġvik, 19 July 2018)' (Chapter 3, n 281) 11.

309 See for example the Alaskan Eskimo Whaling Commission and the Eskimo Walrus Commission, 'Report of the Fifth FiSCAO Meeting on Central Arctic Ocean Fisheries (Ottawa, 24–26 October 2017)' (Chapter 2, n 161) 11, 19.

310 'Chairman's Statement, Fifth FiSCAO Meeting on Central Arctic Ocean Fisheries (Ottawa, 24–26 October 2017)' 2 <https://apps-afsc.fisheries.noaa.gov/documents/Arctic_fish_stocks_fifth_meeting/508_Documents/508_Final_report_of_the_5th_FiSCAO_meeting.pdf > accessed 2 November 2024.

311 'United Nations OHCHR | Status of Ratification – International Covenant on Civil and Political Rights' <https://indicators.ohchr.org/> accessed 8 April 2022.

minorities may not be denied the right to enjoy their own culture and practices. The Human Rights Committee, in its General Comment 23 (1994), specified that the right comprises traditional activities of indigenous peoples such as hunting and fishing.[312] It further notes that safeguarding these rights imposes specific obligations on States. Positive legal measures of protection and measures to ensure the effective participation of minority communities in decisions with the potential to directly affect them are required.[313] If applied strictly, Article 27 ICCPR even suggests a preferential position for indigenous peoples compared to ordinary citizens,[314] but measures aimed at enabling the exercise of these rights can serve as legitimate differentiation.[315] Hence, it may be argued that in order to preserve indigenous culture in particular regions, fishing quotas and other restrictions imposed by law must be adapted accordingly: they must be loosened for indigenous peoples, but tightened for non-indigenous fishers.[316]

Further, ILO Convention No. 169 addresses indigenous peoples fishing rights in various ways, although concerning the CAOF Agreement signatories, its contents are only binding for Norway and Denmark[317] that ratified the convention.[318] Besides the general understanding of preserving and ensuring a peoples' right to enjoy the exercise of their own culture, Article 6 and 7 ILO Convention No. 169 ensure an indigenous peoples' right to have a say in the implementation of such rights. The convention further calls upon governments

---

312 United Nations Office of the High Commissioner for Human Rights, 'CCPR General Comment No. 23: Article 27 (Rights of Minorities), (8 April 1994) – CCPR/C/21/Rev.1/Add.5' para 7 <https://www.refworld.org/docid/453883fc0.html> accessed 8 April 2022.

313 ibid.

314 See General Comment 23: "should not be confused with other personal rights conferred on one and all under the Covenant".

315 United Nations Office of the High Commissioner for Human Rights (Chapter 3, n 312) paras 6.2, 9.

316 'The Fish Site | Indigenous Fishing Rights' <https://thefishsite.com/articles/indigenous-fishing-rights> accessed 8 April 2022.

317 As no reservations in respect to Greenland or the Faroe Islands have been made, these treaties apply to both territories. In fact, a complaint against Denmark was raised concerning the application of ILO Convention No. 169; see International Labour Organisation, 'Report of the Committee Set up to Examine the Representation Alleging Non-Observance by Denmark of the Indigenous and Tribal Peoples Convention, 1989 (No. 169), Made under Article 24 of the ILO Constitution' (2001) <https://www.ilo.org/dyn/normlex/en/f?p=1000:50012:0::NO:50012:P50012_COMPLAINT_PROCEDURE_ID,P50012_LANG_CODE:2507219,en:NO> accessed 7 April 2022.

318 'International Labour Organization | Ratifications of C169 – Indigenous and Tribal Peoples Convention, 1989 (No. 169)' <https://www.ilo.org/dyn/normlex/en/f?p=1000:11300:0::NO:11300:P11300_INSTRUMENT_ID:312314> accessed 8 April 2022.

to explicitly protect the rights of peoples with respect to the natural resources of their lands,[319] which includes the "total environment of the areas which the peoples concerned occupy or otherwise use", hence also waters.[320] Article 23 ILO Convention No. 169 recognizes hunting and fishing by indigenous peoples as an important factor in the preservation of their culture, and encourages governments to ensure their exercise.

Furthermore, by recognizing the unique status of indigenous peoples in international instruments, as *inter alia* in UN Agenda 21,[321] the indigenous peoples' special link to the environment is paid tribute. In this regard, the United Nations Convention on Biological Diversity (CBD) further sets up a specific framework. In principle, the CBD recognizes the close and traditional dependence of many indigenous and local communities embodying traditional lifestyles on biological resources.[322] Article 8(j) CBD specifically calls upon the CBD's contracting parties – which include all parties to the CAOF Agreement except the United States[323] – subject to their national legislation to respect, preserve and maintain indigenous and local communities' knowledge, innovations and practices relevant for the conservation and sustainable use of biological diversity. Further, a wider application with the approval and involvement of the holders of such knowledge, innovations and practices should be promoted.[324] To further foster the inclusion of local residents, similar to para. 15.4(g) Agenda 21, the CBD encourages equitable sharing of benefits arising from the utilization of such knowledge, innovations and practices.[325] Regarding the value and consideration of traditional knowledge, Article 17(2) CBD makes clear that the exchange of information among parties especially includes the exchange of results of indigenous and traditional knowledge. When developing methods of cooperation for the development and use of technologies, indigenous and traditional knowledge should be incorporated

319 See Article 15 ILO Convention No. 169.

320 See Article 13 ILO Convention No. 169.

321 See para. 26.3(a)(iv) Agenda 21. Agenda 21 is a comprehensive plan of action to be taken globally, nationally and locally by UN organizations, governments, and major groups in every area in which human impacts on the environment; see United Nations Conference on Environment and Development (Chapter 3, n 297).

322 See para. 12 Preamble CBD.

323 'CBD | List of Parties' <https://www.cbd.int/information/parties.shtml> accessed 6 April 2022.

324 Similar, Article 10(c) CBD requires the parties to protect and encourage customary use of biological resources in accordance with traditional cultural practices that are compatible with conservation or sustainable use requirements.

325 See para. 12 Preamble CBD.

and is equally important as scientific knowledge.[326] The conference of the parties (COP), the CBD's decision-making body consisting of the governments of the more than 190 contracting parties, further recognized the importance of maintaining cultural identities for maintaining knowledge, innovations and practices of indigenous and local communities.[327] In addition, an Ad Hoc Open-ended Inter-sessional Working Group on Article 8(j) was established to ensure adequate protection of indigenous peoples and effective implementation of Article 8(j) CBD.[328]

1. Indigenous peoples have further specific rights under the United Nations Declaration on the Rights of Indigenous Peoples (UNDRIP).[329] As its name suggests, UNDRIP is not a treaty but a non-binding declaration. Adopted by the UN General Assembly in 2007, it nevertheless enjoys a high level of international acceptance. The declaration contains several clauses that provide for the protection of the rights of indigenous peoples to natural resources. For instance, Article 3 UNDRIP ensures the right to self-determination, which includes the free pursuit of economic, social and cultural development. Article 8(2)(b) UNDRIP encourages States to take effective mechanisms to prevent and redress for any action which has the aim or effect of dispossessing indigenous peoples and individuals of their lands, territories or resources. Article 11 UNDRIP safeguards the practice of indigenous peoples' traditions, which includes fishing practices, as it is the case with Arctic indigenous peoples. The declaration further stipulates the right of indigenous peoples to pass on their respective traditions,[330] and the right to dignity and diversity of their cultures, traditions, histories and aspirations without discrimination.[331] Further, Article 18 and 19 UNDRIP guarantee indigenous peoples' participation rights in decision-making processes for matters that may affect their rights. In order to obtain their free, prior and informed consent before taking any implementing measures that may affect the peoples, there is a duty to consult. Article 20 UNDRIP ensures *inter alia* the right to develop their own means of subsistence, e.g. fisheries, and entitles to just and fair redress where indigenous peoples are deprived from that right. More specifically, Article 26 and Article 32 UNDRIP

326 See Article 18(4) CBD.

327 CBD Conference of the Parties, 'COP 5 Decision 16: Article 8(j) and related provisions (Nairobi, 26 May 2000)' <https://www.cbd.int/decision/cop/default.shtml?id=7158> accessed 28 April 2024.

328 United Nations Office of the High Commissioner for Human Rights (Chapter 3, n 272) 6.

329 'United Nations General Assembly Resolution 61/295, United Nations Declaration on the Rights of Indigenous Peoples (Adopted 13 September 2007)'.

330 See Article 13 UNDRIP.

331 See Article 15 UNDRIP.

entail the right to use and control land and resources, including water, that an indigenous people has traditionally owned or otherwise acquired, hence also fishing grounds, where a people exercises fishing.[332] Further, indigenous peoples have the right to the conservation and protection of the environment and the productive capacity of their lands or territories and resources.[333] This entails the responsibility of States not only to preserve the environment – meaning the air, water, land in or on which people, animals, and plants live – but also to protect it from possible damage. The obligation is designed as an obligation of conduct, as States shall implement assistance and take effective measures to monitor, maintain and restore the health of indigenous peoples[334] and should be considered in the light of the environmental prevention principle, no harm principle and precautionary principle.[335] Although most of the provisions of UNDRIP are not binding, its obligations should also be considered in the context of the implementation of the CAOF Agreement as a means of interpretation under Article 31 (3) (c) VCLT. There should be fair involvement of traditional Arctic communities in both future consultation and decision-making processes to ensure compliance with commitments and to take into account the relationship of indigenous peoples to their territory, environment and traditions.

Concerning the rights of Arctic residents under the CAOF Agreement, all CAOF Agreement participants are parties to the ICCPR and the CBD and are therefore required to respect the foregoing rules. Further, the CAOF Agreement's Preamble specifically recalls UNDRIP. Hence, its provisions should be taken into account.

In the CAOF Agreement itself, the Preamble incorporates the fundamental ideas of the aforementioned international policies regarding Arctic residents, including indigenous peoples. It recognizes their interests in the long-term conservation and sustainable use of living marine resources and in healthy marine

332 The draft version of Article 32 UNDRIP even foresaw a reference to „their" resources, which was later removed. See more on natural resources in the context of indigenous rights and State sovereignty in Stefania Errico, 'The Controversial Issue of Natural Resources: Balancing States' Sovereignty with Indigenous Peoples' Rights' in Stephen Allen and Alexandra Xanthaki (eds), *Reflections on the UN Declaration on the Rights of Indigenous Peoples* (Hart Publishing 2011).

333 See Article 29 UNDRIP.

334 Adriana Giunta, 'Looking Back to Move Forward: The Status of Environmental Rights under the UN Declaration on the Rights of Indigenous Peoples' (2019) 23 International Journal of Human Rights 149, 152.

335 Cf. Nicolas de Sadeleer, *Environmental Principles: From Political Slogans to Legal Rules* (Oxford University Press 2020), 61 et seq.

CAO ecosystems. Further, the importance of involving these residents in the further process is emphasized. According to Article 5(2) CAOF Agreement, representatives of Arctic communities, including indigenous peoples, may participate in bodies that are formed for the implementation of the Joint Program of Scientific Research and Monitoring and other activities referred to in Article 4 CAOF Agreement. Additionally, the Preamble expresses the desire to promote the use of indigenous and local knowledge on living marine resources in the Arctic Ocean and the ecosystems in which these occur as a basis for prospective CAO fisheries conservation and management measures. Further reference to the implementation of this knowledge is made on various points within the Agreement.[336]

With regard to fisheries, the CAOF Agreement does not allow indigenous peoples to be given preferential treatment with regard to certain fishing rights, as proposed in Article 27 ICCPR, specifically. Yet, for the time being, the Agreement only regulates commercial and exploratory fisheries and fisheries for scientific purposes in particular. Fishing rights of indigenous peoples are not explicitly addressed. However, it is argued that subsistence harvesting forms a separate category of fisheries, similar as it is treated by the International Whaling Commission (IWC): the IWC does not classify native subsistence whaling as commercial whaling as the former is not conducted „to maximise catches or profit", and is hence not subject to the moratorium imposed by the IWC.[337] Further, one has to bear in mind that fisheries, if any, will not take place in the near future. Setting a specific TAC and allocating catch quotas in the CAO were therefore also not yet on the agenda. However, it is recommended to consider the preservation of the aforementioned rights at the right time.

Nevertheless, the delicate question remains to what extent indigenous peoples should be granted participation. In some cases, the participation of indigenous peoples must be treated with special care on the national level. In Canada for example, national law obliges to consult or involve indigenous peoples where new measures could influence the status of resources in the Canadian EEZ.[338] Consideration must also be given to the fact that increased participation of Arctic indigenous peoples could be opposed by non-Arctic signatory states, who fear that their own say and role in Agreement issues

336 See Articles 4(4), Article 5(1)(b) CAOF Agreement.

337 'International Whaling Commission | Aboriginal Subsistence Whaling in the Arctic' <https://iwc.int/aboriginal> accessed 28 June 2021.

338 Wegge (Chapter 2, n 21) 336.

will be jeopardised.[339] It is further noted that within the context of the CAOF Agreement, besides participating in implementation committees, Arctic communities cannot acquire membership or observer status, as it is the case e.g. within the Arctic Council. There, they are given the role of "Permanent Participants", a distinct category of membership between members and observers, which the Arctic Council Members must consult prior to any consensus decision-making. Also in other international fora, indigenous peoples are often accorded the status of NGOs.[340] The current possibility of mere indirect inclusion contradicts *inter alia* the proposals of Koivurova and Molenaar or Pharand, who argued for a closer integration of Arctic communities when organizing a prospective arrangement governing activities in the Arctic (Ocean), e.g. broad participation[341] of regional and territorial governments.[342] Yet, it must be noted that both Koivurova et al. and Pharand imagined the issue of fisheries to be regulated within a broader framework by an organization dealing with Arctic issues in all sectors, not within an RFB. Within fisheries arrangements, local communities do not usually have member status. Yet, the law of treaties does not prevent States per se from granting indigenous peoples' organizations a participatory status in a treaty that is at least equal, or goes beyond, the status of permanent participants within the Arctic Council.[343] Technically, depending on the formalities of the respective RFB, at least the achievement of observer status is possible. However, in the CAOF Agreement, no use was made of this possibility, and it was decided against direct participation of Arctic residents including indigenous peoples.

The only way to safeguard participation is hence through engaging in a special body under Article 5(2) CAOF Agreement or to liaise closely with the respective national government,[344] where national legislation provides for participation.[345] This however does not necessarily guarantee effective international representation: usually, indigenous' and local communities' interests do not clash on the international level but with the interests of their respective sovereign. While it is understandable that different views must first be addressed at the national level, international instruments should nevertheless

339 Cf. Molenaar, 'The Oslo Declaration on High Seas Fishing in the Central Arctic Ocean' (Chapter 2, n 58) 429.

340 Koivurova and Molenaar (Chapter 3, n 32) 16.

341 ibid 106.

342 Pharand (Chapter 3, n 127) 192.

343 Koivurova and Molenaar (Chapter 3, n 32) 58.

344 See Molenaar, 'The Oslo Declaration on High Seas Fishing in the Central Arctic Ocean' (Chapter 2, n 58) 429.

345 As is for example suggested by paras 26.3(b), 26.4–26.6 Agenda 21.

provide a solid foundation to ensure effective participation by local communities. It is suggested that these considerations are kept in mind during the implementation of the CAOF Agreement.

4.3 *Interests of Non-participants to the CAOF Agreement*

The question of interests of States that are not party to the CAOF Agreement might not seem to be of significance at first, but is closely tied to the membership policy of the CAOF Agreement. An agreement is only successful if it is effectively implemented – and this depends not only on the acceptance by participants but also by non-participants. An agreement should therefore always take non-participants into account and try to align their interests with those of its members to ensure the effectiveness of the framework in question.

Where the CAOF Agreement and fisheries are concerned, the broader process aimed at including a group of States that would realistically conduct fishing in the CAO with current specific interests. Yet, technically, every State could conduct fishing or research in the CAO pursuant to the freedom of the high seas, although all vessels that wish to do so must pass through coastal State waters of CAOF Agreement participants. Furthermore, it is inherent in fish stocks that they do not respect the political boundaries of States or agreements and are therefore considered a transboundary natural resource. Hence, a stock "cannot be properly managed nor can its habitat be adequately protected in independent jurisdictions without regional, national and international cooperation."[346] That includes coordination not only among the CAOF Agreement Parties but also other States that could develop an interest in the region – especially if commercial fisheries in CAO waters turn out to be possible and profitable. An open membership policy and an appropriate cost-benefit ratio can ensure that States rather accede[347] to the CAOF Agreement and conduct fisheries within the scope of its framework than on a State's own initiative.

Common global interests are the issues of climate change and the status of the environment. Under international law, States have the obligation to ensure sustainable use of resources and implementation of the ecosystem approach.[348]

346 Pharand (Chapter 3, n 127) 175.

347 Similiar, for the UNFS Agreement, cf. Erik Jaap Molenaar, 'Non-Participation in the Fish Stocks Agreement: Status and Reasons' (2011) 26 International Journal of Marine and Coastal Law 195, 228.

348 On the concepts of sustainable development and the ecosystem approach see Chapter 5 Sections 2, 2.1 *infra*; for more national visions on the Arctic, see Richard C Powell and Klaus Dodds, *Polar Geopolitics?: Knowledges, Resources and Legal Regimes* (Edward Elgar Publishing 2014) 93–200.

As far as these are sufficiently implemented in the CAOF Agreement,[349] colliding interests are unlikely.

Alongside other States, NGOs often play an important role in international agreements and are seen as critical components and drivers of transparency to promote the effectiveness of international bodies under certain conditions.[350] As provided for by Article 12 UNFS Agreement,[351] NGOs interested in the issue of CAO fisheries are expected to make requests across three dimensions of transparency: public participation, access to information and access to outcomes.[352] Accordingly, NGOs such as Greenpeace and the Pew Charitable Trust have expressed interest in participating in the drafting process of the CAOF Agreement, but claims of direct participation have been rejected by the Arctic Five.[353] The Arctic NGO Forum, an initiative that aimed at providing a consistent way for NGOs concerned with Arctic environmental issues to get together, exchange ideas and provide advice to the global Arctic community, seems to be no longer active.[354] This would have provided a suitable platform and strengthened the respective NGOs positions. NGOs are forced to revert to other channels, such as direct participation in the Arctic Council[355] or as participants of national delegations to uphold their interests. Either way, at the international stage, interests of NGOs should be kept in mind. In this respect, creating the possibility for NGO participation as observers of the CAOF Agreement or a subsequent RFB could resolve potential conflicts in advance and strengthen the support for such instruments.

---

349 See specifically on the implementation of sustainable development and the ecosystem approach Chapter 5 Sections 2, 2.1 *infra*.

350 On the participation of NGOs in RFBs, see Chapter 3 Sections 3, 3.2 *supra*.

351 Article 12 UNFS Agreement calls on States to provide for transparency in decision-making processes and other RFMA/O activities and states the right of (non-) governmental organizations to participation and access to information.

352 Petersson (Chapter 2, n 161) 1–3, 8.

353 Wegge (Chapter 2, n 21) 335.

354 See'Arctic Forum Foundation | Engaging NGOs <http://eu-arctic-forum.org/fora/engaging-ngos-on-eu-arctic-policy-and-the-oil-and-gas-industry-12-13-november-haparanda-sweden/> accessed 2 November 2024..

355 A list of the twelve non-governmental organizations that are approved as observers to the Arctic Council can be accessed at 'Arctic Council | Nongovernmental Organizations' <https://arctic-council.org/en/about/observers/non-governmental-organizations/> accessed 30 December 2020.

5 Summary

Several motives led to the conclusion of the CAOF Agreement. Especially a collapse of fish stocks, as has happened for example in the Bering Sea "Donut Hole", wanted to be prevented. Also the ongoing overexploitation of fish stocks worldwide and the lack of a comprehensive international legal framework relating to the conservation and sustainable use of marine biodiversity in areas beyond national jurisdiction called for action. As a result, the process of establishing an agreement on CAO fisheries was initiated by the United States in 2007. While initially, there were only meetings between the five Arctic coastal States, which led to complaints from the other Arctic Council states Iceland, Finland and Sweden, after some time, a broader process was initiated. The process welcomed further participants that issued interest in CAO fisheries, including the EU and relevant DWF States, which were referred to as the Other Five. Parallel to ministerial meetings, scientific FiSCAO meetings took place to assists the process, before the CAOF Agreement was finally signed almost ten years later in 2018.

As commercial fisheries in the CAO may be possible at some point, the CAOF Agreement needs to be prepared for accrediting new members. States must therefore have a "real interest" in the fisheries concerned. The concept is not universally defined but needs to be determined by every RFB individually. For the CAOF Agreement, it is submitted that real interest States are States that are interested in fishing in CAO waters, provided this would be possible. Currently, all States or groups of States that have such an interest have been included in the process.

International agreements involve different actors with different interests. Within the CAOF Agreement, three main stakeholders exist: the Arctic Five, the Other Five, and local residents. The grouping of the Arctic Five wants to safeguard their special position as Arctic coastal States. The Arctic Five will likely only favour the commencement of commercial fisheries in the CAOF Agreement Area if their utilization-oriented or conservation-oriented coastal State interests are not at stake. Contrary, the Other Five are probably more inclined to support the commencement of fishing in the CAO, as they may only conduct Arctic fisheries under the CAOF Agreement. Further, they depend on the support of the Arctic coastal States, which will need to grant access to their coastal infrastructure and facilities. Moreover, all States follow national interests that partly vary significantly from each other. In addition, the interests of Arctic local communities should be taken into account. Many residents still practice subsistence harvesting for marine mammals and fish, which makes them directly dependent on renewable resources. Further, the continuous reduction of Arctic sea ice and resulting difficulties in hunting have already led to food shortages, and communities are forced to abandon their traditional lifestyles, causing social issues in addition to the nutritional aspect. Under the CAOF Agreement, the special status of Arctic residents is recognized, but participation is so far only possible indirectly through national delegations or in committees that may be formed by the CAOF Agreement's parties. Direct involvement in decision-making processes is not foreseen. Similarly, this is the case for other non-participants like NGOs. Interests of non-participants should nevertheless be considered in order to safeguard international acceptance of the Agreement. An open membership policy and compliance with international standards are considered helpful tools in this regard.

CHAPTER 4

Managing (Arctic) Fisheries: Interplay of Law and Governance

As outlined above in detail, the earth faces an environmental challenge. Climate change and its effects, like the loss of biodiversity and depletion of resources, are phenomena that, due to their development from local to global issues, can only be addressed with cooperative means. Therefore, international action in the form of transnational or international governance must be taken.[1] Furthermore, the interplay between environmental concerns and resource utilization creates both challenges and opportunities for the international law and governance framework. Various interests of stakeholders need to be considered and aligned. This poses the question of how international management balancing these interests should look like. One suggestion can be found in Garrett Hardin's theory of the "tragedy of the commons".[2]

The regime of high-seas fisheries is often considered as the prime example of the "tragedy of the commons". According to Hardin's theory, a resource that is common property will be overexploited and destroyed by the competing interests of individual users. This can only be countered by strict regulation and enforcement by States through international means or market mechanisms.[3] Commons should however not be confused with resources, which are shareable, "global common"[4] goods that may be governed within the commons.[5] Instead, commons

> applies to resources, and involves a group or community of people, but commons does not denote the resources, the community, a place, or a thing. Commons [are] the institutional arrangement of these elements.[6]

1 Cf. Ottavio Quirico, 'Disentangling Climate Change Governance: A Legal Perspective' (2012) 21 Review of European Community and International Environmental Law 92, 92.

2 See Garrett Hardin, 'The Tragedy of the Commons' (1968) 162 Science 1243.

3 See ibid; cf. Stefano B Longo, Rebecca Clausen and Brett Clark, 'Sea Change', *The tragedy of the commodity: Oceans, fisheries, and aquaculture* (Rutgers University Press 2015) 9.

4 Quirico (Chapter 4, n 1) 93.

5 Brett M Frischmann, Alain Marciano and Giovanni Battista Ramello, 'Retrospectives: Tragedy of the Commons after 50 Years' (2019) 33 Journal of Economic Perspectives 211, 221.

6 Brett M Frischmann, Michael J Madison and Katherine Jo Strandburg, *Governing Knowledge Commons* (Oxford University Press 2014) 2.

 | DOI:10.1163/9789004700673_005

Commons can therefore be described as "institutionalized sharing of resources among members of a community".[7] The logic behind Hardin's theory is considered a solid starting point for deliberating the use and management of shared resources.[8] However, from there, the theory should be developed further.

Hardin's theory is often considered to provide a potential justification for government regulation of shared resources. Yet, voices were raised that the theory neglects the process in community regulation based on communication and cooperation, contradicting the alleged "inevitableness"[9] of the tragedy that Hardin predicts.[10] In this regard, an important distinction must be made: Hardin focuses in his theory on one specific form of governance, open-access sharing.[11] This tradition stems from the understanding, enshrined in Roman law, that fishery resources are *res nullia*, a thing belonging to no one. Open access sharing, aligned with Grotius' theory of the freedom of the high seas,[12] is still incorporated in many Western traditions and indeed, just as Hardin predicted, provoked excess capacity and overcapitalization of world fishing fleets, which lead to conflicts between sustainable conservation and economic interests.[13] As open access entails no property rights, no right to exclude others from the resource in question exist. Under this perspective, the power of commons as an efficient form of governance seems limited. By contrast, in its modern understanding, "commons" includes some form of communal ownership. Only members of the community may access the resource – under certain conditions – and the exclusion of non-members is possible.[14] The modern interpretation thus throws a different light on Hardin's theory and presents a good basis for the management of high seas fishing.

Multiple interrelated factors shape the outcome of management and governance. In order to determine ways towards an ecologically sound economy,

---

7 ibid.

8 Timothy Taylor, 'What Is the Tragedy of the Commons?' *Conversable Economist* (15 August 2012) <https://conversableeconomist.blogspot.com/2012/08/what-is-tragedy-of-commons.html?m=1> accessed 2 April 2022.

9 Hardin (Chapter 4, n 2) 1244.

10 See Ian Angus, 'The Myth of the Tragedy of the Commons' *Climate and Capitalism* (25 August 2008) <http://climateandcapitalism.com/2008/08/25/debunking-the-tragedy-of-the-commons/> accessed 10 August 2021; Frischmann, Marciano and Ramello (Chapter 4, n 5) 218.

11 Frischmann, Marciano and Ramello (Chapter 4, n 5) 221.

12 On the freedom of the high seas, see Chapter 4 Sections 1, 1.2, 1.2.1 *infra*.

13 MJ Fogarty and JS Collie, 'Fisheries Overview' (2009) 2 Encyclopedia of Ocean Sciences 499, 501 <https://www.sciencedirect.com/science/article/pii/B9780123744739007487> accessed 27 May 2020.

14 Frischmann, Marciano and Ramello (Chapter 4, n 5) 221.

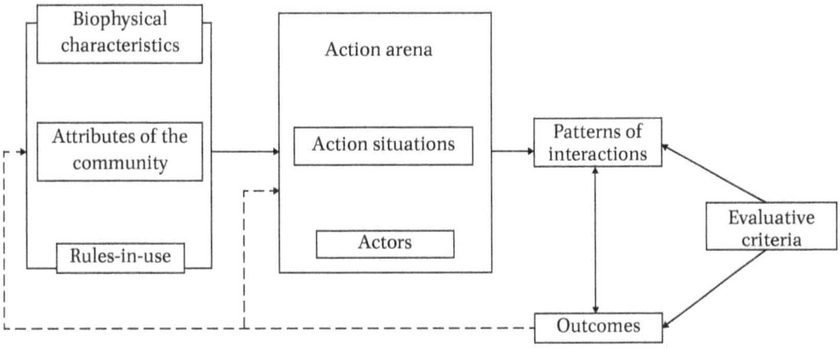

FIGURE 10 Institutional Analysis and Development framework
For description, see text below
SOURCE: FRISCHMANN, MARCIANO AND RAMELLO (CHAPTER 4, N 5) 220

these need to be taken into account to adapt the (partly limited) theory of Hardin – based on immutable factors – to dynamic reality.

The Institutional Analysis and Development (IAD) framework developed by Ostrom et al. gives some guidance to analyse systems that are composed of and depend on variables, therefore being especially appropriate for analyses of "various types of commons and common-pool resources".[15] The IAD groups criteria in external variables (left), the action arena (centre), and outcomes (right). To put this in the context of fisheries, Frischmann et al. give a brief example on lobster fishery:

> The tragedy of the commons allegory makes assumptions about the biophysical characteristics (depletable), community (independent, self-interested rational actors), and rules-in-use (every fisherman for himself); also, it assumes the only actors are the fishermen and the only relevant collective action problem is the prediction of ruinous competition. Viewed through the IAD lens, the empirical shortcomings of Hardin's allegory become clear: lobsters are not purely depletable; as a biological matter, they can reproduce and replenish stocks. The relevant community involves more than just the fishermen. Communication and cooperation are feasible. The rules-in-use are more nuanced than everyone for himself.[16]

15 Elinor Ostrom and Charlotte Hess, *Understanding Knowledge As a Commons: From Theory to Practice* (MIT Press 2006) 43 et seq.

16 Frischmann, Marciano and Ramello (Chapter 4, n 5) 220.

Therefore, the examination of Hardin's theory through the IAD framework shows that much potential lies in the commons, strongly dependant on the variables in question. This holds opportunities for modern, sustainable management of resources, which is also the CAOF Agreement's approach. It is suggested that in order to generate intergenerational equity, which is part of sustainable development,[17] the economy must be integrated in society and culture. Yet, this raises another problem: furthering institutional conditions that currently structure modern economies is considered to bring only short-term success. Hence, environmental policies should be future-oriented and welcome to change.[18] The ideal approach to counteract economic pursuit of endless growth would be a socioeconomic system that operates within ecological limits and enhances the qualitative well-being of people.[19] Yet, this significantly contradicts today's prevailing growth-dependant ideologies. Alternatives to the all-encompassing competitive market system are inconceivable, not least due to political barriers that are too large to overcome.[20] However, the question arises as to which scenario is most unbearable. In this regard, it is agreed with Daly, who states that

> [o]ne might be tempted to declare that such a project would be politically impossible. But the alternative [...] is biophysically impossible. In choosing between tackling a political impossibility and a biophysical impossibility, I would judge the latter to be more impossible and take my chances with the former.[21]

A system should therefore try to orient itself towards ecological limits. However, growth-dependant ideologies like capitalism should not be discarded completely. They may serve as a basic existing and functioning framework on which social-ecologic principles such as social equity, justice, community empowerment and human development need to be based on in order to move towards an ecologically sustainable future. In the context of fishing resources, this means e.g. that seafood production must primarily serve satisfying needs,

17 On sustainable development, see Chapter 5 Sections 2, 2.1 *infra*.

18 Stefano B Longo, Rebecca Clausen and Brett Clark, 'Healing the Rifts', *The tragedy of the commodity: Oceans, fisheries, and aquaculture* (Rutgers University Press 2015) 198.

19 Anthony DM Smith and Serge M Garcia, 'Fishery Management: Contrasts in the Mediterranean and the Atlantic' (2014) 24 Current Biology R810, R811 <https://www.cell.com/current-biology/comments/S0960-9822(14)00859-8> accessed 14 July 2020.

20 Longo, Clausen and Clark (Chapter 4, n 3) 200 et seq.

21 Herman E Daly, 'Economics in a Full World' (2005) 293 Scientific American 100, 102 <https://www.jstor.org/stable/10.2307/26061149> accessed 4 April 2022.

not markets. In order to achieve social justice, democratic organization, where producers are in control of the process and fruits of their labour, needs to be in place, and science and technology should be used to benefit the community. Therefore, a specific, regional approach should be taken. Otherwise, sustainable fisheries management will continue to be undermined and aquaculture will proceed to operate, irrespective of the needs of communities of producers or consumers, hence resulting in said tragedy of the commons.[22] Only in a second step, challenges should involve broader or global institutions, also as many Arctic environmental problems originate outside the Arctic.[23]

In summary, for fisheries management to be sustainable and effective, and in order to prevent a "tragedy of the commons", the global understanding must distance itself from continued and careless exploitation of humans and the biosphere and work in a cooperative manner. It is important to keep in mind that although wide acceptance of a management regime is required, in order to safeguard a sustainable fishing yield, not all States can at all times actively fish managed stocks. Short-term national and economic interests,[24] which currently often prevail over long-term global interests, must be overcome or reconciled with common interests.[25]

The globalisation of issues in managing common resources and their impact on the environment is however not a new phenomenon, but one that has intensified over recent years. The transboundary nature of air pollution was legally considered in the Trail Smelter arbitration case in the 1930s.[26] Twenty years later, the international community dealt with international oil pollution in the oceans.[27] In the 1970s, the consequences of the destruction

22 Longo, Clausen and Clark (Chapter 4, n 3) 201 et seq.

23 See Olav Schram Stokke, 'Environmental Security in the Arctic: The Case for Multilevel Governance' (2011) 66 International Journal 835, 848 <https://www-1jstor-1org-1001lf5ry0424.emedia1.bsb-muenchen.de/stable/pdf/23104396.pdf?ab_segments=0%252Fbasic_SYC-5055%252Ftest&refreqid=excelsior%3A78e2972719085fe2797c466f2e2dd5b3> accessed 11 March 2020.

24 Yet, not all participants are driven by selfish motives. Coastal States might for instance actively engage in RFMAs to create a comprehensive uniform conservation and management standard that is compatible with the standard they have adopted domestically within their EEZ.

25 Matley (Chapter 3, n 37) 106.

26 *Trail Smelter Case (United States v Canada), Awards of 16 April 1938 and 11 March 1941, Reports of International Arbitral Awards Vol III, p 1905.*

27 As a response to destructive practices, in 1954, the International Convention for the Prevention of Pollution of the Sea by Oil (OILPOL) was established, which was later incorporated in the International Convention for the Prevention of Pollution from Ships (MARPOL); on MARPOL, see Chapter 4 Sections, 1, 1.3, 1.3.1 *infra*.

of flora and fauna were recognized. Shortly after, and still ongoing as intense as probably never before, is the critical analysis of the impacts of global environmental threats like climate change. In 1992, the United Nations Conference on Environment and Development (UNCED) agreed on several environmental priorities. This coincided with the first (international) judicial statement acknowledging international environmental obligations: in its 1996 Nuclear Weapons Advisory Opinion, the International Court of Justice (ICJ) finally recognised some sort of international transboundary obligation to safeguard the environment, holding that

> the general obligation of States to ensure that activities within their jurisdiction and control respect the environment of other States or of areas beyond national control is now part of the corpus of international law relating to the environment.[28]

The wording is clearly inspired by Principle 21 of the 1972 Declaration of the United Nations Conference on the Human Environment (Stockholm Declaration)[29] and Principle 2 of the 1992 Rio Declaration on Environment and Development (Rio Declaration)[30] that express that States have a duty "to ensure that activities within their jurisdiction or control do not cause damage to the environment of other States or of areas beyond the limits of national jurisdiction". Since the anchoring in an official judicial statement of an international court, treaty regimes adapted accordingly and established international environmental obligations,[31] and similar statements and judgements became more frequent.[32]

28 *Legality of the Threat or Use of Nuclear Weapons, Advisory Opinion of 8 July 1996, ICJ Reports 1996, p 226* 242.

29 United Nations, 'Report of the United Nations Conference on the Human Environment – Declaration of the United Nations Conference on the Human Environment (Stockholm, 5–16 June 1972) – A/CONF.48/14/Rev.1' <http://www.un-documents.net/aconf48-14r1.pdf> accessed 30 June 2021.

30 United Nations General Assembly, 'Report of the United Nations Conference on Environment and Development (Rio de Janeiro, 3–14 June 1992), Annex I: Rio Declaration on Environment and Development – A/CONF.151/26/Vol.I' <https://www.un.org/en/development/desa/population/migration/generalassembly/docs/globalcompact/A_CONF.151_26_Vol.I_Declaration.pdf> accessed 30 June 2021.

31 See for example the 16th Protocol on Civil Liability and Compensation for Damage Caused by the Transboundary Effects of Industrial Accidents on Transboundary Waters to the 1992 Convention on the Protection and Use of Transboundary Watercourses and International Lakes and to the 1992 Convention on the Transboundary Effects of Industrial Accidents.

32 See Philippe Sands, *Principles of International Environmental Law* (4th edn, Cambridge University Press 2018) 4.

This understanding has also become one of the cornerstones of contemporary governance. Simply stated, governance is "the act or process of governing or overseeing the control and direction of something"[33] and involves a variety of actors and arrangements in the form of a network.[34] In this regard, the equality of participants in the global context is considered particularly important. Governance consists of elements, usually confined to a certain region, that steer behaviour in a certain direction, often through non-binding means. These are, for instance, developed in soft law, as it is the case in the Arctic with established soft law regimes like the Arctic Council, NGO's, and scientific organizations.[35] Governance must consider international treaties, customary international law and State sovereignty. Keeping the different stakeholders in the Arctic and their interests in mind,[36] Arctic governance focuses on the most different issues like territorial sovereignty and the extension of national continental shelves,[37] security, navigation, protection of the environment and also fisheries.

Several States and institutions already have a role in managing Arctic issues, although a regime managing fisheries in the CAO has not been established yet.[38] Also no permanent, single institution responsible for managing the Arctic marine area has been established. In principle, human activities in Arctic areas beyond national jurisdiction are governed by the over-arching legal framework of UNCLOS and a variety of global treaties and competent international organizations regulating specific activities in areas beyond national jurisdiction, such as fishing, shipping, and dumping.[39] The current framework, especially UNCLOS, was however not considered to be sufficient on its own to govern the Arctic Ocean, as the Convention was not formulated with specific regard to

33 'Merriam Webster Dictionary | Governance' <https://www.merriam-webster.com/dictionary/governance> accessed 5 December 2021.

34 Christopher Alcantara and Jen Nelles, 'Indigenous Peoples and the State in Settler Societies: Toward a More Robust Definition of Multilevel Governance' (2014) 44 Publius 183, 188 <https://www-1jstor-1org-10011f5v4013e.emedia1.bsb-muenchen.de/stable/pdf/24734623.pdf?refreqid=excelsior%3Acb3701da0966b67d783128373c9ae7c9> accessed 10 August 2021; see Janelle Knox-Hayes, *The Cultures of Markets: The Political Economy of Climate Governance* (Oxford University Press 2016) 14.

35 Keskitalo, Koivurova and Bankes (Chapter 2, n 78) 2.

36 On the diversity of stakeholders and interests in the context of the CAOF Agreement, see Chapter 3 Section 4 *supra*.

37 Keskitalo, Koivurova and Bankes (Chapter 2, n 78) 7.

38 The protection regime of marine mammals is not considered here.

39 On specific treaties, see Chapter 4 Sections 1 and 2 *infra*. On the development of a comprehensive treaty, see Chapter 3 Section 1 *supra*.

the current circumstances of climate change and the unique consequences of melting ice in Arctic waters.[40]

Fisheries management may differ depending on the type of fish to be managed – migratory,[41] straddling,[42] transboundary[43] or discrete[44] high seas fish. The CAOF Agreement merely refers to "fish stocks" to be managed in CAO waters.[45] However, the management of highly migratory and straddling fish stocks does not differ[46] – in fact, straddling fish stocks, narrowly defined, is a collective term for all fish stocks to be found both within the EEZ and the adjacent high seas.[47] Also, transboundary fish stocks deal with straddling stocks within EEZ only. Therefore, it is relied upon the broad understanding of the FAO that fish stocks in the sense of the CAOF Agreement include all (not mutually exclusive) categories of fish.[48] A distinction for management purposes is therefore not necessary.

The complex task of fisheries management hence involves multiple different aspects that exceed simple management and protection of stocks. A purely legal approach to questions on international fisheries is considered not beneficial. Controversies can only be fully understood in the context of the combined effect of biological and economic factors that influence international fisheries. Simply asking States to follow scientific advice in setting catch limits does not solve emerging management problems: it does not provide States with guidance to act when scientists disagree or when the scientific advice itself turns out to be too optimistic. Further, where economic forces have been ignored, the legal system has proven insufficient to prevent a collapse of fish

40 European Union, 'Debates of the European Parliament (9 October 2008)' 23 <https://www.europarl.europa.eu/sides/getDoc.do?pubRef=-//EP//NONSGML+CRE+20081009+SIT+DOC+PDF+V0//EN&language=EN> accessed 11 March 2022.

41 Fish stocks that are being highly migratory in nature, to be found both within the coastal State EEZ and the adjacent high seas; mainly refers to tuna stocks (see Annex I UNCLOS).

42 All other fish stocks (except anadromous/catadromous stocks) that are to be found both within the coastal State's EEZ and the adjacent high seas.

43 Fish resources crossing the EEZ boundary of one coastal State into the EEZ(s) of one or more other coastal States.

44 Fish stocks to be found exclusively in the high seas.

45 See e.g. Articles 2, 3(1)(a), 4(2) CAOF Agreement.

46 Cf. Gordon R Munro, Annick Van Houtte and Rolf Willmann, 'FAO Fisheries Technical Paper 465: The Conservation and Management of Shared Fish Stocks: Legal and Economic Aspects' (2004) s 4.2 <http://www.fao.org/3/y5438e/y5438e00.htm> accessed 9 May 2020.

47 Trond Bjørndal and Gordon Munro, *The Economics and Management of World Fisheries* (Oxford University Press 2012).

48 Munro, Van Houtte and Willmann (Chapter 4, n 46) s 2.

stocks.[49] Therefore, a combined approach of law and governance, and, based thereupon, specific management is needed.

The present section deals with the current law and governance framework in the Arctic. The legal standard that applies to the CAO (Chapter 4 Section 1) and additional cooperative mechanisms are presented (Chapter 4 Section 2), before possibilities and approaches for governing fisheries are set out (Chapter 4 Section.3).

1 Legal Regime Concerning Fisheries in the CAO

Although no specific Arctic fisheries regime has been established before the CAOF Agreement, the Arctic was not a legal vacuum. Besides treaties on specific issues like the 1973 Agreement on the Conservation of Polar Bears[50] or the 2013 Agreement on Cooperation on Marine Oil Pollution Preparedness and Response in the Arctic,[51] also a legal standard for fisheries existed. In principle, where no specific regime governs fisheries in areas beyond national jurisdiction, the regime of the high seas applies.[52] Fisheries in particular are covered by international fisheries law, with the underlying aim to prevent IUU fishing.[53] International fisheries law is part of general international law or international law of the sea and consists of three interconnected components: it entails substantive norms that prescribe rights and obligations, substantive fisheries standards such as fishing limits or gear restrictions, and institutional arrangements that refer *inter alia* to decision-making within an international body.[54] These entail not only binding treaties like UNCLOS, the UNFS Agreement and FAO instruments, but also general principles and soft-law agreements. Until the ratification of the CAOF Agreement through all signatories, this regime governed Arctic waters. The standard further still applies to States that do not

49 Serdy, 'The Bioeconomics of High Seas Fishing: New Entrants and the Tragedy of the Commons' (Chapter 3, n 107) 4.

50 'Agreement on the Conservation of Polar Bears (Oslo, 15 November 1973) – UNTS Vol. 2898, No. 50540' (Chapter 2, n 245).

51 'Arctic Council Agreement on Cooperation on Marine Oil Pollution Preparedness and Response in the Arctic (Kiruna, 15 May 2013)' <https://oaarchive.arctic-council.org/handle/11374/529> accessed 10 August 2021.

52 On the basics of the regime, see Chapter 4 Sections 1, 1.1, 1.1.1 *infra*.

53 Loctier (Chapter 2, n 137).

54 See Molenaar, 'International Regulation of Central Arctic Ocean Fisheries' (Chapter 2, n 20) 434.

accede to the CAOF Agreement.[55] Whereas the arrangements named mainly establish a jurisdictional framework, the implementation of measures is carried out by the participating States individually or collectively, e.g. through an RFB like the CAOF Agreement.[56] The Agreement implements the obligations under the fisheries regulatory framework and modifies them by setting more specific requirements.[57] Including the current regime of international environmental law, which is considered the basis for environmental fisheries regulations,[58] the following section describes the established framework of key instruments[59] to combat IUU fishing on the high seas that currently applies to the CAO.

1.1 *International Treaties*

Several international treaties apply to the CAO. Whereas the over-arching legal framework of UNCLOS and its implementation agreement, the UNFS Agreement, give answers to most general questions, the 1993 Agreement to Promote Compliance with International Conservation and Management Measures by Fishing Vessels on the High Seas (FAO Compliance Agreement) and the Agreement on Port State Measures to Prevent, Deter and Eliminate Illegal, Unreported and Unregulated Fishing (PSMA) focus on enforcement and compliance. It remains to be mentioned that treaty obligations may vary from State to State, depending on their submission to the respective treaty and the universality of the provisions.

1.1.1 United Nations Convention on the Law of the Sea

UNCLOS, hereinafter also referred to as the Convention, is considered the general legal basis for the protection and use of living and non-living resources of the world's oceans and one of the key frameworks for management in the Arctic. It was established in 1982 and came into force in 1994. As of 2022,

55 However, States that want to conduct fisheries shall either join the CAOF Agreement and conduct fishing according to its regulations, or refrain from fishing in the Agreement Area; cf. Chapter 3 Sections 3, 3.2 *supra*.

56 See Molenaar, 'International Regulation of Central Arctic Ocean Fisheries' (Chapter 2, n 20) 435.

57 On management under the CAOF Agreement, see specifically Chapters 5 and 6 *infra*.

58 Matley (Chapter 3, n 37) 102; see Daniel Bodansky, *The Art and Craft of International Environmental Law* (Harvard University Press 2010) 267 et seq.

59 The FAO provides a comprehensive overview and further information on the framework of international fisheries, see 'FAO | Illegal, Unreported and Unregulated (IUU) Fishing: International Framework' <http://www.fao.org/iuu-fishing/international-framework/en/> accessed 2 May 2020.

there are 168 parties to the Convention including all signatories of the CAOF Agreement except the United States.[60] Although it is frequently acknowledged that the US is already bound by the Convention through customary international law and President Reagan's 1983 Ocean Policy,[61] this is not the same as being a party to the Convention, which subjects States to more extensive obligations under the treaty.[62] Nevertheless, the policy demonstrates that the main inconveniences with the Convention do not directly concern fisheries but deep seabed mining,[63] the impact of accession on US sovereignty and security and enhanced "ocean bureaucracy".[64] This, together with the fact that the United States is a contracting party to the UNCLOS implementation agreement, the UNFS Agreement,[65] shows that being bound by fisheries regulations is not seen as problematic by the United States. However, for management considerations in the CAO, one major weakness of the non-participation of the United States is the unfeasibility of the dispute settlement mechanisms of Part XV UNCLOS between member States and the United States. Effective management becomes challenging: dispute settlement remains possible but is becoming increasingly difficult as a unilateral rather than collective settlement approach must be followed.[66]

UNCLOS does not only determine the high seas and areas beyond national jurisdiction geographically by defining marine boundaries, therefore preventing conflicts about territorial claims, but also sets forth general provisions of natural resource management including fisheries. The Convention provides

60 'United Nations | Oceans and Law of the Sea – Chronological Lists of Ratifications of, Accession and Succession to the Convention and the Related Agreements' <https://shorturl.at/SoJcS> accessed 6 April 2022.

61 United States National Archives, 'Ronald Reagan: Statement on United States Oceans Policy (10 March 1983)' <https://www.reaganlibrary.gov/archives/speech/statement-united-states-oceans-policy> accessed 8 April 2022.

62 Jonathan J Vanecko, 'Time to Ratify UNCLOS; A New Twist on an Old Problem' (Naval War College 2011) 6 <https://apps.dtic.mil/sti/tr/pdf/ADA546081.pdf> accessed 2 November 2024; see Daniel W Gray, 'Changing Arctic: A Strategic Analysis Of United States Arctic Policy And The United Nations Convention On The Law Of The Sea' (Joint Forces Staff College 2013) 72–73 <https://apps.dtic.mil/sti/pdfs/ADA581139.pdf> accessed 4 October 2021.

63 George D Haimbaugh, 'Impact of the Reagan Administration on the Law of the Sea' (1989) 46 Washington and Lee Law Review 151, 153 <https://scholarlycommons.law.wlu.edu/wlulr/vol46/iss1/6> accessed 30 April 2020.

64 John A Duff, 'The United States And The Law Of The Sea Convention: Sliding Back From Accession And Ratification' (2005) 11 Ocean and Coastal Law Journal 1, 30–31 <https://digitalcommons.mainelaw.maine.edu/oclj/vol11/iss1/2/> accessed 2 November 2024.

65 On the UNFS Agreement specifically, see Chapter 4 Sections, 1, 1.1, 1.1.2 *infra*.

66 Barnes (Chapter 2, n 10) 206.

a legal framework for fisheries in both areas under national jurisdiction and waters outside the EEZ[67] on the high seas. Most of its provisions, and hence also its regulations about fisheries management, are provisions of customary international law.[68]

Part V UNCLOS regulates States' rights and obligations within the EEZ in detail. Article 56 UNCLOS sets out the right of States to exploit, conserve and manage natural resources within the EEZ, *inter alia* by determining TAC and MSY quotas.[69] In this regard, concerns about "the extension of coastal state fishery rights, duties, and interests seaward of 200 NM with respect to those fish species that straddle and migrate between the 200 NM zone and the adjacent high seas area" as a form of "creeping jurisdiction" of coastal States are often mentioned.[70] UNCLOS addresses this issue by encouraging the coastal State and the States fishing for such stocks in the adjacent area to agree on conservation measures. States should seek agreement either directly or through appropriate subregional or regional organizations.[71]

Particularly relevant for fisheries and for the CAOF Agreement is Part VII UNCLOS, which deals with the high seas. Article 86 UNCLOS defines the high seas as "all parts of the sea that are not included in the exclusive economic zone, in the territorial sea or in the internal waters of a State, or in the archipelagic waters of an archipelagic State". Article 87 UNCLOS sets forth that the high seas are subject to the freedom of the high seas, meaning that they are generally open to all States for free navigation and fishing. More specifically, the freedom of fishing is manifested in Article 87(e) UNCLOS and specified by Article 116 UNCLOS. Accordingly, the freedom to fish on the high seas is restricted by treaty obligations, the interests of other States, and conservation management duties specified in the following Articles. Thus, States should take measures necessary for the conservation of the living resources of the high seas,[72] alone or through cooperation with other States, e.g. through establishing (S)RFMOs.[73] In this regard, UNCLOS stipulates a duty to

67 The EEZ, the zone between 12 and 200 NM from the shore, is defined in Articles 55 and 57 UNCLOS. Within the EEZ, States enjoy absolute rights over fish and seabed resources, see Articles 56 et seq. UNCLOS.

68 See Roach (Chapter 3, n 5).

69 See Article 61(3) UNCLOS.

70 Barbara Kwiatkowska, 'The High Seas Fisheries Regime: At a Point of No Return?' (1993) 8 International Journal of Marine and Coastal Law 327, 327 <https://brill-com.emedien.ub.uni-muenchen.de/view/journals/estu/8/3/article-p327_1.xml> accessed 2 July 2020; similiarly, see Chapter 3 Sections 4, 4.1.

71 See Article 63(2) UNCLOS.

72 See Article 117 UNCLOS.

73 See Article 118 UNCLOS; similar, see Article 63(2) UNCLOS.

cooperate.[74] Conservation measures should be non-discriminatory, cooperative, and take into account the best scientific evidence available, a fish stocks MSY, environmental and economic factors, the interdependence of species and generally recommended international minimum standards.[75]

Where environmental protection is concerned, UNCLOS' mandate is to preserve the marine environment and foster cooperation among the participating States.[76] Hence, although the Convention "grants states the sovereign right to exploit their natural resources pursuant to their environmental policies", States must act "in accordance with their duty to protect and preserve the marine environment".[77] UNCLOS further allocates coastal States unilateral rights to enforce non-discriminatory regulations where severe climatic conditions and ice coverage create exceptional hazards for navigation – but only within the limits of their EEZ.[78] Every State can hence adopt provisions against the contamination of the environment for economic use, and in ice-covered regions like the Arctic also against contamination by ships and vessels, e.g. by establishing marine protected areas within their EEZ.

One problem of the UNCLOS regime for fisheries management is that it sets up rather general and flexible conservation requirements. Catch levels can easily be set too high for conservation limits, and destructive fishing patterns can be implemented. The regime favours the exhaustion of catch limits[79] and resulting trade of fishing quotas,[80] which is gratefully accepted by fishing States. As an example, during the 1980s, the Soviet Union has traded most of its cod quotas in the Northeast Arctic Sea to Norway in return for much more pelagic species that were under the exclusive management of Norway.[81] Similar trade suggestions have been issued by the United States and the former Soviet Union.[82]

Another problem with managing fisheries under UNCLOS is enforcement. Concerning fisheries management in the Arctic, Koivurova and Molenaar correctly point out that management on a

74 See more on cooperation Chapter 4 Sections, 1, 1.2, 1.2.2 and Chapter 5 Sections 2, 2.2 *infra*.

75 See Article 119 UNCLOS.

76 See PART XII UNCLOS.

77 Weidemann (Chapter 3, n 48) 83; see Article 193 UNCLOS.

78 See Article 234 UNCLOS.

79 Cf. Article 62(2) UNCLOS.

80 Cf. Article 72(1) UNCLOS.

81 Olav Schram Stokke, *Disaggregating International Regimes: A New Approach to Evaluation and Comparison* (MIT Press 2012) 87.

82 See Haimbaugh (Chapter 4, n 63) 185.

> global scale would not provide much operational impact. Also, linking a legally binding instrument for the marine Arctic to [UNCLOS] – even if its spatial scope would be limited to areas beyond national jurisdiction – would not be acceptable to Arctic Ocean coastal states because its negotiation would fall under the UN General Assembly (UNGA); a forum where the five Arctic Ocean coastal states could potentially be confronted by 180-odd states with opposing views and interests.[83]

The UNCLOS regime should hence be considered as a basis, but not a comprehensive framework for contemporary fisheries management – neither in the Arctic, nor elsewhere. Similarly, at the 2008 Ilulissat Meeting, the Arctic States considered the law of the sea to be a "solid foundation for responsible management".[84] Any regime or organization that covers Arctic fisheries, such as the CAOF Agreement, should therefore be based on the provisions of UNCLOS but refine them according to the special needs of the respective issue.

1.1.2 United Nations Fish Stocks Agreement

The Agreement for the Implementation of the Provisions of the United Nations Convention on the Law of the Sea of 10 December 1982 relating to the Conservation and Management of Straddling Fish Stocks and Highly Migratory Fish Stocks of 4 August 1995 (often referred to as Fish Stocks Agreement, hereinafter UNFS Agreement; in the CAOF Agreement "the 1995 Agreement") came into force in 2001. As of 2022, 91 parties, including the EU and, apart from China, all CAOF Agreement signatory States, are parties.[85] Although implementing the provisions of UNCLOS, the UNFS Agreement is an independent agreement. Nevertheless, criticism exists that certain provisions of the UNFS Agreement amend rather than implement UNCLOS and are therefore inconsistent with the Convention. As an example, denying non-members of RFBs the access to fishery resources pursuant to Article 8(4) UNFS Agreement is partly regarded as inconsistent with the right to fish on the high seas pursuant to Article 116 UNCLOS.[86]

83 Koivurova and Molenaar (Chapter 3, n 32) 58.

84 'Arctic Ocean Conference Ilulissat Declaration (Ilulissat, 28 May 2008)' (Chapter 3, n 78).

85 'United Nations | Oceans and Law of the Sea – Chronological Lists of Ratifications of Accession and Succession to the Convention and the Related Agreements' (Chapter 4, n 60).

86 Molenaar, 'Non-Participation in the Fish Stocks Agreement: Status and Reasons' (Chapter 3, n 347) 201.

The UNFS Agreement is considered a "policy keystone"[87] for RFBS, as it is an instrument providing for a framework of rules to manage and ensure compliance and the conservation of straddling and highly migratory fish stocks, which apply to fish stocks both in and beyond national jurisdiction.[88] It provides the basis for RFBS, and hence also the CAOF Agreement, by calling upon relevant coastal States and States fishing for straddling fish stocks or highly migratory fish stocks on the high seas to establish RFBS to set up conservation and management measures for such stocks.[89] Fisheries management and conservation measures can be set up by extending an RFB's mandate or creating a new RFB. The UNFS Agreement sets forth general principles, including the precautionary principle, that need to be considered for such measures.[90] The UNFS Agreement further stipulates prerequisites and functions of RFBS,[91] the aim of making their established measures "compatible"[92] with the UNFS Agreement,[93] and sets up flag States' duties concerning fishing vessels.[94] In order to implement its obligations, the UNFS Agreement primarily relies on RFBS as instruments of cooperation.[95]

The UNFS Agreement further implies a strong duty to cooperate amongst and between participants and non-participants.[96] Most importantly, compliance with the duty to cooperate is a prerequisite for exercising the freedom of fishing on the high seas: only States that agree to cooperate in an RFB or comply with the provisions of an RMFA/O shall have the right to participate in the fisheries in question.[97]

In summary, the UNFS Agreement can be considered a guiding instrument for the management of long-term conservation and sustainable use of straddling and highly migratory fish stocks. Nevertheless, although being much more

---

87 Løbach and others, 'FAO Fisheries and Aquaculture Technical Paper 651: Regional Fisheries Management Organizations and Advisory Bodies' (2020) 7 <https://openknowledge.fao.org/server/api/core/bitstreams/adocb83d-c3b6-4166-8cb5-958dodc6a242/content> accessed 11 May 2024.

88 Cf. Article 3(1) UNFS Agreement.

89 See Article 8(5) UNFS Agreement.

90 See Articles 5 and 6 UNFS Agreement.

91 See Articles 9 and 10 UNFS Agreement.

92 Erik Jaap Molenaar, 'Addressing Regulatory Gaps in High Seas Fisheries' (2005) 20 International Journal of Marine and Coastal Law 533, 546.

93 See *inter alia* Article 7 UNFS Agreement.

94 See Article 18 UNFS Agreement.

95 Cf. *inter alia* Articles 1(1)(d) UNFS Agreement, Article 117 UNCLOS.

96 See especially Articles 20–21 UNFS Agreement, cf. e.g. Articles 7(2), 8(1), 8(3), 8(5), 13, 14, 18(g)(i) UNFS Agreement.

97 Cf. 8(4), 10(b), 17(3) UNFS Agreement.

specific than UNCLOS, it is still considered not specific enough to serve as an instrument for fisheries management on its own. It is therefore advantageous that the agreement provides for the creation of new RFBs or the strengthening of existing ones, so that these bodies can implement specific and effective fisheries management themselves.

1.1.3 FAO Compliance Agreement

The 1993 Agreement to Promote Compliance with International Conservation and Management Measures by Fishing Vessels on the High Seas, the FAO Compliance Agreement, came into force in 2003, ten years after its approval. It has not been widely ratified and counts only around forty parties. From the signatories of the CAOF Agreement, the United States, South Korea, Japan, Norway, the EU, and Canada are parties to the agreement.[98]

The FAO Compliance Agreement aims to enhance the responsibility of flag States over their vessels and to strengthen compliance with international fisheries conservation and management measures. Specifically, flag States should ensure that none of their vessels is fishing on the high seas unless authorised, and that they can effectively exercise their flag State responsibilities to guarantee that their vessels comply with international measures.[99] In principle, the FAO Compliance Agreement applies to all vessels used or intended for fishing on the high seas.[100] "Reflagging" of vessels fishing on the high seas under the flags of States unable or unwilling to enforce international measures for the conservation and management of fish stocks to flags of States with low regulatory standards should be prevented. The FAO Compliance Agreement strongly follows UNCLOS' and the UNFS Agreement's approach of focusing on effective enforcement of measures: enforcement should be ensured, *inter alia,* through the maintenance of records of fishing vessels[101] and international cooperation including the sharing of data.[102]

With respect to the role of RFBs, the FAO Compliance Agreement calls upon States that do not participate in global or regional fisheries management bodies to do so. Alternatively, it proposes to establish mutual assistance arrangements

98 Food and Agriculture Organization of the United Nations, 'Agreement to Promote Compliance with International Conservation and Management Measures by Fishing Vessels on the High Seas (Rome, 24 November 1993) – UNTS Vol. 2221, No. 39486' <https://treaties.un.org/pages/showDetails.aspx?objid=080000028007be1a> accessed 28 June 2021.

99 See *inter alia* Article III FAO Compliance Agreement.

100 See Article II FAO Compliance Agreement.

101 See Article IV FAO Compliance Agreement.

102 See Articles V, VI FAO Compliance Agreement.

to achieve compliance with international conservation and management measures[103] and offers further support to developing States in this regard.[104]

Although barely ratified, when developing new RFBs – also in the Arctic – the FAO Compliance Agreement may serve as a model arrangement for developing minimum requirements for RFBs, especially suitable for areas with predominantly new and exploratory fisheries.[105]

1.1.4 Agreement on Port State Measures

TheAgreement on Port State Measures to Prevent, Deter and Eliminate Illegal, Unreported and Unregulated Fishing, PSMA, is the first binding international agreement to specifically target IUU fishing.[106] The PSMA currently counts 70 parties.[107] Except for China, all parties to the CAOF Agreement are parties to the PSMA. Approved by the FAO in 2009, its objective is to prevent illegally caught fish from entering international markets through ports by applying to fishing vessels intending to enter the port of a State that is different from their flag State. Thus, the PSMA reduces the incentive of such vessels to continue operating while it also blocks fishery products from IUU fishing from reaching national and international markets. The aim of the PSMA should be ensured through regulating the entry and use of ports,[108] regular inspections,[109] and the obligation to share information.[110] With regard to fisheries in the CAO, it is unlikely that the PSMA will apply to the CAO in the foreseeable future, as fishing in CAO waters is not really possible at present. Nevertheless, it provides a necessary regulation in the fight against IUU fishing and could prove helpful for future CAO fisheries.

103 Cf. Preamble, and Article V(3) FAO Compliance Agreement.

104 See Article VII FAO Compliance Agreement.

105 See also Molenaar, 'Addressing Regulatory Gaps in High Seas Fisheries' (Chapter 4, n 92) 545.

106 Food and Agriculture Organization of the United Nations, 'Agreement on Port State Measures to Prevent, Deter and Eliminate Illegal, Unreported and Unregulated Fishing (Rome, 22 November 2009)' <http://extwprlegs1.fao.org/treaty/docs/tre000003E.pdf> accessed 6 April 2022.

107 'FAO | Parties to the PSMA' <https://www.fao.org/port-state-measures/background/parties-psma/en/> accessed 8 April 2022.

108 Part 2 and 3 PSMA.

109 Part 4 PSMA.

110 Cf. Articles 15, 16 PSMA.

1.2 *Customary International Law Standards*

Besides international treaty regimes, customary law standards apply to the CAO. For international fisheries, of special relevance are the freedom of the high seas and the duty to cooperate.

1.2.1 Freedom of the High Seas

As described above,[111] the concept of the freedom of the high seas developed by Dutch scholar Hugo Grotius has become firmly anchored in international law. Overlooking the North Sea from Holland's shore in the early seventeenth century, Grotius initially observed "immense, infinite"[112] waters, "bounded only by the heavens" and impossible to possess,[113] inconceivable to construe otherwise than allowing for navigation, fishing,[114] and trade.[115] Accordingly, in his flagship publication *Mare Liberum*,[116] he declared that the seas represented a shared resource, which allowed for a "common use" to benefit mankind, unappropriable as being common to all.[117] The concept has been included in UNCLOS, where Article 136 UNCLOS stipulates that the area of the high seas and its resources "are the common heritage of mankind". The perception of the freedom of the high seas itself is incorporated in Article 87 UNCLOS. Based thereupon, Article 116 UNCLOS guarantees all States, not only coastal States but also land-locked ones,[118] the right to engage in fishing on the high seas. Although the ICJ has not yet addressed the customary status of any of the provisions of Part VII UNCLOS,[119] the Court has specifically expressed that content of Article 2 of the 1958 Convention on the High Seas[120] dealing with the freedom of the seas, which is now reflected in Articles 86–115 UNCLOS, is customary international law.[121] Crawford supports this finding by stating that

111 See Chapter 3 Section 1 *supra*.
112 Feenstra (Chapter 3, n 4) 81.
113 ibid.
114 ibid 69.
115 ibid 25.
116 Grotius (Chapter 3, n 2); for an English translation, see Feenstra (Chapter 3, n 4).
117 Rossi, 'Tradition, Tendency, Temptation' (Chapter 3, n 30) 1.
118 See Articles 87(1), 69 UNCLOS.
119 Titled "High Seas", Articles 86–120 UNCLOS.
120 'Convention on the High Seas (Geneva, 29 April 1958)' <https://treaties.un.org/pages/ViewDetails.aspx?src=TREATY&mtdsg_no=XXI-2&chapter=21> accessed 12 August 2021.
121 Cf. *Military and Paramilitary Activities in and against Nicaragua (Nicaragua v United States of America), Merits Judgment of 27 June 1986, ICJ Reports 1986*, p 111, paras 212–214.; for an overview on the customary status of UNCLOS provisions see Roach (Chapter 3, n 5).

the "freedom of fishing on the high seas was well established in customary international law".[122]

Claims to sovereignty are expressly forbidden in the context of fishing on the high seas, due to the concept of freedom of the high seas. Rather, States are encouraged to exercise their sovereignty to become members to RFBS, therefore submitting themselves to the applicable rules of the regime.[123] The freedom is further limited by treaty obligations of States, the rights, duties and interests of coastal States in certain fish stocks, and obligations relating to the conservation and management of the living resources of the high seas.[124]

As a result, States have the duty to cooperate.[125] This includes the obligation to restrict fishing activities of their nationals in order to cooperate in the conservation and management of stocks occurring on the high seas[126] and to counteract problems such as the massive waste in fisheries resulting from open access.[127] Where States fail to comply with that duty, they are deprived of their right to exercise the freedom of fishing.[128] Hence, the regime of freedom of fishing is influenced by a range of qualifications. These derive, *inter alia,* from the rights of different international stakeholders, UNCLOS regulations, the principles of the UNFS Agreement and the FAO Compliance Agreement, and specific RFB regulations. Although the original Grotian concept of the freedom of the high seas has hence been significantly modified, it remains a valid and fundamental concept of international law.[129]

1.2.2 Duty to Cooperate

A basis that is essential for the functioning of RBFS is the duty of States to cooperate in the conservation and management of living resources as enshrined in UNCLOS.[130] This duty, in its broadest form,[131] is universally accepted in international law. For instance, the International Tribunal for the Law of the

122 Crawford (Chapter 3, n 5) 305.
123 Lodge and others (Chapter 3, n 185) 70.
124 See Article 116 UNCLOS.
125 On the scope of the customary status of the duty to cooperate, see Chapter 4 Sections, 1, 1.2, 1.2.2 *infra.*
126 See Articles 117, 118 UNCLOS.
127 Food and Agriculture Organization of the United Nations, 'FAO Fisheries Circular No. 853: Marine Fisheries and Law of the Sea: A Decade of Change' (1993) 31 <http://www.fao.org/3/u9345e/u9345e00.pdf> accessed 18 September 2021.
128 Cf. Article 8(4) UNFS Agreement.
129 Lodge and others (Chapter 3, n 185) 70–71.
130 See, *inter alia,* Articles 63, 117 and 118 UNCLOS.
131 Such as e.g. formulated in Article 197 UNCLOS.

Sea (ITLOS) found the duty to cooperate to be a fundamental principle in the prevention of pollution of the marine environment both under UNCLOS and general international law.[132] It contains different obligations. The duty to cooperate imposes a duty to give "due regard to the rights of other States and the needs of conservation for the benefit of all".[133] Further, States are obliged to seek agreement with other States. In particular, they should behave in such a way "that the negotiations are meaningful, which will not be the case when either of them insists upon its own position without contemplating any modification of it".[134] The duty to cooperate further implies the negative obligation not to take unilateral action, whether or not an agreement has been reached. This is particularly important when disputes between States arise or objections to a decision to be taken are raised.[135]

The exact nature of the duty to cooperate depends on the specifics of the regime in question. In the context of fisheries, the duty imposes on a State to engage in multinational management solutions for high sea fish stocks and restrict fishing activities of its nationals[136] regardless of whether conservation and management measures have already been agreed. The duty to cooperate further restricts access to fisheries to States that are either members of an RFB or otherwise agree to apply the conservation and management measures established by such organization or arrangement.[137]

1.3 *Non-binding Soft Law Instruments*

Non-binding legal instruments, commonly referred to as soft law, have a weak reputation compared to binding agreements. However, soft law also has the power to influence international relations, albeit in a more subtle way and only with the strong political will and support of participants. Based on an agreement, although non-binding, soft law establishes mutual accountability

---

132 See *Land Reclamation by Singapore in and Around the Straits of Johor (Malaysia v Singapore), Provisional Measures, Order of 8 October 2003, ITLOS Reports 2003, p 10* [92]; *MOX Plant Case (Ireland v United Kingdom), Provisional Measures, Order of 3 December 2001, ITLOS Reports 2001, p 95* [82].

133 *Fisheries Jurisdiction (United Kingdom v. Iceland), Judgment of 25 July 1974, ICJ Reports 1974, p. 3* (Chapter 3, n 10) para 72; *Fisheries Jurisdiction (Federal Republic of Germany v. Iceland), Judgment of 25 July 1974, ICJ Reports 1974, p. 175* (Chapter 3, n 10) para 64.

134 *North Sea Continental Shelf Cases (Federal Republic of Germany/Denmark; Federal Republic of Germany/Netherlands), Judgement of 20 February 1969, ICJ Reports 1969, p 3* [85a].

135 Lodge and others (Chapter 3, n 185) 70–71.

136 See Articles 117, 118 UNCLOS.

137 See Article 8(4) UNFS Agreement. A more specific consideration of the duty to cooperate can be found at Chapter 5 Sections 2, 2.2 *infra*.

between parties. By concluding an agreement, matters that previously only concerned one party become a matter for several parties. While a binding agreement can establish a claim to compliance with the regulations, a non-binding agreement at least gives one party the opportunity to have a say on the other party's compliance with the regulations. Each party can therefore legitimately expect the other to either comply with the agreement or provide relevant information for the reasons for non-compliance.[138] This creates internal and, if one of the parties turns to the public, external pressure on the non-compliant party.[139] The relevant parties may also claim a moral obligation. Although this may not have the same effect as claims under a binding agreement, which can lead to the imposition of sanctions, there is an impact of soft law on international relations.[140]

Soft-law instruments are an important component in the framework of international fisheries management. The United Nations, as the biggest international comprehensive forum, plays a special role in this regard. The annual report of the UN Secretary General on Oceans and the Law of the Sea provides an overview of regulatory developments in the law of the sea.[141] Additionally, since 2003, the UN General Assembly issues annual resolutions specifically on sustainable fisheries.[142] Priority issues are mainly the formulation of codes of conduct and guidelines, improving existing regulatory regimes and applying eco-system based approaches to fisheries management.[143] Further, the FAO Code of Conduct for Responsible Fisheries (FAO Code of Conduct), FAO

138 Andrei Marmor, 'Soft Law, Authoritative Advice and Non-Binding Agreements' (2019) 39 Oxford Journal of Legal Studies 507, 523 et seq. <https://academic.oup.com/ojls/article/39/3/507/5474953> accessed 11 November 2020.

139 See e.g. on the effectiveness of the concept of "naming and shaming" Astrid Dannenberg, Marcel Lumkowsky, Emily K Carlton and David G Victor, 'Naming and shaming as a strategy for enforcing the Paris Agreement: The role of political institutions and public concern' (2023) 120 Proceedings of the National Academy of Sciences of the United States of America 40 <https://www.pnas.org/doi/epdf/10.1073/pnas.2305075120> accessed 28 April 2024.

140 Andrei Marmor, 'Soft Law, Authoritative Advice and Non-Binding Agreements' (2019) 39 Oxford Journal of Legal Studies 507, 523 et seq. <https://academic.oup.com/ojls/article/39/3/507/5474953> accessed 11 November 2020.

141 See 'United Nations | Oceans and the Law of the Sea in the General Assembly of the United Nations – Reports of the Secretary-General' <https://www.un.org/Depts/los/general_assembly/general_assembly_reports.htm> accessed 18 September 2020.

142 For the latest one, see 'United Nations General Assembly Resolution 76/71, Sustainable Fisheries (Adopted 9 December 2021)'.

143 See 'United Nations | Oceans and the Law of the Sea in the General Assembly of the United Nations – General Assembly Resolutions and Decisions' <https://www.un.org/depts/los/general_assembly/general_assembly_resolutions.htm> accessed 18 September 2020.

Technical Guidelines for Responsible Fisheries, and the International Plan(s) of Action (IPOAs) should form a part of any regime that manages fisheries.[144] Moreover, specifically for Arctic fisheries, in addition to the FAO instruments, the International Maritime Organization's Guidelines and the Arctic Council's Arctic Environmental Protection Strategy are considered relevant.

1.3.1 International Maritime Organization Guidelines and Polar Code

The International Maritime Organization (IMO)[145] was established by the United Nations in 1948 as the first international body devoted exclusively to maritime matters. It consists of 175 member States and three associated members to date. Of the CAOF Agreement signatories, the EU is the only non-member of the organization. Further, multiple intergovernmental and non-governmental organizations are accredited as observers to the organization.[146] IMO's aim is to ensure safe and sustainable shipping in clean oceans, the protection of special areas and particularly sensitive sea areas, to limit and restrict operational discharges and the dumping of wastes at sea, and to mitigate climate change. For this cause, IMO has promoted the adoption of some fifty conventions and protocols, e.g. the International Convention on Safety of Life at Sea (SOLAS)[147] including the instrument of the International Ice Patrol,[148] and the International Convention for the Prevention of Pollution from Ships (MARPOL).[149] It has also adopted more than 1.000 codes and recommendations on maritime safety and security, the prevention of pollution and related matters, with some of them being mandatory under the relevant provisions of SOLAS and MARPOL. IMO works through a number of specialist committees and sub-committees composed of representatives of member States.[150]

144 See also Barnes (Chapter 2, n 10) 212.

145 Until 1982 Inter-Governmental Maritime Consultative Organization.

146 'IMO | Member States, IGOs and NGOs' <https://www.imo.org/en/About/Membership> accessed 6 April 2022.

147 'International Convention for the Safety of Life at Sea (London, 1 November 1974) – UNTS Vol. 1184, No. 18961' <https://treaties.un.org/doc/publication/unts/volume 1184/volume-1184-i-18961-english.pdf> accessed 30 October 2021.

148 See Daniel-Erasmus Khan, 'The International Ice Patrol' in Stefan Lorenzmeier and Hans-Peter Folz (eds), *Recht und Realität* (Nomos 2017) 498 et seq.

149 'International Convention for the Prevention of Pollution from Ships (London, 2 November 1973) – UNTS Vol. 1340, No. 22484' <https://treaties.un.org/doc/Publication/UNTS/Volume 1340/volume-1340-A-22484-English.pdf> accessed 30 October 2021.

150 International Maritime Organization, 'IMO – What It Is' (2013) <https://wwwcdn.imo.org/localresources/en/About/Documents/What it is Oct 2013_Web.pdf> accessed 8 April 2022; General information on the activities of the IMO can be found on 'IMO | IMO and Its Role in Protecting the World's Oceans' <http://www.imo.org/en/MediaCentre/HotTopics/oceans/Pages/default.aspx> accessed 6 May 2020.

IMO's instruments provide useful tools to protect the Arctic marine environment. MARPOL for example recognizes the need for more stringent requirements to manage and protect so-called "Special Areas" that are specifically vulnerable to sea traffic due to their ecology. For example, the Antarctic has been declared a "Special Area" in 1992. This option is still possible for the Arctic and has been partially supported – just as the option of declaring the Arctic a Particularly Sensitive Sea Area (PSSA) by IMO.[151] According to Annex 1(2) of the Revised Guidelines for the Identification and Designation of PSSA, a PSSA is an area

> that needs special protection through action by IMO because of its significance for recognized ecological, socio-economic, or scientific attributes where such attributes may be vulnerable to damage by international shipping activities.[152]

With the precautionary approach in mind,[153] and considering the delicate Arctic environment, designating the Arctic a PSSA would be a useful protective step for the Arctic. Moreover, the Arctic could be declared an "Emission Control Area" under Annex IV MARPOL, which sets up regulations for the prevention of air pollution from ships to enhance further protection.

Regarding the protection of marine biodiversity, IMO adopted measures to prevent the spread of potentially invasive aquatic organisms[154] by the adoption of the International Convention for the Control and Management of Ships' Ballast Water and Sediments,[155] or the 2011 Guidelines for the Control and Management of Ships' Biofouling to Minimize the Transfer of Invasive Aquatic Species.[156] Where climate change is concerned, IMO was the first

151 Federal Foreign Office Germany (Chapter 2, n 250) 14; Federal Foreign Office Germany (Chapter 2, n 89) 20.

152 International Maritime Organization, 'Revised Guidelines for the Identification and Designation of Particularly Sensitive Sea Areas (1 December 2005) – Resolution A.982(24)' <https://wwwcdn.imo.org/localresources/en/KnowledgeCentre/IndexofIMOResolutions/AssemblyDocuments/A.982(24).pdf> accessed 4 April 2022.

153 On the precautionary approach, see specifically Chapter 5 Sections 2, 2.1, 2.1.1 *infra*.

154 On the introduction of non-indigenous and invasive species, see Chapter 2 Sections, 4, 4.2, 4.2.3 *supra*.

155 See 'International Convention for the Control and Management of Ships' Ballast Water and Sediments (London, 13 February 2004) – UNTS No. 55544' <https://treaties.un.org/doc/Publication/UNTS/No Volume/55544/Part/I-55544-080000028053b465.pdf> accessed 15 December 2020.

156 International Maritime Organization, '2011 Guidelines for the Control and Management of Ships' Biofouling to Minimize the Transfer of Invasive Aquatic Species (15 July

international transport sector regulator to adopt binding energy-efficiency requirements that apply to all ships globally.[157] Furthermore, IMO is engaging in global capacity-building projects to support the implementation of regulations and encourage innovation and technology transfer to enhance the quality of new and existing ships and further green technology.[158]

Besides IMO's general instruments, specifically for the Arctic and Antarctic, IMO adopted the International Code for Ships Operating in Polar Waters (Polar Code), a binding instrument under both MARPOL and SOLAS offering comprehensive ship regulations, which entered into force in 2017. The Polar Code aims to cover all shipping related matters like ship design, construction and equipment, operational and training concerns, search and rescue, and the protection of the unique environment and eco-systems of Arctic and Antarctic waters. It includes mandatory[159] and recommendatory[160] provisions.[161]

In summary, IMO's regulations so far focus mainly on the technical requirements of shipping in general, not specifically on fishing. Nevertheless, IMO regulations will be of importance when vessels enter the waters of the CAO.

1.3.2 Arctic Environmental Protection Strategy and Arctic Council Instruments

In June 1991, after discussions on the protection of the Arctic environment, the eight Arctic States Canada, Denmark on behalf of the Faroe Islands and Greenland, Finland, Iceland, Norway, Russia, Sweden and the United States established the Arctic Environmental Protection Strategy (AEPS). The process was initialised by Finland, therefore sometimes referred to as the Finnish initiative or Rovaniemi process,[162] and finalized with large input from Canada. The non-binding legal instrument was intended as a forum for the eight States to deal with issues such as monitoring, assessment, conservation, protection,

2011) – Annex 26 Resolution MEPC.207(62)' <https://wwwcdn.imo.org/localresources/en/OurWork/Environment/Documents/RESOLUTIONMEPC.207%5B62%5D.pdf> accessed 30 June 2021.

157 See Annex VI MARPOL.

158 See 'IMO | IMO and the Sustainable Development Goals' <https://www.imo.org/en/MediaCentre/HotTopics/Pages/SustainableDevelopmentGoals.aspx> accessed 15 December 2020.

159 See part I-A and II-A Polar Code.

160 See part I-B and II-B Polar Code.

161 See 'IMO | Polar Code' <https://www.imo.org/en/ourwork/safety/pages/polar-code.aspx> accessed 2 November 2024.

162 Mark Nuttall, 'Arctic Environmental Protection Strategy' *Climate Policy Watcher* (1 January 2019) <https://www.climate-policy-watcher.org/canadian-arctic/arctic-environmental-protection-strategy.html> accessed 20 February 2020.

emergency preparedness and response in the Arctic.[163] The underlying objective was to establish a charter to promote cooperation[164] and cooperatively combat threats to the Arctic ecosystem that could no longer be faced individually.[165] As part of the strategy, four environmental protection groups were established dealing with the Conservation of Arctic Flora and Fauna (CAFF) – which was later proposed as a managing body of Arctic fisheries[166] –, the Protection of the Arctic Marine Environment (PAME), Emergency Prevention, Preparedness and Response (EPPR) and the Arctic Monitoring and Assessment Programme (AMAP).[167]

AMAP is considered the central element of the AEPS.[168] Its aim is to provide

> reliable and sufficient information on the status of, and threats to, the Arctic environment, and providing scientific advice on actions to be taken in order to support Arctic governments in their efforts to take remedial and preventive actions relating to contaminants and adverse effects of climate change.[169]

The aim should be achieved through monitoring, assessing and reporting on the environmental well-being of the Arctic, while taking into account the cultural and ecological significance of the Arctic for native people.[170] On a political level, the AEPS consisted of ministerial meetings that were held once or twice a year with one representative from each of the eight governments present. Over time, the AEPS process increased in transparency by accrediting observer status to non-Arctic states and (N)GOs.[171]

---

163 Froukje Maria Platjouw, Eirik Hovland Steindal and Trude Borch, 'From Arctic Science to International Law: The Road towards the Minamata Convention and the Role of the Arctic Council' (2018) 9 Arctic Review on Law and Politics 226, 231 <https://arcticreview.no/index.php/arctic/article/view/1234> accessed 12 March 2020.

164 United States Office of Technology Assessment, 'Nuclear Wastes in the Arctic: An Analysis of Arctic and Other Regional Impacts From Soviet Nuclear Contamination – OTA-ENV-632' (1995) 196 <https://digital.library.unt.edu/ark:/67531/metadc39768/m2/1/high_res_d/9504.pdf> accessed 20 February 2020.

165 Philippe Sands (Chapter 4, n 32) 644 et seq.

166 Nuttall (Chapter 4, n 162).

167 Keskitalo, Koivurova and Bankes (Chapter 2, n 78) 5.

168 United States Office of Technology Assessment (Chapter 4, n 164) 196.

169 'AMAP | Arctic Monitoring and Assessment Programme' <https://www.amap.no/> accessed 10 August 2021.

170 United States Office of Technology Assessment (Chapter 4, n 164) 197.

171 Nuttall (Chapter 4, n 162).

At their 1993 meeting in Nuuk, the ministers of the AEPS member States considered broadening the AEPS mandate to focus more on pollution and sustainable development in the Arctic.[172] In the 1996 Inuvik Declaration, the AEPS ministers stressed their full commitment for "the earliest possible establishment of the Arctic Council".[173] Subsequently, in the 1996 Alta Declaration, the eight Arctic States committed to continued implementation, development, and improvement of AEPS programs under the auspices of the Arctic Council,[174] which was subsequently formally established through the Ottawa Declaration of the same year.[175] At the same time, the AEPS working groups were integrated as working groups under the Arctic Council.[176]

Although the Arctic Council lacks the mandate to engage in fisheries management, the suitability of the Arctic Council for managing (central) Arctic Ocean fisheries, either within its framework, e.g. via its working group CAFF, or independently, has been discussed time and again.[177] In fact, there are both reasons for and against. Even though in principle, the Arctic Council has a broad mandate, it has been specified continuously from dealing with "common Arctic issues" that could potentially include all matters except the ones "related to military security",[178] and now focuses on environmental cooperation and sustainable development. In this regard, an additional Sustainable Development Working Group was created. Also, new programs related to environmental protection, such as the Arctic Council Action Plan to Eliminate Pollution in the Arctic, have been adopted, for which a sixth working group has been founded.[179] Furthermore, with the transition from the AEPS, the

172 'Nuuk Declaration on Environment and Development in the Arctic (Nuuk, 16 September 1993)' <https://referenceworks.brill.com/display/entries/ILWO/SIM-032762.xml> accessed 2 November 2024.

173 'Inuvik Declaration (Inuvik, 21 March 1996)' <http://library.arcticportal.org/1272/1/The_Inuvik_Declaration.pdf> accessed 6 May 2020.

174 'Alta Declaration (Alta, 13 June 1997)' <http://library.arcticportal.org/1271/1/The_Alta_Declaration.pdf> accessed 6 May 2021.

175 'Declaration On The Establishment Of The Arctic Council (Ottawa, 19 September 1996)' <https://oaarchive.arctic-council.org/bitstream/handle/11374/85/EDOCS-1752-v2-ACMMCA00_Ottawa_1996_Founding_Declaration.PDF?sequence=5&isAllowed=y> accessed 5 December 2021.

176 Platjouw, Steindal and Borch (Chapter 4, n 163) 231.

177 Koivurova and Molenaar (Chapter 3, n 32) 11.

178 'Declaration On The Establishment Of The Arctic Council (Ottawa, 19 September 1996)' (Chapter 4, n 175).

179 Timo Koivurova, Paula Kankaanpää and Adam Stępień, 'Innovative Environmental Protection: Lessons from the Arctic' (2015) 27 Journal of Environmental Law 285, 291 <https://academic.oup.com/jel/article-abstract/27/2/285/419150> accessed 5 December 2021.

Arctic Council opened up further and is now defined by its distinct category of memberships, which benefits the acceptance of international management. Beside its eight permanent member States and indigenous peoples organizations, intergovernmental organizations, NGO's and other organizations can participate.[180] Nevertheless, the Arctic Council lacks the capacity to adopt legally binding obligations.[181] The institution has to rely on the goodwill of governments to function and can only state non-binding soft law recommendations.[182] Moreover, the Arctic Council (and previously the AEPS) is not a regulatory body backed up by a hard law treaty.[183] However, the Arctic Council can adopt facilitative measures. Possible are measures like using scientific working groups to provide information that can be used in other fora or to generally asses the need for adjustments of the international framework in response to threats to the Arctic ecosystem.[184] CAFF for instance provided a 2008–2011 Arctic Marine Biodiversity Monitoring Plan[185] as part of the Circumpolar Biodiversity Monitoring Programme, and in 2013 it released the scientific Arctic Biodiversity Assessment.[186] Programs like the joint AMAP, CAFF and International Arctic Science Committee's ACIA[187] that deal with the impacts of climate change in the region including impacts on fishing, were introduced.[188] Current

180 See Annex 2, 'Arctic Council Rules of Procedure (Revised Version 2013)' 13 <https://oaarchive.arctic-council.org/bitstream/handle/11374/940/2015-09-01_Rules_of_Procedure_website_version.pdf?sequence=1&isAllowed=y> accessed 10 August 2021.

181 European Union, 'Policy Department B: Fisheries Management And The Arctic In The Context Of Climate Change – Study' (Chapter 2, n 149).

182 Njord Wegge, 'The Political Order in the Arctic: Power Structures, Regimes and Influence' (2011) 47 Polar Record 165, 171 <https://shorturl.at/10MfO> accessed 5 December 2021.

183 Stadtländer (Chapter 2, n 80) 1 et seq.

184 Erik J Molenaar, 'Climate Change and Arctic Fisheries' in E Carina H Keskitalo, Timo Koivurova and Nigel Bankes (eds), *Climate Governance in the Arctic* (Springer 2009) 165.

185 Conservation of Arctic Flora and Fauna (CAFF) Working Group, 'Arctic Marine Biodiversity Monitoring Plan (CBMP-MARINE PLAN) – CAFF Monitoring Series Report No.3' (2011) <https://oaarchive.arctic-council.org/server/api/core/bitstreams/0567a2b3-ca08-4bd5-830c-72d312f128c1/content> accessed 4 December 2024.

186 T et al Barry, 'Arctic Biodiversity Assessment – Scientific Report' (Arctic Council 2013) <https://oaarchive.arctic-council.org/items/b32baf29-d9d7-4c9e-8598-877db37141da> accessed 2 November 2024.

187 Arctic Monitoring and Assessment Programme (AMAP), Conservation of Arctic Flora and Fauna (CAFF) Working Group and International Arctic Science Committee (IASC) (Chapter 2, n 78) 45, 215, 220, 365, 482; similiar, see Keskitalo, Koivurova and Bankes (Chapter 2, n 78) 1.

188 Fourth Arctic Council Ministerial Meeting, 'Arctic Climate Impact Assessment Policy Document (Reykjavík, 24 November 2004)' <https://acia.amap.no/> accessed 30 June 2021.

projects[189] involve, *inter alia,* CAFF's State of the Arctic Marine Biodiversity Report.[190] Moreover, in order to implement ecosystem-based management in the CAO, PAME has teamed up with ICES and PICES forming the joint Working Group on Integrated Ecosystem Assessment for the Central Arctic Ocean with the task to investigate the current state of the CAO.[191]

Although not specifically dealing with fisheries, the Arctic Council therefore provides for an extensive Arctic-related framework, and the reports of the individual working groups serve as a valuable source of information and guidance on Arctic issues.

1.3.3 FAO Code of Conduct and Related Soft-Law Instruments

Not to be confused with the binding FAO Compliance Agreement that deals with compliance with international conservation and management measures by fishing vessels on the high seas,[192] the FAO Code of Conduct for Responsible Fisheries (FAO Code of Conduct)[193] was adopted by the FAO Conference on 31 October 1995 by Resolution 4/95. With its comprehensive, all-encompassing nature, the code addresses governments and stakeholders involved in fisheries and aquaculture. The purpose of the FAO Code of Conduct is to set international standards of behaviour for responsible practices with a view to ensure the effective conservation, management and development of living aquatic resources and due respect for the ecosystem and biodiversity.

The code recognizes the nutritional, economic, social, environmental and cultural importance of fisheries and the interests of all stakeholders of the fishing and aquaculture industries. Additionally, it takes into account the biological characteristics of the resources and their environment and the interests of consumers and other users. These standards should be appropriately implemented at the national, subregional and regional levels and through promoting increased responsible behaviour in the fisheries sector. It is anticipated that these standards and norms will lead to achieving long-term sustainable

189 An overview of Arctic Council projects can be found at https://arctic-council.org/en/projects/.

190 Conservation of Arctic Flora and Fauna (CAFF) Working Group, 'State of the Arctic Marine Biodiversity: Key Findings and Advice for Monitoring' (Chapter 2, n 166).

191 'Arctic Council | Integrated Ecosystem Assessment (IEA) of the Central Arctic Ocean' <https://arctic-council.org/en/projects/iea/> accessed 25 September 2020.

192 See specifically on FAO Compliance Agreement Chapter 4 Sections, 1, 1.3, 1.3.3 *supra.*

193 Food and Agriculture Organization of the United Nations, 'Code of Conduct for Responsible Fisheries (Rome, 31 October 1995)' <https://www.fao.org/fishery/docs/CDrom/aquaculture/a0805e/documents/Code of Conduct for Responsible Fisheries.pdf> accessed 6 April 2022.

outcomes. Where RFBs are concerned, the FAO regards the implementation of the code and the strengthening of RFBs as being intrinsically linked.[194] For fisheries management specifically, Article 7 FAO Code of Conduct suggests specific management measures while following the precautionary approach.

A variety of instruments have been established within the framework of the FAO Code of Conduct to assist fishers, the fishing industry and governments in taking necessary practical steps to implement the various facets of the code, including four international plans of action, IPOA, and two strategies. The CAOF Agreement specifically acknowledges these instruments by recalling the principles and provisions of the FAO Code of Conduct and other relevant FAO instruments in its Preamble. In this regard, the International Plan of Action to Prevent, Deter and Eliminate Illegal, Unreported and Unregulated Fishing (IPOA-IUU) is considered relevant.[195] The IPOA-IUU is, just like the FAO Code of Conduct itself, a voluntary instrument that applies to all States, State entities and fishers. It has been elaborated within the framework of the Code as envisaged by Article 2(d) FAO Code of Conduct.[196] The IPOA-IUU was created specifically as existing international instruments to combat IUU fishing were not effective due to a lack of political will, priorities and capacity to both ratify or accede to agreements and to implement regulations.[197] The IPAO-IUU aims at implementing measures to prevent, deter and eliminate IUU fishing. These measures focus on general and flag State responsibilities, coastal and port State measures, internationally agreed market-related measures, research and RFBs. *Inter alia*, requirements for monitoring, control and surveillance,[198] sanctions and economic incentives,[199] and national plans of action are suggested.[200] Where RFBs are concerned, the IPAO-IUU emphasizes the need for compliance with measures established by RFBs and encourages participants to cooperatively develop specific plans and programs.[201] Due to its level of detail, the plan is suitable as a comprehensive basis for specific management

---

194 'FAO | Code of Conduct for Responsible Fisheries – Illegal, Unreported and Unregulated (IUU) Fishing' <https://www.fao.org/iuu-fishing/international-framework/code-of-conduct-for-responsible-fisheries/en/> accessed 8 April 2022.

195 Food and Agriculture Organization of the United Nations, 'International Plan Of Action To Prevent, Deter And Eliminate Illegal, Unreported And Unregulated Fishing (Rome, 2 March 2001)' <http://www.fao.org/3/y1224e/Y1224E.pdf> accessed 2 May 2020.

196 Cf. Section II(4) IPOA-IUU.

197 See Introduction IPOA-IUU.

198 See Section IV(24) IPAO-IUU.

199 See Section IV(21;23) IPAO-IUU.

200 See Section IV(25–31) IPAO-IUU.

201 See Section IV(78–84) IPAO-IUU.

measures – especially for the further development of the CAOF Agreement as an RFMA[202] with the possibility of establishing an additional RFB.[203]

Another FAO instrument worth mentioning are the FAO Voluntary Guidelines for Flag State Performance (FSP Guidelines).[204] The guidelines were established as another tool to prevent, deter and eliminate IUU fishing. Compliance with the international tasks and obligations of flag states in relation to flagging and control of fishing vessels is ensured through the effective implementation of the FSP responsibilities. For small-scale fisheries specifically, the FAO Voluntary Guidelines for Securing Sustainable Small-Scale Fisheries in the Context of Food Security and Poverty Eradication (SSF Guidelines) were developed to provide complementary guidance in support of the overall principles and provisions of the FAO Code of Conduct.[205] The SSF Guidelines aim at supporting the visibility, recognition and enhancement of the role of small-scale fisheries and contribute to global and national efforts towards food stability. This is to support responsibly managed fisheries and their sustainable, social and economic development. Further, in 2018, the FAO Voluntary Guidelines on the Marking of Fishing Gear (MFG Guidelines) were introduced.[206] The MFG Guidelines address the purpose, principles, scope of application and implementation of a gear marking system and its associated components. This includes reporting, recovery and disposal of abandoned, lost or otherwise discarded fishing gear and its commercial traceability.

In total, the framework of guidelines developed by the FAO provides solid guidance for current and future fisheries management, in anticipation of possible commercial fishing in the CAO and the related establishment of a supplementary RFB.

202 On the classification of the CAOF Agreement, see Chapter 4 Sections 3, 3.3 *infra*.

203 See Article 5(1)(c)(i) CAOF Agreement.

204 Food and Agriculture Organization of the United Nations, 'Voluntary Guidelines for Flag State Performance (Rome, 9 June 2014)' <http://www.fao.org/3/I4577T/i4577t.pdf> accessed 7 May 2020.

205 Food and Agriculture Organization of the United Nations, 'Voluntary Guidelines for Securing Sustainable Small-Scale Fisheries in the Context of Food Security and Poverty Eradication (Rome, 1 June 2014)' <http://www.fao.org/3/a-i4356en.pdf> accessed 7 May 2020.

206 Food and Agriculture Organization of the United Nations, 'Voluntary Guidelines on the Marking of Fishing Gear (Rome, 9 July 2018)' <https://www.fao.org/3/ca3546t/ca3546t.pdf> accessed 8 April 2022.

1.4 *Environmental Legal Standards*

Marine species and their diversity[207] are crucial components for the functioning of our environment. Marine life produces a third of the oxygen we breathe, provides a valuable source of protein and mitigates global climate change.[208] Especially on the high seas, fishing has a negative impact on marine biodiversity.[209] Fortunately, since the end of the 20th century, increasing attention has been given to the environment and its protection. For the high seas, the following instruments in particular are now important for both the protection of marine ecosystems and its species.

1.4.1 Convention on Biological Diversity

As a response to growing threats to species and ecosystems, and inspired by increasing global commitment to sustainable development, the United Nations Environment Programme initiated the creation of the Convention on Biological Diversity[210] in 1988, which was adopted in 1992 and entered into force one year later.[211] The treaty aims at the conservation of biological diversity, sustainable use of its components, and the fair and equitable sharing of benefits arising out of the utilization of genetic resources.[212] As of 2022, it has 196 parties including all signatories of the CAOF Agreement except the United States.[213] The CBD mainly suggests measures for conservation and sustainable use, which should be implemented nationally via revised and updated national biodiversity strategies and action plans[214] and to regularly prepare national reports on the status of implementation.[215]

To enhance effective implementation, the CBD is accompanied by two binding supplementary agreements, the Cartagena Protocol on Biosafety to the Convention on Biological Diversity (Cartagena Protocol)[216] and the Nagoya

207 On biodiversity, see *inter alia* Chapter 5 Sections 2, 2.1, 2.1.2 *infra*.

208 'CBD | What Is Marine and Coastal Biodiversity?' <https://www.cbd.int/marine/intro.shtml> accessed 1 July 2020.

209 Matley (Chapter 3, n 37) 102.

210 'Convention on Biological Diversity (Rio de Janeiro, 5 June 1992) – UNTS Vol. 1760, No. 30619' <https://treaties.un.org/doc/Publication/UNTS/Volume 1760/v1760.pdf> accessed 8 April 2022.

211 'CBD | History of the Convention' <https://www.cbd.int/history/> accessed 12 August 2021.

212 See Article 1 CBD.

213 'CBD | List of Parties' (Chapter 3, n 323).

214 See Article 6 CBD.

215 See Article 26 CBD.

216 'Cartagena Protocol on Biosafety to the Convention on Biological Diversity (Montreal, 29 January 2000) – UNTS Vol. 2226, No. 30619' <https://treaties.un.org/doc/Publication/UNTS/Volume 2226/v2226.pdf> accessed 9 July 2021.

Protocol on Access to Genetic Resources and the Fair and Equitable Sharing of Benefits Arising from their Utilization to the Convention on Biological Diversity (Nagoya Protocol),[217] which entered into force in 2003 and 2014 respectively. Whereas the Cartagena Protocol seeks to protect biological diversity from the potential risks posed by living modified organisms resulting from modern biotechnology, the Nagoya Protocol aims at ensuring fair and equitable sharing of benefits arising from the utilization of genetic resources. Consisting of representatives of all parties to the CBD, the conference of the parties, the COP, serves as the CBD's governing body.[218] Two subsidiary bodies to the CBD exist: the Subsidiary Body for Scientific, Technical and Technological Advice makes recommendations to the COP on scientific and technical issues,[219] and the later established Subsidiary Body on Implementation improves and facilitates effective implementation of CBD goals. Within the framework of the Nagoya Protocol, at the 10th conference of the parties (COP-10) in 2010, a revised and updated Strategic Plan for Biodiversity including the twenty Aichi Biodiversity Targets for the 2011–2020 period was adopted.[220] Based on these recommendations, the UN declared the years of 2011–2020 the United Nations Decade on Biodiversity.[221] The Strategic Plan is part of the 2030 Agenda for Sustainable Development (2030 Agenda) and mutually supportive and reinforcing with the UN Sustainable Development Goals.[222]

The COP has established seven thematic programs of work that correspond to some of the major biomes on the planet. Each program provides a vision and basic principles including a suggested timetable and means for achieving key issues to guide future work. For the Arctic, the thematic program Marine and Coastal Biodiversity applies. Further, to connect the thematic programs,

---

217 'Nagoya Protocol on Access to Genetic Resources and the Fair and Equitable Sharing of Benefits Arising from Their Utilization to the Convention on Biological Diversity (Nagoya, 29 October 2010) – UNTS Vol. 3008, No.30619' <https://treaties.un.org/doc/Publication/UNTS/Volume 3008/v3008.pdf> accessed 8 May 2020.

218 Cf. Article 23 CBD.

219 See Article 25 CBD.

220 CBD Conference of the Parties, 'COP 10 Decision 2: The Strategic Plan for Biodiversity 2011–2020 and the Aichi Biodiversity Targets (Nagoya, 29 October 2010)' <https://www.cbd.int/doc/decisions/cop-10/cop-10-dec-02-en.pdf> accessed 12 August 2021.

221 'United Nations General Assembly Resolution 65/161, Convention on Biological Diversity (Adopted 20 December 2010)'.

222 CBD Conference of the Parties, 'Biodiversity and Sustainable Development – Technical Note (21 October 2016) – UNEP/CBD/COP/13/10/Add.1' para 2 <https://www.cbd.int/doc/meetings/cop/cop-13/official/cop-13-10-add1-en.pdf> accessed 10 August 2021. For the 2030 Agenda and Sustainable Development Goals, see specifically Chapter 4 Sections, 1, 1.4, 1.4.4 infra.

the COP has carved out cross-cutting issues corresponding to the conservation and management measures addressed in Articles 6–20 CBD.[223] With regard to invasive alien species, the COP explicitly recognized the adverse impacts of such species on biological diversity in vulnerable ecosystems like the Arctic.[224] Since they are regarded as the main direct drivers of biodiversity loss, the Supplementary Voluntary Guidance for Avoiding Unintentional Introductions of Invasive Alien Species Associated with Trade in Live Organisms was adopted by the COP in 2018.[225]

Considered particularly relevant for assisting fisheries management in the Arctic are the CBD's cross-cutting issues: these include climate change and biodiversity, the ecosystem approach, sustainable wildlife management and technical and scientific cooperation, traditional knowledge, innovations and practices as well as the subject of protected areas.[226] For the monitoring and assessment of status and trends in, and threats to, Arctic biodiversity, the CBD parties cooperate closely with the Arctic Council working group CAFF through the implementation of the Strategic Plan for Biodiversity 2011–2020 and hopefully continue their contribution towards the implementation of the post-2020 framework by providing relevant reports.[227]

Furthermore, at the COP-10 and COP-11 meetings, the COP requested CBD's Executive Secretary to work with the parties and other governments as well as competent organizations and regional initiatives – such as the FAO and IMO, regional seas conventions and action plans, and, where appropriate, RFBs with regard to fisheries management – to organize a series of (sub)regional workshops. The primary objective was to facilitate the description of ecologically or biologically significant marine areas (EBSAs)[228] as well as additional relevant

223 'CBD | Thematic Programmes and Cross-Cutting Issues' <https://www.cbd.int/programmes/> accessed 12 August 2021.

224 CBD Conference of the Parties, 'COP 14 Decision 11: Invasive Alien Species (Sharm El-Sheikh, 30 November 2018)' 4 <https://www.cbd.int/doc/decisions/cop-14/cop-14-dec-11-en.pdf> accessed 17 January 2022.

225 CBD Conference of the Parties, 'COP 14 Decision 11: Invasive Alien Species (Sharm El-Sheikh, 30 November 2018)' (Chapter 4, n 224).

226 Cf. 'CBD | Thematic Programmes and Cross-Cutting Issues' (Chapter 4, n 223).

227 Cf. Conservation of Arctic Flora and Fauna (CAFF) Working Group, 'Arctic Biodiversity and the Post2020 Framework' (2020) <https://www.cbd.int/api/v2013/documents/CBB01D91-94B7-5DA3-F6FA-F014376CD07E/attachments/212341/CAFF-2.pdf> accessed 4 April 2022.

228 EBSAs are areas that are crucial to the healthy functioning of the global marine ecosystem. EBSA designation does not entail management measures or restrictions on activities but merely recognises the biological or ecological importance of an area. The information used to describe EBSAs can however be of great value for conservation and management, for example to support the case for area-based management tools such as

compatible scientific criteria, which have been agreed on a national and intergovernmental level. Moreover, scientific guidance on the identification of marine areas beyond national jurisdiction should be given. Accordingly, the CBD, in cooperation with CAFF, held the Arctic Regional Workshop to Facilitate the Description of EBSAs in March 2014.[229] Where the CAO is concerned, the working group concluded that there are still significant gaps in data relevant to specific areas in the high seas part beyond national jurisdiction, and declared the marginal ice zone, the seasonal ice cover over the deep parts of the Arctic Ocean and the multi-year ice of the CAO as EBSAs.[230] Therefore, special attention should be given to these parts.

In summary, until not too long ago, agreements focused only narrowly on fisheries conservation, fisheries management and optimum utilisation, and especially did not include broader biodiversity considerations.[231] This changed significantly with the introduction of the CBD and the UNFS Agreement, which now provide a solid basis for the protection of (marine) biodiversity.[232] It should however be kept in mind that treaties like the CBD deal with many more activities than fisheries and therefore enshrine more general obligations.[233] Therefore, they provide a rather loose framework for fishing. By contrast, if obligations were formulated more explicitly, a much smaller extent of overfishing would already breach these obligations and result in much more specific legal consequences.[234] However, the CBD is important as a treaty that ensures the most fundamental conservation of biodiversity.

---

marine protected areas or environmental impact assessments; see 'EBSA | Global Ocean Biodiversity Initiative' <http://gobi.org/ebsas/> accessed 24 May 2021.

229 CBD Conference of the Parties and Conservation of Arctic Flora and Fauna (CAFF) Working Group (Chapter 2, n 126) 1–2.

230 ibid 50.

231 Barnes (Chapter 2, n 10) 210.

232 E.g. Article 2 and Part II 'Convention on the Conservation and Management of Highly Migratory Fish Stocks in the Western and Central Pacific Ocean (Honolulu, 5 September 2000)' <https://www.wcpfc.int/doc/convention-conservation-and-management-highly-migratory-fish-stocks-western-and-central-pacific> accessed 12 August 2021 (WCPFC).

233 See e.g. Article 8(f) CBD stating that States are obliged to "promote the recovery of threatened species, inter alia, through the development and implementation of plans or other management strategies".

234 See e.g. Article 25 WCPFC, compared to Article 8(f) CBD.

1.4.2 Convention on the Conservation of Migratory Species of Wild Animals

The Convention on the Conservation of Migratory Species of Wild Animals (CMS)[235] is a UN adopted environmental treaty that provides a global platform for the conservation and sustainable use of migratory animals and their habitats. It counts 133 member States as of March 2022. From the signatories to the CAOF Agreement, only the EU, Denmark and Norway are party to the CMS.[236] The CMS mobilizes all Range States, namely the States through which migratory animals pass, and hence creates a forum where internationally coordinated comprehensive measures can be arranged. The CMS foresees a listing system where species threatened with extinction are listed on Appendix I, calling for strict protection of the species through, *inter alia,* restoration and conservation of their habitat and diminishing impediments to migration. Species listed in Appendix II are migratory species that are considered to significantly benefit from international cooperation in their conservation. The CMS therefore encourages the conclusion of international or regional protection agreements that may reach from binding treaties to soft-law arrangements.[237] Due to climate change and its cross-sectoral impacts, wildlife conservation regimes like the CMS and fisheries regimes need to be effectively linked. For instance, effective international regulation of both seabird bycatch and fishing effort are needed.[238] For CAO fisheries, due to its species-specific application, the CMS is considered especially helpful when it comes to the individual protection of one species of fish, but not to play a prominent role in Arctic fisheries beyond that.

---

235 'Convention on the Conservation of Migratory Species of Wild Animals (Bonn, 23 June 1979) – UNTS Vol. 1651, No. 28395' <https://treaties.un.org/doc/Publication/UNTS/Volume 1651/v1651.pdf> accessed 12 August 2021.

236 'CMS | Parties and Range States' <https://www.cms.int/en/parties-range-states> accessed 11 November 2020.

237 'CMS | Convention on the Conservation of Migratory Species of Wild Animals' <https://www.cms.int/en/legalinstrument/cms> accessed 12 August 2021.

238 Arie Trouwborst, 'Bird Conservation and Climate Change in the Marine Arctic and Antarctic: Classic and Novel International Law Challenges Converging in the Polar Regions' (2013) 16 Journal of International Wildlife Law and Policy 1, 39 <https://heinonline-org.emedien.ub.uni-muenchen.de/HOL/Page?collection=journals&handle=hein.journals/intwlp16&id=5&men_tab=srchresults> accessed 30 September 2020.

1.4.3 Convention on International Trade in Endangered Species of Wild Fauna and Flora

The Convention on International Trade in Endangered Species of Wild Fauna and Flora (CITES)[239] is an international treaty with the aim to ensure that international trade in specimens of wild animals and plants does not threaten their survival. It was established in 1973 and amended twice in the following ten years. As of 2022, CITES enjoys wide acceptance and counts 184 parties, including all CAOF Agreement signatories.[240] CITES can be joined voluntarily and does not replace national laws despite its binding character. Rather, it provides a framework to be adhered to when implementing the treaty. The trade regulated is diverse, ranging from living animals and plants to a vast array of wildlife products derived from them. Whereas levels of exploitation of some animal and plant species are high, other wildlife species in trade are not endangered. However, CITES considers itself an agreement to ensure the sustainability of trade in species for their future conservation. The species covered by CITES are listed in three appendices, depending on their level of protection.[241]

CITES subjects international trade – import, export, re-export and introduction from the sea – in specimens of selected species to certain controls. All trade has to be authorised through a licensing system, controlled by management authorities designated by the parties.[242] CITES' parties are further obliged to appoint scientific authorities for providing advice on the effects of trade on the status of the species.

None of the fish species currently fished (commercially) in waters adjacent to the CAO, and which therefore have the potential to migrate into CAO waters, are currently listed in the CITES Appendices.[243] As of 2022, CITES is therefore

---

239 'Convention on International Trade in Endangered Species of Wild Fauna and Flora (Washington, 3 March 1973) – UNTS Vol. 993, No. 14537' <https://treaties.un.org/doc/Publication/UNTS/Volume 993/v993.pdf> accessed 8 April 2022.

240 'CITES | List of Contracting Parties' <https://www.cites.org/eng/disc/parties/chronolo.php> accessed 6 April 2022.

241 'CITES | What Is CITES?' <https://www.cites.org/eng/disc/what.php> accessed 11 November 2020.

242 Article VII CITES provides for exemptions and special procedures to the general rules, although a permit or certificate will generally still be required, e.g. for specimens in transit or being transhipped.

243 See e.g. 'Fisheries and Oceans Canada | Fisheries by Species – Atlantic, Quebec and Arctic Regions Commercial Fisheries' <https://www.dfo-mpo.gc.ca/fisheries-peches/commercial-commerciale/atl-arc/index-eng.html> accessed 10 August 2021; 'Alaska Department of Fish and Game | Commercial Fisheries Overview – Arctic Management Area' <https://www.adfg.alaska.gov/index.cfm?adfg=commercialbyareanorthern.main> accessed 12 August 2021.

considered of little relevance for CAO fisheries, although this might change in the future. Should a species become endangered, CITES provides a well-established framework for its future preservation.

1.4.4 2030 Agenda and Sustainable Development Goals

With regard to fisheries and aquaculture, the 2030 Agenda for Sustainable Development (2030 Agenda) including the UN Sustainable Development Goals (SDGs) should play a key role in governance.[244]

The 2030 Agenda was adopted by the UN General Assembly in 2015[245] as a plan of action for people, planet and prosperity, seeking to strengthen universal peace in larger freedom. The Agenda was developed as "a comprehensive, far-reaching and people-centred set of universal and transformative Goals and targets".[246] The 17 SDGs and their 169 targets set up guidance for development actions of governments, international agencies, civil society and other institutions until 2030. Key features are food security, nutrition, sustainable management and use of natural resources. Accordingly, all countries are expected to integrate the three dimensions of sustainable development – economic, social and environmental –,[247] which is currently so urgently needed that UN Secretary-General Guterres declared 2020–2030 as the decade of action to foster implementation.[248]

In the context of the CAOF Agreement, in particular two SDGs are highly relevant. SDG No. 13 calls upon States to take urgent action to combat climate change and its impacts.[249] *Inter alia*, resilience and adaptive capacity to climate-related hazards should be strengthened, and climate change measures should be integrated nationally.[250] For fisheries, SDG No. 14 that deals with the conservation and sustainable use of the oceans, seas and marine resources to

---

244 Food and Agriculture Organization of the United Nations, 'The State of World Fisheries and Aquaculture 2016: Contributing to Food Security and Nutrition for All' (Chapter 1, n 3) 7.

245 'United Nations General Assembly Resolution 70/1, Transforming Our World: The 2030 Agenda for Sustainable Development (Adopted 25 September 2015)'.

246 ibid 2.

247 See more on sustainable development Chapter 5 Sections 2, 2.1 *infra*.

248 United Nations, 'Secretary General Antonio Guterres: Remarks to High-Level Political Forum on Sustainable Development (24 September 2019)' <https://www.un.org/sg/en/content/sg/speeches/2019-09-24/remarks-high-level-political-sustainable-development-forum> accessed 4 April 2022.

249 Acknowledging that the United Nations Framework Convention on Climate Change (UNFCCC) is the primary international, intergovernmental forum for negotiating a global response to climate change.

250 See SDGs No. 13.1, 13.2.

achieve sustainable development is of particular importance and should be considered when managing fisheries under the CAOF Agreement. Accordingly, especially the protection of marine and coastal ecosystems, effective regulation and harvesting in order to end overfishing, IUU fishing and destructive fishing practices by 2020 should be implemented.[251] Further, the increase of scientific knowledge and the development of research capacity should be promoted.[252] As an overarching goal, this is supposed to lead to an end of hunger, achieve food security and improved nutrition and promote sustainable agriculture by 2030.[253]

The 2030 Agenda and SDGs do not set up a binding framework. However, they provide a plan of action, by which sustainable development can be implemented across all sectors step by step. Also for the implementation of the CAOF Agreement, the framework should be taken heed of.

1.4.5 United Nations Framework Convention on Climate Change, Kyoto Protocol and Paris Agreement

The 1994 United Nations Framework Convention on Climate Change (UNFCCC)[254] enjoys nearly global support and binds its 197 members, including all CAOF Agreement signatories,[255] to protect the climate system for the benefit of present and future generations[256] even in the face of scientific uncertainty.[257] It aims at stabilizing greenhouse gas concentrations

> at a level that would prevent dangerous anthropogenic interference[258] with the climate system. Such a level should be achieved within a time frame sufficient to allow ecosystems to adapt naturally to climate change, to ensure that food production is not threatened and to enable economic development to proceed in a sustainable manner.[259]

251 See SDGs No. 14.2, 14.4.
252 See SDG No. 14.a.
253 See SDG No. 2.
254 'United Nations Framework Convention on Climate Change (New York, 9 May 1992) – UNTS Vol. 1771, No. 30822' <https://treaties.un.org/doc/Publication/UNTS/Volume 1771/v1771.pdf> accessed 9 July 2021.
255 'UNFCCC | Parties UNFCCC' <https://unfccc.int/process/parties-non-party-stakeholders/parties-convention-and-observer-states> accessed 6 April 2022.
256 See Article 3(1) UNFCCC.
257 See Article 3(3) UNFCCC.
258 The level of a dangerous anthropogenic interference will be determined by the Intergovernmental Panel on Climate Change, see 'IPCC | Intergovernmental Panel on Climate Change Reports' <https://www.ipcc.ch/reports/> accessed 22 September 2020.
259 See Article 2 UNFCCC.

As the UNFCCC itself merely asks industrialized countries, so called Annex I parties, as the originators of most past and current greenhouse gas emissions to adopt policies and measures on mitigation and to file periodical reports, the UNFCCC is operationalized by the Kyoto Protocol. The Kyoto Protocol[260] counts 192 parties as of 2022, including all signatory States to the CAOF Agreement and the EU except the United States and Canada. The treaty actively addresses industrialized countries and economies in transition to limit and reduce greenhouse gas emissions pursuant to agreed individual targets. Thus, the Kyoto Protocol places a heavier burden on these countries following the principle of "common but differentiated responsibility and respective capabilities" compared to non-Annex I countries or least developed countries.[261] The Kyoto Protocol has been considered effective for reducing worldwide CO_2 emissions.[262] Yet, the initial leap in CO_2 reduction in the protocol's early years can *inter alia* be traced back to the collapse of the Soviet Union, rather than a worldwide large-scale decrease.[263] Furthermore, in 2018, more than 27% of the world's CO_2 emissions arose from Canada and the United States, which are not party to the Kyoto Protocol, questioning the effectiveness of the protocol to significantly reduce CO_2 emissions globally.[264] Also criticized is the international emission permit trade that the protocol allows.[265] Overall, it is understandable why it is sometimes claimed that the agreement only limits the growth of greenhouse gas emissions instead of significantly reducing them[266] – although without the protocol, it can be predicted with certainty that CO_2 emissions

260 'Kyoto Protocol to the United Nations Framework Convention on Climate Change (Kyoto, 11 December 1997) – UNTS Vol. 2303, No. 30822' <https://treaties.un.org/doc/Publication/UNTS/Volume 2303/v2303.pdf> accessed 28 June 2021.

261 'UNFCCC | What Is the Kyoto Protocol?' <https://unfccc.int/kyoto_protocol> accessed 22 September 2020.

262 Yoomi Kim, Katsuya Tanaka and Shunji Matsuoka, 'Environmental and Economic Effectiveness of the Kyoto Protocol' (2020) 15 PLOS ONE 1, 12 et seq. <https://dx.plos.org/10.1371/journal.pone.0236299> accessed 12 November 2020.

263 'The Kyoto Protocol: Climate Change Success or Global Warming Failure?' *Circular Ecology* (4 February 2015) <https://circularecology.com/news/the-kyoto-protocol-climate-change-success-or-global-warming-failure> accessed 12 November 2021.

264 Hannah Ritchie and Max Roser, 'CO_2 Emissions' *Our World in Data* (31 December 2020) <https://ourworldindata.org/co2-emissions> accessed 12 November 2020.

265 See Brian R Copeland and M Scott Taylor, 'Free Trade and Global Warming: A Trade Theory View of the Kyoto Protocol' (2005) 49 Journal of Environmental Economics and Management 205 <https://www.sciencedirect.com/science/article/abs/pii/S0095069604000737> accessed 12 August 2021.

266 'The Kyoto Protocol: Climate Change Success or Global Warming Failure?' (Chapter 4, n 263).

would be at worse levels now, and its existence is yet an important, if not sufficient, tool in the fight against climate change.

Although the Kyoto Protocol remains in force to that day, it has been superseded by another environmental agreement that is considered additionally important for fisheries governance.[267] Based on the UNFCCC, in 2015 at the 21st Conference of the Parties to the UNFCCC, the Paris Agreement[268] was adopted to combat climate change and accelerate and intensify the actions and investments needed for a sustainable low carbon future.[269] It enjoys wide acceptance and all CAOF Agreement signatories are (again)[270] party to it.[271] Its central aim is to limit the increase in the global average temperature to well below 2°C (3,6°F), if possible to 1,5°C (2,7°F) above pre-industrial levels.[272] The Paris Agreement further recognizes that climate change is a fundamental threat to global food security, sustainable development and efforts to eradicate poverty. Governance in the CAO therefore needs to ensure that potential fisheries and aquaculture adapt to the impacts of climate change and improve the resilience of food production systems.[273] At the latest UNFCCC party meeting in Dubai, United Arab Emirates, in 2023, the so-called COP28, the first global stocktake, a process for countries and stakeholders to see where they're collectively making progress towards meeting the goals of the Paris Agreement, was concluded. The finding was that progress has been too slow in all areas

267 Food and Agriculture Organization of the United Nations, 'The State of World Fisheries and Aquaculture 2016: Contributing to Food Security and Nutrition for All' (Chapter 1, n 3) 7.

268 'Paris Agreement (Paris, 12 December 2015) – UNTS Vol. 3156, No. 54113' (Chapter 2, n 96).

269 'UNFCCC | What Is the Paris Agreement?' <https://unfccc.int/process-and-meetings/the-paris-agreement/what-is-the-paris-agreement> accessed 22 September 2020.

270 After the Trump administration withdraw from the Paris Agreement in November 2020, new-elected President Biden rejoined the Agreement in 2021, see The White House, 'Statement of President Biden: Paris Climate Agreement (20 January 2021)' <https://www.whitehouse.gov/briefing-room/statements-releases/2021/01/20/paris-climate-agreement/> accessed 4 October 2021; on the issue, see also Lisa Friedman, 'U.S. Quits Paris Climate Agreement: Questions and Answers' *The New York Times* (4 November 2020) <https://www.nytimes.com/2020/11/04/climate/paris-climate-agreement-trump.html> accessed 16 December 2020.

271 'UNFCCC | Parties Paris Agreement' <https://unfccc.int/process/parties-non-party-stakeholders/parties-convention-and-observer-states?field_partys_partyto_target_id%5B511%5D=511> accessed 24 May 2021.

272 See Article 2(1)(a) Paris Agreement.

273 Cf. Food and Agriculture Organization of the United Nations, 'The State of World Fisheries and Aquaculture 2016: Contributing to Food Security and Nutrition for All' (Chapter 1, n 3) 7.

of climate action – from reducing greenhouse gas emissions and building resilience to climate change to providing financial and technological support to vulnerable countries. Hence, the common understanding was to speed up action in all areas of climate action by 2030. This includes calling on governments to make the transition from fossil fuels to renewable energies such as wind and solar power a key climate commitment.[274] The annual conferences and in particular instruments such as the global stocktake are therefore used to monitor and improve the continuous progress of climate protection measures, which will ultimately – hopefully – also benefit the CAO.

2 Additional Cooperative Arctic Mechanisms

As different fish stocks may be regulated by different RFBS,[275] and certain interdependencies between targeted stocks and associated or dependent stocks exist, cooperation among arrangements is key.[276] Besides the instruments mentioned above, a variety of cooperative mechanisms that deal with Arctic issues exist. These mechanisms should be taken into account when implementing the CAOF Agreement, as cooperation with them is considered helpful to achieve broad acceptance and effective application of the Arctic fisheries agreement.

One of these cooperative mechanisms is OSPAR, a designation composed of the Oslo-Paris Conventions ("OS" for Oslo and "PAR" for Paris) by the fifteen governments of Belgium, Denmark, Finland, France, Germany, Iceland, Ireland, Luxembourg, The Netherlands, Norway, Portugal, Spain, Sweden, Switzerland, the United Kingdom and the EU to protect the marine environment of the North-East Atlantic. OSPAR started in 1972 with the Convention for the Prevention of Marine Pollution by Dumping from Ships and Aircraft concluded in Oslo[277] and was extended by the 1974 Convention[278] for the Prevention of Marine Pollution from Landbased Sources that was concluded in

274 'UNFCCC | UN Climate Change Conference – United Arab Emirates' <https://unfccc.int/cop28> accessed 4 May 2024.

275 See more on different RFBs Chapter 6 Section 1, 1.2 *infra*.

276 Molenaar, 'The Concept of "Real Interest" and Other Aspects of Co-Operation through Regional Fisheries Management Mechanisms' (Chapter 2, n 145) 477.

277 'Convention for the Prevention of Marine Pollution by Dumping from Ships and Aircraft (Oslo, 15 February 1972) – UNTS Vol. 932, No. 13269' <https://treaties.un.org/doc/Publication/UNTS/Volume 932/volume-932-I-13269-English.pdf> accessed 12 August 2021.

278 Not to be confused with the 2015 Paris Agreement.

FIGURE 11 OSPAR Convention Area, divided into Regions I–V
SOURCE: 'OSPAR COMMISSION | THE NORTH-EAST ATLANTIC' <HTTPS://WWW.OSPAR.ORG/CONVENTION/THE-NORTH-EAST-ATLANTIC> ACCESSED 20 MAY 2020

Paris.[279] Updated and extended, these two conventions were unified to create the 1992 Convention for the Protection of the Marine Environment of the North-East Atlantic (OSPAR Convention).[280] In 1998, an annex on biodiversity and ecosystems to cover non-polluting human activities that can adversely affect the sea was additionally adopted.[281] The maritime area that is protected by the OSPAR Convention is set out in Article 1(a) OSPAR Convention and covers Arctic waters and northern parts of the Atlantic Ocean. It is divided into five regions, whereas Region I, the northernmost one, comprises parts of the Arctic Ocean and partially significant ocean fisheries.[282]

279 'Convention for the Prevention of Marine Pollution from Landbased Sources (Paris, 4 June 1974) – UNTS Vol. 1546, No. 26842' <https://treaties.un.org/doc/Publication/UNTS/Volume 1546/volume-1546-I-26842-English.pdf> accessed 12 August 2021.

280 'Convention for the Protection of the Marine Environment of the North-East Atlantic (OSPAR Convention) (Paris, 22 September 1992) – UNTS Vol. 2345, No. 42279' (Chapter 3, n 52).

281 'OSPAR Commission | About' <https://www.ospar.org/about> accessed 20 May 2020.

282 'OSPAR Commission | Region I: Arctic Waters' (Chapter 2, n 125).

Assessments regarding the marine environmental quality, especially in the Arctic sector, are conducted regularly. OSPAR acts mainly through its commission, which consists of representatives of each of the contracting parties.[283] Whereas OSPAR regulates, *inter alia,* oil and gas extraction and works towards the effective implementation of CBD regulations, its mandate does not comprise regulating fisheries. This task is carried out by the NEAFC, which regulatory area is almost congruent to OSPAR's regulatory area. To record their relationship, NEAFC and OSPAR concluded a memorandum of understanding.[284] OSPAR might be of help when it comes to develop integrated, cross-sectoral ecosystem-based ocean management in the Arctic. OSPAR's expertise should therefore be additionally considered when managing CAO fishing.

Attention should also be paid to the Nordic Council. Together with the Nordic Council of Ministers, comprised of executive level representatives from member States, the Nordic Council is a body for formal inter-parliamentary cooperation. Following a proposal of the Danish Prime Minister, in 1952, the Nordic Council was established as a consultation body in which Nordic parliamentarians would meet on a regular basis. It currently consists of 87 representatives from Denmark, Finland, Iceland, Norway, Sweden, the Faroe Islands, Greenland and the Åland Islands.[285] The aim of the Nordic Council is "to make the Nordic region one that people want to live and work in".[286] Hence, its activities focus on sustainable development, social affairs, education, health but also climate and the environment.[287] Fisheries management in the North-East Atlantic is touched upon, but not regulated.[288]

Additionally, following a regional rather than national approach, the Northern Forum is an international organization bringing together Arctic and Northern regions to address common political, environmental and economic issues. It was formally established in 1991 and is composed of sub-national

283 See Article 10 OSPAR Convention.

284 North-East Atlantic Fisheries Commission, 'Memorandum of Understanding between the North-East Atlantic Fisheries Commission and the OSPAR Commission' (2008) <https://www.neafc.org/system/files/opsar_mou.pdf> accessed 2 April 2020.

285 'Nordic Cooperation | The History of the Nordic Council' <https://www.norden.org/en/information/history-nordic-council> accessed 6 April 2022.

286 'Nordic Cooperation | The Nordic Council' <https://www.norden.org/en/information/nordic-council> accessed 5 December 2021.

287 'Nordic Cooperation | Policy Areas' <https://www.norden.org/en/political_areas> accessed 5 December 2021.

288 Henrik Sparholt and others, 'Nordic Working Papers: Report of the 1st Working Group Meeting on Optimization of Fishing Pressure in the Northeast Atlantic (Copenhagen, 20–21 June 2017)' (2019) <http://norden.diva-portal.org/smash/get/diva2:1307971/FULLTEXT01.pdf> accessed 12 April 2022.

or regional governments of Iceland, the United States, Russia, South Korea and Finland.[289] For several decades, the Northern Forum has been successfully implementing initiatives and projects that benefit Northern and Arctic areas and acted as a regional voice on current Arctic issues.[290] Several working groups within the Northern Forum focus on different aspects of Arctic life, like the development of energy, housing and transport, but also the environment and its conservation, although specific focus on fisheries is not made.[291]

Another cooperative northern instrument has been established in 1993. Through the creation of the intergovernmental Barents Euro-Arctic Council (BEAC) and the interregional Barents Regional Council (BRC), cooperation for sustainable development in the Barents Euro-Arctic region has been launched on two levels. Whereas the BEAC, initially established to ensure security in the region around the Barents Sea,[292] meets at foreign minister level of the eight parties Denmark, Finland, Iceland, Norway, Russia, Sweden and the European Commission, the BRC consists of thirteen counties or similar sub-national entities.[293] Both councils established working groups, where the participation of indigenous peoples is possible. Further coordination with the relevant activities of the Nordic Council of Ministers, the Council of the Baltic Sea States, the Arctic Council and the Northern Dimension is envisaged where appropriate.[294] Fisheries are not a main concern, but the focus is on economic cooperation, transport and rescue while safeguarding the environment.

Although, or rather because, these mechanisms do not specifically address fisheries but general Arctic issues, cooperation with these instruments are considered helpful to a comprehensive implementation of the CAOF Agreement in the future.

289 'Northern Forum | UNDP Climate Change Adaptation' <https://www.adaptation-undp.org/partners/northern-forum> accessed 23 May 2020; 'Northern Forum | History' <https://www.northernforum.org/en/the-northern-forum/history> accessed 23 May 2020.

290 'UArctic | New Strategy of Northern Forum' <https://www.uarctic.org/news/2018/4/new-strategy-of-northern-forum/> accessed 23 May 2020.

291 'Northern Forum | Working Groups' <https://www.northernforum.org/en/working-groups> accessed 25 September 2020.

292 Keskitalo, Koivurova and Bankes (Chapter 2, n 78) 6.

293 In Finland: Lapland, Oulu Region, Kainuu and North Karelia; in Norway: Nordland and Troms og Finnmark; in Russia: Arkhangelsk Region, Murmansk Region, Karelia, Komi and Nenets; and in Sweden: Norrbotten and Västerbotten; see 'BEAC | About the Regional Council' <https://barents-council.org/barents-regional-council/about-the-council> accessed 2 November 2024.

294 'Barents Euro-Arctic Cooperation | About Us' (Chapter 3, n 249).

3 Possibilities and Approaches of Governance in Fisheries

Fisheries management is the product of an interplay of law and governance. Therefore, besides considering legal standards, a suitable governance approach should be followed. Considerations include a strictly multilateral approach, for instance by following the organizational structure of the Arctic Council, a unilateral approach, where each State develops some structure of its own, or a mixed approach of a regime that includes States with a specific interest.[295] All approaches have advantages and disadvantages, which will be addressed in the following. Further, the approach of the CAOF Agreement itself is presented.

3.1 *Unilateral vs. Multilateral Approach*

The nature of highly migratory and straddling fish stocks is to migrate between territories, irrespective of the borders between States' EEZs and open waters. Hence, the general conflict when managing such stocks is the clash between the equally important[296] (coastal) States' sovereign fishing rights in their EEZ and the freedom of fishing on the high seas. A management regime for the high seas inevitably puts coastal States in the position of having to adapt their own legal standard in their EEZ in accordance with the management regulations so that a comprehensive standard for fisheries management is achieved. As always, however, an incentive is required for the coastal State to adapt to this standard, which each regime has to find an individual balance for.

Whether a multilateral governance solution rather than a unilateral one is needed should be considered carefully on the basis of protection and conservation of the respective marine environment and biodiversity and the urgency for regulatory action. High urgency is, *inter alia,* suggested where destructive fishing practices are conducted.[297] Similarly, the possible threat to the Arctic marine environment through IUU fishing highlights an urgency to govern fisheries, e.g. through considering broad prohibition of fishing in the CAO. Further, where areas beyond national jurisdiction – therefore common areas – are at stake, it is assumed common interest that challenges like the prevention of IUU fishing and preservation of sensitive ecosystems are addressed in a coordinated, cooperative way rather than by States unilaterally.

Not only multilateral, but also bilateral agreements provide a useful tool to manage fisheries in a certain area. The Russian-Greenlandic mutual fishery

---

295 Concerning the concept of real interest, see Chapter 3 Sections 3, 3.2 *supra*.

296 Cf. Article 7 UNFS Agreement.

297 'United Nations General Assembly Resolution 59/25, Sustainable Fisheries (Adopted 17 November 2004)' paras 66–69.

relations since 1992[298] or the 1988 Agreement between the US and the Soviet Socialist Republics on Mutual Fisheries Relations[299] serve as solid examples. Further, Norway and Russia have long collaborated in fisheries in the Barents Sea. Most prominent is the Joint Norwegian-Russian Fisheries Commission[300] that deals with managing fisheries including the issue of IUU fishing in Russian and Norwegian waters,[301] and was even considered a possible arrangement to govern fisheries in the CAO.[302] Bilateral agreements are well suited for regional, localised fisheries. Such instruments usually provide for cooperation, recognition of access rights and authority to set catch levels.[303] However, due to their limited number of participants, they have difficulties with regulating rights and duties of third States. Yet, these are necessary to consider in a broader international context since third States may provide information on specific fisheries and contribute to improve the availability and quality of information for ecosystem-based fisheries management.[304]

In some cases, increased regional cooperation could encourage fragmentation of legal standards and lead to different levels of protection in different areas,[305] and unilateral management should therefore be pursued. However, for the CAO, the broader cooperative regional approach implemented through the CAOF Agreement is considered most appropriate to address its unique characteristics. It should nevertheless be kept in mind that additional regional arrangements can provide a useful "safety net"[306] of legal protection and should therefore be considered as a future option.

---

298 Barnes (Chapter 2, n 10) 222.

299 Continued by the 'Agreement between the United States of America and the Russian Federation on Cooperation for the Purposes of Preventing, Deterring and Eliminating Illegal, Unreported, and Unregulated Fishing (Portland, 11 September 2015)' <https://2009-2017.state.gov/documents/organization/250927.pdf> accessed 9 July 2021.

300 On the Joint Norwegian-Russian Fisheries Commission, see Chapter 6 Sections 1, 1.2, 1.2.1 *infra*.

301 Geir B Hønneland, 'Autonomy and Regionalisation in the Fisheries Management of Northwestern Russia' (1998) 22 Marine Policy 57, 58 <https://www.sciencedirect.com/science/article/abs/pii/S0308597X97000298?via%3Dihub> accessed 5 December 2024.

302 Molenaar, 'International Regulation of Central Arctic Ocean Fisheries' (Chapter 2, n 20) 452 et seq.

303 Barnes (Chapter 2, n 10) 222.

304 ibid 224.

305 Cf. Nele Matz-Lück and Johannes Fuchs, 'The Impact of OSPAR on Protected Area Management beyond National Jurisdiction: Effective Regional Cooperation or a Network of Paper Parks?' (2014) 49 Marine Policy 155, 163 <http://dx.doi.org/10.1016/j.marpol.2013.12.001> accessed 2 July 2020.

306 See Vylegzhanin, Young and Berkman (Chapter 3, n 62) 6.

3.2 *Multilateral Governance Systems in Fisheries: Regional Fishery Bodies*

International multilateral cooperation may take several forms. As for management involving two or more entities, in fisheries, Regional Fishery Bodies, RFBs, have proven effective for bi- or multilaterally governed areas where fisheries are conducted.[307] In fact, according to the UNFS Agreement[308] and other international bodies,[309] they should be considered the preferable means of cooperation in fisheries. The FAO differentiates RFBs with the power to adopt binding measures on their members, Regional Fishery Management Arrangements, RFMAs – or, if such arrangement additionally provides for the establishment of an organization, Regional Fishery Management Organizations, RFMOs – and RFBs with purely advisory status in areas where RFMA/Os are absent. In some cases, RFBs govern waters under national jurisdiction, while others have management powers over areas beyond national jurisdiction.[310] Where the regulatory area comprises a larger area, RFBs are referred to as Sub-regional Fisheries Management Organizations or Arrangements (SRFMO/As).[311] For convenience only, in this thesis, the terms RFB, RFMA and RFMO are widely used, which are supposed to include the sub-category of SRFMA/Os.[312]

The relationship between international regimes, like RFMAs, and international organizations, like RFMOs, varies depending on the respective definition. While it is sometimes argued that international organizations are constituent elements of international regimes,[313] others make the case for the two being independent of one another, saying that regimes can be institutionalized or not, such as organizations can be regimes, but do not need to

307 See Yoshinobu Takei, 'Current Legal Developments – UN Fish Stocks Agreement: 2006 Review Conference' (2007) 21 International Journal of Marine and Coastal Law 551, 557.

308 See *inter alia* Articles 7(7), 8(1) UNFS Agreement. Further, access to fisheries is limited to participants, see Article 8(4) UNFS Agreement.

309 Cf. Løbach and others (Chapter 4, n 87) 8.

310 'FAO | Regional Bodies Involved in the Management of Deep-Sea Fisheries' <http://www.fao.org/in-action/vulnerable-marine-ecosystems/background/regional-fishery-bodies/en/> accessed 20 February 2021.

311 Cf. 'Chairman's Statement, Third Meeting on Central Arctic Ocean Fisheries (Nuuk, 24–26 February 2014)' (Chapter 3, n 89) 2.

312 The FAO provides a comprehensive overview of RFBs and their competence areas on their website; see 'FAO | Regional Fishery Bodies Map Viewer' <http://www.fao.org/figis/geoserver/factsheets/rfbs.html> accessed 29 January 2022.

313 Robert Owen Keohane, *After Hegemony: Cooperation and Discord in the World Political Economy* (Princeton University Press 1984) 94.

be.[314] While UNCLOS itself lacks a definition, the UNFS Agreement defines an arrangement as

> a cooperative mechanism established in accordance with the Convention and this Agreement by two or more States for the purpose, inter alia, of establishing conservation and management measures in a subregion or region for one or more straddling fish stocks or highly migratory fish stocks.[315]

As both RFMAS and RFMOS are cooperative mechanisms in this regard, and the latter only specializes that the mechanism is arranged as an organization, the term RFB is considered a broad term comprising both RFMAS and RFMOS. The concept of RFBS is further not confined to be used relating to straddling fish stocks or highly migratory fish stocks but also to shared or discrete fish stocks and other categories.[316]

RFBS either manage fish stocks by geographical area, such as e.g. the NEAFC in the North-Eastern part of the Atlantic Ocean, which are referred to as generic RFBS. Where RFBS focus on specific species of fish like deep-sea species or highly migratory species, e.g. the International Commission for the Conservation of Atlantic Tunas (ICCAT) that focuses on tuna,[317] they are called species-specific RFBS.[318] Most RFBS are open both to countries in the region with adjacent waters, the coastal States, and countries with interests in the fisheries concerned, the interest States.[319] RFB's management powers range from adopting binding measures on their members to setting catch and fishing effort limits, technical measures and controlling obligations.[320] Other RFB's only have consultative functions or focus on providing scientific support.[321]

RFBS can bring together countries in a region to provide a valuable forum for dialogue. Experiences can be coordinated and the forum can be used to initiate

---

314 Arthur A Stein, *Why Nations Cooperate: Circumstance and Choice in International Relations* (Cornell University Press 1990) 185.

315 See Article 1(1)(d) UNFS Agreement.

316 Molenaar, 'International Regulation of Central Arctic Ocean Fisheries' (Chapter 2, n 20) 444.

317 On the commission, see Chapter 6 Sections 1, 1.2, 1.2.4 *infra*.

318 Løbach and others (Chapter 4, n 87) 8.

319 See more on the concept of real interest and participation in RFBS at Chapter 3 Sections 3, 3.2 *supra*.

320 'European Commission | Regional Fisheries Management Organisations (RFMOS)' <https://ec.europa.eu/fisheries/cfp/international/rfmo_en> accessed 25 April 2020.

321 Løbach and others (Chapter 4, n 87) 65 et seq., which also provides for a list of advisory RFBS.

or implement important activities related to sustainable fisheries, capacity development and promoting cooperation with partner organizations. Further, they enable effective implementation of the FAO Code of Conduct, which urges all RFBs to participate in the promotion of good fisheries governance.[322] As a matter of principle, RFBs play a central role in ensuring that the provisions of international instruments are implemented.[323] It was for instance discussed whether to establish high seas marine protected areas as a prerogative for RFBs, and, where agreed, suggested for RFB mandates to be taken into account in the discussion on the development of the BBNJ treaty.[324] For fisheries in an international context, they certainly provide a useful management tool.

Global geographic coverage of general and species-specific RFBs per se is almost comprehensive. The coverage of general RFBs specifically, which cover all species of fish occurring in a certain area, is not quite complete yet, but is approaching completeness.[325] Where the central part of the Arctic Ocean is concerned, no exhaustive RFB has previously covered this high seas portion.[326] Only the southern part of the CAO overlaps with the NEAFC Convention Area.[327]

322 Food and Agriculture Organization of the United Nations, 'Report of the Fifth Meeting of the Regional Fishery Body Secreteriats Network (RSN-5), (Rome, 7 and 13 June 2014)' 17 <http://www.fao.org/3/a-i4210e.pdf> accessed 20 February 2020.

323 Food and Agriculture Organization of the United Nations, 'Report of the Meeting of the High-Level Panel of External Experts in Fisheries (Rome, 26–27 January 1998)' para 26 et seq. <http://www.fao.org/3/w9887e/w9887e.htm> accessed 16 June 2020; Judith Swan, 'FAO Fisheries Circular No. 995: Decision-Making in Regional Fishery Bodies or Arrangements: The Evolving Role of RFBs and International Agreement on Decision-Making Processes' (2004) <http://www.fao.org/3/y5357e/y5357e07.htm#bm7> accessed 2 April 2022; Food and Agriculture Organization of the United Nations, 'The State of World Fisheries and Aquaculture 2002' 63 et seq. <http://www.fao.org/3/a-y7300e.pdf> accessed 16 June 2020.

324 'United Nations General Assembly Resolution 69/292, Development of an International Legally Binding Instrument under UNCLOS on the Conservation and Sustainable Use of Marine Biological Diversity of Areas beyond National Jurisdiction (Adopted 19 June 2015)'; United Nations General Assembly, 'Report of the Resumed Review Conference on the Agreement for the Implementation of UNCLOS Provisions (New York, 23–27 May 2016) – A/CONF.210/2016/5' para 53 <https://documents-dds-ny.un.org/doc/UNDOC/GEN/N16/244/06/PDF/N1624406.pdf?OpenElement> accessed 4 April 2022.

325 Stefán Ásmundsson, 'Regional Fisheries Management Organisations (RFMOs): Who Are They, What Is Their Geographic Coverage on the High Seas and Which Ones Should Be Considered as General RFMOs, Tuna RFMOs and Specialised RFMOs?' (2016) 7 <https://www.cbd.int/doc/meetings/mar/soiom-2016-01/other/soiom-2016-01-fao-19-en.pdf> accessed 10 August 2021.

326 Cf. European Union, 'Policy Department B: Fisheries Management And The Arctic In The Context Of Climate Change – Study' (Chapter 2, n 149).

327 On the CAOF Agreement Area, see Chapter 2 Section 3 *supra*.

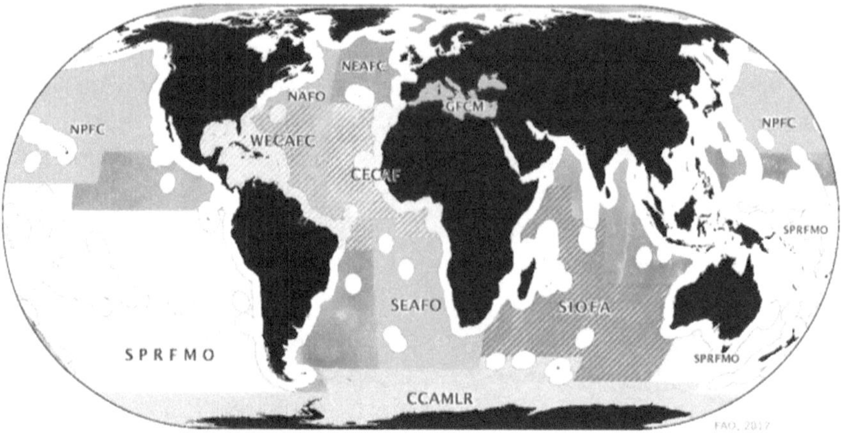

FIGURE 12 Regulatory areas of RFBs with the mandate to manage deep-sea fisheries within areas beyond national jurisdiction
SOURCE: FOOD AND AGRICULTURE ORGANIZATION OF THE UNITED NATIONS, 'REPORT OF THE TECHNICAL WORKSHOP ON DEEP-SEA FISHERIES AND VULNERABLE MARINE ECOSYSTEMS IN THE EASTERN CENTRAL ATLANTIC (DAKAR, 8–10 NOVEMBER 2016)' 5 <HTTPS://OPENKNOWLEDGE.FAO.ORG/SERVER/API/CORE/BITSTREAMS/D82C934B-E7FB-452B-BA91-4E00ACDB0BE8/CONTENT> ACCESSED 18 DECEMBER 2024

Although RFBs are considered the best multilateral instrument for managing international fisheries, they also have drawbacks. In addition to the general problem of the absence or inexperience of effective mechanisms, such as control and monitoring systems to enforce conservation and management measures,[328] there are further common problems of RFBs that should be considered, especially with regard to the implementation of the CAOF Agreement as an RFB.

One of the biggest issues is the geographical gaps in coverage. Most areas on the high seas are not covered by comprehensive RFBs that have legal authority to regulate fishing in the area. This triggers unregulated high seas fisheries in these areas adjacent to regulated areas. An imbalance of fisheries conducted and inconsistency of regulatory standards are often the result. As a long-term approach, effective RFBs should be widely in place, and compliance with their rules by all countries fishing in a given area or for a certain species should be

328 Food and Agriculture Organization of the United Nations, 'Report of the Meeting of the High-Level Panel of External Experts in Fisheries (Rome, 26–27 January 1998)' (Chapter 4, n 323) para 28.

ensured.[329] Similarly, the coverage of members is a common issue. RFB rules apply only to member States. Vessels flying flags of non-member States, including vessels flying flags of convenience, are not regulated by RFBs in RFB waters. Although RFB member countries can apply some sanctions on uncooperative non-member countries such as trade restrictions and import bans of certain types of fish products, the lack of control over non-member State's fleets is an enormous loophole in the regional fisheries management scheme. Measures are constantly at risk to be undermined by countries not party to the RFB.[330] Furthermore, while member States' fishing fleets are generally bound by the rules adopted by an RFB, enforcement of the rules is usually almost entirely left to each individual member State, making RFBs fully dependent on the good faith efforts of their members. States may additionally choose not to be bound by some of these rules, influenced by national political pressures and priorities. As an example, in the past, RFB members did often not provide information in time or did not report catches at all. Furthermore, even if RFB member States are willing to enforce rules, in order to circumvent restrictions, ship owners are free to transfer their vessels to flags of convenience.[331] This makes it difficult to implement and adhere to a uniform standard in an RFB regulatory area.

Another aspect is the ineffectiveness of quotas. A common task of RFBs is to set fishing quotas in the respective regulated area. These quotas are often without effect as they go far beyond the advice of scientists and are sometimes based on the number of the historically largest fishing opportunities, even though the fish stocks subject to the quotas have declined or are depleted.[332] Furthermore, RFBs often lack enforcement capacity. This relates first to the low enforcement mandates of RFBs, as many identify their role as research arm and advisor rather than decision-maker and enforcer. There is no comprehensive international agreement on the management authority of RFBs. A stronger overall organization and a clear mandate have been called for to stabilise RFBs. The problem was improved with the introduction of the UNFS Agreement and

329 Deep Sea Conservation Coalition, 'A Net with Holes: The Regional Fisheries Management System' (2004) 2 <http://www.savethehighseas.org/publicdocs/RFMO.pdf> accessed 20 February 2020.

330 Food and Agriculture Organization of the United Nations, 'Report of the Meeting of the High-Level Panel of External Experts in Fisheries (Rome, 26–27 January 1998)' (Chapter 4, n 323) para 28; Deep Sea Conservation Coalition (Chapter 4, n 329) 3.

331 Food and Agriculture Organization of the United Nations, 'Report of the Meeting of the High-Level Panel of External Experts in Fisheries (Rome, 26–27 January 1998)' (Chapter 4, n 323) para 28.

332 Deep Sea Conservation Coalition (Chapter 4, n 329).

additional instruments that clarified the role of RFBs, but should always be considered when the effectiveness of an RFB is questioned.[333] Second, in some cases, the lack of financial resources further hampered the execution of tasks, and as a result, decisions of RFBs were not operational.[334]

Moreover, as in most international bodies, the decision-making process is a common issue. Most RBFs require consensus to adopt regulations. As a result, decision-making is slow and decisions are often diluted to meet the lowest common denominator. Issues such as lack of political will, different national agendas, economic priorities and time horizons, and scientific uncertainties further hamper decision-making. Most of these problems are caused by a broader, heterogeneous membership consisting of both coastal States and DWF States, naturally following different interests.[335] There is further criticism that the process is not transparent and reforms are difficult to implement as they are addressed so slowly.[336] Also, the frequency of annual meetings, compared to e.g. monthly meetings of some US RFBs, was considered too low to take adequate and realistic management decisions.[337]

In summary, RFBs should be aware of the gaps in reporting and coverage of members, make decisions based on science, and consider their practical implications achieved through joint decision-making and enforcement of those decisions. All weaknesses and common problems of RFBs should be prepared for and taken into account in the implementation of the Agreement.

3.3 *Classification of the CAOF Agreement*

On the international stage, it was noticed early that potential Arctic fisheries need specific regulation. Many options were discussed, *inter alia* whether a hard law or soft law approach should be taken, the spatial scope of existing RFBs should be adjusted, an RFMO dealing with Arctic fisheries should be established,[338] a comprehensive treaty system similar to the Antarctic treaty

333 Cf. Swan (Chapter 4, n 323) s 1.2.

334 Food and Agriculture Organization of the United Nations, 'Report of the Meeting of the High-Level Panel of External Experts in Fisheries (Rome, 26–27 January 1998)' (Chapter 4, n 323) para 28.

335 Organisation for Economic Co-Operation and Development, 'Strengthening Regional Fisheries Management Organisations' (2009) 111 et seq. <https://read.oecd.org/10.1787/9789264073326-en?format=pdf> accessed 31 March 2022.

336 Deep Sea Conservation Coalition (Chapter 4, n 329).

337 Food and Agriculture Organization of the United Nations, 'Report of the Meeting of the High-Level Panel of External Experts in Fisheries (Rome, 26–27 January 1998)' (Chapter 4, n 323) para 28.

338 Papastavridis (Chapter 2, n 156) 359.

would be suitable, or an implementing agreement under UNCLOS should be created.[339] Pharand for example, already in 1991, issued the proposal of an Arctic treaty with the aim of creating a regional Arctic Council. Although not specifically focusing on fisheries – maybe due to the low likelihood of fisheries in the area at that time – Arctic cooperation in the fields of protection of the environment (including global warming and the marine environment) and on the conservation of living resources (including the involvement of Arctic native residents, with a special focus on the coordination of scientific research) were key issues.[340] Similarly, Koivurova and Molenaar developed a model agreement for the WWF.[341] The model is based upon the review of other instruments, e.g. OSPAR and the Antarctic Treaty, and focuses strongly on the Arctic Council. Yet, it proposes a varying structure, varying members, and to implement a two-tier system of addressing key principles in its main instrument and detailed substantive matters in its annexes or protocols.[342] The authors suggested a tailor-made regional legally binding instrument that gives due regard to established general principles and considerations, being overarching and "conducive to integrated, cross-sectoral ecosystem-based oceans management".[343] A new comprehensive international legal regime to govern the Arctic Ocean equivalent to the Antarctic treaty was nevertheless already waived by the Arctic Five in their 2008 Ilulissat Declaration.[344] Such a regime would likely have left much to be desired both in terms of flexibility across issues and adaptability over time.[345] Nevertheless, although the CAOF Agreement turned out to be not part of a comprehensive agreement managing the Arctic marine area, it is a multilateral regional binding agreement specifically dealing with Arctic fisheries.

Also the categorisation of the CAOF Agreement was unclear, specifically, whether it constitutes an RFMA or RFMO. According to the UNFS Agreement, an arrangement is a cooperative mechanism established in accordance with UNCLOS and the UNFS Agreement by two or more States for the purpose, *inter alia*, of establishing (sub)regional conservation and management measures

339 Koivurova and Molenaar (Chapter 3, n 32) 79 et seq.
340 Pharand (Chapter 3, n 127) 163.
341 Koivurova and Molenaar (Chapter 3, n 32) para 88 et seq.
342 Barnes (Chapter 2, n 10) 227.
343 Koivurova and Molenaar (Chapter 3, n 32) 87.
344 'Arctic Ocean Conference Ilulissat Declaration (Ilulissat, 28 May 2008)' (Chapter 3, n 78).
345 See also Oran R Young, 'Arctic Tipping Points: Governance in Turbulent Times' (2012) 41 AMBIO 75, para 82 <https://link.springer.com/article/10.1007/s13280-011-0227-4> accessed 5 December 2021.

for one or more straddling or highly migratory fish stocks.[346] Therefore, with regard to the designation of the Agreement, the CAOF Agreement is considered to constitute an RFMA: the CAOF Agreement is a multilateral instrument, established in accordance with UNCLOS and the UNFS Agreement[347] by eleven signatories,[348] for the purpose of preventing unregulated fishing of all fish stocks in the high seas portion of the CAO[349] through the application[350] of precautionary conservation and management measures.[351] Indications in the Agreement's Preamble further support this finding. The CAOF Agreement's Preamble contains a sequence of secondary clauses, often referred to as *considérants*,[352] that have a visualizing character and outline the status quo of the environmental, economic and political situation in central Arctic waters and explain the drafting States' motivations and intentions. However, a binding element expressing concrete rights or obligations is missing. Hence, the preamble serves the classic function of an introductory and explanatory part of the treaty[353] that is not legally binding.[354] Yet, it can well be considered for the Agreement's interpretation[355] and definition of its object and purpose.[356] Therefore, the references contained in the Preamble which refer to "*additional* regional or subregional fisheries management organizations

346 Article 1(d) UNFS Agreement.
347 See multiple references throughout this work.
348 Cf. Article 9(1) CAOF Agreement.
349 Cf. Article 2 CAOF Agreement.
350 See Articles 3(3), 5(1)(d) CAOF Agreement.
351 For a more detailled analysis on the nature of the CAOF Agreement, see Schatz, Proelß and Liu (Chapter 2, n 41) para 238 et seq.; Molenaar, 'Participation in the Central Arctic Ocean Fisheries Agreement' (Chapter 2, n 23) 162.
352 Makane Moïse Mbengue, 'Preamble', *Max Planck Encyclopedia of Public International Law* (2006), para. 1.
353 Cf. Rainer Lagoni, 'Preamble' in Alexander Proelß (ed), *United Nations Convention on the Law of the Sea: A Commentary* (Nomos 2017) 3.
354 Liav Orgad, 'The Preamble in Constitutional Interpretation' (2010) 8 International Journal of Constitutional Law 714, 722–726.
355 Cf. *Case Concerning the Application of the Convention of 1902 Governing the Guardianship of Infants (Netherlands v Sweden), Judgement of 28 November 1958, ICJ Reports 1958, p 55* [67]; World Trade Organization, 'Report of the Appellate Body: United States – Prohibition of Certain Shrimp and Shrimp Products (12 October 1998) – WT/DS58/AB/R' <https://docs.wto.org/dol2fe/Pages/FE_Search/FE_S_S009-DP.aspx?language=E&CatalogueIdList=58544&CurrentCatalogueIdIndex=0&FullTextSearch=> accessed 6 April 2021; *Beagle Channel Arbitration (Argentina v Chile), Award of 18 February 1977, Reports of International Arbitral Awards, Volume XXI, p 53* [19].
356 According to Article 31(2) VCLT, the context for the purpose of the interpretation of a treaty shall comprise, in addition to the text, its preamble. Further, although preambular paragraphs might not be binding themselves, a State is obliged to refrain from acts which

or arrangements"[357] and "*additional* conservation and management measures"[358] [emphasis added] that may be established supplementary to the CAOF Agreement and its conservation and management measures are considered to substantiate the conclusion that the CAOF Agreement constitutes an RFMA. As the definition of arrangement provided by the UNFS Agreement does not request a binding instrument but refers to "cooperative mechanism", already the 2015 Oslo Declaration and Draft of the CAOF Agreement arguably qualify as an RFMA.[359]

The creation of an RFMA was not intended from the outset, but presents the result of an evolving process. During the process of establishing the CAOF Agreement, it was not clear how the negotiations would turn out. Most delegations viewed the process as aiming to create less than an RFMA or RFMO, although the issue was probably not discussed in plenary at all in the early sessions. It is therefore unlikely that the Parties aimed to provide the text of the Agreement with the necessary requirements for such a body. Rather, the agreement evolved over time into an RFMA and no party intervened.[360]

4 Summary

The international law standard in Arctic waters presents itself as a compilation of internationally binding and non-binding instruments, customary law and soft-law approaches. It is not surprising that a comprehensive marine Arctic instrument was requested from various sides in order to work with a less ramified legal standard. At least for fisheries, this has been approached by the CAOF Agreement.

Until the entry into force of the CAOF Agreement, UNCLOS and the UNFS Agreement settled – and still settle for non-signatories – most issues concerning the high seas and fisheries in general. They are supported by the customary principle of the freedom of the high seas. The customary duty to cooperate further demands cooperation in all matters. For compliance, the FAO Compliance

would defeat the object and purpose of a treaty when it has signed the treaty or expressed its consent to be bound otherwise, see Article 18 VCLT.

357 See Preamble and Articles 5(1)(c)(i), 13(3), 14(1), 14(3).

358 See Preamble; cf. Articles 3(5), 5(1)(c)(ii).

359 Molenaar, 'The December 2015 Washington Meeting on High Seas Fishing in the Central Arctic Ocean' (Chapter 3, n 96) 11.

360 See, in great detail, Molenaar, 'The CAOF Agreement: Key Issues of International Fisheries Law' (Chapter 2, n 20) 468, 470 et seq.

Agreement and the PSMA are of help. Additional soft-law instruments developed by the IMO, under the Arctic Council regime or by the FAO give guidance on how to regulate specific fisheries issues and may be useful for the further development of the CAOF Agreement or affiliated arrangements. International environmental instruments like the CBD, the UN SDGs or the CMS, which deal mostly with climate change, the protection of biodiversity and the conservation and sustainable use of species, include broader biodiversity considerations and safeguard a general environmental approach. Cooperation in Arctic issues, not necessarily only fisheries related, may be sought through established mechanisms.

The foregoing section shows that there are basic regulations for fishing on the high seas. However, the main problem is that these regulations are inconsistent for the Arctic. Furthermore, not all States that want to fish in the Arctic are parties to all agreements. Therefore, a standard exists in which the respective obligations of the States differ, sometimes significantly. This shows why the CAOF Agreement is necessary: the existing gap of inconsistency needs to be closed in order to ensure effective protection of fish stocks and the environment.

Not only a legal standard, also a suitable governance approach should be followed. In international fisheries, States mostly opt for the multilateral instrument of an RFB. Likewise, the CAOF Agreement adopted the approach and is considered to present an RFMA with the task to implement management measures. The following section will consider how the CAOF Agreement performs concerning the specific elements and approaches that an RFMA should entail.

CHAPTER 5

Substantive Standards and Principles of Fisheries Management in the CAO

Although fishing opportunities in the CAO are currently scarce, it cannot be ruled out that there will be significant fishing in the area in the not too distant future. Climatic changes and the enormous size of the high seas pocket of the Arctic Ocean and nearby fisheries, on the nose and tail of the Grand Banks in the Northwest Atlantic, may create many possible fishing areas.[1] But where there is a potential for fishing, there is also a potential for unsustainable overfishing. When fishing is conducted extensively and exceeds the MSY, the adult fish population is reduced and not enough fish are left to breed and replenish their numbers. In the long term, overfishing leads to the depletion of fish from oceans and an imbalance of the oceanic ecosystem.[2]

Besides overfishing, IUU fishing and destructive fishing methods that damage the ecosystem are the main reasons for unsustainable fisheries.[3] These are driven by overcapacity.[4] The FAO describes overcapacity as "a long run phenomenon that exists when the potential output that could exist under normal operating conditions is different from a target level of production in fishery".[5] The potential of overcapacity must be reduced through long-lasting management that limits the number of participants in fisheries and relies on regulative schemes.[6] Otherwise, fishing effort and capacity tend to exceed the limit

1 Koivurova and Molenaar (Chapter 3, n 32) 76.

2 Griffin Smith, 'Overfishing' *The Earth Times* (10 January 2012) <http://www.earthtimes.org/encyclopaedia/environmental-issues/overfishing/> accessed 1 December 2020.

3 ibid.

4 Smith and Garcia (Chapter 4, n 19) R811; Food and Agriculture Organization of the United Nations, 'Report of the Expert Consultation on Catalysing the Transition Away from Overcapacity in Marine Capture Fisheries (Rome, 15–18 October 2002)' s 1.2 <https://openknowledge.fao.org/server/api/core/bitstreams/02864203-7c15-468b-b1d8-b649fb59bf80/content> accessed 2 November 2024.

5 Food and Agriculture Organization of the United Nations, 'Report of the Expert Consultation on Catalysing the Transition Away from Overcapacity in Marine Capture Fisheries (Rome, 15–18 October 2002)' (Chapter 5, n 4) s 1.2.

6 See Dominique F Gréboval, 'The Measurement and Monitoring of Fishing Capacity: Introduction and Major Considerations' <https://www.fao.org/4/y4849e/y4849e02.htm#fn1> accessed 2 November 2024.

 | DOI:10.1163/9789004700673_006

where sustainable conservation of stocks and a profitable fishing industry can coexist.[7]

Fisheries management is therefore considered a solution to counteract the potential „tragedy of the commons“[8] caused by overfishing, IUU fishing and destructive fishing methods. Traditionally,[9] this is done by concluding an agreement that either establishes new or strengthens existing RFBs.[10] When concluding an agreement in an international environmental context, additional attention must be given to the difficulty of accommodating multiple stakeholders and non-legal factors such as science, politics and moral codes.[11] Scientific consensus has proven to be conducive to agreements.[12] Another factor favouring the conclusion of an agreement is growing public interest: it is, among other things, raised where new or unknown risks occur or a catastrophic event happens, which may trigger governments to take action – just as the melting of ice in the Arctic encouraged the CAOF Agreement signatories to form an agreement.[13] Establishing the Agreement as a new RFMA that sets up fisheries management measures can therefore be regarded as the first step in combating Arctic IUU fishing and overfishing.

The fundamental goal of fisheries management is to maximize the benefits of the fish stock that is being managed. Since stocks usually exceed national boundaries, a geopolitical component is added and multiple stakeholders get involved. As already mentioned, an arrangement or institution that channels fisheries management is seen as helpful in promoting a compromise among these stakeholders. Additionally, where possible, a regional or local approach should be followed. Each management institution or arrangement further

7 Smith and Garcia (Chapter 4, n 19) R811; Cf. Food and Agriculture Organization of the United Nations, 'The State of World Fisheries and Aquaculture 2016: Contributing to Food Security and Nutrition for All' (Chapter 1, n 3) 180, 186.

8 See specifically in the introductory part of Chapter 3 *supra*.

9 As an example, for the improvement of the British white herring fisheries, and better regulation of the trade thereof, and for preventing frauds and impositions in the management of the same, in 1750, his Majesty's Royal Charter incorporated the Society of the Free British Fishery, who had the power to make by-laws on fisheries; see King George the Second, *His Majesty's Royal Charter for Incorporating the Society of the Free British Fishery* (1750) <https://catalog.hathitrust.org/Record/008604519> accessed 2 April 2022.

10 Cf. Food and Agriculture Organization of the United Nations, 'Report of the Expert Consultation on Catalysing the Transition Away from Overcapacity in Marine Capture Fisheries (Rome, 15–18 October 2002)' (Chapter 5, n 4) s 6.2.3.

11 Philippe Sands (Chapter 4, n 32) 6.

12 ibid.

13 See Robert W Hahn and Kenneth R Richards, 'The Internationalization of Environmental Regulation' (1989) 30 Harvard International Law Journal 421, 432.

necessitates supporting infrastructure. Research facilities and scientists enable management by determining the present condition of the managed stock, assessing the interaction of current management with these stocks, and provide advice on how future management will affect the sustainability of the species managed. Various fields like biology, stock dynamics, oceanography, ecosystem considerations, economics and sociology need to be considered. Further, data reporting and collection and enforcement systems need to be set up. Moreover, a consolidated management authority, consisting of one or more committees or panels responsible for decision-making, is advantageous. This assigns every player in the system with a unique task: scientists need to be capable of explaining, in a clear and concise manner, the interaction between the fishery and the stock and possible consequences of multiple management alternatives. Fishers need to report data accurately and in a timely manner. Data managers are assigned the task of arranging effective and manageable data collection instruments, and managers and enforcement agencies need to work closely to encourage uniform, fair and consistent enforcement of management plans among all participants.[14] If the knowledge used for management decisions is poor, if the economic and social impacts cause significant political problems for governments, and if people are reluctant to comply, management will most likely not be successful. Thus, transparent and participatory decision-making processes are another key management aspect.[15] Therefore, it becomes clear why a transboundary fisheries management system like an RFB must ensure that the RFB parties share a common interest and explicit objective for the conservation and management of shared fish stocks. In addition, strong links between the RFB and other international fora in order to receive high political consideration should be established. RFBs should further be based on dynamic economic models[16] so that they are flexible to respond to different management challenges in a timely and effective manner.[17]

Influenced by these considerations, regulations adapting measures for marine areas tend to follow common principles that have either traditionally proven effective or have evolved over the years as necessary for successful

14 TP Smith and MP Sissenwine, 'Fishery Management' (2001) 2 Encyclopedia of Ocean Sciences 1014, 514 et seq. <https://www.sciencedirect.com/sdfe/pdf/download/eid/3-s2.0-B9780123744739004598/first-page-pdf> accessed 27 May 2020.

15 DC Wilson and BJ McCay, 'Fishery Management, Human Dimension' (2001) 2 Encyclopedia of Ocean Sciences 1023, 527 <https://www.sciencedirect.com/sdfe/pdf/download/eid/3-s2.0-B9780123744739004604/first-page-pdf> accessed 4 April 2022.

16 Bjørndal and Munro (Chapter 4, n 47) 256.

17 Munro, Van Houtte and Willmann (Chapter 4, n 46) s 3.6.2.

FIGURE 13 Stepwise fisheries management process
SOURCE: FLEWWELLING (CHAPTER 5, N 19) S 3.3

management.[18] These form the substantial part of an overarching guiding framework, created by Flewwelling and the FAO, to provide additional assistance in developing appropriate fisheries management strategies and overcoming difficulties in their implementation.[19] Fisheries management measures are therefore based on three associated components, namely:

- Data gathering, which comprises the collection of data on biological, economic and social aspects of the fisheries and basic information on fishers, boats and gear;
- Decision-making (or fisheries management planning); and,
- Implementation; the monitoring, control and surveillance aspect of fisheries management involving both government officials and members of the fisheries community and industry.[20]

A management process, which might be applied periodically as a review process of the foregoing process, can thereby be described as follows:

As the CAOF Agreement constitutes a fisheries management measure itself, this framework can also be applied to the Agreement. Therefore, the following section outlines how the different components of the process are addressed within the CAOF Agreement. The subgroups "input", "analysis" and "advice" are dealt with under the subject of scientific research (Chapter 5 Section 1). "Advice" is again addressed in relation to the principles of fisheries management (Chapter 5 Section 2), alongside "decision-making", "management planning" and "implementation". Specific interim measures as part of the implementation process will be presented in the subsequent Chapter 6.

---

18 Principles of fisheries management will be addressed in detail under Chapter 5 Section 2 *infra*.

19 P Flewwelling, 'FAO Fisheries Technical Paper 338: An Introduction to Monitoring, Control and Surveillance Systems for Capture Fisheries' (1994) s 1 <http://www.fao.org/3/V4250E/V4250E00.htm#toc> accessed 20 July 2020; similar but more specifically, see Food and Agriculture Organization of the United Nations, 'FAO Fisheries and Aquaculture Report No. 881: Report of the Technical Consultation on International Guidelines for the Management of Deep-Sea Fisheries in the High Seas (Rome, 4–8 February and 25–29 August 2008)' para 21 <http://www.fao.org/documents/card/en/c/b02fc35e-a0c4-545a-86fb-4fc340e13b52> accessed 2 December 2020.

20 Flewwelling (Chapter 5, n 19) s 3.3.

1 Scientific Research

In line with the precautionary approach,[21] science plays a fundamental[22] yet dynamic role in fisheries management.[23] Accordingly, scientific research should focus on assessing the impacts of climate change and general environmental stressors on managed stocks.[24] The same applies within the context of the CAOF Agreement. In the time between consultations on and the possible establishment of an additional RFB managing fisheries,[25] the Agreement focuses on providing scientific advice through scientific research in order to be able to develop the best management measures possible. This is particularly relevant as there are significant gaps in scientific knowledge on fisheries and ecosystem data in the CAO.[26] For example, for the central part of the Arctic, there was not only little, but rather no winter data at all before the 2019–2020 MOSAiC expedition.[27]

In general, any State can conduct research individually or collectively in the Arctic according to the principle of the freedom of the high seas.[28] Both options have advantages and should be conducted in parallel. Coordinated, collective research allows for a broader understanding of the ecosystems and their ability and capacity to sustain fishing and other activities,[29] while research conducted by each State individually enhances the independence of research. Similarly, the CAOF Agreement encourages the Parties to conduct scientific research under the framework of the Joint Program of Scientific Research and Monitoring that is to be put in place by the Parties while not

21 See specifically on the precautionary approach Chapter 5 Sections 2, 2.1, 2.1.1 *infra*.

22 See Wilson and McCay (Chapter 5, n 15) 1023 et seq.

23 Cf. wording of Articles 5(b) and 6(3)(a), 6(3)(b), 6(7) UNFS Agreement, that request management measures to be based on the „best scientific [information/evidence] available", and Article 6(5) UNFS Agreement, stating that measures shall be revised "regularly in the light of new information".

24 See Rosemary Rayfuse, 'Addressing Climate Change Impacts in Regional Fisheries Management Organizations', *Strengthening International Fisheries Law in an Era of Changing Oceans* (Hart Publishing 2019) 268.

25 As foreseen by Article 5(1)(i) CAOF Agreement; see more on this possibility Chapter 6 Sections 1, 1.1 *infra*.

26 See e.g. 'Report of the Fifth FiSCAO Meeting on Central Arctic Ocean Fisheries (Ottawa, 24–26 October 2017)' (Chapter 2, n 161) 6 et seq.

27 See 'Video: Expedition Arktis – Ein Jahr. Ein Schiff. Im Eis.' ARD – *Das Erste* (16 November 2020) <https://www.daserste.de/information/reportage-dokumentation/erlebnis-erde/videos/expedition-arktis-video-100.html> accessed 11 December 2020.

28 See Articles 87(1)(f), 238 et seq. UNCLOS.

29 Barnes (Chapter 2, n 10) 225.

undermining marine scientific research that may be conducted under UNCLOS.[30] Additionally, research should be carried out under the Parties' national scientific programs and established programs that are already conducting research in the Arctic.[31]

Therefore, the importance of scientific research and its foundations within the framework of the CAOF Agreement will be briefly discussed first, before the various scientific research activities within the Agreement are presented.

1.1 *Significance of Scientific Research in Fisheries Management*

In line with the concept of sustainable development and the precautionary approach,[32] States are urged to make greater use of scientific advice in fisheries management in the development, adoption and implementation of conservation and management measures.[33] Such advice is generated through a longer-lasting process of data collection and scientific research.[34] In this regard, data collected through accurate and reliable reporting and monitoring of catches is considered fundamental for scientific stock assessment and the implementation of the ecosystem approach to fisheries management.[35]

Further, the likelihood of achieving agreement is said to increase with greater scientific consensus about the cause and seriousness of the relevant issue.[36] Traditionally, the existence of compelling (scientific) evidence was therefore a prerequisite.[37] However, fortunately, the consolidation of the precautionary approach[38] in environmental law has shifted away from the requirement of compelling scientific evidence,[39] which now means action can be taken even

---

30 See Articles 3(2), 3(7), 4 CAOF Agreement.

31 See Article 3(2), 4(4) CAOF Agreement.

32 On sustainable development in general, see Chapter 5 Sections 2, 2.1 *infra*. Specifically on the precautionary approach, see Chapter 5 Sections 2, 2.1, 2.1.1 *infra*.

33 See inter alia 'United Nations General Assembly Resolution 74/18, Sustainable Fisheries (Adopted 10 December 2019)' 12.

34 See e.g. the creation of the Minamata Convention on Mercury, which has been shaped through scientific and political input of the Arctic Council and its working group AMAP; see Platjouw, Steindal and Borch (Chapter 4, n 163) 229.

35 'United Nations General Assembly Resolution 73/125, Sustainable Fisheries (Adopted 11 December 2018)' 2; 'United Nations General Assembly Resolution 74/18, Sustainable Fisheries (Adopted 10 December 2019)' 2.

36 Hahn and Richards (Chapter 5, n 13) 432.

37 Philippe Sands (Chapter 4, n 32) 6.

38 On the precautionary approach, see Chapter 5 Sections 2, 2.1, 2.1.1 *infra*.

39 See e.g. Preamble 'Vienna Convention for the Protection of the Ozone Layer (Vienna, 22 March 1985) – UNTS Vol. 1513, No. 26164' <https://treaties.un.org/doc/Treaties/1988/09/19880922 03-14 AM/Ch_XXVII_02p.pdf> accessed 9 July 2021; Preamble 'Montreal Protocol on Substances That Deplete the Ozone Layer (Montreal, 16 September 1987) – UNTS Vol.

in cases of scientific uncertainty or consensus on possible environmental harm.[40] However, the precautionary approach also requests decision-making to be based on obtaining and sharing the best scientific information available. Scientific data collection and research programs should conduct environmental (impact) assessments (EIA),[41] which are best carried out in a cooperative manner,[42] thus fulfilling the duty to cooperate.[43] Furthermore, EIAs are considered a useful tool for implementing the prevention principle.[44] Also the ICJ held that

> it may now be considered a requirement under general international law to undertake an environmental assessment where there is a risk that the proposed industrial activity may have a significant adverse impact in a transboundary context, in particular, on a shared resource.[45]

Nevertheless, there are different views on the level of proof required for scientific evidence or information. The United States, for example, requires "hard

---

1522, No.26369' <https://treaties.un.org/doc/Treaties/1989/01/19890101 03-25 AM/Ch_XXVII_02_ap.pdf> accessed 9 July 2021 Article 3(3) UNFCCC, Preamble and Article 2(3) Kyoto Protocol, Articles 5(c) and 6 UNFS Agreement, Preamble Paris Agreement; and Preamble and Article 1 'Cartagena Protocol on Biosafety to the Convention on Biological Diversity (Montreal, 29 January 2000) – UNTS Vol. 2226, No. 30619' (Chapter 4, n 216).

40 See ITLOS decisions requiring a similar standard of "prudence and caution", e.g. *Southern Bluefin Tuna (New Zealand v Japan; Australia v Japan), Provisional Measures, Order of 27 August 1999, ITLOS Reports 1999, p 280* [77]; *Land Reclamation by Singapore in and Around the Straits of Johor (Malaysia v. Singapore), Provisional Measures, Order of 8 October 2003, ITLOS Reports 2003, p. 10* (Chapter 4, n 132) para 99; *MOX Plant Case (Ireland v. United Kingdom), Provisional Measures, Order of 3 December 2001, ITLOS Reports 2001, p. 95* (Chapter 4, n 132); see Philippe Sands (Chapter 4, n 32) 6.

41 See also Article 206 UNCLOS. For EIA within the precautionary approach, see Chapter 5 Sections 2, 2.1, 2.1.1, 2.1.1.1 *infra*.

42 See Neil Craik, 'The Duty to Cooperate in the Customary Law of Environmental Impact Assessment' (2020) 69 International and Comparative Law Quarterly 239, ss 240, 259 <https://www.cambridge.org/core/journals/international-and-comparative-law-quarterly/article/abs/duty-to-cooperate-in-the-customary-law-of-environmental-impact-assessment/AB1F146A96DB6DAE9B38DE669E20ADCE> accessed 12 August 2021.

43 See specifically on the duty to cooperate Chapter 4 Sections, 1, 1.2, 1.2.2 *supra* and Chapter 5 Sections 2, 2.2 *infra*.

44 Maksim Lavrik, 'Customary Norms, General Principles of International Environmental Law, and Assisted Migration as a Tool for Biodiversity Adaptation to Climate Change' (2022) 4 Jus Cogens 99 <https://doi.org/10.1007/s42439-022-00055-8> accessed 4 May 2024; on the distinction of the principles, see Chapter 5 Sections 2, 2.1, 2.1.1, 2.1.1.1 *infra*.

45 *Case Concerning Pulp Mills on the River Uruguay (Argentina v Uruguay), Judgement of 20 April 2010, ICJ Reports 2010, p 14* [204].

science" to be necessary, fearing that the scientific basis will otherwise be weakened.[46] The EU, on the other hand, relies on a broader margin of appreciation in the identification of scientific evidence and focuses on early risk assessment beyond the traditional use of EIA.[47] In the CAOF Agreement, a "sound"[48] scientific basis is required before commercial fishing may be allowed in CAO waters.[49] Based on the various aspects of research in the Agreement that are discussed in detail below, it is argued that "sound" research means that the research is compiled over a longer period of time by several independent sources using several methods and is therefore particularly reliable.

1.2 *Basis of Scientific Research Activities under the CAOF Agreement*

Article 3(4) CAOF Agreement sets up certain basic prerequisites for scientific research activities, involving the catching of fish, in the course of interim measures, hence until a possible new RFB is created. In this respect, in line with the rationale of Article 18(a)[50] VCLT,[51] States conducting scientific research activities shall ensure that the Agreement's objective, the prevention of both commercial and exploratory unregulated fishing and the protection of healthy marine ecosystems,[52] are not undermined. In this regard, the provision encourages the Parties to inform each other about their plans for authorising scientific research activities, which can be seen as part of a code of conduct. As a rather fragile construct depending on the Parties goodwill, the CAOF Agreement is based on trust and cooperation without which its implementation would not be possible. The exchange of information among the Parties

46 Christian Gollier and Nicolas Treich, 'Decision-Making Under Scientific Uncertainty: The Economics of the Precautionary Principle' (2003) 27 The Journal of Risk and Uncertainty 77, 77.

47 Philippe Sands (Chapter 4, n 32) 7.

48 See Article 5(1)(d)(iii) CAOF Agreement.

49 This has already been supported by most States beforehand. See for instance the United States, United States Congress (Chapter 2, n 163); North Pacific Fishery Management Council (Chapter 2, n 17); Inuit Circumpolar Council, 'Kitigaaryuit Declaration (Kitigaaryuit, 24 July 2014)' (Chapter 3, n 300); or the EU that urged to "prevent fisheries developing in a regulatory vacuum", see European Union, 'Communication from the Commission to the European Parliament and the Council – The European Union and the Arctic Region (20 November 2008) – COM/2008/0763 Final' (Chapter 2, n 80).

50 Article 18(a) VCLT stipulates that a State is obliged to refrain from acts which would defeat the object and purpose of a treaty when it has signed the treaty.

51 'Vienna Convention on the Law of Treaties (Vienna, 23 May 1969) – UNTS Vol. 1155, No. 18232' <https://treaties.un.org/doc/publication/unts/volume1155/volume-1155-i-18232-english.pdf> accessed 9 July 2021.

52 See Article 2 CAOF Agreement.

on when and how fishing (for scientific purposes) will be conducted is a necessary tool to keep the character of conducting fishing in the CAO exceptional. Further, in that way, research activities by different States can be combined and, as a result, improved. In addition, considering the difficult conditions in the Arctic, collaborations regarding material and cost sharing are beneficial for all participants. This renders the exchange of information and research results attractive for everyone involved.

1.3 *Joint Program of Scientific Research and Monitoring*

The collection and assessment of data is essential for determining fisheries management measures,[53] but time-consuming. Furthermore, the harsh conditions in the Arctic make it even more difficult to evaluate scientific information. Frequently criticised was that there are still significant data gaps on certain key parts of the Arctic Ocean beyond national jurisdiction[54] and on certain Arctic species and their response to environmental change.[55] Soon, it became apparent that a mechanism for collecting and sharing specific data exceeding voluntary collaboration had to be established.[56]

Prior to the conclusion of the CAOF Agreement, the ten negotiating parties had the understanding that multiple research steps had to be taken. They first agreed on designing a mapping program, where mapping refers to "initial data collection and analysis in the High Seas CAO to create a snapshot of the diversity, distributions and relative abundances of fishes and invertebrates, and their supporting or reliant ecosystem components (e.g., habitats and food web)". Further, a monitoring program should be designed, where monitoring involves "data collection to assess temporal variability in species abundances and supporting ecosystem components over time".[57] This understanding was put into practice: prior to the fourth FiSCAO meeting in 2017 in Tromsø,

53 Cf. wording of Articles 5(b), 6(3)(a), 6(3)(b), and 6(7) UNFS Agreement, that request management measures to be based on the "best scientific [information/evidence] available", and Article 6(5) UNFS Agreement, stating that measures shall be revised "regularly in the light of new information".

54 CBD Conference of the Parties and Conservation of Arctic Flora and Fauna (CAFF) Working Group (Chapter 2, n 126) 50.

55 'Report of the First FiSCAO Meeting on Central Arctic Ocean Fisheries (Anchorage, 15–17 June 2011)' (Chapter 2, n 161) 2.

56 See e.g. 'Report of the Third FiSCAO Meeting on Central Arctic Ocean Fisheries (Seattle, 14–16 April 2015)' (Chapter 3, n 92) 9 et seq.; 'Report of the Fifth FiSCAO Meeting on Central Arctic Ocean Fisheries (Ottawa, 24–26 October 2017)' (Chapter 2, n 161) 39.

57 'Chairman's Statement, Fifth FiSCAO Meeting on Central Arctic Ocean Fisheries (Ottawa, 24–26 October 2017)' (Chapter 3, n 310) 1.

participants collected existing data and analyses of the CAO available from scientific organizations of the negotiating parties, which allowed for a broader scientific analysis of the CAO environment and identified the priorities for research and monitoring gaps.[58] The fifth FiSCAO meeting in 2018 assessed the development of methods and data and proposed several options for the way forward. *Inter alia*, implementing a specific working group or delegating the task to an existing one was suggested, which culminated in the Joint Program of Scientific Research and Monitoring (JPSRM).[59]

In addition, the process identified resource needs. These included human resources, vessels and equipment for mapping and monitoring. Preliminary cost estimates for these tasks were provided, including example budgets, based on experiences with similar programs of the participants.[60] In line with Article 119(2) UNCLOS,[61] the approach of the negotiating parties to the CAOF Agreement was to create a mechanism of collecting, sharing, and hosting data protocols while striking a balance between making these data available for assessment and protecting the respective ownership rights.[62] As a result, the JPSRM was established and implemented in the CAOF Agreement.

As a basis for the JPSRM, Article 4(1) CAOF Agreement encourages the Parties to facilitate cooperation in scientific activities with the goal of increasing knowledge of the living marine resources of the CAO and the ecosystems in which they occur. The JPSRM is outlined in more detail in the following paragraphs of the same article, in particular the aspect of how scientific data are collected and evaluated within the program. Since collaboration can vary in form and shape, the program allows for everything from financial support to sharing equipment to exchanging scientific knowledge – in short, anything that helps to increase knowledge about the CAO ecosystem and its living marine resources.

---

58 'Report of the Fourth FiSCAO Meeting on Central Arctic Ocean Fisheries (Tromsø, 26–28 September 2016)' (Chapter 2, n 134) 81.

59 'Report of the Fifth FiSCAO Meeting on Central Arctic Ocean Fisheries (Ottawa, 24–26 October 2017)' (Chapter 2, n 161) 19.

60 ibid 20–26.

61 Article 119(2) UNCLOS encourages States, when dealing with the conservation of fish stocks on the high seas, to contribute and exchange available scientific information, catch and fishing effort statistics, and other data relevant to the conservation on a regular basis.

62 'Report of the Fifth FiSCAO Meeting on Central Arctic Ocean Fisheries (Ottawa, 24–26 October 2017)' (Chapter 2, n 161) 27.

1.3.1 Outline of the Program

According to Article 4(2) CAOF Agreement, the Parties should establish the JPSRM within two years of the entry into force of the Agreement and thus by June 2023. In this regard, the wording "the Parties agree to establish" leaves no room for an optional establishment. The JPSRM is to be organized by the Parties as a scientific advisory body and is supposed to continue the work conducted previously by the scientific FiSCAO meetings. The aim of creating such program is, concurrent with the Agreement's objective,[63] to improve the understanding of the ecosystems in the Agreement Area while fishing in the CAO is still unlikely. Its main tasks are the mapping of the ecosystem, monitoring of long-term trends and to identify infrastructure and resource needs in order to reduce scientific uncertainty.[64]

In this respect, Article 4(2) CAOF Agreement addresses the central issue of the Agreement. Fisheries agreements usually deal with actual fisheries, not only potential fisheries. It is therefore crucial to first establish whether there are fish in CAO waters at all and, if this is actually the case, what types of stocks exist. As of 2022, likely due to the difficult accessibility of the area, little scientific evidence could be gathered supporting the existence of specific fish stocks.

Second, where it is found that fish stocks exist, it is to determine whether these stocks exist in the CAO only now or will likely exist in these waters in the future. Climate change in particular can have a major impact in this regard. Stocks existing in specific areas at present might not be living in the same areas in the future. For instance, already an increase of 2–4°C (3,6–7,2°F) in water temperature might cause the movement of an entire stock towards waters up to 16° latitude away from their original habitat.[65]

Third, the program should identify whether harvesting fish stocks is possible. The fact that stocks might be identified does not necessarily mean that they can be harvested, e.g. due to their habitat being inaccessible because it's too deep, or the ice cover is too thick, or the technical features are not sufficient.

Fourth, if harvesting is possible, it must be determined whether it is possible on a sustainable basis.[66] The goal of sustainability is addressed at several

63 See Article 2 CAOF Agreement: "The objective of this Agreement is to prevent unregulated fishing in the high seas portion of the central Arctic Ocean through the application of precautionary conservation and management measures as part of a long-term strategy to safeguard healthy marine ecosystems and to ensure the conservation and sustainable use of fish stocks."

64 See Gold (Chapter 2, n 143) s 15.

65 See Rose (Chapter 2, n 161) 1528 et seq.

66 For sustainable development, see specifically Chapter 5 Sections 2, 2.1 *infra*.

points throughout the Agreement. Reference is made to sustainable management and sustainable use of fish stocks.[67] In this regard, sustainable can be interpreted as a means of, or relating to, harvesting or using a resource so that the resource is not depleted or permanently damaged.[68] In the CAO, harvesting may only be permitted up to the level of sustainability. Defining this level will be the key issue for fisheries in CAO waters, on which all Parties will want to have a say. The harvesting of fish stocks must therefore take into account a stock's quantity, distribution and development. Fishing overcapacity is a considerable issue in this regard. The fact that IUU fishing leads to excess fishing capacity is "rather obvious [...]: the more vessels, the less fish, the larger the tendency to engage in IUU fishing so as to preserve adequate return on fishing activities", whereas IUU fishing in turn is often related to insufficient control or inappropriate management schemes.[69] This means that the level of fishing must commensurate with the sustainability of fish stocks, which can be managed by ongoing capacity assessment and management plans, the establishment of target levels or by creating incentives for voluntary reduction.[70] The FAO's voluntary International Plan of Action for the Management of Fishing Capacity (IPOA-CAPACITY), which was elaborated within the framework of the FAO Code of Conduct, can provide further guidance in this regard.[71] The IPOA-CAPACITY calls on States and RFBs facing an overcapacity problem to first limit fishing capacity to current levels and gradually reduce it for affected fisheries. In the long run, growth in capacity undermining long-term sustainability objectives should be avoided.[72] The plan suggests strategies,[73] principles and approaches.[74] Urgent actions are promoted in Part III IPOA-CAPACITY,

67 See e.g. Preamble, Article 2, Article 3(1)(a), Article 5(1)(c) CAOF Agreement, and reference to sustainable marine ecosystems in general in the Preamble.

68 'Merriam Webster Dictionary | Sustainable' <https://www.merriam-webster.com/dictionary/sustainable> accessed 5 December 2021.

69 Dominique F Gréboval, 'International Plan of Action for the Management of Fishing Capacity and Selected Issues Pertaining to Illegal, Unreported and Unregulated Fishing' (2000) <http://www.fao.org/3/y3274e/y3274e0f.htm> accessed 6 August 2020.

70 'United Nations General Assembly Resolution 73/125, Sustainable Fisheries (Adopted 11 December 2018)' 23; United Nations General Assembly, 'Report of the Resumed Review Conference on the Agreement for the Implementation of UNCLOS Provisions (New York, 23–27 May 2016) – A/CONF.210/2016/5' 37; 'United Nations General Assembly Resolution 64/72, Sustainable Fisheries (Adopted 4 December 2009)' 14.

71 Food and Agriculture Organization of the United Nations, 'International Plan of Action for the Management of Fishing Capacity (Rome, 22 July 1998)' <http://www.fao.org/3/X3170E/x3170e04.htm> accessed 6 April 2022.

72 See para. 7 IPOA-CAPACITY.

73 See para. 8 IPOA-CAPACITY.

74 See para. 9 IPOA-CAPACITY.

followed by mechanisms to promote implementation.[75] When determining the question as to whether harvesting is possible on a sustainable basis within the JPSRM, these considerations should be taken into account – not least because the Agreement recalls relevant FAO instruments.[76]

Fifth and last, under the JPSRM, the Parties should determine the possible impacts of sustainable fishing in the CAO on the ecosystems of the Agreement Area. This issue will likely be touched upon already when determining the sustainability of harvesting, as the existence of living resources is closely linked to the ecosystem. However, impacts on the ecosystems should be separately dealt with and anticipated before taking action is too late, thus following the recurring pre-emptive and preventive approach of the CAOF Agreement.[77]

These five aspects of the program form the basis of a comprehensive mechanism. However, the mechanism must also be implemented. According to Article 4(3) CAOF Agreement, this task is entrusted to the Parties as guardians of the Agreement. They should guide the development, coordination and implementation of the JPSRM. The Parties are therefore encouraged to actively and cooperatively establish the program, implement it and adapt it to achieve sustainable fishing in the CAO at any point.

Article 4(4) CAOF Agreement requests the Parties to ensure that the JPSRM takes into account the work of relevant scientific and technical organizations, bodies and programs, as well as indigenous and local knowledge. Relevant organizations likely refer to organizations that are able to contribute to collect pertinent data, e.g. ICES, PICES or relevant working groups of the Arctic Council.[78] In doing that, the provision implements references made in the Preamble that recall UNDRIP, the importance of involving indigenous peoples and communities and their interests in the long-term conservation and sustainable use of Arctic living marine resources and in healthy marine ecosystems, and the use of their knowledge of these resources and the ecosystems of the CAO.[79] Similar reference is also made in Article 5(2) CAOF Agreement, where the Parties are encouraged to form committees or similar bodies in which representatives of Arctic communities, including Arctic indigenous peoples, may

75 Part IV IPOA-CAPACITY.

76 See Preamble CAOF Agreement.

77 Concerning the anticipatory nature of the CAOF Agreement, see Chapter 5 Sections 2, 2.1, 2.1.1 *infra*.

78 Relevant programs are presented at Chapter 5 Sections 1, 1.6, 1.6.2 *infra*.

79 General references to make use of scientific knowledge while conducting research and taking it as a basis for fisheries conservation and management are further made in the Preamble, Articles 2(2), 5(1)(b) and (c), 5(d)(iii) and Article 5(2) CAOF Agreement.

participate to promote the implementation of the Agreement and the JPSRM. Overall, Article 4(4) CAOF Agreement ensures the transfer of knowledge and cooperation among diverse actors. In particular, it is important to see that the Parties have acknowledged that local communities and their long experience in the region can provide a wealth of knowledge that will likely be useful for the future program.

1.3.2 Data Sharing Protocol

As part of the JPSRM, Article 4(5) CAOF Agreement encourages the Parties to adopt a data sharing protocol and share relevant data, thus furthering strong cooperation among the participants on a scientific level. Data reporting is considered a critical component in monitoring fisheries and is vital for better stock assessments, implementation of the ecosystem approach and enforcement to meet compliance efforts.[80] A lack of data and insufficient data reporting represent key challenges in estimating stocks and defining precautionary reference points for stocks rebuilding.[81] The CAOF Agreement successfully counteracts this issue by implementing data sharing provisions from the start.

The data sharing protocol under the CAOF Agreement is to be adopted within two years of the entry into force of the Agreement. This creates a defined time frame for the Parties to conduct research and process and prepare data that can be presented within a protocol to the other Parties and help to conduct further research. In order to prevent double workload, it might be even more effective if such a protocol is shared among the Parties at an earlier point, and includes information on what kind of research is carried out and in what manner. Nevertheless, it is reasonable that research must be coordinated (individually) first. Further, where multiple States or organizations collect similar data, this data can be compared, which in itself serves as a first review step. In any case, in order to maintain national interests, the time frame of two years seems adequate to allow for trial-and-error expeditions of each State. Once the data protocol is implemented, data can be shared almost immediately.

Further, Article 4(5) CAOF Agreement requests the CAOF Agreement Parties to share relevant data. Data may be considered relevant where they serve the

---

80 Daniela Diz and others, 'Summary of the Resumed Review Conference of the UN Fish Stocks Agreement (24–28 May 2010)' (2010) 7 Earth Negotiations Bulletin 65, 12 <http://www.iisd.ca/oceans/rfsaic/> accessed 30 May 2020.

81 Catherine Wahlén and others, 'Summary of the Resumed Review Conference of the UN Fish Stocks Agreement (23–27 May 2016)' (2016) 7 Earth Negotiations Bulletin 71, 12 <https://enb.iisd.org/events/resumed-unfsa-review-conference/summary-report-23-27-may-2016> accessed 5 December 2024.

object and purpose of the JPSRM: either where they serve the improvement of the understanding of the ecosystems of the Agreement Area, or are of help for determining whether fish stocks that could be harvested on a sustainable basis might exist in the Agreement Area now or in the future, or for determining the possible impacts of such fisheries on the ecosystems of the Agreement Area.[82] The data should be shared directly or via relevant scientific and technical organizations, bodies, and programs,[83] including ICES and PICES,[84] in accordance with the data protocol. It is expected that the data protocol will specify the requirements for the data to be used, such as the origin of the data, i.e. who collected and transmitted it, how it is processed and what its content is.

1.4 *Joint Scientific Meetings*

Pursuant to Article 4(6) CAOF Agreement, the Parties shall hold joint scientific meetings to present the results of their research, review the best available scientific information, and provide timely scientific advice to meetings of the Parties. In the context of cooperation, meetings play an important role as they establish a forum for the Parties to openly discuss the research conducted. Parties can learn from successes and mistakes of other Parties and adjust and carry out their research in a more effective way. Furthermore, for the successful operation of the JPSRM, reviewing the best available scientific information is considered key. Such review can help to implement additional programs, serve as a basis for ongoing research and improve research in general. The insights gained through open discussions can afterwards be used to provide concrete advice in the meetings of the Parties.

The scientific meetings should take place at least every two years. This time frame seems appropriate as long as a certain information exchange through the data protocol is ensured more frequently. Pursuant to the Agreement, the scientific meetings should take place at least two months before the meetings of the Parties, which are also to be conducted every two years.[85] This timeframe is considered necessary for the Parties to be able to submit (new) scientific advice and to prepare the data collected so that it can be presented at the meetings of the Parties at least two months later.

Scientific meetings under the CAOF Agreement may be held in person or by other means. This modern approach is welcomed as it leaves it up to the Parties to decide how to organise the meetings. As has been shown in recent

82 See Article 4(2) CAOF Agreement.

83 See same reference in Article 4(4) CAOF Agreement.

84 Relevant programs are presented at Chapter 5, Sections 1, 1.6, 1.6.2 *infra*.

85 See Article 5(1) CAOF Agreement.

years during the COVID-19 pandemic, video call meetings provide an option to meet digitally without consuming resources, money and time.

Article 4(6) CAOF Agreement further provides that the Parties shall adopt terms of reference and other procedures for the functioning of the joint scientific meetings. These will surely increase the effectiveness of the meetings and serve as an opportunity to implement further programs and cooperative activities like working groups or task forces and to adopt general organizational terms. Article 4(6) CAOF Agreement foresees the terms to be established within two years of the entry into force of the Agreement by June 2023 and as such just in time before the first scientific meeting and general meeting of the Parties should take place.

1.5 *Marine Scientific Research under UNCLOS*

Article 3(7) CAOF Agreement states that apart from Article 3(4),[86] nothing in the CAOF Agreement shall be interpreted to restrict the entitlements of the Parties in relation to marine scientific research as reflected in UNCLOS.

As a matter of principle, UNCLOS guarantees States the right and freedom to conduct marine scientific research on the high seas.[87] Most importantly, Articles 255–257 UNCLOS stipulate the right of all States to conduct scientific marine research in areas beyond national jurisdiction, and States shall facilitate such research and assist marine scientific research vessels by, for example, giving access to their harbours and promoting assistance. Articles 258–265 UNCLOS describe scientific research installations or equipment in the marine environment, enabling the establishment of safety zones around scientific research installations. Article 263 UNCLOS deals with responsibility and liability in the context of research, and Articles 264–265 UNCLOS present the settlement of disputes and interim measures pending such settlement.

However, it is debated whether scientific research requirements established by an RFB in relation to fisheries take precedence over respective UNCLOS provisions. Article 4 UNFS Agreement makes clear that this is not the case:[88] research within the framework of an RFB does not exempt States from complying with the general rules set up by UNCLOS. The bottom line is that research can be conducted in parallel as long as the basic UNCLOS rules are followed. Also under the CAOF Agreement, an RFB itself, research activities under

86 Article 3(4) CAOF Agreement states that conducting scientific research in the CAO may not undermine the prevention of unregulated fishing in the Agreement Area but ensure the protection of healthy marine ecosystems.

87 See Articles 87(1)(f), 238 UNCLOS.

88 See in detail Schatz, Proelß and Liu (Chapter 2, n 41) 230 et seq.

UNCLOS should be carried out in parallel with respective research activities taken under the CAOF Agreement.

1.6 *Supplementary Research Activities in the Marine Arctic*

According to the CAOF Agreement, Parties shall additionally conduct scientific research under their respective national programs[89] and take into account, especially under the JPSRM, the work of relevant scientific and technical organizations, bodies and programs.[90] In fact, although the Arctic is a remote area, research has been and is being carried out there, albeit not on a large scale.

While the history of indigenous peoples in the Arctic goes back several thousand years, it was not until the 18th century that serious scientific exploration of the Arctic began. One major step for both multidisciplinary but also multinational polar research was the first International Polar Year (IPY) in 1882, which was initiated to organize various stations of eleven countries around the northern polar region. During one year, different observations using identical devices and methods were simultaneously performed. The IPY focused on studying weather at high northern latitudes, it effects on the global climate, ice drift far from the coast, and geomagnetic phenomena around the northern magnetic pole. Scientists coordinated national programs, organized expeditions and created winter camps and observatories at transpolar points of major significance for science. Results were published in the following years in 36 large volumes. These data formed the basis for further long-term research on physical processes on the planet. Based thereupon, the second IPY took place in 1932 with more than forty countries and new technology involved.[91] The approach continued with the International Geophysical Year, also referred to as the third IPY, in 1957 with 67 nations participating. In 2007, with the active involvement of more than 60 nations and participants from numerous scientific disciplines and institutions, the fourth IPY was conducted, representing the most comprehensive and sophisticated effort undertaken in polar research so far.[92] Therefore, over the years, a factual basis for cooperative research in the field of Arctic fisheries has been created.

---

89 See Article 3(2) CAOF Agreement.

90 See Article 4(4) CAOF Agreement.

91 OM Raspopov, IA Kuz'min and EP Kharin, 'The 50th Anniversary of International Geophysical Year (1957–1958): From the First International Polar Year (1882–1883) to the International Heliophysical Year (2007–2008) and International Polar Year (2007–2009)' (2007) 47 Geomagnetism and Aeronomy 1, 1–2 <https://link-springer-com.emedien.ub.uni-muenchen.de/article/10.1134/S001679320701001X> accessed 24 March 2022.

92 United States National Research Council and Polar Research Board, 'Lessons and Legacies of International Polar Year 2007–2008' (2012) 9 <https://ebookcentral-1proquest-1com-1008395e10318.emedia1.bsb-muenchen.de/lib/bsb/detail.action?docID=3564278#> accessed 24 March 2022.

The legal basis for Arctic research activities is the right and freedom to conduct marine scientific research on the high seas.[93] However, the space to conduct research freely is restricted by the Arctic coastal States' EEZs. It is recalled, however, that the Arctic States have committed themselves to developing international cooperation and promoting freedom of scientific research in marine areas. Research should further be consistent with both the States interests and the interests of local and indigenous Arctic peoples.[94] Cooperation on scientific activities in the Arctic should be promoted not only on Arctic high seas, but also in areas under national jurisdiction.[95] Therefore, the Parties should not only carry out national and cooperative research activities, but additional research programs must be considered.

1.6.1 National Research Activities

Many States have long been setting up research institutes to deal with Arctic research or even strategies for such research. In the following, the strategies of three States with different backgrounds will be presented:[96] Germany, as a State part of an association of States, Norway, as a coastal State, and China, as a DWF State.

Germany, indirect party to the Agreement via the EU, is engaged in polar research through the Alfred-Wegener-Institut (AWI) that collects long-term polar data. Among other things, it operates the research icebreaker Polarstern,[97] and, jointly with France, the research aircrafts Polar 5, Polar 6 and the Arctic research station AWIPEV.[98] Germany is further involved in

93 See Articles 87(1)(f), 238 UNCLOS.

94 Federal Foreign Office Germany (Chapter 2, n 250) 9; Federal Foreign Office Germany (Chapter 2, n 89) 29.

95 See Article 1 of the 2017 Arctic Council Agreement on Enhancing International Arctic Scientific Cooperation that engages the parties to 'enhance cooperation in Scientific Activities in order to increase effectiveness and efficiency in the development of scientific knowledge about the Arctic'. The geographic scope defined in Annex I thereby refers to areas under the jurisdiction of the participating States; see 'Arctic Council Agreement on Enhancing International Arctic Scientific Cooperation (Fairbanks, 11 May 2017)' <https://oaarchive.arctic-council.org/handle/11374/1916> accessed 9 July 2021.

96 For a detailed account of activities, see 'Report of the First FiSCAO Meeting on Central Arctic Ocean Fisheries (Anchorage, 15–17 June 2011)' (Chapter 2, n 161) 3–8; 'Report of the Second FiSCAO Meeting on Central Arctic Ocean Fisheries (Tromsø, 28–31 October 2013)' (Chapter 2, n 161) 13 et seq.

97 See more on the MOSAiC expedition conducted on the Polarstern at Chapter 7 *infra*.

98 Federal Foreign Office Germany (Chapter 2, n 89) 27.

Arctic research through a number of routes: through the Federal Institute for Geosciences and Natural Resources, which researches structures in the earth crust; the International Arctic Science Committee; research programs of the EU; and through its participation in the Nordic Council, Arctic Council and the European Polar Board.[99] In addition, Germany issued a research strategy paper named Rapid Climate Change in the Arctic: Polar Research as a Global Responsibility,[100] in line with the Federal Government's research program MARE:N – Coastal, Marine and Polar Research for Sustainability.[101]

Norway has a long tradition of national research expeditions. In 1893, the Norwegian researcher Fridtjof Nansen set out with a team of explorers and scientists to study the Arctic Ocean on a research vessel. After three years, they returned with new knowledge that significantly shaped our concepts and understanding of the Arctic Ocean.[102] To continue this heritage, a unique comprehensive Arctic research collaboration of ten Norwegian research institutions, the Nansen Legacy, was established. It provides joint scientific knowledge of the marine environment and resources of the Barents Sea and adjacent Arctic Basin through the 21st century as a basis for sustainable management. Studies touch upon various fields and include the investigation of fish populations. *Inter alia*, variations of fish species, the predictability of temperature and fish stocks in the Barents Sea, their seasonal dynamics and spatial distribution are investigated. From 2018 to 2022, the Nansen Legacy will conduct 15 scientific cruises and spend at least 350 days in the northern Barents Sea and adjacent Arctic Ocean.[103] Great contributions to research in the Arctic are expected from this expedition – also findings that can be important for future measures under the CAOF Agreement.

China's focus in polar research was primarily on Antarctica,[104] and Chinese Arctic projects have only recently received more funding and

99 Federal Foreign Office Germany (Chapter 2, n 250) 9 et seq.

100 Bundesministerium für Bildung und Forschung / Federal Ministry of Education and Research (BMBF), 'Rapid Climate Change in the Arctic: Polar Research as a Global Responsibility' (2012) <http://www.bmbf.de> accessed 5 August 2020.

101 Federal Ministry of Education and Research Germany, 'Mare:N – Coastal, Marine and Polar Research for Sustainability – German Federal Government Research Program' (2020) <https://www.foerderinfo.bund.de/SharedDocs/Publikationen/de/bmbf/FS/31356_Mare_N_en.pdf?__blob=publicationFile&v=4> accessed 2 November 2024.

102 Reigstad, Eldevik and Gerland (Chapter 2, n 187).

103 Nansen Legacy, 'Annual Report' (2019) 4, 12, 17, 26–29, 32, 40 <https://arvenetternansen.com/wp-content/uploads/2020/06/Nansen-Legacy-AR2019-web.pdf> accessed 22 July 2021.

104 See Anne Marie Brady, 'China's Rise in Antarctica?' (2010) 50 Asian Survey 759, 761 et seq. <https://www.jstor.org/stable/10.1525/as.2010.50.4.759> accessed 25 March 2022.

attention – however, with great interest.[105] This can be attributed to China's shift in its position to a global power: China's economic rise in the late 1970s gave it political confidence to demand being involved in regional governance worldwide, including the Arctic. Moreover, understandably, China increasingly feels and fears the impact of Arctic climate change on agriculture or rising sea levels, which threaten the coastal centres of its economy.[106] China regularly conducts Arctic explorations on its scientific icebreakers Xue Long 1 and Xue Long 2.[107] It further formulated an Arctic strategy in 2018, which emphasizes the importance of scientific research, environmental protection, sea passages and natural resources in the area.[108] In fact, China has successfully implemented a wide independent Arctic scientific research program.[109] In building its Arctic identity, the country emphasized its right to conduct scientific research and to explore and exploit natural resources, including fish, in the high Arctic waters, and formed international partnerships with other nations interested in monitoring Arctic climate and environmental changes. In 2020, besides national research centres like the Polar Research Institute of China in Shanghai, China operated research stations on Svalbard and Iceland, an overseas land satellite receiving station in Sweden, and planned to collaborate with Finland to establish a joint research centre for Arctic space observation and data sharing services.[110]

1.6.2 Cooperative Research Activities

Apart from national research activities, cooperative research has also increased over time. Regimes like the Arctic Council or the European Polar Board conduct

105 Linda Jakobson, 'Analysis Brief: Northeast Asia Turns Its Attention to the Arctic' *National Bureau of Asian Research* (17 December 2012) <https://www.nbr.org/publication/northe ast-asia-turns-its-attention-to-the-arctic/#:~:text=Linda Jakobson%2C Director of the,%2C Japan%2C and South Korea.> accessed 5 August 2021.

106 Michael Evan Goodsite and others, 'The Role of Science Diplomacy: A Historical Development and International Legal Framework of Arctic Research Stations under Conditions of Climate Change, Post-Cold War Geopolitics and Globalization/Power Transition' (2016) 6 Journal of Environmental Studies and Sciences 645, 646 <https://link-springer-com.emedien.ub.uni-muenchen.de/article/10.1007/s13412-015-0329-6> accessed 25 March 2022.

107 Malte Humpert, 'China Reveals Details of Newly Designed Heavy Icebreaker' *High North News* (16 December 2019) <https://www.highnorthnews.com/en/china-reveals-deta ils-newly-designed-heavy-icebreaker> accessed 5 August 2020.

108 State Council of the People's Republic of China (Chapter 3, n 236).

109 Frédéric Lasserre, Linyan Huang and Olga V. Alexeeva, 'China's Strategy in the Arctic: Threatening or Opportunistic?' (2017) 53 Polar Record 31, 32.

110 Kopra (Chapter 3, n 235).

specific research, e.g. through working groups or action groups.[111] Further, in the IPY 2007, international researchers from all around the world operated expeditions and collected extensive amounts of data about the Arctic (and Antarctic) region.[112] Cooperation with Arctic indigenous residents has also been improved, and technical innovations through remote sensing now enable comprehensive and uninterrupted data collection via satellites and aircraft, especially where in-person data collection is too complex.[113]

Article 4(4) CAOF Agreement requests the Agreement's Parties to take into account "the work of relevant scientific and technical organizations, bodies and programs". In the scientific meetings during the CAOF Agreement's establishment process, it was agreed that existing scientific bodies and (sub)Arctic working groups like the Pacific Arctic Group,[114] Arctic Council working groups, ICES, PICES and the joint Barents Sea Norwegian-Russian survey,[115] could provide support for data monitoring and research, and can hence be considered as such bodies. In addition, links should be established between the Agreement's bodies and these groups to avoid duplication of effort and to share data.[116] Currently, there are a number of cooperative research activities conducted by such bodies and programs in the Arctic worth mentioning.

1.6.2.1 *International Council for the Exploration of the Sea and North Pacific Marine Science Organization*

Within the establishment process of the CAOF Agreement, delegations were unsure as to whether the Agreement should have its own scientific body or rely on existing bodies.[117] While European delegations mainly considered ICES

111 'Arctic Council | Working Groups' <https://arctic-council.org/en/about/working-groups/> accessed 22 May 2020; 'European Polar Board | Action Groups' <http://www.europeanpolarboard.org/activities/action-groups/> accessed 30 June 2021.

112 See United States National Research Council and Polar Research Board (Chapter 5, n 92).

113 'National Snow and Ice Data Center | Studying Arctic Climate' <https://nsidc.org/cryosphere/arctic-meteorology/studying.html> accessed 17 January 2022.

114 The Pacific Arctic Group is a group of institutes and individuals organized under the International Arctic Science Committee having a Pacific perspective on Arctic science, see 'PAG Arctic Portal | The Pacific Arctic Group' <https://pag.arcticportal.org/> accessed 18 December 2021.

115 D Protozorkevich and GI van der Meeren, 'Survey Report from the Joint Norwegian/Russian Ecosystem Survey in the Barents Sea and Adjacent Waters (August-October 2019)' (2020) <https://www.hi.no/resources/IMR-PINRO-Report-2019-survey.pdf> accessed 18 December 2020.

116 'Report of the Fourth FiSCAO Meeting on Central Arctic Ocean Fisheries (Tromsø, 26–28 September 2016)' (Chapter 2, n 134) 30–31.

117 See e.g. ibid 31.

as the most appropriate body, other delegations favoured PICES to include a Pacific perspective on the issue.[118] The findings of ICES and PICES were regularly discussed among the negotiating parties, and representatives of both organizations have participated in the meetings.[119] Although a separate scientific institution, the JPSRM, in which all Parties may participate equally, was ultimately chosen, both organizations appear suitable to assist in providing a scientific basis for the CAOF Agreement.

ICES is an intergovernmental marine science organization. Its roots date back to 1902, where ICES was established by the exchange of letters between participating countries. Multiple years later, the 1964 ICES Convention gave the institution legal foundation and full international status.[120] ICES' twenty parties include all CAOF Agreement parties except the EU and the three Asian States South Korea, Japan and China.[121] ICES aims to provide impartial evidence on the state and sustainable use of the oceans and seas. Its goal is to improve and distribute the scientific understanding of marine ecosystems. The knowledge acquired should then guide States to produce innovative advice on how to achieve conservation, management and sustainability goals, which is seen as particularly useful for the conservation-oriented CAOF Agreement. Not far away from the CAO, ICES work focuses on all living resources in mostly the North Atlantic Ocean as well as the adjacent North Sea and Baltic Sea. Research is carried out in a collaborative and coordinated manner within a network of almost 6000 scientists in laboratories and institutes of the ICES member countries, which favours the approach to gain comprehensive knowledge. Through strategic partnerships, ICES work extends into the Arctic, the Mediterranean Sea, the Black Sea and the North Pacific Ocean.[122]

The North Pacific Marine Science Organization, nicknamed PICES for a Pacific ICES, is an intergovernmental scientific organization that was founded

118 Molenaar, 'The CAOF Agreement: Key Issues of International Fisheries Law' (Chapter 2, n 20) 454.

119 See 'Report of the Second FiSCAO Meeting on Central Arctic Ocean Fisheries (Tromsø, 28–31 October 2013)' (Chapter 2, n 161) 4,9,16; 'Report of the Fourth FiSCAO Meeting on Central Arctic Ocean Fisheries (Tromsø, 26–28 September 2016)' (Chapter 2, n 134) 6, 10, 22–23; 'Chairman's Statement, Fifth FiSCAO Meeting on Central Arctic Ocean Fisheries (Ottawa, 24–26 October 2017)' (Chapter 3, n 310).

120 'Convention for the International Council for the Exploration of the Sea (Copenhagen, 12 September 1964) – UNTS Vol. 652, No. 9344' <https://treaties.un.org/doc/Publication/UNTS/Volume 652/v652.pdf> accessed 9 April 2022.

121 'ICES | Our History' <https://www.ices.dk/about-ICES/who-we-are/Pages/Our-history.aspx> accessed 19 November 2020.

122 'ICES | Who We Are' <https://www.ices.dk/about-ICES/who-we-are/Pages/Who-we-are.aspx> accessed 20 May 2020.

in 1992. Its present members partly coincide with the CAOF Agreement parties and are Canada, China, Japan, the Republic of Korea, the Russian Federation and the United States. PICES promotes and coordinates scientific research mainly in the temperate and sub-Arctic region of the North Pacific Ocean and its adjacent seas, especially northward from 30°N latitude.[123] The organization follows a multidisciplinary approach: standing committees are concerned with biological oceanography, fishery science, physical oceanography and climate and marine environmental quality but also monitoring and data management. Specialist groups regularly exchange ideas in joint scientific sessions at annual meetings. PICES has further joined forces with other international organizations, e.g. ICES, many times.[124]

ICES and PICES are considered to be of great value for managing CAO fisheries, especially for determining the status of fish stocks in the CAO. If fishing should be possible in the CAO in the future, various interests[125] must be weighed up simply and decisively as to whether and under what specific conditions commercial fishing should be allowed.[126] In this regard, compelling scientific evidence gathered by scientific institutions can lead the way. As has been suggested by individual States[127] in the Oslo Declaration[128] and offered by the two organizations themselves,[129] the findings of ICES and PICES in assessing sustainable fisheries in the CAO should be implemented, whilst management should be left to the CAOF Agreement.

1.6.2.2 *Arctic Council Working Groups*

The Arctic Council has made an effort in developing scientific research in the Arctic. It uses scientific working groups to provide information that can be used

123 'North Pacific Marine Science Organization | About Us – PICES' <https://meetings.pices.int/about> accessed 30 June 2021.

124 'North Pacific Marine Science Organization | Journey to PICES' <https://meetings.pices.int/about/history> accessed 30 June 2021.

125 On the opposing interests, see Chapter 3 Section 4 *supra*.

126 On the circumstances of authorizing commercial fishing, see Chapter 6 Section 1 *infra*.

127 North-East Atlantic Fisheries Commission, 'Proposal by Norway on a Request to ICES to Provide Assessments of the Status of the Ecosystem in a Portion of the High Seas of the Central Arctic Ocean (12–14 November 2019) – AM 2019–44' <https://www.neafc.org/system/files/AM-2019-44_Proposal-by-Norway_Request-to-ICES-assessment-status-of-ecosystem-CAO.pdf> accessed 10 August 2021.

128 'Declaration Concerning the Prevention of Unregulated High Seas Fishing in the Central Arctic Ocean (Oslo, 16 July 2015)' (Chapter 2, n 22).

129 International Council for the Exploration of the Sea, 'Minutes from the Meeting of the ICES Science Committee (SCICOM) (8 and 13 September 2019) – ICES CM 2019/SCICOM:02' 17 et seq. <www.ices.dkinfo@ices.dk> accessed 23 July 2020.

in other fora, e.g. the CAFF 2008–2011 Arctic Biodiversity Marine Monitoring Plan,[130] which was part of the Circumpolar Biodiversity Monitoring Programme, or generally to assess the need for adjustments of the international framework in response to threats to the Arctic ecosystem.[131] In 2013, CAFF released the Arctic Biodiversity Assessment. The report contains the best available scientific information shaped by traditional ecological knowledge on the status and trends of Arctic biodiversity and accompanying policy recommendations for biodiversity conservation.[132] Especially through its working group AMAP, the role of the Arctic Council changed from simply being "a supplier of Arctic data and knowledge to being a key data supplier, coordinator, and broker of scientific knowledge".[133] Programs like the joint AMAP, CAFF and International Arctic Science Committee's Arctic Climate Impact Assessment that deal with the impacts of climate change on the region, including impacts on fishing, were established.[134] Current projects[135] include CAFF's State of the Arctic Marine Biodiversity Report.[136] Furthermore, in order to implement ecosystem-based management in the CAO, PAME, ICES and PICES cooperatively developed the joint Working Group on Integrated Ecosystem Assessment for the Central Arctic Ocean to investigate the current state of the CAO. The working group's objective is to provide scientific advice and identify appropriate authorities to deal with issues like possible future CAO fisheries and the Arctic's ecosystem sensitivity and vulnerability to shipping-related activities.[137] In addition, representatives of PAME and CAFF working groups participated in FiSCAO meetings and were thus also involved in scientific research in the CAO.[138]

130 Conservation of Arctic Flora and Fauna (CAFF) Working Group, 'Arctic Marine Biodiversity Monitoring Plan (CBMP-MARINE PLAN) – CAFF Monitoring Series Report No.3' (Chapter 4, n 185).

131 Molenaar, 'Climate Change and Arctic Fisheries' (Chapter 4, n 184) 165.

132 Barry (Chapter 4, n 186).

133 Platjouw, Steindal and Borch (Chapter 4, n 163) 233.

134 Fourth Arctic Council Ministerial Meeting (Chapter 4, n 188); Arctic Monitoring and Assessment Programme (AMAP), Conservation of Arctic Flora and Fauna (CAFF) Working Group and International Arctic Science Committee (IASC) (Chapter 2, n 78).

135 An overview of Arctic Council projects can be found at 'Arctic Council | Projects' <https://arctic-council.org/en/projects/> accessed 9 July 2021.

136 Conservation of Arctic Flora and Fauna (CAFF) Working Group, 'State of the Arctic Marine Biodiversity: Key Findings and Advice for Monitoring' (Chapter 2, n 166).

137 'Arctic Council | Integrated Ecosystem Assessment (IEA) of the Central Arctic Ocean' (Chapter 4, n 191).

138 'Chairman's Statement, Fifth FiSCAO Meeting on Central Arctic Ocean Fisheries (Ottawa, 24–26 October 2017)' (Chapter 3, n 310).

1.6.2.3 *Scientific Experts on Fish Stocks in the Central Arctic Ocean*

As part of the process of establishing the CAOF Agreement, scientific experts on fish stocks in the CAO, referred to as FiSCAO, met regularly in parallel with the Arctic Five negotiating meetings and contributed in large part to the creation of the CAOF Agreement. The meetings were initiated as a concurrent scientific cooperation to support policy discussions and negotiations.

In general, FiSCAO meetings tried to deliver scientific answers to questions that came up in the negotiation process.[139] During the first meeting of the Arctic Five in Oslo in 2010, the question on the status of science arose. The first FiSCAO meeting, held in Anchorage in 2011, came to the conclusion that no urgency concerning the status of science existed, as baseline data needed to be established first. In 2013, the Arctic Five met for the second time, and wondered about the prospects for commercial fisheries in Arctic areas beyond national jurisdiction. The 2013 FiSCAO meeting established that more knowledge about fish stocks and the environment had to be gathered, and commercial fisheries are unlikely to be possible in CAO waters so far. Whereas the Arctic Five meeting in 2014 in Nuuk led to an agreement on the text for the Oslo Declaration, the 2015 meeting of FiSCAO scientists in Seattle resulted in the publication of a status of knowledge report and created the framework for a science plan.[140] In summary, in the first three meetings from 2011–2015, FiSCAO produced status and gap reports and a draft framework for research, monitoring and the JPSRM. At the fourth meeting in 2016, a plan for synthesising knowledge, science and monitoring was developed, as well as a framework for an implementation plan. At the fifth meeting in Ottawa in 2017, a concrete implementation plan was developed,[141] showing the intertwining of policy and legal decisions and science for the management of CAO fisheries.

FiSCAO findings are considered to have paved the way for scientific research under the CAOF Agreement. Based on the efforts of FiSCAO, ICES and PICES agreed to join forces to coordinate activities related to the CAOF Agreement. A joint paper outlining the potential contributions of the two organizations has already been submitted to the CAOF Agreement signatories. The paper is also expected to contribute to the negotiations on a new, long-awaited legal instrument on marine biodiversity in areas beyond national jurisdiction under UNCLOS,[142] where ICES and PICES suggested providing a platform where

---

139 For an overview of the drafting process and conducted meetings, see Chapter 3 Section 2 *supra*.

140 Gold (Chapter 2, n 143) 12–14.

141 ibid.

142 On the creation oft he BBNJ treaty, see Chapter 3 Section 1 *supra*.

other experts can participate. ICES, PICES and NOAA further plan to conduct a joint pilot study on data hosting and exchange protocols using the fish distribution dataset developed during the fourth FiSCAO meeting, following the recommendations of the fifth FiSCAO meeting.[143] FiSCAO was not formally instructed to convene further meetings after its fifth meeting in October 2017 and no formally agreed arrangements were made for the timeframe leading up to the entry into force of the CAOF Agreement.[144] However, with the establishment of the Provisional Scientific Coordinating Group (PSCG) under the CAOF Agreement at the beginning of the implementation process in 2020, the FiSCAO body became more or less superfluous.[145] Nevertheless, its research forms the basis for any research that has been and will be carried out within the framework of the Agreement.[146]

1.6.3 Additional Research Programs

The Agreement encourages the Parties to take into account the work of relevant scientific and technical programs when conducting research.[147] Since successful evaluation is based on reliable data, including data collected in the past, existing data collection and evaluation tools should be considered as relevant programs in this regard.

Fisheries are considered from both global and regional perspectives. Therefore, fisheries statistical programs need to be coherent and consistent. Thus, it is proposed that common regional or interregional standards defining internationally recognised terms are applied. To coordinate statistical programs of RFBs, NGOs and other bodies in the fisheries statistic sector, the FAO's Coordinating Working Party on Fishery Statistics (CWP) introduced a Handbook of Fisheries Statistics Standards that includes internationally applied concepts, definitions, classifications and data exchange protocols that should be applied nationally as a logical extension of the international

143 International Council for the Exploration of the Sea (Chapter 5, n 129) 17 et seq.

144 See also Molenaar, 'The CAOF Agreement: Key Issues of International Fisheries Law' (Chapter 2, n 20) 455.

145 'European Commission | The EU Joins Forces with Nine Countries for Future Science-Based Management of the High Seas of the Central Arctic Ocean (13 February 2020)' (Chapter 3, n 19).

146 See also 'Report of the 1st Meeting of the Provisional Scientific Coordinating Group (PSCG) of the Agreement to Prevent Unregulated High Seas Fisheries in the Central Arctic Ocean (Ispra, 11–13 February 2020)' <https://apps-afsc.fisheries.noaa.gov/documents/Arctic_fish_stocks_fifth_meeting/13200_109215706.pdf> accessed 25 March 2022.

147 See Article 4(4) CAOF Agreement.

standard.[148] The CWP currently consist of 19 participating organizations including ICCAT, ICES, NEAFC, NASCO and NAFO.[149] Whenever fisheries statistics are concerned, it seems reasonable to take into account the standards agreed upon by the main stakeholders responsible for fisheries statistics.

Furthermore, with technological development, entirely new ways of researching the depths of the Arctic Ocean are available, including research on the effects of climate change on fish stocks.[150] In order to estimate the likelihood of a stock migrating to CAO waters, the FAO provides a map of marine resources and fisheries that marks identified fish stocks and makes it possible to study the migration behaviour of fish stocks under changed circumstances in their current habitat.[151] Therefore, this instrument appears to be a useful tool to support scientific research and management under the CAOF Agreement.

2 Principles of Fisheries Management

When adopting measures for marine areas, regimes usually follow common principles that have been either traditionally proven effective or evolved as being necessary for successful management over the years.[152] These include the protection and conservation of the ecosystem (later developed into the ecosystem approach),[153] the implementation of the precautionary principle

148 'FAO | Coordinating Working Party on Fishery Statistics (CWP) – The CWP Handbook of Fishery Statistics' <http://www.fao.org/cwp-on-fishery-statistics/handbook> accessed 12 August 2021.

149 'FAO | Coordinating Working Party on Fishery Statistics (CWP) – Background' <http://www.fao.org/cwp-on-fishery-statistics/background/en/> accessed 10 August 2021.

150 Briney (Chapter 2, n 27).

151 'FAO | FIRMS Stocks and Fisheries Map Viewer' <http://firms.fao.org/firms/stocks-fisheries-map-viewer> accessed 28 June 2021.

152 For an overview of marine treaty provisions, see Annex I, Koivurova and Molenaar (Chapter 3, n 32) 111 et. seq.

153 See e.g. Article III NAFO Convention, see 'Convention on Cooperation in the Northwest Atlantic Fisheries (Ottawa, 24 October 1987) – UNTS Vol. 1135, No. 17799' <https://treaties.un.org/doc/Publication/UNTS/Volume1135/volume-1135-I-17799-English.pdf> accessed 12 August 2021; First Joint Ministerial Meeting of the Helsinki and OSPAR Commissions, 'Statement on the Ecosystem Approach to the Management of Human Activities (Bremen, 25–26 June 2003)' <https://www.ospar.org/site/assets/files/1232/jmm_annex05_ecosystem_approach_statement.pdf> accessed 9 July 2021; Article 4(2) NEAFC Convention, see 'Convention on Future Multilateral Cooperation in North-East Atlantic Fisheries (London, 18 November 1980) – UNTS Vol. 1285, No. 21173' <https://treaties.un.org/doc/Publication/UNTS/Volume 1285/volume-1285-A-21173-English.pdf> accessed 12 August 2021; Article 2 'Protocol on Environmental Protection to the Antarctic Treaty

or approach[154] and the duty to cooperate,[155] the conduction of impact assessments,[156] decision-making based on the best scientific evidence available,[157] and sustainable management in general.[158] Most of them find their basis in the UNFS Agreement. Likewise, the concept of sustainability is embedded in the founding mandates of most RFBs. Furthermore, the three main common policy approaches of fisheries bodies to sustainable fisheries management nowadays are the execution of the ecosystem approach to fisheries and aquaculture, the application of the precautionary approach, and science-based decision-making.[159]

Accordingly, the following interrelated concepts and principles should form the basis of a modern RFB:

- Sustainable development including the use of general principles such as the precautionary approach and ecosystem approach;
- The right and duty to cooperate;
- Efficient decision-making procedures, including transparency and stakeholder participation;
- Effective mechanisms for compliance and enforcement including the peaceful settlement of disputes; and
- Compatibility between conservation and management measures adopted for areas under national jurisdiction and those established in the adjacent high seas.[160]

(Madrid, 4 October 1991) – UNTS Vol. 2941, No. 5778' <https://treaties.un.org/doc/Publication/UNTS/Volume 2941/v2941.pdf>; Article 5 UNFS Agreement; Article II(3) CAMLR Convention.

154 See Article 4(3) Barcelona Convention, see 'Convention for the Protection of the Mediterranean Sea Against Pollution (Barcelona, 16 February 1976) – UNTS Vol. 1102, No. 16908' <https://treaties.un.org/doc/Publication/UNTS/Volume 1102/volume-1102-I-16908-English.pdf> accessed 12 August 2021; First Joint Ministerial Meeting of the Helsinki and OSPAR Commissions (Chapter 5, n 153).

155 See e.g. Article 5 UNFS Agreement; Article III NAFO Convention; Article 4(2) NEAFC Convention; Article 4(3) 1995 Barcelona Convention.

156 See e.g. Article 5 UNFS Agreement.

157 See e.g. Article 5 UNFS Agreement; Art. 2(3)(b) OSPAR Convention; cf. Article 3 Protocol on Environmental Protection to the Antarctic Treaty.

158 See e.g. Article 5 UNFS Agreement; Article II(3) CAMLR Convention.

159 Food and Agriculture Organization of the United Nations, 'Report of the Fifth Meeting of the Regional Fishery Body Secreteriats Network (RSN-5), (Rome, 7 and 13 June 2014)' (Chapter 4, n 322) 17; 'FAO | Regional Bodies Involved in the Management of Deep-Sea Fisheries' (Chapter 4, n 310).

160 See United Nations, 'Resumed Review Conference on the Agreement Relating to the Conservation and Management of Straddling Fish Stocks and Highly Migratory Fish Stocks (New York, 24–28 May 2010)' 1–2 <https://www.un.org/depts/los/convention_agreements/reviewconf/FishStocks_EN_B.pdf> accessed 8 April 2022; Henriksen, Hønneland and Sydnes (Chapter 3, n 171) 195.

For a modern marine environmental arrangement like the CAOF Agreement, it is considered key to implement and follow the aforementioned concepts to guarantee sustainable fisheries management. In the following section, the scope of these principles and how the CAOF Agreement has implemented them will be presented. Subsequently, an overview of common fisheries management problems that a fisheries arrangement can and should avoid through preventive action is provided.

2.1 *Sustainable Development*

As fisheries deal with renewable resources, sustainability is not new to international fisheries agreements, but has only evolved over time into an overarching concept in fisheries management. Since management always takes place over a period of time, progress and developments are naturally included in this concept. Nevertheless, the meaning and legal status of the resulting concept of sustainable development is not yet clear, and sustainable development has often been understood as an "all-encompassing concept" including everything that benefits nature, people and future generations.[161] On the international stage, sustainable development, and with it the term sustainability itself, was coined by the World Commission on Environment and Development, known as the Brundtland Commission.[162] In its Our Common Future Report from 1987, the Commission defines sustainable development as

> development that meets the needs of the present without compromising the ability of future generations to meet their own needs" and "involves a progressive transformation of economy and society". It "requires that the adverse impacts on the quality of air, water, and other natural elements are minimized so as to sustain the ecosystem's overall integrity".[163]

In the broadest sense, sustainable development aims at promoting harmony among human beings and between humanity and nature.[164] Therefore, two

161 Nico Schrijver, *The Evolution of Sustainable Development in International Law: Inception, Meaning and Status* (Martinus Nijhoff 2008) 24.

162 Michael Ben-Eli, 'Sustainability: Definition and Five Core Principles – A New Framework' (The Sustainability Laboratory 2015) 2 <https://www.sustainabilitylabs.org/ecosystem-restoration/wp-content/uploads/2015/08/Sustainability-The-Five-Core-Principles.pdf> accessed 2 Novemeber 2024.

163 World Commission on Environment and Development, 'Report: Our Common Future' (1987) 41 et seq. <http://www.un-documents.net/our-common-future.pdf> accessed 6 April 2022.

164 ibid 57.

basic interests must be taken into account: on the one hand, present needs must be satisfied, and on the other hand, development must be limited to the satisfaction of essential needs in order to have enough for future generations to meet their own essential needs. Hence, the prevailing definition of sustainability emphasizes cross-generational equity. This raises further difficulties, as the needs of future generations are not easy to determine.[165] In fact, unfortunately, it has already happened that societies have not been able to meet the basic needs of their people in the future, mostly through overexploiting resources.[166] This particularly risks marginalising indigenous peoples whose livelihoods heavily rely on the continued quality of their land[167] and environment.[168]

An alternative definition considers sustainability as the desired equilibrium between a population's ability to reach its full potential without causing irreversible, adverse impacts on the carrying capacity of its environment.[169] A set of potentially measurable key variables is provided to facilitate the determination of that desired balance. This entails a non-declining flow of resources, aligning the world's economy with nature's regeneration capacity, ensuring biodiversity, and maximizing degrees of freedom and potential self-realization of all humans without any individual or group adversely affecting others.[170] Similar, the United Nations' understanding of sustainable development has three dimensions, namely sustainable economic growth, social inclusion, and the protection of the environment and the global commons.[171]

As a principle, sustainability or sustainable development emerged in the run-up to UNCED and was most likely first mentioned as such in a treaty in the preamble of the 1994 Agreement on the European Economic Area.[172] Over

165 Ben-Eli (Chapter 5, n 162) 3.

166 See e.g. B Saragih, 'Economic Value of Non-Timber Forest Products among Paser Indigenous People of East Kalimantan' (Leiden University 2011) <https://openaccess.leidenuniv.nl/handle/1887/18078> accessed 19 December 2020.

167 See more on traditional communities and their relationship towards the environment Chapter 3, Sections, 4, 4.2 *supra*.

168 World Commission on Environment and Development (Chapter 5, n 163) 41 et seq.; cf. Pharand (Chapter 3, n 127) 177–178.

169 Ben-Eli (Chapter 5, n 162) 3.

170 Ben-Eli (Chapter 5, n 162).

171 United Nations System Task Team, 'Thematic Think Piece on the Post-2015 UN Development Agenda: Global Governance and Governance of the Global Commons in the Global Partnership for Development beyond 2015' (2013) 8 <https://www.un.org/en/development/desa/policy/untaskteam_undf/thinkpieces/24_thinkpiece_global_governance.pdf> accessed 1 September 2021.

172 'Agreement on the European Economic Area (Brussels, 17 March 1993)' <https://www.efta.int/media/documents/legal-texts/eea/the-eea-agreement/Main Text of the Agreement/EEAagreement.pdf> accessed 10 August 2021.

the years, it has been established as an international legal concept and is now commonly found in international and national instruments, especially in those with an environmental character, including treaty law and jurisprudence.[173] In particular, Principle 27 Rio Declaration,[174] Chapter 39 of Agenda 21,[175] and the 2030 Agenda, most of all SDG No. 14,[176] are prominent examples. In the context of fisheries, the concept has been promulgated as a general principle especially by the UNFS Agreement that requires measures to "ensure long-term sustainability" of fish stocks.[177] The annual UN General Assembly Resolutions on Sustainable Fisheries provide further guidance on how to achieve sustainable fisheries, e.g. the latest 2021 Resolution 76/71.[178] Although increasingly established at national and international levels, the implementation of sustainable development has not always improved over time[179] and the need for continuous development is emphasised.

While there may be disagreement on the exact definition of sustainable development, there is agreement that it contains several components that can be divided into concepts or principles. The New Delhi Declaration of Principles of International Law Relating to Sustainable Development (New Delhi Declaration), adopted by the International Law Association in 2002, plays a major role in this regard. The document was circulated at the 2002 World Summit on Sustainable Development (WSSD) in Johannesburg,[180] which was in turn addressed in UN General Assembly Resolution 57/253.[181] The 2002 WSSD also furthered the Plan of the Implementation of the World Summit on

173 Philippe Sands (Chapter 4, n 32) 217 et seq.

174 United Nations General Assembly, 'Report of the United Nations Conference on Environment and Development (Rio de Janeiro, 3–14 June 1992), Annex I: Rio Declaration on Environment and Development – A/CONF.151/26/Vol.I' (Chapter 4, n 30).

175 United Nations Conference on Environment and Development (Chapter 3, n 297); World Commission on Environment and Development (Chapter 5, n 163) s 1(2).

176 'United Nations General Assembly Resolution 70/1, Transforming Our World: The 2030 Agenda for Sustainable Development (Adopted 25 September 2015)' 23.

177 See Article 5(a) UNFS Agreement.

178 'United Nations General Assembly Resolution 76/71, Sustainable Fisheries (Adopted 9 December 2021)'.

179 United Nations General Assembly, 'Resolutions and Decisions Adopted by the General Assembly during Its Nineteenth Special Session (23–28 June 1997) – A/S-19/33' 6 <https://undocs.org/A/S-19/33> accessed 30 June 2021.

180 United Nations, 'World Summit on Sustainable Development (Johannesburg, 26 August-4 September 2002), ILA New Delhi Declaration of Principles of International Law Relating to Sustainable Development – A/CONF.199/8' <http://www2.ecolex.org/server2neu.php/libcat/docs/LI/MON-070850.pdf> accessed 30 June 2021.

181 'United Nations General Assembly Resolution 57/253, World Summit on Sustainable Development (Adopted 20 December 2002)'.

Sustainable Development (Johannesburg Plan of Implementation),[182] which entails specific advice on how to implement the sustainable development principles established by the New Delhi Declaration.

The New Delhi Declaration presents seven interrelated principles of international law that relate to sustainable development, with human beings as the centre of concern,[183] and which largely align with the content of sustainable development presented in the Rio Declaration and Agenda 21, namely:

(1) *The duty of States to ensure sustainable use of natural resources,* derived from a State's sovereignty over its natural resources and the initial negative obligation not to cause irreparable damage to the territories of other States, which later turned into the positive obligation to ensure that natural resources are used in a sustainable manner;

(2) *The principle of equity and the eradication of poverty,* including both intergenerational equity (the right of future generations to enjoy an appropriate level of common inheritance) and intergenerational equality (the right of all peoples within the present generation to have fair access to the present generation's entitlement on the earth's natural resources);

(3) *The principle of common but differentiated responsibilities,* which evolved from the notion of the common heritage of mankind and is a particular manifestation of the general principle of equity in international law. This includes the shared responsibility of States to protect the environment and the need to take into account different circumstances, particularly in relation to each State's contribution to the development of a particular problem and its ability to prevent, reduce and control a respective threat;

(4) *The principle of the precautionary approach to human health, natural resources and ecosystems* as a central concept of sustainable development; meaning that human activities that can significantly harm human health, natural resources or ecosystems should be avoided, even in the case of scientific uncertainty;

---

182 United Nations, 'Report of the World Summit on Sustainable Development (Johannesburg, 26 August-4 September 2002) – A/CONF.199/20' 6 et seq. <https://digitallibrary.un.org/record/478154/files/A_CONF.199_20-EN.pdf> accessed 4 April 2022.

183 See United Nations, 'World Summit on Sustainable Development (Johannesburg, 26 August–4 September 2002), Plan of Implementation of the World Summit on Sustainable Development – A/CONF.199/L.7' s 31 <https://www.un.org/esa/sustdev/documents/WSSD_POI_PD/English/WSSD_PlanImpl.pdf> accessed 4 April 2022.

(5) *The principle of public participation and access to information and justice,* including the effective protection of the human right to hold and express opinions and to seek, receive and impart ideas. It also implies the opportunity to participate in official socio-economic development decision-making processes and activities that directly affect and impact peoples' lives and well-being;

(6) *The principle of good governance,* that, *inter alia,* commits States and international organizations (as administrative authorities) to adopt democratic and transparent decision-making procedures and financial accountability to combat corruption, to respect the principle of due process in their procedures, the rule of law and human rights and to implement a public procurement approach, both on a domestic and international level; and

(7) *The principle of integration and interrelationship,* which is to be applied in particular in relation to human rights and social, economic and environmental objectives, e.g. through considering the use of sustainability or integrated impact assessments as a basis for economic development decisions, including decisions about policies, plans, programs or projects.[184]

Looking at the CAOF Agreement in terms of implementing sustainability, the sustainable approach ties back to the Preamble, which mentions sustainability several times as one of the foundations of the Agreement. Some of the seven partly-correlating principles set out in the New Delhi Declaration are explicitly mentioned and prioritized in the CAOF Agreement, while others are only briefly addressed.

Omnipresent is the obligation of the Parties to ensure the sustainable use of fish stocks.[185] Furthermore, it is requested that management should be sustainable.[186] The inclusion of the principle of equity must be considered in two parts. First, intra-generational equity can be deducted from the relatively open

184 United Nations, 'World Summit on Sustainable Development (Johannesburg, 26 August–4 September 2002), ILA New Delhi Declaration of Principles of International Law Relating to Sustainable Development – A/CONF.199/8' (Chapter 5, n 180); The Center for International Sustainable Development Law (CISDL), 'Legal Working Paper on The Principles of International Law Related to Sustainable Development' (2005) <https://www.cisdl.org/wp-content/uploads/2018/05/International-sustainable-development-law-2002.pdf> accessed 2 November 2024, providing a commentary on the principles established.

185 See Preamble and Articles 2, 4(2), 5(1)(c), 13(3) CAOF Agreement.

186 See Article 3(1)(a) CAOF Agreement.

access to membership[187] in the Agreement. Inter-generational equity is not explicitly mentioned, but can be linked to the future-oriented approach of the CAOF Agreement. Second, the principle of common but differentiated responsibilities is taken into account, *inter alia*, by recognizing "the special responsibilities and special interests of the central Arctic Ocean coastal States in relation to the conservation and sustainable management of fish stocks in the central Arctic Ocean",[188] although less emphasis is placed on poverty reduction as the original intent of this principle. The precautionary approach[189] and the ecosystem approach[190] are further addressed several times in the Agreement. Also mentioned is the principle of public participation, with special attention to indigenous and local communities, focusing on the consideration of local and indigenous knowledge rather than on the granting of decision-making rights.[191] Transparent decision-making procedures as part of the principle of good governance are only briefly addressed.[192] Where the principle of integration and interrelationship is concerned, the Agreement refers to a decision to be made "on the basis of the scientific information" derived from established programs.[193]

In summary, while some areas still have room for improvement, overall, the elements of sustainability as defined in the New Delhi Declaration have been mostly well integrated into the CAOF Agreement. In the following, the most important components of sustainability, namely the precautionary approach and the ecosystem approach, and their implementation in the Agreement are examined in more detail.

2.1.1 Precautionary Approach

The precautionary approach is considered a component of sustainable development based on a prospective element. Regulations dealing with climate change, such as the CAOF Agreement, usually contain such an element: as it depends on several factors, it is not possible to make a safe prediction about the environmental situation in several years in specific areas. However, an approximate idea is needed in order to take action. This is where the precautionary approach comes into play: the approach seeks to provide a starting point for

187 On participation in the CAOF Agreement, see Chapter 3 Section 3 *supra*.
188 See Preamble CAOF Agreement.
189 See Preamble, Articles 2, 5(1)(c) CAOF Agreement.
190 See Preamble and Articles 2, 3(4), 4(1), 4(2), 5(1)(c), 5(1)(d)(ii), 13(3) CAOF Agreement.
191 See Preamble and Articles 4(4), 5(1)(b), 5(2) CAOF Agreement.
192 See Article 6 CAOF Agreement.
193 See Article 5(1)(c) CAOF Agreement.

action so that relevant agreements can be critically analysed within the framework of this approach. Adjustments must be made, and changes incorporated promptly if a regime does not provide for efficient protection of its respective subject, e.g. the environment.

The very creation of the CAOF Agreement reflects the anticipatory approach. Previously, fishing was conducted before it was regulated. For the Arctic, however, "at that stage, it could be too late".[194] In response, the Agreement is the first fisheries agreement ever in place before fishery in the regulatory area has occurred and is therefore strongly based on predictions. Hence, the precautionary approach fulfils a theoretical and practical function within the Agreement. First, the CAOF Agreement as a fisheries management tool itself can be theoretically measured against the approach. The approach has been introduced as the precautionary approach or precautionary principle in international environmental law but has not yet evolved to a solid basic tool for generally analysing international agreements. However, the example of the present agreement could promote the approach as an indispensable legal threshold for international environmental agreements. Second, it could be hypothetically assessed how the precautionary approach is translated into practical measures that may be implemented under the CAOF Agreement. However, since the CAOF Agreement just recently entered into force and thus no measures have yet been taken under the Agreement, only how the CAOF Agreement itself has implemented the precautionary approach can be determined.

2.1.1.1 *Development and Definition of the Precautionary Approach*

Although widely used in international law and politics, several uncertainties concerning different aspects of the precautionary approach remain: there is no unanimity regarding the (legal) definition of the precautionary approach, its legal quality as a rule, general principle of law or principle of customary law, and regarding its scope and substance. While some consider the precautionary approach unscientific and an obstacle to progress, others see it as a necessary approach to protect human health and the environment. Different actors apply different definitions depending on the degree of scientific uncertainty needed for authorities to take action. Although there is broad consensus among experts that the precautionary approach does not prescribe explicit measures, e.g. a ban of specific actions, there is no common opinion on how to determine when precautionary measures should be taken.[195]

194 Loctier (Chapter 2, n 137).

195 Didier Bourguignon, 'The Precautionary Principle: Definitions, Applications and Governance' (European Parliament 2016) 4–22 <https://www.europarl.europa.eu/thinktank/en/document.html?reference=EPRS_IDA(2015)573876> accessed 10 August 2021; see

Moreover, there is ongoing discussion about the meaning of the expressions "principle" and "approach" in relation to precaution.[196] In the international law context, "principle" is mostly used as the theoretical basis of precaution whereas "approach" is referred to in the context of its practical application. The distinction is further sometimes made to express one's opinion as to whether the principle has acquired the status of a general principle of law, a customary rule of international law or remains some sort of concept only. Nevertheless, both terms are closely related and applied interchangeably many times.[197] The expression "precautionary approach" has for instance been used in international settings to refer to the precautionary principle: the English version of Principle 15 Rio Declaration refers to the word "approach", whereas the Spanish version uses "principio".[198] Unless expressly mentioned otherwise, in this thesis, both expressions will be used synonymously.

Apart from these terminological uncertainties, doubts also remain over the legal substance of the approach.[199] In rather general terms, the ICJ has held that the "general obligation of States to ensure that activities within their jurisdiction and control respect the environment of other States or of areas beyond national control is now part of the corpus of international law relating to the environment."[200] In fact, this rationale is also reflected in Article 194(2) UNCLOS. The approach has partly even been declared as being part of customary international law,[201] as State practice and *opinio iuris* have been

Yoshinobu Takei, *Filling Regulatory Gaps in High Seas Fisheries: Discrete High Seas Fish Stocks, Deep-Sea Fisheries, and Vulnerable Marine Ecosystems* (Brill | Nijhoff 2013) 258.

196 See different perceptions at Alexander Proelß, 'Prinzipien Des Internationalen Umweltrechts' in Alexander Proelß (ed), *Internationales Umweltrecht* (De Gruyter 2017) 90 et seq. with further references.

197 World Commission on the Ethics of Scientific Knowledge and Technology, 'The Precautionary Principle' (2005) 22–23 <https://unesdoc.unesco.org/ark:/48223/pf0000139578> accessed 4 April 2022.

198 ibid 23.

199 On the origin and varying defintions of the precautionary principle, see Bourguignon (Chapter 5, n 195) 4 et seq.; World Commission on the Ethics of Scientific Knowledge and Technology (Chapter 5, n 197) 12 et seq.

200 *Case Concerning Pulp Mills on the River Uruguay (Argentina v. Uruguay), Judgement of 20 April 2010, ICJ Reports 2010, p. 14* (Chapter 5, n 45) para 193; *Legality of the Threat or Use of Nuclear Weapons, Advisory Opinion of 8 July 1996, ICJ Reports 1996, p. 226* (Chapter 4, n 121) para 29.

201 Cf. *MOX Plant Case (Ireland v United Kingdom), Provisional Measures, Order of 3 December 2001, ITLOS Reports 2001, p 95, Separate Opinion of Judge Wolfrum.*

considered sufficient in this regard.[202] At least in the context of environmental law, unanimity seems to prevail that the principle has acquired the status of a well-established rule of international law. Due to its wide adoption in international treaties, especially environmental treaties,[203] it has been noted that "the principle has been progressively consolidated in international environmental law, and so it has since become a full-fledged and general principle of international law".[204] However, a precise assignment to one of the three main sources of international law[205] is not made.

The lowest common denominator for the substance of a definition of the precautionary principle is provided by Principle 15 Rio Declaration: "(w)here there are threats of serious or irreversible damage, lack of full scientific certainty shall not be used as a reason for postponing cost-effective measures to prevent environmental degradation". This also implies that "the benefit of doubt is given to nature: *in dubio pro natura*."[206] Necessary condition for the application of the approach is therefore (a certain degree of) uncertainty. The applicability of the precautionary approach is hence limited where risks are established with certainty. In this case, the prevention principle[207] should be applied to avert harm.[208]

202 Cf. *North Sea Continental Shelf Cases (Federal Republic of Germany/Denmark; Federal Republic of Germany/Netherlands), Judgement of 20 February 1969, ICJ Reports 1969, p. 3* (Chapter 4, n 134) para 77.

203 E.g. CBD and the UNFCCC, Article 191(2) Treaty on the Functioning of the European Union, and national legislations. Additional case law can be found at Bourguignon (Chapter 5, n 195) 10.

204 ibid 6.

205 Cf. Article 38(1) Statute of the International Court of Justice; see 'Charter of the United Nations and Statute of the International Court of Justice (San Francisco, 1945)' <https://treaties.un.org/doc/Publication/CTC/uncharter.pdf> accessed 9 April 2022.

206 Arie Trouwborst, 'International Nature Conservation Law and the Adaptation of Biodiversity to Climate Change: A Mismatch?' (2009) 21 Journal of Environmental Law 419, 425 <https://www.jstor.org/stable/44248707> accessed 2 April 2022; Similarly, see United Nations, 'Resumed Review Conference on the Agreement Relating to the Conservation and Management of Straddling Fish Stocks and Highly Migratory Fish Stocks (New York, 24–28 May 2010)' (Chapter 5, n 160) 1.

207 See e.g. Article 4(2)(c) 'Basel Convention on the Control of Transboundary Movements of Hazardous Wastes and Their Disposal (Basel, 22 March 1989) – UNTS Vol. 1673, No. 28911' <https://treaties.un.org/doc/Publication/UNTS/Volume 1673/v1673.pdf> accessed 9 July 2021; Article 191(2) Treaty on the Functioning of the European Union; Article 2(2) and paras. 17, 20 of European Union, 'Decision No 1386/2013/EU of the European Parliament and of the Council on a General Union Environment Action Programme to 2020 "Living Well, within the Limits of Our Planet" (20 November 2013) – L354/171' <https://eur-lex.europa.eu/legal-content/EN/TXT/PDF/?uri=CELEX:32013D1386&from=EN> accessed 9 July 2021.

208 Bourguignon (Chapter 5, n 195) 6.

Further, it is submitted that precaution entails that

> the proponent of activities which might lead to either significant, serious or irreversible harm is obliged to take measures (or permit measures to be taken) to prevent this damage (including halting the proposed activities), even if there is a lack of full scientific certainty as to the existence and severity of the risk.[209]

Therefore, for the precautionary approach to apply, harm or damage must be imminent. In particular, the principle should be applied in the case of significant adverse harm.[210] However, the respective degree of harm cannot be defined unequivocally, but must be determined individually for each case. Serving as an indicator, the extent of harm is most often inversely proportionate to the likelihood of risk for precaution to be triggered: both the likelihood of a risk to be high or low and whether the consequences, should the harm occur, are severe or minor, are decisive. Precaution is for instance recommended when there is a high risk of possible harm, or when there is a lower risk of serious and irreversible harm. Where precious goods are endangered, e.g. where human lives are concerned, the probability for the harm to occur may be minimal but might nevertheless meet the threshold and trigger the need for precaution.[211] Yet, it is worth noting that whether the precautionary approach needs to be applied remains a case-by-case decision based on careful consideration of the specific circumstances at hand.[212] Further, a specific action can be declared sustainable at one point in time, but not in another: for instance, in fisheries, especially when dealing with migratory species, changes in migration patterns or the introduction of new technology[213] can develop

---

209 The Center for International Sustainable Development Law (CISDL) (Chapter 5, n 184) 12.

210 Cf. *Responsibilities and Obligations of States Sponsoring Persons and Entities with Respect to Activities in the Area, Advisory Opinion of 1 February 2011, ITLOS Reports 2011, p 10* [116, 146–147]; 'Convention on Environmental Impact Assessment in a Transboundary Context (Espoo, 25 February 1991) – UNTS Vol. 1989, No. 34028' para 7 Preamble <https://treaties.un.org/doc/Treaties/1991/02/1991022508-29PM/Ch_XXVII_04p.pdf> accessed 12 August 2021; *Southern Bluefin Tuna (New Zealand v. Japan; Australia v. Japan), Provisional Measures, Order of 27 August 1999, ITLOS Reports 1999, p. 280* (Chapter 5, n 40) para 77.

211 The Center for International Sustainable Development Law (CISDL) (Chapter 5, n 184) 13.

212 Proelß (Chapter 5, n 196) 90 et seq.

213 Bjørndal and Munro (Chapter 4, n 47) 234 et seq.

significant harm through overfishing, which easily alters the need for the application of precautionary measures.[214]

Put simply, the precautionary approach is about risk management. In this regard, three capacities are of vital importance. The basis is the requirement for scientific research to establish different reference points.[215] In addition, there must be a willingness to accept established scientific advice and set an acceptable level of risk politically. Furthermore, when measures have been determined, compliance with these measures must be ensured throughout the management system of a managing authority, e.g. an RFB, and by the member States.[216]

In the context of fisheries, the precautionary approach has been considered a general principle by Article 5(c) UNFS Agreement. Further, Article 6 UNFS Agreement urges States to "apply the precautionary approach widely to conservation, management and exploitation of straddling fish stocks and highly migratory fish stocks in order to protect the living marine resources and preserve the marine environment". Also, the precautionary principle has become established as a general principle in fisheries management through its inclusion in several international fisheries agreements[217] either through amendments or through direct implementation where new agreements have been introduced.[218] As a matter of principle, the implementation of the precautionary approach in adopting fisheries management and conservation measures has become more important over time. A broad implementation of the approach both through RFBs and at national levels has been suggested.[219] The FAO High-Level Panel of External Experts in Fisheries encourages RFBs to be "proactive and anticipate crises which might confront them in the future".[220]

214 Bourguignon (Chapter 5, n 195) 15.

215 See specifically on scientific research and scientific evidence Chapter 5 Sections 1, 1.1 *supra*.

216 Henriksen, Hønneland and Sydnes (Chapter 3, n 171) 201.

217 Takei (Chapter 4, n 307) 554; Wahlén and others (Chapter 5, n 81) 4; Schatz, Proelß and Liu (Chapter 2, n 41) 218; see extensively Jon M Van Dyke, 'The Evolution and International Acceptance of the Precautionary Principle' in David D Caron and Harry N Scheiber (eds), *Bringing New Law to Ocean Waters* (Brill | Nijhoff 2004).

218 See e.g. Principles 6.5 and 7.5. FAO Code of Conduct; Articles 5(c), 6 WCPFC; Article 3 'Convention on the Conservation and Management of Fishery Resources in the South East Atlantic Ocean (Windhoek, 20 April 2001) – UNTS Vol. 2221, No. 39489' <https://treaties.un.org/pages/showDetails.aspx?objid=080000028007bd54> accessed 12 August 2021.

219 See Swan (Chapter 4, n 323) s 3.1.

220 Food and Agriculture Organization of the United Nations, 'Report of the Meeting of the High-Level Panel of External Experts in Fisheries (Rome, 26–27 January 1998)' (Chapter 4, n 323) para 32.

The need for continuous adaptation of mandates, structures and policies for better responses to the challenges facing world fisheries was emphasised.[221] In general, the more sophisticated the research, management and enforcement systems in place, the greater the diversity of options for applying the precautionary approach.[222]

Article 6 UNFS Agreement further gives special guidance for the application and implementation of the precautionary approach in fisheries. In summary,

- A wide application when taking measures is requested;[223]
- Caution shall be exercised where information is uncertain, unreliable or inadequate; yet, the absence of adequate scientific information shall not be used as an excuse for postponing or failing to take suitable measures;[224]
- Decision-making shall be based on obtaining and sharing the best scientific information available, and risk and uncertainty shall be taken into account[225] and approached with improved techniques;[226]
- Stock-specific reference points, in regard to a harvesting limit within which the stocks can reproduce, a maximum sustainable yield, and target reference points to meet management objectives[227] shall be determined, and in terms of enforcement, ensured that these are not exceeded;[228]
- Data collection and research programs to conduct environmental impact assessments shall be developed, and where harm to the environment may be caused, plans shall be adopted;[229]
- Review measures shall be implemented where a stock's status is of concern;[230]
- Cautious conservation and management measures for new or exploratory fish stocks shall be adopted and remain in force until sufficient data

221 Food and Agriculture Organization of the United Nations, 'Report of the Second Meeting of FAO and Non-FAO Regional Fishery Bodies or Arrangements (Rome, 20–21 February 2001)' 25 <http://www.fao.org/3/a-y0593e.pdf> accessed 16 June 2020.

222 Cf. Food and Agriculture Organization of the United Nations, 'Technical Guidelines for Responsible Fisheries No. 2: Precautionary Approach to Capture Fisheries and Species Introductions' (1996) para 87 <http://www.fao.org/3/a-w3592e.pdf> accessed 18 June 2021.

223 Article 6(1) UNFS Agreement.

224 Article 6(2) UNFS Agreement.

225 Article 6(3)(c) UNFS Agreement.

226 Article 6(3)(a) UNFS Agreement.

227 Article 6(3)(b), Annex II UNFS Agreement.

228 Article 6(4) UNFS Agreement.

229 Article 6(3)(d) UNFS Agreement.

230 Article 6(5) UNFS Agreement.

about the impact on the long-term sustainability of such stocks are available;[231] and

- Emergency management measures where a natural phenomenon or fishing activities significantly and adversely impact a stock's status or its sustainability[232] shall be adopted.

The New Delhi Declaration[233] follows a similar approach except that it additionally demands accountability for harm caused.[234] It calls for precautionary measures to be transparent and based on independent, up-to-date scientific judgment. Yet, they should not result in economic protectionism. Clear structures should be established, which involve all interested parties, including non-State actors, in the consultation process. Further, appropriate review of measures by a judicial or administrative body should be available.[235]

Both specifications, those established by Article 6 UNFS Agreement and by the New Delhi Declaration, can be used as a guideline for the implementation of the precautionary approach in the CAOF Agreement.

2.1.1.2 *Implementation in the CAOF Agreement*

As all CAOF Agreement signatories are parties to the UNFS Agreement, and the United States that generally disagrees with the precautionary principle being customary international law[236] did not object to the provisions of precaution in the UNFS Agreement,[237] it is submitted that the CAOF Agreement must apply the precautionary approach in light of how it is suggested by the UNFS Agreement and completed by the New Delhi Declaration as an internationally

231 Article 6(6) UNFS Agreement.

232 Article 6(7) UNFS Agreement.

233 For the principles established by the New Delhi Declaration, see Chapter 5 Sections 2, 2.1 *supra*.

234 United Nations, 'World Summit on Sustainable Development (Johannesburg, 26 August-4 September 2002), ILA New Delhi Declaration of Principles of International Law Relating to Sustainable Development – A/CONF.199/8' (Chapter 5, n 180) s 5.

235 ibid.

236 See for instance World Trade Organization, 'European Communities – Measures Affecting the Approval and Marketing of Biotech Products – Reports of the Panel (29 September 2006) – WT/DS291-293/R' paras 7.81–7.82 <https://www.worldtradelaw.net/document.php?id=reports/wtopanels/ec-biotech(panel).pdf&mode=download> accessed 17 December 2021.

237 The US only made a declaration concerning dispute settlement, cf. 'United Nations Treaty Collection | Status of Treaties: Agreement for the Implementation of the Provisions of UNCLOS Relating to the Conservation and Management of Straddling Fish Stocks and Highly Migratory Fish Stocks (New York, 4 August 1995)' <https://treaties.un.org/Pages/ViewDetails.aspx?src=TREATY&mtdsg_no=XXI-7&chapter=21&clang=_en> accessed 1 July 2021.

accepted UN document. In fact, the CAOF Agreement performs well in terms of implementing the components set up by Article 6 UNFS Agreement:

First, the UNFS Agreement requests a wide application of the approach. Although the insertion of the word "widely" in Article 6(1) UNFS Agreement caused significant disagreement between DWF States and coastal States[238] – most likely due to the fact that DWF States were concerned that the concept would be adopted by coastal States as an "open licence to adopt moratoria as a new management norm"[239] – a wide approach is highly appreciated as a basis for taking comprehensive measures of precaution.[240] Against this standard, the CAOF Agreement has excellently implemented the precautionary principle. The agreement has a strong anticipatory character, and reliance on scientific predictions is the basis of almost every article. The approach is also reflected in the objective of the Agreement: according to Article 2 CAOF Agreement, the Agreements' main goal is to "prevent unregulated fishing" in the Agreement Area, whereas the wording "prevent" is considered to display a direct link to the precautionary approach. Consequently, the broad application of the principle requested by the UNFS Agreement is followed.

As further provided for in the UNFS Agreement,[241] the implementation of the precautionary approach under the CAOF Agreement shall be achieved by the application of precautionary conservation and management measures.[242] The measures are part of a long-term strategy.[243] Similar references to a precautionary, future-oriented approach are explicitly mentioned throughout the Agreement.[244] Uncertainty about what the situation in the Arctic in a few years might be like is constantly present. Whereas on the one hand, the continuous melting of Arctic sea ice is now an increasingly substantiated fact[245] – by 2100, the CAO will likely have open-water conditions between 3 months up to

238 UN Fish Stocks Agreement Review Conference, 'Summary of the Fifth Substantive Session (24 July-4 August 1995): Part II – Conservation and Management of Straddling and Highly Migratory Fish Stocks' (1995) 7 Earth Negotiations Bulletin 54 <https://enb.iisd.org/vol07/0754012e.html> accessed 30 May 2020.

239 UN Fish Stocks Agreement Review Conference, 'Summary of the Fifth Substantive Session (24 July-4 August 1995): Conservation and Management Gains' (1995) 7 Earth Negotiations Bulletin 54 <https://enb.iisd.org/vol07/0754029e.html> accessed 30 May 2020.

240 Cf. World Commission on the Ethics of Scientific Knowledge and Technology (Chapter 5, n 197) 15.

241 See Article 6(6) UNFS Agreement.

242 See Article 2 CAOF Agreement. The measures are *inter alia* specified in Article 3 CAOF Agreement.

243 See Preamble and Article 2 CAOF Agreement.

244 See Preamble, Articles 2, 5(1)(c) CAOF Agreement.

245 Liu, Chen and Feng (Chapter 2, n 13) 1153.

nearly 8 months on average[246] – there is, on the other hand, very little reliable data on the development of marine ecosystems in the Arctic region. Although most studies register the moving of fish to regions further north,[247] it is unclear whether the Arctic environment may serve as a long-term, adequate habitat for species. To continue activities in the long run, the application of precautionary conservation and management measures are therefore necessary.

The precautionary approach as framed by the UNFS Agreement further demands that the absence of adequate scientific information should not be used as an excuse to exercise suitable measures. Information should be shared and decision-making based on the best scientific information available. The CAOF Agreement equally satisfies this demand. Among other things, the Agreement refers to "the best available scientific information",[248] "all available scientific information"[249] and "scientific information derived from the Joint Program of Scientific Research and Monitoring"[250] to be used as a basis for taking decisions. Completeness of information is not required before action is to be taken. Information should be shared, *inter alia*, in meetings and via data sharing protocols.[251]

Precaution demands uncertainty to be approached with improved techniques. Whereas within the CAOF Agreement, no specific techniques are mentioned, the JPSRM established by Article 4 CAOF Agreement provides a basis for modern and improved data collection. In line with the prerequisites of the UNFS Agreement, data collection focuses especially on assessing the impact of fisheries and management on the environment.[252]

---

246 Alex Crawford and others, 'Arctic Open-Water Periods Are Projected to Lengthen Dramatically by 2100' (2021) 2 Communications Earth & Environment 1, 4 <https://doi.org/10.1038/s43247-021-00183-x> accessed 12 August 2021.

247 Olga Wassmann, Paul, Reigstad, Marit, Haug, Tore, Rudels, Bert, Carroll, Michael L., Hop, Haakon, Gabrielsen, Geir Wing, Falk-Petersen, Stig, Denisenko, Stanislav G., Arashkevich, Elena, Slagstad, Dag, Pavlova, 'Food Webs and Carbon Flux in the Barents Sea' (2006) 71(2) Progress in Oceanography 232; Hansen, 'Snow Crab (Chionoecetes Opilio) in the Barents Sea. Diet, Biology and Management' (Chapter 2, n 207) 46.

248 Article 4(6) CAOF Agreement.

249 Article 5(1)(a) CAOF Agreement.

250 Article 5(1)(c) CAOF Agreement.

251 Cf. Article 4(5), 4(6) CAOF Agreement.

252 See Article 4(2) CAOF Agreement: The JPSRM is established with the "aim of improving their understanding of the ecosystems of the Agreement Area and, in particular, of determining whether fish stocks might exist in the Agreement Area now or in the future that could be harvested on a sustainable basis and the possible impacts of such fisheries on the ecosystems of the Agreement Area". Determinations shall, *inter alia*, take into account "relevant fisheries management and ecosystem considerations, including the precautionary approach and potential adverse impacts of fishing on the ecosystems"

The UNFS Agreement's conception of the precautionary approach further foresees stock-specific reference points[253] to be determined and compliance with these reference points to be enforced. Stock reference points, rather than keeping a maximum sustainable yield, were intentionally implemented as a more conservative approach and clear commitment to the precautionary approach.[254] The CAOF Agreement establishes a qualified abstention on unregulated commercial fishing in the Agreement Area[255] as the strictest form of setting reference points. As commercial fisheries under the CAOF Agreement are to be conducted pursuant to measures established by a new or existing RFB,[256] the current identification of further specific stock reference points is considered premature and should be left to a potential RFB entrusted with managing CAO commercial fisheries. The importance of continuously adopting a precautionary approach to commercial fishing in these waters was further emphasised. As such, a determination of reference points should always take into account both the current and potential future situation and therefore be reviewed and adjusted from time to time.[257] With regard to the enforcement of compliance with reference points, the Agreement refers several times to the importance of ensuring compliance with the abstention.[258] However, no specific enforcement measures are mentioned, other than the approach of exercising some degree of cooperative coordination among the Parties.[259]

Review measures required by the UNFS Agreement are provided for in Articles 4(6), 5(1)(a) and (b) CAOF Agreement.[260]

The CAOF Agreement further implements cautious conservation and management measures for exploratory fishing.[261] As exploratory fishing means

---

and "consider, inter alia, whether the distribution, migration and abundance of fish in the Agreement Area would support a sustainable commercial fishery" (see Article 5(1)(c) CAOF Agreement).

253 Reference points are benchmarks that scientists and managers use to compare the current status of a stock or fishery to a desirable (or undesirable) state, and hence help to determine the success of the harvest strategy; see PEW Charitable Trust, 'Reference Points: Measuring Success in Fisheries Management' (2016) 1 <https://www.pewtrusts.org/~/media/assets/2016/09/referencepts_brief_v6.pdf> accessed 19 December 2020.

254 Diz and others (Chapter 5, n 80) 12.

255 See Articles 3(1), 5(1)(c) CAOF Agreement.

256 See Articles 3(1), 5(1)(c)(i) CAOF Agreement.

257 See Inuit Circumpolar Council, 'Kitigaaryuit Declaration (Kitigaaryuit, 24 July 2014)' (Chapter 3, n 300) para 21.

258 Cf. Article 3(1), 3(3)–3(5) CAOF Agreement.

259 Cf. Article 3(4), 3(6) CAOF Agreement.

260 On review of the CAOF Agreement, see specifically Chapter 6 Section 4 *infra*.

261 See Article 5(1)(d) CAOF Agreement.

"fishing for the purpose of assessing the sustainability and feasibility of future commercial fisheries by contributing to scientific data relating to such fisheries",[262] it is suggested that these measures remain in force until commercial fishing becomes possible or even stay in force simultaneously.[263]

No specific emergency measures, requested by the UNFS Agreement, are foreseen by the CAOF Agreement. Nevertheless, it must be considered that the Agreement itself constitutes an emergency measure in response to a natural phenomenon, the melting of sea ice in the CAO: should the ice layer continue to melt, allowing fish stocks to move further north, and should commercial fishing therefore theoretically be possible in CAO waters, the CAOF Agreement provides a framework of various steps to be taken to meet management needs.

In conclusion, the CAOF Agreement has implemented the precautionary approach very well in theory. Time will tell whether this also holds true for its practical application.

2.1.2 Ecosystem Approach

Sometimes referred to as part of a precautionary approach towards the ecosystem,[264] the ecosystem approach has become a significant concept itself and is therefore dealt with separately.

2.1.2.1 *Development and Definition of the Ecosystem Approach*

Overexploitation of natural resources over hundreds of years has widely disrupted the equilibrium within ecological systems. Already in 1982, the UN General Assembly claimed in their World Charter for Nature that

> Lasting benefits from nature depend upon the maintenance of essential ecological processes and life support systems, and upon the diversity of life forms, which are jeopardized through excessive exploitation and habitat destruction by man.[265]

Damage, unsustainable development and the failure to invest and reinvest in their productivity, health and sustainability led to the degradation of

262 Article 1(e) CAOF Agreement.

263 North-East Atlantic Fisheries Commission, 'Procedures and Standards for PECMAS' Consideration of Proposals for Exploratory Fishing Pursuant to Rec. 19:2014 (11 November 2015)' <www.neafc.org> accessed 2 April 2020.

264 See Principle No. 4 New Delhi Declaration.

265 'United Nations General Assembly Resolution 37/7, World Charter for Nature (Adopted 28 October 1982)'.

ecosystems worldwide.[266] The decline of biodiversity as part of every ecosystem[267] is destroying the world just as much as climate change.[268] Organisms respond to modifications and substantial stress resulting from climate change by variations in temperature or weather patterns, and species and ecosystems gradually shift their distributions.[269]

Sir David Attenborough notes in this regard:

> Often I find that while people are familiar with the problem of climate change, they know less about the loss of nature that's happening around us. We should be in no doubt, "biodiversity loss", the destruction of nature, is as grave an issue as climate change. They both work together to destabilise the world we rely upon.[270]

In order to counteract such destruction, maintaining the health of marine ecosystems is therefore considered one of the most important objectives when managing marine areas.

In respect of fisheries, with the application of the precautionary approach, the ecosystem approach also found its way into RFB conventions[271] and has developed to be "generally accepted by the international community".[272] The approach is usually mentioned in the context of sustainable development and alongside the precautionary approach. For a long time, intensive monitoring of the quality of the marine environment was mostly carried out regionally. The results of the status of the environment were published in periodic reports providing solid information that might be used by RFBs in ecosystem-based management of fisheries.[273] However, progress has been made in the application

266 'CBD| Ecosystem Restoration' <https://www.cbd.int/restoration/> accessed 17 January 2022.

267 Cf. Article 2 CBD, which describes biological diversity as ":the variability among living organisms from all sources including, *inter alia*, terrestrial, marine and other aquatic ecosystems and the ecological complexes of which they are part: this includes diversity within species, between species and of ecosystems."

268 'Biodiversity: The Loss of Nature, Interview with David Attenbrough (Published 28 September 2020)' <https://www.instagram.com/p/CFrRYBxH_pF/> accessed 28 May 2021.

269 Trouwborst (Chapter 5, n 206) 419–421.

270 'Biodiversity: The Loss of Nature, Interview with David Attenbrough (Published 28 September 2020)' (Chapter 5, n 268).

271 Wahlén and others (Chapter 5, n 81) 12.

272 Molenaar and Caddell (Chapter 3, n 13) 426.

273 Food and Agriculture Organization of the United Nations, 'Report of the Second Meeting of FAO and Non-FAO Regional Fishery Bodies or Arrangements (Rome, 20–21 February 2001)' (Chapter 5, n 221) 2.

of the ecosystem approach. Although the overall implementation and application of the concept still leaves room for improvement,[274] ecosystem-based fisheries management has become one of the key aspects in managing fisheries.[275] The approach has been prominently supported, *inter alia,* by the annual UN General Assembly Resolutions on Sustainable Fisheries,[276] which have widely been adopted by consensus, reflecting the possible existence of *opinio juris*[277]with respect to the application of the ecosystem approach.[278] While few RFB treaties refer directly to the term "ecosystem approach", most contain wording that can be interpreted as referring to the approach. Thus, for example, many treaties contain references to the protection of marine ecosystems and biodiversity in the marine environment, or to the impacts of fisheries on species of the same ecosystem. In addition, most of them refer directly or indirectly to the precautionary approach. For instance, some RFBs established measures on preventing negative impacts on vulnerable marine ecosystems[279] or revised their instruments to accommodate the approach.[280] However, due to the complexity of the ecosystem approach, few fisheries management tools have implemented and applied comprehensive ecosystem concerns but rather focus on regulating species that are targeted by specific fisheries.

One of the first RFB treaties to implement the ecosystem approach was the CAMLR Convention.[281] According to the treaty, management ideally takes

274 CBD Conference of the Parties, 'COP 9 Decision 7: Ecosystem Approach (Bonn, 9 October 2008)' <https://www.cbd.int/doc/decisions/cop-09/cop-09-dec-07-en.pdf> accessed 17 January 2022.

275 Takei (Chapter 4, n 307) 554 et seq.

276 Starting from 2003, until currently up to 2021; 'United Nations General Assembly Resolution 58/14, Sustainable Fisheries (Adopted 24 November 2003)'; 'United Nations General Assembly Resolution 76/71, Sustainable Fisheries (Adopted 9 December 2021)'.

277 Cf. *Military and Paramilitary Activities in and against Nicaragua (Nicaragua v United States of America), Merits Judgment of 27 June 1986, ICJ Reports 1986, p 14* [188]; *Legality of the Threat or Use of Nuclear Weapons, Advisory Opinion of 8 July 1996, ICJ Reports 1996, p. 226* (Chapter 4, n 121) para 68 et seq.

278 Daniela Diz Pereira Pinto, 'Fisheries Management in Areas beyond National Jurisdiction' in David Freestone (ed), *Legal Aspects of Sustainable Development* (13th edn, Brill | Nijhoff 2012) 48.

279 Guidance for identifying vulnerable marine ecosystems and assessing significant adverse impacts is provided by the FAO, see Food and Agriculture Organization of the United Nations, 'FAO Fisheries and Aquaculture Report No. 881: Report of the Technical Consultation on International Guidelines for the Management of Deep-Sea Fisheries in the High Seas (Rome, 4–8 February and 25–29 August 2008)' (Chapter 5, n 19) para 42 et seq.

280 Løbach and others (Chapter 4, n 87) 14–15.

281 'Convention on the Conversation of Antarctic Marine Living Resources (Canberra, 20 May 1980)' (Chapter 2, n 68).

into account all the delicate and complex relationships between organisms and physical processes, e.g. currents and sea temperature, that are part of a marine ecosystem. This is undoubtedly a complex task. Local fishing conditions should be given much consideration so that regional impacts can be addressed in a more specific, customized manner.[282] Further, the implementation of the ecosystem approach should not only consider targeted species, but expand to a more holistic management to protect related or dependent species and also take into account bycatch and discards[283] to maintain the ecological sustainability of all species within an ecosystem.[284] In this regard, a common approach is important. In the discussions on the establishment of the BBNJ Treaty, which focuses on the protection of biodiversity as part of ecosystems, delegations had emphasised that

> the principle of the common heritage of mankind was a bedrock for achieving the goal of conserving and sustainably using marine biological diversity of areas beyond national jurisdiction.[285]

However, similar to the precautionary approach, there is no universally accepted definition of the ecosystem approach in international law, probably due to its constantly developing nature. Most instruments focus on the application of the approach rather than providing a definition. For instance, the UNFS Agreement merely refers to ecosystem considerations that should be taken into account: these may include the minimization of discards, conservation of species belonging to the same ecosystem and associated or dependent species, the protection of the marine environment including habitats of special concern, and biological diversity.[286] Further, the participants of the 2006 UN Review Conference of the UNFS Agreement outline that area-based tools should be implemented, and that States should "protect habitats, marine

---

282 William WL Cheung and others, 'Modelling Future Oceans: The Present and Emerging Future of Fish Stocks and Fisheries' in Richard Caddell and Erik J Molenaar (eds), *Strengthening International Fisheries Law in an Era of Changing Oceans* (Hart Publishing 2019) 23.

283 Wahlén and others (Chapter 5, n 81) 4; see Molenaar and Caddell (Chapter 3, n 13) 426–427.

284 'CCAMLR | Ecosystem Approach' <http://archive.ccamlr.org/pu/E/sc/eco-app-intro.htm> accessed 12 June 2020.

285 United Nations General Assembly, 'Intergovernmental Conference on an International Legally Binding Instrument under UNCLOS: Statement by the President of the Conference at the Closing of the Third Session (New York, 19–30 August 2019) – A/CONF.232/2019/10' 2 <https://undocs.org/a/conf.232/2019/10> accessed 8 April 2022.

286 Cf. Articles 5, 6 UNFS Agreement.

biodiversity and vulnerable marine ecosystems, on a case-by-case basis in accordance with the best available scientific information, the precautionary approach and international law".[287]

Although a universally accepted definition remains absent, there seems to be relatively broad consensus on the crucial elements of the approach.[288] Most sources agree that the ecosystem approach entails comprehensive, integrated management of human activities, rather than simply managing the ecosystem.[289] There is further agreement that the approach is based on the best available knowledge on components, structure and dynamics of ecosystems with the aim of satisfying human needs in a way that does not compromise an ecosystem's integrity or health.[290]

The UN General Assembly calls upon States to apply the ecosystem approach in accordance with paragraph 30(d) of the Johannesburg Plan of Implementation.[291] This paragraph refers to the Reykjavik Declaration on Responsible Fisheries in the Marine Ecosystem and Decision V/6 of the COP to the CBD (Decision V/6), which both promote the adoption of the ecosystem approach.[292] Section A Decision V/6 describes the approach, similar to the

---

287 Takei (Chapter 4, n 307) 555.

288 Cf. Sarah Ryan Enright and Ben Boteler, 'The Ecosystem Approach in International Marine Environmental Law and Governance' in TG O'Higgins, Manuel Lago and Theodore H DeWitt (eds), *Ecosystem-Based Management, Ecosystem Services and Aquatic Biodiversity* (Springer 2020) 335 <https://doi.org/10.1007/978-3-030-45843-0_17> accessed 23 November 2020.

289 See for instance annual UNGA Resolutions on Oceans and the Law of the Sea, inter alia 'United Nations General Assembly Resolution 61/222, Oceans and the Law of the Sea (Adopted 20 December 2006)' para 119(b); 'United Nations General Assembly Resolution 74/19, Oceans and the Law of the Sea (Adopted 10 December 2019)' para 196(b).

290 See Trouwborst (Chapter 5, n 206) 425; Jake Rice and others, 'ICES Cooperative Research Report No. 273: Guidance on the Application of the Ecosystem Approach to Management of Human Activities in the European Marine Environment' (2005) 4 <https://www.ices.dk/sites/pub/Publication Reports/Forms/DispForm.aspx?ID=35965> accessed 8 April 2022; OSPAR Commission, 'Annual Report 2002–2003, Volume 2' (2003) 16 <https://www.ospar.org/documents?v=6955> accessed 8 April 2022; simplified see CBD Conference of the Parties, 'COP 5 Decision 6: Ecosystem Approach (Nairobi, 26 May 2000)' s A(1) <https://www.cbd.int/decisions/cop/5/6> accessed 12 August 2021; in more detail, see United Nations General Assembly, 'Report on the Work of the United Nations Open-Ended Informal Consultative Process on Oceans and the Law of the Sea at Its Seventh Meeting (17 July 2006) – A/61/156' para 6 <https://undocs.org/en/A/61/156> accessed 23 November 2021.

291 'United Nations General Assembly Resolution 64/72, Sustainable Fisheries (Adopted 4 December 2009)' 19.

292 Food and Agriculture Organization of the United Nations, 'Reykjavik Declaration on Responsible Fisheries in the Marine Ecosystem (Included in Appendix I, Report of the

description provided above, to be "a strategy for the integrated management of land, water and living resources that promotes conservation and sustainable use in an equitable way", with reference to the definition of ecosystem in Article 2 CBD. Accordingly, ecosystem refers to "a dynamic complex of plant, animal and micro-organism communities and their non-living environment interacting as a functional unit". In light of the CBD, the ecosystem approach is hence the „primary framework for action" under the CBD.[293]

Based on the Malawi Principles[294] that were established in a CBD Workshop on the Ecosystem Approach in 1998,[295] Section B Decision V/6 further presents twelve interlinked, complementary principles of the ecosystem approach, which provide a good orientation with regard to the specific content of the approach.[296] Principle 1 notes that the objectives of management are a matter of societal choice, and that both cultural and biological diversity should be taken into account as central components of the approach. Management should be decentralized where appropriate (Principle 2), and actual or potential effects of managing activities on adjacent and other ecosystems should be considered (Principle 3). The approach should be followed within its functional, temporal and spatial limits while considering the economic context of management measures and the limits of ecosystems (Principles 4–7) and applied long-term, also embracing change (Principles 8–9). Principles 10 and 11 highlight that the ecosystem approach "should seek the appropriate balance between, and integration of, conservation and use of biological diversity" and "consider all forms of relevant information, including scientific and indigenous and local knowledge, innovations and practices". Management should further involve all relevant sectors of society and scientific disciplines (Principle 12).

Reykjavik Conference on Responsible Fisheries in the Marine Ecosystem (Reykjavik, 1–4 October 2001))' <http://www.fao.org/fishery/docs/DOCUMENT/reykjavik/y2198t00_dec.pdf> accessed 10 August 2021; 'COP 5 Decision 23: Annex III. Decisions Adopted by the Conference of the Parties to the Convention on Biological Diversity at Its Fifth Meeting (Nairobi, 15–26 May 2000)' (2000) <https://www.cbd.int/doc/decisions/COP-05-dec-en.pdf> accessed 3 June 2020.

293 'CBD | Ecosystem Approach' <https://www.cbd.int/ecosystem/> accessed 17 January 2022.

294 See SM Garcia and others, 'FAO Fisheries Technical Paper 443: The Ecosystem Approach to Fisheries' (2003) Annex 1 <http://www.fao.org/3/Y4773E/y4773e00.htm#Contents> accessed 28 March 2022; Enright and Boteler (Chapter 5, n 219) 342.

295 CBD Conference of the Parties, 'COP 4 Item 13: Report of the Workshop on the Ecosystem Approach (Lilongwe, 26–28 March 1998)' 7 et seq.

296 CBD Conference of the Parties, 'COP 5 Decision 6: Ecosystem Approach (Nairobi, 26 May 2000)' (Chapter 5, n 290) s B.

Section C Decision V/6 provides operational guidance for the application of the ecosystem approach and its principles.[297]

2.1.2.2 *Implementation in the CAOF Agreement*

All parties to the CAOF Agreement are also parties to the CBD. Therefore, the decisions of the COP are also binding to them. The elaboration of the ecosystem approach under Decision V/6 can hence serve as a reference for defining the scope of the ecosystem approach and its implementation in the CAOF Agreement.

In general, the CAOF Agreement satisfies the standard developed in Decision V/6. The CAOF Agreement refers to the ecosystem on various occasions, although the phrase "ecosystem approach" is not used. The CAOF Agreement mentions the importance of healthy marine ecosystems and their protection,[298] and that knowledge about and the understanding of ecosystems should be increased.[299] Closest to referencing the approach is the wording in Article 5(1)(c) CAOF Agreement, stating that "ecosystem considerations, including the precautionary approach and potential adverse impacts of fishing on the ecosystems" should be taken into account. However, given the various facets of the ecosystem approach, the wording is not a necessary requirement showing that the approach has been implemented. Rather, the fundamental objective of the Agreement is in line with the ecosystem approach, namely to ensure the conservation and sustainable use of living marine resources in healthy marine ecosystems.[300]

As parts of an ecosystem, both cultural and biological diversity should be taken into account.[301] Again, the CAOF Agreement does not explicitly mention biological or cultural diversity, but refers to indigenous and local knowledge and considers that this knowledge meets the needs of diverse cultures.[302] However, there is a lack of references to biodiversity and how it can be considered individually depending on social sectors. Merely "healthy marine ecosystems"[303] are mentioned. This is disappointing in a way, especially considering that the ecosystem approach is not clearly outlined and the insufficient

297 ibid C.

298 Cf. Preamble and Articles 2, 3(4), 5(1)(d)(ii), 13(3) CAOF Agreement.

299 Cf. Article 4(1), 4(2) CAOF Agreement.

300 Cf. Preamble, Articles 2, 3(1), 3(3) 3(6), 5(1)(c)(ii), 5(1)(d), 13(3) CAOF Agreement.

301 See Principle 1 Decision V/6.

302 On the consideration of this knowledge, see Chapter 3, Sections, 4, 4.2, 4.2.2 *supra*.

303 See Articles 2, 3(4), 13 (3) CAOF Agreement.

protection of biodiversity in areas outside national jurisdiction is an evident problem.[304]

Although the CAOF Agreement participants take decisions jointly,[305] States are encouraged to implement conservation and management measures themselves. States are ultimately the actors that authorise commercial fishing[306] and exploratory fishing,[307] conduct research under their national programs,[308] monitor the conduct of vessels entitled to fly the flags of non-parties,[309] and manage fish stocks within national jurisdiction.[310] Hence, in accordance with Principle 2 Decision V/6, the CAOF Agreement adopts a decentralized approach, as the Agreement's measures are to be carried out individually by each State rather than by an institutional body.

The ecosystem approach further requires States to take anticipatory action by considering the impacts of future management measures on adjacent and other ecosystems.[311] In the Agreement, this is implemented by the JPSRM. According to Article 4(2) CAOF Agreement, the aim of the JPSRM is to determine "possible impacts of such fisheries on the ecosystems of the Agreement Area". These considerations form part of the basis for deciding whether commercial fishing should be permitted in the Agreement Area.[312] Although specific reference to adjacent ecosystems is missing in the Agreement, it is noted that scientific research activities in the Agreement Area should "not undermine the prevention of unregulated commercial and exploratory fishing and the protection of healthy marine ecosystems",[313] thus referring to multiple ecosystems, including adjacent ones. This reasoning is supported by the fact that the Agreement further emphasizes the importance to safeguard the "compatibility of conservation and management measures for fish stocks that occur in areas both within and beyond national jurisdiction" in order to "ensure conservation and management of those stocks in their entirety".[314]

To identify potential management gains, ecosystems need to be understood and managed in an economic context. Market distortions that adversely affect

304 On the creation of the BBNJ treaty, see Chapter 3 Section 1 *supra*.
305 On decision-making, see Chapter 5 Sections 2, 2.3 *infra*.
306 See Article 3(1) CAOF Agreement.
307 See Articles 3(3), 5(1)(d)(iii)–(v) CAOF Agreement.
308 See Article 3(2) CAOF Agreement.
309 See Article 8(2) CAOF Agreement.
310 See Article 3(6) CAOF Agreement.
311 See Principle 3 Decision V/6.
312 Cf. Article 5(1)(c) CAOF Agreement.
313 See Article 3(4) CAOF Agreement.
314 See Article 3(6) CAOF Agreement.

biodiversity should be reduced and incentives to promote biodiversity should be aligned in a way that creates equity between those who benefit and those who bear the costs of conserving the ecosystem.[315] Therefore, an approach that benefits the ecosystem must include fair and equitable distribution and sharing of benefits.[316] Typically, at present, only a few States benefit from governance: for example, the continued proliferation and fragmentation of international law in the atmospheric commons and the resulting competition between several different sub-regimes raises concerns that these work "systematically to the overall advantage and interests of the most powerful States, whose consent is essential for the functioning of the system".[317] The application of Principle 4 Decision V/6 is intended to prevent the occurrence of such inequalities. Yet, the CAOF Agreement does not directly implement this approach. In this regard, however, it should be borne in mind that the Agreement only provides a framework for potential fisheries. Commercial activities, if any, are likely to be carried out under an additional agreement. Substantial benefits such as a share in the TAC of certain fisheries do not yet exist. It is therefore expected that the ideas of Principle 4 Decision V/6 will be implemented in an additional, more economically oriented arrangement.

Ecosystems should be managed within the functional, spatial and temporal limits of the ecosystem and consider contextual effects.[318] In this regard, the CAOF Agreement only makes reference in respect to the bearing capacity of an ecosystem by limiting exploratory fishing in "duration, scope and scale to minimize impacts on fish stocks and ecosystems".[319]

The principles further request an integrated management approach.[320] Based on modelling studies and experience, under the ecosystem approach, a single strategy in fisheries management was considered "inadequate to meet the ecological, economic and social objectives that must be addressed for successful ecosystem-based management."[321] Involving industry, conservation,

---

315 See Principle 4 Decision V/6.

316 Cf. CBD Conference of the Parties, 'COP 10 Decision 2: The Strategic Plan for Biodiversity 2011–2020 and the Aichi Biodiversity Targets (Nagoya, 29 October 2010)' (Chapter 4, n 220) Strategic Goal D.

317 Peter H Sand and Jonathan B Wiener, 'Towards a New International Law of the Atmosphere?' (2016) 2 Goettingen Journal of International Law 195, 10 et seq.

318 See Principles 5–7 Decision V/6.

319 See Article 5(1)(d)(ii) CAOF Agreement.

320 See Principles 1, 12 Decision V/6.

321 EA Fulton and others, 'An Integrated Approach Is Needed for Ecosystem Based Fisheries Management: Insights from Ecosystem-Level Management Strategy Evaluation' (2014) 9 PLOS ONE 1, 14 <https://journals.plos.org/plosone/article?id=10.1371/journal.pone.0084242> accessed 14 July 2020.

communities, managers and scientists in a multi-level management approach was expected to achieve social, economic and environmental goals more effectively.[322] The CAOF Agreement considers different stakeholders at different levels. Reference is made to national (individual) obligations and international (collective) obligations.[323] In addition, the Agreement identifies the Parties, traditional and local communities, and scientific and technical organizations, institutions and programs as different stakeholders, all of which should be taken into account when determining actions under the Agreement.

In line with Principle 8 Decision V/6, Article 2 CAOF Agreement makes clear that conservation and management measures are "part of a long-term strategy". Similar reference can be found in the Preamble. No explicit reference is made to the inclusion of changed circumstances. However, it should be noted that the Agreement is formulated with an open-outcome approach and does not focus on any particular development. This adaptive management approach alone can be seen as embracing change.

A balance should be sought between the conservation and use of biological diversity and its integration.[324] In marine management, the terms conservation and sustainable use are usually used side by side,[325] which may sound contradictory: how can something be conserved when it is used? This highlights the difficulties of fisheries management, or resource management and use in general, in maintaining a delicate balance between exploitation and preservation of the status quo. In the CAOF Agreement, the two components – use and conservation – are also usually referenced jointly.[326] Instructions to balance both interests are not explicitly mentioned, but certain interdependence is indicated, among other things, by making exploration measures, i.e. the use of resources, dependent on conservation and management measures.[327]

Lastly, all forms of relevant information, including scientific knowledge, indigenous and local knowledge, innovations and practices should be

322 ibid.

323 See e.g. within the JPSRM, Article 4 CAOF Agreement.

324 See Principle 10 Decision V/6.

325 See e.g. 'United Nations General Assembly Resolution 72/249, International Legally Binding Instrument under UNCLOS on the Conservation and Sustainable Use of Marine Biological Diversity of Areas beyond National Jurisdiction (Adopted 24 December 2017)' paras 1–2; 'United Nations General Assembly Resolution 64/72, Sustainable Fisheries (Adopted 4 December 2009)'; 'United Nations General Assembly Resolution 59/25, Sustainable Fisheries (Adopted 17 November 2004)'.

326 Cf. Preamble, Articles 2, 13(3) CAOF Agreement; reference to "conservation" and "sustainable management" in Preamble and Articles 3(1)(a), 3(6), CAOF Agreement.

327 See Article 3(3) CAOF Agreement.

considered.[328] Throughout the CAOF Agreement, the use of both scientific knowledge and indigenous and local knowledge is promoted.[329]

In summary, when assessing the CAOF Agreement in light of the CBD principles, specific references are missing that could have been easily implemented and could have promoted the importance of the ecosystem approach, e.g. a consideration of adverse impacts on adjacent and other ecosystems. Nevertheless, overall the CAOF Agreement implements most elements of the ecosystem approach well. Thus, in addition to the precautionary approach, the additional important component of sustainable development is anchored in CAO fisheries management.

2.2 *Duty to Cooperate*

The Arctic harbours a certain number of discovered and yet untapped resources. Since parts of the Arctic Ocean belong to the high seas and do not fall within the sovereignty sphere of any State, these are classified as "natural resources that occur in areas under the jurisdiction of more than one State or fully or partly in areas beyond the limits of national jurisdiction" and hence as shared resources.[330] However, as Arctic waters border sovereign States and multiple stakeholders are involved, and fish stocks often occur transboundary, political discussions on how to best manage and use these resources in the region are on the agenda. In this context, international and national strategies for the Arctic tend to be built on the essential idea of cooperation. In this regard, Sir David Attenborough notes that "the time for nationalism is over. Internationalism has to be what we must look forward to", and in this respect, equality in what nations take from the world's resources must be improved.[331] Hence, there is a need for international cooperation, especially for the management of fish on the high seas and organisms that migrate across jurisdictional boundaries.[332] With regard to law, this need has developed into the international duty to cooperate.

---

328 See Principle 11 Decision V/6.

329 Cf. Preamble, Articles 4(4), 5(1)(b) CAOF Agreement.

330 Sharelle Hart, 'IUCN Environmental Policy and Law Paper No. 72 – Shared Resources: Issues of Governance' (2008) 1 <https://portals.iucn.org/library/sites/library/files/documents/EPLP-072.pdf> accessed 30 March 2022.

331 'Interview with David Attenbrough and Michael Palin (Published 13 October 2020)' <https://www.instagram.com/p/CGR5tF-Hfiz/> accessed 29 May 2021.

332 Trouwborst (Chapter 5, n 206) 423; for the Arctic specifically, see Inuit Circumpolar Conference, *Principles and Elements for a Comprehensive Arctic Policy* (Centre for Northern Studies and Research 1992) 53.

2.2.1 Development and Definition of the Duty to Cooperate

The duty to cooperate is an established concept in customary international law.[333] In the context of fisheries, a State's obligation to cooperate in the management of straddling stocks is first mentioned throughout UNCLOS[334] and further strengthened by the UNFS Agreement, which basically presents a holistic implementation of the duty to cooperate.[335] Most important, wherever an RFB exists, compliance with the duty to cooperate is a prerequisite for exercising the freedom of fishing on the high seas:[336] only States that agree to cooperate in an RFB or comply with the provisions of an RFB may participate in the fisheries in the area at stake.[337]

Also the UN General Assembly emphasizes in its annual Resolutions on Sustainable Fisheries that States have an obligation

> to cooperate in the conservation and management of living marine resources" and should recognize "the importance of coordination and cooperation at the global, regional, subregional as well as national levels in the areas, inter alia, of marine scientific research, data collection, information-sharing, capacity-building and training for the conservation, management and sustainable development of marine living resources".[338]
>
> The resolutions especially urge States to "strengthen and enhance cooperation among existing and developing regional fisheries management organizations and arrangements in which they participate, including increased communication and further coordination of measures".[339]

The preference for cooperative rather than individual management in fisheries has proven to be beneficial: for example, contrary to what had been feared,

333 On the customary character of the obligation, see Chapter 4 Sections 1, 1.2, 1.2.2 *supra*.

334 See Articles 116(c)–120 (especially Articles 117 and 118), 197, 200, 201 UNCLOS, cf. e.g. Articles 61(2), 63, 64, 66(4), 69(3), 70(4) UNCLOS.

335 See especially Articles 20–21 UNFS Agreement, cf. e.g. Articles 7(2), 8(1), 8(3), 8(5), 13, 14, 18(g)(i) UNFS Agreement.

336 Henriksen, Hønneland and Sydnes (Chapter 3, n 171) 8; Rosemary Rayfuse, 'Countermeasures and High Seas Fisheries Enforcement' (2004) 51 Netherlands International Law Review 41, 54.

337 Cf. 8(4), 10(b), 17(3) UNFS Agreement.

338 See e.g. 'United Nations General Assembly Resolution 64/72, Sustainable Fisheries (Adopted 4 December 2009)' Preamble, para 99; 'United Nations General Assembly Resolution 74/18, Sustainable Fisheries (Adopted 10 December 2019)' Preamble, para 166.

339 See e.g. 'United Nations General Assembly Resolution 64/72, Sustainable Fisheries (Adopted 4 December 2009)' Preamble, para 99; 'United Nations General Assembly Resolution 74/18, Sustainable Fisheries (Adopted 10 December 2019)' Preamble, para 166.

cooperative management under a cartel led to higher potential profits than under open access (with potential closure of the fishery). Further, with regard to sustainability, simulations have shown that the benefits of such international cooperation far exceed the returns of a competitive open access fishery over a period of several decades. The presence of several competing fishing operations in deep-sea fisheries, on the other hand, has in many cases led to partial or complete depletion of the respective stock. Moreover, where participants were allocated a comparatively small zone to fish, aggressive fishing was carried out when the stock moved into the allocated fishing zone.[340] As regards Norwegian spring spawning herring for example, while cooperation resulted in an optimal stock at a very high and sustainable level, open access nearly caused the extinction of the stock.[341] Similarly, in the high seas enclave between Russian and American zones, the "Donut Hole",[342] the two coastal States and a few DWF States overexploited Alaskan pollock resources, as cooperative management of the straddling stocks was non-existent.[343]

Since compliance with the duty to cooperate paves the way for participation in fisheries, a determination of the specific content of that duty must be made. In the context of fisheries, the duty to cooperate originates in general principles of international law that were developed when dealing with the governance of the exploitation of transboundary resources. It consists of several components, the collaborative element being the intrinsic one in all related duties. It embodies, *inter alia*, the duty of conservation, which goes hand in hand with the duty to adopt appropriate conservation measures[344] that arises from the exhaustibility of fish stocks and applies to all States and thus to all vessels fishing in all areas of the high seas. As a result, the duty to cooperate can be described as

> a natural corollary of the duty to conserve a shared natural resource in that conservation of an open access regime will only be possible where all exploiting states agree on, and implement, measures to regulate their exploitation.[345]

340 Bjørndal and Munro (Chapter 4, n 47) 243–244.
341 ibid 245.
342 More specifically on the "Donut Hole" issue see Chapter 3 Section 1 *supra*.
343 Munro, Van Houtte and Willmann (Chapter 4, n 46) s 4.2.
344 See Article 117 UNCLOS.
345 Rayfuse, 'Countermeasures and High Seas Fisheries Enforcement' (Chapter 5, n 336) 54.

Pursuant to UNCLOS, where States whose nationals exploit identical living resources or different living resources in the same area, cooperation should take place either through entering into negotiations with a view to taking the measures necessary for the conservation of the living resources concerned or by the establishment of (S)RFMOs.[346] Similarly, the UNFS Agreement supports the same approach.[347] Further, the UNFS Agreement sets forth different fields of cooperation, such as international, subregional and regional cooperation in enforcement,[348] cooperation in regard to developing States[349] and dispute settlement.[350]

The core element of the duty to cooperate is compliance by not only RFB member States but also non-member States with the measures adopted by the RFBs including the prohibition of fishing: where RFBs regulate fisheries in a certain area, the duty to cooperate within the UNFS Agreement implies, more specifically than the duty described in UNCLOS, that States with a real interest fishing for the stocks on the high seas and relevant coastal States should become members of this RFB or agree to comply with measures established elsewhere.[351] States that do not agree to the application of the relevant measures are still obliged to fulfil their duty to cooperate according to Article 17(2) UNFS Agreement. Hence, they must not authorise their vessels to fish for straddling or highly migratory fish stocks subjected to measures established by such RFB. In order to safeguard broad compliance with the measures, State parties should nevertheless encourage non-parties to the UNFS Agreement to become parties and to adopt laws and regulations consistent with its provisions.[352] As part of their duty to cooperate, RFB members should exchange information with respect to the activities of fishing vessels flying the flags of non-member States that are engaged in fishing operations for the relevant stocks.[353] They should take legitimate measures to deter activities of vessels that undermine the effectiveness of (sub)regional conservation and management measures.[354] Therefore, it becomes clear that pursuant to the UNFS Agreement, the tool for cooperative management in fisheries is an RFB.

346 See Article 118 UNCLOS.
347 See Article 8 UNFS Agreement.
348 See Articles 20, 21 UNFS Agreement.
349 See Articles 24–26 UNFS Agreement.
350 See Article 28 UNFS Agreement.
351 See Article 8(3) UNFS Agreement.
352 See Article 33(1) UNFS Agreement.
353 See Article 17(4) UNFS Agreement.
354 See Articles 17(4), 33(2) UNFS Agreement.

Cooperative, comprehensive management also relates to the fish stocks themselves. The term "in their entirety" in Article 7(2) UNFS Agreement, which replaced the initial wording "overall", suggests that when establishing appropriate conservation and management measures, States must take into account fish stocks throughout their geographical migration range.[355] In this regard, the chairman of the second session of the UN Conference on Straddling Fish Stocks and Highly Migratory Fish Stocks mentioned that

> [t]he biological nature and distribution of these stocks necessitate compatible and coherent management measures over their entire range. In this respect, fish know no boundaries, and at different times during their life cycles, they may be found both within areas of national jurisdiction and on the high seas.[356]

In response to breaches of the duty to cooperate, RFBs have adopted a range of actions to be taken, including the denial of landings and transhipments, adoption of trade measures, taking of diplomatic action and the inspection of non-member vessels within their ports.[357] A breach of the obligation to cooperate might not always invoke the other members' right to board, inspect and possibly arrest.[358] Yet, breaches that undermine the effectiveness of RFB conservation and management measures may well incite such action.[359]

2.2.2 Implementation in the CAOF Agreement

The CAOF Agreement largely incorporates the duty to cooperate as outlined above. In fact, the CAOF Agreement as such, as an RFB, is already a means of cooperation requested by the UNFS Agreement. The CAOF Agreement specifically mentions cooperation in different contexts. The Preamble addresses cooperation by underlining

> the importance of ensuring cooperation and coordination between the Parties and the NEAFC and other relevant mechanisms for fisheries

355 Oude Elferink (Chapter 2, n 64) 5 et seq.

356 United Nations General Assembly, 'United Nations Conference on Straddling Fish Stocks and Highly Migratory Fish Stocks, Second Session (New York, 12–30 July 1993), Chairman Statement Held on 12 July 1993 – A/CONF.164/11' (Chapter 2, n 64) 3.

357 For a comprehensive overview, see Rayfuse, 'Countermeasures and High Seas Fisheries Enforcement' (Chapter 5, n 336) 57.

358 See e.g. Articles 19(b), 20(6), 21, 22 UNFS Agreement.

359 Rayfuse, 'Countermeasures and High Seas Fisheries Enforcement' (Chapter 5, n 336) 57.

> management that are established and operated in accordance with international law, as well as with relevant international bodies and programs.

Particular emphasis is placed on the importance of cooperation and coordination between the Parties and the NEAFC, as the latter has competence to adopt conservation and management measures in part of the high seas portion of the CAO.[360] The original reference to "scientific"[361] bodies was removed from the text in order to broaden the scope of cooperation to include bodies such as the Arctic Council and the OSPAR Commission. This was considered helpful for the comprehensive implementation of an ecosystem approach to marine governance, also for the development of the broad BBNJ treaty process.[362]

With reference to Article 7 UNFS Agreement, Article 3(6) CAOF Agreement highlights the need for cooperation between coastal State Parties and other Parties to ensure the compatibility of conservation and management measures for transboundary fish stocks – namely fish stocks that occur in areas within and beyond national jurisdiction in or adjacent to the CAOF Agreement Area. This approach is intended to ensure the conservation and management of these stocks in their entirety. The Parties shall further facilitate cooperation in scientific activities[363] and cooperate in fulfilling obligations that they are subject to under international law and other existing treaties.[364]

On other occasions, the CAOF Agreement implies cooperation more subtly. For instance, the JPSRM as a joint program is established on the basis of cooperation.[365] Decisions on (interim) conservation and management measures are made by the Parties jointly,[366] and the review and implementation of the Agreement should be conducted collectively.[367] Furthermore, where Parties intend to authorise scientific research activities involving the catching of fish in the Agreement Area, they must inform each other of such plans.[368]

Moreover, the formation of committees or similar bodies to promote implementation of the CAOF Agreement[369] is based on cooperation. Where

360 On the issue of overlapping regulatory areas, see Chapter 2 Section 3 *supra*.

361 Cf. 'Report of the Third FiSCAO Meeting on Central Arctic Ocean Fisheries (Seattle, 14–16 April 2015)' (Chapter 3, n 92) 16.

362 Molenaar, 'The CAOF Agreement: Key Issues of International Fisheries Law' (Chapter 2, n 20) 454,459.

363 See Article 4(1) CAOF Agreement.

364 See Article 14(1) CAOF Agreement.

365 Cf. Article 4 CAOF Agreement.

366 Cf. Articles 3(1)(b), 5(1)(d), 6 CAOF Agreement.

367 See Article 5 CAOF Agreement.

368 See Article 3(4) CAOF Agreement.

369 As foreseen by Article 5(6) CAOF Agreement.

non-parties are concerned, the Parties should encourage them to take measures in accordance with the Agreement and to deter the activities of vessels entitled to fly the flags of non-parties that undermine the effective implementation of the CAOF Agreement.[370] In addition, cooperation with Arctic residents and their communities should be achieved through inclusion.[371]

In summary, the CAOF Agreement, as a fisheries management arrangement, is a construct of cooperation that continues to implement the duty to cooperate throughout. Although some obligations are to be fulfilled by each State individually,[372] the ten Parties are supposed to address substantive issues[373] in a cooperative manner.

2.3 *Decision-Making Procedures*

Effective decision-making procedures are another fundamental element of RFBs. Consolidated governance in RFBs does not always lead to more effective fisheries management. The unwillingness of member States to delegate sufficient decision-making power and responsibility to an international authority hinders efficient processes.[374] Where effective decision-making procedures are missing, conflicts have to be resolved in court, as it was for example the case in a dispute submitted to ITLOS: the tribunal was asked to decide on TAC limits because the contracting parties to the Commission for the Conservation of Southern Bluefin Tuna could not reach an agreement on such limits.[375] Further, older RFMOs that have not focused on establishing effective decision-making procedures still struggle to respond to the urgency of conservation and management and to implement the adoption of precautionary and ecosystem approaches. In part, this was linked to the lack of political will of some members, or more general, the will to agree.[376] Hence, this underlines the statement that "an RFMO is only as good as its members"[377] – or their effort to reach a mutual decision.

---

370 See Article 8 CAOF Agreement.

371 See Preamble CAOF Agreement.

372 Such as the authorisation of vessels to conduct commercial or exploratory fishing according to Article 3(1) and (3) CAOF Agreement.

373 See Article 6(3) CAOF Agreement.

374 Food and Agriculture Organization of the United Nations, 'Report of the Meeting of the High-Level Panel of External Experts in Fisheries (Rome, 26–27 January 1998)' (Chapter 4, n 323) para 28.

375 *Southern Bluefin Tuna (New Zealand v. Japan; Australia v. Japan), Provisional Measures, Order of 27 August 1999, ITLOS Reports 1999, p. 280* (Chapter 5, n 40).

376 See Swan (Chapter 4, n 323) s 2.1.

377 Wahlén and others (Chapter 5, n 81) 11.

2.3.1 Development and Definition of Efficient Decision-Making Procedures

RFBs developed from fulfilling advisory functions to performing regulatory functions with the power to adopt binding decisions on conservation and management measures. Additionally, progressive decision-making activity could be detected in most RFBs.[378]

In fisheries decision-making processes, various types of decisions need to be made in various fields, such as membership, finance and administration, work programs, priorities and the establishment of working groups, committees or other subsidiary bodies. Furthermore, RFBs will have to decide on research priorities, liaison with other bodies, implementation of international instruments, meeting attendance by observes and dispute settlement. Most RFBs are organized institutionally and hence consist of different working bodies, e.g. a commission, council, scientific committee, standing committees and working groups[379] that are all more or less involved in decision-making.[380]

The UNFS Agreement, as a framework agreement, does not lay down many preconditions for decision-making. Article 6(3)(a) UNFS Agreement states that in implementing the precautionary approach, States must "improve decision-making for fishery resource conservation and management by obtaining and sharing the best scientific information available and implementing improved techniques for dealing with risk and uncertainty". States should "agree on decision-making procedures which facilitate the adoption of conservation and management measures in a timely and effective manner",[381] and "efficient and expeditious decision-making procedures" to prevent disputes.[382]

For specification, several objectives for regulatory RFBs regarding the decision-making process on management measures are suggested.[383]

First, in line with the UNFS Agreement,[384] decisions should be taken promptly, efficiently and in accordance with current and future needs.[385] Prompt decisions increase the chances of reacting quickly and purposefully to developments. Irreversible changes can thus be avoided.

378 Swan (Chapter 4, n 323) s 2.2.
379 See e.g. NAFO and ICCAT.
380 Swan (Chapter 4, n 323) s 2.2.
381 See Article 10(j) UNFS Agreement.
382 See Article 28 UNFS Agreement.
383 Swan (Chapter 4, n 323) s 2.2.
384 See Articles 10(j), 28 UNFS Agreement.
385 Swan (Chapter 4, n 323) s 2.2.

Second, binding decisions must be issued to the greatest extent possible.[386] Opting-out provisions, according to which a State raising a qualified objection is not bound by a decision, are problematic in this respect.[387] RFBs usually either provide for objections to decisions or, in order to prevent objections, require unanimous agreement among all members for decisions to be taken.[388] As often experienced in the context of the UN Security Council, the exercise of such rights of objection or the refusal to take a unanimous decision inherently inhibits decisions and development. Such obstacles should be avoided wherever possible in order to prevent blocked measures and irreversible consequences, especially in the field of international environmental law, where community interests are supposed to take precedence over national interests. Majority voting instead of consensus-based decision-making may serve as a helpful instrument here.[389]

Third, as decision-making should be based on science, economics and other values,[390] institutional mechanisms must be applied. The transfer of clear and standardized information important for decision-making should be ensured, and internationally agreed concepts be implemented.[391] As an example, the Commission for the Conservation of Antarctic Marine Living Resources (CCAMLR) applies the precautionary approach within decision-making processes as follows:

> CCAMLR collects the data it can, then weighs up the extent and effect of the uncertainties and gaps in such data before making a management decision. The approach aims to minimise the risk of long-term adverse effects rather than delaying decisions until all necessary data are available.[392]

Specifically in the light of sustainable development, the New Delhi Declaration urges that decision-making processes should always endorse a precautionary approach to risk management and include the adoption of appropriate transparent precautionary measures that are based on independent, up-to-date

386 ibid.
387 Henriksen, Hønneland and Sydnes (Chapter 3, n 171) 205.
388 Swan (Chapter 4, n 323) s 2.2.
389 Schatz, Proelß and Liu (Chapter 2, n 41) 231 et seq.
390 Philippe Sands (Chapter 4, n 32) 6 et seq.
391 Swan (Chapter 4, n 323) ss 2.1, 2.2, 3.
392 'CCAMLR | Ecosystem Approach' (Chapter 5, n 284).

scientific judgment.[393] Data collection, analysis and dissemination of information on status and trends of fisheries and fishery resources support such an implementation.[394]

Fourth, transparency in decision-making is one of the most important concepts to implement. This begins with access requirements. For example, during the negotiation process of the UNFS Agreement, it was criticised that membership in RFBs was like a "select club", often dependent on a certain financial contribution. It is submitted that transparency can only be achieved through public scrutiny of the decision-making process. However, it must be kept in mind that even if an RFB is willing to open its "secret deliberations" to a selected circle, the necessary funds have to be raised to gain access, which is difficult for some less prosperous actors, e.g. NGOs.[395]

Fifth, effective decision-making should include some kind of analysis or evaluation of the effectiveness of existing decision-making processes and allow for adaptation.[396] In this regard, performance indicators for self-evaluation would be helpful and have already been considered. However, defining indicators that are generally applicable to all RFBs is very difficult, as RFBs differ, *inter alia*, in terms of their mandate, species coverage, the economic situation of members or governance systems.[397] Nevertheless, it is argued that addressing decision-making in whatever form shapes effective decision-making processes.

Lastly, efficient dispute settlement mechanisms[398] should be in place where a decision or the process of decision-making is disputed.[399]

---

393 United Nations, 'World Summit on Sustainable Development (Johannesburg, 26 August-4 September 2002), ILA New Delhi Declaration of Principles of International Law Relating to Sustainable Development – A/CONF.199/8' (Chapter 5, n 180) s 5.

394 Swan (Chapter 4, n 323) s 3.1.

395 UN Fish Stocks Agreement Review Conference, 'Summary of the Fifth Substantive Session (24 July-4 August 1995): Failings and Set-Backs' (1995) 7 Earth Negotiations Bulletin 54 <https://enb.iisd.org/vol07/0754030e.html> accessed 30 May 2020; Food and Agriculture Organization of the United Nations, 'Report of the Meeting of the High-Level Panel of External Experts in Fisheries (Rome, 26–27 January 1998)' (Chapter 4, n 323) para 30.

396 Cf. Swan (Chapter 4, n 323) ss 2.1, 2.3; Henriksen, Hønneland and Sydnes (Chapter 3, n 171) 207.

397 Food and Agriculture Organization of the United Nations, 'Report of the Second Meeting of FAO and Non-FAO Regional Fishery Bodies or Arrangements (Rome, 20–21 February 2001)' (Chapter 5, n 221) 3.

398 Specifically on dispute settlement, see Chapter 5 Sections 2, 2.4, 2.4.2 *infra*.

399 See Henriksen, Hønneland and Sydnes (Chapter 3, n 171) 207–208; Swan (Chapter 4, n 323) s 2.2.

In summary, the effectiveness of decision-making depends first on the willingness of stakeholders to consent. This willingness depends on the extent to which scientific information is relied upon and shared. In this way, a common ground is created that facilitates agreement. In addition, the transparency and swiftness of the process, the review of procedures and possible periodic adjustments are crucial to increase effectiveness. Further, effective dispute resolution should be ensured.

2.3.2 Implementation in the CAOF Agreement

As the CAOF Agreement just recently entered into force, and decisions within the framework have not yet been taken, decision-making cannot be practically assessed so far. However, it can be reviewed whether the envisaged process theoretically provides a basis for efficient decision-making.

Whereas the CAOF Agreement implements most of the approaches mentioned, it also suffers from a couple of weaknesses.

The CAOF Agreement's principal decision-making body is the meeting of the Parties. Meetings shall take place every two years or more frequently.[400] Further, to assist implementation of the Agreement, the Agreement foresees the formation of committees or similar bodies in which representatives of Arctic communities may participate.[401] This revives the promises made in the Preamble to involve and consider the interests of Arctic residents, including Arctic indigenous peoples, when dealing with the conservation and sustainable use of living marine resources in healthy marine ecosystems in the Arctic Ocean. In that way, although depending on the will of the Parties to form such bodies, local Arctic residents get the chance to guide the practical application of measures not only during its active implementation but also its determination by voting for or against measures in the interest of their respective communities. Advice should be provided by the scientific meetings under the JPSRM, which should take place at least two months prior to the meeting of the Parties.[402]

In the CAOF Agreement, the provisions on the JPSRM address speed and efficiency of decisions by the request "to provide timely scientific advice" to the meetings of the Parties.[403] This enables responsiveness to future needs, as the meeting of the Parties takes decisions and does not merely make

400 See Article 5(1) CAOF Agreement.
401 See Article 5(2) CAOF Agreement.
402 See Article 4(6) CAOF Agreement.
403 See Article 4(6) CAOF Agreement.

recommendations. The sooner scientific advice is passed on, the sooner final decisions can be made.

It was recommended that binding decisions should be made where possible. Within the CAOF Agreement, this matter is more complex. The issue of decision-making procedures was one of the difficult points of discussion on the way to the Agreement.[404] Several procedures were proposed during the negotiations. Among others, it was suggested that decisions on substantive matters be taken by a three-fourths majority vote, including at least three of the Arctic Five, where consensus could not be reached. A separate procedure should have been applied for commercial fishing issues, allowing coastal States to delay the start of commercial fishing for up to two years. Another proposal called for a veto right for the Arctic Five. Both suggestions were rejected by the Other Five, who opposed any kind of special role of the Arctic Five in decision-making. Finally, at their sixth meeting, the Parties agreed on a single decision-making procedure for substantive issues as part of a package deal.[405] As a result, all Parties are now formally on equal footing concerning decision-making under the Agreement. With regard to procedural matters, the final text of the Agreement provides for such decisions to be taken by a majority of the Parties,[406] which promotes progress rather than risking important decisions being blocked due to (possibly less crucial) procedural issues. This leaves enough room for discussions on substantive issues to be decided by consensus.[407] Consensus is considered to refer to the absence of any formal objection made at the time the decision in question was taken,[408] although not necessarily reflecting "unanimity" of opinion on the substantive matter.[409] Hence, by opting for consensus in decision-making, the Parties' possibility to

404 'Chairman's Statement, Fourth Meeting on Central Arctic Ocean Fisheries (Tórshavn, 29 November – 1 December 2016)' (Chapter 2, n 238) 2.

405 Molenaar, 'Participation in the Central Arctic Ocean Fisheries Agreement' (Chapter 2, n 23)(Chapter 3, n 32) 158.

406 See Article 6(1) CAOF Agreement.

407 See Article 6(2) CAOF Agreement.

408 In relation to decisions on the interpretation of treaties, see United Nations General Assembly, 'Report of the International Law Commission, Sixty-Sixth Session (5 May–6 June and 7 July–8 August 2014) – A/69/10, Supplement No. 10' 214 et seq. <https://documents-dds-ny.un.org/doc/UNDOC/GEN/G14/134/72/PDF/G1413472.pdf?OpenElement> accessed 4 April 2022.

409 United Nations Office of Legal Affairs, 'Comments on Some Procedural Questions' (2009) s Consensus in UN practice General, para 8 <https://legal.un.org/ola/media/GA_RoP/GA_RoP_EN.pdf> accessed 18 June 2021.

raise objections reflects a *de facto* veto right to decisions.[410] There is no specific procedure on objections to decisions under the CAOF Agreement, only for objections to the duration of the CAOF Agreement.[411] Therefore, it is assumed that similar prerequisites for raising an objection within decision-making processes apply, i.e. the objection must be issued by the legal representative of the Party, transmitted to the competent authority – presumably the meeting of the Parties as the CAOF Agreements' decision-making body – and should preferably be in writing. However, although broad acceptance of a decision taken by consensus is guaranteed, such a decision is problematic as it reflects the lowest common denominator of the Parties' position and may become relatively meaningless, even though it might be binding.[412]

The CAOF Agreement provides for decisions by consensus only for questions of substance.[413] An issue is considered to be substantial if a contracting Party considers it to be essential.[414] Therefore, the contracting Parties may individually determine when this is the case.[415] This broad approach can hamper swift decision-making. Nevertheless, the option ensures that all Parties and their concerns are taken seriously and that no Party is given the feeling of being secondary. This is particularly important when considering the issue of the Artic Five in relation to the Other Five.[416]

As regards the reliance on scientific evidence for decision-making that is requested by the UNFS Agreement, the CAOF Agreement indicates that decisions within the JPSRM under Article 4 CAOF Agreement should include and be based on scientific information and knowledge provided by relevant scientific and technical organizations, bodies and programs, as well as indigenous and local communities. Specifically, the Parties should take a decision on probably the most important question under the Agreement – whether sustainable commercial fishing in the CAOF Agreement Area will be possible, whether a

410 Cf. Molenaar, 'The CAOF Agreement: Key Issues of International Fisheries Law' (Chapter 2, n 20) 470.

411 See Article 13(2) CAOF Agreement.

412 Cf. United Nations Office of Legal Affairs (Chapter 5, n 409) s Consensus in UN practice General, para 21.

413 See Article 6(1) and (2) CAOF Agreement.

414 See Article 6(3) CAOF Agreement.

415 Similiar to e.g. Article VIII 'Convention for the Conservation of Anadromous Stocks in the North Pacific Ocean (Moscow, 11 February 1992)' <https://www.npafc.org/wp-content/uploads/Public-Documents/Handbook/Handbook-3rd-E-Convention-Only-English.pdf> accessed 2 November 2024.

416 On the relationship of the Arctic Five and the Other Five, see Chapter 3 Sections 3, 3.1 *supra*.

new RFB should be established, and whether additional or different interim conservation and management measures should be initiated – based on the scientific information derived from the JPSRM, national scientific programs and other relevant sources.[417]

Transparency through accreditation of different members or observers to the Agreement could have been implemented in a better way. (N)GOs are currently only allowed to participate through members' delegations.[418] Furthermore, even though the Preamble emphasises the importance of involving Arctic residents, representatives of Arctic communities are only allowed to participate in committees or similar bodies that – optionally – can be formed by the Parties.[419]

The CAOF Agreement contains no reference to a periodic review of decision-making. Only the implementation of the Agreement and available scientific information is to be reviewed.[420] However, it is considered likely that once decisions are made under the Agreement, the process will be reviewed to some extent.

The CAOF Agreement also provides for dispute-settlement,[421] which will be looked at in more detail separately.[422]

The Agreement therefore contains most elements that are considered to support effective decision-making, but leaves room for improvement of the process. Greater involvement of (N)GOs is desirable, should decisions, especially concerning commercial or exploratory fishing, be made. In particular, it will be interesting to see how the requirement to take decisions of substance by consensus will affect the content and quality of future decisions.

2.4 *Compliance and Dispute Settlement*

Effective fisheries management often faces implementation and enforcement problems rather than a lack of regulation. Compliance and enforcement, including the peaceful settlement of disputes, are hence considered key concepts of fisheries management. Almost inevitable in a management process involving several actors are disagreements that may arise sooner or later. Parties are therefore well advised to additionally include dispute resolution arrangements as a preventive measure.

---

417 See Article 5(1)(c) CAOF Agreement.

418 On participation of NGOs, see Chapter 3, Sections 3, 3.2 and Chapter 3, Section 4, 4.3 *supra*.

419 See Article 5(2) CAOF Agreement.

420 See Articles 5(1)(a), 5(1)(b), 4(6) CAOF Agreement.

421 See Article 7 CAOF Agreement.

422 See specifically on dispute settlement Chapter 5 Sections 2, 2.4, 2.4.2 *infra*.

2.4.1 Compliance and Enforcement

Creating a fully-fledged legal order requires not only substantive norms, but also their implementation: the most well designed laws can only be effective if they are respected by all parties and their enforcement is successful. Nevertheless, compliance with legal regimes does not necessarily correspond with its effectiveness: if standards are set too low and are met, less progress can be made than if ambitious targets are set and these are only partially met.[423] Therefore, in a first step, realistic goals must be defined. In a second step, after establishing precise rules, compliance with these rules is necessary to achieve progress within a regime.

2.4.1.1 *Aspects of Compliance and Enforcement*

There are two general approaches on how to deal with compliance. Strict compliance enforcement or an institutional design approach, where compliance is managed rather than enforced, can be followed. The strict enforcement approach presumes that "States are rational utility maximizers" who "will violate treaties if the benefits of violation outweigh the costs". Therefore, States must be compelled to comply by coercion, usually through the imposition of sanctions. Contrary, the managing institutional design approach considers States to generally comply with norms "unless there are strong countervailing circumstances". Hence, where a State does not comply with norms, this "results from lack of capacity or clarity rather than from wilful disobedience".[424] The approach aims at facilitating overall compliance and organizational effectiveness by focusing on the particular causes of non-compliance. RFBs often follow the managing approach, yet, the models are not mutually exclusive and elements of both can be found in international fisheries agreements nowadays.[425] In general, it can be said that the effectiveness of an agreement strongly depends on the will of the parties to act in conformity with established regulations.[426]

Rooted in customary norms of State responsibility[427] that set up the consequences of unlawful action,[428] compliance control has been implemented

423 Tim Stephens, 'International Courts and Environmental Governance', *International courts and environmental protection* (Cambridge University Press 2009) 63.

424 Bodansky (Chapter 4, n 58) 236.

425 Matley (Chapter 3, n 37) 108 et seq.; cf. Janine Grabs, *Selling Sustainability Short?* (Cambridge University Press 2020) 14.

426 Wahlén and others (Chapter 5, n 81) 11.

427 See *Case Concerning the Factory at Chorzów (Claim for Indemnity), Judgement of 26 July 1927, Publications of the Permanent Court of International Justice Series A – No 9* 21; *Corfu Channel Case (United Kingdom of Great Britain and Northern Ireland v Albania), Judgement of 9 April 1949, ICJ Reports 1949, p 4* 23.

428 Cf. Article 1 International Law Commission, 'Draft Articles on Responsibility of States for Internationally Wrongful Acts (1 November 2001) – A/56/10, Supplement No. 10' <https://www.refworld.org/docid/3ddb8f804.html> accessed 9 July 2021.

in most international environmental agreements by now. Initially, provisions with environmental character were enforceable through conventional means of State responsibility and dispute settlement. The development of these norms resulted in refined multilateral environmental agreements establishing institutions that deal with enforcement and compliance issues of their respective regime themselves. These tend to integrate judicial elements while retaining several general international compliance mechanisms.[429]

In fisheries, compliance is considered an important tool to combat IUU fishing.[430] In this regard, the UN General Assembly encourages States to

> establish and undertake cooperative surveillance and enforcement activities in accordance with international law to strengthen and enhance efforts to ensure compliance with conservation and management measures, and prevent and deter illegal, unreported and unregulated fishing.[431]

UNCLOS entails certain actions that may be taken to ensure compliance with and enforcement of UNCLOS provisions[432] including conservation measures.[433] Furthermore, the UNFS Agreement specifically sets up a general duty to ensure compliance by stating that a State whose vessels fish on the high seas "shall take such measures as may be necessary to ensure that vessels flying its flag comply with subregional and regional conservation and management measures",[434] which are specified in the subsequent paragraphs of the same Article and further throughout the UNFS Agreement.[435] Additionally, States are obliged to cooperate in compliance and enforcement of the conservation and management measures adopted internationally[436] and (sub) regionally.[437]

429 Stephens (Chapter 5, n 423) 64 et seq.

430 Papastavridis (Chapter 2, n 156) 359.

431 'United Nations General Assembly Resolution 73/125, Sustainable Fisheries (Adopted 11 December 2018)' para 114.

432 Cf. Articles 153(4) and (5), 162(2)(a), 217 UNCLOS.

433 Cf. Article 117 UNCLOS.

434 See Article 18(1) UNFS Agreement. A similar duty exists in regard to vessels that do not fish on the high seas but fly the flag of a respective State, see Article 19(1) UNFS Agreement.

435 Cf. Articles 9–23 UNFS Agreement.

436 See Article 20(1) UNFS Agreement.

437 See Article 21 UNFS Agreement.

The FAO considers that compliance is anchored in the precautionary approach, as the approach involves assessing the feasibility and reliability of fisheries management options. This assessment takes into account the possibility of implementing and ensuring compliance with the respective management options. Furthermore, it includes the implementation of detailed compliance instructions and enforcement tactics such as contingency rules and sanctions for non-compliance.[438] The 1993 FAO Compliance Agreement is considered to be of special relevance in this regard.[439] It follows UNCLOS' and the UNFS Agreement's approach of focusing on the effective enforcement of measures. Although not all CAOF Agreement Parties are parties to this agreement, the FAO Compliance Agreement is considered to present minimum requirements of compliance for (future) RFBs. These are international cooperation, achieved e.g. through data sharing, and enhanced participation of States in RFBs, control of vessels and generally the approach of a wide enforcement of measures through flag State responsibility.[440] Suggested enforcement tools include port State control measures, flag State measures like fishing vessels' registration, and measures by third States, including inspections at sea. Private actors play a key role in this regard.[441] In addition, the formulation of clearer obligations for those providing support services to fishing vessels is considered helpful in ensuring compliance with the rules against IUU fishing at all levels.[442] Furthermore, fairness, non-discrimination and transparency should be applied for ensuring compliance,[443] both among parties but also in regard to non-participants. Contracting parties should for instance adhere to the established rules themselves in order to legitimize management measures to

438 Food and Agriculture Organization of the United Nations, 'Technical Guidelines for Responsible Fisheries No. 2: Precautionary Approach to Capture Fisheries and Species Introductions' (Chapter 5, n 222) paras 35–36, 39.

439 Food and Agriculture Organization of the United Nations, 'Agreement to Promote Compliance with International Conservation and Management Measures by Fishing Vessels on the High Seas (Rome, 24 November 1993) – UNTS Vol. 2221, No. 39486' (Chapter 4, n 98).

440 See more on the FAO Compliance Agreement Chapter 4 Sections 1, 1.1, 1.1.3 *supra*.

441 See Carmino Massarella, 'Ensuring Compliance with Fisheries Regulations by Private Actors' in Richard Caddell and Erik J Molenaar (eds), *Strengthening International Fisheries Law in an Era of Changing Oceans* (Hart Publishing 2019).

442 See Richard Caddell, George Leloudas and Bariş Soyer, 'Emerging Regulatory Responses to IUU Fishing' in Richard Caddell and Erik J Molenaar (eds), *Strengthening International Fisheries Law in an Era of Changing Oceans* (Hart Publishing 2019).

443 See Robin Churchill, 'International Trade Law Aspects of Measures to Combat IUU and Unsustainable Fishing' in Richard Caddell and Erik J Molenaar (eds), *Strengthening International Fisheries Law in an Era of Changing Oceans* (Hart Publishing 2019).

non-contracting parties that require the latter to prevent their vessels from fishing on certain stocks.[444] Adjacent experienced regimes could assist in implementing compliance processes,[445] as IUU fishing often involves a transnational component, especially concerning the sale of fish caught under IUU circumstances. Illegal fishing activities and other kinds of transnational maritime crimes such as drug smuggling, trafficking in persons and piracy further caught the attention of international law enforcement instruments such as the UN Office on Drugs and Crime, the International Organization for Migration, the ILO and the International Criminal Police Organization INTERPOL. The institutions' distinctive capacities in preventing and investigating transnational criminal action and legal prosecution provide a helpful set-up for ensuring enforcement of and compliance with IUU fishing regulations.[446]

Despite existing compliance and enforcement regimes, preventive enforcement or voluntary compliance is undeniably most beneficial. In fisheries, the understanding of the usefulness of measures or laws and the acceptance by fishermen as direct stakeholders serve as the basis for a commitment to measures. It should be kept in mind that most fishermen engage in fishing for their survival in a harsh business and working environment. Bureaucratic controls, especially if they appear at first glance to have little practical use, therefore benefit from being well explained and appropriate.[447] Enforcement resources can then be channelled towards more bothersome areas. In a second step, where enforcement is still challenging, legal measures including sanctions can be applied.[448]

2.4.1.2 *Implementation in the CAOF Agreement*

Also for the CAOF regime, compliance and support are crucial for its success. Above all, support from the Arctic coastal States is of particular importance: when the ice melts, fishing can be carried out in their waters first. The CAOF Agreement opted for a rather soft management compliance approach instead of a strict enforcement approach, built on trust rather than on coercion. In contrast to the FAO proposals, the current text does not provide for sanctions or penalties – although this would have been somewhat premature

444 Cf. Henriksen, Hønneland and Sydnes (Chapter 3, n 171) 130.

445 Papastavridis (Chapter 2, n 156) 360.

446 Olav Schram Stokke, 'Management Options for High Seas Fisheries: Making Regime Complexes More Effective' in Richard Caddell and Erik Jaap Molenaar (eds), *Strengthening International Fisheries Law in an Era of Changing Oceans* (Hart Publishing 2019) 60.

447 Flewwelling (Chapter 5, n 19) s 2.

448 ibid 3.2.

anyway, given the current circumstances in the CAO, which do not allow for fishing any time soon.

Similar to the specifications of the UNFS Agreement,[449] the CAOF Agreement contains compliance obligations both for the Parties and their own actions and in relation to non-participants. Article 3(5) CAOF Agreement urges Parties to ensure compliance with interim measures. These include the interim measures established by Article 3, but also possible newly-established interim measures in the context of the discussion on the establishment of a new RFB for managing fishing in the Agreement Area. The Agreement further requests the Parties to ensure that their scientific research activities involving the catching of fish in the Agreement Area "do not undermine" the objective of the Agreement.[450] In relation to non-parties, similar to the provisions in the UNFS Agreement[451] and the FAO Compliance Agreement,[452] Article 8(1) CAOF Agreement requests the Parties to encourage non-parties to act in accordance with the provisions of the Agreement.

Article 8(2) CAOF Agreement encourages Parties to actively prevent actions that may be detrimental to the objective of the Agreement. In this regard, measures to deter activities carried out by vessels entitled to fly flags of non-parties that undermine the effective implementation of the Agreement shall be taken. In this way, the Agreement can find broad acceptance even if only a few States have ratified it and ensure step by step that its purpose is preserved. Nevertheless, specific compliance and enforcement tools are missing in the CAOF Agreement. The trust-based, rather loose approach to compliance may be appropriate for the early stages of the Agreement. However, the approach will have to be reconsidered at the latest when TAC quotas for CAO fisheries are allocated, probably under a new agreement.

2.4.2 Dispute Settlement

Although an agreement is based on mutual consent, it may leave room for interpretation and cause disputes between the parties. An important part of ensuring compliance with established provisions is therefore the ability to resolve disagreements over the application or interpretation of provisions between parties. Hence, an international agreement should provide a mechanism for the peaceful and efficient resolution of disputes.

449 Cf. e.g. Articles 7(2)(a), 17(4), 18(1), 33 UNFS Agreement.
450 See Article 3(4) CAOF Agreement.
451 See Article 33 UNFS Agreement.
452 See Article VIII FAO Compliance Agreement.

In the context of fisheries, Article IX FAO Compliance Agreement motivates parties to resolve disputes expeditiously and provides for choosing between various bodies such as the ICJ, ITLOS Tribunal or an arbitral tribunal as a dispute settlement forum. To further improve enforcement, the possibility of mandatory, compulsory dispute settlement[453] has been included in international fisheries agreements over the years.[454]

The CAOF Agreement provides for dispute settlement regulations in its Article 7. Therefore, the provisions relating to the settlement of disputes set forth in Part VIII UNFS Agreement apply, irrespective of party affiliation, *mutatis mutandis* to any dispute between the CAOF Agreement Parties relating to the interpretation or application of the CAOF Agreement. It is noted that the notion of "shall", often used throughout the Agreement, has not been used within Article 7 (not "shall apply" but "apply"). It is assumed that when it comes to the settlement of disputes, a strict dispute settlement mechanism that does not leave room for interpretation is advantageous. This follows the current trend of implementing compulsory dispute settlement clauses in RFB regulatory frameworks.

Part VIII (Articles 27 et seq.) UNFS Agreement sets up the obligation to settle disputes by peaceful means. Further, in order to prevent disputes from arising, States shall cooperate through efficient and expeditious decision-making procedures within the respective RFB,[455] which the CAOF Agreement has implemented in its Articles 6 and 4. The UNFS Agreement specifically addresses the sub-category of technical disputes.[456] Accordingly, Parties have the possibility to refer a technical dispute to an ad hoc expert panel established by them. As for the exact procedure of dispute settlement, the UNFS Agreement refers to the provisions relating to the settlement of disputes set out in Part XV UNCLOS. These shall apply, *mutatis mutandis*, to any dispute between States parties to the UNFS Agreement concerning its interpretation or application[457] and the interpretation or application of a subregional, regional or global fisheries agreement that they are parties to,[458] regardless of whether the parties concerned are parties to UNCLOS. In order to ensure the functioning of established systems, States are also explicitly encouraged to make provisional arrangements of a practical nature pending the resolution of a dispute.[459]

453 See e.g. Article 32 WCPFC, Article XV NAFO Convention.
454 Schatz, Proelß and Liu (Chapter 2, n 41) 236 with further references.
455 See Article 28 UNFS Agreement.
456 See Article 30 UNFS Agreement.
457 See Article 30(1) UNFS Agreement.
458 See Article 30(2) UNFS Agreement.
459 See Article 31 UNFS Agreement.

The referenced Part XV UNCLOS provides detailed regulations for dispute settlement. Similar to the UNFS Agreement, UNCLOS establishes the conflicting parties' obligation to settle disputes by any peaceful means of their choice.[460] Where these means do not lead to the settlement of a dispute,[461] or a time-limit set for the settlement expires,[462] the procedures provided for in Part XV UNCLOS shall apply.[463] This should only not be the case if the parties to the dispute have agreed through a general, regional or bilateral agreement or otherwise that disputes be submitted to a procedure that entails a binding decision.[464] Further, UNCLOS sets up an obligation to exchange views,[465] and one of the conflicting parties may invite the respective other party to submit the dispute to conciliation.[466] Article 287(1) UNCLOS leaves the parties the choice of submitting their dispute to ITLOS, the ICJ, an arbitral tribunal constituted in accordance with Annex VII UNCLOS or a special arbitral tribunal constituted in accordance with Annex VIII UNCLOS. The choice should be communicated by means of a written declaration "[w]hen signing, ratifying or acceding to this Convention or at any time thereafter".[467] For disputes involving scientific or technical matters, similar to Article 30 UNFS Agreement, Article 289 UNCLOS provides for the possibility of scientific or technical experts to sit with the respective court or tribunal. Reflecting the precautionary approach, UNCLOS provides that, pending a final decision, interim measures may be taken to safeguard the respective rights of the parties to the dispute or to prevent serious harm to the marine environment.[468] In preliminary proceedings, the judicial body in question may determine *proprio motu* whether the claim constitutes an abuse of a legal process or whether it is unfounded at first sight,[469] which might conclude the proceedings. To obtain final clarification of a matter, decisions of the chosen court or tribunal shall be final and binding between the parties.[470] Section 3 Part XV UNCLOS[471] contains limitations on the applicability[472] of

460 See Articles 278 and 279 UNCLOS.
461 See Article 281(a) UNCLOS.
462 See Article 281(b) UNCLOS.
463 Cf. Article 286 UNCLOS.
464 See Article 282 UNCLOS.
465 See Article 283 UNCLOS.
466 See Article 284 UNCLOS.
467 See Article 287(1) UNCLOS.
468 See Article 290 UNCLOS; as a continuation of the approach, see Article 292 UNCLOS.
469 See Article 294 UNCLOS.
470 See Article 296 UNCLOS.
471 See Articles 297–299 UNCLOS.
472 See Article 297 UNCLOS.

Section 2,[473] in cases concerning the exercise of sovereign rights or jurisdiction by coastal States and optional exceptions to the applicability of Section 2.[474] Article 299 UNCLOS gives the parties the right to agree on a procedure or to settle disputes amicably in these cases.

In general, this framework should be applied where disputes under the CAOF Agreement occur. The advantage of having a pre-existing framework, and perhaps one of the reasons why the Parties agreed to refer to UNFS Agreement/UNCLOS dispute settlement rules, is certainly that it is a comprehensive and proven system. Jurisprudence and interpretation have contributed to the smooth functioning of the system. It allows disputing parties to choose between various experienced international law bodies that are specialised in matters of the law of the sea, such as ITLOS and the ICJ, or who are familiar with specific economic issues that may frequently arise in fisheries, such as arbitral tribunals. It is particularly welcomed that technical disputes can be decided by an ad hoc expert panel.[475] Provisional measures allow for effective implementation of the precautionary approach and prevent disputes from paralysing the functioning of the CAOF Agreement framework.

In summary, the CAOF Agreement is well prepared for possible disputes. A minor suggestion for improvement would be the implementation of a multilayered dispute resolution procedure that, in addition to judicial dispute resolution, provides for a review of decisions by a panel of experts.[476]

2.5 *Compatibility of the CAOF Agreement with Existing Regulations*

Compatibility of national fisheries and legislative purposes with RFB objectives and international legal obligations is considered to strengthen and increase the effectiveness of RFBs.[477] Compatibility in the context of the CAOF Agreement involves two aspects: first, compatibility of the Agreement with the existing legal framework of the CAO, and second, compatibility of conservation and management measures for areas under national jurisdiction and areas on the adjacent high seas.

473 See Articles 286–296 UNCLOS.

474 See Article 298 UNCLOS.

475 See Article 30 UNFS Agreement.

476 See Schatz, Proelß and Liu (Chapter 2, n 41) 236; cf. Swan (Chapter 4, n 323) s 2.3; Henriksen, Hønneland and Sydnes (Chapter 3, n 171) s 207.

477 Organisation for Economic Co-Operation and Development (Chapter 4, n 335) 17, 96.

2.5.1 Compatibility of the CAOF Agreement with the Existing Legal Framework in the CAO

As regards the first issue, clauses on the relationship of an international agreement towards other laws and regulations are a common feature of most international instruments. For instance, the UNFS Agreement stipulates that "[n]othing in this Agreement shall prejudice the rights, jurisdiction and duties of States under the Convention".[478] Where RFBs are concerned, when establishing a new RFB, States shall agree on "the relationship between the work of the new organization or arrangement and the role, objectives and operations of any relevant existing fisheries management organizations or arrangements".[479]

The CAOF Agreement also entails such clauses. Within the CAOF Agreement, the Preamble recalls the principles and provisions of treaties and other international instruments relating to marine fisheries that already apply to the high seas portion of the CAO. These include the provisions contained in UNCLOS, the UNFS Agreement, relevant instruments adopted by the FAO such as the FAO Code of Conduct, and UNDRIP. More specifically, Article 14 CAOF Agreement addresses the relation of the CAOF Agreement to other agreements. The first section deals with the obligations stemming from relevant provisions of international law, including those reflected in UNCLOS and the UNFS Agreement. The Parties recognize that they are and will continuously be bound by these obligations. Further, the Parties recognize the vital importance of continuous cooperation when fulfilling these obligations. The Parties agree to acknowledge said obligations even if the CAOF Agreement expires, or the CAOF Agreement is terminated and no other Agreement establishing an RFB for managing fisheries in the CAOF Agreement Area has been established. Hence, Article 14(1) CAOF Agreement can be considered a provision of last resort to preserve the essence of the CAOF Agreement. It must not be forgotten that the CAOF Agreement and its existence are sustained by the political will of the Parties. Its continuation depends on the support of the Parties in sixteen years after its entry into force. A lot can change between now and then, especially with regard to national interests and the political positions of States. Although States should follow the general rules of international law, should no additional fisheries management agreement be concluded in the CAO, the provision serves as a fall-back clause to remind States to adhere to the international legal standard that existed prior to the entry into force of the CAOF Agreement.

---

478 See Article 4 UNFS Agreement.

479 See Article 9(1)(c) UNFS Agreement.

The second section of Article 14 CAOF Agreement deals with the positions of the Parties. Therefore, nothing in the CAOF Agreement shall prejudice a Party's position with respect to its rights and obligations under international law. This ensures that national interests can continue to be pursued and that there is no need to subjugate any individual party to group interests. At the same time, the essential interests agreed by the Parties and set out in the CAOF Agreement are preserved. Furthermore, the Parties' positions on matters relating to the law of the sea shall remain unaffected. This includes any position that relates to the exercise of rights and jurisdiction in the Arctic Ocean. It is not surprising that this last section of Article 14(2) CAOF Agreement has been a key element for achieving consensus on the Agreement.[480] Territorial claims in the Arctic are still on the agenda. Not only the issue of controversial continental shelf claims in the North Pole area,[481] but also in relation to Svalbard are regularly discussed issues.[482] Further, one Party to the CAOF Agreement, the United States, has not ratified UNCLOS. Although they comply with most regulations and recognize them as part of customary international law, the US supports positions in the field of international maritime law that deviate from

480 Cf. Molenaar, 'Participation in the Central Arctic Ocean Fisheries Agreement' (Chapter 2, n 23) 154.

481 A good overview provides Irena Valková, 'Claiming the Arctic: On the Legal Geography of the Northernmost Sovereignty Dispute' (2017) 7 The Polar Journal 143 <https://www.tandfonline.com/doi/full/10.1080/2154896X.2017.1310489> accessed 8 July 2020; similar Rossi, 'Tradition, Tendency, Temptation' (Chapter 3, n 30) 3 et seq.; for in-depth studies, including a chronology of legally relevant events and a selection of essential materials see Kristina Schönfeldt, *The Arctic in International Law and Policy* (Hart Publishing 2017).

482 For an overview, see Torbjørn Pedersen, 'The Svalbard Continental Shelf Controversy: Legal Disputes and Political Rivalries' (2006) 37 Ocean Development & International Law 339 <http://content.ebscohost.com/ContentServer.asp?T=P&P=AN&K=21806539&S=R&D=bsu&EbscoContent=dGJyMNXb4kSeprY4yOvqOLCmsEieprzssa24TLCWxWXS&ContentCustomer=dGJyMPGrtk6zp7BNuePfgeyx44Dt6fIA> accessed 8 July 2020; see the submissions from Norway and Russia to the Commission for the Etension of the Continental Shelf: Government of Norway, 'Continental Shelf Submission of Norway in Respect of Areas in the Arctic Ocean, the Barents Sea and the Norwegian Sea – Executive Summary' (2006) <https://www.un.org/depts/los/clcs_new/submissions_files/nor06/nor_exec_sum.pdf> accessed 5 December 2021; Commission on the Limits of the Continental Shelf, 'Outer Limits of the Continental Shelf beyond 200 Nautical Miles from the Baselines: Submission to the Commission on the Limits of the Continental Shelf by the Russian Federation' <https://www.un.org/depts/los/clcs_new/submissions_files/submission_rus.htm> accessed 8 July 2020; for an analysis of consequences see Christopher R Rossi, 'Terra Nullius and the "unique" International Problem of Svalbard', *Sovereignty and Territorial Temptation–The Grotian Tendency* (Cambridge University Press 2017).

the view of the majority of States.[483] It is probably for this reason that Article 14(2) CAOF Agreement refers to a Party's position with respect to "its rights and obligations" rather than referring generally to UNCLOS rights and obligations.

Article 14(3) CAOF Agreement regulates similar issues with regard to the rights and obligations of the Parties. Nothing in the Agreement shall prejudice the Parties' rights, jurisdiction and duties under relevant provisions of international law as reflected in UNCLOS and the UNFS Agreement. Specific reference is made to the right to propose and therefore initiate negotiations on the establishment of one or multiple RFBs for the Agreement Area. This right is explicitly foreseen in Article 5(1)(c) CAOF Agreement and is internationally more generally defined by Articles 118 UNCLOS and more specifically by Article 8(2) UNFS Agreement. With regard to other provisions and obligations, the Preamble already explicitly highlights the importance of ensuring cooperation and coordination with NEAFC and other relevant fisheries management mechanisms, international bodies and programs, most likely relating to ICCAT, JointFish and NASCO. Alignment with these mechanisms with overlapping regulatory areas or in close proximity to the CAOF Agreement Area may play an important role if commercial fishing in CAO waters becomes possible.[484]

Article 14(4) CAOF Agreement makes clear that the Agreement may not alter the Parties' rights and obligations arising from other agreements. This shall however only be the case where these agreements are compatible with the CAOF Agreement and where the rights and obligations of one Party do not affect the enjoyment of rights or the performance of CAOF Agreement obligations by other Parties. It is understood that a Party would not conclude the CAOF Agreement if it contradicts its existing obligations. Yet, in any event, the provision clarifies that in this case the later established CAOF Agreement takes precedence over any conflicting rights and obligations stemming from other agreements.

The last part of Article 14(4) CAOF Agreement deals with the role and mandate of other agreements, setting forth that the Agreement shall neither undermine nor conflict with the role and mandate established by an existing international mechanism that relates to fisheries management. When

483 See Duff (Chapter 4, n 64); Will Schrepferman, 'Hypocri-Sea: The United States' Failure to Join the UN Convention on the Law of the Sea' *Harvard International Review* (31 October 2019) <https://hir.harvard.edu/hypocri-sea-the-united-states-failure-to-join-the-un-convention-on-the-law-of-the-sea-2/> accessed 8 July 2020.

484 On the discussion on the implementation of measures regarding commercial fishing, see Chapter 6 Section 1 *infra*.

interpreting the CAOF Agreement, and conflicts about roles and mandates arise, the interpretation should aim to be in conformity with other mandates and roles.

In summary, by establishing specific rules for the relationship between other international instruments and the CAOF Agreement, a good basis has been created to avoid conflicts of norms from the outset.

2.5.2 Compatibility of Conservation and Management Measures within and beyond Areas under National Jurisdiction

Pursuant to Article 7 UNFS Agreement, besides being compatible with the existing legal framework, conservation and management measures should be compatible within and beyond areas under national jurisdiction. The matter was one of the most controversially discussed issues during the inter-sessional meetings of the founding conference of the UNFS Agreement.[485] Coastal States supported the idea of an extension of jurisdiction over the adjacent waters on the high seas,[486] which was rejected by DWF States, recalling the freedom of the high seas.[487] A compromise was agreed upon, which is now embodied in Article 7(1) UNFS Agreement, stating that compatibility should be achieved

> [w]ithout prejudice to the sovereign rights of coastal States for the purpose of exploring and exploiting, conserving and managing the living marine resources within areas under national jurisdiction as provided for in the Convention, and the right of all States for their nationals to engage in fishing on the high seas in accordance with the Convention.

Article 7(1)(a) UNFS Agreement, similar to Article 63(2) UNCLOS, calls upon the relevant coastal States and the States whose nationals fish for straddling stocks in the adjacent high seas to agree on necessary conservation measures of such stocks on the high seas. Pursuant to subsection (b), similar to Article 64(1) UNCLOS, said States shall cooperate in ensuring the conservation and promotion of the objective of optimum utilisation of highly migratory stocks in areas within and beyond national jurisdiction.

---

485 David J Doulman, 'FAO Fisheries Circular No. 898: Structure and Process of the 1993–1995 United Nations Conference on Straddling Fish Stocks and Highly Migratory Fish Stocks' (1995) s 4 <http://www.fao.org/3/v9929e/v9929E00.htm> accessed 26 November 2021.

486 Some States are still opposed to the concept of compatibility, as they believe it undermines the rights of coastal States in their EEZs; see Serdy, 'Postmodern International Fisheries Law, or We Are All Coastal States Now' (Chapter 3, n 108) 404.

487 Diz Pereira Pinto (Chapter 5, n 278) 94.

The UNFS Agreement further sets up the duty of coastal States and States fishing on the high seas to cooperate to achieve compatibility of conservation and management measures regarding straddling fish stocks and highly migratory fish stocks established for the high seas and those adopted for areas under national jurisdiction.[488] Agreement over such measures should be reached within a reasonable period of time.[489] Otherwise, dispute settlement procedures may be invoked[490] and provisional measures may be obtained.[491] Coastal States should further inform States fishing on the high seas in the region[492] or other interested States[493] of measures they have adopted within areas under national jurisdiction.

Furthermore, compatibility between conservation and management measures adopted for areas under national jurisdiction and those established in the adjacent high seas should always be considered in the light of the ecosystem approach.[494] This is reasonable, since the latter aims to protect fish stocks in their entirety within an ecosystem that naturally extends beyond the boundaries of the EEZs and the high seas.[495] Rather than considering only the effects of conservation and management measures in their area of application, compatible conservation and management measures must consider the effects of measures on a stock throughout its geographical range.[496]

In order to implement the duty in practice, different approaches can be taken. One option is that the measures are set up by the coastal State within its EEZ, and since the measures on the high seas must be compatible, these determinations are also adopted for the high seas. The coastal State hence sets the standard of measures for both within and beyond areas of national jurisdiction. Another option for RFB members is to establish such measures collectively as a group, and for compatibility reasons, this standard should be applied in coastal States' EEZs.[497] Whereas the latter option might give the impression that DWF States thus intervene in coastal States sovereign rights to a large extent, one must bear in mind that usually, coastal States are part of adjacent RFBs and will therefore naturally be included in taking a decision on

488 See Article 7(2) UNFS Agreement.
489 See Article 7(3) UNFS Agreement.
490 See Article 7(4) UNFS Agreement.
491 See Article 7(5) and (6) UNFS Agreement.
492 See Article 7(7) UNFS Agreement.
493 See Article 7(8) UNFS Agreement.
494 See Article 7(2)(d) and (f) UNFS Agreement.
495 See Diz Pereira Pinto (Chapter 5, n 278) 87,91.
496 Oude Elferink (Chapter 2, n 64) 10.
497 Munro, Van Houtte and Willmann (Chapter 4, n 46) s 4.1.2.

measures. An excellent example for pursuing the duty described, even before it was embedded in the UNFS Agreement, is the Convention on the Conservation and Management of Pollock Resources in the Central Bering Sea:[498] The agreement resulted from the joint action of coastal States and DWF States to establish a comprehensive standard in order to conquer overfishing on the high seas area of the "Donut Hole" surrounded by Russian and US EEZS.[499]

The CAOF Agreement contains specific reference to the compatibility of conservation and management measures in areas within and beyond national jurisdiction. With reference to Article 7 UNFS Agreement, pursuant to Article 3(6) CAOF Agreement,

> coastal States Parties and other Parties shall cooperate to ensure the compatibility of conservation and management measures for fish stocks that occur in areas both within and beyond national jurisdiction in the central Arctic Ocean in order to ensure conservation and management of those stocks in their entirety.

The Agreement further implicitly addresses the duty established by the UNFS Agreement. Among other things, Article 14(1) CAOF Agreement recognizes the binding nature of the duties of the UNFS Agreement and the importance of fulfilling them cooperatively. Article 14(3) CAOF Agreement further notes that nothing shall prejudice the rights, jurisdiction and duties of any Party under the UNFS Agreement – therefore also the duty to ensure compatibility of conservation and management measures set up by Article 7 UNFS Agreement. Additionally, various references to the duty to cooperate, as the underlying element[500] of the duty to ensure compatibility, are mentioned in the CAOF Agreement.[501] Furthermore, also the inclusion of the ecosystem approach implies a quest for compatibility of measures within an entire ecosystem to maintain the sustainability of fish stocks, both within and beyond areas of national jurisdiction.[502]

498 'Convention on the Conservation and Management of Pollock Resources in the Central Bering Sea (Washington D.C., 16 June 1994)' (Chapter 3, n 27).

499 Diz Pereira Pinto (Chapter 5, n 278) 95; see Robin R Churchill and AV Lowe, *The Law of the Sea* (3rd edn, Manchester University Press 1999) 306–307.

500 See e.g. Article 7(1)(b) UNFS Agreement.

501 On the duty to cooperate, see specifically Chapter 5 Sections 2, 2.2 *infra*.

502 On the implementation of the ecosystem approach in the CAOF Agreement, see Chapter 5 Sections 2, 2.1, 2.1.2, 2.1.2.2 *supra*.

The obligation for coastal States to inform fishing States about measures adopted within areas under their respective national jurisdiction, foreseen by Article 7(7) and (8) UNFS Agreement, is not specifically included in the CAOF Agreement. Article 5(1)(d)(iv) and (v) CAOF Agreement merely obliges Parties to notify other Parties of their plans for exploratory fishing in the Agreement Area and to report the results of such fishing. According to Article 3(4) CAOF Agreement, the same should apply to scientific research activities in the Agreement Area.

Although the process of compatibility could be further fleshed out by informing Parties of national activities in coastal States' EEZs, the CAOF Agreement has sufficiently addressed the obligation to ensure compatibility through explicit reference to Article 7 UNFS Agreement and several implicit references. As far as recent developments are concerned, the Arctic coastal States have not expressed the intention to bring their EEZ policies in line with those of the CAOF Agreement. However, it is important to note that there is limited potential for conflict since currently, little or no fishing in the EEZ areas adjacent to the CAO is conducted. Furthermore, the two explicit existing EEZ fisheries policies by the US[503] and Canada[504] are both compatible with the objectives of the CAOF Agreement.[505]

2.6 *Lessons Learned from Common Problems in Fisheries Management*

When it comes to defining or adapting Arctic fisheries management, attention should also be given to international RFB's experiences.[506] International agreements represent a compromise reached by all participants involved in the drafting process. Therefore, such regimes are never flawless, and some common issues remain. These must be disclosed and carefully considered when managing fisheries, so that adaptions can be made accordingly.[507] A critical element in strengthening RFB performance is the ability to learn from experiences of the past, as they may be particularly helpful in avoiding traps or dead ends that may impede the process of implementation. Then again, processes

503 North Pacific Fishery Management Council (Chapter 2, n 17).

504 'Government of Canada | News Release: Minister Aglukkaq Announces the Signature of the Beaufort Sea Integrated Fisheries Management Framework (17 October 2014)' (Chapter 3, n 220).

505 Zou and Huntington (Chapter 3, n 117) 133.

506 'First International Meeting on the Establishment of the South Pacific Regional Fisheries Management Organisation (Wellington, 14–17 February 2006) – SP/01/Inf5' (Chapter 3, n 193) para 13.

507 Matley (Chapter 3, n 37) 102.

may have been adopted that have proven successful.[508] A new fisheries management arrangement should therefore keep defects in mind and try to counteract their occurrence through implementing best practices.

In the field of fisheries, States should not rely on UNCLOS to solve all problems. *Inter alia*, the question of coastal States fishing rights in areas beyond the EEZ on the high seas was part of the "unfinished agenda"[509] of UNCLOS.[510] As a combined result of the lack of a coherent regime, ineffective management and cooperation, increased capitalization, excessive fleet sizes and unsustainable fishing practices, straddling and highly migratory fish stocks were overfished and IUU fishing increased. The implementation of the UNFS Agreement in 1995 ameliorated the situation. The Agreement dealt with highly migratory stocks, consolidated UNCLOS vaguely formulated duty to cooperate and introduced a detailed precautionary approach.[511] Yet, the regime lags behind its possibilities, especially concerning its normative development.[512] The concept established by the UNFS Agreement to either comply with measures adopted by RFBS in a certain area or refrain from fishing in those grounds is still not universally accepted.[513] UNCLOS further provides only limited guidance on the responsibilities of flag States in relation to fisheries. A binding agreement on a set of clearly defined flag States' responsibilities was hence requested,[514] exceeding the FAO Voluntary Guidelines for Flag State Performance. Flag State responsibility and enforcement is still very much based on trust, with the result that low-control States fail to restrict fishing companies from owning and operating flags of convenience vessels. This means that vessels fly the flag of a country other than the country of ownership, therefore creating a "continuous circle of non-compliant behaviour".[515] A genuine link between the vessel and the

508 Organisation for Economic Co-Operation and Development (Chapter 4, n 335) 17.

509 James Harrison and Elisa Morgera, 'Article 63 – Stocks Occurring within the Exclusive Economic Zones of Two or More Coastal States or Both within the Exclusive Economic Zone and in an Area beyond and Adjacent to It' in Alexander Proelß (ed), *United Nations Convention on the Law of the Sea: A Commentary* (Nomos 2017) para 4.

510 Kwiatkowska (Chapter 4, n 70) 327.

511 Matley (Chapter 3, n 37) 105.

512 Robin Churchill, 'The LOSC Regime for Protection of the Marine Environment-Fit for the Twenty-First Century?' in Rosemary Rayfuse (ed), *Research Handbook on International Marine Environmental Law* (Edward Elgar Publishing 2015) 29 et seq.

513 Cf. Camille Goodman, 'The Regime for Flag State Responsibility in International Fisheries Law – Effective Fact, Creative Fiction, or Further Work Required?' (2009) 23 Australian and New Zealand Maritime Law Journal 157, 164 et seq.

514 ibid 169.

515 ibid 164.

State is missing,[516] and the problem is aggravated as States are not rigorously inspecting these vessels landing at their ports.[517] In this context, it should be mentioned that operators of IUU vessels often conduct fishing operations in remote high seas areas where management measures are lacking, particularly in waters under developing coastal State jurisdiction, which have difficulties to undermine such fishing activities. Naturally, the vessels' owners also seek to avoid detection. Means include deceptive business practices like the creation of interlaced corporate arrangements to impede investigators, a frequent change of names and call signs of their vessels and reflagging vessels in States with open registries.[518] Port State Control systems have improved this issue, but the problem still exists. Additionally, international rules and procedures on this matter are not implemented adequately by all States. To tackle these issues, it is *inter alia* suggested to establish minimum standard guidelines for the authorisation of organizations acting on behalf of the administration and to create a system of flag State self-assessment regarding the State's ability to give effect to regulations.[519] A more visible control system, like the one in effect in the South Pacific region, might also be efficient: under the Niue Treaty on Cooperation in Fisheries Surveillance and Law Enforcement in the South Pacific Region,[520] based on Article 73 UNCLOS, States are encouraged to share their assets in fisheries surveillance and law enforcement activities, including boarding, inspection and seizure of vessels.[521] Further suggested is the listing of problem vessels on IUU vessel lists.[522]

Recent developments of management oversight, government regulations and traceability of fishing activities on the seas are good steps in countering

516 ibid 159 et seq.

517 'WWF | Fishing Problems: Poor Fisheries Management' <https://wwf.panda.org/our_work/oceans/problems/fisheries_management/> accessed 1 July 2020; cf. Matley (Chapter 3, n 37) 107.

518 Food and Agriculture Organization of the United Nations, 'Technical Guidelines for Responsible Fisheries No. 9: Implementation of the International Plan of Action to Prevent, Deter and Eliminate Illegal, Unreported and Unregulated Fishing' (2002) 17 <http://www.fao.org/3/a-y3536e.pdf> accessed 3 July 2020.

519 Goodman (Chapter 5, n 513) 159 et seq.

520 'Niue Treaty on Cooperation in Fisheries Surveillance and Law Enforcement in the South Pacific Region (Honiara, 9 July 1992)' <https://www.ffa.int/system/files/NiueTreaty_0.pdf> accessed 12 April 2022.

521 Transform Aqorau, 'Illegal Fishing and Fisheries Law Enforcement in Small Island Developing States: The Pacific Islands Experience' (2000) 15 International Journal of Marine and Coastal Law 37, 54 et seq. <https://brill-com.emedien.ub.uni-muenchen.de/view/journals/estu/15/1/article-p37_2.xml> accessed 3 July 2020.

522 Matley (Chapter 3, n 37) 115 et seq.

overfishing. Yet, fisheries regulations and enforcement measures often lack efficiency, and fishing capacity and efforts are not administered adequately. The fact that fishing activities take place in areas far away from regulators makes it even harder to enforce regulations.[523] On the one hand, the current inadequacy of regulations is a problem for fisheries, in particular regarding regulations that aim at making high seas fisheries sustainable. On the other hand, the lack of implementation of existing agreements or of their enforcement, often co-related to a lack of political will, poses difficulties to effective management. Absence of transparency and traceability favours customers to purchase fish from unsustainable fisheries. Scientific advice on fish quotas and catch limits is not followed in a sufficient way.[524] Unfortunately, in this regard, the principle applies that "the weaker the governance of a country, the likelier and more serious the incidence of IUU fishing."[525]

The existing difficulties in implementing the commitments make it rather unattractive for a large number of States to join an RFB. Sadly, this contributes to maintaining the membership policy that only States with a real interest should be included, thus excluding States that seek support for environmental reasons.[526] Moreover, an agreement that sets stricter requirements for the protection of the marine environment will meet stronger resistance if no economic benefits are foreseen, e.g. an effective financing mechanism to cover the additional costs and technology transfer.[527] An agreement must keep this in mind and strike a balance between obligations and benefits to create an incentive for States to join an agreement or to comply with it.

For fish spawning grounds and the deep sea, which are specifically vulnerable to overfishing, it is further problematic that very few protected areas and no-take zones, where fishing is banned or strictly regulated exist. An extension of these zones could provide essential safe refuges enabling young fish to grow to maturity and reproduce before being caught.[528]

Fortunately, the regime of international fisheries is a flexible and dynamic system. In contrast to other areas of environmental law, the regime is able to assimilate developments relatively quickly by revision or adaption. Fast-track

---

523 'WWF | Fishing Problems: Poor Fisheries Management' (Chapter 5, n 517).

524 ibid.

525 'FAO | GLOBEFISH: Catch Documentation Schemes: Practices and Applicability in Combating IUU Fishing' <http://www.fao.org/in-action/globefish/fishery-information/resource-detail/en/c/426994/> accessed 29 January 2022.

526 See on the discussion about the criterion of real interest Chapter 3 Sections 3, 3.2 *supra*.

527 Cf. Matz-Lück and Fuchs (Chapter 4, n 305) 163 et seq.

528 'WWF | Fishing Problems: Poor Fisheries Management' (Chapter 5, n 517).

or automatic entry-into-force provisions facilitate such adaption.[529] The issues mentioned should therefore be taken into account when it comes to implementing and further shaping the framework for fisheries in the CAO.

3 Summary

The CAOF Agreement was initiated to prevent IUU fishing in the high seas portion of the CAO. The objective should be achieved "through the application of precautionary conservation and management measures as part of a long-term strategy to safeguard healthy marine ecosystems and to ensure the conservation and sustainable use of fish stocks".[530]

Scientific research is considered the basis of fisheries management measures not only generally, but also in the CAOF Agreement. In this regard, the CAOF Agreement foresees the establishment of the JPSRM, a joint program that coordinates the research conducted under the Agreement with the aim of improving the understanding of the ecosystems of the Agreement Area. In particular, it should be determined whether fish stocks in this area might exist now or in the future that could be harvested on a sustainable basis. In addition, the possible impacts of such fisheries on CAO ecosystems should be assessed. A data sharing protocol and joint scientific meetings will assist the scientific progress. Furthermore, additional research activities that have been conducted or are conducted in the CAO nationally or cooperatively, e.g. by ICES, PICES, or the work conducted in the FiSCAO meetings, should be taken into account.

Contemporary fisheries management bodies should meet several requirements. Accordingly, a state-of-the-art RFB should be based on sustainable development, cooperation, and the application of precautionary conservation and management measures. It should provide for effective decision-making procedures and mechanisms for compliance and enforcement including the peaceful settlement of disputes. Additionally, compatibility between conservation and management measures adopted for areas under national jurisdiction and those established in the adjacent high seas should be ensured. The CAOF Agreement satisfactorily implements sustainable development, including the precautionary approach, the duty to cooperate and references to the compatibility of conservation and management measures. Nevertheless, there are shortcomings in the implementation of the ecosystem approach,

529 Matley (Chapter 3, n 37) 108.
530 See Article 2 CAOF Agreement.

where biodiversity conservation could have been addressed more specifically, and concerning decision-making processes, where transparency could be increased. Also, the prerequisite of taking most decisions by consensus might cause problems in the future. Whereas dispute settlement mechanisms largely meet the recommended standard, specific compliance and enforcement measures should be implemented if and when an additional RFB regulating fisheries in the CAO is established.

CHAPTER 6

Interim Conservation and Management Measures under the CAOF Agreement

Where there is no fully developed governance regime and knowledge of fish stocks in a particular area is limited, interim measures are a useful tool to secure initial conservation objectives. These remain in place until sufficient data has been collected and an agreement has been reached on longer-term conservation and management measures.[1]

This idea is enshrined in Article 6(6) UNFS Agreement, which states that

> [f]or new or exploratory fisheries, States shall adopt as soon as possible cautious conservation and management measures, including, *inter alia*, catch limits and effort limits. Such measures shall remain in force until there are sufficient data to allow assessment of the impact of the fisheries on the long-term sustainability of the stocks, whereupon conservation and management measures based on that assessment shall be implemented.

Furthermore, according to the precautionary approach, even where an RFB exists, measures must be taken to prevent IUU fishing.[2] In this regard, the 2006 Review Conference on the UNFS Agreement recommended that States should agree on interim measures pending the establishment of RFBs.[3] The 2015 Oslo Declaration takes the same approach. It states that although international law obliges States to cooperate with each other concerning the conservation and management of living marine resources in high seas areas and to implement the precautionary approach, it would be "desirable to implement appropriate

1 See 'First International Meeting on the Establishment of the South Pacific Regional Fisheries Management Organisation (Wellington, 14–17 February 2006) – SP/01/Inf5' (Chapter 3, n 193) paras 2–3.

2 Takei (Chapter 4, n 307) 557.

3 UN Fish Stocks Agreement Review Conference, 'Summary Report of the UN Fish Stocks Agreement Review Conference (22–26 May 2006)' (2006) 7 Earth Negotiations Bulletin 61, 3 <https://enb.iisd.org/events/un-fish-stocks-agreement-review-conference/summary-report-22-26-may-2006> accessed 16 June 2021.

 | DOI:10.1163/9789004700673_007

interim measures to deter unregulated fishing in the future in the high seas portion of the central Arctic Ocean."[4]

Already in the past, fisheries have been managed whilst RFBs were being established. In order to safeguard the object and purpose of an envisaged full-fledged governance structure, which will likely take multiple years to be established, and to prevent this process from being jeopardized by IUU fisheries, interim measures were adopted.[5] Interim measures can take various forms. For instance, the so-called Majuro Declaration, which was issued during the establishment of the Western and Central Pacific Fisheries Commission, sets up certain obligations – interim measures – for participating States: *inter alia*, parties should work cooperatively in negotiations, exchange data and financially support established monitoring control and surveillance measures. Similar measures were adopted in the consolidation process of the Southern Indian Ocean Fisheries Agreement[6] and in the run-up of the establishment of the South Pacific Regional Fisheries Management Organisation (SPRFMO).[7] Also during consultations on the South East Atlantic Fisheries Organization, flag State responsibilities were laid down in an interim agreement.[8] Furthermore, in the context of the Review Conference of the UNFS Agreement in 2010, interim measures for the implementation of UN General Assembly Resolutions 61/105 and 64/72 regarding bottom trawling and deep sea gill netting were requested.[9]

As far as the most effective content of interim measures is concerned, the first international meeting on the establishment of the SPRFMO can further provide guidance. Accordingly, interim measures should generally follow international best practice, i.e. be based on the best available scientific information, and follow the precautionary principle. Scientific working groups were suggested as a good way to guide science and provide scientific advice. Standards could be developed for data collection, review and assessment, reporting, storage, access, stock assessment and guidance. Yet, it was emphasised that interim arrangements should exceed mere data collection. Among

4 'Declaration Concerning the Prevention of Unregulated High Seas Fishing in the Central Arctic Ocean (Oslo, 16 July 2015)' (Chapter 2, n 22).

5 'First International Meeting on the Establishment of the South Pacific Regional Fisheries Management Organisation (Wellington, 14–17 February 2006) – SP/01/Inf5' (Chapter 3, n 193) para 1.

6 ibid 4.

7 Tang (Chapter 3, n 62) 223 et seq.

8 'First International Meeting on the Establishment of the South Pacific Regional Fisheries Management Organisation (Wellington, 14–17 February 2006) – SP/01/Inf5' (Chapter 3, n 193) para 4.

9 Diz and others (Chapter 5, n 80) 5.

other things, cooperation with RFBs with adjacent regulatory areas should be taken into account, and controversies should be re-addressed from time to time. In general, a sustainable approach should be followed, ensuring compatibility with subsequent permanent measures, possibly through transitional norms.[10] As a matter of course, further international standards established by UNCLOS, the UNFS Agreement, FAO guidelines and IPOAs, among others, should be adhered to.[11]

Where multiple players are involved, various views must be aligned in a timely process in order to establish both conventional and interim measures. A voluntary statement has therefore been suggested to present a good format for interim measures.[12] This simplifies the possibility of reaching an agreement and does not require the time and effort needed for consultations on a binding fisheries management regime. As an expression of their commitment, in line with Article 18 UNFS Agreement and the FAO Compliance Agreement, participants shall contribute to the success of a binding agreement through financial help or by providing resources. Participants are further expected to refrain from actions that could undermine management and conservation objectives.[13]

In summary, interim measures should follow the concept of sustainability, including the precautionary approach, foster cooperation, and include concepts of data collection, e.g. through creating scientific working groups. Their duration should be limited, they should be periodically reviewed and provide for a swift transition to subsequent permanent measures.

Based thereupon, the basis for the interim measures of the CAOF Agreement can be found in the 2015 Oslo Declaration. Therein, the Arctic Five agreed on the following:

- "We will authorize our vessels to conduct commercial fishing in this high seas area only pursuant to one or more regional or subregional fisheries management organizations or arrangements that are or may be established to manage such fishing in accordance with recognized international standards.
- We will establish a joint program of scientific research with the aim of improving understanding of the ecosystems of this area and promote cooperation with relevant scientific bodies, including but not limited to the

10 See 'First International Meeting on the Establishment of the South Pacific Regional Fisheries Management Organisation (Wellington, 14–17 February 2006) – SP/01/Inf5' (Chapter 3, n 193) paras 5–8, 10, 18, 29–33, 40.

11 ibid 9, 16, 36.

12 ibid 11–12.

13 ibid 15–16.

International Council for the Exploration of the Sea (ICES) and the North Pacific Marine Science Organization (PICES).
- We will promote compliance with these interim measures and with relevant international law, including by coordinating our monitoring, control and surveillance activities in this area.
- We will ensure that any non-commercial fishing in this area does not undermine the purpose of the interim measures, is based on scientific advice and is monitored, and that data obtained through any such fishing is shared."[14]

Although the Arctic Five had the opportunity in the Oslo Declaration to define the exact conditions under which future high seas fishing may begin, they only laid down general obligations.[15] These general commitments have also been implemented in the CAOF Agreement. Article 3 CAOF Agreement further specifies interim conservation and management measures for fishing.[16] The Parties are encouraged to ensure compliance with interim measures[17] and to cooperate to ensure the compatibility of conservation and management measures, including interim measures for fish stocks that occur in areas both within and beyond national jurisdiction in the CAO.[18] Where specific interim measures are concerned, Article 3 CAOF Agreement distinguishes between measures for commercial fishing (Chapter 6 Section 1)[19] and non-commercial fishing, which can again be distinguished in scientific research activities (Chapter 6 Sections 2, 2.1)[20] and exploratory fishing (Chapter 6 Sections 2, 2.2).[21] The CAOF Agreement additionally entails provisions on the Agreement's (and interim measures') duration (Chapter 6 Section 3), review (Chapter 6 Section 4) and transition to a hypothetical new arrangement (Chapter 6 Section 5) that are further looked at. Lastly, suggestions for subsequent conservation and management measures are made (Chapter 6 Section 6).

14 'Declaration Concerning the Prevention of Unregulated High Seas Fishing in the Central Arctic Ocean (Oslo, 16 July 2015)' (Chapter 2, n 22).
15 Molenaar, 'PPP: The CAOF Agreement: Key Issues of International Fisheries Law' (Chapter 3, n 102).
16 Fishing in the context of the CAOF Agreement is defined broadly, meaning "searching for, attracting, locating, catching, taking or harvesting fish or any activity that can reasonably be expected to result in the attracting, locating, catching, taking or harvesting of fish", enabling seamless protection of fish; see Article 1(c) CAOF Agreement.
17 See Article 3(5) CAOF Agreement.
18 See Article 3(6) CAOF Agreement.
19 See Article 3(1) CAOF Agreement.
20 See Article 3(2),(4) and (7) CAOF Agreement.
21 See Article 3(3) CAOF Agreement.

1 Measures regarding Commercial Fishing

Article 3(1) CAOF Agreement describes the circumstances under which a vessel may engage in commercial fishing in the Agreement Area. Commercial fishing in Article 3(1) refers to "fishing for commercial purposes".[22] The vessel must be authorised by one of the Parties and hence fly the flag of the respective authorising State. Furthermore, commercial fishing is only allowed within the framework of established measures.[23] The term "only pursuant to" in Article 3(1) CAOF Agreement confirms the exceptional nature of the activity.

Article 3(1)(a) CAOF Agreement specifies that commercial fishing is only allowed where conservation and management measures for the sustainable management of fish stocks have been adopted by one or more (S)RFMA/Os that have been or may be established. This underlines the precautionary approach of the CAOF Agreement, which should be included in interim measures.[24] As one of the key aspects of the Oslo Declaration, the CAOF Agreement does not impose a general moratorium, but only a moratorium on unregulated commercial fishing.[25] Except under the auspices of RFBs with a mandate to allow for commercial fishing,[26] commercial fishing is banned from the area,[27] constituting a temporary qualified abstention or "a fisheries management measure in the form of a non-allocation of fishing opportunities (quota or TAC of zero) itself".[28] Parties may therefore allow for commercial fishing under certain circumstances. Although this poses a slightly higher risk to Arctic fish stocks and ecosystems, the Parties have deliberately chosen not to impose a moratorium:[29] the requirement in the CAOF Agreement to take decisions by consensus[30] could have posed a real threat to the lifting of an imposed moratorium if

---

22 See Article 1(d) CAOF Agreement.

23 Article 3(1)(a) and (b) CAOF Agreement.

24 On the suggested content of interim measures, see introductory Chapter 6 *supra*.

25 Molenaar, 'International Regulation of Central Arctic Ocean Fisheries' (Chapter 2, n 20) 451–454.

26 The Oslo Declaration refers, *inter alia*, explicitly to the NEAFC. For potential RFBs, see Chapter 6 Sections 1, 1.2 *infra*.

27 In line with what is suggested by the FAO, see Food and Agriculture Organization of the United Nations, 'FAO Fisheries and Aquaculture Report No. 881: Report of the Technical Consultation on International Guidelines for the Management of Deep-Sea Fisheries in the High Seas (Rome, 4–8 February and 25–29 August 2008)' (Chapter 5, n 19) para 63.

28 Schatz, Proelß and Liu (Chapter 2, n 41) 220.

29 The Parties possibly had the situation of the International Whaling Commission (IWC) in mind: the IWC requires a three-fourths majority for taking decisions. Due to that requirement, States interested in commercial whaling, although sustainable exploitation would have been respected, could not lift an IWC moratorium imposed on commercial whaling.

30 On decision-making under the CAOF Agreement, see Chapter 5 Sections 2, 2.3, 2.3.2 *supra*.

a State opposed such a decision, thus giving a single State the power to block the start of CAO fisheries.[31]

Article 3(1)(a) CAOF Agreement names the possibility of an established RFB to adopt measures. Even before the CAOF Agreement, it was explicitly stated that in order to ensure effective management, it would be necessary either to reform an existing RFB or to create a new one. While reformation risks introducing existing difficulties and failures into the reformed institution, a new institution would have a high enforcement capacity but a lack of experience. It was unclear which solution would better address the difficulties of overcapacity, political tensions and IUU fishing in the CAO. Whereas the EU and Iceland favoured the establishment of a new arrangement, Russia was against such establishment, and both positions found supporters among the Parties.[32] Although the CAOF Agreement itself did not finally decide on this issue, it expressly foresees the possibility – not the obligation – to establish an additional (S)RFMO or (S)RFMA responsible for managing (commercial) fishing in the Agreement Area.[33] The possibility to reform an existing RFB was not further pursued.

Consequently, as commercial fishing in the central part of the high seas portion of the Arctic Ocean seems feasible,[34] although not in the near future,[35] the management of such fishing will either be transferred to a newly established or an existing RFB. Another possibility is to conduct commercial fishing according to interim conservation and management measures adopted by the CAOF Agreement's Parties. All scenarios will be addressed in the following.

1.1 *Commercial Fishing as a Management and Conservation Measure Authorised by a Newly Established RFB*

According to Article 3(1)(a) CAOF Agreement, a newly established RFB might allow for commercial fishing as part of conservation and management measures. Such establishment is foreseen in Article 5(1)(c)(i) CAOF Agreement, which is considered the trigger clause of the Agreement, dealing with one of the

31 Molenaar, 'International Regulation of Central Arctic Ocean Fisheries' (Chapter 2, n 20) 454–455; 462; see Molenaar, 'The CAOF Agreement: Key Issues of International Fisheries Law' (Chapter 2, n 20) 195; Schatz, Proelß and Liu (Chapter 2, n 41) 225.

32 'Notes of phone call with Maya Gold, Canadian Representative in Consultations for the CAOF Agreement, on 19 September 2019, on file with the author'.

33 See Article 5(1)(c)(i) CAOF Agreement.

34 Van Pelt and others (Chapter 3, n 298) s 79.

35 See Molenaar, 'The CAOF Agreement: Key Issues of International Fisheries Law' (Chapter 2, n 20) 468.

central questions of the treaty.[36] In fact, it entails two types of triggers: Parties should determine whether to commence negotiations to establish one or more additional RFBs for managing fishing in the CAOF Agreement Area. The decision should further be subject to another determination: beforehand, it should be decided whether the distribution, migration and abundance of fish in the Agreement Area would support sustainable commercial fisheries. The decision should be based on scientific information derived from the JPSRM, from national scientific programs and from other relevant sources, "taking into account relevant fisheries management and ecosystem considerations, including the precautionary approach and potential adverse impacts of fishing on the ecosystems".[37] Pursuant to Article 3(1)(a) CAOF Agreement, such a newly established RFB could then allow commercial fishing.

Initially, the drafters of the CAOF Agreement did not favour the creation of a new framework at all – not even of the CAOF Agreement itself. The 2008 Ilulissat Declaration stated that there was "no need to develop a new comprehensive international legal regime" that governs the Arctic Ocean, as an extensive framework would already be in place forming a solid foundation for responsible management by the Arctic Five.[38] The underlying idea was to maintain a balance between surveillance and trust. The Arctic Five declared to count on "cooperation, which is based on mutual trust and transparency".[39] However, it is noted that the Ilulissat Declaration was not specifically concerned with the regulation of living resources but rather with general management in the Arctic. The United States slightly deviated from the view issued in the Ilulissat Declaration, saying that "international fishing treaties and agreements provide a framework for establishing rules", and RFBs are appropriate fora for their implementation.[40] This is interpreted as the US declaring that the international framework is not sufficient and that new rules would have to be created by new international bodies. Further, this consideration initially led to the creation of the CAOF Agreement as a first, rather general RFB for CAO fisheries. Nevertheless, the CAOF Agreement's Parties opted to decide on the creation of an additional RFB only at a later point in time and within the framework of the

36 ibid 461, 472–473; cf. David A Balton and Andrei Zagorski, 'Implementing Marine Management in the Arctic Ocean' (Russian International Affairs Council; Wilson Center; Polar Institute 2020) 437 <https://www.wilsoncenter.org/publication/implementing-marine-management-arctic-ocean> accessed 10 August 2021.

37 See Article 5(1)(c) CAOF Agreement.

38 'Arctic Ocean Conference Ilulissat Declaration (Ilulissat, 28 May 2008)' (Chapter 3, n 78).

39 ibid.

40 United States Congress (Chapter 2, n 163) 2.

Agreement. Commercial fisheries seemed unlikely in the near future and there was no perceived need to establish an additional RFB immediately.[41] Most delegations considered the establishment of the CAOF Agreement "as part of a "stepwise" process in advance of possibly establishing one or more additional regional fisheries management organizations or arrangements for this area".[42] The Other Five even took the view that the establishment of an additional RFB should not be considered an option but be pursued in any case[43] – which is not surprising considering that, unlike the Arctic Five with their EEZs, fishing in the Arctic would realistically only be possible for these States if it was authorised by such a new body. Thus, the creation of an additional RFB in the form of an RFMA or RFMO was not considered necessary yet, but was seen as a future option, which was implemented in Article 5(1)(c)(i) CAOF Agreement.

The conditions under which a decision to initiate negotiations on the establishment of an additional RFB will be taken was one of the sensitive points of discussion on the way to the CAOF Agreement.[44] In the final text, Article 3(1)(a) CAOF Agreement sets up the prerequisite that the respective RFB must be "operated in accordance with international law to manage such fishing in accordance with recognized international standards". In this regard, international law presumably refers to UNCLOS, the UNFS Agreement and general international law. Recognized international standards likely include the FAO Code of Conduct and similar accepted instruments, as mentioned in the Preamble of the Agreement.[45] Although during the drafting process, the wording was changed from "modern international standards"[46] to "recognized international standards",[47] it is assumed[48] that this comprises generally recommended international minimum standards[49] including "key obligations of

41 'Declaration Concerning the Prevention of Unregulated High Seas Fishing in the Central Arctic Ocean (Oslo, 16 July 2015)' (Chapter 2, n 22).

42 'Chairman's Statement, Fourth Meeting on Central Arctic Ocean Fisheries (Tórshavn, 29 November – 1 December 2016)' (Chapter 2, n 238) 1.

43 Molenaar, 'The CAOF Agreement: Key Issues of International Fisheries Law' (Chapter 2, n 20) 469.

44 'Chairman's Statement, Fourth Meeting on Central Arctic Ocean Fisheries (Tórshavn, 29 November – 1 December 2016)' (Chapter 2, n 238) 2.

45 See Schatz, Proelß and Liu (Chapter 2, n 41) 223.

46 'Chairman's Statement, Third Meeting on Central Arctic Ocean Fisheries (Nuuk, 24–26 February 2014)' (Chapter 3, n 89) 2.

47 'Declaration Concerning the Prevention of Unregulated High Seas Fishing in the Central Arctic Ocean (Oslo, 16 July 2015)' (Chapter 2, n 22) 2.

48 As similarly referred to in Articles 119(1)(a), 61(3) UNCLOS Article 5(b), 10(c), 30(5) UNFS Agreement.

49 Ryder (Chapter 2, n 244) 5.

international fisheries law, such as ecosystem and precautionary approaches to fisheries management, with specific attention to new and exploratory fisheries."[50] This is in line with the established requirement that interim measures should include sustainable management considerations such as the precautionary approach.

Nevertheless, after the CAOF Agreement's establishment the question still remains whether fish stocks and fishing possibilities, e.g. the declining ice coverage that creates new fishing areas, justify the creation of a new RFB. As commercial fishing is conceivable in the CAO,[51] it is assumed that a decision on whether to establish an additional RFB in the area will have to be taken sooner or later. In this context, it must be considered whether the establishment of an RFMA or an RFMO for CAO fisheries is deemed more beneficial. The relationship between international regimes, like RFMAs, and international organizations, like RFMOs, varies depending on the respective definition. The term RFMA is considered to refer to an RFB with the power to adopt binding measures for its members, while an RFMO is considered to be an RFMA which agreement provides for the establishment of an organization.[52] But can meaningful regimes even operate and function without the backup of international organizations, either new or existing ones? Considering history and experience, a general rule can be set up: "If States care for the effective operation of the regime, they will opt for a strong organization; if they prefer a weak regime, they will opt for a weak organization or no organization at all."[53] In principle, where more than two or possibly three States are involved in a fishery, the establishment of an RFMO has been considered necessary.[54] Also for Arctic fisheries, the establishment of an RFMO as a strong managing organization has been supported from various sides.[55]

Indeed, the creation of an RFMO to strengthen a fisheries management system like the existing RFMA, the CAOF Agreement, seems appropriate for other reasons, although some of them also apply to RFMAs. Among other things, a new RFMO that deals exclusively with fisheries in the CAO bears the advantage

50 Molenaar, 'International Regulation of Central Arctic Ocean Fisheries' (Chapter 2, n 20) 462.

51 Van Pelt and others (Chapter 3, n 298) s 79.

52 For a definition of RFMA and RFMO see Chapter 4 Sections 3, 3.2 *supra*.

53 Winfried Lang, 'Regimes and Organizations in the Labyrinth of International Institutions' in Karl Zemanek and Konrad Ginther (eds), *Völkerrecht zwischen normativem Anspruch und politischer Realität: Festschrift für Karl Zemanek zum 65. Geburtstag* (Duncker & Humblot 1994) 289.

54 Rayfuse, 'Countermeasures and High Seas Fisheries Enforcement' (Chapter 5, n 336) 55.

55 Papastavridis (Chapter 2, n 156) 359.

of being unencumbered. While it is likely that a new RFB would be based on the CAOF Agreement, this is not necessarily the case. Membership structure, decision-making processes or policies can be adapted to the needs that have evolved over the years that the CAOF Agreement has been in force. The organizational construct of an RFMO format further supports the regime. Also, distraction is not to be expected: likely, a new RFB that is established based on Article 5(1)(c)(i) CAOF Agreement will deal only with fisheries in the CAO without other major fields of duty, can thus be structured and arranged more easily, and focus its resources on such fisheries only. In this regard, a new RFB does not have to be created from scratch. An analysis of advantages and disadvantages of existing RFBs can provide helpful guidance in how to structure a new organization, based on years of experience.[56] However, the establishment of an RFB, especially an RFMO, is always a heavy measure that takes up a lot of resources in terms of time, money and manpower, and represents a certain administrative burden. One factor that should especially be kept in mind is the duration of negotiations. Already the creation of the CAOF Agreement took more than ten years from the first tangible ideas to the start of implementation. Admittedly, the CAOF Agreement established a basis for future specific management, including the creation of an additional RFB. However, one can imagine that the establishment of specific fisheries measures such as the allocation of TACs and the setting of quotas could take a reasonable amount of time – not to mention the creation of an organizational structure, including possible new members such as interest States attracted by new commercial opportunities.

In summary, an RFMO as a complementary, institutionalized RFB to the CAOF Agreement presents itself as a good solution for managing commercial fisheries in the CAO – provided that the circumstances of the ecosystem support a sustainable commercial fishery.

In order to assess the latter issue, Article 5(1)(c) CAOF Agreement requests the Parties to consider matters like the distribution, migration and abundance of fish in the Agreement Area. The provision stresses the anticipatory character of the Agreement, being the first fisheries agreement in place before fishing in the regulatory area has occurred. It is still unclear whether specific fish stocks reside in the Agreement Area, and if they do, whether the taking of species is possible on a commercial level without undermining the sustainable approach of the Agreement. In line with the suggestions for elements of interim measures,[57] it further underlines the scientific approach that the Agreement is based

56 See more on challenges of RFBs Chapter 5 Sections 2, 2.6 *supra*.

57 On the elements of interim measures, see introductory Chapter 6 *supra*.

on. When determining the level of commerciality, the distribution of possible fish stocks, their migration routes and patterns and their occurrence in CAO waters should be taken into account as indicating factors. Considerations should be made on the basis of the scientific information derived from the JPSRM, national scientific programs and other relevant sources, likely similar to the sources mentioned under Article 5(1)(b) CAOF Agreement. As required for interim measures, Article 5(1)(c) CAOF Agreement reiterates the crucial importance of the information prepared by the JPSRM for critical decisions in the implementation process of the Agreement. As commercial fishing cannot be allowed until the findings of the JPSRM are available, and the JPSRM may be established within a period of two years after the Agreement has entered into force,[58] commercial fishing under the Agreement is unlikely to occur any sooner.

As another aspect, the Parties should take into account relevant fisheries management and ecosystem considerations. In this regard, considerations on the ecosystem should recognize the complex interactions among ecosystem components.[59] They likely include the issues of ocean temperature, nutrient and energy content of the habitat and species inhabiting the area including considering the ecological pyramid.[60] Further, the precautionary approach and potential adverse impacts of fishing on the ecosystems should be taken into account.[61] This is in line with the aim of the Agreement to support the conservation of the ecosystem in all respects and thus to take action and prevent negative impacts. In principle, the precautionary approach[62] as part of customary international law[63] should always be considered when acting within the scope of environmental agreements. Potential adverse impacts are part of precautionary considerations, as these should consider all beneficial and harmful factors and their potential consequences. However, it makes sense to

58 See Article 4(2) CAOF Agreement.

59 North Pacific Fishery Management Council (Chapter 2, n 17) 4.

60 On the ecological conditions in the CAO, see especially Chapter 2 Section 4 *supra*.

61 See Article 5(1)(c) CAOF Agreement.

62 On the precautionary approach, see Chapter 5 Sections 2, 2.1, 2.1.1 *supra*.

63 Cf. *Corfu Channel Case (United Kingdom of Great Britain and Northern Ireland v Albania), Judgement on the Merits, 9 April 1949: ICJ Reports 1949, 4* 22–23; *Advisory Opinion on Responsibilities and Obligations of States Sponsoring Persons and Entities with Respect to Activities in the Area, 1 February 2011, ITLOS Case No. 17* (Chapter 5, n 210) paras 125–135; *Case Concerning Pulp Mills on the River Uruguay (Argentina v Uruguay), Judgement of 20 April 2010, ICJ Reports 2010, 14* [164]; United Nations Convention on Environmental Impact Assessment in a Transboundary Context (Espoo Convention) (Chapter 5, n 210) Preamble para 7.

stress the significance of encompassing such considerations, as detrimental, possibly irreversible impacts are to be avoided at all costs – it is better to be safe than sorry. Adverse impacts include effects of fishing on the food chain, e.g. an impaired reproduction of fish stocks that leads to an increased production of another predatory species higher in the food chain, resulting in narrowing down the number of another stock to an unsustainable level, or water pollution by fishing boats and icebreakers that enter the region. For instance, the pollution of CAO water by Russian rivers, increased inflow of water and anticipated ocean acidification might lead to a decrease of fisheries in the CAO.[64] Further impacts are fish interchanges, in whose pace the maritime industry could play a role: ships assist in transferring exotic marine species from other ecosystems in ballast water tanks or on the wetted surface of hulls as biofouling.[65] Further possible scenarios are collisions of ships with marine mammals or surface and underwater noises negatively impacting marine life.[66] All in all, the Arctic is a very delicate ecosystem, and no one knows for sure what effects an intrusion in the CAO might have in the long run. It is therefore even more important that developments in the CAO are carefully observed and assessed, so that a determination on the possibility of commercial sustainable fisheries can be made.

To sum up, since scientific knowledge about the Arctic is rather limited, the future option of establishing an additional RFB was kept on the table but immediately not pursued.[67] In fact, there is no concrete evidence on what species are living in CAO waters, on their abundance or their lifecycle. Based on current knowledge, it is unlikely that the area itself harbours fish, but that stocks that currently exist further south of the CAO are migrating north into the area and finding new habitat in Arctic waters.[68] Technology is developing, but at present, the vessels entering the Agreement Area are only equipped as

64 Molenaar, 'International Regulation of Central Arctic Ocean Fisheries' (Chapter 2, n 20) 431.

65 Chris Ware and others, 'Climate Change, Non-Indigenous Species and Shipping: Assessing the Risk of Species Introduction to a High-Arctic Archipelago' (2014) 20 Diversity and Distributions 10, 11 <http://doi.wiley.com/10.1111/ddi.12117> accessed 11 March 2020; Wisz and others (Chapter 2, n 193) 262.

66 Aldo Chircop, 'The Use of IMO Instruments for Marine Conservation on the High Seas' in Robert C Beckman and others (eds), *High Seas Governance: Gaps and Challenges* (Brill | Nijhoff 2019) 126.

67 'Notes of phone call with Maya Gold, Canadian Representative in Consultations for the CAOF Agreement, on 19 September 2019, on file with the author'.

68 On the ecological development of fish in the Arctic, see specifically Chapter 2 Sections, 4, 4.2 *supra*.

icebreakers without fishing capabilities.[69] Therefore, at the moment, the focus is on science and trying to understand the CAO ecosystem. However, the possibility of establishing an additional body, if circumstances allow, has been included in the Agreement. If such a new body is created, it may establish measures for commercial fishing under the CAOF Agreement.

1.2 *Commercial Fishing as a Management and Conservation Measure Authorised by Existing RFBs*

Apart from the possibility to conduct commercial fishing in accordance with measures adopted by a newly established RFB, Article 3(1)(a) CAOF Agreement allows for commercial fishing pursuant to conservation and management measures for the sustainable management of fish stocks adopted by one or more existing RFBs.

Originally, as discussed above,[70] there were different views on what arrangement should manage fisheries in the central part of the Arctic Ocean. Back in 2008, the EU mentioned the need for a framework, but extending the mandate of existing management organizations such as the NEAFC was preferred to creating a new body.[71] Also Barnes suggested that it would be easiest if an existing RFMO was reformed, as existing expertise could be used.[72] Although these suggestions were made before the CAOF Agreement was finally established and were likely referring to the discussion on the initial creation of the CAOF Agreement itself, the essential considerations can be taken into account in assessing the possibility of an existing RFB to allow for commercial fishing in the Agreement Area.

The extensive experience of such a body would be a great advantage for CAO commercial fisheries if they were regulated by an already established RFB. Even though active leadership in this area would be new, no familiarisation of an organizational structure is required.[73] CAO fisheries could be

---

69 See e.g. Conservation of Arctic Flora and Fauna (CAFF) Working Group, 'State of the Arctic Marine Biodiversity: Key Findings and Advice for Monitoring' (Chapter 2, n 166) 17; Struzik, 'Welcome to the Arctic Ocean, Mysterious Fish' (Chapter 2, n 111); Drinkwater, Mueter and Saitoh (Chapter 2, n 122) 2294; European Union, 'Policy Department B: Fisheries Management And The Arctic In The Context Of Climate Change – Study' (Chapter 2, n 149) 83; Rose (Chapter 2, n 161) 1528.

70 See the discussion in Chapter 6 Sections 1, 1.1 *supra*.

71 European Union, 'Communication from the Commission to the European Parliament and the Council – The European Union and the Arctic Region (20 November 2008) – COM/2008/0763 Final' (Chapter 2, n 80) 7 et seq.

72 Barnes (Chapter 2, n 10) 228.

73 ibid.

swiftly implemented along other regulatory areas into an entrenched regime. Moreover, a high number of member States and entities within the existing RFB can ensure broad acceptance of CAO fisheries regulations, which is the ultimate goal of preventing IUU fishing, whereas a new RFB would necessarily take time to gain international acceptance.

Apart from advantages and disadvantages that support measures to be taken by an existing RFB for CAO fisheries, a significant task is to identify the existing body that would be most suitable for and capable of such management. In this regard, Article 3(1)(a) CAOF Agreement sets up the prerequisite that the respective (S)RFMA/O must be "operated in accordance with international law to manage such fishing in accordance with recognized international standards". Therefore, it must not actively manage fishing in accordance with international standards but have the ability to manage fishing in such a way.[74] As stated before, recognized international standards are considered to comprise generally recommended international minimum standards including key obligations of international fisheries law, such as the ecosystem and precautionary approach.[75]

Some sort of link to the central Arctic is considered a necessary characteristic of potential RFBs. Hence, only RFBs with either a regulatory area that is in geographical proximity to the CAO or RFBs that manage specific stocks that occur close to the northern polar region are considered: small adjustments to a regulatory area are considered relatively easy, while large changes to the regulatory area involving newly accessible areas such as the Arctic are considered difficult to implement.[76] However, the greatest difficulty would be to justify the extension of the regulatory competence or the agreement area to States that are not party to the respective RFB, but also to members of these RFBs that are not party to the CAOF Agreement. Although it is not necessary that the parties to the CAOF Agreement are parties to a potential RFB, this might strengthen the support for such body and avoid conflicts with e.g. measures adopted under the CAOF Agreement.

There are several RFB regulatory areas that are geographically defined,[77] some of which share a water border or overlap with the CAOF Agreement Area.

74 Molenaar, 'International Regulation of Central Arctic Ocean Fisheries' (Chapter 2, n 20) 451–454.

75 On the determination of recognized international standards in Article 3(1)(a) CAOF Agreement, see Chapter 6 Sections 1, 1.1 *supra*.

76 Koivurova and Molenaar (Chapter 3, n 32) 74 et seq.

77 See Figure 14 *infra*.

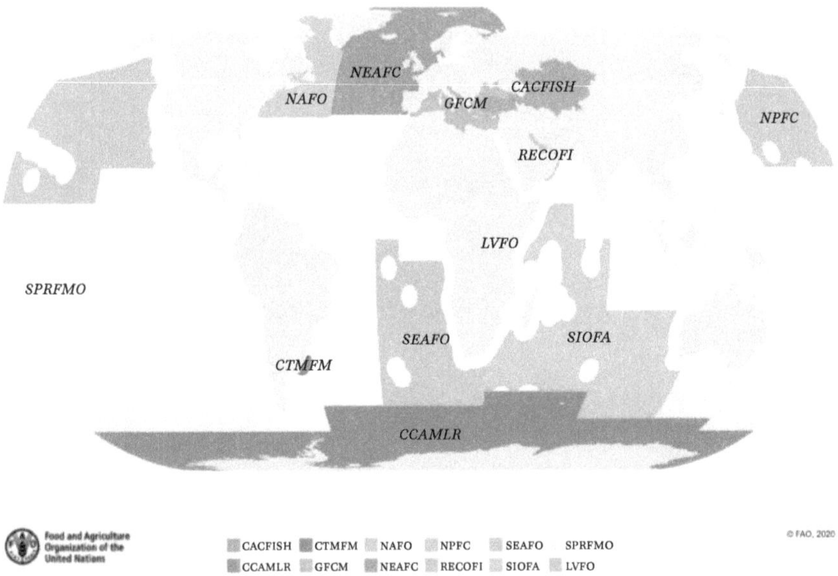

FIGURE 14 Generic RFBs
SOURCE: LØBACH AND OTHERS (CHAPTER 4, N 87) 10

Additionally, there are RFB areas that are more vaguely defined depending on the occurrence of certain species of fish.[78]

Some fisheries management bodies operate in geographical proximity to the Agreement Area. Nevertheless, although an RFB might be competent to regulate most fishery resources in an area near the CAO, e.g. NAFO in the Northwest Atlantic,[79] it is considered unlikely that an RFB's regulatory area is extensively expanded. Hence, only RFBs that either already have a mandate in (parts of) the CAO or manage stocks that have the potential to migrate into CAO waters are considered here.

1.2.1 Joint Norwegian-Russian Fisheries Commission

The Joint Norwegian-Russian Fisheries Commission, also referred to as JointFish, was initially established by Norway and the Soviet Union in 1976[80] and manages the commercially most important fish stocks[81] of both

78 See Figure 15 *infra*.
79 Cf. Article 1(f)(i) NAFO Convention; see 'Convention on Cooperation in the Northwest Atlantic Fisheries (Ottawa, 24 October 1987) – UNTS Vol. 1135, No. 17799' (Chapter 5, n 153).
80 Henriksen, Hønneland and Sydnes (Chapter 3, n 171) 131.
81 Mostly cod, haddock and capelin.

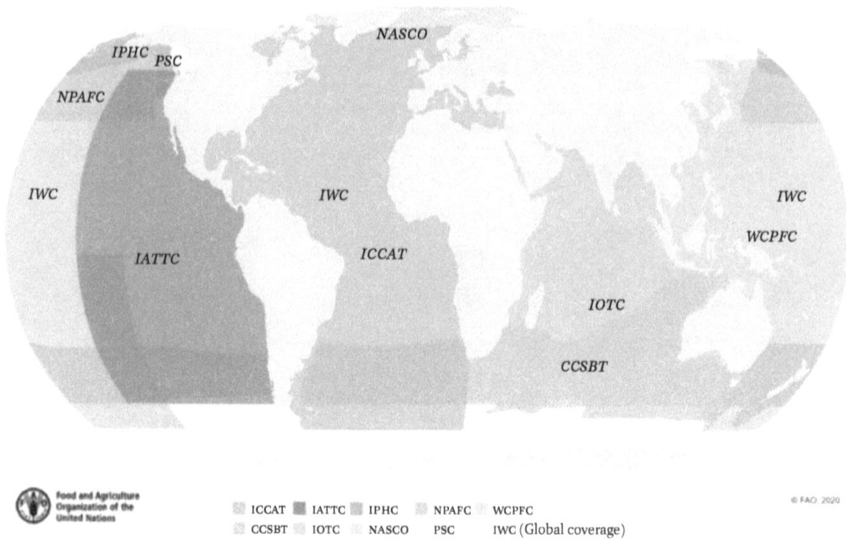

FIGURE 15 Species-specific RFBs
SOURCE: FLEWWELLING (CHAPTER 5, N 19) S 3.3

participating countries in the Barents Sea and the Norwegian Sea. The two parties, Russia and Norway, cooperate on the basis of annual JointFish meetings, in relation to scientific assessments, fisheries regulations and enforcement and control. JointFish has set up TAC quotas for shared stocks throughout their entire range, covering the parties' EEZs, the fisheries protection zone around Svalbard, and the Barents Sea "loophole".[82] TAC quotas are further exchanged in bilateral negotiations with third countries, traditionally with the Faroe Islands and the EU.[83] Where sustainable fisheries are concerned, the parties have developed monitoring and research activities in the northern seas to provide the basis for scientific advice on sustainable management. All monitoring data and research results from joint investigations are coordinated and quality assured by ICES, which provides subsequent management advice.[84]

In order to regulate fishing in the CAO, JointFish must be "operated in accordance with international law".[85] In this regard, in the past, there has been

82 For visualization purposes, see map of the high seas pockets in the Arctic (Figure 7) at Chapter 3 Section 1 *supra*.

83 Henriksen, Hønneland and Sydnes (Chapter 3, n 171) 9, 135.

84 'Joint Fish | Research – Cooperation' <https://www.jointfish.com/eng/RESEARCH/COOPERATION.html> accessed 8 April 2022.

85 See Article 3(1)(a) CAOF Agreement.

criticism of the implementation of the provisions of the UNFS Agreement. Above all, the regime has been accused of exceeding quotas – in 2006, Norway estimated Russian overfishing at around 20.000 to 30.000 tonnes annually[86] – and of lacking transparency. Consequently, Norway allowed for Norwegian counties to appoint representatives to the joint commission to enhance transparency.[87] Nowadays, JointFish refers to "sustainable management of marine resources, benefiting the fishing fleet in the Barents Sea for current and future generations" to be conducted.[88]

The Parties to the CAOF Agreement have ensured that the CAOF Agreement itself does not make any determinations regarding JointFish's status as an RFMA or RFMO or its regulatory scope, which were both points on which the Parties disagreed.[89] However, as the scope of JointFish is not spatially restricted but includes the "entire range" of a species,[90] it can be interpreted as including CAO waters. JointFish may hence potentially manage Arctic fisheries.[91] Yet, one drawback of JointFish is that with only Russia and Norway as members, it does not provide a multinational forum. The regime was put in place and still functions as a bilateral arrangement. Although it would be possible to increase the number of members – potentially by all States with a real interest[92] in CAO fisheries – and to extend measures to CAO waters, should the managed species migrate northwards, it is questionable whether this artificially inflates the rather simple structure of JointFish. In any case, the fact that the only two parties to JointFish, Russia and Norway, are also Parties to the CAOF Agreement already indicates their support for a multilateral rather than a bilateral approach to CAO fisheries management. It is therefore unlikely that the two States will allow commercial fisheries in CAO waters solely under the guidance of JointFish.[93] Nevertheless, it is on JointFish to decide on future measures and their scope of application.

---

86 Geir Hønneland, 'Norway and Russia in the Barents Sea – Cooperation and Conflict in Fisheries Management' (2007) 20 Russian Analytical Digest 9, 11 <https://css.ethz.ch/content/dam/ethz/special-interest/gess/cis/center-for-securities-studies/pdfs/RAD-20-9-11.pdf> accessed 17 November 2020.

87 See Henriksen, Hønneland and Sydnes (Chapter 3, n 171) 140 et seq.

88 'Joint Fish | The Fisheries Commission' <https://www.jointfish.com/eng/THE-FISHERIES-COMMISSION/ABOUT-THE-WEBSITE.html> accessed 17 November 2020.

89 See discussion in relation to the Agreement Area at Chapter 2 Section 3 *supra*.

90 Henriksen, Hønneland and Sydnes (Chapter 3, n 171) 143.

91 See also Schatz, Proelß and Liu (Chapter 2, n 41) 203, 213.

92 On the concept of real interest, see Chapter 3 Sections 3, 3.2 *supra*.

93 See also Molenaar, 'The Oslo Declaration on High Seas Fishing in the Central Arctic Ocean' (Chapter 2, n 58) 428.

1.2.2 North Atlantic Salmon Conservation Organization

The North Atlantic Salmon Conservation Organization (NASCO) manages stocks of Atlantic salmon which migrate beyond areas of fisheries jurisdiction of the North Atlantic coastal States. NASCO's regulatory area[94] overlaps spatially with NAFO's and NEAFC's regulatory areas.

Created in 1983, the conventional-based inter-governmental organization focuses on the objective to conserve, restore, enhance and rationally manage wild Atlantic salmon. NASCO has seven parties: Canada, Denmark (in respect of the Faroe Islands and Greenland), the European Union, the United Kingdom, Norway, the Russian Federation and the United States. France, in respect of St. Pierre & Miquelon, attends NASCO's meetings as an observer. Iceland withdrew from NASCO in 2009 due to financial considerations, but will presumably rejoin the RFB when their financial situation improves. Hence, six of the ten CAOF Agreement parties are parties to NASCO. Further, forty-four NGOs are accredited as observers.[95]

NASCO is strongly following the precautionary approach and has developed a range of precautionary agreements and guidelines.[96] NASCO's management is successful and has led to a reduction in salmon harvests throughout the North Atlantic. Within the organization, there is a strong willingness to take enforcement action against illegal fishing from third countries. NASCO has also done much to coordinate and promote enforcement measures by port States as an effective means against the landing of illegal catch. These factors indicate that NASCO might successfully be adapted to accommodate new salmon fisheries in Arctic waters. The functioning organizational structure with a clear distribution of tasks and experience in research coordination can provide a solid basis for future measures. Technically, NASCO could regulate salmon throughout much of FAO Major Fishing Area 18 (Arctic Ocean),[97] if NASCO's three regional commissions, the North American Commission, the North-East Atlantic Commission, and the West Greenland Commission, are restructured.[98] Yet, NASCO is built upon the concept that fishing for salmon beyond areas of fisheries jurisdiction, and in most areas of the North Atlantic, beyond

94 See Article I NASCO Convention; see 'Convention for the Conservation of Salmon in the North Atlantic Ocean (Reykjavik, 2 March 1982) – UNTS Vol. 1338, No. 22433' <https://treaties.un.org/doc/Publication/UNTS/Volume 1338/v1338.pdf> accessed 12 August 2021.

95 'NASCO | The North Atlantic Salmon Conservation Organization – About' <https://nasco.int/about/> accessed 19 November 2021.

96 ibid.

97 See 'FAO | FAO Major Fishing Areas: Arctic Sea (Major Fishing Area 18)' (Chapter 2, n 15).

98 Barnes (Chapter 2, n 10) 218.

12 NM of the baselines, is prohibited.[99] As this understanding is considered the cornerstone of the organization, a deviation in terms of extending the scope of regulation to CAO high seas seems unlikely.

1.2.3 North-East Atlantic Fisheries Commission

As the name suggests, the North-East Atlantic Fisheries Commission (NEAFC) is an RFMO regulating fisheries in the North-East Atlantic with the objective to ensure the long-term conservation and optimum utilisation of fishery resources in the NEAFC Convention Area.[100] Contracting parties are the CAOF Agreement parties Denmark (in respect of the Faroe Islands and Greenland), the European Union, Iceland, Norway, and the Russian Federation. Cooperating non-contracting parties are the Bahamas, Canada, Curaçao, Liberia, New Zealand and Panama. Despite the United States' proximity to the NEAFC's regulatory area, they are not party to the NEAFC Convention.

The area covered by the NEAFC Convention stretches from the southern tip of Greenland east to the Barents Sea, and from the North Pole south to Portugal.[101] In the high seas areas beyond national jurisdiction in the CAO, the NEAFC is the regional body responsible for the Atlantic sector and part of the only regime that significantly overlaps with the CAOF Agreement Area.[102] In this regard, to prevent conflicts, the Preamble of the CAOF Agreement underlines "the importance of ensuring cooperation and coordination between the Parties and the [NEAFC], which has competence to adopt conservation and management measures in part of the high seas portion of the central Arctic Ocean". Additionally, Article 14(4) CAOF Agreement states that the Agreement "shall neither undermine nor conflict with the role and mandate of any existing international mechanism relating to fisheries management".[103]

As the North-East Atlantic is one of the most abundant fishing areas in the world, the NEAFC regularly makes binding recommendations and has adopted conservation and management measures for multiple different fish stocks in several parts. For instance, in accordance with the FAO Agreement on Port State Measures, the NEAFC has adopted port state control procedures that

---

99 See Articles 1, 2 'Convention for the Conservation of Salmon in the North Atlantic Ocean (Reykjavik, 2 March 1982) – UNTS Vol. 1338, No. 22433' (Chapter 6, n 94).

100 See Article 2 NEAFC Convention; 'Convention on Future Multilateral Cooperation in North-East Atlantic Fisheries (London, 18 November 1980) – UNTS Vol. 1285, No. 21173' (Chapter 5, n 153).

101 See Article 1(a) NEAFC Convention.

102 See 16 *supra*.

103 See specifically on the overlap of the CAOF Agreement Area and NEAFC's regulatory area Chapter 2 Section 3 *supra*.

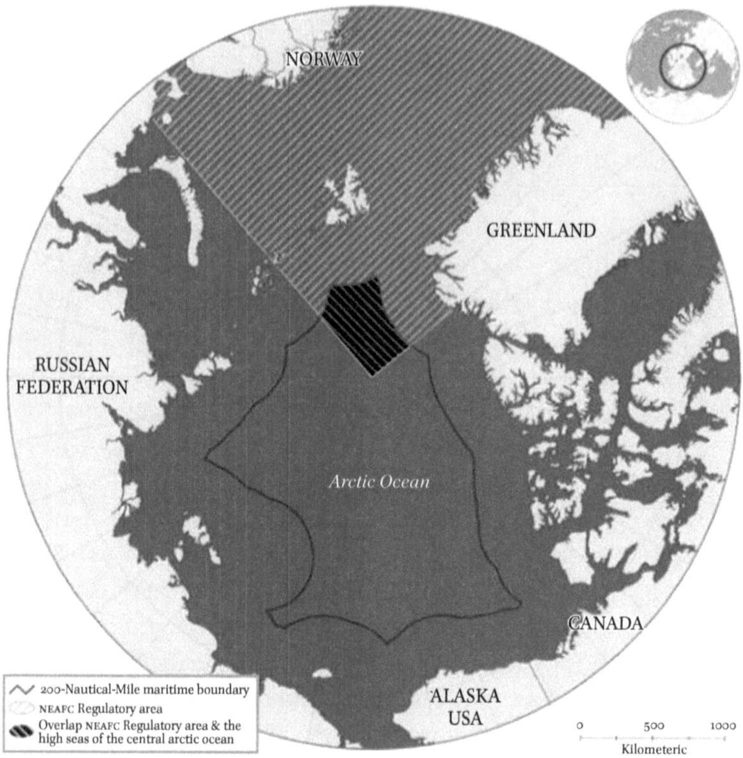

FIGURE 16 CAOF Agreement Area and NEAFC Regulatory Area with overlap
SOURCE: BALTON, 'IMPLEMENTING THE NEW ARCTIC FISHERIES AGREEMENT' (CHAPTER 3, N 26) 436

apply to the use of ports of NEAFC Convention parties by foreign fishing vessels with catches of fishery resources on board that have either been caught in the NEAFC Convention area by such vessels or that have not been previously landed or transhipped in a port.[104] In addition, the NEAFC has taken measures, such as closing areas to bottom fishing, to protect other components of the marine ecosystem from possible negative impacts of fishing. In this way, the NEAFC contributes to the implementation of the ecosystem approach to fisheries and the protection of marine biodiversity.

104 Annual reports on compliance with regulatory instruments, primarily the NEAFC Scheme of Control and Enforcement, and on inspection activities on the high seas and in ports in the NEAFC Convention Area can be accessed at 'NEAFC | Compliance' <https://www.neafc.org/compliance> accessed 31 March 2022.

According to Article 14 NEAFC Convention, the NEAFC should seek information and advice from ICES in order to enhance ocean governance. Based thereupon, the NEAFC does not undertake scientific work itself. NEAFC's conservation and management measures, including those related to other parts of the marine ecosystem, rely on ICES for scientific advice. In this regard, ICES takes a scientific role only but closely cooperates with the NEAFC,[105] e.g. through regular bilateral meetings to discuss long-term developments such as multispecies consultation, possible climatic effects and other ecosystem considerations. The NEAFC also promotes sustainability of deep-sea fisheries, in particular with the aim of focusing attention on rapidly changing or increasing fisheries.[106]

In the discussion on whether an existing RFB should be reformed to govern Arctic Ocean fisheries, most supporters of a reformation considered the NEAFC to be the best option.[107] Now, when it comes to considering an RFB that could allow for fishing in CAO waters, the NEAFC is still in play. It can either allow for fishing in the section of its regulatory area that overlaps with the CAOF Agreement Area. Further, as amendments of the NEAFC Convention are possible,[108] its geographical regulatory area could also be adapted to cover more parts of the Arctic high seas. Additionally, most States that conduct fishing activities in the Arctic region are already members to the RFB, and Canada is a non-contracting Party. For both reasons, therefore, a closer look should be taken at the structure and work of the NEAFC.

The subjects of NEAFC regulation are fishery resources. These are defined in Article 1(b) NEAFC Convention. Fishery resources include all resources of fish, molluscs, crustaceans and – contrary to the CAOF Agreement[109] – sedentary species, excluding in so far as they are dealt with by other international agreements, highly migratory species listed in Annex I UNCLOS, and anadromous

105 For the relationship between NEAFC and ICES, see North-East Atlantic Fisheries Commission, 'Memorandum of Understanding between the North-East Atlantic Fisheries Commission and the International Council for the Exploration of the Sea' (2019) <https://www.neafc.org/system/files/ices_mou-2019.pdf> accessed 2 April 2020.

106 North-East Atlantic Fisheries Commission, 'Submission by the North-East Atlantic Fisheries Commission Regarding the Report of the Secretary-General of the United Nations on Oceans and the Law of the Sea, Pursuant to General Assembly Resolution 72/124' (2019) 1–2 <https://www.neafc.org/compliance> accessed 2 April 2020.

107 See e.g. Barnes (Chapter 2, n 10) 228.

108 See Article 19 NEAFC Convention.

109 For the notion of fish in the sense of the CAOF Agreement, see Chapter 2 Sections 4, 4.2, 4.2.4 *supra*.

stocks. In this respect, the subject matter of the NEAFC Convention does not differ significantly from the subject matter of the CAOF Agreement.

As for the NEAFC's organizational structure, a commission with legal personality, consisting of not more than two representatives of each contracting party, has been established.[110] Its main task is to make recommendations concerning both fisheries conducted in areas beyond national jurisdiction of contracting parties[111] and within areas under the jurisdiction of a contracting party where the contracting party in question so requests.[112] Where specific measures are concerned, based on Article 7 NEAFC Convention, so far, the NEAFC Commission has set TAC limits, allocated these to the contracting parties, and adopted a range of technical measures. Measures were directed at conserving deep-sea fish species, both target resources and by-catch species, and address the effects of bottom fisheries on other components of the marine ecosystem, *inter alia* by area closures to protect vulnerable marine ecosystems.[113]

The NEAFC system allows for objections and withdrawals of consent to adopted recommendations.[114] This usually impedes the effective enforcement of measures and makes the regime dependent on the willingness of its contracting parties, although the imposition of sanctions for breaches of regulatory measures is provided for in Article 15 NEAFC Convention. Yet, the NEAFC is quite successful in implementing and monitoring its compliance measures. Reasons could be the members' political cooperation, common interests of coastal States and the NEAFC due to common fisheries in EEZ areas and areas beyond national jurisdiction, and a comparatively small regulatory area.[115]

Within the NEAFC, a strong degree of control is given to coastal States.[116] Yet, with the increase of fishing interests and evolvement of possibilities in the Arctic, greater uncertainty exists about how coastal States will manage fisheries, especially how these States will pursue national fishing interests within the NEAFC.[117]

Concerning the CAOF Agreement, the NEAFC "welcomes" the Agreement's conclusion but noted that

---

110 Cf. Article 3 NEAFC Convention.

111 See Article 5(1) NEAFC Convention.

112 See Article 6(1) NEAFC Convention.

113 Cf. 'FAO | Vulnerable Marine Ecosystems Database: NEAFC Regulatory Area 2013' <https://www.fao.org/fishery/en/vme/vme_neafc_regulatory_1/2013> accessed 4 October 2020.

114 See Articles 12 and 13 NEAFC Convention.

115 Barnes (Chapter 2, n 10) 215.

116 See Tang (Chapter 3, n 62) 229.

117 Barnes (Chapter 2, n 10) 216.

> Parties to that agreement underline the importance of ensuring cooperation and coordination between them and this Commission, which has the competence to adopt conservation and management measures in a portion of the high seas of the central Arctic Ocean.[118]

Several conservation and management measures are currently applicable in the NEAFC Convention Area, and partly therefore also in the CAO. These include a control and enforcement scheme covering fishing authorisations and vessel registration requirements, record-keeping and reporting obligations. Additionally applicable are a mandatory vessel monitoring system and inspection system at sea, port controls, infringement prosecution procedures and measures to combat IUU fishing. Further, measures regarding the protection of vulnerable marine ecosystems and deep-sea fisheries, and annual regulations on a series of fish stocks are in place.[119] In addition, the NEAFC introduced a new electronic reporting system. The system will allow detailed up-to-date information of fishing activities in the NEAFC Convention area – therefore also in parts of the CAOF Agreement Area – and will be available to fisheries inspectors of all contracting parties. NEAFC's contracting parties are instructed to roll out the system over the coming years.[120] For the CAO specifically, Norway proposed that the NEAFC should request ICES to periodically provide information on and assessments of the status of the marine ecosystem in central Arctic waters, which shall be coordinated with scientific activities under the CAOF Agreement.[121]

Although the NEAFC is making an effort, its management has not been extraordinarily effective so far: many of the fish stocks exploited still remain unregulated. These even triggered assumptions as to "whether the recent focus on ecosystem management is a way of diverting attention from these stocks".[122]

In summary, the NEAFC is an established RFMO with a regulatory area geographically close to the CAOF Agreement Area and even overlaps with it in

118 North-East Atlantic Fisheries Commission, 'Statement Regarding the Conclusion of the Negotiations on the Agreement to Prevent Unregulated High Seas Fisheries in the Central Arctic Ocean' (2018) <https://www.neafc.org/system/files/NEAFC-statement_Central-Arctic-Ocean-Agreement.pdf> accessed 2 April 2022.

119 ibid.

120 'Press Release from the 2018 Annual Meeting of the North-East Atlantic Fisheries Commission', p. 1 <www.neafc.org,> accessed 5 April 2019.

121 North-East Atlantic Fisheries Commission, 'Proposal by Norway on a Request to ICES to Provide Assessments of the Status of the Ecosystem in a Portion of the High Seas of the Central Arctic Ocean (12–14 November 2019) – AM 2019–44' (Chapter 5, n 127).

122 Henriksen, Hønneland and Sydnes (Chapter 3, n 171) 130.

a small part. An adjustment of the NEAFC regulatory area is not specifically foreseen by the NEAFC Convention, but also not prohibited.[123] Its regulatory competences have neither been exceptional nor detrimental but leave room for improvement. When considered as an RFB adopting management measures for CAO fishing, the position of the CAOF Agreement parties that are non-contracting parties to the NEAFC Convention can be problematic. Canada for instance is not a full member to the NEAFC Convention, and the United States are also non-participants. It is expected that non-members tend to disapprove of allowing commercial fishing in CAO waters by the NEAFC, *inter alia* as this potentially decreases their own TAC allocated by a possible new CAO RFB. Similarly, the NEAFC regime may be unattractive to non-coastal States or DWF States like China or South Korea due to NEAFC's practices of giving preferential treatment to coastal States when establishing and allocating TAC quotas for straddling fish stocks.[124] In a nutshell, it is argued that there are better options than extending the NEAFC regulatory area and allocating the NEAFC with fisheries management in the CAO.

1.2.4 Species-Specific RFBs

Besides the RFBs presented, RFBs dealing with specific species should be considered. If the regulated species were to migrate northwards, the specific range of the RFB may also adapt and extend to waters further north, up to or near the CAO.

In this regard, another body that comes into question is the International Pacific Halibut Commission (IPHC), which focuses on the conservation and preservation of the fishery of Pacific halibut of the Northern Pacific Ocean and Bering Sea.[125] However, the IPHC Convention limits the convention area to the waters off the west coasts of Canada and the United States, including the south and west coasts of Alaska, within the respective maritime areas where either State exercises exclusive fisheries jurisdiction.[126] Similar to NASCO, it is unlikely that the IPHC will expand its area to the high seas, although halibut may migrate towards northern waters.

123 Koivurova and Molenaar (Chapter 3, n 32) 73.

124 ibid 56, 76.

125 See Article I IPHC Convention; 'Protocol Amending the Convention between the United States of America and Canada for the Preservation of the Halibut Fishery of the Northern Pacific Ocean and Bering Sea (29 March 1979)' <https://shorturl.at/qwoRk> accessed 21 December 2020.

126 See Article I(3) IPHC Convention.

Theoretically, also the International Whaling Commission and the North Atlantic Marine Mammal Commission that cover the same area as the CAOF Agreement are possible RFBS to adopt measures. However, as the treaty subjects differ from the definition of fish in the CAOF Agreement, they are not further considered as RFBS adopting conservation and management measures for the sustainable management of fish stocks under Article 3(1)(a) CAOF Agreement.

Other possible regimes that can be addressed are the Convention on the Conservation and Management of Pollock Resources in the Central Bering Sea that manages Alaskan pollock in a small part of the high seas area of the Bering Sea[127] and the North Pacific Anadromous Fish Commission, focusing on different salmon species in the North Pacific Ocean and its adjacent seas, partly the Bering sea.[128] It has already happened to some extent that the species and stocks managed by these arrangements migrate to northern waters towards the CAO. Although unlikely, it will be interesting to see if and how the regulatory areas of these RFBS change and adapt to further prospective migrations and how this affects management in the CAO.

From the current point of view, the International Commission for the Conservation of Atlantic Tunas, ICCAT, is considered to be the RFB most likely to adopt, or rather extend fisheries conservation and management measures to the CAO. ICCAT has the objective to ensure conservation of tunas and tuna-like species in the Atlantic Ocean and adjacent seas,[129] hence meeting both the interests of coastal States and DWF nations.[130] Yet, it must be noted that most tuna species are located in the southern part of the Atlantic Ocean, and no specific plans for Arctic waters have been developed by ICCAT so far.[131] The objective of ICCAT is to study the populations of tuna and tuna-like fish, including research on the abundance, biometrics and ecology of the fish, the oceanography of their environment and the impact of natural and human factors on their abundance. In doing so, ICCAT should investigate and evaluate information to ensure that populations of tuna and tuna-like species in the

127 See Article I 'Convention on the Conservation and Management of Pollock Resources in the Central Bering Sea (Washington D.C., 16 June 1994)' (Chapter 3, n 27).

128 'Convention for the Conservation of Anadromous Stocks in the North Pacific Ocean (Moscow, 11 February 1992)' (Chapter 5, n 415).

129 See Article I ICCAT Convention; International Commission for the Conservation of Atlantic Tunas, 'Basic Texts' (2019) 5 <https://www.iccat.int/documents/commission/basictexts.pdf> accessed 8 April 2022.

130 Serdy, 'Postmodern International Fisheries Law, or We Are All Coastal States Now' (Chapter 3, n 108) 387.

131 Barnes (Chapter 2, n 10) 216.

regulatory area are maintained at levels that allow the maximum sustainable catch, and ensure the effective exploitation of those fish in a manner consistent with that catch.[132]

Some aspects should be considered, especially in view of the fact that both ICCAT and a newly established RFB could simultaneously allow commercial fishing in the CAO. ICCAT has 52 contracting parties as of 2022,[133] and as such provides for a considerable number of members – members that want to have a slice of the cake, namely a share in the fisheries. Furthermore, sound conservation and management strategies that have been developed need to be reconciled with modern approaches to fisheries management.[134] In this regard, ICCATs management was harshly criticized in the past: catch quotas were continuously set far higher than its own scientists recommend, and considered a "disgrace" and half-hearted attempt at sustainable fisheries management and a disrespectful affront to science.[135] ICCAT's lack of progress on key conservation measures was considered disappointing, and concern was raised about

> ICCAT's continued failure to adopt measures that are critical to the sustainable management and sound conservation of ICCAT-managed fisheries and protected living marine resources.[136]

ICCAT's management failings were largely attributed to a lack of compliance of contracting parties, cooperating non-contracting parties, and other entities.[137] Although most of the challenges ICCAT faces were regarded as simple to fix if these entities developed the political will to fully implement and adhere to the wording and spirit of the rules and recommendations of ICCAT,[138] there

132 See Article IV(1),(2)(b) ICCAT Convention.

133 'ICCAT | Contracting Parties' <https://www.iccat.int/en/contracting.html> accessed 8 April 2022.

134 International Commission for the Conservation of Atlantic Tunas, 'Report of the Independent Performance Review of ICCAT' (2009) <https://www.iccat.int/Documents/Other/PERFORM_ REV_TRI_LINGUAL.pdf> accessed 5 December 2021.

135 'WWF | Tuna Commission Comes up with "a Disgrace, Not a Decision"' <https://www.wwf.eu/?151021/Tuna-commission-comes-up-with-quota-disgrace-not-a-decisionquot> accessed 22 May 2020.

136 'NOAA Fisheries | Statement by John Henderschedt, United States Commissioner to the International Commission for the Conservation of Atlantic Tunas (21 November 2018)' <https://www.fisheries.noaa.gov/leadership-message/statement-john-henderschedt-united-states-commissioner-international-commission> accessed 22 May 2020.

137 International Commission for the Conservation of Atlantic Tunas (Chapter 6, n 134) 2.

138 ibid.

are good reasons to be cautious about the potential for ICCAT to effectively manage Arctic fisheries.[139]

In summary, the RFBs presented provide certain structures that theoretically enable fisheries management in the Arctic. However, if fishing is really commercially viable, it seems to make more sense to establish a new body for fisheries management. In any case, this decision is up to the parties to the CAOF Agreement.

1.3 *Commercial Fishing as an Interim Measure under the CAOF Agreement as Decided by the Parties*

Another possibility to conduct commercial fishing is presented in Article 3(1)(b) CAOF Agreement: commercial fishing in the Agreement Area may be conducted pursuant to interim conservation and management measures that may be established by the Parties in accordance with Article 5(1)(c)(ii) CAOF Agreement. According to the latter provision, where ecosystem considerations lead to the conclusion that sustainable commercial fisheries are possible, the Parties should decide whether to adopt additional or other interim conservation and management measures for the stocks concerned in the Agreement Area. This should only be pursued once negotiations on whether to establish an additional RFB[140] have commenced and once mechanisms to ensure the sustainability of fish stocks have been agreed upon. As referred to in Article 3(1)(b) CAOF Agreement, these provisional measures are a prerequisite for vessels flying the flag of one of the Parties to engage in commercial fishing activities in the Agreement Area. The classification of the measures as interim measures indicates that the Parties did not consider it a mere possibility, but assumed that another fisheries arrangement – whether already in existence or one that has yet to be created – would adopt actual rather than provisional conservation and management measures for commercial fisheries in the CAO. In the meantime, interim measures serve to protect the object and purpose of the CAOF Agreement, which is to prevent IUU fishing in the central part of the Arctic Ocean,[141] and the Parties are directed to comply with these measures.[142]

In order to determine whether commercial fisheries may be authorised as an interim measure by the Parties, the same fisheries management and ecosystem considerations that are relevant for commercial fisheries to be allowed

139 See also Bjørndal and Munro (Chapter 4, n 47) 247 et seq.

140 See Article 5(1)(c)(i) CAOF Agreement.

141 See Article 2 CAOF Agreement.

142 See Article 3(5) CAOF Agreement.

for as a management and conservation measure authorised by a newly established CAO RFB[143] should be applied.[144]

In summary, the authorisation of commercial fishing in the CAO is a deliberate, step-by-step process that must meet several requirements. Developments in the Arctic ecosystem are unpredictable and interventions by fisheries in the ecosystem should be well thought through as they may have irreversible effects. It is therefore considered appropriate that the authorisation of commercial fishing under the CAOF Agreement retains its exceptional character as an interim measure.

2 Measures regarding Non-commercial Fishing

The Parties to the CAOF Agreement made a key commitment to refrain from unregulated high seas fishing. The interim measure in Article 3(1) CAOF Agreement, however, only restricts commercial fishing. Although not explicitly mentioned in the Agreement, in line with Ryder, it is submitted that the limitations imposed by the provision "do not apply to subsistence, scientific, recreational, or other types of non-commercial fishing"[145] that may take place in the Agreement Area.[146] Non-commercial fishing might be conducted under different conditions and does therefore not contradict the commitment. The CAOF Agreement differentiates two categories of non-commercial fishing, namely scientific research activities or exploratory fishing. The latter is defined as "fishing for the purpose of assessing the sustainability and feasibility of future commercial fisheries by contributing to scientific data relating to such fisheries".[147] Exploratory fishing is hence considered different from fishing for scientific purposes, but the two types of fishing are inevitably interlinked. Fishing for subsistence purposes is not expressly mentioned in the CAOF Agreement, but considered to be non-commercial, similar to common practice.[148] Both possibilities to conduct fishing, either for scientific purposes or as exploratory fishing, are further looked at.

143 Regarding specific considerations, see Chapter 6 Sections 1, 1.1 *supra*.
144 See Article 5(1)(c) CAOF Agreement.
145 Ryder (Chapter 2, n 244) 4.
146 Similiar, see Molenaar, 'International Regulation of Central Arctic Ocean Fisheries' (Chapter 2, n 20) 451.
147 See Article 1(e) CAOF Agreement.
148 As treated for instance by the IWC; see 'International Whaling Commission | Aboriginal Subsistence Whaling in the Arctic' (Chapter 3, n 337).

2.1 *Fishing for Scientific Purposes*

Scientific research activities, which may include the catching of fish,[149] should be carried out under the CAOF Agreement to provide clarity on the CAO ecosystem and existing fish stocks. They are considered the basis for deciding on further activities in the CAO. Scientific research should be conducted in the interim "until there are sufficient data to allow assessment of the impact of the fisheries on the long-term sustainability of the stocks, whereupon conservation and management measures based on that assessment shall be implemented"[150] and an additional RFB for managing fisheries in the CAO might be established.[151] Article 3(2) CAOF Agreement encourages the Parties to conduct scientific research under the framework of the JPSRM established according to Article 4 CAOF Agreement and under further relevant scientific programs. Moreover, the activities may not undermine the object and purpose of the CAOF Agreement, and the Parties should cooperate through informing each other about their plans for authorising such activities.[152]

2.2 *Exploratory Fishing*

The UNFS Agreement calls on States to adopt precautionary conservation and management measures as soon as possible in order to obtain sufficient catch data to assess the impact of fishing on the long-term sustainability of the stocks concerned and on the surrounding ecosystem.[153] Accordingly, appropriate measures, like exploratory fishing, can be taken to support the gradual development of the fishery and its possible transition to commercial management. Regulating new fisheries from the outset, first as exploratory fisheries, provides an excellent opportunity to implement the precautionary approach and to "secure a culture of proactive and ecologically sensitive management" for future fisheries.[154]

Indeed, the precautionary approach should be applied to exploratory fisheries, as it should be applied to interim measures in general. Furthermore, where a fishery is not fully managed, additional and ongoing research requirements

---

149 See Article 3(4) CAOF Agreement.

150 See Article 6(6) UNFS Agreement.

151 See Article 5(1)(c) CAOF Agreement.

152 See Article 3(4) CAOF Agreement. Scientific research in the CAO and under the CAOF Agreement is addressed in detail under Chapter 5 Section 1 supra.

153 See Article 6(6) UNFS Agreement.

154 Richard Caddell, 'Precautionary Management and the Development of Future Fishing Opportunities: The International Regulation of New and Exploratory Fisheries' (2018) 33 International Journal of Marine and Coastal Law 199, 199, 258 <https://brill.com/view/journals/estu/33/1/article-p199_199.xml?language=en> accessed 10 August 2021.

are needed to ensure that the fishery remains exploratory, rather than focusing on collecting commercially valuable data and operating as a *de facto* commercial fishery. As no specific international standard for exploratory fishing has been established yet, the CCAMLR's measures on exploratory fishing can be relied on for guidance.[155] Defining and adapting catch limits, gear usage, data-collection requirements and fishing areas are considered reference points in this regard.[156] The framework within which appropriate action is possible can be delineated by analysing past or existing agreements and their experience with specific limits.

Under the CAOF Agreement, exploratory fishing, as defined in Article 1(e) CAOF Agreement, may be conducted "only pursuant to conservation and management measures established by the Parties on the basis of Article 5, paragraph 1(d)".[157] This enables the Parties to establish measures under the CAOF Agreement itself, independent of the establishment or engagement of another RFB. The term "only pursuant to" in Article 3(3) CAOF Agreement states an exception and defines the limits of legality rather than, conversely, determining illegality. The Agreement thus provides for a temporary qualified abstention from fishing until measures for exploratory fishing are in place. This is welcomed in view of the precautionary environmental approach of the Agreement: prevention is better than cure, especially when irreversible measures that may lead to the depletion of a stock may be taken.

The referenced Article 5(1)(d) CAOF Agreement demands for the establishment of conservation and management measures for exploratory fishing in the CAO within a limited time frame of three years after the entry into force of the Agreement, thus by June 2024. This deviates from all other time frames within the Agreement, which refer to a period of two years[158] or a much longer period.[159] One possible explanation for setting the timeframe of three years is

155 See e.g. Commission for the Conservation of Antarctic Marine Living Resources (CCAMLR), 'Conservation Measure 21–02 (2011) – Exploratory Fisheries' <https://www.ccamlr.org/sites/default/files/21-02.pdf> accessed 10 August 2021; Commission for the Conservation of Antarctic Marine Living Resources (CCAMLR), 'Conservation Measure 21–02 (2019) – Exploratory Fisheries' <https://www.ccamlr.org/sites/default/files/21-02_33.pdf> accessed 10 August 2021; for more specific measures on exploratory fishing, see 'CCAMLR | Browse Conservation Measures' <https://www.ccamlr.org/en/conservation-and-management/browse-conservation-measures> accessed 10 August 2021.

156 Caddell (Chapter 6, n 154) 259–260.

157 See Article 3(3) CAOF Agreement.

158 For instance, the time limit in which meetings of the Parties and joint scientific meetings shall take place, see Articles 4(2), 4(6), 5(1) CAOF Agreement.

159 E.g. 16 years duration of the Agreement, five year succession periods, see Article 13(1) and (2) CAOF Agreement.

that such measures should only be established after a meeting of the Parties and a joint scientific meeting have taken place. This can ensure that sufficient scientific information is available to establish effective measures for exploratory fishing. Further, the provision allows for an occasional amendment of measures by the Parties. This ensures effective measures that can adapt to new circumstances.

Article 5(1)(d) CAOF Agreement is further divided into five subparagraphs that specify, non-conclusively, the content of the measures established by the provision.

According to Article 5(1)(d)(i) CAOF Agreement, measures for exploratory fishing shall not undermine the objective of the CAOF Agreement, namely the prevention of unregulated fishing in the Agreement Area.[160] This basic idea of refraining from acts that would be contrary to the object and purpose of a treaty when a State has signed or consented to be bound by the treaty is codified in Article 18 VCLT and is a generally accepted principle in international and national law as an expression of the principle of good faith.[161] Despite the established nature of the concept, the drafters of the Agreement apparently wanted to emphasise the importance of the objective of the Agreement and in particular the exceptional nature of CAO fishing.

In accordance with the requirements proposed for exploratory fishing measures in general, pursuant to Article 5(1)(d)(ii) CAOF Agreement, exploratory fishing shall be limited in time, scope and scale. Impacts on fish stocks and ecosystems should be minimised, as healthy and sustainable marine ecosystems play a crucial role for food and nutrition.[162] In this regard, it could be helpful to base the determination of factors on empirical values derived from similar exploratory fisheries in other areas. Special features including the condition of a stock's habitat, water temperature, diet, reproduction and life cycle are factors that can be taken into account.[163] In accordance with the Agreement,

160 See Article 2 CAOF Agreement.

161 See Paul Gragl and Malgosia Fitzmaurice, 'The Legal Character of Article 18 of the Vienna Convention on the Law of Treaties' (2019) 68 International & Comparative Law Quarterly 699 <https://www.cambridge.org/core/journals/international-and-comparative-law-quarterly/article/abs/legal-character-of-article-18-of-the-vienna-convention-on-the-law-of-treaties/C5B1C5E68EF8DE46E348371271A9B589#access-block> accessed 5 December 2024.

162 See reference in Preamble CAOF Agreement.

163 Cf. Ned W Pankhurst and Philip L Munday, 'Effects of Climate Change on Fish Reproduction and Early Life History Stages' (2011) 62 Marine and Freshwater Research 1015, 1023 <www.publish.csiro.au/journals/mfr> accessed 30 November 2020; Richard A Barnes, 'The Capacity of Property Rights to Accommodate Social-Ecological Resilience'

exploratory fishing should further be subject to the standard requirements set forth in the data sharing protocol that should be adopted under the JPSRM.[164]

Article 5(1)(d)(iii) CAOF Agreement sets up the criteria for authorising exploratory fishing by a Party. The authorisation must be based on sound scientific research and be consistent with the JPSRM and national scientific programs. The first criterion is already taken into account by the preceding subparagraph (ii), which requires that exploratory fishing shall be based on standard requirements laid down in the data sharing protocol. Due to the interconnectedness of the CAOF Agreement's provisions on science, data and measures, it is expected that sound scientific research also forms the basis for the data sharing protocol. For the same reasons, the second requirement, namely compliance with the JPSRM and national scientific programs, is doubly secured: it is expected that sound scientific data are derived from the JPSRM or national programs that provide, likely exclusively, the available data. Hence, derived data stems from the program and must, in a last step, only be designated to be scientifically valuable in order to form the basis of sound scientific research under 5(1)(d)(iii) CAOF Agreement.

Another requirement for the authorisation of exploratory fishing by the Parties is set up by Article 5(1)(d)(iv) CAOF Agreement. The provision requires that an authorisation may only be granted if the authorising Party has notified the other Parties of its plans for exploratory fishing and they have been given the opportunity to express their agreement or disagreement with these plans. This underlines the cooperative spirit of the Agreement and the exceptional nature of the exercise of fishing in the CAO. Although the Parties are not given an instrument to prevent exploratory fisheries authorised by one of the Parties, mutual control and communication is seen as a first step to ensure compliance with the Agreement and to allow participation in activities so that they can be conducted cooperatively.

Once exploratory fishing has been authorised in accordance with Article 5(1)(d) CAOF Agreement, supervision is mandatory for successful implementation. Therefore, in line with the precautionary approach, subparagraph (v) requires adequate monitoring of exploratory fishing by the authorising Party. The term "adequately" leaves room for interpretation. Adequate monitoring, in the sense of the other provisions of the Agreement, is understood to mean maintaining control over activities by recording data on who is conducting exploratory

(2013) 18 Ecology and Society 6, 2 <http://www.ecologyandsociety.org/vol18/iss1/art6/> accessed 10 August 2021.

164 See Article 5(1)(d)(ii) and 4(5) CAOF Agreement. On the JPSRM, see Chapter 5 Sections 1, 1.3 *supra*.

fisheries, when, how often, with what technique and, more general, to what extent. Further, Article 5(1)(d)(v) CAOF Agreement requests that the results of such fishing are reported to the other Parties. This ensures transparency and strengthens members' confidence in the activities carried out.

3 Duration of Interim Measures and of the CAOF Agreement

The measures envisaged under Article 3 CAOF Agreement have one thing in common: they are not intended to be implemented permanently, but during the transitional period from the entry into force of the CAOF Agreement until sufficient data are available to assess the impact of fisheries on the long-term sustainability of stocks,[165] and, possibly, a new RFB managing CAO fisheries is established.

The starting point is therefore the entry into force of the Agreement. Article 11(1) CAOF Agreement states that the Agreement should enter into force 30 days after the depositary[166] received all instruments of ratification, acceptance or approval of or accession to the Agreement, depending on the particular internal process of the ten signatories listed in Article 9(1) CAOF Agreement.[167] It was refrained to follow an initial, quite common suggestion that the deposit of such instruments by a qualified majority of States – e.g. the Arctic Five – would be sufficient for the treaty to enter into force.[168] The current arrangement had the disadvantage to potentially prolong the process of enactment and jeopardise the entry into force of the Agreement if only one signatory refrained from depositing such an instrument. However, fortunately, by June 2021, all signatories have submitted instruments of ratification to the Agreement, and the Agreement entered into force on 25 June 2021.[169]

165 See Article 6(6) UNFS Agreement.

166 According to Article 15(1) CAOF Agreement, the depositary for this Agreement shall be Canada. It can be considered a neutral Party mediating between the Russian Federation, the United States, and the EU, who generally represent the most diverging views.

167 Cf. Articles 2(b), 24 VCLT. For a State acceding to the Agreement pursuant to Article 10(2) CAOF Agreement, Article 11(2) CAOF Agreement provides that the treaty enters into force 30 days after the deposit of an instrument of accession for that State.

168 See Molenaar, 'The CAOF Agreement: Key Issues of International Fisheries Law' (Chapter 2, n 20) 474–475.

169 'Arctic Council | An Introduction to: The International Agreement to Prevent Unregulated Fishing in the High Seas of the Central Arctic Ocean' (25 June 2021) <https://arctic-council.org/en/news/introduction-to-international-agreement-to-prevent-unregulated-fishing-in-the-high-seas-of-the-central-arctic-ocean/> accessed 30 June 2021; 'European

Naturally, in order to enable the implementation of certain measures, the Agreement must continue to be into force and hence binding on the respective Parties. The binding nature may be omitted through withdrawal from the Agreement. In the context of international law, withdrawal from a treaty must be considered an *ultima ratio*, exceptional to the overarching general principle of *pacta sunt servanda* enshrined in Article 26 VCLT.[170] Yet, including a denunciation or withdrawal clause in a treaty likely increases the number of ratifications of that treaty and encourages States to make broader commitments than in the absence of such clause. Then again, exit clauses that have few, easily fulfilled preconditions can further complicate future cooperation and harm a State's incentive to invest the resources necessary to comply with the treaty. The fact that most treaties do not provide for the enforcement of the imposition of financial or other sanctions further complicates the problem. Accordingly, a delicate balance must be found:

> [O]ptimal exit rules must deter opportunistic invocations of exit clauses by harnessing (…) compliance-inducing mechanisms as the reputational consequences of withdrawal, exclusions from benefits available to treaty members, and extra-treaty sanctions or incentives.[171]

Although Article 42(2) VCLT foresees the possibility to withdraw from a treaty,[172] including a clause regulating withdrawal in a treaty is recommended in order to leave control of the process and the ability to ensure the stability of an agreement after withdrawal to the treaty regime and the remaining parties. With regard to the CAOF Agreement, Article 12 CAOF Agreement constitutes such clause. The provision allows the Parties to withdraw from the Agreement at any time by giving six months' written notice. Similar to most withdrawal clauses,[173] it does not require the withdrawing Party to provide a justification for its decision to leave the agreement and is thus a simple withdrawal clause. It also does not attach any negative consequences to the withdrawal. A possible

---

Union | Arctic: Agreement to Prevent Unregulated Fishing Enters into Force (25 June 2021)' (Chapter 2, n 59).

170 Carmen Moldovan, 'BREXIT and the International Law on Treaty Withdrawal' (2018) 5 EURINT 257, 257 et seq. <http://cse.uaic.ro/eurint/proceedings/index_htm_files/EURINT2018_MOL.pdf> accessed 9 July 2020.

171 Laurence R Helfer, 'Exiting Treaties' (2005) 91 Virginia Law Review 1579, 1599 et seq.

172 Articles 54 et seq., 65 et seq. VCLT provide for the prerequisites and procedure of withdrawal. A treaty may also contain no information on termination and it may not be possible to withdraw from a contract, cf. Article 56 VCLT.

173 Cf. Helfer (Chapter 6, n 171) 1598.

threat could have been the exclusion from participation in possible (commercial) fisheries in the Agreement Area. While it would have been certainly very effective in preventing withdrawals, it is highly unlikely that the Agreement would have included such a clause, as the Parties certainly did not want to let the opportunity of commercial fishing slip away. Article 12 CAOF Agreement further stipulates that the withdrawal of a Party shall have no adverse effect with respect to the continued application of the CAOF Agreement between the remaining Parties. In accordance with Article 43 VCLT, withdrawal does further not affect the obligation of the withdrawing Party to fulfil commitments contained in the CAOF Agreement to which it would otherwise be subject to under international law. This includes existing agreements signed by the withdrawing party and the (customary) standard of international law that applies to the CAO and to which Parties and non-parties alike must adhere.

The Agreement shall initially remain in force for 16 years[174] and will hence stay into force until at least 2037. The implementation of such a "sunset clause"[175] has evolved rather late in the Agreement's establishment process.[176] The exact duration of 16 years was chosen more or less arbitrarily in the last minutes of the last meeting and prompted Russia to agree to the Agreement.[177] A time frame was chosen that would allow for optimal implementation of the Agreement, research, evaluation of scientific findings and a decision on the establishment of another RFB. At the same time, the duration would not allow too much time to pass to analyse the agreement and incorporate possible countermeasures. Timeframe proposals went from five years – which was considered as being too short to acquire actual reliable scientific results in the first years of the Agreement being in force, considering the recent technological developments and research possibilities – to 30 years, inspired by the initial duration period of 30 years of the Antarctic Treaty.[178] 16 years was considered a compromise for enabling both efficient research and leaving room for a potential course correction, although this was considered to be possible

174 See Article 13(1) CAOF Agreement.

175 Cf. United Nations General Assembly, 'Report of the Resumed Review Conference on the Agreement for the Implementation of UNCLOS Provisions (New York, 23–27 May 2016) – A/CONF.210/2016/5' (Chapter 4, n 324) para 49.

176 Molenaar, 'Participation in the Central Arctic Ocean Fisheries Agreement' (Chapter 2, n 23)160.

177 'Notes of phone call with Maya Gold, Canadian Representative in Consultations for the CAOF Agreement, on 19 September 2019, on file with the author'.

178 Cf. Article XII(2)(a) Antarctic Treaty.

to be conducted also in a slightly shorter timeframe.[179] While a short and flexible term allows for easy adjustments, it also has the disadvantage that the continuation of the respective agreement can be deviated from without further ado. Especially where conditions, as in the polar regions, and thus political interests are in flux, agreements are at risk. In that context, it is noted that "long-time observers know that the uncharted waters of polar politics can constantly surprise".[180]

After the expiration of the initial period of 16 years, the CAOF Agreement will remain in force for successive five-year extension periods,[181] unless a party objects.[182] In international law, the concept of objections is governed by Articles 19–23 VCLT, in the most commonly used context of an objection to a reservation that a party has made to a treaty. If the issue of objection is not regulated, the validity of an agreement between the different parties is at risk. Hence, unlike withdrawal, objection to the continuation of the CAOF Agreement may lead to the termination of the Agreement.

Sub-paragraphs (a) and (b) of Article 13(2) CAOF Agreement specify two possibilities for objection. According to Article 13(2)(a) CAOF Agreement, an objection may be presented formally at the last meeting of the Parties[183] before the expiration of the initial period of 16 years[184] or any following extension period of five years.[185] Formal in this sense usually refers to a communication with legal significance that is attributable to the respective State,[186] e.g. through issuance by diplomatic channels, i.e. the representative of the respective State, and within the procedural framework of the respective agreement.[187] As

179 Cf. 'Notes of phone call with Maya Gold, Canadian Representative in Consultations for the CAOF Agreement, on 19 September 2019, on file with the author'.

180 Klaus Dodds, 'In 30 Years the Antarctic Treaty Becomes Modifiable, and the Fate of a Continent Could Hang in the Balance' *The Conversation* (12 July 2018) <https://theconversation.com/in-30-years-the-antarctic-treaty-becomes-modifiable-and-the-fate-of-a-continent-could-hang-in-the-balance-98654> accessed 9 July 2020.

181 For initial proposals on the procedure for extension, see Molenaar, 'Participation in the Central Arctic Ocean Fisheries Agreement' (Chapter 2, n 23) 160.

182 See Article 13(2) CAOF Agreement.

183 Cf. Article 5(1)(a) CAOF Agreement.

184 See Article 13(1) CAOF Agreement.

185 See Article 13(2) CAOF Agreement.

186 Cf. in relation to objections to reservations International Law Commission, 'Guide to Practice on Reservations to Treaties' (2011) s 7 <https://legal.un.org/ilc/texts/instruments/english/draft_articles/1_8_2011.pdf> accessed 8 April 2022.

187 Cf. Christian Eckart, *Promises of States under International Law* (Hart Publishing 2012) s E A Note on Notification et seq. <https://books.google.de/books?id=HY56BAAAQBAJ&dq=formal+notification+international+law&hl=de&source=gbs_navlinks_s> accessed 10 July 2020.

Article 13(2)(a) CAOF Agreement does not require the objection to be in writing as foreseen by Article 13(2)(b) CAOF Agreement, it is assumed that a formal objection under Article 13(2)(a) CAOF Agreement does not need to be in written form. This seems useful, considering the format under which an objection may be presented: the objection must be filed at the last meeting of the Parties, the decision-making body, which further ensures that the objection and a Party's concerns that led to the filing of the objection can be discussed in a forum with all Parties involved. This provides an opportunity to clarify issues, which may even lead to a withdrawal of the objection. The other possibility for States to object to the duration of the CAOF Agreement is provided for in Article 13(2)(b) CAOF Agreement. Under this provision, an objection must be formal, in written form, sent to the depositary Canada,[188] and is only possible if issued no later than six months prior to the expiration of the respective period of the Agreement being into force. This second option bears the advantage that in the event of serious concerns that raise doubts about the effectiveness of the Agreement, an objection to the continued validity of the Agreement is still possible after the last meeting of the Parties: considering that the Parties meet at least every two years,[189] and the extension period of the duration of the Agreement is five years, it is possible that the last meeting of the Parties took place one year prior to the expiration of the extension period. The provision thus leaves room to respond to changing circumstances. However, it is problematic that such an objection cannot be dealt with in a forum with all Parties, unlike an objection made under Article 13(2)(a) CAOF Agreement. This means that the possibility of removing doubts or amending certain provisions about which the objecting Party is concerned is almost exhausted and only possible by forwarding the communication to all other Parties. It is confidently assumed that the provision of Article 13(2)(b) CAOF Agreement will never be used. However, if a State objects on the basis of Article 13(2)(b) CAOF Agreement, it is hoped that a procedure to inform the Parties of the objection will be followed and that discussions will be initiated between all Parties.

Although the Agreement does not regulate it precisely, it is still hoped that after an objection, the Agreement will not simply cease to be in force, but only the process of its automatic renewal will be inhibited. A common approach that preserves the Agreement and removes existing doubts would be desirable in this regard.

188 See Article 15(1) CAOF Agreement.

189 See Article 5(1) CAOF Agreement.

4 Review of the CAOF Agreement

In terms of sustainable management and in line with what is required for interim measures, the CAOF Agreement, as a modern agreement dealing with a dynamic issue such as fisheries, provides for a regular review of the Agreement and its implementation. In this regard, pursuant to Article 5(1) CAOF Agreement, the Parties shall meet every two years or more frequently if they so decide. The timeframe is aligned with the timeframe for the joint scientific meetings,[190] which will be held two months prior to the review meetings. This underlines the Agreement's currently most important task of conducting research and gathering scientific evidence on fish stocks in the CAO. The provision also leaves it open for the Parties to meet more frequently if circumstances so require. This serves as a useful tool for effective management as it allows for an immediate collective response to a possible change of circumstances.

In addition to deciding whether to establish a new RFB and under what circumstances to allow commercial fishing,[191] and establishing conservation and management measures for exploratory fisheries,[192] Article 5(1)(a) and (b) CAOF Agreement contains issues that the Parties should address at their meetings.

Article 5(1)(a) CAOF Agreement sets up the task to review the implementation of the Agreement that has taken place up to the review meeting. In this regard, a high degree of implementation by the Parties presents the first step towards a functioning enforcement of the Agreement's provisions and purpose. Therefore, it must initially be ensured that the CAOF Agreement has been fully implemented by the Parties. Lack of implementation has to be identified and analysed so that obstacles that occurred during the implementation process can be removed. Further, the Parties should, where appropriate, consider any issues, including objections, relating to the duration of the Agreement.[193] The Agreement can only serve its purpose while being in force, or a similar arrangement is in place. Disagreement on this issue among the Parties can endanger the Agreement's validity and should be discussed – and hopefully resolved – with priority. Only at a later point in time, when the Agreement has been developed further, issues such as stock assessments, catch limits and quota allocations might need to be reviewed periodically and adjusted so that

190 See Article 4(6) CAOF Agreement.

191 See Article 5(1)(c) CAOF Agreement; see also Chapter 6 Section 1 *supra*.

192 See Article 5(1)(d) CAOF Agreement; see also Chapter 6 Sections 2, 2.2 *supra*.

193 See Article 13(2) CAOF Agreement.

climate-induced changes in stock abundance and distribution are properly taken into account.[194]

Article 5(1)(b) CAOF Agreement provides that the Parties review all scientific information available. As no commercially viable fishery is expected to be possible in the high seas portion of the CAO in the near future,[195] the focus is currently on pursuing research and collecting scientific data. The Parties should specifically review the scientific data developed by the JPSRM,[196] which should be forwarded to the Parties' review meetings with advice from the Parties' joint scientific meetings.[197] Further, scientific information that has been developed through national scientific programs should be reviewed. The same applies to information gathered through other relevant sources. Likely, this refers to data collected by scientific and technical organizations, bodies and programs[198] like ICES and PICES,[199] and which shall include indigenous and local knowledge.[200] The repeated reference to indigenous and local knowledge suggests that the drafters of the Agreement wanted to emphasize participation of indigenous and local communities as mentioned in the Preamble, respect towards them, and stress the importance and benefit of obtaining scientific evidence from multiple sources to best assess the scientific situation in the CAO. Nevertheless, it should be noted that a comprehensive reassessment of information during review meetings would make joint scientific meetings, which are provided for in Article 4(6) CAOF Agreement, more or less superfluous. It should be clear that the joint scientific meetings serve to pre-filter all scientific information collected by all kinds of organizations and programs. The data processed in this way can then be used as a basis for discussion at the official (review) meetings of the Parties under Article 5(1)(b) CAOF Agreement.

---

194 See Rayfuse, 'Addressing Climate Change Impacts in Regional Fisheries Management Organizations' (Chapter 5, n 24) 268.

195 Molenaar, 'The CAOF Agreement: Key Issues of International Fisheries Law' (Chapter 2, n 20) 468.

196 See Article 4 CAOF Agreement.

197 See Article 4(6) CAOF Agreement.

198 Likely referring to Article 4(5) CAOF Agreement.

199 Cf. 'Declaration Concerning the Prevention of Unregulated High Seas Fishing in the Central Arctic Ocean (Oslo, 16 July 2015)' (Chapter 2, n 22).

200 Similar, see Article 4(4) CAOF Agreement.

5 Possible Transition to a New Agreement

The CAOF Agreement is a fisheries management measure itself. Article 13(3) CAOF Agreement makes further clear that it is also an interim measure: the Article provides for a transition from the CAOF Agreement to a new definitive agreement.[201] As by their very nature, interim measures are of a provisional character only, the CAOF Agreement is designed to become obsolete and to be replaced by a new one, provided that this new agreement creates an additional RFB managing fishing in the Agreement Area. It should further be based on the same values as the CAOF Agreement, meaning it must safeguard healthy marine ecosystems and ensure the conservation and sustainable use of fish stocks in the Agreement Area.[202] This ensures that the aim and level of protection is similar to the current CAOF Agreement, and an additional agreement does not lead to a regulatory gap in the CAO. The Parties shall provide for an effective transition, paying tribute to possible transitional frictions associated with the legal change itself. Van Alstine describes these "legal transition costs" as arising from "the need to learn about the content of new legal norms and the uncertainty and error costs that flow from the loss of the accrued experience with the old legal regime as well as from contending with doubts about the new one".[203] Yet, transition should not be viewed exclusively in negative terms. Rather, sensitivity to transition costs should be shown by considering the material benefits including the alignment of new legal regimes.[204] It is therefore suggested that an effective transition from the CAOF Agreement to a new agreement under Article 13(3) CAOF Agreement refers to a transition within a reasonable time frame, one that considers the characteristics of the Parties concerned, and which implements the knowledge and research results acquired during the duration period of the CAOF Agreement. The core task when establishing an additional agreement is to pursue the achievements of the CAOF Agreement, correct possible mistakes, and maintain at least the same level of protection of fish stocks that is guaranteed by the CAOF Agreement.

---

201 The establishment of such new regime is foreseen as an option in Article 5(1)(c)(i) CAOF Agreement.

202 See Article 2 CAOF Agreement, which entails the objective of the CAOF Agreement in the exact same wording as the prerequisites stipulated in Article 13(3) CAOF Agreement.

203 Michael P Van Alstine, 'Treaty Law and Legal Transition Costs' (2002) 77 Chicago-Kent Law Review 1303, 1303.

204 ibid 1304.

6 Suggested Subsequent Measures

The CAOF Agreement is an agreement suitable for managing fisheries in its early stages. Determining specific fisheries management measures that may be applied subsequently to interim measures will most likely be the task of a newly generated RFB. Nevertheless, it can do no harm to already look at possible measures, which could also be beneficial for determining advanced interim measures. Learning from existing international cooperative or national best practices is considered helpful in this regard.[205]

When establishing an effective management system dealing with the execution of fisheries, multiple factors need to be considered. Year-class failure and hence stock propagation occurs partly, but likely not primarily, due to climate-related factors. Therefore, the development and potential yield in biomass of commercial stocks will in most cases depend on effective rational management – i.e. a management policy aimed at increasing the abundance of stocks through reduced fishing mortalities and protection of juveniles – or, for instance, by ensuring an increase in the abundance of many demersal fish stocks.[206] The CAOF Agreement pursues this idea by introducing a qualified abstention for commercial fishing in the CAO, but effective specific management comprises more than that.

Specific management strategies, that might be taken into account as a further step in the CAOF Agreement's management process, range from granting open access with or without fisheries closure to monopoly control to a cartel option, where an abundant migratory fish stock is managed under international fisheries management and each participating State receives a share of the total catch.[207] The joint US Resolution that initiated the establishment of the CAOF Agreement requested that a possible new agreement should establish catch and bycatch limits, harvest allocations, regulations on observers, monitoring, data collection and reporting, enforcement, and additional features necessary for sustaining future Arctic fish stocks.[208] As an example for such measures, the 2008 EU Marine Strategy Framework Directive (the

205 See 'First International Meeting on the Establishment of the South Pacific Regional Fisheries Management Organisation (Wellington, 14–17 February 2006) – SP/01/Inf5' (Chapter 3, n 193) para 13.

206 Arctic Monitoring and Assessment Programme (AMAP), Conservation of Arctic Flora and Fauna (CAFF) Working Group and International Arctic Science Committee (IASC) (Chapter 2, n 78) 720.

207 Bjørndal and Munro (Chapter 4, n 47) 241–242.

208 United States Congress (Chapter 2, n 163) 2.

Directive) aims to protect the marine environment of the waters within the EU more effectively.[209] The Directive establishes a framework within which EU Member States shall take necessary measures to achieve or maintain good environmental status in the marine environment by 2020,[210] while considering regional cooperation in regard of the transboundary nature of the marine environment.[211] The determination is supplemented by qualitative descriptors for determining good environmental status in Annex I. Annex V and VI provide special guidance for monitoring programs and programs of measures. Every EU Member State is required to establish a unique and specific strategy for its own waters, which is reviewed every six years.[212] It focuses on cooperation and follows an adaptive management approach. The cyclical process starts with an initial assessment of targets, indicators and objectives, followed by monitoring and measuring programs and the implementation of the respective marine strategy. Subsequently, different elements of the process are carefully reviewed, before the process starts again.[213] In 2020, the EU issued a report on the implementation of the Directive to display the preliminary findings.[214] Overall, the Directive is considered a useful tool to better understand the pressures and impacts of human activities on the sea and their implications for marine biodiversity, species habitats, and the ecosystems they sustain.[215] This approach can be an incentive for further management under the CAOF Agreement. The Directive can be used as a guidance tool for exercising governance over fisheries in the Arctic marine area, also regarding compatibility of measures by the Agreement and coastal State measures.

---

209 European Union, 'Directive 2008/56/EC Establishing a Framework for Community Action in the Field of Marine Environmental Policy (Marine Strategy Framework Directive) (17 June 2008) – OJ L 164/19' <https://eur-lex.europa.eu/legal-content/EN/TXT/PDF/?uri=CELEX:32008L0056&from=EN> accessed 20 January 2022.

210 See Article 1(1) Directive.

211 See Article 3(5) Directive. Accordingly, good environmental status means that ecologically diverse and dynamic oceans and seas which are clean, healthy and productive are provided, the marine environment is sustainably used, and the potential for uses and activities by current and future generations is ensured.

212 See No. 11 Preamble, Articles 5 et seq., 17(2) Directive.

213 'European Commission | Our Oceans, Seas and Coast – EU Coastal and Marine Policy' <https://ec.europa.eu/environment/marine/eu-coast-and-marine-policy/marine-strategy-framework-directive/index_en.htm> accessed 20 January 2020.

214 European Commission, 'Report on the Implementation of the Marine Strategy Framework Directive (Brussels, 25 June 2020) – COM(2020) 259 Final' <https://dx.doi.org/10.2771/21854> accessed 25 November 2020.

215 'European Commission | More Protection for Our Seas and Oceans Is Needed, Report Finds (25 June 2020)' <https://ec.europa.eu/commission/presscorner/detail/en/IP_20_1160> accessed 25 November 2020.

Further, the application of area-based management tools,[216] e.g. the designation of closed areas, marine protected areas and marine reserves, are considered effective tools for the conservation and management of some fish stocks.[217] More general, the employment of input controls is an additionally favoured mechanism, such as the implementation of gear restriction and fishing seasons. As input controls have however failed to reduce excess fishing and might even contribute to a destructive race to catch fish, they can only be recommended conditionally.[218]

Most specific measures include the allocation of catch shares. The question of how to best distribute such shares must however be addressed carefully. Effort controls in one region tend to lead to effort leakage into another region. This is especially the case where individual fisheries with comparable gear and high market substitutability with sector species are concerned.[219] In this regard, quota mechanisms have proven to be highly effective and are used mostly in fisheries management. As an example, New Zealand controls how much fish can be taken from the ocean instead of focusing on effort. A quota management system defines a yearly TAC limit for every fish stock or a certain species of fish, shellfish or seaweed from a particular area. The ever-growing information on the health of fish enables the setting of TACs for sustainable fisheries. The TAC is set to allow the maximum sustainable catch from a fish stock while deducting natural variation and is shared between the different users of the fishery. Recreational and customary fishing and other fishing-related mortality are taken into account. The total allowable commercial catch (TACC) remains, which limits the amount of fish that can be caught by commercial fishers. Quota owners get an annual catch entitlement, which can be bought and sold. There are limits on how much quota people can own. The so-called aggregation limits can be placed on a whole species or an individual stock. The quota management system requires regular reporting from fishers and licensed fish receivers that help monitoring the TAC, TACC and accuracy

216 See e.g. No. 11 CBD Aichi Targets: "By 2020, at least 17 per cent of terrestrial and inland water areas, and 10 per cent of coastal and marine areas, especially areas of particular importance for biodiversity and ecosystem services, are conserved through effectively and equitably managed, ecologically representative and well connected systems of protected areas and other effective area-based conservation measures, and integrated into the wider landscapes and seascapes."

217 Takei (Chapter 4, n 307) 555.

218 Barnes (Chapter 6, n 163) 11.

219 Cunningham, Bennear and Smith (Chapter 3, n 192) 344.

of fisheries reporting.[220] This system of private property-based fishing rights is used to remove inefficiency from marine commercial fisheries and secure indigenous fishing rights.[221]

The same model that saved Iceland from a Cod crisis might be equally applied to CAO waters to benefit potential Arctic fisheries: Iceland's Marine Research Institute sets fishing limits for its fleet in order to keep fish populations healthy, and the Directorate of Fisheries calculates vessel limits based on their allocated quota. It is considered a "unique opportunity not to repeat the mistakes of the past".[222] Three important steps should be followed. Catches should be tracked, scientific limits need to be set up, and where incomprehensible developments occur, less should be caught. The Directorate collected data as soon as they received the mandate of managing fisheries in the 1980s, developed a data base and opened access to it a couple of years later. Independent, certified weighers create reliable data by registering catches into ministry databases that are updated every couple of hours. When a vessel surpasses its limits, the real-time data capture notifies authorities. Prompt action, like the imposition of fines, the confiscation of illegal gear and detention of repeat offenders is therefore possible.[223]

To sum up, for effective monitoring and enforcement, based on these examples, fisheries management should rely on science-based fishing limits and shared quotas. It should deposit data in a central system, and make detailed catch information public in real-time. Establishing a region-wide system that can handle day-to-day catches would create optimal conditions for effective and sustainable fisheries management.

As for scientific data, NEMURO might provide guidance in future fisheries management, especially as the CAOF Agreement is particularly science-based. The prototype lower trophic level ecosystem model for the North Pacific Ocean, named the North Pacific Ecosystem Model for Understanding Regional Oceanography (NEMURO), was developed by the PICES MODEL Task Team. PICES promoted an international science program on Climate Change and Carrying Capacity (CCCC) in the temperate and subarctic regions of the North Pacific Ocean, with ecosystem modelling being one of the five key research activities defined by the CCCC Implementation Panel. The PICES CCCC

220 'New Zealand Government | Fisheries NZ – Quota Management System' <https://www.mpi.govt.nz/law-and-policy/legal-overviews/fisheries/quota-management-system/> accessed 1 July 2020.

221 Barnes (Chapter 6, n 163) 11.

222 Turner (Chapter 1, n 4).

223 ibid.

MODEL Task Team was given the role to implement the CCC program through encouraging, facilitating and coordinating modelling activities among the member nations. At the first Workshop on Modelling in 1996, efforts leading to a standardization of models within the CCC program were dismissed based on the assumption that diversity favoured advances in the region. Two years later, the workshop participants changed their view and agreed that "Models with different state variables and mathematical formulations would be impossible to compare, and [...] comparison protocols are necessary to tackle the problem."[224] This led to the proposal of a workshop on the development of a prototype model and comparison protocols, which ended up in the International Workshop to Develop a Prototype Lower Trophic Level Ecosystem Model for Comparison of Different Marine Ecosystems in the North Pacific in 2000.[225] NEMURO became the *de facto* lower trophic level model used by PICES to examine questions concerning the effect of climate change on marine ecosystems shortly after the first workshop in 1996 that took place in Nemuro, Japan.[226] Following the development of NEMURO, the PICES MODEL Task Team developed a bioenergetic fish growth model to serve as input for the plankton densities generated by the NEMURO model, which resulted in the NEMURO.FISH (NEMURO For Including Saury and Herring) model. These two basic models were then modified to address their specific systems and questions. Both assert to provide a strong basis for developing versions of the model employable to other locations, new species and community types, and offer answers to climate change and variability issues. The first NEMURO workshop initiated an extensive dialog between modellers, plankton biologists, oceanographers, and fisheries scientists that led to multiple scientific publications[227] and still offers a framework for prospective studies on the variability of marine ecosystems in relation to global change.[228] The models are hence the result of

224 David L Eslinger and others, 'Model Task Team Workshop Report – Final Report of the International Workshop to Develop a Prototype Lower Trophic Level Ecosystem Model for Comparison of Different Marine Ecosystems in the North Pacific' (2000) 2 <https://pices.int/publications/scientific_reports/Report15/MODEL.pdf> accessed 1 July 2021.

225 ibid.

226 'PICES | Materials of the 2000 NEMURO Model Workshop' <https://pices.int/members/task_teams/Disbanded_task_teams/MODEL_materials/mws1.html> accessed 30 June 2021.

227 Michio J Kishi and others, 'A Review of the NEMURO and NEMURO.FISH Models and Their Application to Marine Ecosystem Investigations' (2011) 67 Journal of Oceanography 3, 4 <https://www.pmel.noaa.gov/foci/publications/2011/kish0728.pdf> accessed 8 April 2022.

228 Michio J Kishi and others, 'NEMURO-a Lower Trophic Level Model for the North Pacific Marine Ecosystem' (2007) 202 Ecological Modelling 12, 20 <https://www.sciencedirect.com/science/article/abs/pii/S0304380006004534> accessed 8 April 2022.

an international, multidisciplinary research effort.[229] This cooperative, interdisciplinary approach focusing on climate change and variability and their effects on ecosystems is considered to perfectly meet the approach of the CAOF Agreement and should find consideration in the ongoing management process.

One means to reduce the potential of overcapacity, a problem that significantly contributes to worldwide overfishing,[230] is the issuance of authorisations of vessels to fish in a specific area, similar and related to the process of the distribution of TAC quotas. These permits are subject to fixed reporting requirements that allow identification, such as the name of the vessel, registration number and port of registry, details of the owner and the vessel capacity, including the type of fishing carried out. Where further catch requirements are concerned, it is suggested that the participants notify other participants prior to catching fish of their intention to fish, establish a detailed reporting system of fish prior to landing in port, and regulate bycatch.[231] More specifically, as an example, catch limits including trigger TACs for exploratory fisheries were suggested as possible interim measures in the first meeting on the establishment of the SPRFMO. Further suggested were capacity limitations referring to the number of vessels and total gross registered tonnage, and spatial and temporal measures like banning certain gear types or the provisional closing of spawning areas.[232] Use can be made of catch documentation schemes (CDS), which are market-based monitoring tools developed to combat IUU fishing open to use by RFBs or other (inter)national bodies. In accordance with para. 68 of the 2013 UN General Assembly Resolution on Sustainable Fisheries, the FAO Committee on Fisheries developed voluntary guidelines for CDS. Thereafter, a CDS is a system that

> tracks and traces fish from the point of capture through unloading and throughout the supply chain. A CDS records and certifies information that identifies the origin of fish caught and ensures they were harvested in a manner consistent with relevant national, regional and international

229 Kishi and others (Chapter 6, n 227) 4.

230 Smith and Garcia (Chapter 4, n 19) R811; Cf. Food and Agriculture Organization of the United Nations, 'The State of World Fisheries and Aquaculture 2016: Contributing to Food Security and Nutrition for All' (Chapter 1, n 3) 180, 186.

231 'First International Meeting on the Establishment of the South Pacific Regional Fisheries Management Organisation (Wellington, 14–17 February 2006) – SP/01/Inf5' (Chapter 3, n 193) paras 22–25.

232 ibid 34.

conservation and management measures. The objective of the CDS is to combat IUU fishing by limiting access of IUU fish and fishery products to markets.[233]

Multilateral and unilateral CDS exist, with the only unilateral CDS in place today being the EU's Catch Certification Scheme introduced by the so-called EU-IUU Directive[234] that covers nearly all caught marine wild fish traded by non-EU countries into the EU market. In the international context, where multilateral IUU fishing is concerned, it is recommended to opt for multilateral CDS. Successful examples for multilateral CDS in place are the CDS covering Southern Bluefin tuna, introduced in 2010 by the Commission for the Conservation of Southern Bluefin Tuna, and the CDS covering Atlantic Bluefin tuna, introduced in 2008 by ICCAT. In both cases, the implementation of CDS has proven to be the most efficient enforcement mechanism suitable to target and eliminate underreporting.[235]

Certainly, these considerations are not only helpful for determining interim measures at an advanced stage under the CAOF Agreement but should also be kept in mind when it comes to determine definitive specific measures for fishing by an additional RFB.

7 Summary

The interim measures provided for under the CAOF Agreement reflect the overriding objective of the Agreement to prevent unregulated fishing in the CAO. They set up a qualified abstention for commercial fishing in the Agreement Area. Non-commercial fishing, including scientific research activities and exploratory fishing, may also only be conducted under strict circumstances, mainly within the framework of or dependant on the outcome of the JPSRM and further scientific programs, thus respecting the concept of sustainability

233 Food and Agriculture Organization of the United Nations, 'Report of the Expert Consultation on Catch Documentation Schemes (CDS) (Rome, 21–24 July 2015)' 11 <http://www.fao.org/3/i5063e/i5063e.pdf> accessed 14 May 2020.

234 European Union, 'Council Regulation (EC) No 1005/2008 Establishing a Community System to Prevent, Deter and Eliminate Illegal, Unreported and Unregulated Fishing (29 September 2008) – OJ L 286, 29.10.2008, p.1' <https://eur-lex.europa.eu/legal-content/EN/TXT/PDF/?uri=CELEX:02008R1005-20110309&from=EN> accessed 11 August 2020.

235 'FAO | GLOBEFISH: Catch Documentation Schemes: Practices and Applicability in Combating IUU Fishing' (Chapter 5, n 525).

and applying the precautionary approach to fisheries management. In addition, further requirements of interim measures are satisfactorily implemented: the Agreement provides for the formation of representative committees or similar bodies, and includes provisions on the duration of measures, review and transition.

CHAPTER 7

Current Developments

After ratification by all signatories, the CAOF Agreement entered into force on 25 June 2021.[1] But even before the CAOF Agreement has entered into force, the Parties have agreed to start working on its implementation, in particular on the JPSRM. The nine signatory States and the EU held a meeting from 11–13 February 2020 in Ispra. Around forty scientists participated in the first meeting of the Provisional Scientific Coordinating Group (PSCG) that was established in the context of the Agreement.[2] Participants discussed the current status of scientific knowledge, ways and methods to determine fish species in the Agreement Area, and how to access the harsh marine Arctic in general.[3] The EU has further taken a leading role in implementing the scientific commitments made under the Agreement: funding from the European Maritime and Fisheries Fund gives researchers the opportunity to collect data on ecosystems in the CAO.[4]

As outlined above, one of the main objectives of the CAOF Agreement is to gather data through scientific research. An example for recent research is the AWI's Multidisciplinary[5]drifting Observatory for the Study of Arctic Climate, the MOSAiC expedition.[6] In September 2019, the German research icebreaker Polarstern set sail from Tromsø. In October 2019, it became deliberately frozen into the ice north of Siberia, and drifted north and west for thousands of miles through Arctic marine waters until it landed back in Germany in October

1 'Arctic Council | An Introduction to: The International Agreement to Prevent Unregulated Fishing in the High Seas of the Central Arctic Ocean' (Chapter 6, n 169).

2 'European Commission | The EU Joins Forces with Nine Countries for Future Science-Based Management of the High Seas of the Central Arctic Ocean (13 February 2020)' (Chapter 3, n 19).

3 'Report of the 1st Meeting of the Provisional Scientific Coordinating Group (PSCG) of the Agreement to Prevent Unregulated High Seas Fisheries in the Central Arctic Ocean (Ispra, 11–13 February 2020)' (Chapter 5, n 146).

4 'European Commission | The EU Joins Forces with Nine Countries for Future Science-Based Management of the High Seas of the Central Arctic Ocean (13 February 2020)' (Chapter 3, n 19).

5 See 'MOSAiC | Main Scientific Focus Areas' <https://mosaic-expedition.org/science/scientific-focus-areas/> accessed 31 March 2022.

6 An enlightening overview of the mission is provided by an ARD documentation, see 'Video: Expedition Arktis – Ein Jahr. Ein Schiff. Im Eis.' (Chapter 5, n 27); generally on the expedition, see 'MOSAiC | The Mission' <https://mosaic-expedition.org/science/mission/> accessed 31 March 2022.

 | DOI:10.1163/9789004700673_008

2020.[7] The Polarstern was the first modern research icebreaker close to the North Pole, just 156 km (97 miles) away, conducting research in Arctic waters in polar winter. Entirely in line with the multinational approach of the CAOF Agreement, 600 researchers from twenty countries were involved.[8] The mission was initiated due to insufficient knowledge about the status of and developments in Arctic waters – a problem that is well known to the CAOF Agreement parties. The data previously available were considered "not a solid and robust enough basis for the important political decisions we have to take".[9] Despite harsh conditions, the aim of the mission to gather in-depth information about the Arctic and especially its relation to climate change was successfully completed. It was noted that the mission constitutes a "historic milestone for Arctic research" and the information collected would be "invaluable in helping scientists understand the region".[10] With regard to the CAOF Agreement, the scientific data collected is expected to be particularly important for the future of fishing in CAO waters, as the qualified fishing abstention set out in the CAOF Agreement is tied to scientific findings. An important factor in this could be that the MOSAiC researchers were able to catch fish in CAO waters for the first time. Professor Leijonalm, who participated in the MOSAiC expedition, explains why this is of great importance:

> We will be able to analyse its stomach, its stable isotopes, its fatty acids. [...] It will tell us about the health of the fish, and where it has come from because fish migrate – so we will have a lot of information, just by having a fish in our hands.

Therefore, the findings of this and future expeditions will help to answer the core question of the CAOF Agreement – whether fishing in the CAO can be conducted on a sustainable basis, or whether the central waters of the Arctic Ocean should remain untouched for the years ahead.

Despite all efforts, only time will tell whether the Parties will stick to their progressive goals and continue to cooperate, as recent developments put this to the test: while "for the last 25 years, Arctic leadership has been able

---

7 'MOSAiC | The Expedition' <https://mosaic-expedition.org/expedition/> accessed 11 December 2021.

8 Henry Fountain, 'After a Year in the Ice, the Biggest-Ever Arctic Science Mission Ends' *The New York Times* (12 October 2020).

9 Henry Fountain, 'Scientists to Drift With Arctic Ice to Study Climate Change' *The New York Times* (19 September 2019) <https://www.nytimes.com/2019/09/19/climate/mosaic-expedition-arctic.html?searchResultPosition=10> accessed 11 December 2020.

10 Fountain, 'After a Year in the Ice, the Biggest-Ever Arctic Science Mission Ends' (Chapter 7, n 8).

to navigate the winds of change" due to "a bubble around the Arctic, keeping other tensions out",[11] this bubble burst recently at the end of February 2022 when Russian troops invaded Ukraine.[12] As a result, for instance,[13] all other Arctic Council members announced that they would temporarily suspend their participation in all meetings of the Council and its subsidiary bodies.[14] Further, all other members of the Barents Euro Council announced that they would suspend activities involving Russia in the Barents Euro-Arctic cooperation.[15] Against this background, with regard to the CAOF Agreement, it can only be hoped that the implementation of the Agreement, and in particular its objective to prevent IUU fishing, will continue to be pursued by all Parties.

---

11 Gloria Dickie and Timothy Gardner, 'Arctic Council in Upheaval over Russia as Climate Change Transforms Region' *Reuters* (3 March 2022) <https://www.reuters.com/world/arctic-council-countries-halt-meetings-over-russias-invasion-ukraine-2022-03-03/> accessed 25 March 2022.

12 Cf. *Allegations of Genocide under the Convention on the Prevention and Punishment of the Crime of Genocide (Ukraine v Russian Federation) – Request for the Indication of Provisional Measures, ICJ Order of 16 March 2022, General List No 182*; 'United Nations General Assembly Resolution ES-11/1, Aggression against Ukraine (Adopted 2 March 2022)'; European Court of Human Rights, 'Press Release: Decision of the Court on Requests for Interim Measures in Individual Applications Concerning Russian Military Operations on Ukrainian Territory (4 March 2022) – ECHR 073 (2022)'.

13 More general, see Andreas Raspotnik and Andreas Østhagen, 'The End of an Exceptional History: Re-Thinking the EU-Russia Arctic Relationship' *E-International Relations* (23 March 2022) <https://www.e-ir.info/2022/03/23/the-end-of-an-exceptional-history-re-thinking-the-eu-russia-arctic-relationship/> accessed 25 March 2022.

14 United States Department of State, 'Joint Statement on Arctic Council Cooperation Following Russia's Invasion of Ukraine (3 March 2022)' <https://www.state.gov/joint-statement-on-arctic-council-cooperation-following-russias-invasion-of-ukraine/> accessed 25 March 2022.

15 'European External Action Service | Barents Euro-Arctic Cooperation: Joint Statement of the European Union, Finland, Denmark, Iceland, Norway and Sweden on Suspending Activities with Russia' (9 March 2022) <https://eeas.europa.eu/headquarters/headquarters-homepage/112462/barents-euro-arctic-cooperation-joint-statement-european-union-finland-denmark-iceland-norway_en> accessed 25 March 2022.

CHAPTER 8

Conclusion

This concluding chapter recaps the main points developed in the thesis (Chapter 8 Section 1) and examines possible implications of the CAOF Agreement for public international law (Chapter 8 Section 2). More specifically, two fundamental questions will be addressed: first, whether the CAOF Agreement sets up a new threshold for RFBs (Chapter 8 Sections 2, 2.1), and second, whether the establishment of the CAOF Agreement heralds the end of the time-honoured concept of the freedom of the high seas (Chapter 8 Sections 2, 2.2).

1 The CAOF Agreement: a Fisheries Management Approach to a Unique Scenario

Although several States are involved in managing the Arctic region, a comprehensive and binding management regime governing fisheries in the central part of the Arctic Ocean had not been established before the CAOF Agreement. In particular, the lack of such regime has posed a potential threat to the protection of the particularly fragile Arctic marine environment. Commercially viable fisheries in the high sea parts of the CAO are absent. However, with rapidly developing opportunities in the Arctic Ocean, the 2018 CAOF Agreement comes in the nick of time to address upcoming challenges.

The area covered by the Agreement encompasses only the central high seas part of the Arctic Ocean. It is surrounded by waters within which Canada, Denmark in respect of Greenland, Norway, the Russian Federation and the United States, also referred to as the Arctic Five, exercise fisheries jurisdiction. Ongoing climate change is transforming the fragile region: temperatures are constantly increasing, and as a result, Arctic sea ice is melting. This in turn leads to changes in the food web and environment for both aquatic animals and native communities. It is assumed that there are currently only few fish stocks present in the CAO. However, as temperatures rise in the Arctic marine area, fish stocks are gradually moving north to colder areas, opening up new opportunities for fisheries and other activities requiring regulation.[1]

1 See Chapter 2 *supra*.

 DOI:10.1163/9789004700673_009

Even before the conclusion of the CAOF Agreement, with respect to fisheries, the area at stake was governed by a whole series of rather general rules: international binding and non-binding instruments, customary law and soft-law approaches. Until the CAOF Agreement entered into force, and still for non-participants, UNCLOS and the UNFS Agreement settle most issues concerning the high seas and fisheries in general. These are complemented by the customary principle of the freedom of the high seas. The FAO Compliance Agreement and the PSMA are setting up a framework for compliance. Additional soft-law instruments developed by the IMO, under the Arctic Council regime or by the FAO give guidance on how to regulate specific fisheries issues. International environmental instruments like the CBD, the United Nations SDGs, or the CMS include broader biodiversity considerations and safeguard a general environmental approach. The customary duty to cooperate further demands cooperation in all matters, which may be sought through established mechanisms. Specifically for fisheries, the multilateral instrument of an RFB is considered the most appropriate cooperative governance approach. Likewise, the CAOF Agreement has adopted the approach and is structured as an RFMA.[2]

Initiated by the United States in 2007, the establishment of the CAOF Agreement was motivated by the ongoing overexploitation of fish stocks worldwide and the lack of a comprehensive international legal framework relating to the conservation and sustainable use of marine biodiversity in areas beyond national jurisdiction. Its objective is to prevent IUU fishing, to safeguard healthy marine ecosystems, and to ensure the conservation and sustainable use of fish stocks in the central part of the Arctic Ocean. At the beginning of the negotiation process, meetings were conducted among the five Arctic coastal States only. This understandably met with criticism from the remaining Arctic Council States Iceland, Finland and Sweden. As a result, after some time, a broader process was initiated. Further participants that showed interest in CAO fisheries, including the EU and relevant DWF States, together referred to as the Other Five, got involved. Parallel to ministerial meetings, scientific FiSCAO meetings took place to assist the process, before the CAOF Agreement was signed in 2018. The CAOF Agreement enables new members to accede when they have a real interest in the fisheries concerned, meaning, where they are interested in fishing in CAO waters, provided this would be possible. This broad approach is welcomed as it allows all future CAO fisheries to be regulated under the CAOF Agreement.[3]

---

2 See Chapter 4 *supra*.

3 See Chapter 3 Sections 1–3 *supra*.

Within the CAOF Agreement, the three most important stakeholders are the Arctic Five, the Other Five, and local residents. Among them, there was consensus that an Agreement should be created and implemented that restricts fishing in the Arctic high seas for the time being. Apart from that, they all pursued different goals that had to be reconciled in the negotiation process. The Arctic Five are in an advantageous position due to their vicinity to the Arctic high seas. They have the possibility to conduct fishing within their adjacent maritime zones and under the CAOF Agreement within the high seas portion of the CAO. Their aim was to extend some kind of prerogative arising from their special position to the CAOF Agreement. By contrast, the Other Five are in a less advantageous position – they may only conduct Arctic fisheries under the CAOF Agreement and depend on the support of the Arctic coastal States, as the latter will need to grant access to their coastal fisheries infrastructure. Therefore, different views are expected on the timing and conditions of the commencement of fishing under the CAOF Agreement. Further, Arctic residents are likely to support commercial fisheries, if at all, only if they continue to benefit from an exemption. Many still practice subsistence harvesting of marine mammals and fish, which makes them directly dependent on renewable resources. In addition, the continuous decline of sea ice in the Arctic and the associated difficulties in hunting have already led to food shortages, forcing communities to consider abandoning their traditional way of life. Traditional communities should therefore be treated as competent partners in addressing international issues, and their traditions and customs should be part of any Arctic renewable resource management regime. This is particularly the case as traditional communities' need for fish – and hence involving them – will certainly not lead to excessive overfishing. Under the CAOF Agreement, the participation of Arctic residents is dependent on their relationship with their national State: they may only indirectly participate through national delegations or in committees that may be established by the CAOF Agreement's Parties.[4]

The CAOF Agreement is an RFB, more specifically an RFMA. As such, the CAOF Agreement comprises specific elements and approaches that characterize an RFB as a fisheries management tool. Science forms the basis for such management. Consequently, in a first step, the CAOF Agreement focuses on conducting scientific research. In order to acquire comprehensive data, scientific knowledge about fish stocks and the CAO ecosystem shall be obtained from different sources, especially from the CAOF Agreement's own scientific

4 See Chapter 3 Section 4 *supra*.

program, the JPSRM, but also national and international programs. The findings obtained will be decisive for answering some of the key questions of the Agreement. Among other things, they will help to determine whether sustainable fisheries in the CAO are at all possible and whether a new RFB, an (S)RFMA or (S)RFMO, should be established in this context. In this way, the CAOF Agreement and especially the science conducted under its framework substantially contribute to tackle the consequences of climate change not only in the Arctic. Expected consequences must be presented to the largest public audience possible so that awareness is created and subsequent action to conquer these consequences is taken. Planck noted[5] in this regard that a

> new scientific truth does not tend to establish itself by convincing its opponents and them declaring themselves converted, but rather by the gradual extinction of the opponents and the familiarisation of the younger generation with the truth from the outset.[6]

Modern fisheries management comprises further requirements. These are sometimes better and sometimes worse implemented in the Agreement. The CAOF Agreement implements the concept of sustainability, including the precautionary approach, and the duty to cooperate to a satisfying extent. It further incorporates regulations on the compatibility of conservation and management measures. However, the decision-making processes under the Agreement should be improved through more transparency, e.g. through enhanced participation of NGOs. Due to diverging interests, the requirement that most decisions are taken by consensus, although being a standard clause, could further hamper decision-making. Also, specific references to firmly anchor the ecosystem approach could have been implemented. Whereas dispute settlement mechanisms largely meet the recommended standard, the standard of compliance and enforcement measures should be reconsidered when fishing might be allowed either under the CAOF Agreement or a newly established RFB.[7]

5 'Max Planck: Vorträge Und Erinnerungen' *Die Zeit* (17 February 1984) <https://www.zeit.de/1984/08/vortraege-und-erinnerungen?utm_referrer=https%3A%2F%2Fwww.google.com%2F> accessed 22 December 2020.

6 Original quote in German: "Eine neue wissenschaftliche Wahrheit pflegt sich nicht in der Weise durchzusetzen, dass ihre Gegner überzeugt werden und sich als bekehrt erklären, sondern vielmehr dadurch, dass die Gegner allmählich aussterben und dass die heranwachsende Generation von vornherein mit der Wahrheit vertraut gemacht wird."

7 See Chapter 5 *supra*.

Whereas the establishment of the CAOF Agreement was the first step in conquering IUU fishing in the CAO, interim measures provided for under the CAOF Agreement are the second step. In line with the precautionary approach, interim measures under the CAOF Agreement foresee setting a qualified abstention for commercial fishing in the Agreement Area. One prerequisite for commercial fishing to be conducted is the possibility of sustainable fishing. Non-commercial fishing including scientific research activities, exploratory fishing and subsistence fisheries, may widely also be conducted under strict circumstances only, namely within the framework of or dependant on the outcome of joint and national scientific programs.[8]

The CAOF Agreement lives up to its claim to prevent IUU fishing. But will this framework be expedient? Nansen, the famous Norwegian Arctic researcher, noted correctly that it "is not so much where we stand as in what direction we are moving."[9] Hence, the success of the Agreement depends on its realisation by the Parties. First of all, the CAOF Agreement needed to come into force, which happened in June 2021. In the period between signature and ratification, the current international law standard applied to the CAO, which merely provided fragmented protection. But even now that the Agreement has entered into force, the measures and procedures it provides for, which are in principle useful to combat IUU fishing, must be implemented. It is assumed that both the implementation process and reaching a decision on specific fisheries measures under the Agreement itself or an additional RFB could be challenging. Further regulation will be needed as, after all, the Agreement was created mainly to avoid issues, not necessarily to solve them. Especially if commercially viable fisheries may be conducted, it is likely that economic motives will be pursued, and cooperation put to a test. The Parties should be prepared for such developments by taking cooperative, consequent and binding decisions while aiming for sustainable fisheries.

Furthermore, the application of additional measures under different instruments may be a suitable means to enhance protection of the Arctic fish and ecosystem. Areas within the CAO but also in other parts of the Arctic could be designated as protected areas,[10] such as under the IMO Guidelines for the

---

8 See Chapter 6 *supra*.

9 Government of Norway, "Norway's Arctic Policy (Speech of Minister Vidar Helgesen, Brussels, 15 June 2015)" <https://www.regjeringen.no/en/aktuelt/arctic_policy/id2422677/> accessed 4 April 2022.

10 See M Rabaut, A Cliquet and F Maes, 'Marine Protected Areas: International Framework, State of the Art, the Belgian Situation' (2004) <https://www.vliz.be/imisdocs/publications/57792.pdf> accessed 12 April 2022.

Identification and Designation of Particularly Sensitive Sea Areas,[11] under the CBD,[12] by the OSPAR Commission,[13] or even as natural heritage.[14] Given the rapidity and uncertainty of climate change impacts and the consequent need to act swiftly, the Agreement could also be part of a universal international legally binding instrument to implement adaptive resource management.[15] Furthermore, regarding the current progress in the negotiations on the BBNJ treaty, in addition to its genuine function, the CAOF Agreement might be part of a broader framework for marine protection in areas beyond national jurisdiction in the near future.

2 Implications for Public International Law: New Fisheries Management Standard and the End of the High Seas?

Based on a scientifically founded, anticipatory approach, the CAOF Agreement, for the first time ever, establishes a fisheries management regime before fisheries in the management area took place. This gives rise to two fundamental questions: first, whether the CAOF Agreement introduces a new threshold for RFBs and second, since the CAOF Agreement establishes regulations for one of the last pristine marine areas on earth, the question as to whether the Agreement heralds the end of Grotius fundamental concept of the freedom of the high seas.

2.1 *Evolvement of a New International Standard for RFBs?*

Today, ocean governance inevitably addresses environmental issues, especially as the environmental component and the protection of global commons as dimensions of sustainable development are key aspects for achieving coherence in global governance.[16] Therefore, a question that often arises in this

---

11 International Maritime Organization, 'Revised Guidelines for the Identification and Designation of Particularly Sensitive Sea Areas (1 December 2005) – Resolution A.982(24)' (Chapter 4, n 152).

12 See, *inter alia,* Article 8(a) CBD.

13 See Annex V OSPAR Convention.

14 See Article 2 'UNESCO Convention Concerning the Protection of the World Cultural and Natural Heritage (Paris, 16 November 1972) – UNTS Vol. 1037, No. 15511' <https://treaties.un.org/doc/Publication/UNTS/Volume 1037/v1037.pdf> accessed 12 August 2021.

15 Cf. Ekaterina Uryupova, 'Why Do We Need a Shared Pan-Arctic Fisheries Governance Complex?' *The Arctic Institute* (27 April 2021) <https://www.thearcticinstitute.org/need-shared-pan-arctic-fisheries-governance-complex/> accessed 25 March 2022.

16 United Nations System Task Team (Chapter 5, n 171) 8.

context is whether the prospects for ecological management of the commons point to the arrival of a new international (customary) standard,[17] a "paradigm-shifting development in which new rules and doctrines of customary international law emerge with unusual rapidity and acceptance".[18] To come straight to the point: no doubts, the Agreement's anticipatory approach is highly innovative, yet unique. The CAOF Agreement is the first fisheries agreement ever to be in place before actual fisheries in the respective agreement area have occurred. With good reason, the Agreement is therefore referred to as "historic".[19] Nevertheless, the CAOF Agreement is not considered to ring in such a development. Due to the limited number of Parties to the CAOF Agreement and regional limitation of the regulatory area, the CAOF Agreement is considered too small to provide significant *opinio iuris* and State practice to form a new rule of customary law. Also, no regional custom is established, as the Agreement does not set-up a "paradigm-shifting" new substantive standard in a certain field: rather, existing standards are collectively applied in the Agreement in an unprecedented way. Nevertheless, the anticipatory methodology of the Agreement, influenced by region-specific developments, can be a guideline for further agreements in (relatively) pristine areas if applied carefully.[20] Admittedly, areas as untouched as the CAO are probably only found in outer space and the deep sea. Yet, the approach of the Agreement can be applied also to areas where resources are newly exploited or serve as a model when revising existing agreements with regard to new activities – not necessarily fisheries. Furthermore, building on the Arctic Council's large-scale science-based assessments useful for both influencing policy and building a common understanding of threats and indicative solutions,[21] the reliance on and involvement of research in the Agreement is remarkable. Currently, in international law, the issue of research is entirely regulated by each individual international agreement, and limited guidance on the standard of scientific research that must be met for taking decisions exists. Although the Agreement does not provide a comprehensive framework, its broad approach to research, involving programs under the Agreement and additional bodies,

17 Christopher R Rossi, 'Conclusions on the Future of the Global Commons', *Sovereignty and Territorial Temptation–The Grotian Tendency* (Cambridge University Press 2017) 281.

18 Milena Sterio, 'Humanitarian Intervention Post-Syria: A Grotian Moment?' (2014) 20 ILSA Journal of International & Comparative Law 343, 343 <https://nsuworks.nova.edu/ilsajournal/vol20/iss2/6> accessed 5 December 2021.

19 Dickie (Chapter 3, n 155).

20 Koivurova, Kankaanpää and Stępień (Chapter 4, n 179) 310.

21 See ibid 311.

and the condition to base decisions on scientific evidence excellently illustrate a threshold for environmental research. Additionally, the Agreement is a good example of the general need to use regional agreements for the introduction of area-based management tools.[22] This is especially the case, as no international legally binding instrument under UNCLOS on the conservation and sustainable use of marine biodiversity of areas beyond national jurisdiction has been established yet.

2.2 *The End of Grotius' Freedom of the High Seas?*

The Grotian idea of *mare liberum* considers the high seas to be common to all, impossible to possess, and allowing for common use of its resources.[23] Due to its natural law foundations, it claims general validity both in space and time. In view of enhanced global governance, however, the question arises to what extent this idea might be outdated and whether it has become a mere exception, announcing the end of the high seas.

In fact, over time, the original concept has been influenced by and modified *inter alia* UNCLOS regulations, the principles of the UNFS Agreement and the FAO Compliance Agreement, and specific RFB regulations. As a result, nowadays, the freedom of the high seas can only be exercised under certain conditions. Especially the lure of global governance imposes specific limits on the freedom. Also fisheries in the Arctic Ocean are now fully governed – the EEZs by their respective coastal State, and the remaining high seas parts by the CAOF Agreement – which impose certain conditions on exercising the freedom to fish. Therefore, it can be argued that the modern interpretation of the concept is slowly shifting away from the original concept.[24]

But does the modern understanding of the concept really differ so much from the original understanding? Grotius himself distinguished between different ways of using the commons. While the right of innocent passage may not be restricted because it does not take anything away from the commons, Grotius held that the use of exhaustible commons – such as fish – may indeed be limited.[25] Furthermore, with increasing governance and thus more and more stakeholders involved, does a shared freedom not necessarily has to

22 Cf. United Nations General Assembly, 'Report of the Resumed Review Conference on the Agreement for the Implementation of UNCLOS Provisions (New York, 23–27 May 2016) – A/CONF.210/2016/5' (Chapter 4, n 324) paras 52–53.

23 See specifically on the freedom of the high seas Chapter 4 Sections, 1, 1.2, 1.2.1 *supra* and Chapter 3 Section 1 *supra*.

24 See also Lodge and others (Chapter 3, n 185) 70–71.

25 Cf. Feenstra (Chapter 3, n 4) 93–95.

adapt to developments and accept the restriction of individual freedom? Is this not all the more the case when the freedom to use resources concerns exhaustible resources? It is argued that precisely the looming problem of overfishing, which Grotius, who spoke of "infinite" seas, could not have been aware of at that time, requires control through regulation and hence a modification of the concept.

Restrictions per se therefore appear reasonable and in line with the original concept. However, another aspect is considered problematic: increasing global governance over shared resources is claimed to be only in line with the Grotian concept where resources are actually shared among all. Nevertheless, it seems that the shift from the original understanding of the freedom of the high seas is "moderated not by the penchant to share resources but to divide them".[26] Geo-spatial races appear to be invitational, encompassing the most proximate, well-situated States that are capable of exercising their territorial tendency to enclose.[27] In this regard, Rossi concludes:

> Though they pledge cooperation, they compete; though they compete, they unite to exclude all others; when they see no need to unite, they act unilaterally. In concert, they render indeterminate the future interests of the global commons.[28]

Hence, what remains of the concept is that the commons are not assigned to one or more sovereigns. Through governance beyond States, on a multilateral level, they retain their status as fundamentally commons. In fact, clarity on sovereignty is withheld mainly to avoid responsibility for sovereignty while gaining ad hoc access to territorial benefits such as resources, including fisheries.[29] The CAOF Agreement takes a similar approach, as it does not allocate the Agreement area to one or more States, but allows the extraction of its fishery resources. Problematic in this regard is that due to the lack of common responsibility, contemporary conservation principles such as the precautionary and ecosystem approach, and tools such as marine protected areas lack broad incorporation and leave large areas of the global commons without a regional agreement. Fragmented, unspecified regulatory frameworks on global common goods further benefit territorial temptation.[30] Nevertheless, shared

26 Rossi, 'Conclusions on the Future of the Global Commons' (Chapter 8, n 17) 288.
27 ibid; see Rossi, 'Tradition, Tendency, Temptation' (Chapter 3, n 30) 8.
28 Rossi, 'Conclusions on the Future of the Global Commons' (Chapter 8, n 17) 288.
29 ibid 288 et seq.
30 United Nations System Task Team (Chapter 5, n 171) 6 et seq.

governance of the commons, foreseen by the freedom of the high seas, is difficult to implement in the context of global governance due to the large number of stakeholders.

As a result, the concept of the freedom of the high seas must be interpreted in the context of the development of international law and globalisation: with increasing governance, it was necessary for the concept to adapt to a dynamic framework and be limited over time. However, it is highly questionable whether the current practice of over-using the commons is covered by the freedom of the high seas. So has the rule coined by Grotius become the exception? This is not the case. The spirit of the rule still exists, albeit in a modified form. It is held in accordance with Rossi, that "[p]erhaps portions of the tradition no longer fit where they once did, having been lifted out or reconstructed from an imagined past in pursuit of a wishfully preferred future."[31]

31 Rossi, 'Conclusions on the Future of the Global Commons' (Chapter 8, n 17) 291.

Bibliography

Treaties and Legal Declarations

'Agreement between the Government of Norway, the Government of Iceland and the Government of the Russian Federation Concerning Certain Aspects of Cooperation in the Area of Fisheries (Saint Petersburg, 15 May 1999) – UNTS Vol. 2073, No. 35869 ' <https://treaties.un.org/doc/Publication/UNTS/Volume 2073/v2073.pdf> accessed 7 April 2022.

'Agreement between the United States of America and the Russian Federation on Cooperation for the Purposes of Preventing, Deterring and Eliminating Illegal, Unreported, and Unregulated Fishing (Portland, 11 September 2015)' <https://2009-2017.state.gov/documents/organization/250927.pdf> accessed 9 July 2021.

'Agreement For The Implementation Of The Provisions Of UNCLOS Relating To The Conservation And Management Of Straddling Fish Stocks And Highly Migratory Fish Stocks (New York, 4 August 1995) – UNTS Vol. 2167, No. 37924' <https://documents-dds-ny.un.org/doc/UNDOC/GEN/N95/274/67/PDF/N9527467.pdf?OpenElement> accessed 1 July 2021.

'Agreement on Fisheries between the European Economic Community, of the One Part, and the Government of Denmark and the Home Government of the Faroe Islands, of the Other Part (Brussels, 15 March 1977) – OJ L 226/12' <https://eur-lex.europa.eu/LexUriServ/LexUriServ.do?uri=CELEX:21977A0315(01):EN:HTML> accessed 30 June 2021.

'Agreement on Fisheries between the European Economic Community and the Kingdom of Norway (Brussels, 29 August 1980) – OJ L 226/48' <https://eur-lex.europa.eu/LexUriServ/LexUriServ.do?uri=CELEX:21980A0227(05):EN:HTML> accessed 30 June 2021.

'Agreement on the Conservation of Polar Bears (Oslo, 15 November 1973) – UNTS Vol. 2898, No. 50540' <https://treaties.un.org/pages/showDetails.aspx?objid=0800000280363c19> accessed 30 June 2021.

'Agreement on the European Economic Area (Brussels, 17 March 1993)' <https://www.efta.int/media/documents/legal-texts/eea/the-eea-agreement/Main Text of the Agreement/EEAagreement.pdf> accessed 10 August 2021.

'Agreement to Prevent Unregulated High Seas Fisheries in the Central Arctic Ocean (Ilulissat, 3 October 2018)' <https://www.dfo-mpo.gc.ca/international/documents/pdf/EN-CAO.pdf> accessed 9 July 2021.

'Alta Declaration (Alta, 13 June 1997)' <http://library.arcticportal.org/1271/1/The_Alta_Declaration.pdf> accessed 6 May 2021.

'Antarctic Treaty (Washington, 1 December 1959) – UNTS Vol. 402, No. 5778' <https://treaties.un.org/doc/Publication/UNTS/Volume402/volume-402-I-5778-English.pdf> accessed 4 April 2022.

'Arctic Council Agreement on Cooperation on Marine Oil Pollution Preparedness and Response in the Arctic (Kiruna, 15 May 2013)' <https://oaarchive.arctic-council.org/handle/11374/529> accessed 10 August 2021.

'Arctic Council Agreement on Enhancing International Arctic Scientific Cooperation (Fairbanks, 11 May 2017)' <https://oaarchive.arctic-council.org/handle/11374/1916> accessed 9 July 2021.

'Arctic Council Nuuk Declaration (Nuuk, 12 May 2011)' <https://oaarchive.arctic-council.org/handle/11374/92> accessed 12 March 2022.

'Arctic Ocean Conference Ilulissat Declaration (Ilulissat, 28 May 2008)' <https://cil.nus.edu.sg/wp-content/uploads/2017/07/2008-Ilulissat-Declaration.pdf> accessed 14 April 2022.

'Basel Convention on the Control of Transboundary Movements of Hazardous Wastes and Their Disposal (Basel, 22 March 1989) – UNTS Vol. 1673, No. 28911' <https://treaties.un.org/doc/Publication/UNTS/Volume 1673/v1673.pdf> accessed 9 July 2021.

'Cartagena Protocol on Biosafety to the Convention on Biological Diversity (Montreal, 29 January 2000) – UNTS Vol. 2226, No. 30619' <https://treaties.un.org/doc/Publication/UNTS/Volume 2226/v2226.pdf> accessed 9 July 2021.

'Charter of the United Nations and Statute of the International Court of Justice (San Francisco, 1945)' <https://treaties.un.org/doc/Publication/CTC/uncharter.pdf> accessed 9 April 2022.

'Convention for the Conservation of Anadromous Stocks in the North Pacific Ocean (Moscow, 11 February 1992)' <https://www.npafc.org/wp-content/uploads/Public-Documents/Handbook/Handbook-3rd-E-Convention-Only-English.pdf> accessed 2 November 2024.

'Convention for the Conservation of Salmon in the North Atlantic Ocean (Reykjavik, 2 March 1982) – UNTS Vol. 1338, No. 22433' <https://treaties.un.org/doc/Publication/UNTS/Volume 1338/v1338.pdf> accessed 12 August 2021.

'Convention for the International Council for the Exploration of the Sea (Copenhagen, 12 September 1964) – UNTS Vol. 652, No. 9344' <https://treaties.un.org/doc/Publication/UNTS/Volume 652/v652.pdf> accessed 9 April 2022.

'Convention for the Prevention of Marine Pollution by Dumping from Ships and Aircraft (Oslo, 15 February 1972) – UNTS Vol. 932, No. 13269' <https://treaties.un.org/doc/Publication/UNTS/Volume 932/volume-932-I-13269-English.pdf> accessed 12 August 2021.

'Convention for the Prevention of Marine Pollution from Landbased Sources (Paris, 4 June 1974) – UNTS Vol. 1546, No. 26842' <https://treaties.un.org/doc/Publication/UNTS/Volume 1546/volume-1546-I-26842-English.pdf> accessed 12 August 2021.

'Convention for the Protection of the Marine Environment of the North-East Atlantic (OSPAR Convention) (Paris, 22 September 1992) – UNTS Vol. 2345, No. 42279' <https://treaties.un.org/doc/Publication/UNTS/Volume 2354/v2354.pdf> accessed 12 August 2021.

'Convention for the Protection of the Mediterranean Sea Against Pollution (Barcelona, 16 February 1976) – UNTS Vol. 1102, No. 16908' <https://treaties.un.org/doc/Publication/UNTS/Volume 1102/volume-1102-I-16908-English.pdf> accessed 12 August 2021.

'Convention on Biological Diversity (Rio de Janeiro, 5 June 1992) – UNTS Vol. 1760, No. 30619' <https://treaties.un.org/doc/Publication/UNTS/Volume1760/v1760.pdf> accessed 8 April 2022.

'Convention on Cooperation in the Northwest Atlantic Fisheries (Ottawa, 24 October 1987) – UNTS Vol. 1135, No. 17799' <https://treaties.un.org/doc/Publication/UNTS/Volume 1135/volume-1135-I-17799-English.pdf> accessed 12 August 2021.

'Convention on Environmental Impact Assessment in a Transboundary Context (Espoo, 25 February 1991) – UNTS Vol. 1989, No. 34028' <https://treaties.un.org/doc/Treaties/1991/02/19910225 08-29 PM/Ch_XXVII_04p.pdf> accessed 12 August 2021.

'Convention on Future Multilateral Cooperation in North-East Atlantic Fisheries (London, 18 November 1980) – UNTS Vol. 1285, No. 21173' <https://treaties.un.org/doc/Publication/UNTS/Volume 1285/volume-1285-A-21173-English.pdf> accessed 12 August 2021.

'Convention on International Trade in Endangered Species of Wild Fauna and Flora (Washington, 3 March 1973) – UNTS Vol. 993, No. 14537' <https://treaties.un.org/doc/Publication/UNTS/Volume 993/v993.pdf> accessed 8 April 2022.

'Convention on the Conservation and Management of Fishery Resources in the South East Atlantic Ocean (Windhoek, 20 April 2001) – UNTS Vol. 2221, No. 39489' <https://treaties.un.org/pages/showDetails.aspx?objid=080000028007bd54> accessed 12 August 2021.

'Convention on the Conservation and Management of Highly Migratory Fish Stocks in the Western and Central Pacific Ocean (Honolulu, 5 September 2000)' <https://www.wcpfc.int/doc/convention-conservation-and-management-highly-migratory-fish-stocks-western-and-central-pacific> accessed 12 August 2021.

'Convention on the Conservation and Management of Pollock Resources in the Central Bering Sea (Washington D.C., 16 June 1994)' <https://www.ecolex.org/details/treaty/convention-on-the-conservation-and-management-of-pollock-in-the-central-bering-sea-tre-001217/> accessed 12 August 2021.

'Convention on the Conservation of Migratory Species of Wild Animals (Bonn, 23 June 1979) – UNTS Vol. 1651, No. 28395' <https://treaties.un.org/doc/Publication/UNTS/Volume 1651/v1651.pdf> accessed 12 August 2021.

'Convention on the Conversation of Antarctic Marine Living Resources (Canberra, 20 May 1980)' <https://www.ccamlr.org/en/organisation/camlr-convention-text>.

'Convention on the High Seas (Geneva, 29 April 1958)' <https://treaties.un.org/pages/ViewDetails.aspx?src=TREATY&mtdsg_no=XXI-2&chapter=21> accessed 12 August 2021.

'Declaration Concerning the Prevention of Unregulated High Seas Fishing in the Central Arctic Ocean (Oslo, 16 July 2015)' <https://www.regjeringen.no/globalassets/departementene/ud/vedlegg/folkerett/declaration-on-arctic-fisheries-16-july-2015.pdf> accessed 10 August 2021.

'Declaration on Cooperation in the Barents Euro-Arctic Region (Kirkenes, 11 January 1993)' <https://barents-council.org/files/459_doc_KirkenesDeclaration.pdf> accessed 2 November 2024.

'Declaration On The Establishment Of The Arctic Council (Ottawa, 19 September 1996)' <https://oaarchive.arctic-council.org/bitstream/handle/11374/85/EDOCS-1752-v2-ACMMCA00_Ottawa_1996_Founding_Declaration.PDF?sequence=5&isAllowed=y> accessed 5 December 2021.

European Union, 'Directive 2008/56/EC Establishing a Framework for Community Action in the Field of Marine Environmental Policy (Marine Strategy Framework Directive) (17 June 2008) – OJ L 164/19' <https://eur-lex.europa.eu/legal-content/EN/TXT/PDF/?uri=CELEX:32008L0056&from=EN> accessed 20 January 2022.

Food and Agriculture Organization of the United Nations, 'Agreement on Port State Measures to Prevent, Deter and Eliminate Illegal, Unreported and Unregulated Fishing (Rome, 22 November 2009)' <http://extwprlegs1.fao.org/treaty/docs/tre000003E.pdf> accessed 6 April 2022.

Food and Agriculture Organization of the United Nations, 'Agreement to Promote Compliance with International Conservation and Management Measures by Fishing Vessels on the High Seas (Rome, 24 November 1993) – UNTS Vol. 2221, No. 39486' <https://treaties.un.org/pages/showDetails.aspx?objid=080000028007be1a> accessed 28 June 2021.

Food and Agriculture Organization of the United Nations, 'Code of Conduct for Responsible Fisheries (Rome, 31 October 1995)' <https://www.fao.org/fishery/docs/CDrom/aquaculture/a0805e/documents/Code of Conduct for Responsible Fisheries.pdf> accessed 6 April 2022.

Food and Agriculture Organization of the United Nations, 'International Plan of Action for the Management of Fishing Capacity (Rome, 22 July 1998)' <http://www.fao.org/3/X3170E/x3170e04.htm> accessed 6 April 2022.

Food and Agriculture Organization of the United Nations, 'International Plan Of Action To Prevent, Deter And Eliminate Illegal, Unreported And Unregulated Fishing (Rome, 2 March 2001)' <http://www.fao.org/3/y1224e/Y1224E.pdf> accessed 2 May 2020.

Food and Agriculture Organization of the United Nations, 'Reykjavik Declaration on Responsible Fisheries in the Marine Ecosystem (Included in Appendix I, Report of the Reykjavik Conference on Responsible Fisheries in the Marine Ecosystem (Reykjavik, 1–4 October 2001))' <http://www.fao.org/fishery/docs/DOCUMENT/reykjavik/y2198t00_dec.pdf> accessed 10 August 2021.

Food and Agriculture Organization of the United Nations, 'Voluntary Guidelines for Flag State Performance (Rome, 9 June 2014)' <http://www.fao.org/3/I4577T/i4577t.pdf> accessed 7 May 2020.

Food and Agriculture Organization of the United Nations, 'Voluntary Guidelines for Securing Sustainable Small-Scale Fisheries in the Context of Food Security and Poverty Eradication (Rome, 1 June 2014)' <http://www.fao.org/3/a-i4356en.pdf> accessed 7 May 2020.

Food and Agriculture Organization of the United Nations, 'Voluntary Guidelines on the Marking of Fishing Gear (Rome, 9 July 2018)' <https://www.fao.org/3/ca3546t/ca3546t.pdf> accessed 8 April 2022.

'International Convention for the Control and Management of Ships' Ballast Water and Sediments (London, 13 February 2004) – UNTS No. 55544' <https://treaties.un.org/doc/Publication/UNTS/No Volume/55544/Part/I-55544-080000028053b465.pdf> accessed 15 December 2020.

'International Convention for the Prevention of Pollution from Ships (London, 2 November 1973) – UNTS Vol. 1340, No. 22484' <https://treaties.un.org/doc/Publication/UNTS/Volume 1340/volume-1340-A-22484-English.pdf> accessed 30 October 2021.

'International Convention for the Safety of Life at Sea (London, 1 November 1974) – UNTS Vol. 1184, No. 18961' <https://treaties.un.org/doc/publication/unts/volume 1184/volume-1184-i-18961-english.pdf> accessed 30 October 2021.

International Labour Organisation, 'Indigenous and Tribal Peoples Convention No. 169 (Geneva, 27 June 1989)' <https://www.ilo.org/dyn/normlex/en/f?p=NORMLEXPUB:12100:0::NO::P12100_ILO_CODE:C169> accessed 7 April 2020.

International Law Commission, 'Draft Articles on Responsibility of States for Internationally Wrongful Acts (1 November 2001) – A/56/10, Supplement No. 10' <https://www.refworld.org/docid/3ddb8f804.html> accessed 9 July 2021.

International Maritime Organization, '2011 Guidelines for the Control and Management of Ships' Biofouling to Minimize the Transfer of Invasive Aquatic Species (15 July 2011) – Annex 26 Resolution MEPC.207(62)' <https://wwwcdn.imo.org/localresources/en/OurWork/Environment/Documents/RESOLUTIONMEPC.207%5B62%5D.pdf> accessed 30 June 2021.

International Maritime Organization, 'Revised Guidelines for the Identification and Designation of Particularly Sensitive Sea Areas (1 December 2005) – Resolution A.982(24)' <https://wwwcdn.imo.org/localresources/en/KnowledgeCentre/IndexofIMOResolutions/AssemblyDocuments/A.982(24).pdf> accessed 4 April 2022.

Inuit Circumpolar Council, 'Kitigaaryuit Declaration (Kitigaaryuit, 24 July 2014)' <https://iccalaska.org/wp-icc/wp-content/uploads/2016/01/2014-Kitigaarguit-Declaration-Final-Signed.pdf > accessed 2 November 2024.

Inuit Circumpolar Council, 'Utqiaġvik Declaration (Utqiaġvik, 19 July 2018)' <https://www.arctictoday.com/wp-content/uploads/2018/07/2018-Utigavik-Declaration.pdf> accessed 8 April 2020.

'Inuvik Declaration (Inuvik, 21 March 1996)' <http://library.arcticportal.org/1272/1/The_Inuvik_Declaration.pdf> accessed 6 May 2020.

'Kyoto Protocol to the United Nations Framework Convention on Climate Change (Kyoto, 11 December 1997) – UNTS Vol. 2303, No. 30822' <https://treaties.un.org/doc/Publication/UNTS/Volume 2303/v2303.pdf> accessed 28 June 2021.

'Montreal Protocol on Substances That Deplete the Ozone Layer (Montreal, 16 September 1987) – UNTS Vol. 1522, No.26369' <https://treaties.un.org/doc/Treaties/1989/01/19890101 03-25 AM/Ch_XXVII_02_ap.pdf> accessed 9 July 2021.

'Nagoya Protocol on Access to Genetic Resources and the Fair and Equitable Sharing of Benefits Arising from Their Utilization to the Convention on Biological Diversity (Nagoya, 29 October 2010) – UNTS Vol. 3008, No.30619' <https://treaties.un.org/doc/Publication/UNTS/Volume 3008/v3008.pdf> accessed 8 May 2020.

'Niue Treaty on Cooperation in Fisheries Surveillance and Law Enforcement in the South Pacific Region (Honiara, 9 July 1992)' <https://www.ffa.int/system/files/Niue Treaty_0.pdf> accessed 12 April 2022.

'Nuuk Declaration on Environment and Development in the Arctic (Nuuk, 16 September 1993)' <https://referenceworks.brill.com/display/entries/ILWO/SIM-032762.xml > accessed 2 November 2024.

'Paris Agreement (Paris, 12 December 2015) – UNTS Vol. 3156, No. 54113' <https://treaties.un.org/doc/Treaties/2016/02/20160215 06-03 PM/Ch_XXVII-7-d.pdf> accessed 5 April 2022.

'Protocol Amending the Convention between the United States of America and Canada for the Preservation of the Halibut Fishery of the Northern Pacific Ocean and Bering Sea (29 March 1979)' <https://www.ecolex.org/details/treaty/protocol-amending-the-convention-between-the-united-states-of-america-and-canada-for-the-preservation-of-the-halibut-fishery-of-the-northern-pacific-ocean-and-the-bering-sea-1979-tre-151686/> accessed 21 December 2020.

'Protocol on Environmental Protection to the Antarctic Treaty (Madrid, 4 October 1991) – UNTS Vol. 2941, No. 5778' <https://treaties.un.org/doc/Publication/UNTS/Volume 2941/v2941.pdf>.

'Treaty on the Functioning of the European Union (Consolidated Version) (Lissabon, 1 December 2009)' <https://eur-lex.europa.eu/legal-content/EN/TXT/PDF/?uri=CELEX:12012E/TXT&from=EN> accessed 9 July 2021.

'Treaty Relating to Spitsbergen (Svalbard) (9 February 1920)' <https://www.spitzbergen.de/wp-content/uploads/2020/01/Spitsbergen-treaty_English.pdf> accessed 2 March 2021.

'UNESCO Convention Concerning the Protection of the World Cultural and Natural Heritage (Paris, 16 November 1972) – UNTS Vol. 1037, No. 15511' <https://treaties.un.org/doc/Publication/UNTS/Volume 1037/v1037.pdf> accessed 12 August 2021.

United Nations, 'Report of the United Nations Conference on the Human Environment – Declaration of the United Nations Conference on the Human Environment (Stockholm, 5–16 June 1972) – A/CONF.48/14/Rev.1' <http://www.un-documents.net/aconf48-14r1.pdf> accessed 30 June 2021.

'United Nations Convention on the Law of the Sea (Montego Bay, 10 December 1982) – UNTS Vol. 1833, No. 31363' <https://treaties.un.org/doc/Publication/UNTS/Volume 1833/volume-1833-A-31363-English.pdf> accessed 30 March 2022.

'United Nations Framework Convention on Climate Change (New York, 9 May 1992) – UNTS Vol. 1771, No. 30822' <https://treaties.un.org/doc/Publication/UNTS/Volume 1771/v1771.pdf> accessed 9 July 2021.

'Vienna Convention for the Protection of the Ozone Layer (Vienna, 22 March 1985) – UNTS Vol. 1513, No. 26164' <https://treaties.un.org/doc/Treaties/1988/09/19880922 03-14 AM/Ch_XXVII_02p.pdf> accessed 9 July 2021.

'Vienna Convention on the Law of Treaties (Vienna, 23 May 1969) – UNTS Vol. 1155, No. 18232' <https://treaties.un.org/doc/publication/unts/volume 1155/volume-1155-i-18232-english.pdf> accessed 9 July 2021.

Cases

Allegations of Genocide under the Convention on the Prevention and Punishment of the Crime of Genocide (Ukraine v Russian Federation) – Request for the Indication of Provisional Measures, ICJ Order of 16 March 2022, General List No 182.

Beagle Channel Arbitration (Argentina v Chile), Award of 18 February 1977, Reports of International Arbitral Awards, Volume XXI, p 53.

Case Concerning Pulp Mills on the River Uruguay (Argentina v Uruguay), Judgement of 20 April 2010, ICJ Reports 2010, p 14.

Case Concerning the Application of the Convention of 1902 Governing the Guardianship of Infants (Netherlands v Sweden), Judgement of 28 November 1958, ICJ Reports 1958, p 55.

Case Concerning the Continental Shelf (Libyan Arab Jamahiriya v Malta), Judgment of 3 June 1985, ICJ Reports 1985, p 13.

Case Concerning the Factory at Chorzów (Claim for Indemnity), Judgement of 26 July 1927, Publications of the Permanent Court of International Justice Series A – No 9.

Corfu Channel Case (United Kingdom of Great Britain and Northern Ireland v Albania), Judgement of 9 April 1949, ICJ Reports 1949, p 4.

Fisheries Jurisdiction (Federal Republic of Germany v Iceland), Judgment of 25 July 1974, ICJ Reports 1974, p 175.

Fisheries Jurisdiction (United Kingdom v Iceland), Judgment of 25 July 1974, ICJ Reports 1974, p 3.

Land Reclamation by Singapore in and Around the Straits of Johor (Malaysia v Singapore), Provisional Measures, Order of 8 October 2003, ITLOS Reports 2003, p 10.

Legality of the Threat or Use of Nuclear Weapons, Advisory Opinion of 8 July 1996, ICJ Reports 1996, p 226.

Military and Paramilitary Activities in and against Nicaragua (Nicaragua v United States of America), Merits Judgment of 27 June 1986, ICJ Reports 1986, p 14

MOX Plant Case (Ireland v United Kingdom), Provisional Measures, Order of 3 December 2001, ITLOS Reports 2001, p 95, Separate Opinion of Judge Wolfrum

MOX Plant Case (Ireland v United Kingdom), Provisional Measures, Order of 3 December 2001, ITLOS Reports 2001, p 95.

North Sea Continental Shelf Cases (Federal Republic of Germany/Denmark; Federal Republic of Germany/Netherlands), Judgement of 20 February 1969, ICJ Reports 1969, p 3.

Responsibilities and Obligations of States Sponsoring Persons and Entities with Respect to Activities in the Area, Advisory Opinion of 1 February 2011, ITLOS Reports 2011, p 10

Southern Bluefin Tuna (New Zealand v Japan; Australia v Japan), Provisional Measures, Order of 27 August 1999, ITLOS Reports 1999, p 280.

Trail Smelter Case (United States v Canada), Awards of 16 April 1938 and 11 March 1941, Reports of International Arbitral Awards Vol III, p 1905.

Reports and Official Documents

Arctic Centre University of Lapland, 'Strategic Assessment of Development of the Arctic – Assessment Conducted for the European Union' (2014) <http://library.arcticportal.org/1905/> accessed 10 August 2021.

'Arctic Council Rules of Procedure (Revised Version 2013)' <https://oaarchive.arctic-council.org/bitstream/handle/11374/940/2015-09-01_Rules_of_Procedure_website_version.pdf?sequence=1&isAllowed=y> accessed 10 August 2021.

Arctic Monitoring and Assessment Programme (AMAP), 'Arctic Pollution Issues: A State of the Arctic Environment Report' (1997) <https://www.amap.no/documents/download/68/inline> accessed 10 August 2021.

Arctic Monitoring and Assessment Programme (AMAP), 'AMAP Assessment Report: Arctic Pollution Issues' (1998) <https://www.amap.no/documents/doc/amap-assessment-report-arctic-pollution-issues/68> accessed 10 August 2021.

Arctic Monitoring and Assessment Programme (AMAP), Conservation of Arctic Flora and Fauna (CAFF) Working Group and International Arctic Science Committee (IASC), 'Arctic Climate Impact Assessment' (2005) <http://www.amap.no/documents/doc/arctic-arctic-climate-impact-assessment/796> accessed 10 August 2021.

ARCTIS, 'Russian Federation Policy for the Arctic from 2008 to 2020 (English Translation)' (2009) <http://www.arctis-search.com/Russian+Federation+Policy+for+the+Arctic+to+2020> accessed 10 August 2021.

Ásmundsson S, 'Regional Fisheries Management Organisations (RFMOs): Who Are They, What Is Their Geographic Coverage on the High Seas and Which Ones Should Be Considered as General RFMOs, Tuna RFMOs and Specialised RFMOs?' (2016) <https://www.cbd.int/doc/meetings/mar/soiom-2016-01/other/soiom-2016-01-fao-19-en.pdf> accessed 10 August 2021.

Balton DA and Zagorski A, 'Implementing Marine Management in the Arctic Ocean' (Russian International Affairs Council; Wilson Center; Polar Institute 2020) <https://www.wilsoncenter.org/publication/implementing-marine-management-arctic-ocean> accessed 10 August 2021.

Barber D and others, 'An Open Letter from International Scientists' (2012) <https://www.pewtrusts.org/~/media/legacy/oceans_north_legacy/page_attachments/international-arctic-scientist-letter-with-sigs-522012.pdf?la=en> accessed 10 August 2021.

Barry T et al., 'Arctic Biodiversity Assessment – Scientific Report' (Arctic Council 2013) <https://oaarchive.arctic-council.org/items/b32baf29-d9d7-4c9e-8598-877db37141da> accessed 2 November 2024.

Ben-Eli M, 'Sustainability: Definition and Five Core Principles – A New Framework' (The Sustainability Laboratory 2015) < https://www.sustainabilitylabs.org/ecosystem-restoration/wp-content/uploads/2015/08/Sustainability-The-Five-Core-Principles.pdf> accessed 2 Novemeber 2024.

Bourguignon D, 'The Precautionary Principle: Definitions, Applications and Governance' (European Parliament 2016) <https://www.europarl.europa.eu/thinktank/en/document.html?reference=EPRS_IDA(2015)573876> accessed 10 August 2021.

Bowen D, Rice J and Trumble RJ, 'MSC Final Report and Determination for Alaska Pollock – Bering Sea-Aleutian Islands' (MRAG Americas 2015) <https://cert.msc.org/FileLoader/FileLinkDownload.asmx/GetFile?encryptedKey=v5NA0jNkiUZRzn52Lf/KM5Ylxb3g6nRc8mRKhTsxOdE4pwpZXgAkpouYs6bJWuLB> accessed 10 August 2021.

CBD Conference of the Parties, 'Biodiversity and Sustainable Development – Technical Note (21 October 2016) – UNEP/CBD/COP/13/10/Add.1' <https://www.cbd.int/doc/meetings/cop/cop-13/official/cop-13-10-add1-en.pdf> accessed 10 August 2021.

CBD Conference of the Parties, 'COP 10 Decision 2: The Strategic Plan for Biodiversity 2011–2020 and the Aichi Biodiversity Targets (Nagoya, 29 October 2010)' <https://www.cbd.int/doc/decisions/cop-10/cop-10-dec-02-en.pdf> accessed 12 August 2021.

CBD Conference of the Parties, 'COP 14 Decision 11: Invasive Alien Species (Sharm El-Sheikh, 30 November 2018)' <https://www.cbd.int/doc/decisions/cop-14/cop-14-dec-11-en.pdf> accessed 17 January 2022.

CBD Conference of the Parties, 'COP 4 Item 13: Report of the Workshop on the Ecosystem Approach (Lilongwe, 26–28 March 1998)'.

CBD Conference of the Parties, 'COP 5 Decision 6: Ecosystem Approach (Nairobi, 26 May 2000)' <https://www.cbd.int/decisions/cop/5/6> accessed 12 August 2021.

CBD Conference of the Parties, 'COP 5 Decision 16: Article 8(j) and related provisions (Nairobi, 26 May 2000)' <https://www.cbd.int/decision/cop/default.shtml?id=7158> accessed 28 April 2024.

CBD Conference of the Parties, 'COP 6 Decision 23: Alien Species That Threaten Ecosystems, Habitats or Species (The Hague, 7 – 19 April 2002)' <https://www.cbd.int/doc/decisions/cop-06-dec-23-en.pdf> accessed 10 August 2021.

CBD Conference of the Parties, 'COP 9 Decision 7: Ecosystem Approach (Bonn, 9 October 2008)' <https://www.cbd.int/doc/decisions/cop-09/cop-09-dec-07-en.pdf> accessed 17 January 2022.

CBD Conference of the Parties and Conservation of Arctic Flora and Fauna (CAFF) Working Group, 'Arctic Regional Workshop to Facilitate the Description of Ecologically or Biologically Significant Marine Areas (Helsinki, 3–7 March 2014)' <https://www.cbd.int/doc/meetings/mar/ebsaws-2014-01/official/ebsaws-2014-01-05-en.pdf> accessed 10 August 2021.

'Chairman's Statement, Fifth FiSCAO Meeting on Central Arctic Ocean Fisheries (Ottawa, 24–26 October 2017)' <https://apps-afsc.fisheries.noaa.gov/documents/Arctic_fish_stocks_fifth_meeting/508_Documents/508_Final_report_of_the_5th_FiSCAO_meeting.pdf > accessed 2 November 2024.

'Chairman's Statement, Fifth Meeting on Central Arctic Ocean Fisheries (Reykjavik, 15–18 March 2017)' <https://2017-2021.state.gov/remarks-and-releases-bureau-of-oceans-and-international-environmental-and-scientific-affairs/meeting-on-high-seas-fisheries-in-the-central-arctic-ocean-5/#fn1> accessed 2 November 2024.

'Chairman's Statement, Fourth Meeting on Central Arctic Ocean Fisheries (Tórshavn, 29 November – 1 December 2016)' <https://apps-afsc.fisheries.noaa.gov/documents/Arctic_fish_stocks_fifth_meeting/508_Documents/508_Chairman_s%20Statement%20from%20Torshavn%20Meeting%202016.pdf> accessed 2 November 2024.

'Chairman's Statement, Sixth Meeting on Central Arctic Ocean Fisheries (Washington D.C., 28–30 November 2017)' <https://oceanconservancy.org/wp-content/uploads/2017/11/Chairmans-Statement-from-Washington-Meeting-2017.pdf> accessed 10 August 2021.

'Chairman's Statement, Third Meeting on Central Arctic Ocean Fisheries (Nuuk, 24–26 February 2014)' <http://www.pewtrusts.org/~/media/assets/2014/09/arcticnationsagreetoworkoninternationalfisheries-accord.pdf?la=it> accessed 10 August 2021.

Cochrane K and others, 'FAO Fisheries and Aquaculture Technical Paper 530: Climate Change Implications for Fisheries and Aquaculture' (2009) <http://www.lis.edu.es/uploads/07483fb7_72a2_45ca_b8e7_48bf74072fd3.pdf> accessed 24 April 2020.

Commission for the Conservation of Antarctic Marine Living Resources (CCAMLR), 'Conservation Measure 21–02 (2011) – Exploratory Fisheries' <https://www.ccamlr.org/sites/default/files/21-02.pdf> accessed 10 August 2021.

Commission for the Conservation of Antarctic Marine Living Resources (CCAMLR), 'Conservation Measure 21–02 (2019) – Exploratory Fisheries' <https://www.ccamlr.org/sites/default/files/21-02_33.pdf> accessed 10 August 2021.

Commission on the Limits of the Continental Shelf, 'Outer Limits of the Continental Shelf beyond 200 Nautical Miles from the Baselines: Submission to the Commission on the Limits of the Continental Shelf by the Russian Federation' <https://www.un.org/depts/los/clcs_new/submissions_files/submission_rus.htm> accessed 8 July 2020.

Conservation of Arctic Flora and Fauna (CAFF) Working Group, 'Arctic Flora and Fauna: Status and Conservation' (2001) <https://oaarchive.arctic-council.org/bitstream/handle/11374/169/Arctic_Flora_Fauna_Status_Trends_2001%281%29.pdf?sequence=1&isAllowed=y> accessed 4 April 2022.

Conservation of Arctic Flora and Fauna (CAFF) Working Group, 'Arctic Marine Biodiversity Monitoring Plan (CBMP-MARINE PLAN) – CAFF Monitoring Series Report No.3' (2011) <https://oaarchive.arctic-council.org/server/api/core/bitstreams/0567a2b3-ca08-4bd5-830c-72d312f128c1/content> accessed 4 December 2024.

Conservation of Arctic Flora and Fauna (CAFF) Working Group, 'State of the Arctic Marine Biodiversity: Key Findings and Advice for Monitoring' (2017) <https://oaarchive.arctic-council.org/handle/11374/1945> accessed 4 April 2022.

Conservation of Arctic Flora and Fauna (CAFF) Working Group, 'Arctic Biodiversity and the Post2020 Framework' (2020) <https://www.cbd.int/api/v2013/documents/CBB01D91-94B7-5DA3-F6FA-F014376CD07E/attachments/212341/CAFF-2.pdf> accessed 4 April 2022.

'COP 5 Decision 23: Annex III. Decisions Adopted by the Conference of the Parties to the Convention on Biological Diversity at Its Fifth Meeting (Nairobi, 15–26 May 2000)' (2000) <https://www.cbd.int/doc/decisions/COP-05-dec-en.pdf> accessed 3 June 2020.

Deep Sea Conservation Coalition, 'A Net with Holes: The Regional Fisheries Management System' (2004) <http://www.savethehighseas.org/publicdocs/RFMO.pdf> accessed 20 February 2020.

'Denmark, Greenland and the Faroe Islands: Kingdom of Denmark Strategy for the Arctic 2011–2020' (2011) <http://library.arcticportal.org/1890/1/DENMARK.pdf> accessed 13 April 2022.

'Deputy Secretary's Meeting with Canadian Resource Minister Lunn in Greenland, Cable to the U.S. Secretary of State (11 June 2008) – Ref.08COPENHAGEN338' <https://wikileaks.org/plusd/cables/08COPENHAGEN338_a.html> accessed 11 September 2020.

'Deputy Secretary's Meeting with Norwegian Fm Stoere in Greenland, Cable to the U.S. Secretary of State (11 June 2008) – Ref 08COPENHAGEN337' <https://wikileaks.org/plusd/cables/08COPENHAGEN337_a.html> accessed 11 September 2020.

Doulman DJ, 'FAO Fisheries Circular No. 898: Structure and Process of the 1993–1995 United Nations Conference on Straddling Fish Stocks and Highly Migratory Fish Stocks' (1995) <http://www.fao.org/3/v9929e/v9929E00.htm> accessed 26 November 2021.

Eslinger DL and others, 'Model Task Team Workshop Report – Final Report of the International Workshop to Develop a Prototype Lower Trophic Level Ecosystem Model for Comparison of Different Marine Ecosystems in the North Pacific' (2000) <https://pices.int/publications/scientific_reports/Report15/MODEL.pdf> accessed 1 July 2021.

European Commission, 'Commission Regulation (EC) No 1010/2009 Laying down Detailed Rules for the Implementation of Council Regulation (EC) No 1005/2008 (22 October 2009) – OJ L 280/5' <https://eur-lex.europa.eu/legal-content/EN/TXT/PDF/?uri=CELEX:32009R1010&from=DE> accessed 12 August 2021.

European Commission, 'Joint Communication – A Stronger EU Engagement for a Peaceful, Sustainable and Prosperous Arctic (13 October 2021) – JOIN(2021) 27 Final' <https://www.ipcc.ch/report/ar6/wg1/> accessed 25 March 2022.

European Commission, 'Joint Communication – Developing a European Union Policy towards the Arctic Region: Progress since 2008 and next Steps (2012) – JOIN(2012) 19 Final' <https://op.europa.eu/de/publication-detail/-/publication/70245d63-201c-47e8-9091-d5c07b96d964> accessed 5 December 2021.

European Commission, 'Letter from the Director General for Maritime Affairs and Fisheries (MARE) – Subject: Snow Crab Fisheries in the NEAFC Regulatory Area (5 August 2015)' <https://www.politico.eu/wp-content/uploads/2017/06/SPOLITICO-17061514340.pdf> accessed 8 September 2020.

European Commission, 'Report on the Implementation of the Marine Strategy Framework Directive (Brussels, 25 June 2020) – COM(2020) 259 Final' <https://dx.doi.org/10.2771/21854> accessed 25 November 2020.

European Commission, 'North-East Atlantic: Important Agreements on Conservation and Enforcements Measures' (21 November 2018) <https://ec.europa.eu/oceans-and-fisheries/news/north-east-atlantic-important-agreements-conservation-and-enforcements-measures-2018-11-21_en> accessed 5 December 2021.

European Court of Human Rights, 'Press Release: Decision of the Court on Requests for Interim Measures in Individual Applications Concerning Russian Military Operations on Ukrainian Territory (4 March 2022) – ECHR 073 (2022)'.

European Economic and Social Committee, 'Opinion: An Integrated European Union Policy for the Arctic (14 December 2016) – JOIN (2016) 21 Final, REX/470' <https://eur-lex.europa.eu/legal-content/EN/TXT/PDF/?uri=CELEX:52016AE4426&rid=4>.

European Parliament, 'Report on an Integrated European Union Policy for the Arctic (2017) – A8-0032/2017' <https://www.europarl.europa.eu/doceo/document/A-8-2017-0032_EN.html> accessed 29 January 2022.

'European Parliament Parliamentary Questions, VP/HR – EU Policy on the Arctic and the Successor to the Special Advisor/Ambassador at Large for the Arctic (17 April 2019)' <https://www.europarl.europa.eu/doceo/document/P-8-2019-001961_EN.html> accessed 25 March 2022.

'European Parliament Resolution on an Integrated European Union Policy for the Arctic (16 March 2017) – P8_TA(2017)0093' <http://www.inuitcircumpolar.com/uploads/3/0/5/4/30542564/> accessed 23 April 2021.

'European Parliament Resolution on Arctic Governance (9 October 2008) – P6_TA(2008)0474' <https://www.europarl.europa.eu/sides/getDoc.do?type=TA&language=EN&reference=P6-TA-2008-474> accessed 10 August 2021.

'European Parliament Resolution on the EU Strategy for the Arctic (12 March 2014) – P7_TA(2014)0236' <https://eur-lex.europa.eu/legal-content/EN/TXT/PDF/?uri=CELEX:52014IP0236&from=EN> accessed 29 January 2022.

European Union, 'Act Concerning the Conditions of Accession and the Adjustments to the Treaties on Which the European Union Is Founded, Protocol No 3 – on the Sami People (29 August 1994) – 11994N/PRO/03' <https://eur-lex.europa.eu/legal-content/BG/TXT/?uri=CELEX:11994N/PRO/03> accessed 6 April 2021.

European Union, 'Communication from the Commission to the European Parliament and the Council – The European Union and the Arctic Region (20 November 2008) – COM/2008/0763 Final' <https://eur-lex.europa.eu/legal-content/EN/TXT/?uri=celex:52008DC0763> accessed 5 December 2021.

European Union, 'Council Conclusions on the Arctic: Foreign Affairs Council (20 June 2016) – 10400/16' <http://data.consilium.europa.eu/doc/document/ST-10400-2016-INIT/en/pdf> accessed 4 April 2022.

European Union, 'Council Regulation (EC) No 1005/2008 Establishing a Community System to Prevent, Deter and Eliminate Illegal, Unreported and Unregulated Fishing (29 September 2008) – OJ L 286, 29.10.2008, p.1' <https://eur-lex.europa.eu/legal-content/EN/TXT/PDF/?uri=CELEX:02008R1005-20110309&from=EN> accessed 11 August 2020.

European Union, 'Debates of the European Parliament (9 October 2008)' <https://www.europarl.europa.eu/sides/getDoc.do?pubRef=-//EP//NONSGML+CRE+20081009+SIT+DOC+PDF+V0//EN&language=EN> accessed 11 March 2022.

European Union, 'Decision No 1386/2013/EU of the European Parliament and of the Council on a General Union Environment Action Programme to 2020 "Living Well, within the Limits of Our Planet" (20 November 2013) – L354/171' <https://eur-lex.europa.eu/legal-content/EN/TXT/PDF/?uri=CELEX:32013D1386&from=EN> accessed 9 July 2021.

European Union, 'Opinion of the European Committee of the Regions – Union Policy for the Arctic (8 February 2017) – OJ C 207/17' <https://eur-lex.europa.eu/legal-content/EN/TXT/PDF/?uri=CELEX:52016AR4295&from=NL> accessed 23 April 2020.

European Union, 'Press Release: The Arctic Merits the European Union's Attention – First Step towards an EU Arctic Policy (20 November 2008) – IP/08/1750' <http://europa.eu/rapid/press-release_IP-08-1750_en.htm> accessed 12 August 2021.

European Union, 'Policy Department: The Outcome of the Ninth Arctic Council Ministerial Meeting' (2015) <http://www.arctic-council.org/index.php/en/about-us/arctic-council/observers> accessed 23 April 2020.

European Union, 'Policy Department B: Fisheries Management And The Arctic In The Context Of Climate Change – Study' (2015) <http://www.europarl.europa.eu/RegData/etudes/STUD/2015/563380/IPOL_STU(2015)563380_EN.pdf> accessed 10 August 2021.

Federal Foreign Office Germany, 'Guidelines of the Germany Arctic Policy – Assume Responsibility, Seize Opportunities' (2013) <https://www.arctic-office.de/fileadmin/user_upload/www.arctic-office.de/PDF_uploads/Germanys_Arctic_policy_guidelines.pdf> accessed 4 April 2022.

Federal Foreign Office Germany, 'Germany's Arctic Policy Guidelines – Assuming Responsibility, Creating Trust, Shaping the Future' (2019) <https://www.arctic-office.de/fileadmin/user_upload/www.arctic-office.de/PDF_uploads/Germany_s_Arctic_Policy_Guidelines_2019_Web.pdf> accessed 2 Novmeber 2024.

Federal Ministry of Education and Research Germany, 'Rapid Climate Change in the Arctic: Polar Research as a Global Responsibility' (2012) <https://www.fona.de/medien/pdf/Rapid_Climate_Change_in_the_Arctic.pdf> accessed 10 August 2021.

Federal Ministry of Education and Research Germany, 'Mare:N – Coastal, Marine and Polar Research for Sustainability – German Federal Government Research Program' (2020) <https://www.foerderinfo.bund.de/SharedDocs/Publikationen/de/bmbf/FS/31356_Mare_N_en.pdf?__blob=publicationFile&v=4> accessed 2 November 2024.

'First International Meeting on the Establishment of the South Pacific Regional Fisheries Management Organisation (Wellington, 14–17 February 2006) – SP/01/Inf5' <http://www.sprfmo.int/assets/Meetings/Meetings-before-2013/International-Consultations-2006-to-2009/IntCons-1-2006-Wellington-New-Zealand/SPRFMO-InfConf-1-2006-Interim-Measures.pdf> accessed 20 July 2020.

First Joint Ministerial Meeting of the Helsinki and OSPAR Commissions, 'Statement on the Ecosystem Approach to the Management of Human Activities (Bremen, 25–26

June 2003)' <https://www.ospar.org/site/assets/files/1232/jmm_annex05_ecosystem_approach_statement.pdf> accessed 9 July 2021.

Flewwelling P, 'FAO Fisheries Technical Paper 338: An Introduction to Monitoring, Control and Surveillance Systems for Capture Fisheries' (1994) <http://www.fao.org/3/V4250E/V4250E00.htm#toc> accessed 20 July 2020.

Food and Agriculture Organization of the United Nations, 'FAO Fisheries and Aquaculture Report No. 881: Report of the Technical Consultation on International Guidelines for the Management of Deep-Sea Fisheries in the High Seas (Rome, 4–8 February and 25–29 August 2008)' <http://www.fao.org/documents/card/en/c/b02fc35e-a0c4-545a-86fb-4fc340e13b52> accessed 2 December 2020.

Food and Agriculture Organization of the United Nations, 'Report of the Expert Consultation on Catalysing the Transition Away from Overcapacity in Marine Capture Fisheries (Rome, 15–18 October 2002)' <https://openknowledge.fao.org/server/api/core/bitstreams/02864203-7c15-468b-b1d8-b649fb59bf80/content> accessed 2 November 2024.

Food and Agriculture Organization of the United Nations, 'Report of the Expert Consultation on Catch Documentation Schemes (CDS) (Rome, 21–24 July 2015)' <http://www.fao.org/3/i5063e/i5063e.pdf> accessed 14 May 2020.

Food and Agriculture Organization of the United Nations, 'Report of the Fifth Meeting of the Regional Fishery Body Secreteriats Network (RSN-5), (Rome, 7 and 13 June 2014)' <http://www.fao.org/3/a-i4210e.pdf> accessed 20 February 2020.

Food and Agriculture Organization of the United Nations, 'Report of the Meeting of the High-Level Panel of External Experts in Fisheries (Rome, 26–27 January 1998)' <http://www.fao.org/3/w9887e/w9887e.htm> accessed 16 June 2020.

Food and Agriculture Organization of the United Nations, 'Report of the Second Meeting of FAO and Non-FAO Regional Fishery Bodies or Arrangements (Rome, 20–21 February 2001)' <http://www.fao.org/3/a-y0593e.pdf> accessed 16 June 2020.

Food and Agriculture Organization of the United Nations, 'Report of the Technical Workshop on Deep-Sea Fisheries and Vulnerable Marine Ecosystems in the Eastern Central Atlantic (Dakar, 8–10 November 2016)' <https://openknowledge.fao.org/server/api/core/bitstreams/d82c934b-e7fb-452b-ba91-4e00acdb0be8/content> accessed 18 December 2024.

Food and Agriculture Organization of the United Nations, 'The State of World Fisheries and Aquaculture 2002' <http://www.fao.org/3/a-y7300e.pdf> accessed 16 June 2020.

Food and Agriculture Organization of the United Nations, 'The State of World Fisheries and Aquaculture 2016: Contributing to Food Security and Nutrition for All' <https://www.fao.org/3/i5555e/i5555e.pdf> accessed 5 December 2021.

Food and Agriculture Organization of the United Nations, 'The State of World Fisheries and Aquaculture 2020: Sustainability in Action' <https://doi.org/10.4060/ca922 9en> accessed 4 April 2022.

Food and Agriculture Organization of the United Nations, 'FAO Fisheries Circular No. 853: Marine Fisheries and Law of the Sea: A Decade of Change' (1993) <http://www .fao.org/3/u9345e/u9345e00.pdf> accessed 18 September 2021.

Food and Agriculture Organization of the United Nations, 'Technical Guidelines for Responsible Fisheries No. 2: Precautionary Approach to Capture Fisheries and Species Introductions' (1996) <http://www.fao.org/3/a-w3592e.pdf> accessed 18 June 2021.

Food and Agriculture Organization of the United Nations, 'Technical Guidelines for Responsible Fisheries No. 9: Implementation of the International Plan of Action to Prevent, Deter and Eliminate Illegal, Unreported and Unregulated Fishing' (2002) <http://www.fao.org/3/a-y3536e.pdf> accessed 3 July 2020.

Fourth Arctic Council Ministerial Meeting, 'Arctic Climate Impact Assessment Policy Document (Reykjavík, 24 November 2004)' <https://acia.amap.no/> accessed 30 June 2021.

Garcia SM and others, 'FAO Fisheries Technical Paper 443: The Ecosystem Approach to Fisheries' (2003) <http://www.fao.org/3/Y4773E/y4773e00.htm#Contents> accessed 28 March 2022.

Government of Canada, 'Canada's Northern Strategy: Our North, Our Heritage, Our Future' (2009) <https://publications.gc.ca/collections/collection_2009/ainc-inac /R3-72-2008.pdf> accessed 2 November 2024.

Government of Finland, 'Finland's Strategy for the Arctic Region (Prime Minister's Office Publications 8/2010)' (2010) <https://arcticportal.org/images/stories/pdf/J08 10_Finlands.pdf> accessed 14 April 2022.

Government of Finland, 'Finland's Strategy for the Arctic Region 2013 – Government Resolution on 23 August 2013 (Prime Minister's Office Publications 16/2013)' (2013) <https://vnk.fi/documents/10616/1093242/J1613_Finland's+Strategy+for+the+Arctic+Region.pdf/cf80d586-895a-4a32-8582-435f60400fd2?version=1.0> accessed 14 April 2022.

Government of Japan, 'Japan's Arctic Policy (Provisional Translation)' (2015) <https://www8.cao.go.jp/ocean/english/arctic/pdf/japans_ap_e.pdf> accessed 7 April 2022.

Government of Norway, 'Continental Shelf Submission of Norway in Respect of Areas in the Arctic Ocean, the Barents Sea and the Norwegian Sea – Executive Summary' (2006) <https://www.un.org/depts/los/clcs_new/submissions_files/nor06/nor_exec _sum.pdf> accessed 5 December 2021.

Government of Norway, 'Norway's Arctic Policy (Speech of Minister Vidar Helgesen, Brussels, 15 June 2015)' <https://www.regjeringen.no/en/aktuelt/arctic_policy /id2422677/> accessed 4 April 2022.

Gréboval DF, 'International Plan of Action for the Management of Fishing Capacity and Selected Issues Pertaining to Illegal, Unreported and Unregulated Fishing' (2000) <http://www.fao.org/3/y3274e/y3274e0f.htm> accessed 6 August 2020.

Gréboval DF, 'The Measurement and Monitoring of Fishing Capacity: Introduction and Major Considerations' <https://www.fao.org/4/y4849e/y4849e02.htm#fn1> accessed 2 November 2024.

Hart S, 'IUCN Environmental Policy and Law Paper No. 72 – Shared Resources: Issues of Governance' (2008) <https://portals.iucn.org/library/sites/library/files/documents/EPLP-072.pdf> accessed 30 March 2022.

Intergovernmental Panel on Climate Change, 'Climate Change 2007: Synthesis Report – Contribution of Working Groups I, II and III to the Fourth Assessment Report' (2007) <https://www.ipcc.ch/site/assets/uploads/2018/02/ar4_syr_full_report.pdf> accessed 26 March 2020.

Intergovernmental Panel on Climate Change, 'Climate Change 2013: The Physical Science Basis – Contribution of Working Group I to the Fifth Assessment Report of the Intergovernmental Panel on Climate Change' (2013) <https://www.ipcc.ch/site/assets/uploads/2018/02/WG1AR5_all_final.pdf> accessed 4 April 2022.

Intergovernmental Panel on Climate Change, 'Climate Change 2014: Synthesis Report-Summary for Policymakers' (2014) <https://www.ipcc.ch/site/assets/uploads/2018/02/AR5_SYR_FINAL_SPM.pdf> accessed 26 March 2020.

Intergovernmental Panel on Climate Change, 'Special Report 2018: Global Warming of 1.5°C – Summary for Policymakers' (2018) <https://www.ipcc.ch/sr15/chapter/spm/> accessed 8 April 2022.

Intergovernmental Panel on Climate Change, 'Special Report 2019: The Ocean and Cryosphere in a Changing Climate' (2019) <https://www.ipcc.ch/srocc/chapter/summary-for-policymakers/> accessed 4 April 2022.

Intergovernmental Panel on Climate Change, 'Climate Change 2022: Impacts, Adaptation and Vulnerability – Working Group II Contribution to the Sixth Assessment Report ' (2022) <https://www.ipcc.ch/report/ar6/wg2/downloads/report/IPCC_AR6_WGII_SummaryForPolicymakers.pdf> accessed 13 April 2022.

International Commission for the Conservation of Atlantic Tunas, 'Report of the Independent Performance Review of ICCAT' (2009) <https://www.iccat.int/Documents/Other/PERFORM_ REV_TRI_LINGUAL.pdf> accessed 5 December 2021.

International Commission for the Conservation of Atlantic Tunas, 'Basic Texts' (2019) <https://www.iccat.int/documents/commission/basictexts.pdf> accessed 8 April 2022.

International Council for the Exploration of the Sea, 'Minutes from the Meeting of the ICES Science Committee (SCICOM) (8 and 13 September 2019) – ICES CM 2019/SCICOM:02' <www.ices.dkinfo@ices.dk> accessed 23 July 2020.

International Labour Organisation, 'Report of the Committee Set up to Examine the Representation Alleging Non-Observance by Denmark of the Indigenous and Tribal Peoples Convention, 1989 (No. 169), Made under Article 24 of the ILO Constitution' (2001) <https://www.ilo.org/dyn/normlex/en/f?p=1000:50012:0::NO:50012:P50012_COMPLAINT_PROCEDURE_ID,P50012_LANG_CODE:2507219,en:NO> accessed 7 April 2022.

International Law Commission, 'Guide to Practice on Reservations to Treaties' (2011) <https://legal.un.org/ilc/texts/instruments/english/draft_articles/1_8_2011.pdf> accessed 8 April 2022.

International Maritime Organization, 'IMO – What It Is' (2013) <https://wwwcdn.imo.org/localresources/en/About/Documents/What it is Oct 2013_Web.pdf> accessed 8 April 2022.

Inuit Circumpolar Council, 'A Circumpolar Inuit Declaration on Sovereignty in the Arctic' (2009) <https://iccalaska.org/wp-icc/wp-content/uploads/2016/01/Signed-Inuit-Sovereignty-Declaration-11x17.pdf> accessed 7 April 2020.

Inuit Circumpolar Council, 'Inuit Arctic Policy' (2010) <http://library.arcticportal.org/1898/1/g100765_Inuit_Arctic_Policy-June02.pdf> accessed 25 April 2020.

King George the Second, *His Majesty's Royal Charter for Incorporating the Society of the Free British Fishery* (1750) <https://catalog.hathitrust.org/Record/008604519> accessed 2 April 2022.

Lackenbauer PW and Dean R, 'Canada's Northern Strategy under Prime Minister Stephen Harper: Key Speeches and Documents, 2005–15' (2016) <www.sju.ca/cfpf> accessed 13 April 2020.

Larsen JN and Fondahl G, 'Arctic Human Development Report' (2015) <http://urn.kb.se/resolve?urn=urn:nbn:se:norden:org:diva-3809> accessed 5 December 2021.

Løbach T and others, 'FAO Fisheries and Aquaculture Technical Paper 651: Regional Fisheries Management Organizations and Advisory Bodies' (2020) <https://openknowledge.fao.org/server/api/core/bitstreams/ad0cb83d-c3b6-4166-8cb5-958d0dc6a242/content> accessed 11 May 2024.

Mcbride MM and others, 'Joint Norwegian-Russian Environmental Status 2013: Report on the Barents Sea Ecosystem Part II' (2016) <https://www.barentsportal.com/barentsportal/index.php/en/joint-norwegian-russian-environmental-status-2013-report-on-the-barents-sea-ecosystem-part-ii-complete-report-published-2016> accessed 5 December 2021.

McKenzie CH and others, 'ICES Cooperative Research Report No. 335: Alien Species Alert: Didemnum Vexillum Kott, 2002: Invasion, Impact, and Control' (2017) <http://doi.org/10.17895/ices.pub.2138> accessed 20 January 2020.

Ministry of Oceans and Fisheries of the Republic of Korea, 'Policy Framework for the Promotion of Arctic Activities of the Republic of Korea 2018–2022' (2019) <http://www.koreapolarportal.or.kr/data/Policy_Framework_for_the_Promotion_of_Arctic_Activities_of_the_Republic_of_Korea-2018-2022.pdf> accessed 7 April 2022.

Munro GR, Van Houtte A and Willmann R, 'FAO Fisheries Technical Paper 465: The Conservation and Management of Shared Fish Stocks: Legal and Economic Aspects' (2004) <http://www.fao.org/3/y5438e/y5438e00.htm> accessed 9 May 2020.

Nansen Legacy, 'Annual Report' (2019) <https://arvenetternansen.com/wp-content/uploads/2020/06/Nansen-Legacy-AR2019-web.pdf> accessed 22 July 2021.

National Oceanic and Atmospheric Administration, 'Fisheries of the United States Exclusive Economic Zone Off Alaska; Fisheries of the Arctic Management Area; Bering Sea Subarea' (2009) 74 Federal Register 56734 <https://www.federalregister.gov/documents/2009/11/03/E9-26452/fisheries-of-the-united-states-exclusive-economic-zone-off-alaska-fisheries-of-the-arctic-management>.

National Oceanic and Atmospheric Administration, 'Fisheries of the United States Exclusive Economic Zone Off Alaska; Fisheries of the Arctic Management Area; Bering Sea Subarea' (2009) 74 Federal Register 27498 <https://www.govinfo.gov/content/pkg/FR-2009-06-10/pdf/FR-2009-06-10.pdf> accessed 6 April 2021.

National Oceanic and Atmospheric Administration, 'Arctic Report Card 2018: Effects of Persistent Arctic Warming Continue to Mount' (2018) <www.arctic.noaa.gov/Report-Card> accessed 27 March 2020.

National Oceanic and Atmospheric Administration, 'Arctic Report Card 2019: Arctic Ecosystems and Communities Are Increasingly at Risk Due to Continued Warming and Declining Sea Ice' (2019) <www.arctic.noaa.gov/Report-Card> accessed 27 March 2020.

National University of Singapore Centre for International Law, 'Workshop on the "Conservation and Sustainable Use of Marine Biological Diversity of Areas beyond National Jurisdiction: Preparing for the PrepCom" – Executive Summary' (2016) <https://cil.nus.edu.sg/wp-content/uploads/2015/10/BBNJ-Workshop-Executive-Summary-Final.pdf> accessed 2 November 2024.

Natural Resources Defense Council, 'NRDC Is Reviving Our Oceans' (2013) <https://www.nrdc.org/sites/default/files/reviving-our-oceans-FS.pdf> accessed 8 April 2022.

North-East Atlantic Fisheries Commission, 'Procedures and Standards for PECMAS' Consideration of Proposals for Exploratory Fishing Pursuant to Rec. 19:2014 (11 November 2015)' <www.neafc.org> accessed 2 April 2020.

North-East Atlantic Fisheries Commission, 'Proposal by Norway on a Request to ICES to Provide Assessments of the Status of the Ecosystem in a Portion of the High Seas of the Central Arctic Ocean (12–14 November 2019) – AM 2019–44' <https://www.neafc.org/system/files/AM-2019-44_Proposal-by-Norway_Request-to-ICES-assessment-status-of-ecosystem-CAO.pdf> accessed 10 August 2021.

North-East Atlantic Fisheries Commission, 'Statement by the EU Regarding the EU's Contribution to the Implementation of the International Agreement to Prevent Unregulated High Seas Fisheries in the Central Arctic Ocean (12–14 November 2019) – AM 2019–95' <https://www.neafc.org/system/files/AM-2019-95_EU-statement-on-Arctic_Final.pdf> accessed 10 August 2021.

North-East Atlantic Fisheries Commission, 'Memorandum of Understanding between the North-East Atlantic Fisheries Commission and the OSPAR Commission' (2008) <https://www.neafc.org/system/files/opsar_mou.pdf> accessed 2 April 2020.

North-East Atlantic Fisheries Commission, 'Statement Regarding the Conclusion of the Negotiations on the Agreement to Prevent Unregulated High Seas Fisheries in the Central Arctic Ocean' (2018) <https://www.neafc.org/system/files/NEAFC-statement_Central-Arctic-Ocean-Agreement.pdf> accessed 2 April 2022.

North-East Atlantic Fisheries Commission, 'Memorandum of Understanding between the North-East Atlantic Fisheries Commission and the International Council for the Exploration of the Sea' (2019) <https://www.neafc.org/system/files/ices_mou-2019.pdf> accessed 2 April 2020.

North-East Atlantic Fisheries Commission, 'Submission by the North-East Atlantic Fisheries Commission Regarding the Report of the Secretary-General of the United Nations on Oceans and the Law of the Sea, Pursuant to General Assembly Resolution 72/124' (2019) <https://www.neafc.org/compliance.> accessed 2 April 2020.

North Pacific Fishery Management Council, 'Fishery Management Plan for Fish Resources of the Arctic Management Area' (2009) <https://www.npfmc.org/wp-content/PDFdocuments/fmp/Arctic/ArcticFMP.pdf> accessed 5 December 2021.

Northwest Atlantic Fisheries Organization, 'Report of the Working Group on Allocation of Fishing Rights to Contracting Parties of NAFO and Chartering of Vessels Between Contracting Parties (Halifax, 13–15 April 1999)' <https://www.nafo.int/Portals/0/PDFs/gc/1999/GC-99-004.pdf> accessed 6 March 2020.

'Norwegian Directorate of Fisheries | (Utgått) Forskrift Om Forbud Mot Fangst Av Snøkrabbe, J-280-2014 [(Expired) Regulation Concerning Ban of Catching of Snow Crab)]' <https://www.fiskeridir.no/Yrkesfiske/Regelverk-og-reguleringer/J-meldinger/Utgaatte-J-meldinger/J-280-2014> accessed 8 September 2020.

Norwegian Ministries, 'Norway's Arctic Strategy – between Geopolitics and Social Development' (2017) <https://www.regjeringen.no/contentassets/fad46f0404e14b2a9b551ca7359c1000/arctic-strategy.pdf> accessed 13 April 2020.

Norwegian Ministry of Foreign Affairs, 'Decree No. 6 of 1977 Relative to the Fishery Protection Zone of Svalbard' <http://extwprlegs1.fao.org/docs/html/nor12764.htm> accessed 2 March 2021.

Norwegian Ministry of Foreign Affairs, 'The Norwegian Government's High North Strategy' (2006) <https://www.regjeringen.no/globalassets/upload/ud/vedlegg/strategien.pdf> accessed 13 April 2022.

Norwegian Ministry of Foreign Affairs, 'New Building Blocks in the North – The next Step in the Government's High North Strategy' (2009) <https://www.regjeringen.no/globalassets/upload/ud/vedlegg/nordomradene/new_building_blocks_in_the_north.pdf> accessed 22 April 2020.

Norwegian Ministry of Foreign Affairs, 'Norway's Arctic Policy – Creating Value, Managing Resources, Confronting Climate Change and Fostering Knowledge. Developments in the Arctic Concern Us All' (2014) <https://www.regjeringen.no/globalassets/departementene/ud/vedlegg/nord/nordkloden_en.pdf> accessed 13 April 2020.

Norwegian Parliament, 'Skriftlig Spørsmål Fra Helga Pedersen (A) Til Fiskeriministeren [Written Question from Helga Pedersen (A) to the Fisheries Minister]' (2017) <https://www.stortinget.no/no/Saker-og-publikasjoner/Sporsmal/Skriftlige-sporsmal-og-svar/Skriftlig-sporsmal/?qid=68730> accessed 8 September 2020.

Organisation for Economic Co-Operation and Development, 'Strengthening Regional Fisheries Management Organisations' (2009) <https://read.oecd.org/10.1787/9789264073326-en?format=pdf> accessed 31 March 2022.

OSPAR Commission, 'Annual Report 2002–2003, Volume 2' (2003) <https://www.ospar.org/documents?v=6955> accessed 8 April 2022.

Parliament of Iceland Althingi, 'Parliamentary Resolution on Iceland's Arctic Policy (Reykjavík, 28 March 2011)' <http://library.arcticportal.org/1861/> accessed 10 August 2021.

PEW Charitable Trust, 'Reference Points: Measuring Success in Fisheries Management' (2016) <https://www.pewtrusts.org/~/media/assets/2016/09/referencepts_brief_v6.pdf> accessed 19 December 2020.

'Preventing Unregulated Commercial Fishing in the Central Arctic Ocean (CAO) – A Compilation of Reports from Meetings of Experts in Shanghai (China), Incheon (Korea) & Sapporo (Japan)' (2017) <https://oceanconservancy.org/wp-content/uploads/2018/09/Preventing-Unregulated-Commercial-Fishing-CAO.pdf> accessed 23 July 2020.

Protection of the Arctic Marine Environment (PAME) Working Group, 'PAME Factsheet Series 13/18: Central Arctic Ocean LME' (2016) <https://www.pame.is/index.php/document-library/ecosystem-approach-to-management-documents/large-marine-ecosystems/398-13-central-arctic-ocean-lme/file> accessed 12 March 2020.

Protozorkevich D and van der Meeren GI, 'Survey Report from the Joint Norwegian/Russian Ecosystem Survey in the Barents Sea and Adjacent Waters (August-October 2019)' (2020) <https://www.hi.no/resources/IMR-PINRO-Report-2019-survey.pdf> accessed 18 December 2020.

Rabaut M, Cliquet A and Maes F, 'Marine Protected Areas: International Framework, State of the Art, the Belgian Situation' (2004) <https://www.vliz.be/imisdocs/publications/57792.pdf> accessed 12 April 2022.

'Report, SAO Meeting (Ilulissat, 28–29 April 2010)' <https://oaarchive.arctic-council.org/bitstream/handle/11374/979/SAO_report_illulissat_Apr_2010.pdf?sequence=1&isAllowed=y> accessed 12 March 2020.

'Report, SAO Meeting (Narvik, 28–29 November 2007)' <https://oaarchive.arctic-council.org/bitstream/handle/11374/380/ACSAO-NO02_Narvik_FINAL_Report.pdf?sequence=1&isAllowed=y> accessed 11 March 2020.

'Report of the 1st Meeting of the Provisional Scientific Coordinating Group (PSCG) of the Agreement to Prevent Unregulated High Seas Fisheries in the Central Arctic Ocean (Ispra, 11–13 February 2020)' <https://apps-afsc.fisheries.noaa.gov/documents/Arctic_fish_stocks_fifth_meeting/13200_109215706.pdf> accessed 25 March 2022.

'Report of the Fifth FiSCAO Meeting on Central Arctic Ocean Fisheries (Ottawa, 24–26 October 2017)' <https://archive.fisheries.noaa.gov/afsc/Arctic_fish_stocks_fifth_meeting/pdfs/Final_report_of_the_5th_FiSCAO_meeting.pdf> accessed 10 August 2021.

'Report of the First FiSCAO Meeting on Central Arctic Ocean Fisheries (Anchorage, 15–17 June 2011)' <https://archive.fisheries.noaa.gov/afsc/Arctic_fish_stocks_third_meeting/First Meeting Sci Experts Arctic Fisheries 30 Aug 2011.pdf> accessed 10 August 2021.

'Report of the Fourth FiSCAO Meeting on Central Arctic Ocean Fisheries (Tromsø, 26–28 September 2016)' <https://apps-afsc.fisheries.noaa.gov/documents/Arctic_fish_stocks_fourth_meeting/508_Documents/508_FourthFiSCAOreportfinalJan26_2017.pdf> accessed 2 November 2024.

'Report of the Second FiSCAO Meeting on Central Arctic Ocean Fisheries (Tromsø, 28–31 October 2013)' <https://archive.fisheries.noaa.gov/afsc/Arctic_fish_stocks_third_meeting/Report of 2nd Scientific Meeting on Arctic Fish Stocks 28 31 October 2013.pdf> accessed 10 August 2021.

'Report of the Third FiSCAO Meeting on Central Arctic Ocean Fisheries (Seattle, 14–16 April 2015)' <https://www.research.kobe-u.ac.jp/gsics-pcrc/sympo/20151218/documents/03Ocean/03Ocean_03Science2015.pdf> accessed 10 August 2021.

Rice J and others, 'ICES Cooperative Research Report No. 273: Guidance on the Application of the Ecosystem Approach to Management of Human Activities in the European Marine Environment' (2005) <https://www.ices.dk/sites/pub/Publication Reports/Forms/DispForm.aspx?ID=35965> accessed 8 April 2022.

Sparholt H and others, 'Nordic Working Papers: Report of the 1st Working Group Meeting on Optimization of Fishing Pressure in the Northeast Atlantic (Copenhagen, 20–21 June 2017)' (2019) <http://norden.diva-portal.org/smash/get/diva2:1307971/FULLTEXT01.pdf> accessed 12 April 2022.

State Council of the People's Republic of China, 'China's Arctic Policy' (2018) <http://english.www.gov.cn/archive/white_paper/2018/01/26/content_281476026660336.htm> accessed 12 August 2021.

Struzik E, 'Fire and Ice: Arctic Responses to Climate Change and Lessons for the Rest of Canada' (2019) <https://ppforum.ca/wp-content/uploads/2019/06/ArcticResponsesToClimateChangeAndLessonsForTheRest-of-PPF-JUNE2019-EN.pdf> accessed 12 March 2022.

Swan J, 'FAO Fisheries Circular No. 995: Decision-Making in Regional Fishery Bodies or Arrangements: The Evolving Role of RFBs and International Agreement on Decision-Making Processes' (2004) <http://www.fao.org/3/y5357e/y5357e07.htm#bm7> accessed 2 April 2022.

The Center for International Sustainable Development Law (CISDL), 'Legal Working Paper on The Principles of International Law Related to Sustainable Development' (2005) <https://www.cisdl.org/wp-content/uploads/2018/05/International-sustainable-development-law-2002.pdf> accessed 2 November 2024.

The White House, 'Statement of President Biden: Paris Climate Agreement (20 January 2021)' <https://www.whitehouse.gov/briefing-room/statements-releases/2021/01/20/paris-climate-agreement/> accessed 4 October 2021.

The White House, 'United States National Security Presidential Directive NSPD-66 on Arctic Region Policy' (2009) <https://fas.org/irp/offdocs/nspd/nspd-66.htm> accessed 2 April 2022.

The White House, 'National Security Strategy' (2010) <http://unipd-centrodirittiumani.it/public/docs/USA_NSS_2010.pdf> accessed 5 December 2021.

The White House, 'United States National Strategy for the Arctic Region' (2013) <https://obamawhitehouse.archives.gov/sites/default/files/docs/nat_arctic_strategy.pdf> accessed 22 April 2021.

UN Fish Stocks Agreement Review Conference, 'Summary of the Fifth Substantive Session (24 July-4 August 1995): Conservation and Management Gains' (1995) 7 Earth Negotiations Bulletin 54 <https://enb.iisd.org/vol07/0754029e.html> accessed 30 May 2020.

UN Fish Stocks Agreement Review Conference, 'Summary of the Fifth Substantive Session (24 July-4 August 1995): Failings and Set-Backs' (1995) 7 Earth Negotiations Bulletin 54 <https://enb.iisd.org/vol07/0754030e.html> accessed 30 May 2020.

UN Fish Stocks Agreement Review Conference, 'Summary of the Fifth Substantive Session (24 July-4 August 1995): Part II – Conservation and Management of Straddling and Highly Migratory Fish Stocks' (1995) 7 Earth Negotiations Bulletin 54 <https://enb.iisd.org/vol07/0754012e.html> accessed 30 May 2020.

UN Fish Stocks Agreement Review Conference, 'Summary Report of the UN Fish Stocks Agreement Review Conference (22–26 May 2006)' (2006) 7 Earth Negotiations Bulletin 61 <https://enb.iisd.org/events/un-fish-stocks-agreement-review-conference/summary-report-22-26-may-2006> accessed 16 June 2021.

United Nations, 'Fourth Session of the BBNJ Intergovernmental Conference: Letter from the President of the General Assembly (9 March 2020)' <https://www.un.org/bbnj/sites/www.un.org.bbnj/files/bbnj-letter-from-president-of-the-bbnj-conference.pdf> accessed 4 February 2022.

United Nations, 'Letter from the President of the BBNJ Intergovernmental Conference to Delegations (10 September 2020)' <https://www.un.org/bbnj/sites/www.un.org.bbnj/files/intersessional_work_-_bbnj_president_letter_to_delegations.pdf> accessed 11 December 2020.

United Nations, 'Press Release: Indigenous Peoples Must Be Part of High-Level Decision- Making, Speakers Stress, Calling for Observer Status in General Assembly, as Permanent Forum Continues (26 April 2019)' <https://www.un.org/press/en/2019/hr5435.doc.htm> accessed 5 December 2021.

United Nations, 'Report of the World Summit on Sustainable Development (Johannesburg, 26 August-4 September 2002) – A/CONF.199/20' <https://digitallibrary.un.org/record/478154/files/A_CONF.199_20-EN.pdf> accessed 4 April 2022.

United Nations, 'Resumed Review Conference on the Agreement Relating to the Conservation and Management of Straddling Fish Stocks and Highly Migratory Fish Stocks (New York, 24–28 May 2010)' <https://www.un.org/depts/los/convention_agreements/reviewconf/FishStocks_EN_B.pdf> accessed 8 April 2022.

United Nations, 'Secretary General Antonio Guterres: Remarks to High-Level Political Forum on Sustainable Development (24 September 2019)' <https://www.un.org/sg/en/content/sg/speeches/2019-09-24/remarks-high-level-political-sustainable-development-forum> accessed 4 April 2022.

United Nations, 'Updated Programme of the BBNJ Intersessional Work (9 November 2020)' <https://www.un.org/bbnj/fr/node/963> accessed 11 December 2020.

United Nations, 'World Summit on Sustainable Development (Johannesburg, 26 August-4 September 2002), ILA New Delhi Declaration of Principles of International Law Relating to Sustainable Development – A/CONF.199/8' <http://www2.ecolex.org/server2neu.php/libcat/docs/LI/MON-070850.pdf> accessed 30 June 2021.

United Nations, 'World Summit on Sustainable Development (Johannesburg, 26 August–4 September 2002), Plan of Implementation of the World Summit on Sustainable Development – A/CONF.199/L.7' <https://www.un.org/esa/sustdev/documents/WSSD_POI_PD/English/WSSD_PlanImpl.pdf> accessed 4 April 2022.

United Nations, 'Textual Proposals Submitted by Delegations by 20 February 2020, for Consideration at the Fourth Session of the Intergovernmental Conference on an International Legally Binding Instrument under UNCLOS – A/CONF.232/2020/3' (2020) <https://www.un.org/bbnj/sites/www.un.org.bbnj/files/textual_proposals_compilation_article-by-article_-_15_april_2020.pdf> accessed 13 August 2020.

United Nations Conference on Environment and Development, 'Agenda 21 (Rio de Janerio, 3–14 June 1992)' <https://sustainabledevelopment.un.org/content/documents/Agenda21.pdf> accessed 7 April 2022.

United Nations General Assembly, 'Draft Decision: Intergovernmental Conference on an International Legally Binding Instrument under the United Nations Convention on the Law of the Sea (9 June 2021) – A/75/L96' <https://www.undocs.org/en/A/75/L.96> accessed 28 June 2021.

United Nations General Assembly, 'Intergovernmental Conference on an International Legally Binding Instrument under UNCLOS: Statement by the President of the Conference at the Closing of the Third Session (New York, 19–30 August 2019) – A/CONF.232/2019/10' <https://undocs.org/a/conf.232/2019/10> accessed 8 April 2022.

United Nations General Assembly, 'Report of the International Law Commission, Sixty-Sixth Session (5 May–6 June and 7 July–8 August 2014) – A/69/10, Supplement No. 10' <https://documents-dds-ny.un.org/doc/UNDOC/GEN/G14/134/72/PDF/G1413472.pdf?OpenElement> accessed 4 April 2022.

United Nations General Assembly, 'Report of the Resumed Review Conference on the Agreement for the Implementation of UNCLOS Provisions (New York, 23–27 May 2016) – A/CONF.210/2016/5' <https://documents-dds-ny.un.org/doc/UNDOC/GEN/N16/244/06/PDF/N1624406.pdf?OpenElement> accessed 4 April 2022.

United Nations General Assembly, 'Report of the United Nations Conference on Environment and Development (Rio de Janeiro, 3–14 June 1992), Annex I: Rio Declaration on Environment and Development – A/CONF.151/26/Vol.I' <https://www.un.org/en/development/desa/population/migration/generalassembly/docs/globalcompact/A_CONF.151_26_Vol.I_Declaration.pdf> accessed 30 June 2021.

United Nations General Assembly, 'Report on the Work of the United Nations Open-Ended Informal Consultative Process on Oceans and the Law of the Sea at Its Seventh Meeting (17 July 2006) – A/61/156' <https://undocs.org/en/A/61/156> accessed 23 November 2021.

United Nations General Assembly, 'Resolutions and Decisions Adopted by the General Assembly during Its Nineteenth Special Session (23–28 June 1997) – A/S-19/33' <https://undocs.org/A/S-19/33> accessed 30 June 2021.

United Nations General Assembly, 'United Nations Conference on Straddling Fish Stocks and Highly Migratory Fish Stocks, Second Session (New York, 12–30 July 1993), Chairman Statement Held on 12 July 1993 – A/CONF.164/11' <https://documents-dds-ny.un.org/doc/UNDOC/GEN/N93/403/51/pdf/N9340351.pdf?OpenElement> accessed 3 September 2021.

'United Nations General Assembly Resolution 37/7, World Charter for Nature (Adopted 28 October 1982)'.

'United Nations General Assembly Resolution 57/253, World Summit on Sustainable Development (Adopted 20 December 2002)'.

'United Nations General Assembly Resolution 58/14, Sustainable Fisheries (Adopted 24 November 2003)'.

'United Nations General Assembly Resolution 59/25, Sustainable Fisheries (Adopted 17 November 2004)'.

'United Nations General Assembly Resolution 61/222, Oceans and the Law of the Sea (Adopted 20 December 2006)'.

'United Nations General Assembly Resolution 61/295, United Nations Declaration on the Rights of Indigenous Peoples (Adopted 13 September 2007)'.

'United Nations General Assembly Resolution 64/71, Oceans and the Law of the Sea (Adopted 4 December 2009)'.

'United Nations General Assembly Resolution 64/72, Sustainable Fisheries (Adopted 4 December 2009)'.

'United Nations General Assembly Resolution 65/161, Convention on Biological Diversity (Adopted 20 December 2010)'.

'United Nations General Assembly Resolution 69/292, Development of an International Legally Binding Instrument under UNCLOS on the Conservation and Sustainable Use of Marine Biological Diversity of Areas beyond National Jurisdiction (Adopted 19 June 2015)'.

'United Nations General Assembly Resolution 70/1, Transforming Our World: The 2030 Agenda for Sustainable Development (Adopted 25 September 2015)'.

'United Nations General Assembly Resolution 72/249, International Legally Binding Instrument under UNCLOS on the Conservation and Sustainable Use of Marine Biological Diversity of Areas beyond National Jurisdiction (Adopted 24 December 2017)'.

'United Nations General Assembly Resolution 73/125, Sustainable Fisheries (Adopted 11 December 2018)'.

'United Nations General Assembly Resolution 74/18, Sustainable Fisheries (Adopted 10 December 2019)'.

'United Nations General Assembly Resolution 74/19, Oceans and the Law of the Sea (Adopted 10 December 2019)'.

'United Nations General Assembly Resolution 76/71, Sustainable Fisheries (Adopted 9 December 2021)'.

'United Nations General Assembly Resolution ES-11/1, Aggression against Ukraine (Adopted 2 March 2022)'.

United Nations General Assmebly, 'Official Records of the 56th Plenary Meeting (New York, 4 December 2009) – A/64/PV.56' <https://digitallibrary.un.org/record/672710/files/A_64_PV.56-EN.pdf>.

United Nations Office for Ocean Affairs and the Law of the Sea, 'The Law of the Sea: Baselines: National Legislation With Illustrative Maps' (1989) <https://www.un.org/depts/los/LEGISLATIONANDTREATIES/PDFFILES/publications/E.89.V.10.pdf> accessed 29 March 2021.

United Nations Office of Legal Affairs, 'Comments on Some Procedural Questions' (2009) <https://legal.un.org/ola/media/GA_RoP/GA_RoP_EN.pdf> accessed 18 June 2021.

United Nations Office of the High Commissioner for Human Rights, 'CCPR General Comment No. 23: Article 27 (Rights of Minorities), (8 April 1994) – CCPR/C/21/Rev.1/Add.5' <https://www.refworld.org/docid/453883fc0.html> accessed 8 April 2022.

United Nations Office of the High Commissioner for Human Rights, 'Leaflet No. 10: Indigenous Peoples and the Environment' (2008) <https://www.ohchr.org/Documents/Publications/GuideIPleaflet10en.pdf> accessed 6 April 2020.

United Nations System Task Team, 'Thematic Think Piece on the Post-2015 UN Development Agenda: Global Governance and Governance of the Global Commons in the Global Partnership for Development beyond 2015' (2013) <https://www.un.org/en/development/desa/policy/untaskteam_undf/thinkpieces/24_thinkpiece_global_governance.pdf> accessed 1 September 2021.

United States Congress, 'Senate Joint Resolution No.17 (4 October 2007) – 122 STAT. 1569' <https://www.congress.gov/bill/110th-congress/senate-joint-resolution/17/text> accessed 8 April 2022.

United States Department of State, 'Joint Statement on Arctic Council Cooperation Following Russia's Invasion of Ukraine (3 March 2022)' <https://www.state.gov/joint-statement-on-arctic-council-cooperation-following-russias-invasion-of-ukraine/> accessed 25 March 2022.

United States Department of State, 'Public Notice 2237: Exclusive Economic Zone and Maritime Boundaries; Notice of Limits' (1995) 60 Federal Register 43825 <https://www.govinfo.gov/content/pkg/FR-1995-08-23/pdf/95-20794.pdf> accessed 28 March 2021.

United States National Archives, 'Ronald Reagan: Statement on United States Oceans Policy (10 March 1983)' <https://www.reaganlibrary.gov/archives/speech/statement-united-states-oceans-policy> accessed 8 April 2022.

United States National Research Council and Polar Research Board, 'Lessons and Legacies of International Polar Year 2007–2008' (2012) <https://ebookcentral-1proquest-1com-1008395e10318.emedia1.bsb-muenchen.de/lib/bsb/detail.action?docID=3564278#> accessed 24 March 2022.

United States Office of Technology Assessment, 'Nuclear Wastes in the Arctic: An Analysis of Arctic and Other Regional Impacts From Soviet Nuclear Contamination – OTA-ENV-632' (1995) <https://digital.library.unt.edu/ark:/67531/metadc39768/m2/1/high_res_d/9504.pdf> accessed 20 February 2020.

United States Senate, 'Hearing: Defending U.S. Economic Interests in the Changing Arctic: Is There a Strategy? (112. Congress, First Session, 27 July 2011)' <https://www.govinfo.gov/content/pkg/CHRG-112shrg72568/pdf/CHRG-112shrg72568.pdf> accessed 10 December 2021.

Walday M, 'European Environment Agency: Europe's Biodiversity – Biogeographical Regions and Seas: The Arctic Ocean' (2008) <https://www.eea.europa.eu/publications/report_2002_0524_154909/regional-seas-around-europe/arctic_ocean.pdf/view> accessed 4 April 2022.

World Commission on Environment and Development, 'Report: Our Common Future' (1987) <http://www.un-documents.net/our-common-future.pdf> accessed 6 April 2022.

World Commission on the Ethics of Scientific Knowledge and Technology, 'The Precautionary Principle' (2005) <https://unesdoc.unesco.org/ark:/48223/pf0000139578> accessed 4 April 2022.

World Trade Organization, 'European Communities – Measures Affecting the Approval and Marketing of Biotech Products – Reports of the Panel (29 September 2006)–WT/DS291-293/R'<https://www.worldtradelaw.net/document.php?id=reports/wtopanels/ec-biotech(panel).pdf&mode=download> accessed 17 December 2021.

World Trade Organization, 'Report of the Appellate Body: United States – Prohibition of Certain Shrimp and Shrimp Products (12 October 1998) – WT/DS58/AB/R' <https://docs.wto.org/dol2fe/Pages/FE_Search/FE_S_S009-DP.aspx?language=E&CatalogueIdList=58544&CurrentCatalogueIdIndex=0&FullTextSearch=> accessed 6 April 2021.

Books

Balton DA, 'The Bering Sea Doughnut Hole Convention: Regional Solution, Global Implications' in Olav Schram Stokke (ed), *Governing High Seas Fisheries: The Interplay of Global and Regional Regimes* (Oxford University Press 2001).

Balton DA, 'Considering Future Arctic Fisheries' in Myron H Nordquist, Tomas H Heidar and John Norton Moore (eds), *Changes in the Arctic Environment and the Law of the Sea* (Martinus Nijhoff Publishers 2010).

Balton DA, 'Implementing the New Arctic Fisheries Agreement' in Tomas Heidar (ed), *New Knowledge and Changing Circumstances in the Law of the Sea* (Brill | Nijhoff 2020).

Bjørndal T and Munro G, *The Economics and Management of World Fisheries* (Oxford University Press 2012).

Bodansky D, *The Art and Craft of International Environmental Law* (Harvard University Press 2010).

Caddell R, Leloudas G and Soyer B, 'Emerging Regulatory Responses to IUU Fishing' in Richard Caddell and Erik J Molenaar (eds), *Strengthening International Fisheries Law in an Era of Changing Oceans* (Hart Publishing 2019).

Cheung WW and others, 'Modelling Future Oceans: The Present and Emerging Future of Fish Stocks and Fisheries' in Richard Caddell and Erik J Molenaar (eds), *Strengthening International Fisheries Law in an Era of Changing Oceans* (Hart Publishing 2019).

Chircop A, 'The Use of IMO Instruments for Marine Conservation on the High Seas' in Robert C Beckman and others (eds), *High Seas Governance: Gaps and Challenges* (Brill | Nijhoff 2019).

Churchill R, 'The LOSC Regime for Protection of the Marine Environment-Fit for the Twenty-First Century?' in Rosemary Rayfuse (ed), *Research Handbook on International Marine Environmental Law* (Edward Elgar Publishing 2015).

Churchill R, 'International Trade Law Aspects of Measures to Combat IUU and Unsustainable Fishing' in Richard Caddell and Erik J Molenaar (eds), *Strengthening International Fisheries Law in an Era of Changing Oceans* (Hart Publishing 2019).

Churchill RR and Lowe AV, *The Law of the Sea* (3rd edn, Manchester University Press 1999).

Crawford J, *Brownlie's Principles of Public International Law* (9th edn, Oxford University Press 2019).

de Sadeleer N, *Environmental Principles: From Political Slogans to Legal Rules* (2nd edn, Oxford University Press 2020).

Diz Pereira Pinto D, 'Fisheries Management in Areas beyond National Jurisdiction' in David Freestone (ed), *Legal Aspects of Sustainable Development* (13th edn, Brill | Nijhoff 2012).

Eckart C, *Promises of States under International Law* (Hart Publishing 2012) <https://books.google.de/books?id=HY56BAAAQBAJ&dq=formal+notification+international+law&hl=de&source=gbs_navlinks_s> accessed 10 July 2020.

Enright SR and Boteler B, 'The Ecosystem Approach in International Marine Environmental Law and Governance' in TG O'Higgins, Manuel Lago and Theodore H DeWitt (eds), *Ecosystem-Based Management, Ecosystem Services and Aquatic Biodiversity* (Springer 2020) <https://doi.org/10.1007/978-3-030-45843-0_17> accessed 23 November 2020.

Errico S, 'The Controversial Issue of Natural Resources: Balancing States' Sovereignty with Indigenous Peoples' Rights' in Stephen Allen and Alexandra Xanthaki (eds), *Reflections on the UN Declaration on the Rights of Indigenous Peoples* (Hart Publishing 2011).

Fedyakov VV. and Naumov AD, 'Marine Bivalvia of the Arctic Ocean' in Yvonne Herman (ed), *The Arctic Seas* (Springer US 1989).

Feenstra R, *Hugo Grotius Mare Liberum 1609–2009 – Original Latin Text and English Translation* (Brill | Nijhoff 2009) <https://brill.com/view/title/16983> accessed 8 July 2020.

Frischmann BM, Madison MJ and Strandburg KJ, *Governing Knowledge Commons* (Oxford University Press 2014).

Grabs J, *Selling Sustainability Short?* (Cambridge University Press 2020).

Grotius H, *Mare Liberum: Sive de Iure Quod Batavis Competit Ad Indicana Commercia Dissertatio* (Lodewijk Elzevir 1609).

Guilfoyle D, 'Article 87 – Freedom of the High Seas' in Alexander Proelß (ed), *United Nations Convention on the Law of the Sea: A Commentary* (Nomos 2017).

Hansen HSB, 'The Challenging Barents Sea Snow Crab' in Svein Rottem and Ida Soltvedt (eds), *Arctic Governance Volume 2: Energy, Living Marine Resources and Shipping* (IB Tauris 2018).

Harrison J and Morgera E, 'Article 63 – Stocks Occurring within the Exclusive Economic Zones of Two or More Coastal States or Both within the Exclusive Economic Zone and in an Area beyond and Adjacent to It' in Alexander Proelß (ed), *United Nations Convention on the Law of the Sea: A Commentary* (Nomos 2017).

Heidar T, 'The Legal Framework for High Seas Fisheries in the Central Arctic Ocean' in Myron H Nordquist, John Norton Moore and Ronán Long (eds), *International Marine Economy: Law and Policy*, vol 20 (Brill | Nijhoff 2017).

Heininen L, 'Northern Geopolitics: Actors, Interests and Processes in the Circumpolar Arctic' in Richard C Powell and Klaus Dodds (eds), *Polar Geopolitics?: Knowledge, Resources and Legal Regimes* (Edward Elgar Publishing 2014).

Henriksen T, Hønneland G and Sydnes A, *Law and Politics in Ocean Governance-The UN Fish Stocks Agreement and Regional Fisheries Management Regimes* (Brill | Nijhoff 2006).

Hince B, *The Antarctic Dictionary: A Complete Guide to Antarctic English* (CSIRO Publishing 2000) <https://books.google.de/books?id=upcoFJXWT38C&hl=de> accessed 2 September 2020.

Hong S-Y and Van Dyke JM, 'Publications on Ocean Development' in Jon M Van Dyke (ed), *Maritime Boundary Disputes, Settlement Processes, and the Law of the Sea* (Brill | Nijhoff 2009).

Huntington HP and others, 'A New Perspective on Changing Arctic Marine Ecosystems: Panarchy Adaptive Cycles in Pan-Arctic Spatial and Temporal Scales' in Salvatore Aricò (ed), *Ocean Sustainability in the 21st Century* (Cambridge University Press 2015).

Inuit Circumpolar Conference, *Principles and Elements for a Comprehensive Arctic Policy* (Centre for Northern Studies and Research 1992).

Keohane RO, *After Hegemony: Cooperation and Discord in the World Political Economy* (Princeton University Press 1984).

Keskitalo ECH, Koivurova T and Bankes N, 'Climate Governance in the Arctic: Introduction and Theoretical Framework' in Timo Koivurova, E Carina H Keskitalo and Nigel Bankes (eds), *Climate Governance in the Arctic* (Springer 2009).

Khan D-E, 'The International Ice Patrol' in Stefan Lorenzmeier and Hans-Peter Folz (eds), *Recht und Realität* (Nomos 2017).

Knox-Hayes J, *The Cultures of Markets: The Political Economy of Climate Governance* (Oxford University Press 2016).

Lagoni R, 'Preamble' in Alexander Proelß (ed), *United Nations Convention on the Law of the Sea: A Commentary* (Nomos 2017).

Lalonde S, 'Donat Pharand – The Arctic Scholar' in Suzanne Lalonde and Ted L McDorman (eds), *International Law and Politics of the Arctic Ocean: Essays in Honor of Donat Pharand*, vol 44 (Brill | Nijhoff 2015).

Lang W, 'Regimes and Organizations in the Labyrinth of International Institutions' in Karl Zemanek and Konrad Ginther (eds), *Völkerrecht zwischen normativem Anspruch und politischer Realität: Festschrift für Karl Zemanek zum 65. Geburtstag* (Duncker & Humblot 1994).

Lodge MW and others, 'Recommended Best Practices for Regional Fisheries Management Organizations – Report of an Independent Panel to Develop a Model for Improved Governance by Regional Fisheries Management Organizations' (Chatham House 2007) <https://repository.oceanbestpractices.org/bitstream/handle/11329/1456/39374297.pdf?sequence=1&isAllowed=y> accessed 2 November 2024.

Longo SB, Clausen R and Clark B, 'Healing the Rifts', *The tragedy of the commodity: Oceans, fisheries, and aquaculture* (Rutgers University Press 2015).

Longo SB, 'Sea Change', *The tragedy of the commodity: Oceans, fisheries, and aquaculture* (Rutgers University Press 2015).

Massarella C, 'Ensuring Compliance with Fisheries Regulations by Private Actors' in Richard Caddell and Erik J Molenaar (eds), *Strengthening International Fisheries Law in an Era of Changing Oceans* (Hart Publishing 2019).

Matley H, 'Developments in International Fisheries Law and Their Contribution to Improving the Effectiveness of RFMOs and Other Environmental Regimes' in Neil Craik and others (eds), *Global Environmental Change and Innovation in International Law* (Cambridge University Press 2018).

Molenaar EJ, 'Climate Change and Arctic Fisheries' in E Carina H Keskitalo, Timo Koivurova and Nigel Bankes (eds), *Climate Governance in the Arctic* (Springer 2009).

Molenaar EJ, 'Arctic Fisheries Management' in Erik J Molenaar, Alex G Oude Elferink and Donald R Rothwell (eds), *The Law of the Sea and the Polar Regions: Interactions between global and regional regimes* (Koninklijke Brill NV 2013).

Molenaar EJ, 'International Regulation of Central Arctic Ocean Fisheries' in Myron H Nordquist, John Norton Moore and Ronán Long (eds), *Challenges of the Changing Arctic: Continental Shelf, Navigation, and Fisheries* (Brill | Nijhoff 2016).

Molenaar EJ, 'Participation in the Central Arctic Ocean Fisheries Agreement' in Akiho Shibata and others (eds), *Emerging Legal Orders in the Arctic-The Role of Non-Arctic Actors* (Routledge 2019).

Molenaar EJ, 'Participation in Regional Fisheries Management Organizations' in Richard Caddell and Erik J Molenaar (eds), *Strengthening International Fisheries Law in an Era of Changing Oceans* (Hart Publishing 2019).

Molenaar EJ, 'The CAOF Agreement: Key Issues of International Fisheries Law' in Tomas Heidar (ed), *New Knowledge and Changing Circumstances in the Law of the Sea* (Brill | Nijhoff 2020).

Molenaar EJ and Caddell R, 'Options and Pathways to Strengthen International Fisheries Law in an Era of Changing Oceans', *Strengthening International Fisheries Law in an Era of Changing Oceans* (Hart Publishing 2019).

Nuttall M, Christensen TR and Siegert M, *The Routledge Handbook of the Polar Regions* (Routledge 2018).

Orrego Vicuña F, *The Changing International Law of High Seas Fisheries* (Cambridge University Press 1999).

Ostrom E and Hess C, *Understanding Knowledge As a Commons: From Theory to Practice* (MIT Press 2006).

Philippe Sands, *Principles of International Environmental Law* (4th edn, Cambridge University Press 2018).

Powell RC and Dodds K, *Polar Geopolitics?: Knowledges, Resources and Legal Regimes* (Edward Elgar Publishing 2014).

Proelß A, 'Prinzipien Des Internationalen Umweltrechts' in Alexander Proelß (ed), *Internationales Umweltrecht* (De Gruyter 2017).

Rayfuse R, 'Article 118 – Cooperation of States in the Conservation and Management of Living Resources' in Alexander Proelß (ed), *United Nations Convention on the Law of the Sea: A Commentary* (Nomos 2017).

Rayfuse R, 'Regulating Fisheries in the Central Arctic Ocean: Much Ado About Nothing?' in Niels Vestergaard and others (eds), *Arctic Marine Resource Governance and Development* (Springer 2018).

Rayfuse R, 'Addressing Climate Change Impacts in Regional Fisheries Management Organizations', *Strengthening International Fisheries Law in an Era of Changing Oceans* (Hart Publishing 2019).

Rossi CR, 'Conclusions on the Future of the Global Commons', *Sovereignty and Territorial Temptation–The Grotian Tendency* (Cambridge University Press 2017).

Rossi CR, 'Problems of Governance: The Arctic and the Club Within the Club', *Sovereignty and Territorial Temptation–The Grotian Tendency* (Cambridge University Press 2017).

Rossi CR, 'Terra Nullius and the "unique" International Problem of Svalbard', *Sovereignty and Territorial Temptation–The Grotian Tendency* (Cambridge University Press 2017).

Rossi CR, 'Tradition, Tendency, Temptation', *Sovereignty and Territorial Temptation–The Grotian Tendency* (Cambridge University Press 2017).

Schönfeldt K, *The Arctic in International Law and Policy* (Hart Publishing 2017).

Schram Stokke O, *Disaggregating International Regimes: A New Approach to Evaluation and Comparison* (MIT Press 2012).

Schrijver N, *The Evolution of Sustainable Development in International Law: Inception, Meaning and Status* (Martinus Nijhoff 2008).

Serdy A, 'Quota Trading in International Fisheries Commissions: An Idea Whose Time Has Come?', *The New Entrants Problem in International Fisheries Law* (Cambridge University Press 2016).

Serdy A, 'The Bioeconomics of High Seas Fishing: New Entrants and the Tragedy of the Commons', *The New Entrants Problem in International Fisheries Law* (Cambridge University Press 2016).

Serdy A, *The New Entrants Problem in International Fisheries Law* (Cambridge University Press 2016).

Stein AA, *Why Nations Cooperate: Circumstance and Choice in International Relations* (Cornell University Press 1990).

Stephens T, 'International Courts and Environmental Governance', *International courts and environmental protection* (Cambridge University Press 2009).

Stokke OS, 'Management Options for High Seas Fisheries: Making Regime Complexes More Effective' in Richard Caddell and Erik Jaap Molenaar (eds), *Strengthening International Fisheries Law in an Era of Changing Oceans* (Hart Publishing 2019).

Takei Y, *Filling Regulatory Gaps in High Seas Fisheries: Discrete High Seas Fish Stocks, Deep-Sea Fisheries, and Vulnerable Marine Ecosystems* (Brill | Nijhoff 2013).

Tanaka Y, *The International Law of the Sea* (Cambridge University Press 2015).

Tang J, 'Conservation of Marine Living Resources in the Central Arctic Ocean: Five Arctic Coastal States' Initiatives' in Myron H Nordquist, John Norton Moore and Ronán Long (eds), *International Marine Economy: Law and Policy*, vol 20 (Brill | Nijhoff 2017).

Van Dyke JM, 'The Evolution and International Acceptance of the Precautionary Principle' in David D Caron and Harry N Scheiber (eds), *Bringing New Law to Ocean Waters* (Brill | Nijhoff 2004).

Van Ittersum JM, 'Hugo Grotius: The Making of a Founding Father of International Law' in Anne Orford and Florian Hoffmann (eds), *The Oxford Handbook of the Theory of International Law* (Oxford University Press 2016).

Weidemann L, *International Governance of the Arctic Marine Environment* (Springer 2014).

Journals

Alcantara C and Nelles J, 'Indigenous Peoples and the State in Settler Societies: Toward a More Robust Definition of Multilevel Governance' (2014) 44 Publius 183

<https://www-1jstor-1org-10011f5v4013e.emedia1.bsb-muenchen.de/stable/pdf/24734623.pdf?refreqid=excelsior%3Acb3701da0966b67d783128373c9ae7c9> accessed 10 August 2021.

Alvain S and others, 'Rapid Climatic Driven Shifts of Diatoms at High Latitudes' (2013) 132 Remote Sensing of Environment 195 <http://dx.doi.org/10.1016/j.rse.2013.01.014> accessed 10 August 2021.

Aqorau T, 'Illegal Fishing and Fisheries Law Enforcement in Small Island Developing States: The Pacific Islands Experience' (2000) 15 International Journal of Marine and Coastal Law 37 <https://brill-com.emedien.ub.uni-muenchen.de/view/journals/estu/15/1/article-p37_2.xml> accessed 3 July 2020.

Årthun M, Eldevik T and Smedsrud LH, 'The Role of Atlantic Heat Transport in Future Arctic Winter Sea Ice Loss' (2019) 32 Journal of Climate 3327 < https://journals.ametsoc.org/view/journals/clim/32/11/jcli-d-18-0750.1.xml> accessed 2 November 2024.

Balton DA, 'Strengthening the Law of the Sea: The New Agreement on Straddling Fish Stocks and Highly Migratory Fish Stocks' (1996) 27 Ocean Development & International Law 125 <https://www.tandfonline.com/doi/abs/10.1080/00908329609546078> accessed 10 August 2021.

Barnes RA, 'International Regulation of Fisheries Management in Arctic Waters' (2011) 54 German Yearbook of International Law 193 <https://papers.ssrn.com/sol3/papers.cfm?abstract_id=3676485> accessed 2 November 2024.

Barnes RA, 'The Capacity of Property Rights to Accommodate Social-Ecological Resilience' (2013) 18 Ecology and Society 6 <http://www.ecologyandsociety.org/vol18/iss1/art6/> accessed 10 August 2021.

'Besitzergreifung von Spitzbergen (Svalbard) Durch Norwegen' (1925) 31 Geographische Zeitschrift 300 <https://www.jstor.org/stable/27811470?seq=4#metadata_info_tab_contents> accessed 10 August 2021.

Block BA and others, 'Tracking Apex Marine Predator Movements in a Dynamic Ocean' (2011) 475 Nature 86 <http://dx.doi.org/10.1038/nature10082> accessed 10 August 2021.

Brady AM, 'China's Rise in Antarctica?' (2010) 50 Asian Survey 759 <https://www.jstor.org/stable/10.1525/as.2010.50.4.759> accessed 25 March 2022.

Caddell R, 'Precautionary Management and the Development of Future Fishing Opportunities: The International Regulation of New and Exploratory Fisheries' (2018) 33 International Journal of Marine and Coastal Law 199 <https://brill.com/view/journals/estu/33/1/article-p199_199.xml?language=en> accessed 10 August 2021.

Calizza E, Costantini ML and Rossi L, 'Effect of Multiple Disturbances on Food Web Vulnerability to Biodiversity Loss in Detritus-Based Systems' (2015) 6 Ecosphere 1 <http://doi.wiley.com/10.1890/ES14-00489.1> accessed 10 August 2021.

Chachamovich E and others, 'Suicide Among Inuit: Results From a Large, Epidemiologically Representative Follow-Back Study in Nunavut' (2015) 60 Canadian Journal of Psychiatry 268.

Chan FT and others, 'Climate Change Opens New Frontiers for Marine Species in the Arctic: Current Trends and Future Invasion Risks' (2019) 25 Global Change Biology 25 <https://onlinelibrary.wiley.com/doi/abs/10.1111/gcb.14469> accessed 12 August 2021.

Christiansen JS, Mecklenburg CW and Karamushko OV., 'Arctic Marine Fishes and Their Fisheries in Light of Global Change' (2014) 20 Global Change Biology 352 <https://onlinelibrary.wiley.com/doi/full/10.1111/gcb.12395> accessed 12 August 2021.

Chu C, Mandrak NE and Minns CK, 'Potential Impacts of Climate Change on the Distributions of Several Common and Rare Freshwater Fishes in Canada' (2005) 11 Diversity and Distributions 299 <http://doi.wiley.com/10.1111/j.1366-9516.2005.00153.x> accessed 12 August 2021.

Conde Pérez E and Yaneva ZV, 'The European Arctic Policy in Progress' (2016) 10 Polar Science 441 <https://linkinghub.elsevier.com/retrieve/pii/S1873965216300536> accessed 12 August 2021.

Cook E and others, 'Marine Biosecurity: Protecting Indigenous Marine Species' (2016) 5 Research and Reports in Biodiversity Studies 1 <https://www.researchgate.net/publication/290474067_Marine_biosecurity_protecting_indigenous_marine_species> accessed 12 August 2021.

Copeland BR and Taylor MS, 'Free Trade and Global Warming: A Trade Theory View of the Kyoto Protocol' (2005) 49 Journal of Environmental Economics and Management 205 <https://www.sciencedirect.com/science/article/abs/pii/S0095069604000737> accessed 12 August 2021.

Craik N, 'The Duty to Cooperate in the Customary Law of Environmental Impact Assessment' (2020) 69 International and Comparative Law Quarterly 239 <https://www.cambridge.org/core/journals/international-and-comparative-law-quarterly/article/abs/duty-to-cooperate-in-the-customary-law-of-environmental-impact-assessment/AB1F146A96DB6DAE9B38DE669E20ADCE> accessed 12 August 2021.

Crawford A and others, 'Arctic Open-Water Periods Are Projected to Lengthen Dramatically by 2100' (2021) 2 Communications Earth & Environment 1 <https://doi.org/10.1038/s43247-021-00183-x> accessed 12 August 2021.

Cullis-Suzuki S and Pauly D, 'Failing the High Seas: A Global Evaluation of Regional Fisheries Management Organizations' (2010) 34 Marine Policy 1036 <https://www.sciencedirect.com/science/article/abs/pii/S0308597X10000540>accessed12August 2021.

Cunningham S, Bennear LS and Smith MD, 'Spillovers in Regional Fisheries Management: Do Catch Shares Cause Leakage?' (2016) 92 Land Economics 344

<https://papers.ssrn.com/sol3/papers.cfm?abstract_id=2467161> accessed 12 August 2021.

Daly HE, 'Economics in a Full World' (2005) 293 Scientific American 100 <https://www.jstor.org/stable/10.2307/26061149> accessed 4 April 2022.

Dannenberg A, Lumkowsky M, Carlton EK and Victor DG, 'Naming and shaming as a strategy for enforcing the Paris Agreement: The role of political institutions and public concern' (2023) 120 Proceedings of the National Academy of Sciences of the United States of America 40 <https://www.pnas.org/doi/epdf/10.1073/pnas.2305075120> accessed 28 April 2024.

De Lucia V, 'The Question of the Common Heritage of Mankind and the Negotiations Towards a Global Treaty on Marine Biodiversity in Areas Beyond National Jurisdiction: No End in Sight?' (2020) 16 McGil International Journal of Sustainable Development Law & Policy 138 <https://www.ssrn.com/abstract=3542384> accessed 17 January 2022.

de Rivera CE and others, 'Potential for High-Latitude Marine Invasions along Western North America' (2011) 17 Diversity and Distributions 1198 <http://doi.wiley.com/10.1111/j.1472-4642.2011.00790.x> accessed 20 January 2020.

Dickson B and others, 'Rapid Freshening of the Deep North Atlantic Ocean over the Past Four Decades' (2002) 416 Nature 832 <http://www.nature.com/articles/416832a> accessed 17 January 2022.

Diz D and others, 'Summary of the Resumed Review Conference of the UN Fish Stocks Agreement (24–28 May 2010)' (2010) 7 Earth Negotiations Bulletin 65 <http://www.iisd.ca/oceans/rfsaic/> accessed 30 May 2020.

Dodds K, 'The Ilulissat Declaration (2008): The Arctic States, "Law of the Sea," and Arctic Ocean' (2013) 33 SAIS Review of International Affairs 45.

Drinkwater KF, Mueter FJ and Saitoh S-I, 'Shifting Boundaries of Water, Ice, Flora, Fauna, People, and Institutions in the Arctic and Subarctic' (2017) 75 ICES Journal of Marine Science 2293 <https://academic.oup.com/icesjms/article-abstract/75/7/2293/5256682> accessed 15 January 2020.

Duff JA, 'The United States And The Law Of The Sea Convention: Sliding Back From Accession And Ratification' (2005) 11 Ocean and Coastal Law Journal 1 <https://digitalcommons.mainelaw.maine.edu/oclj/vol11/iss1/2/> accessed 2 November 2024.

Edelist D and others, 'Restructuring the Sea: Profound Shifts in the World's Most Invaded Marine Ecosystem' (2013) 19 Diversity and Distributions 69.

Fogarty MJ and Collie JS, 'Fisheries Overview' (2009) 2 Encyclopedia of Ocean Sciences 499 <https://www.sciencedirect.com/science/article/pii/B9780123744739007487> accessed 27 May 2020.

Frischmann BM, Marciano A and Ramello GB, 'Retrospectives: Tragedy of the Commons after 50 Years' (2019) 33 Journal of Economic Perspectives 211.

Fulton EA and others, 'An Integrated Approach Is Needed for Ecosystem Based Fisheries Management: Insights from Ecosystem-Level Management Strategy Evaluation' (2014) 9 PLOS ONE 1 <https://journals.plos.org/plosone/article?id=10.1371/journal.pone.0084242> accessed 14 July 2020.

Giunta A, 'Looking Back to Move Forward: The Status of Environmental Rights under the UN Declaration on the Rights of Indigenous Peoples' (2019) 23 International Journal of Human Rights 149.

Gjerde KM, Clark NA and Harden-Davies HR, 'Building a Platform for the Future: The Relationship of the Expected New Agreement for Marine Biodiversity in Areas beyond National Jurisdiction and the UN Convention on the Law of the Sea' (2019) 33 Ocean Yearbook Online 3 <https://brill.com/view/journals/ocyo/33/1/article-p1_1.xml> accessed 5 December 2021.

Gollier C and Treich N, 'Decision-Making Under Scientific Uncertainty: The Economics of the Precautionary Principle' (2003) 27 The Journal of Risk and Uncertainty 77.

Goodman C, 'The Regime for Flag State Responsibility in International Fisheries Law – Effective Fact, Creative Fiction, or Further Work Required?' (2009) 23 Australian and New Zealand Maritime Law Journal 157.

Goodsite ME and others, 'The Role of Science Diplomacy: A Historical Development and International Legal Framework of Arctic Research Stations under Conditions of Climate Change, Post-Cold War Geopolitics and Globalization/Power Transition' (2016) 6 Journal of Environmental Studies and Sciences 645 <https://link-springer-com.emedien.ub.uni-muenchen.de/article/10.1007/s13412-015-0329-6> accessed 25 March 2022.

Gragl P and Fitzmaurice M, 'The Legal Character of Article 18 of the Vienna Convention on the Law of Treaties' (2019) 68 International & Comparative Law Quarterly 699 <https://www.cambridge.org/core/journals/international-and-comparative-law-quarterly/article/abs/legal-character-of-article-18-of-the-vienna-convention-on-the-law-of-treaties/C5B1C5E68EF8DE46E348371271A9B589#access-block> accessed 5 December 2024.

Hahn RW and Richards KR, 'The Internationalization of Environmental Regulation' (1989) 30 Harvard International Law Journal 421.

Haimbaugh GD, 'Impact of the Reagan Administration on the Law of the Sea' (1989) 46 Washington and Lee Law Review 151 <https://scholarlycommons.law.wlu.edu/wlulr/vol46/iss1/6> accessed 30 April 2020.

Häkkinen S and Rhines PB, 'Decline of Subpolar North Atlantic Circulation during the 1990s' (2004) 304 Science 555 <https://www-jstor-org.emedien.ub.uni-muenchen.de/stable/3836715?seq=1#metadata_info_tab_contents> accessed 7 September 2020.

Hansen B, Turrell WR and Østerhus S, 'Decreasing Overflow from the Nordic Seas into the Atlantic Ocean through the Faroe Bank Channel since 1950' (2001) 411 Nature 927 <http://www.nature.com/articles/35082034> accessed 7 September 2020.

Hansen HSB, 'Three Major Challenges in Managing Non-Native Sedentary Barents Sea Snow Crab (Chionoecetes Opilio)' (2016) 71 Marine Policy 38 <http://dx.doi.org/10.1016/j.marpol.2016.05.013> accessed 5 December 2021.

Harada N, 'Review: Potential Catastrophic Reduction of Sea Ice in the Western Arctic Ocean: Its Impact on Biogeochemical Cycles and Marine Ecosystems' (2016) 136 Global and Planetary Change 1 <http://dx.doi.org/10.1016/j.gloplacha.2015.11.005> accessed 5 December 2021.

Hardin G, 'The Tragedy of the Commons' (1968) 162 Science 1243.

Haug T and others, 'Future Harvest of Living Resources in the Arctic Ocean North of the Nordic and Barents Seas: A Review of Possibilities and Constraints' (2017) 188 Fisheries Research 38 <https://linkinghub.elsevier.com/retrieve/pii/S0165783616304131> accessed 5 December 2021.

Hawkings JR and others, 'Large Subglacial Source of Mercury from the Southwestern Margin of the Greenland Ice Sheet' (2021) 14 Nature Geoscience 496 <http://www.nature.com/articles/s41561-021-00753-w> accessed 26 May 2021.

Helfer LR, 'Exiting Treaties' (2005) 91 Virginia Law Review 1579.

Hoberg EP and others, 'Arctic Biodiversity: From Discovery to Faunal Baselines – Revealing the History of a Dynamic Ecosystem' (2003) 89 Journal of Parasitology 84 <https://www.researchgate.net/publication/285855224_Arctic_biodiversity_From_discovery_to_faunal_baselines_-_Revealing_the_history_of_a_dynamic_ecosystem> accessed 1 March 2022.

Hollowed AB, Planque B and Loeng H, 'Potential Movement of Fish and Shellfish Stocks from the Sub-Arctic to the Arctic Ocean' (2013) 22 Fisheries Oceanography 355 <http://doi.wiley.com/10.1111/fog.12027> accessed 6 March 2020.

Hønneland G, 'Norway and Russia in the Barents Sea – Cooperation and Conflict in Fisheries Management' (2007) 20 Russian Analytical Digest 9 <https://css.ethz.ch/content/dam/ethz/special-interest/gess/cis/center-for-securities-studies/pdfs/RAD-20-9-11.pdf> accessed 17 November 2020.

Hønneland GB, 'Autonomy and Regionalisation in the Fisheries Management of Northwestern Russia' (1998) 22 Marine Policy 57 <https://www.sciencedirect.com/science/article/abs/pii/S0308597X97000298?via%3Dihub> accessed 5 December 2024.

Humphreys MP, 'Climate Sensitivity and the Rate of Ocean Acidification: Future Impacts, and Implications for Experimental Design' (2017) 74 ICES Journal of Marine Science 934.

Hunt GL and others, 'Climate Impacts on Eastern Bering Sea Foodwebs: A Synthesis of New Data and an Assessment of the Oscillating Control Hypothesis' (2011) 68 ICES Journal of Marine Science 1230 <https://academic.oup.com/icesjms/article-abstract/68/6/1230/703602> accessed 15 January 2020.

Jakobson L, 'China Prepares for an Ice-Free Arctic' (2010) 2 SIPRI Insights on Peace and Security 1 <http://news.xinhuanet.com/ziliao/2006->.

Jakobsson M and others, 'The Early Miocene Onset of a Ventilated Circulation Regime in the Arctic Ocean' (2007) 447 Nature 986 <https://www.researchgate.net/publication/4669106_The_Early_Miocene_onset_of_a_ventilated_circulation_regime_in_the_Arctic_Ocean> accessed 30 June 2021.

Jones MC and Cheung WWL, 'Multi-Model Ensemble Projections of Climate Change Effects on Global Marine Biodiversity' (2015) 72 ICES Journal of Marine Science 741 <http://www.iobis.org/> accessed 10 December 2020.

Kaiser BA, Kourantidou M and Fernandez L, 'A Case for the Commons: The Snow Crab in the Barents' (2018) 210 Journal of Environmental Management 338 <https://doi.org/10.1016/j.jenvman.2018.01.007> accessed 5 December 2021.

Kim Y, Tanaka K and Matsuoka S, 'Environmental and Economic Effectiveness of the Kyoto Protocol' (2020) 15 PLOS ONE 1 <https://dx.plos.org/10.1371/journal.pone.0236299> accessed 12 November 2020.

Kishi MJ and others, 'NEMURO-a Lower Trophic Level Model for the North Pacific Marine Ecosystem' (2007) 202 Ecological Modelling 12 <https://www.sciencedirect.com/science/article/abs/pii/S0304380006004534> accessed 8 April 2022.

Kishi MJ and others, 'A Review of the NEMURO and NEMURO.FISH Models and Their Application to Marine Ecosystem Investigations' (2011) 67 Journal of Oceanography 3 <https://www.pmel.noaa.gov/foci/publications/2011/kish0728.pdf> accessed 8 April 2022.

Koivurova T, Kankaanpää P and Stępień A, 'Innovative Environmental Protection: Lessons from the Arctic' (2015) 27 Journal of Environmental Law 285 <https://academic.oup.com/jel/article-abstract/27/2/285/419150> accessed 5 December 2021.

Kral MJ, 'Suicide and Suicide Prevention among Inuit in Canada' (2016) 61 Canadian Journal of Psychiatry. Revue canadienne de psychiatrie 688 <http://www.ncbi.nlm.nih.gov/pubmed/27738249> accessed 8 April 2020.

Kuersten A, 'The Arctic Five Versus the Arctic Council' (2016) 2016 Arctic Yearbook 389 <https://papers.ssrn.com/sol3/papers.cfm?abstract_id=2861269> accessed 8 April 2022.

Kwiatkowska B, 'The High Seas Fisheries Regime: At a Point of No Return?' (1993) 8 International Journal of Marine and Coastal Law 327 <https://brill-com.emedien.ub.uni-muenchen.de/view/journals/estu/8/3/article-p327_1.xml> accessed 2 July 2020.

Lasserre F, Huang L and Alexeeva O V., 'China's Strategy in the Arctic: Threatening or Opportunistic?' (2017) 53 Polar Record 31.

Lavrik M, 'Customary Norms, General Principles of International Environmental Law, and Assisted Migration as a Tool for Biodiversity Adaptation to Climate Change'

(2022) 4 Jus Cogens 99 <https://doi.org/10.1007/s42439-022-00055-8> accessed 4 May 2024.

Liu D, 'The 2015 Oslo Declaration on Arctic High Seas Fisheries: The Starting Point Towards Future Fisheries Management in the Central Arctic Ocean' (2017) 2017 Arctic Yearbook 1 <https://arcticyearbook.com/images/yearbook/2017/Scholarly_Papers/21_The_2015_Oslo_Declaration_on_Arctic_High_Seas_Fisheries.pdf> accessed 6 March 2020.

Liu X, Chen H and Feng T, 'Multi-Scale Change Analysis Of Sea Ice Extent In Arctic' (2018) XLII–3 The International Archives of the Photogrammetry, Remote Sensing and Spatial Information Sciences 1153 <https://doi.org/10.5194/isprs-archives-XLII-3-1153-2018> accessed 5 December 2021.

Ma J, Hung H and Macdonald RW, 'The Influence of Global Climate Change on the Environmental Fate of Persistent Organic Pollutants: A Review with Emphasis on the Northern Hemisphere and the Arctic as a Receptor' (2016) 146 Global and Planetary Change 89 <http://dx.doi.org/10.1016/j.gloplacha.2016.09.011> accessed 5 December 2021.

Marmor A, 'Soft Law, Authoritative Advice and Non-Binding Agreements' (2019) 39 Oxford Journal of Legal Studies 507 <https://academic.oup.com/ojls/article/39/3/507/5474953> accessed 11 November 2020.

Matz-Lück N and Fuchs J, 'The Impact of OSPAR on Protected Area Management beyond National Jurisdiction: Effective Regional Cooperation or a Network of Paper Parks?' (2014) 49 Marine Policy 155 <http://dx.doi.org/10.1016/j.marpol.2013.12.001> accessed 2 July 2020.

McLoughlin S, 'The Breakup History of Gondwana and Its Impact on Pre-Cenozoic Floristic Provincialism' (2001) 49 Australian Journal of Botany 271 <https://www.publish.csiro.au/bt/bt00023> accessed 8 April 2022.

Melnychuk MC and others, 'Can Catch Share Fisheries Better Track Management Targets?' (2012) 13 Fish and Fisheries 267 <http://doi.wiley.com/10.1111/j.1467-2979.2011.00429.x> accessed 14 July 2020.

Moldovan C, 'BREXIT and the International Law on Treaty Withdrawal' (2018) 5 EURINT 257 <http://cse.uaic.ro/eurint/proceedings/index_htm_files/EURINT2018_MOL.pdf> accessed 9 July 2020.

Molenaar EJ, 'The Concept of "Real Interest" and Other Aspects of Co-Operation through Regional Fisheries Management Mechanisms' (2000) 15 International Journal of Marine and Coastal Law 475.

Molenaar EJ, 'Addressing Regulatory Gaps in High Seas Fisheries' (2005) 20 International Journal of Marine and Coastal Law 533.

Molenaar EJ, 'Managing Biodiversity in Areas beyond National Jurisdiction' (2007) 22 International Journal of Marine and Coastal Law 89.

Molenaar EJ, 'Non-Participation in the Fish Stocks Agreement: Status and Reasons' (2011) 26 International Journal of Marine and Coastal Law 195.

Molenaar EJ, 'Fisheries Regulation in the Maritime Zones of Svalbard' (2012) 27 International Journal of Marine and Coastal Law 3.

Molenaar EJ, 'Arctic Fisheries Conservation and Management: Initial Steps of Reform of the International Legal Framework' (2013) 1 The Yearbook of Polar Law Online 427.

Molenaar EJ, 'The Oslo Declaration on High Seas Fishing in the Central Arctic Ocean' (2015) 2015 Arctic Yearbook 427.

Molnár PK and others, 'Fasting Season Length Sets Temporal Limits for Global Polar Bear Persistence' (2020) 10 Nature Climate Change 732 <http://www.nature.com/articles/s41558-020-0818-9> accessed 5 August 2020.

Navarro LM and others, 'Monitoring Biodiversity Change through Effective Global Coordination' (2017) 29 Current Opinion in Environmental Sustainability 158.

Örebech P, Sigurjonsson K and McDorman TL, 'The 1995 United Nations Straddling and Highly Migratory Fish Stocks Agreement: Management, Enforcement and Dispute Settlement' (1998) 13 International Journal of Marine and Coastal Law 119.

Orgad L, 'The Preamble in Constitutional Interpretation' (2010) 8 International Journal of Constitutional Law 714.

Østhagen A, 'Managing Conflict at Sea: The Case of Norway and Russia in the Svalbard Zone' (2018) 9 Arctic Review on Law and Politics 100.

Østhagen A and Raspotnik A, 'Crab! How a Dispute over Snow Crab Became a Diplomatic Headache between Norway and the EU' (2018) 98 Marine Policy 58.

Oude Elferink AG, 'The Impact of Article 7(2) of the Fish Stocks Agreement on the Formulation of Conservation and Management Measures for Straddling and Highly Migratory Fish Stocks' (1999) 4 FAO Legal Papers Online 1 <https://www.fao.org/documents/card/fr/c/04b8e10e-bd4f-4072-9057-daae852e4c8f/> accessed 3 September 2020.

Overland JE and Wang M, 'When Will the Summer Arctic Be Nearly Sea Ice Free?' (2013) 40 Geophysical Research Letters 2097.

Pankhurst NW and Munday PL, 'Effects of Climate Change on Fish Reproduction and Early Life History Stages' (2011) 62 Marine and Freshwater Research 1015 <www.publish.csiro.au/journals/mfr> accessed 30 November 2020.

Papastavridis E, 'Fisheries Enforcement on the High Seas of the Arctic Ocean: Gaps, Solutions and the Potential Contribution of the European Union and Its Member States' (2018) 33 International Journal of Marine and Coastal Law 324.

Pedersen T, 'The Svalbard Continental Shelf Controversy: Legal Disputes and Political Rivalries' (2006) 37 Ocean Development & International Law 339 <https://shorturl.at/C4XzZ> accessed 8 July 2020.

Pedersen T, 'Debates over the Role of the Arctic Council' (2012) 43 Ocean Development and International Law 146.

Petersson MT, 'Transparency in Global Fisheries Governance: The Role of Non-Governmental Organizations' (2022) 136 Marine Policy 104128 <https://doi.org/10.1016/j.marpol.2020.104128> accessed 8 April 2022.

Pharand D, 'The Case for an Arctic Region Council and a Treaty Proposal' (1992) 23 Revue générale de droit 163.

Platjouw FM, Steindal EH and Borch T, 'From Arctic Science to International Law: The Road towards the Minamata Convention and the Role of the Arctic Council' (2018) 9 Arctic Review on Law and Politics 226 <https://arcticreview.no/index.php/arctic/article/view/1234> accessed 12 March 2020.

Quirico O, 'Disentangling Climate Change Governance: A Legal Perspective' (2012) 21 Review of European Community and International Environmental Law 92.

Raspopov OM, Kuz'min IA and Kharin EP, 'The 50th Anniversary of International Geophysical Year (1957–1958): From the First International Polar Year (1882–1883) to the International Heliophysical Year (2007–2008) and International Polar Year (2007–2009)' (2007) 47 Geomagnetism and Aeronomy 1 <https://link-springer-com.emedien.ub.uni-muenchen.de/article/10.1134/S001679320701001X> accessed 24 March 2022.

Rastrick SSP and others, 'Using Natural Analogues to Investigate the Effects of Climate Change and Ocean Acidification on Northern Ecosystems' (2018) 75 ICES Journal of Marine Science 2299 <https://academic.oup.com/icesjms/article/75/7/2299/5133274> accessed 10 December 2020.

Raustiala K, 'States, NGOs, and International Environmental Institutions' (1997) 41 International Studies Quarterly 719 <http://www.jstor.org/stable/2600859> accessed 4 August 2022.

Rayfuse R, 'Countermeasures and High Seas Fisheries Enforcement' (2004) 51 Netherlands International Law Review 41.

Rayfuse R, 'Protecting Marine Biodiversity in Polar Areas beyond National Jurisdiction' (2008) 17 Review of European Community and International Environmental Law 3.

Roach JA, 'Today's Customary International Law of the Sea' (2014) 45 Ocean Development and International Law 239.

Rose GA, 'Capelin (Mallotus Villosus) Distribution and Climate: A Sea "Canary" for Marine Ecosystem Change' (2005) 62 ICES Journal of Marine Science 1524 <https://academic.oup.com/icesjms/article-lookup/doi/10.1016/j.icesjms.2005.05.008> accessed 5 December 2021.

Rossi CR, 'The Club within the Club: The Challenge of a Soft Law Framework in a Global Arctic Context' (2015) 5 Polar Journal 8.

Sand PH and Wiener JB, 'Towards a New International Law of the Atmosphere?' (2016) 2 Goettingen Journal of International Law 195.

Scafetta N and Mazzarella A, 'The Arctic and Antarctic Sea-Ice Area Index Records versus Measured and Modeled Temperature Data' (2015) 2015 Advances in Meteorology 481834 <http://dx.doi.org/10.1155/2015/481834> accessed 27 March 2020.

Schatz V, 'Incorporation of Indigenous and Local Knowledge in Central Arctic Ocean Fisheries Management' (2019) 10 Arctic Review on Law and Politics 130.

Schatz V, Proelß A and Liu N, 'The 2018 Agreement to Prevent Unregulated High Seas Fisheries in the Central Arctic Ocean: A Critical Analysis' (2019) 34 International Journal of Marine and Coastal Law 195.

Serdy A, 'Postmodern International Fisheries Law, or We Are All Coastal States Now' (2011) 60 International and Comparative Law Quarterly 387 <https://www.cambridge.org/core/product/identifier/S002058931100008X/type/journal_article> accessed 5 December 2021.

Silber GK and Adams JD, 'Vessel Operations in the Arctic, 2015–2017' (2019) 6 Frontiers in Marine Science 573 <https://www.frontiersin.org/article/10.3389/fmars.2019.00573/full> accessed 29 May 2020.

Smith ADM and Garcia SM, 'Fishery Management: Contrasts in the Mediterranean and the Atlantic' (2014) 24 Current Biology R810 <https://www.cell.com/current-biology/comments/S0960-9822(14)00859-8> accessed 14 July 2020.

Smith TP and Sissenwine MP, 'Fishery Management' (2001) 2 Encyclopedia of Ocean Sciences 1014 <https://www.sciencedirect.com/sdfe/pdf/download/eid/3-s2.0-B9780123744739004598/first-page-pdf> accessed 27 May 2020.

Stadtländer CTK-H, 'A Book Review on International Governance of the Arctic Marine Environment: With Particular Emphasis on High Seas Fisheries' (2014) 1 Frontiers in Marine Science 10.

Sterio M, 'Humanitarian Intervention Post-Syria: A Grotian Moment?' (2014) 20 ILSA Journal of International & Comparative Law 343 <https://nsuworks.nova.edu/ilsajournal/vol20/iss2/6> accessed 5 December 2021.

Stokke OS, 'Environmental Security in the Arctic: The Case for Multilevel Governance' (2011) 66 International Journal 835 <https://shorturl.at/ZDNbT> accessed 11 March 2020.

Strong C and others, 'On the Definition of Marginal Ice Zone Width' (2017) 34 Journal of Atmospheric and Oceanic Technology 1565 <www.ametsoc.org/PUBSReuseLicenses> accessed 1 March 2021.

Takei Y, 'Current Legal Developments – UN Fish Stocks Agreement: 2006 Review Conference' (2007) 21 International Journal of Marine and Coastal Law 551.

Trouwborst A, 'International Nature Conservation Law and the Adaptation of Biodiversity to Climate Change: A Mismatch?' (2009) 21 Journal of Environmental Law 419 <https://www.jstor.org/stable/44248707> accessed 2 April 2022.

Trouwborst A, 'Bird Conservation and Climate Change in the Marine Arctic and Antarctic: Classic and Novel International Law Challenges Converging in the Polar

Regions' (2013) 16 Journal of International Wildlife Law and Policy 1 <https://heinonline-org.emedien.ub.uni-muenchen.de/HOL/Page?collection=journals&handle=hein.journals/intwlp16&id=5&men_tab=srchresults> accessed 30 September 2020.

Valková I, 'Claiming the Arctic: On the Legal Geography of the Northernmost Sovereignty Dispute' (2017) 7 The Polar Journal 143 <https://www.tandfonline.com/doi/full/10.1080/2154896X.2017.1310489> accessed 8 July 2020.

Van Alstine MP, 'Treaty Law and Legal Transition Costs' (2002) 77 Chicago-Kent Law Review 1303.

Van Pelt TI and others, 'The Missing Middle: Central Arctic Ocean Gaps in Fishery Research and Science Coordination' (2017) 85 Marine Policy 79.

Vermeij GJ, 'When Biotas Meet: Understanding Biotic Interchange' (1991) 253 Science 1099.

Vilhjálmsson H, 'Capelin Biology and Ecology Capelin (Mallotus Villosus) in the Iceland-East Greenland-Jan Mayen Ecosystem' (2002) 59 ICES Journal of Marine Science 870.

Vylegzhanin AN, Young OR and Berkman PA, 'The Central Arctic Ocean Fisheries Agreement as an Element in the Evolving Arctic Ocean Governance Complex' (2020) 118 Marine Policy 104001.

Wahlén C and others, 'Summary of the Resumed Review Conference of the UN Fish Stocks Agreement (23–27 May 2016)' (2016) 7 Earth Negotiations Bulletin 71 <https://enb.iisd.org/events/resumed-unfsa-review-conference/summary-report-23-27-may-2016> accessed 5 December 2024.

Walsh JE and others, 'A Database for Depicting Arctic Sea Ice Variations Back to 1850' (2017) 107 Geographical Review 89.

Wang M and Overland JE, 'A Sea Ice Free Summer Arctic within 30 Years?' (2009) 36 Geophysical Research Letters 1.

Ware C and others, 'Climate Change, Non-Indigenous Species and Shipping: Assessing the Risk of Species Introduction to a High-Arctic Archipelago' (2014) 20 Diversity and Distributions 10 <http://doi.wiley.com/10.1111/ddi.12117> accessed 11 March 2020.

Wassmann, Paul, Reigstad, Marit, Haug, Tore, Rudels, Bert, Carroll, Michael L., Hop, Haakon, Gabrielsen, Geir Wing, Falk-Petersen, Stig, Denisenko, Stanislav G., Arashkevich, Elena, Slagstad, Dag, Pavlova O, 'Food Webs and Carbon Flux in the Barents Sea' (2006) 71(2) Progress in Oceanography 232.

Wegge N, 'The Political Order in the Arctic: Power Structures, Regimes and Influence' (2011) 47 Polar Record 165 <https://shorturl.at/1dJCe> accessed 5 December 2021.

Wegge N, 'The Emerging Politics of the Arctic Ocean: Future Management of the Living Marine Resources' (2015) 51 Marine Policy 331.

Wilson DC and McCay BJ, 'Fishery Management, Human Dimension' (2001) 2 Encyclopedia of Ocean Sciences 1023 <https://www.sciencedirect.com/sdfe/pdf/download/eid/3-s2.0-B9780123744739004604/first-page-pdf> accessed 4 April 2022.

Wilson E, 'Mare Liberum and Opinio Iuris: A Grotian Reading of the North Sea Continental Shelf Cases' (2002) 2 Monash University Law Review 299 <http://www.austlii.edu.au/au/journals/MonashULawRw/2002/13.pdf> accessed 3 September 2020.

Wisz MS and others, 'Arctic Warming Will Promote Atlantic-Pacific Fish Interchange' (2015) 5 Nature Climate Change 261 <http://www.iobis.org> accessed 11 March 2020.

Yoon S and others, 'Potential Habitat for Chum Salmon (Oncorhynchus Keta) in the Western Arctic Based on a Bioenergetics Model Coupled with a Three-Dimensional Lower Trophic Ecosystem Model' (2015) 131 Progress in Oceanography 146 <http://dx.doi.org/10.1016/j.pocean.2014.12.009> accessed 5 December 2021.

Young OR, 'Arctic Tipping Points: Governance in Turbulent Times' (2012) 41 AMBIO 75 <https://link.springer.com/article/10.1007/s13280-011-0227-4> accessed 5 December 2021.

Young TK, Revich B and Soininen L, 'Suicide in Circumpolar Regions: An Introduction and Overview' (2015) 74 International Journal of Circumpolar Health 27349 <https://doi.org/10.3402/ijch.v74.27349> accessed 8 April 2020.

Zou L and Huntington HP, 'Implications of the Convention on the Conservation and Management of Pollock Resources in the Central Bering Sea for the Management of Fisheries in the Central Arctic Ocean' (2018) 88 Marine Policy 132 <https://doi.org/10.1016/j.marpol.2017.11.019> accessed 4 April 2022.

Articles, Blogposts and Other Individual Contributions

Abdelhamid A, 'Climate Change Deniers vs Climate Scientists – Who's Right on Arctic Sea Ice?' *PlanetSave* (25 July 2016) <https://planetsave.com/2016/07/25/climate-change-deniers-vs-climate-scientists-whos-right-arctic-sea-ice/> accessed 30 June 2021.

Angus I, 'The Myth of the Tragedy of the Commons' *Climate and Capitalism* (25 August 2008) <http://climateandcapitalism.com/2008/08/25/debunking-the-tragedy-of-the-commons/> accessed 10 August 2021.

Årthun M, 'The Arctic Sea Ice Extent May Increase despite the World Getting Warmer' *The Nansen Legacy* (6 May 2019) <https://arvenetternansen.com/2019/05/06/arctic-sea-ice-extent-may-increase-despite-the-world-getting-warmer/> accessed 10 August 2021.

Balton DA, 'No. 9 | The Arctic Fisheries Agreement Enters into Force' *Polar Points* (25 June 2021) <https://www.wilsoncenter.org/blog-post/no-9-arctic-fisheries-agreement-enters-force> accessed 30 June 2021.

Blanchfield M, 'Clinton Rebukes Canada on Arctic Meeting' *The Globe and Mail* (29 March 2010) <https://www.theglobeandmail.com/news/politics/clinton-rebukes-canada-on-arctic-meeting/article1210187/> accessed 10 August 2021.

Briney A, 'Arctic Ocean or Arctic Seas' *ThoughtCo.* (6 November 2019) <https://www.thoughtco.com/arctic-seas-overview-1435183> accessed 10 August 2021.

Carroll R, 'Arctic Time Capsule from 2018 Washes up in Ireland as Polar Ice Melts' *The Guardian* (5 November 2020) <https://www.theguardian.com/world/2020/nov/05/arctic-time-capsule-from-2018-washes-up-in-ireland-as-polar-ice-melts> accessed 10 August 2021.

Casteleyn MC, 'China and the Arctic: An Opportunity for the U.S.' (Air University–Maxwell AFB, AL 2017) <https://apps.dtic.mil/sti/citations/AD1038063> accessed 2 November 2024.

Cereceda R, 'How Summer 2019 Was Hellish for the Arctic, the Frontline of Climate Change and Global Warming' *Euronews* (24 September 2019) <https://www.euronews.com/2019/09/18/how-2019-was-hellish-for-the-arctic-the-frontline-of-climate-change-and-global-warming> accessed 10 August 2021.

Dickie G, 'International Accord Bans Fishing in Central Arctic Ocean, Spurs Science' *The New Humanitarian – Oceans Deeply* (4 December 2017) <https://deeply.thenewhumanitarian.org/oceans/community/2017/12/01/an-app-and-volunteer-army-are-improving-local-tidal-flood-forecasts> accessed 20 October 2020.

Dickie G and Gardner T, 'Arctic Council in Upheaval over Russia as Climate Change Transforms Region' *Reuters* (3 March 2022) <https://www.reuters.com/world/arctic-council-countries-halt-meetings-over-russias-invasion-ukraine-2022-03-03/> accessed 25 March 2022.

Dodds K, 'In 30 Years the Antarctic Treaty Becomes Modifiable, and the Fate of a Continent Could Hang in the Balance' *The Conversation* (12 July 2018) <https://theconversation.com/in-30-years-the-antarctic-treaty-becomes-modifiable-and-the-fate-of-a-continent-could-hang-in-the-balance-98654> accessed 9 July 2020.

Dupont N, 'Polar Cod Have Become Larger in the Barents Sea over the Last 30 Years' *The Nansen Legacy* (3 July 2020) <https://arvenetternansen.com/2020/07/03/polar-cod-have-become-larger-in-the-barents-sea-over-the-last-30-years/> accessed 22 July 2020.

Engilbertsson V, 'Energy Dynamics and Recruitment of Icelandic Capelin' (University of Iceland 2014) <https://skemman.is/bitstream/1946/19866/1/MS_ritgerd_vidar.pdf> accessed 5 December 2021.

Fountain H, 'Scientists to Drift With Arctic Ice to Study Climate Change' *The New York Times* (19 September 2019) <https://www.nytimes.com/2019/09/19/climate/mosaic-expedition-arctic.html?searchResultPosition=10> accessed 11 December 2020.

Fountain H, 'Global Warming Is Driving Polar Bears Toward Extinction, Researchers Say' *The New York Times* (20 July 2020) <https://www.nytimes.com/2020/07/20/climate/polar-bear-extinction.html?searchResultPosition=5> accessed 11 December 2020.

Fountain H, 'The Arctic Is Shifting to a New Climate Because of Global Warming' *The New York Times* (14 September 2020) <https://www.nytimes.com/2020/09/14/climate/arctic-changing-climate.html?searchResultPosition=2> accessed 11 December 2020.

Fountain H, 'After a Year in the Ice, the Biggest-Ever Arctic Science Mission Ends' *The New York Times* (12 October 2020).

Friedman L, 'U.S. Quits Paris Climate Agreement: Questions and Answers' *The New York Times* (4 November 2020) <https://www.nytimes.com/2020/11/04/climate/paris-climate-agreement-trump.html> accessed 16 December 2020.

Gibbens S, 'The Arctic Ocean, Explained' *National Geographic* (29 March 2019) <https://www.nationalgeographic.com/environment/oceans/reference/arctic-ocean/> accessed 5 December 2021.

Gramling C, '4 Ways to Put the 100-Degree Arctic Heat Record in Context' *Science News* (1 July 2020) <https://www.sciencenews.org/article/climate-new-high-temperature-heat-record-arctic-siberia-context> accessed 4 September 2020.

Gray DW, 'Changing Arctic: A Strategic Analysis Of United States Arctic Policy And The United Nations Convention On The Law Of The Sea' (Joint Forces Staff College 2013) <https://apps.dtic.mil/sti/pdfs/ADA581139.pdf> accessed 4 October 2021.

Grønnestad KS, 'What Is the Arctic?' *BarentsWatch* (21 January 2016) <https://www.barentswatch.no/en/articles/Hva-er-Arktis/> accessed 5 December 2021.

Hansen HSB, 'Snow Crab (Chionoecetes Opilio) in the Barents Sea. Diet, Biology and Management' (UiT The Arctic University of Norway 2015) <https://munin.uit.no/bitstream/handle/10037/7746/thesis.pdf?sequence=2&isAllowed=y> accessed 14 April 2022.

Hathaway O, 'Reengaging on Treaties and Other International Agreements (Part I): President Donald Trump's Rejection of International Law' *Just Security* (2 October 2020) <https://www.justsecurity.org/72656/reengaging-on-treaties-and-other-international-agreements-part-i-president-donald-trumps-rejection-of-international-law/> accessed 13 April 2021.

Huffines E, 'Most Large Ships Transiting Arctic Use New Routes That Help Protect Environment and Communities' *The Pew Charitable Trusts* (20 May 2020) <https://shorturl.at/oMgNc> accessed 11 December 2020.

Humpert M, 'China Reveals Details of Newly Designed Heavy Icebreaker' *High North News* (16 December 2019) <https://www.highnorthnews.com/en/china-reveals-details-newly-designed-heavy-icebreaker> accessed 5 August 2020.

Isaacson A, 'Extreme Research Shows How Arctic Ice Is Dwindling' *National Geographic* (1 January 2016) <https://www.nationalgeographic.com/magazine/2016/01/arctic-ice-environment/> accessed 5 December 2021.

Jacobsen M, 'Denmark's Strategic Interests in the Arctic: It's the Greenlandic Connection, Stupid!' *The Arctic Institute* (4 May 2016) <https://www.thearcticinstitute.org/denmark-interests-arctic-greenland-connection/> accessed 13 April 2020.

Jakobson L, 'Analysis Brief: Northeast Asia Turns Its Attention to the Arctic' *National Bureau of Asian Research* (17 December 2012) <https://www.nbr.org/publication/northeast-asia-turns-its-attention-to-the-arctic/#:~:text=Linda Jakobson%2C Director of the,%2C Japan%2C and South Korea> accessed 5 August 2021.

Kelly M, 'Movement of Marine Life Follows Speed and Direction of Climate Change' *Princeton University* (12 September 2013) <https://www.princeton.edu/news/2013/09/12/movement-marine-life-follows-speed-and-direction-climate-change#:~:text=Details of the surveys revealed,38 miles north per decade> accessed 8 April 2022.

Kopra S, 'China and Its Arctic Trajectories: The Arctic Institute's China Series 2020' *The Arctic Institute* (17 March 2020) <https://www.thearcticinstitute.org/china-arctic-trajectories-the-arctic-institute-china-series-2020/> accessed 5 August 2020.

Loctier D, 'Protecting Life in the Arctic Seas' *Euronews* (20 March 2020) <https://www.euronews.com/2019/10/10/protecting-life-in-the-arctic-seas> accessed 12 August 2020.

Matthews L, 'Did Native Peoples Live in Harmony with Nature? It' s Complicated.' *Mises Wire* (10 April 2020) <https://mises.org/wire/did-native-peoples-live-harmony-nature-its-complicated> accessed 4 April 2022.

'Max Planck: Vorträge Und Erinnerungen' *Die Zeit* (17 February 1984) <https://www.zeit.de/1984/08/vortraege-und-erinnerungen?utm_referrer=https%3A%2F%2Fwww.google.com%2F> accessed 22 December 2020.

Mbengue MM, 'Preamble' *Max Planck Encyclopedia of Public International Law* (2006) <https://opil.ouplaw.com/view/10.1093/law:epil/9780199231690/law-9780199231690-e1456?prd=EPIL> accessed 8 April 2022.

Michael Byers, 'Rules for the North Pole' *The New York Times* (18 August 2011) <https://www.nytimes.com/2011/08/19/opinion/19iht-edbyers19.html> accessed 10 January 2020.

Molenaar EJ, 'The December 2015 Washington Meeting on High Seas Fishing in the Central Arctic Ocean' *The JCLOS Blog* (5 February 2016) < https://research-portal.uu.nl/en/publications/the-december-2015-washington-meeting-on-high-seas-fishing-in-the-> accessed 2 November 2024.

Nuttall M, 'Arctic Environmental Protection Strategy' *Climate Policy Watcher* (1 January 2019) <https://www.climate-policy-watcher.org/canadian-arctic/arctic-environmental-protection-strategy.html> accessed 20 February 2020.

Østhagen A, 'Swimming Away! Arctic Fisheries and International Cooperation' *The Arctic Institute* (22 October 2019) <https://www.thearcticinstitute.org/swimming-away-arctic-fisheries-international-cooperation/> accessed 14 September 2020.

Raspotnik A and Østhagen A, 'The End of an Exceptional History: Re-Thinking the EU-Russia Arctic Relationship' *E-International Relations* (23 March 2022) <https://www.e-ir.info/2022/03/23/the-end-of-an-exceptional-history-re-thinking-the-eu-russia-arctic-relationship/> accessed 25 March 2022.

Reigstad M, Eldevik T and Gerland S, 'The Nansen Legacy' *The Nansen Legacy* (11 April 2019) <https://arvenetternansen.com/2019/04/11/the-nansen-legacy/> accessed 22 July 2020.

Revkin AC, 'Arctic Climate Change Revealed in a Luxury Cruise and Haunting Wreck' *Dot Earth New York Times Blog* (23 September 2016) <https://dotearth.blogs.nytimes.com/2016/09/23/arctic-change-revealed-in-a-luxury-cruise-and-a-haunting-wreck/?searchResultPosition=3> accessed 11 December 2020.

Ritchie H and Roser M, 'CO_2 Emissions' *Our World in Data* (31 December 2020) <https://ourworldindata.org/co2-emissions> accessed 12 November 2020.

Ryder S, 'The Declaration Concerning the Prevention of Unregulated High Seas Fishing in the Central Arctic Ocean' *The University of Calgary Faculty of Law Blog* (31 July 2015) <https://ablawg.ca/2015/07/31/the-declaration-concerning-the-prevention-of-unregulated-high-seas-fishing-in-the-central-arctic-ocean/> accessed 27 November 2020.

Saragih B, 'Economic Value of Non-Timber Forest Products among Paser Indigenous People of East Kalimantan' (Leiden University 2011) <https://openaccess.leidenuniv.nl/handle/1887/18078> accessed 19 December 2020.

Schrepferman W, 'Hypocri-Sea: The United States' Failure to Join the UN Convention on the Law of the Sea' *Harvard International Review* (31 October 2019) <https://hir.harvard.edu/hypocri-sea-the-united-states-failure-to-join-the-un-convention-on-the-law-of-the-sea-2/> accessed 8 July 2020.

Shankman S, 'Arctic Report Card 2019: Extreme Ice Loss, Dying Species as Global Warming Worsens' *Inside Climate News* (10 December 2019) <https://insideclimatenews.org/news/10122019/arctic-report-card-2019-bering-sea-ice-extent-greenland-melt-permafrost-indigenous-impact> accessed 20 January 2020.

Smith G, 'Overfishing' *The Earth Times* (10 January 2012) <http://www.earthtimes.org/encyclopaedia/environmental-issues/overfishing/> accessed 1 December 2020.

Struzik E, 'Welcome to the Arctic, Fish' *Hakai Magazine* (16 August 2016) <https://www.hakaimagazine.com/article-long/welcome-arctic-fish?utm_content=buffer2ad70&utm_medium=social&utm_source=twitter.com&utm_campaign=buffer> accessed 4 August 2022.

Struzik E, 'Welcome to the Arctic Ocean, Mysterious Fish' *The New Humanitarian – Oceans Deeply* (12 May 2017) <https://deeply.thenewhumanitarian.org/oceans/articles/2017/05/12/welcome-to-the-arctic-ocean-mysterious-fish-2> accessed 8 April 2022.

Sullivan W, 'Expert Says Arctic Ocean Will Soon Be an Open Sea' *The New York Times* (20 February 1969) <https://timesmachine.nytimes.com/timesmachine/1969/02/20/77442757.html?pageNumber=20> accessed 11 December 2020.

Taylor T, 'What Is the Tragedy of the Commons?' *Conversable Economist* (15 August 2012) <https://conversableeconomist.blogspot.com/2012/08/what-is-tragedy-of-commons.html?m=1> accessed 2 April 2022.

'The Kyoto Protocol: Climate Change Success or Global Warming Failure?' *Circular Ecology* (4 February 2015) <https://circularecology.com/news/the-kyoto-protocol-climate-change-success-or-global-warming-failure> accessed 12 November 2021.

Turner B, 'Iceland Offers a Model for Arctic Fisheries Management' *The New Humanitarian–Arctic Deeply* (9 December 2016) <https://deeply.thenewhumanitarian.org/arctic/articles/2016/12/09/iceland-offers-a-model-for-arctic-fisheries-management> accessed 20 October 2020.

'UK Arctic Policy after Brexit: What Might Change?' *Over the Circle* (13 January 2019) <https://overthecircle.com/2019/01/13/uk-arctic-policy-after-brexit-what-might-change/> accessed 14 September 2020.

Uryupova E, 'Why Do We Need a Shared Pan-Arctic Fisheries Governance Complex?' *The Arctic Institute* (27 April 2021) <https://www.thearcticinstitute.org/need-shared-pan-arctic-fisheries-governance-complex/> accessed 25 March 2022.

'US Climate Objections Sink Arctic Council Accord in Finland' *BBC News* (7 May 2019) <https://www.bbc.com/news/world-europe-48185793> accessed 7 May 2021.

Vanecko JJ, 'Time to Ratify UNCLOS; A New Twist on an Old Problem' (Naval War College 2011) <https://apps.dtic.mil/sti/tr/pdf/ADA546081.pdf> accessed 2 November 2024.

'We Don't Survive – We Live Here!' *Arctic Anthropology* (27 September 2019) <https://arcticanthropology.org/2019/09/27/we-dont-survive-we-live-here/> accessed 10 August 2021.

Yeager BB, 'The Ilulissat Declaration: Background and Implications for Arctic Governance' (2008) <https://www.arctic-report.net/wp-content/uploads/2012/01/2008.11-Ilulissat-Background-and-Implications.pdf> accessed 4 April 2022.

Yerkes A, 'Whose Fish? Looking at Svalbard's Fisheries Protection Zone ' *The Polar Connection* (4 December 2016) <https://polarconnection.org/svalbard-fisheries-protection-zone/> accessed 2 March 2021.

Zischka K and others, 'Marine Biodiversity Beyond National Jurisdiction – Australia's Continuing Role' (2017) <https://d3n8a8pro7vhmx.cloudfront.net/edonsw/pages/5428/attachments/original/1513316783/Marine_BBNJ_Report_%28FINAL%29.pdf?1513316783> accessed 11 December 2021.

Miscellaneous

'Alaska Department of Fish and Game | Commercial Fisheries Overview – Arctic Management Area' <https://www.adfg.alaska.gov/index.cfm?adfg=commercialbyareanorthern.main> accessed 12 August 2021.

'AMAP | Arctic Monitoring and Assessment Programme' <https://www.amap.no/> accessed 10 August 2021.

'Arctic Council | An Introduction to: The International Agreement to Prevent Unregulated Fishing in the High Seas of the Central Arctic Ocean' (25 June 2021) <https://arctic-council.org/en/news/introduction-to-international-agreement-to-prevent-unregulated-fishing-in-the-high-seas-of-the-central-arctic-ocean/> accessed 30 June 2021.

'Arctic Council | Integrated Ecosystem Assessment (IEA) of the Central Arctic Ocean' <https://arctic-council.org/en/projects/iea/> accessed 25 September 2020.

'Arctic Council | Nongovernmental Organizations' <https://arctic-council.org/en/about/observers/non-governmental-organizations/> accessed 30 December 2020.

'Arctic Council | Projects' <https://arctic-council.org/en/projects/> accessed 9 July 2021.

'Arctic Council | Working Groups' <https://arctic-council.org/en/about/working-groups/> accessed 22 May 2020.

'Arctic Forum Foundation | Engaging NGOs <http://eu-arctic-forum.org/fora/engaging-ngos-on-eu-arctic-policy-and-the-oil-and-gas-industry-12-13-november-haparanda-sweden/> accessed 2 November 2024.

'Arctic Ocean Diversity | Sea-Bottom Diversity: An Overview of the Benthic Realm' <http://www.arcodiv.org/SeaBottom_overview.html> accessed 17 January 2022.

'Barents Euro-Arctic Cooperation | About Us' <https://www.barentscooperation.org/en/About> accessed 30 June 2021.

'BEAC | About the Regional Council' <https://barents-council.org/barents-regional-council/about-the-council > accessed 2 November 2024.

'Biodiversity: The Loss of Nature, Interview with David Attenbrough (Published 28 September 2020)' <https://www.instagram.com/p/CFrRYBxH_pF/> accessed 28 May 2021.

'Cambridge English Dictionary | Fishing' <https://dictionary.cambridge.org/dictionary/english/fishing> accessed 5 July 2019.

'CBD | Ecosystem Approach' <https://www.cbd.int/ecosystem/> accessed 17 January 2022.

'CBD | History of the Convention' <https://www.cbd.int/history/> accessed 12 August 2021.

'CBD | List of Parties' <https://www.cbd.int/information/parties.shtml> accessed 6 April 2022.

'CBD | Thematic Programmes and Cross-Cutting Issues' <https://www.cbd.int/programmes/> accessed 12 August 2021.

'CBD | What Is Marine and Coastal Biodiversity?' <https://www.cbd.int/marine/intro.shtml> accessed 1 July 2020.

'CBD| Ecosystem Restoration' <https://www.cbd.int/restoration/> accessed 17 January 2022.

'CCAMLR | Browse Conservation Measures' <https://www.ccamlr.org/en/conservation-and-management/browse-conservation-measures> accessed 10 August 2021.

'CCAMLR | Ecosystem Approach' <http://archive.ccamlr.org/pu/E/sc/eco-app-intro.htm> accessed 12 June 2020.

'CITES | List of Contracting Parties' <https://www.cites.org/eng/disc/parties/chronolo.php> accessed 6 April 2022.

'CITES | What Is CITES?' <https://www.cites.org/eng/disc/what.php> accessed 11 November 2020.

'CMS | Convention on the Conservation of Migratory Species of Wild Animals' <https://www.cms.int/en/legalinstrument/cms> accessed 12 August 2021.

'CMS | Parties and Range States' <https://www.cms.int/en/parties-range-states> accessed 11 November 2020.

'Conserve Energy Future | Various Tundra Animals' <https://www.conserve-energy-future.com/various-tundra-animals.php> accessed 22 December 2021.

'EBSA | Global Ocean Biodiversity Initiative' <http://gobi.org/ebsas/> accessed 24 May 2021.

'European Commission | More Protection for Our Seas and Oceans Is Needed, Report Finds (25 June 2020)' <https://ec.europa.eu/commission/presscorner/detail/en/IP_20_1160> accessed 25 November 2020.

'European Commission | Our Oceans, Seas and Coast – EU Coastal and Marine Policy' <https://ec.europa.eu/environment/marine/eu-coast-and-marine-policy/marine-strategy-framework-directive/index_en.htm> accessed 20 January 2020.

'European Commission | Protecting the Ocean, Time for Action: High Ambition Coalition on Biodiversity Beyond National Jurisdiction' <https://ec.europa.eu/oceans-and-fisheries/ocean/international-ocean-governance/protecting-ocean-time-action_de> accessed 6 April 2022.

'European Commission | Regional Fisheries Management Organisations (RFMOs)' <https://ec.europa.eu/fisheries/cfp/international/rfmo_en> accessed 25 April 2020.

'European Commission | The EU Joins Forces with Nine Countries for Future Science-Based Management of the High Seas of the Central Arctic Ocean (13 February 2020)' <https://www.europarl.europa.eu/cmsdata/196428/Trawler%20February%202020.pdf> accessed 2 November 2024.

'European External Action Service | Barents Euro-Arctic Cooperation: Joint Statement of the European Union, Finland, Denmark, Iceland, Norway and Sweden on Suspending

Activities with Russia' (9 March 2022) <https://eeas.europa.eu/headquarters/headquarters-homepage/112462/barents-euro-arctic-cooperation-joint-statement-european-union-finland-denmark-iceland-norway_en> accessed 25 March 2022.

'European Polar Board | Action Groups' <http://www.europeanpolarboard.org/activities/action-groups/> accessed 30 June 2021.

'European Union | Arctic: Agreement to Prevent Unregulated Fishing Enters into Force (25 June 2021)' <https://ec.europa.eu/oceans-and-fisheries/news/arctic-agreement-prevent-unregulated-fishing-enters-force-2021-06-25_en> accessed 25 March 2022.

'FAO | Code of Conduct for Responsible Fisheries – Illegal, Unreported and Unregulated (IUU) Fishing' <https://www.fao.org/iuu-fishing/international-framework/code-of-conduct-for-responsible-fisheries/en/> accessed 8 April 2022.

'FAO | Coordinating Working Party on Fishery Statistics (CWP) – Background' <http://www.fao.org/cwp-on-fishery-statistics/background/en/> accessed 10 August 2021.

'FAO | Coordinating Working Party on Fishery Statistics (CWP) – The CWP Handbook of Fishery Statistics' <http://www.fao.org/cwp-on-fishery-statistics/handbook> accessed 12 August 2021.

'FAO | FAO Major Fishing Areas: Arctic Sea (Major Fishing Area 18)' <http://www.fao.org/fishery/area/Area18/en> accessed 5 December 2021.

'FAO | FIRMS Stocks and Fisheries Map Viewer' <http://firms.fao.org/firms/stocks-fisheries-map-viewer> accessed 28 June 2021.

'FAO | GLOBEFISH: Catch Documentation Schemes: Practices and Applicability in Combating IUU Fishing' <http://www.fao.org/in-action/globefish/fishery-information/resource-detail/en/c/426994/> accessed 29 January 2022.

'FAO | Illegal, Unreported and Unregulated (IUU) Fishing: International Framework' <http://www.fao.org/iuu-fishing/international-framework/en/> accessed 2 May 2020.

'FAO | Parties to the PSMA' <https://www.fao.org/port-state-measures/background/parties-psma/en/> accessed 8 April 2022.

'FAO | Regional Bodies Involved in the Management of Deep-Sea Fisheries' <http://www.fao.org/in-action/vulnerable-marine-ecosystems/background/regional-fishery-bodies/en/> accessed 20 February 2021.

'FAO | Regional Fishery Bodies Map Viewer' <http://www.fao.org/figis/geoserver/factsheets/rfbs.html> accessed 29 January 2022.

'FAO | Vulnerable Marine Ecosystems Database: NEAFC Regulatory Area 2013' <https://www.fao.org/fishery/en/vme/vme_neafc_regulatory_1/2013> accessed 4 October 2020.

'FishBase | Search' <https://www.fishbase.se/search.php> accessed 9 July 2021.

'Fisheries and Oceans Canada | Fisheries by Species – Atlantic, Quebec and Arctic Regions Commercial Fisheries' <https://www.dfo-mpo.gc.ca/fisheries-peches/commercial-commerciale/atl-arc/index-eng.html> accessed 10 August 2021.

Gold M, 'Negotiating the International Agreement to Prevent Unregulated Fishing in the High Seas of the Central Arctic Ocean (Arctic Biodiversity Congress, 10 October 2018)' (2018) <https://www.arcticbiodiversity.is/index.php/program/presentations2018/402-the-cao-fishing-agreement-negotiations-and-next-steps-maya-gold/file> accessed 23 July 2020.

'Government of Canada | Canada's Arctic and Northern Policy Framework' <https://www.rcaanc-cirnac.gc.ca/eng/1560523306861/1560523330587#s4> accessed 13 April 2020.

'Government of Canada | International Agreement to Prevent Unregulated High Seas Fisheries in the Central Arctic Ocean' <http://www.dfo-mpo.gc.ca/international/arctic-arctique-eng.htm> accessed 5 December 2021.

'Government of Canada | Marine Biodiversity in Areas beyond National Jurisdictions: New International Treaty Negotiation' (25 July 2018) <https://shorturl.at/rFO3s> accessed 11 December 2020.

'Government of Canada | News Release: Minister Aglukkaq Announces the Signature of the Beaufort Sea Integrated Fisheries Management Framework (17 October 2014)' <https://www.canada.ca/en/news/archive/2014/10/minister-aglukkaq-announces-signature-beaufort-sea-integrated-fisheries-management-framework.html> accessed 29 November 2021.

'Government of Canada | Snow Crab' <https://www.dfo-mpo.gc.ca/species-especes/profiles-profils/snow-crab-crabe-neiges-atl-eng.html> accessed 5 December 2021.

'Greenpeace | Expedition Launch: Arctic Under Pressure – Greenpeace Heads to Arctic to Investigate Urgent Ocean Threats' <https://wayback.archive-it.org/9650/20200403092926/http://p3-raw.greenpeace.org/international/en/news/features/arctic-under-pressure120510/> accessed 29 January 2022.

'Henry George Liddell, Robert Scott: A Greek-English Lexicon | Ἀρκτικός' <http://www.perseus.tufts.edu/hopper/text?doc=Perseus%3Atext%3A1999.04.0057%3Aentry%3D%2315193&redirect=true> accessed 2 September 2021.

'ICCAT | Contracting Parties' <https://www.iccat.int/en/contracting.html> accessed 8 April 2022.

'ICES | Our History' <https://www.ices.dk/about-ICES/who-we-are/Pages/Our-history.aspx> accessed 19 November 2020.

'ICES | Who We Are' <https://www.ices.dk/about-ICES/who-we-are/Pages/Who-we-are.aspx> accessed 20 May 2020.

'IMO | IMO and Its Role in Protecting the World's Oceans' <http://www.imo.org/en/MediaCentre/HotTopics/oceans/Pages/default.aspx> accessed 6 May 2020.

'IMO | IMO and the Sustainable Development Goals' <https://www.imo.org/en/MediaCentre/HotTopics/Pages/SustainableDevelopmentGoals.aspx> accessed 15 December 2020.

'IMO | Member States, IGOs and NGOs' <https://www.imo.org/en/About/Membership> accessed 6 April 2022.

'IMO | Polar Code' <https://www.imo.org/en/ourwork/safety/pages/polar-code.aspx> accessed 2 November 2024.

'International Labour Organization | Ratifications of C169 – Indigenous and Tribal Peoples Convention, 1989 (No. 169)' <https://www.ilo.org/dyn/normlex/en/f?p=1000:11300:0::NO:11300:P11300_INSTRUMENT_ID:312314> accessed 8 April 2022.

'International Whaling Commission | Aboriginal Subsistence Whaling in the Arctic' <https://iwc.int/aboriginal> accessed 28 June 2021.

'Interview with David Attenbrough and Michael Palin (Published 13 October 2020)' <https://www.instagram.com/p/CGR5tF-Hfiz/> accessed 29 May 2021.

'IPCC | Intergovernmental Panel on Climate Change Reports' <https://www.ipcc.ch/reports/> accessed 22 September 2020.

'Joint Fish | Research – Cooperation' <https://www.jointfish.com/eng/RESEARCH/COOPERATION.html> accessed 8 April 2022.

'Joint Fish | The Fisheries Commission' <https://www.jointfish.com/eng/THE-FISHERIES-COMMISSION/ABOUT-THE-WEBSITE.html> accessed 17 November 2020.

'Marine Conservation Institute | Marine Protection by Country: High Seas' <http://www.mpatlas.org/map/high-seas/> accessed 23 July 2020.

'MarineBio Conservation Society | Ocean Geography' <http://marinebio.org/oceans/geography/> accessed 5 December 2021.

'Merriam Webster Dictionary | Governance' <https://www.merriam-webster.com/dictionary/governance> accessed 5 December 2021.

'Merriam Webster Dictionary | Sustainable' <https://www.merriam-webster.com/dictionary/sustainable> accessed 5 December 2021.

'Ministry of Foreign Affairs of Denmark | Conference in Ilulissat, Greenland: Landmark Political Declaration on the Future of the Arctic' <https://fnnewyork.um.dk/en/denmark/denmarks-engagement-with-the-un/statements/newsdisplaypage/?newsid=3d153209-5740-4b81-ba8b-f89cd39ca4fc> accessed 12 August 2021.

Molenaar EJ, 'PPP: The CAOF Agreement: Key Issues of International Fisheries Law' (2018), on file with the author).

'MOSAiC | Main Scientific Focus Areas' <https://mosaic-expedition.org/science/scientific-focus-areas/> accessed 31 March 2022.

'MOSAiC | The Expedition' <https://mosaic-expedition.org/expedition/> accessed 11 December 2021.

'MOSAiC | The Mission' <https://mosaic-expedition.org/science/mission/> accessed 31 March 2022.

'NASA Earth Observatory | World of Change: Arctic Sea Ice' <https://earthobservatory.nasa.gov/world-of-change/sea_ice.php> accessed 9 July 2021.

'NASCO | The North Atlantic Salmon Conservation Organization – About' <https://nasco.int/about/> accessed 19 November 2021.

'National Snow and Ice Data Center | Arctic People' <https://nsidc.org/cryosphere/arctic-meteorology/arctic-people.html> accessed 10 August 2021.

'National Snow and Ice Data Center | Arctic Sea Ice News & Analysis, 16 July 2020: Siberian Downward Slide' <http://nsidc.org/arcticseaicenews/> accessed 23 July 2020.

'National Snow and Ice Data Center | Charctic Interactive Sea Ice Graph' <https://nsidc.org/arcticseaicenews/charctic-interactive-sea-ice-graph/> accessed 9 July 2021.

'National Snow and Ice Data Center | Climate Change in the Arctic' <https://nsidc.org/cryosphere/arctic-meteorology/climate_change.html> accessed 12 August 2021.

'National Snow and Ice Data Center | Climate vs. Weather' <https://nsidc.org/cryosphere/arctic-meteorology/climate_vs_weather.html> accessed 12 August 2021.

'National Snow and Ice Data Center | Effects of Arctic Weather and Climate' <https://nsidc.org/cryosphere/arctic-meteorology/effects_of_climate_weather.html> accessed 5 December 2021.

'National Snow and Ice Data Center | Factors Affecting Arctic Weather and Climate' <https://nsidc.org/cryosphere/arctic-meteorology/factors_affecting_climate_weather.html> accessed 29 January 2022.

'National Snow and Ice Data Center | Studying Arctic Climate' <https://nsidc.org/cryosphere/arctic-meteorology/studying.html> accessed 17 January 2022.

'National Snow and Ice Data Center | What Is the Arctic?' <https://nsidc.org/cryosphere/arctic-meteorology/arctic.html> accessed 5 December 2021.

'NEAFC | Becoming a Contracting Party' <https://www.neafc.org/becomingacp> accessed 10 August 2021.

'NEAFC | Compliance' <https://www.neafc.org/compliance> accessed 31 March 2022.

'New Zealand Government | Fisheries NZ – Quota Management System' <https://www.mpi.govt.nz/law-and-policy/legal-overviews/fisheries/quota-management-system/> accessed 1 July 2020.

'NOAA Fisheries | Alaska Snow Crab' <https://www.fisheries.noaa.gov/species/alaska-snow-crab> accessed 5 December 2021.

'NOAA Fisheries | Statement by John Henderschedt, United States Commissioner to the International Commission for the Conservation of Atlantic Tunas (21 November 2018)' <https://www.fisheries.noaa.gov/leadership-message/statement-john-henderschedt-united-states-commissioner-international-commission> accessed 22 May 2020.

'Nordic Cooperation | Policy Areas' <https://www.norden.org/en/political_areas> accessed 5 December 2021.

'Nordic Cooperation | The History of the Nordic Council' <https://www.norden.org/en/information/history-nordic-council> accessed 6 April 2022.

'Nordic Cooperation | The Nordic Council' <https://www.norden.org/en/information/nordic-council> accessed 5 December 2021.

'Nordregio | Indigenous Population in the Arctic' <https://archive.nordregio.se/en/Maps/01-Population-and-demography/Indigenous-population-in-the-Arctic/index.html> accessed 5 December 2021.

'North Pacific Marine Science Organization | About Us – PICES' <https://meetings.pices.int/about> accessed 30 June 2021.

'North Pacific Marine Science Organization | Journey to PICES' <https://meetings.pices.int/about/history> accessed 30 June 2021.

'Northern Dimension Institute | About ND' <http://www.northerndimension.info/northern-dimension> accessed 30 June 2021.

'Northern Forum | History' <https://www.northernforum.org/en/the-northern-forum/history> accessed 23 May 2020.

'Northern Forum | UNDP Climate Change Adaptation' <https://www.adaptation-undp.org/partners/northern-forum> accessed 23 May 2020.

'Northern Forum | Working Groups' <https://www.northernforum.org/en/working-groups> accessed 25 September 2020.

'Notes of Phone Call with Erik J. Molenaar, Assistant Professor of Law, Economics and Governance at Utrecht University and EU Representative in Consultations for the CAOF Agreement, on 16 October 2020, on File with the Author'.

'Notes of phone call with Maya Gold, Canadian Representative in Consultations for the CAOF Agreement, on 19 September 2019, on file with the author'.

'OSPAR Commission | About' <https://www.ospar.org/about> accessed 20 May 2020.

'OSPAR Commission | Region I: Arctic Waters' <https://www.ospar.org/convention/the-north-east-atlantic/i> accessed 20 May 2020.

'OSPAR Commission | The North-East Atlantic' <https://www.ospar.org/convention/the-north-east-atlantic> accessed 20 May 2020.

'PAG Arctic Portal | The Pacific Arctic Group' <https://pag.arcticportal.org/> accessed 18 December 2021.

'PICES | Materials of the 2000 NEMURO Model Workshop' <https://pices.int/members/task_teams/Disbanded_task_teams/MODEL_materials/mws1.html> accessed 30 June 2021.

'Polar Bear Range States | National Management' <https://polarbearagreement.org/polar-bear-management/national-management> accessed 5 December 2021.

'Polar Bears in Canada | Guided Hunting in Canada' <https://www.polarbearscanada.ca/en/management/harvest/sport-hunting-in-canada> accessed 8 April 2022.

'The Fish Site | Indigenous Fishing Rights' <https://thefishsite.com/articles/indigenous-fishing-rights> accessed 8 April 2022.

'UArctic | New Strategy of Northern Forum' <https://www.uarctic.org/news/2018/4/new-strategy-of-northern-forum/> accessed 23 May 2020.

'UNFCCC | Parties Paris Agreement' <https://unfccc.int/process/parties-non-party-stakeholders/parties-convention-and-observer-states?field_partys_partyto_target_id%5B511%5D=511> accessed 24 May 2021.

'UNFCCC | Parties UNFCCC' <https://unfccc.int/process/parties-non-party-stakeholders/parties-convention-and-observer-states> accessed 6 April 2022.

'UNFCCC | UN Climate Change Conference – United Arab Emirates' <https://unfccc.int/cop28> accessed 4 May 2024.

'UNFCCC | What Is the Kyoto Protocol?' <https://unfccc.int/kyoto_protocol> accessed 22 September 2020.

'UNFCCC | What Is the Paris Agreement?' <https://unfccc.int/process-and-meetings/the-paris-agreement/what-is-the-paris-agreement> accessed 22 September 2020.

'United Nations | Intergovernmental Conference on Marine Biodiversity of Areas Beyond National Jurisdiction' <https://www.un.org/bbnj/> accessed 6 April 2022.

'United Nations | Maritime Space: Maritime Zones and Maritime Delimitation – Canada' <https://www.un.org/Depts/los/LEGISLATIONANDTREATIES/STATEFILES/CAN.htm> accessed 2 March 2021.

'United Nations | Maritime Space: Maritime Zones and Maritime Delimitation – Denmark' <https://www.un.org/Depts/los/LEGISLATIONANDTREATIES/STATEFILES/DNK.htm> accessed 2 March 2021.

'United Nations | Maritime Space: Maritime Zones and Maritime Delimitation – Norway' <https://www.un.org/Depts/los/LEGISLATIONANDTREATIES/STATEFILES/NOR.htm> accessed 2 March 2021.

'United Nations | Maritime Space: Maritime Zones and Maritime Delimitation – Russian Federation' <https://www.un.org/Depts/los/LEGISLATIONANDTREATIES/STATEFILES/RUS.htm> accessed 2 March 2021.

'United Nations | Maritime Space: Maritime Zones and Maritime Delimitation – United States' <https://www.un.org/Depts/los/LEGISLATIONANDTREATIES/STATEFILES/USA.htm> accessed 2 March 2021.

'United Nations | Oceans and Law of the Sea – Chronological Lists of Ratifications of Accession and Succession to the Convention and the Related Agreements' <https://shorturl.at/twUHg> accessed 6 April 2022.

'United Nations | Oceans and the Law of the Sea in the General Assembly of the United Nations – General Assembly Resolutions and Decisions' <https://www.un.org/depts/los/general_assembly/general_assembly_resolutions.htm> accessed 18 September 2020.

'United Nations | Oceans and the Law of the Sea in the General Assembly of the United Nations – Reports of the Secretary-General' <https://www.un.org/Depts/los/general_assembly/general_assembly_reports.htm> accessed 18 September 2020.

'United Nations OHCHR | Status of Ratification – International Covenant on Civil and Political Rights' <https://indicators.ohchr.org/> accessed 8 April 2022.

'United Nations Treaty Collection | Status of Treaties: Agreement for the Implementation of the Provisions of UNCLOS Relating to the Conservation and Management of Straddling Fish Stocks and Highly Migratory Fish Stocks (New York, 4 August 1995)' <https://treaties.un.org/Pages/ViewDetails.aspx?src=TREATY&mtdsg_no=XXI-7&chapter=21&clang=_en> accessed 1 July 2021.

'Video: Expedition Arktis – Ein Jahr. Ein Schiff. Im Eis.' *ARD – Das Erste* (16 November 2020) <https://www.daserste.de/information/reportage-dokumentation/erlebnis-erde/videos/expedition-arktis-video-100.html> accessed 11 December 2020.

'VisitNordic | Arctic Circle Map' <https://www.visitnordic.com/en/article/arctic-circle-map> accessed 4 May 2024.

'WWF | Fishing Problems: Poor Fisheries Management' <https://wwf.panda.org/our_work/oceans/problems/fisheries_management/> accessed 1 July 2020.

'WWF | Tuna Commission Comes up with "a Disgrace, Not a Decision"' <https://www.wwf.eu/?151021/Tuna-commission-comes-up-with-quota-disgrace-not-a-decisionquot> accessed 22 May 2020.

Index

www.ingramcontent.com/pod-product-compliance
Lightning Source LLC
Chambersburg PA
CBHW051355240926
51852CB00001B/38
9789004700666